OXFORD MONOGRAPHS IN INTERNATIONAL LAW

Overlapping Individual and Interstate Claims in International Law

OXFORD MONOGRAPHS IN INTERNATIONAL LAW

The aim of this series is to publish important and original pieces of research on all aspects of international law. Topics that are given particular prominence are those which, while of interest to the academic lawyer, also have important bearing on issues which touch the actual conduct of international relations. Nonetheless the series is wide in scope and includes monographs on the history and philosophical foundations of international law.

RECENT TITLES IN THE SERIES

The Identity of Governments in International Law
Niko Pavlopoulos

Access to Courts for Asylum Seekers and Refugees
State Obligations under the 1951 Refugee Convention
Emma Dunlop

Gravity at the International Criminal Court
Admissibility and Prosecutorial Discretion
Priya Urs

International Law Obligations on Climate Change Mitigation
Benoit Mayer

Coastal State Jurisdiction over Living Resources in the Exclusive Economic Zone
Camille Goodman

International Law and Corporate Actors in Deep Seabed Mining
Joanna Dingwall

The Concept of an International Organization in International Law
Lorenzo Gasbarri

Necessity and Proportionality and the Right of Self-Defence in International Law
Chris O'Meara

Neutrality in Contemporary International Law
James Upcher

Geographical Change and the Law of the Sea
Kate Purcell

Statehood and the State-Like in International Law
Rowan Nicholson

Overlapping Individual and Interstate Claims in International Law

JESSICA HOWLEY

OXFORD
UNIVERSITY PRESS

OXFORD
UNIVERSITY PRESS

Great Clarendon Street, Oxford, OX2 6DP,
United Kingdom

Oxford University Press is a department of the University of Oxford.
It furthers the University's objective of excellence in research, scholarship,
and education by publishing worldwide. Oxford is a registered trade mark of
Oxford University Press in the UK and in certain other countries

Published in the United States of America by Oxford University Press
198 Madison Avenue, New York, NY 10016, United States of America

British Library Cataloguing in Publication Data

Data available

Library of Congress Control Number: 2024932020

ISBN 978–0–19–287146–6

DOI: 10.1093/oso/9780192871466.001.0001

The manufacturer's authorised representative in the EU for product safety is
Oxford University Press España S.A. of El Parque Empresarial San Fernando
de Henares, Avenida de Castilla, 2 – 28830 Madrid (www.oup.es/en or
product.safety@oup.com). OUP España S.A. also acts as importer into Spain
of products made by the manufacturer.

To my family

Series Editors' Preface

The conferral by States on individuals of a right to initiate proceedings before an international court or tribunal against a State in breach of an international obligation creates the potential for overlapping individual and State claims against the same State in international adjudicative fora. An individual may in principle be entitled to claim against the respondent State in that international court or tribunal for breach of that international obligation. At the same time, on the basis of the same facts, the individual's State of nationality or another State may in principle also be entitled to claim against the same respondent State in the same or a different international court or tribunal for breach of the same or a different international obligation. Regardless, moreover, of any conferral on individuals of a right to proceed in an international adjudicative forum, the same facts may give rise in principle both to a claim by an individual in a municipal court for what at root is a State's breach of an international obligation and to a claim by the individual's State of nationality or another State in an international court or tribunal against the same responsible State. Each of these scenarios raises the possibility that conduct of some form by either the individual or State claimant, including but not limited to the bringing of a claim, may affect in some way the claim of the other, rendering that claim inadmissible, depriving it of substance on the merits, or influencing the form or, in the case of compensation, quantum of any remedy.

It is in this sort of scenario that Jessica Howley's *Overlapping Individual and Interstate Claims in International Law* focuses. The book examines the extent to which, in the light of conduct by either the individual or State claimant, each of a selection of secondary rules of international law may serve to bar procedurally, deprive of merit, or affect the remedy granted in a factually overlapping claim by the other claimant. These rules are the requirement to exhaust local remedies; the respective rules in Article 222(*c*) of the CARICOM Treaty and Article 27(1) of the ICSID Convention; the rule barring claims on the ground of *res judicata*; the rule against double recovery; the rule barring claims that have been waived; and the circumstances precluding the wrongfulness of consent, countermeasures, and self-defence. The claims in question are mostly those in international adjudicative fora, although attention is paid in some contexts to claims by individuals in municipal courts. Dr Howley concludes that all of the rules considered may, given certain conduct by the individual or State claimant, operate in practice to preclude in whole or in part the overlapping claim of the other claimant. She suggests further in policy terms that at least some of these rules may strike an inappropriate balance between the interests of claimant and respondent States, on the one hand, and the interests of individual claimants, on the other, and that international human rights law may offer a useful counterbalance.

Overlapping Individual and Interstate Claims in International Law is a tour de force. It is wide-ranging, learned, rigorous, and at times provocative. Its analyses of the international legal institution of diplomatic protection and the concept of the identity of claims are especially rich and intriguing. It will reward reading by all international lawyers, from the 'high doctrinal' scholar to the 'nuts and bolts' practitioner before international courts and tribunals.

RO'K, CR
Milan and Oxford
April 2024

Acknowledgements

This book is based on a DPhil completed at the University of Oxford in 2019.

The advice and comments of the two supervisors I had—Professors Vaughan Lowe and Dapo Akande—were enormously helpful and greatly improved my thesis. I am deeply indebted to them both for their guidance over many years. I am also grateful for the comments of examiners who have read my work: Sir Frank Berman, Professor Catherine Redgwell, and Professor Christian Tams. Their suggestions helped me to refine the object, structure, and argumentation of the original thesis, and provided direction for its transformation into a manuscript.

Many friends and colleagues have read drafts at various stages in the book's development. I am particularly indebted to Lawrence Hill-Cawthorne, Thomas Liefländer, Miles Jackson, Martins Paparinskis, Cecily Rose, Xavier-Baptiste Ruedin, and Benjamin Spagnolo for their comments and for various discussions relating to the legal points arising from my research. Megan Donaldson, Catherine Harwood, and Francesco Messineo took on the mammoth task of reading the entirety of the book manuscript and provided comprehensive and thoughtful notes. Their suggestions have made this book much better than it would otherwise have been.

I have benefited from discussions on many issues with numerous other colleagues during the course of my studies and thereafter, including Faculty and students attending the University of Oxford Public International Law Research Seminar, and attendees at the various conferences at which I have presented aspects of the work contained herein. My thanks to them all.

The Rhodes Trust and the University of Oxford Faculty of Law provided funding that enabled me to carry out the initial research, and Magdalen College provided me with beautiful surrounds and much support. Professional mentors have provided counsel and care throughout the years. The staff at OUP have been brilliant, kind, and patient.

Finally, this book would not have been possible without friends and family. Thank you, in particular, to my parents, for all of the opportunities they gave me; to Charlotte and Kristen for unwavering belief, optimism, and moments of levity; to Joshua for steadfast support and love; and to Eleanor, my light and joy. This book is for you.

Disclaimer

The views expressed herein are those of the author and do not necessarily reflect the views of any institution with which the author is or has been affiliated, including the United Nations.

Contents

Table of Cases and Statutory Instruments

INTERNATIONAL CASES

Eritrea-Ethiopa Claims Commission

International Court of Justice

International Criminal Court

International Military Tribunal at Nuremberg

International Tribunal for the Law of the Sea

Investor–State decisions

Iran–US Claims Tribunal

Mixed arbitral tribunals

Other arbitral cases and correspondence

Permanent Court of International Justice

United Nations Compensation Commission

World Trade Organization

REGIONAL AND HUMAN RIGHTS DECISIONS

African Commission on Human and Peoples' Rights

Caribbean Court of Justice

Central American Court of Justice

East African Court of Justice

Eastern Caribbean Supreme Court

Economic Community of West African States Community Court of Justice

European Court of Human Rights and European Commission on Human Rights

European Court of Justice

Inter-American Court of Human Rights and Inter-American Commission on Human Rights

MERCOSUR

Southern African Development Community Tribunal

Treaty body decisions

DOMESTIC CASES

Australia

Austria

Belgium

Canada

France

Germany

Italy

Japan

Netherlands

Peru

Senegal

Singapore

South Korea

Switzerland

United Kingdom

United States

NATIONAL AND REGIONAL INSTRUMENTS AND RELATED MATERIAL

Australia

Brazil

Canada

China

Economic Community of West African States

European Union

Islamic Republic of Iran

Japan

League of Arab States

New Zealand

Russian Federation

Singapore

Southern African Development Community

United Kingdom

United States

Table of Abbreviations

ILC ARTICLES

ARSIWA	ILC, *Articles on Responsibility of States for Internationally Wrongful Acts (with commentaries)*, as reproduced in James Crawford, *The International Law Commission's Articles on State Responsibility: Introduction, Text and Commentaries* (CUP 2002) (footnote references to *ARSIWA* refer to this version of the *Articles*)
DADP	ILC, *Draft Articles on Diplomatic Protection, with commentaries* (2006) 2(2) ILCYB 22
DAEAC	ILC, *Draft Articles on the Effects of Armed Conflicts on Treaties, with commentaries* (2011) 2(2) ILCYB 108
DARIO	ILC, *Draft Articles on the Responsibility of International Organizations, with commentaries* (2011) 2(2) ILCYB 46

TREATIES AND RELATED INTERNATIONAL INSTRUMENTS

Access Agreement	Memorandum of Understanding with Canada on Access to Medicines (US–Canada) (16 July 2004), available: <http://www.ustr.gov/archive/assets/Trade_Sectors/Intellectual_Property/asset_upload_file426_6319.pdf>
Achmea Declaration	Declaration of the Representatives of the Member States on the Legal Consequences of the Judgment of the Court of Justice in Achmea and on Investment Protection in the European Union (15 January 2019), available: <https://ec.europa.eu/info/publications/190117-bilateral-investment-treaties_en>
AfCHPR	African Charter on Human and Peoples' Rights (adopted 27 June 1981, entered into force 21 October 1986) (1988) 1520 UNTS 217
AfCHPR Protocol	Protocol to the African Charter on Human and Peoples' Rights on the Establishment of an African Court on Human and Peoples' Rights (adopted 9 June 1998, entered into force 25 January 2004) OAU Doc OAU/LEG/EXP/AFCHPR/PROT(III)
AmCHR	American Convention on Human Rights (adopted 22 November 1969, entered into force 18 July 1978) (1979) 1144 UNTS 123
Anglo–Austrian (1920)	Agreement concerning the Settlement of Enemy Debts Referred to in Section 3 and the Annex Thereto of Part X of the Peace Treaty of Saint-Germain (signed 27 August and 2 October 1920) (1922) 12 LNTS 414
Anglo–Austrian (1930)	Agreement between Austria and Great Britain, and New Zealand and India in regard to the Liquidation of Austrian Properties and Exchange of Notes (signed 15 March 1930) (1931) 113 LNTS 395

Anglo–Austrian (1931)	Agreement between Great Britain and Austria relating to the Provisional Dissolution of the Anglo-Austrian Mixed Arbitral Tribunal (signed 14 July 1931) (1931) 123 LNTS 383
Anglo–Bulgaria	Agreement between the United Kingdom and Bulgaria relating to the Provisional Dissolution of the Anglo-Bulgarian Mixed Arbitral Tribunal (signed 17 June 1927) (1927) 67 LNTS 239
Anglo–German (1929)	Agreement regarding the Liquidation of German Properties and Exchange of Notes (signed 28 December 1929) (1929) 102 LNTS 49
Anglo–German (1932)	Agreement regarding the Dissolution of the Anglo-German Mixed Arbitral Tribunal and Exchange of Notes (26 July 1932) (1932) 133 LNTS 99
Anglo–Turkish	Exchange of Notes regarding the settlement of claims against the Turkish Government in respect of outstanding judgments pronounced by the Anglo-Turkish Mixed Arbitral Tribunal constituted in virtue of Part 3, Section 5 of the Treaty of Lausanne, together with notes exchanged (signed 23 March 1944) (1945) 2 UNTS 227
Australia–Germany	Agreement regarding the release of Property Rights and Interests of German Nationals subject to the Charge created in pursuance of the Treaty of Versailles and Exchange of Notes (signed 17 January 1930) (1930) 107 LNTS 325
Austria PT	State Treaty for the re-establishment of an independent and democratic Austria (adopted 15 May 1955, entered into force 27 July 1955) (1955) 217 UNTS 223
Austria–US	Agreement between the Austrian Federal Government and the Government of the United States of America concerning the Austrian Fund 'Reconciliation, Peace and Cooperation' (Reconciliation Fund) (with annexes) (signed 24 October 2000, entered into force 1 December 2000) (2004) 2162 UNTS 3
Belgium–Austria	Convention between Belgium and Austria for the Final Settlement of the Questions resulting from Sections III and IV of Part X of the Treaty of Saint-Germain (signed 16 January 1930) (1930) 104 LNTS 231
Belgium–Germany	Agreement for the Final Settlement of the Questions resulting from Sections III to VII of Part X of the Treaty of Versailles (signed 18 January 1930) (1930) 104 LNTS 223
Bulgaria PT	Treaty of Peace with Bulgaria (adopted 10 February 1947, entered into force 15 September 1947) (1949) 41 UNTS 21
Bulgarian Settlement	Agreement between Belgium, Great Britain and Northern Ireland, Canada, Australia, New Zealand, Union of South Africa, India, France, Greece, Italy, Japan, Poland, Portugal, Roumania, Czechoslovakia, Yugoslavia and Bulgaria regarding the Settlement of Bulgarian Reparations, with Final Clause and Declarations annexed thereto (signed 20 January 1930) (1930) 112 LNTS 361

Burma PT	Treaty of Peace with Burma (adopted 5 November 1954) (1956) 251 UNTS 202
CAC	United Nations Convention against Corruption (adopted 31 October 2003, entered into force 14 December 2005) (2005) 2349 UNTS 41
CACJ Statute	Statute of the Central American Court of Justice (adopted 10 December 1992, entered into force 2 February 1994) (1995) 34 ILM 921
CAFTA	Central America–Dominican Republic–United States Free Trade Agreement (5 August 2004), available: <http://www.ustr.gov/trade-agreements/free-trade-agreements/cafta-dr-dominican-republic-central-america-fta/final-text>
Canada–France	Exchange of notes constituting an agreement for the settlement of Canada's claim in respect of military relief and the claim of France in respect of French vessels requisitioned by Canada during the war (Ottawa, 26 June and 4 July 1951) (1956) 233 UNTS 101
Canada–Japan	Arrangement regarding the settlement of certain Canadian claims (signed 5 September 1961) (1963) 451 UNTS 47
CARICOM Treaty	The Revised Treaty of Chaguaramas Establishing the Caribbean Community, including the CARICOM Single Market and Economy (adopted 5 July 2001, entered into force 1 January 2006) (2006) 2259 UNTS 293
Cartagena Agreement	The Andean Subregional Integration Agreement (Cartagena Agreement) (1969) 8 ILM 910 (as amended), updated codified text available: <https://wits.worldbank.org/GPTAD/PDF/archive/Cartagena.pdf>
Cartagena Protocol	Protocol Amending the Treaty Creating the Court of Justice of the Cartagena Agreement (adopted 28 May 1996, entered into force 25 August 1999), available in English: <https://wits.worldbank.org/GPTAD/PDF/annexes/Cartagena%20justicetreaty.pdf>
CEDAW	Convention on the Elimination of All Forms of Discrimination against Women (adopted 18 December 1979, entered into force 3 September 1981) (1990) 1249 UNTS 13
CEDAW Protocol	Optional Protocol to the Convention on the Elimination of All Forms of Discrimination against Women (adopted 6 October 1999, entered into force 22 December 2000) (2003) 2131 UNTS 83
CERD	International Convention on the Elimination of All Forms of Racial Discrimination (adopted 21 December 1965, entered into force 4 January 1969) (1971) 660 UNTS 195
Chicago Convention	Convention on International Civil Aviation (adopted 7 December 1944, entered into force 4 April 1947) (1948) 15 UNTS 295
COMESA Treaty	Treaty establishing the Common Market for Eastern and Southern Africa (adopted 11 May 1993, entered into force 8 December 1994) (1993) 33 ILM 1067

CPED	International Covention for the Protection of All Persons from Enforced Disappearance (adopted 20 December 2006, entered into force 23 December 2010) (2010) 2716 UNTS 3
CRC Protocol	Optional Protocol to the Convention on the Rights of the Child on a communications procedure (adopted 19 December 2011, entered into force 14 April 2014) (2014) 2983 UNTS 135
CRPD Protocol	Optional Protocol to the Convention on the Rights of Persons with Disabilities (adopted 13 December 2006, entered into force 3 May 2008) (2011) 2518 UNTS 283
CSD	Claims Settlement Declaration (Declaration of the Democratic and Popular Republic of Algeria Concerning the Settlement of Claims by the Government of the United States of America and the Government of the Islamic Republic of Iran), included in the Algiers Accords (19 January 1981) (1981) 20 ILM 223, also available: <http://www.iusct.net/General%20Documents/2-Claims%20Settlement%20Declaration.pdf>
CWC	Convention on the Prohibition of the Development, Production, Stockpiling and Use of Chemical Weapons and on their Destruction (Chemical Weapons Convention) (signed 3 Septmber 1992, entered into force 29 April 1997) (1997) 1975 UNTS 45
EAC Treaty	Treaty for the Establishment of the East African Community (adopted 30 November 1999, entered into force 7 July 2000) (2003) 2144 UNTS 255
ECHR	European Convention for the Protection of Human Rights and Fundamental Freedoms (as amended) (adopted 4 November 1951, entered into force 3 September 1953) (1955) 213 UNTS 221
ECHR Protocol 1	Protocol to the Convention for the Protection of Human Rights and Fundamental Freedoms (signed 20 March 1952, entered into force 18 May 1954) ETS 9
EECC Agreement	Agreement between Ethiopia and Eritrea (12 December 2000) (Eritrea– Ethiopia Claims Commission), available: <https://pcacases.com/web/sendAttach/786>
ECOWAS Treaty	Revised Treaty of the Economic Community of West African States (ECOWAS) (adopted 24 July 1993, entered into force 23 August 1995) (2010) 2373 UNTS 233
ECOWAS Protocol	Supplementary Protocol A/SP.1/01/05 Amending the Preamble and Articles 1, 2, 9 and 30 of Protocol A/P.1/7/91 relating to the Community Court of Justice and Article 4 paragraph 1 of the English Version of the Said Protocol (19 January 2005), available: <http://www.courtecowas.org/site2012/pdf_files/supplementary_protocol.pdf>
ECT	Energy Charter Treaty (adopted 17 December 1994, entered into force 16 April 1998) (2002) 2080 UNTS 95
EU–Russia PA	Agreement on partnership and cooperation establishing a partnership between the European Communities and their Member States, of the one part, and the Russian Federation, of the other part (signed 24 June 1994, entered into force 1 December 1997) (1998) 2007 UNTS 343

Finland PT	Treaty of Peace with Finland (adopted 10 February 1947, entered into force 15 September 1947) (1950) 48 UNTS 203
General Declaration	Declaration of the Government of the Democratic and Popular Republic of Algeria (General Declaration), included in the Algiers Accords (19 January 1981) (1981) 20 ILM 223, also available: <http://www.iusct.net/General%20Documents/1-General%20Declaration%E2%80%8E.pdf>
Genocide Convention	Convention on the Prevention and Punishment of the Crime of Genocide (adopted 9 December 1948, entered into force 12 January 1951) (1957) 278 UNTS 1950
Germany–France	Agreement regarding the Discontinuance of the Liquidation of German Property (signed 31 December 1929) (1929) 106 LNTS 93
Germany–Poland (1929)	Agreement regarding the Settlement of Claims, with Final Protocol (signed 31 October 1929) (1931) 124 LNTS 345
Germany–Poland (1931)	Agreement between the German and Polish Governments, concerning the Termination of the Functions of the German-Polish Mixed Arbitral Tribunal (1 December 1931) (1933) 141 LNTS 315
Germany–Romania	Convention for the purpose of terminating the existing Financial Disputes between the two countries with Final Protocol and Exchange of Notes (signed 10 November 1928 and 6 December 1928) (1929) 91 LNTS 101
Germany–US	Agreement between the Government of the Federal Republic of Germany and the Government of the United States of America concerning the establishment of the Foundation 'Remembrance, Responsibility and the Future' (with annexes and joint statement) (signed 17 July 2000, entered into force 19 October 2000) (2003) 2130 UNTS 249
Greece–Japan	Arrangement regarding settlement of certain Greek claims (signed 20 September 1966) (1967) 609 UNTS 103
Gut Dam Agreement	Agreement concerning the establishment of an International Arbitral Tribunal to dispose of United States claims relating to Gut Dam (signed 25 March 1965) (1967) 607 UNTS 141
Hague Agreement	Final discharge of financial obligations of Austria (signed 20 January 1930) (1930) 104 LNTS 413
Hungary–Italy (1927)	Agreement between Hungary and Italy for the Friendly Settlement of Certain Claims from Italian Nationals Submitted to the Italio-Hungarian Mixed Arbitral Tribunal (signed 21 May 1927) (1928) 74 LNTS 47
Hungary–Italy (1932)	Convention between Hungary and Italy on the Mixed Arbitral Tribunal set up in Application of Article 239 of the Treaty of Peace of Trianon (signed 12 November 1932) (1933) 142 LNTS 95
Hungary PT	Treaty of Peace with Hungary (adopted 10 February 1947, entered into force 15 September 1947) (1949) 41 UNTS 135

IACtHR RoP	Rules of Procedure of the Inter-American Court of Human Rights (2009), available: <https://www.corteidh.or.cr/reglamento.cfm?lang=en>
ICCPR	International Covenant on Civil and Political Rights (adopted 16 December 1966, entered into force 23 March 1976) (1983) 999 UNTS 171
ICCPR Protocol	Optional Protocol to the International Covenant on Civil and Political Rights (adopted 16 December 1966, entered into force 23 March 1976) (1983) 999 UNTS 171
ICC RoPE	Rules of Procedure and Evidence of the International Criminal Court (2019), available: <https://www.icc-cpi.int/sites/default/files/Publications/Rules-of-Procedure-and-Evidence.pdf>
ICESCR Protocol	Optional Protocol to the International Covenant on Economic, Social and Cultural Rights (adopted 10 December 2008, entered into force 5 May 2013) (2013) 2922 UNTS 29
ICPMW	International Convention on the Protection of the Rights of All Migrant Workers and Members of their Families (adopted 18 December 1990, entered into force 1 July 2003) (2004) 2220 UNTS 3
ICSFT	International Convention for the Suppression of the Financing of Terrorism (adopted 9 December 1999, entered into force 10 April 2002) (2004) 2178 UNTS 197
ICSID	Convention on the Settlement of Investment Disputes between States and Nationals of Other States (adopted 18 March 1965, entered into force 14 October 1966) (1968) 575 UNTS 159
Intra-MERCOSUR Investment Protocol	Protocol of Cooperation and Facilitation of Intra-MERCOSUR Investments (2017), English translation available: <https://edit.wti.org/document/show/b7f1b612-2a53-4496-9917-be1d04c10ed6>
Italy–Germany	Agreements between Germany and Italy regarding questions connected with Articles 296 and 297 of the Treaty of Versailles (signed 1 September 1927) (1927) 67 LNTS 425
Italy PT	Treaty of Peace with Italy (adopted 10 February 1947, entered into force 15 September 1947) (1950) 49 UNTS 3
ITLOS Rules	ITLOS: Rules of the Tribunal (17 March 2009), available: <https://www.itlos.org/fileadmin/itlos/documents/basic_texts/Itlos_8_E_17_03_09.pdf>
IUSCT RoP	Iran–US Claims Tribunal Rules of Procedure (3 May 1983), available: <http://www.iusct.net/General%20Documents/5-TRIBUNAL%20RULES%20OF%20PROCEDURE.pdf>
Japan–Czechoslovakia	Protocol relating to the restoration of normal relations (signed 13 February 1957) (1958) 300 UNTS 119
Japan PT	Treaty of Peace with Japan (adopted 8 September 1951, entered into force 28 April 1952) (1952) 136 UNTS 45
MTA	Agreement on Maritime Transport (France–Algeria) (adopted 24 July 1967, entered into force 25 September 1967) (1972) 821 UNTS 393

Mauritius Convention	United Nations Convention on Transparency in Treaty-based Investor–State Arbitration (adopted 10 December 2014, entered into force 18 October 2017) (2015) 54 ILM 747
NAAEC	North American Agreement on Environmental Cooperation (adopted 13 September 1993, entered into force 1 January 1994) (1993) 32 ILM 1480
NAFTA	North American Free Trade Agreement (adopted 17 December 1992, entered into force 1 January 1994) (1993) 32 ILM 296, 612
NY Convention	Convention on the Recognition and Enforcement of Foreign Arbitral Awards (adopted 10 June 1958, entered into force 7 June 1959) (1959) 330 UNTS 3
OAS Charter	Charter of the Organization of American States (signed 30 April 1948, entered into force 13 December 1951) (1952) 119 UNTS 3
Olivos Protocol	The Olivos Protocol for the Settlement of Disputes in MERCOSUR (adopted 18 February 2002, entered into force 1 January 2004) (2003) 42 ILM 2
Prize Court Convention	Convention (XII) Relative to the Creation of an International Prize Court (adopted 18 October 1907, not in force) 205 CTS 381
Rapallo Agreement	German—Russian Agreement (signed at Rapallo, 16 April 1922) (1923) 19 LNTS 248
Romania PT	Treaty of Peace with Roumania (adopted 10 February 1947, entered into force 15 September 1947) (1949) 42 UNTS 3
SADC Treaty	Treaty of the Southern African Development Community (adopted 17 August 1992, entered into force 5 October 1993) (1993) 32 ILM 116, as amended; consolidated text available: <http://www.sadc.int/files/5314/4559/5701/Consolidated_Text_of_the_SADC_Treaty_-_scanned_21_October_2015.pdf>
SADC Protocol	Protocol on Tribunal in the Southern African Development Community (adopted 7 August 2000, entered into force 14 August 2011), available <https://www.sadc.int/sites/default/files/2021-08/Protocol_on_the_Tribunal_and_Rules_thereof2000.pdf >
SADCT RoP	Rules of Procedure of the Southern African Development Community Tribunal (2000), available: <http://www.sadc.int/files/1413/5292/8369/Protocol_on_the_Tribunal_and_Rules_thereof2000.pdf>
Sequestration Removal Agreement	Removal of sequestration over proceeds from the liquidation of German property in Japan (adopted 12 September 1924) (1926) 59 LNTS 17
SLA	Softwood Lumber Agreement (US–Canada) (12 September 2006), available: <http://www.international.gc.ca/controls-controles/assets/pdfs/softwood/SLA-en.pdf>
Tegucigalpa Protocol	Tegucigalpa Protocol to the Charter of the Organization of Central American States (signed 13 December 1991, entered into force 23 July 1992) (1992) 1695 UNTS 382

Termination Agreement	Agreement for the termination of Bilateral Investment Treaties between the Member States of the European Union (signed 29 May 2020, entered into force 29 August 2020), available: <https://eur-lex.europa.eu/legal-content/EN/TXT/PDF/?uri=CELEX:22020A0529(01)&from=EN>
TEU	Consolidated version of the Treaty on European Union (2016) 59 Official Journal C 202, p. 13, available: <http://eur-lex.europa.eu/collection/eu-law/treaties.html>
TFEU	Consolidated version of the Treaty on the Functioning of the European Union (2016) 59 Official Journal C 202, p. 47, available: <http://eur-lex.europa.eu/collection/eu-law/treaties.html>
Thailand–Japan Settlement	Agreement concerning settlement of 'Special Yen Problem' (signed 9 July 1955) (1956) 230 UNTS 13
Treaty of Neuilly-sur-Seine	Treaty of Peace between the British Empire, France, Italy, Japan and the United States (the Principal Applied and Associated Powers), and Belgium, China, Cuba, Czechoslovakia, Greece, the Hedjaz, Poland, Portugal, Roumania, the Serb-Croat-Slovene State, Siam, and Bulgaria (signed 27 November 1919) 226 CTS 332
Treaty of Paris	Treaty of Paris between the United States and Spain (signed 10 December 1898), 30 Stat 1754, reproduced Coleman Phillipson, *Termination of War and Treaties of Peace* (Unwin 1916), 418–22
Treaty of St-Germain-en-Laye	Treaty of Peace between the British Empire, France, Italy, Japan and the United States (the Principal Applied and Associated Powers), and Belgium, China, Cuba, Czechoslovakia, Greece, Nicaragua, Panama, Poland, Portugal, Roumania, the Serb-Croat-Slovene State, Siam, and Austria (signed 10 September 1919) 226 CTS 8
Treaty of Trianon	Treaty of Peace between the Allied and Associated Powers and Hungary (signed 4 June 1920) (1921) 6 UNTS 187
Treaty of Versailles	Treaty of Peace between the British Empire, France, Italy, Japan and the United States (the Principal Applied and Associated Powers), and Belgium, Bolivia, Brazil, China, Cuba, Czechoslovakia, Ecuador, Guatemala, Haiti, the Hedjaz, Honduras, Liberia, Nicaragua, Panama, Peru, Poland, Portugal, Roumania, the Serb-Croat-Slovene State, Siam, and Uruguay and Germany (signed 28 June 1919) 225 CTS 188
Trianon Settlement Treaty (TST)	Agreements relating to the obligations resulting from the Treaty of Trianon, including Agreement I (Concerning the arrangements between Hungary and

	the Creditor Powers) and Agreement II (Concerning the settlement of questions relating to the agrarian reforms and Mixed Arbitral Tribunals) (signed 28 April 1930) (1931) 121 LNTS 69
UK–Austria	Money and Property Agreement (with exchange of notes) (signed 30 June 1952) (1952) 138 UNTS 152
UK/France/US/Italy/Germany	Agreement relating to certain libraries and properties in Italy (signed 30 April 1953) (1953) 175 UNTS 89
UK–Germany	Agreement between Germany and Great Britain concerning the Liquidation of Germany's Restitution Obligations and Protocol (signed 5 January 1924 and 19 March 1924) (1924) 36 LNTS 366
UNCAT	Convention against Torture and Other Cruel, Inhuman or Degrading Treatment or Punishment (adopted 10 December 1984, entered into force 26 June 1987) (1987) 1465 UNTS 85
UNC	Charter of the United Nations (adopted 26 June 1945, entered into force 24 October 1945), available: <https://www.un.org/en/charter-united-nations/>
UNCLOS	United Nations Convention on the Law of the Sea (adopted 10 December 1982, entered into force 16 November 1994) (1982) 1833 UNTS 397
USMCA	United States–Mexico–Canada Agreement (adopted 30 November 2018, entered into force 1 July 2020), available: < https://ustr.gov/trade-agreements/free-trade-agreements/united-states-mexico-canada-agreement/agreement-between>
US–Austria	Agreement (with appendix) concerning the disposition of certain United States property in Austria (signed 26 September 1955) (1957) 272 UNTS 31
US–France	Agreement respecting maritime claims and litigation (signed 14 March 1949) (1951) 84 UNTS 225
US–Germany Settlement	Agreement regarding the settlement of the claim of the United States of America for post-war economic assistance (other than surplus property) to Germany (signed 27 February 1953) (1955) 224 UNTS 13
US–Iceland Settlement	Agreement regarding the settlement of claims of Icelandic insurance companies (adopted 23 November 1956) (1957) 281 UNTS 361
US–Iraq	Claims Settlement Agreement between the Government of the United States of America and the Republic of Iraq (signed 2 September 2010), available: <https://www.state.gov/documents/organization/166949.pdf>
US–Japan (Awa Maru)	Agreement for settlement of the Awa Maru claim (signed 14 April 1949) (1951) 89 UNTS 141

US–Japan (Amami Islands)	Agreement (with annex, exchange of notes and agreed official minutes) concerning the Amami Islands (signed 24 December 1953) (1955) 222 UNTS 193
US–Libya	Claims Settlement Agreement between the United States of America and the Great Socialist People's Libyan Arab Jamahiriya (signed 14 August 2008), available: <https://www.justice.gov/sites/default/files/pages/attachments/2014/06/18/settlement_agreement.pdf>
US–Norway	Agreement regarding settlement for lend-lease, military relief, and claims (with exchange of notes) (signed 24 February 1948) (1949) 34 UNTS 155
US–UK Interpretation	Exchange of Notes constituting an Agreement Interpreting the Agreement (II) on Settlement of Intergovernmental Claims, annexed to Memorandum of the Governments of the US and the UK pursuant to Joint Statement of December 6, 1945, regarding Settlement for Lend-lease, Reciprocal Aid, Surplus War Property, and Claims (Washington, 19 and 28 February 1947) (1951) 89 UNTS 368
US–UK Settlement	Exchange of Notes (with annex) constituting an agreement relating to claims for damages relating to acts of armed forces personnel (London, 29 February and 28 March 1944) (1948) 15 UNTS 413
VCCR	Vienna Convention on Consular Relations (adopted 24 April 1963, entered into force 19 March 1967) (1969) 596 UNTS 261
VCDR	Vienna Convention on Diplomatic Relations (adopted 18 April 1961, entered into force 24 April 1964) (1965) 500 UNTS 95
VCLT	Vienna Convention on the Law of Treaties (adopted 23 May 1969, entered into force 27 January 1980) (1980) 1155 UNTS 331

STATUTES AND ADMINISTRATIVE MEASURES

ASR	Autonomous Sanctions Regulations (2011) (Australia)
ATPA	Andean Trade Preference Act 19 USC §3201 (US)
ATS	Alien Tort Statute 28 USC §1350 (US)
BelSEUER	Republic of Belarus (Sanctions) (EU Exit) Regulations 2019 (UK)
CIFA	Model Cooperation and Investment Facilitation Agreement (Brazil), English text available: <https://investmentpolicy.unctad.org/international-investment-agreements/treaty-files/4786/download>
EO	Executive Order (US)
EO 12283	Executive Order 12283 (19 January 1981)
EO 13288	Executive Order 13288 (6 March 2003)

EO 13304	Executive Order 13304 (28 May 2003)
EO 13405	Executive Order 13405 (16 June 2006)
EO 13469	Executive Order 13469 (25 July 2008)
EO 13477	Executive Order 13477 (31 October 2008)
EO 13551	Executive Order 13551 (1 September 2010)
EO 13553	Executive Order 13553 (28 September 2010)
EO 13566	Executive Order 13566 (25 February 2011)
EO 13572	Executive Order 13572 (29 April 2011)
EO 13573	Executive Order 13573 (18 May 2011)
EO 13660	Executive Order 13660 (6 March 2014)
EO 13661	Executive Order 13661 (16 March 2014)
EO 13662	Executive Order 13662 (20 March 2014)
EO 13685	Executive Order 13685 (19 December 2014)
EO 13687	Executive Order 13687 (2 January 2015)
EO 13692	Executive Order 13692 (8 March 2015)
EO 13722	Executive Order 13722 (15 March 2016)
EO 13810	Executive Order 13810 (20 September 2017)
EO 13818	Executive Order 13818 (21 December 2017)
EO 13846	Executive Order 13846 (6 August 2018)
EO 13851	Executive Order 13851 (27 November 2018)
EO 14014	Executive Order 14014 (10 February 2021)
EO 14033	Executive Order 14033 (8 June 2021)
EO 14038	Executive Order 14038 (9 August 2021)
EU Dec 2010/638/CFSP	EU Council Decision 2010/638/CFSP (25 October 2010)
EU Dec 2010/788/CFSP	EU Council Decision 2010/788/CFSP (20 December 2010)
EU Dec 2011/137/CFSP	EU Council Decision 2011/137/CFSP (28 February 2011)
EU Dec 2012/285/CFSP	EU Council Decision 2012/285/CFSP (31 May 2012)
EU Dec 2012/642/CFSP	EU Council Decision 2012/642/CFSP (15 October 2012)
EU Dec 2013/255/CFSP	EU Council Decision 2013/255/CFSP (31 May 2013)
EU Dec 2014/119/CFSP	EU Council Decision 2014/119/CFSP (5 March 2014)
EU Dec 2014/145/CFSP	EU Council Decision 2014/145/CFSP (17 March 2014)
EU Dec 2014/499/CFSP	EU Council Decision 2014/499/CFSP (25 July 2014)
EU Dec (CFSP) 2015/1333	EU Council Decision (CFSP)2015/1333 (31 July 2015)
EU Dec 2015/1836/CFSP	EU Council Decision 2015/1836/CFSP (12 October 2015)
EU Dec 2017/667/CFSP	EU Council Decision 2017/667(CFSP) (6 April 2017)
EU Dec 2018/655/CFSP	EU Council Decision 2018/655(CFSP) (26 April 2018)
EU Dec 2018/900/CFSP	EU Council Decision 2018/900(CFSP) (25 June 2018)
EU Dec (CFSP) 2019/1720	EU Council Decision (CFSP) 2019/1720 (14 October 2019)
EU Dec CFSP 2019/1894	EU Council Decision CFSP 2019/1894 (11 November 2019)
EU Dec (CFSP)2021/482	EU Council Decision (CFSP)2021/482 (22 March 2021)
EU Dec CFSP 2021/1277	EU Council Decision CFSP 2021/1277 (30 July 2021)
EU Dec CFSP 2021/2208	EU Council Decision CFSP 2021/2208 (13 December 2021)
EU Dec (CFSP) 2022/329	EU Council Decision (CFSP) 2022/329 (25 February 2022)
EU Dec (CFSP)2022/578	EU Council Decision (CFSP)2022/578 (8 April 2022)
EU Reg 1294/1999	EU Council Regulation 1294/1999 (15 June 1999)

EU Reg 2580/2001	EU Council Regulation 2580/2001 (27 December 2001)
EU Reg 101/2011	EU Council Regulation 101/2011 (4 February 2011)
EU Reg 2011/235/CFSP	EU Council Regulation 2011/235/CFSP (12 April 2011)
EU Reg 267/2012	EU Council Regulation 267/2012 (23 March 2012)
EU Reg 2015/1861	EU Council Regulation 2015/1861 (18 October 2015)
EU Reg 2016/44	EU Council Regulation 2016/44 (18 January 2016)
EU Reg 2017/1509	EU Council Regulation 2017/1509 (30 August 2017)
EU Reg 2017/2063	EU Council Regulation 2017/2063 (13 November 2017)
EU Reg 2019/796	EU Council Regulation 2019/796 (17 May 2019)
EU Reg 2020/1998	EU Council Regulation 2020/1998 (7 December 2020)
GuineaSEUER	Guinea (Sanctions) (EU Exit) Regulations 2019 (UK)
JVCFOA	Justice for Victims of Corrupt Foreign Officials Act (2017) (Canada)
Magnitsky Act	Global Magnitsky Human Rights Accountability Act (2016) 22 USC §2656 (US)
NicSEUER	Nicaragua (Sanctions) (EU Exit) Regulations 2020 (UK)
RSR	Russia Sanctions Regulations 2022 (NZ)
RussSEUER	Russia (Sanctions) (EU Exit) Regulations 2019 (UK)
SEMBelR (Canada)	Special Economic Measures (Belarus) Regulations (2023)
SEMIR (Canada)	Special Economic Measures (Iran) Regulations (2010)
SEMRR (Canada)	Special Economic Measures (Russia) Regulations (2014)
SEMSR (Canada)	Special Economic Measures (Syria) Regulations (2011)
SEMZR (Canada)	Special Economic Measures (Zimbabwe) Regulations (2008)
UnDrillAEMedSEUER	Unauthorised Drilling Activities in the Eastern Mediterranean (Sanctions) (EU Exit) Regulations 2020 (UK)
USIFCPA	Iran Freedom and Counter-Proliferation Act (2012) 22 USC §8801 (US)

JOURNAL AND CASE CITATIONS

Annals AAPSS	Annals of the American Academy of Political and Social Science
AC	Appeal Cases (UK)
AHRLJ	African Human Rights Law Journal
AfJICL	African Journal of International and Comparative Law
AHRLR	African Human Rights Law Reports
AIAJ	Asian International Arbitration Journal
AJIL	American Journal of International Law
Ams LF	Amsterdam Law Forum
Arb Int	Arbitration International
Ariz JICL	Arizona Journal of International and Comparative Law
AUILR	American University International Law Review
Aust Rev I & EL	Austrian Review of International and European Law
Aust YBIA	Austrian Yearbook on International Arbitration
BCDRIAR	BCDR International Arbitration Review
BerkJIL	Berkley Journal of International Law

BYBIL	British Yearbook of International Law
BFSP	British and Foreign State Papers
Camb JI & CL	Cambridge Journal of International and Comparative Law
CCR	Constitutional Court Review
Ch	Law Reports, Chancery Division (UK)
CLR	Commonwealth Law Reports (Australia)
Colum J L & Soc Probs	Columbia Journal of Law and Social Problems
Colum LR	Columbia Law Review
Corn ILJ	Cornell International Law Journal
CYBP & PIL	Czech Yearbook of Public & Private International Law
Denv J Int L & Pol	Denver Journal of International Law & Policy
DR	Decisions and Reports of the European Commission on Human Rights
Duke Env L & Pol For	Duke Environmental Law & Policy Forum
ECHR	Reports of Judgments and Decisions of the European Court of Human Rights
ECR	European Court Reports
EHRR	European Human Rights Reports
EJIL	European Journal of International Law
EWCA	Court of Appeal of England and Wales
EWHC	High Court of England and Wales
EYBIEL	European Yearbook of International Economic Law
FCR	Federal Court Reports (Australia)
GAR	Global Arbitration Review
Geo Wash ILR	George Washington International Law Review
Hague JRL	Hague Journal on the Rule of Law
Hast I & CLR	Hastings International & Comparative Law Review
Harv ILJ	Harvard International Law Journal
Harv LJ	Harvard Law Journal
Harv LR	Harvard Law Review
Hornsby's	Edmund Hornsby, *Report of the Mixed Commission on Private Claims, established under the convention between Great Britain and the United States of America of the 8th February 1853: with the judgments of the commissioners and umpire* (Harrison & Sons, 1856)
HRLR	Human Rights Law Review
IA Rep	International Arbitration Reporter
IAYBkHR	Inter-American Yearbook on Human Rights
ICC	International Chamber of Commerce
ICSID Rep	ICSID Reports
ICSID Rev-FILJ	ICSID Review—Foreign Investment Law Journal
ICLQ	International & Comparative Law Quarterly
IDIA	Annuaire de l'institut de droit international
Ind JGLS	Indiana Journal of Global Legal Studies
Int L Forum	International Law FORUM du droit international

ILA Conf Rep	ILA Reports of Conferences
ILCYB	Yearbook of the International Law Commission
ILDC	Oxford Reports on International Law in Domestic Courts
ILM	International Legal Materials
ILPr	International Litigation Procedure
ILR	International Law Reports
Iran–USCTR	Iran–US Claims Tribunal Reports
ISQ	International Studies Quarterly
JC & SL	Journal of Conflict and Security Law
JIA	Journal of International Arbitration
JICJ	Journal of International Criminal Justice
JIDS	Journal of International Dispute Settlement
JIEL	Journal of International Economic Law
JWIT	Journal of World Investment and Trade
KB	Law Reports, King's Bench Division (UK)
LPICT	Law and Practice of International Courts and Tribunals
Loy LAI & CLR	Loyola of Los Angeles International & Comparative Law Review
Martens	*Nouveau Recueil Général de Traités et Autres Actes Relatifs aux Rapports de Droit International, Continuation du Grand Recueil de G. Fr. Martens* par Heinrich Triepel, Troisième Série (Librarie Theodor Weicher, 1927)
Minn LR	Minnesota Law Review
Moore's	John Bassett Moore, *History and Digest of the International Arbitrations to which the US has been a Party* (GPO, 1898)
MULR	Melbourne University Law Review
NDLR	Notre Dame Law Review
NDWP	Notre Dame Working Paper
Nord JIL	Nordic Journal of International Law
NwULRColl	Northwestern University Law Review Colloquy
NYUJ Legis & Pub Pol	New York University Journal of Legislation & Public Policy
Op Juris	Opinio Juris Blog <http://opiniojuris.org/>
ÖZ	Österreische Zeitschrift für öffentliches Recht und Völkerrecht
PolYBIL	Polish Yearbook of International Law
RDIP & P	Rivista di Diritto Internazionale Privato e Processuale
RdC	Recueil des Cours (Collected Courses of the Hague Academy of International Law)
Rep	Report
RPUNO	Repertory of Practice of United Nations Organs
SAYIL	South African Yearbook of International Law
SCC	Stockholm Chamber of Commerce
SCLR	Santa Clara Law Review
SDILJ	San Diego International Law Journal
Sel Dec HRC	Selected Decisions of the Human Rights Committee
SMULR	Southern Methodist University Law Review

SYBIL	Singapore Year Book of International Law
TAM	Recueil des Décisions des Tribunaux Arbitraux Mixtes
Tul JICL	Tulane Journal of International and Comparative Law
Tul LR	Tulane Law Review
UCLAJILFA	UCLA Journal of International Law & Foreign Affairs
UNRIAA	United Nations Reports of International Arbitral Awards
UNSWLJ	University of New South Wales Law Journal
UNYB	United Nations Yearbook
Virg JIL	Virginia Journal of International Law
VJTL	Vanderbilt Journal of Transnational Law
Wash LR	Washington Law Review
WLR	Weekly Law Reports (UK)
WWR	Western Weekly Reports (Canada)
YBkECHR	Yearbook of the European Convention on Human Rights
YLJ	Yale Law Journal
ZfaöRV	Zeitschrift für ausländisches öffentliches Recht und Völkerrecht

BOOK AND PUBLISHER ABBREVIATIONS

CUP	Cambridge University Press
HLS	Harvard Law School
Man UP	Manchester University Press
MPEPIL	Rüdiger Wolfrum (ed), Max Planck Encyclopaedia of Public International Law (Online) (OUP) <www.mpepil.com>
OUP	Oxford University Press
Stan UP	Stanford University Press
YUP	Yale University Press

OTHER ABBREVIATIONS

AB	Appellate Body of the World Trade Organization
ACommHPR	African Commission on Human and Peoples' Rights
ACtHPR	African Court on Human and Peoples' Rights
ALI	American Law Institute
Andean Court	Court of the Andean Subregional Integration Community
BCCA	British Columbia Court of Appeal
BCJ	Benelux Court of Justice
BGH	Bundesgerichtshof (Federal Supreme Court, Germany)
BIICL	British Institute of International and Comparative Law
BIT	Bilateral Investment Treaty
BVerfG	Bundesverfassungsgericht (Federal Constitutional Court, Germany)
CARICOM	Caribbean Community
CA	Court of Appeal
CAT	Committee Against Torture
CACJ	Central American Court of Justice
CCJ	Caribbean Court of Justice

CFI	Court of First Instance
Cl Comm	Claims Commission
Civ Ct	Civil Court
CJ	Court of Justice
COMESA	Common Market for Eastern and Southern Africa
Conc Comm	Conciliation Commission
Cons d'Etat	Conseil d'Etat
Counter-Mem	Counter-Memorial
Cour Cass	Cour de Cassation
CTS	Consolidated Treaty Series
DC	District Court
DoS	Department of State (US)
DPRK	Democratic People's Republic of Korea (North Korea)
DRC	Democratic Republic of the Congo
EAC	East African Community
EC	European Commission
ECFR	European Council on Foreign Relations
ECJ	European Court of Justice
ECommHR	European Commission on Human Rights
ECOWAS	Economic Community of West African States
ECSC	Eastern Caribbean Supreme Court
ECtHR	European Court of Human Rights
EEA	European Economic Area
EECC	Eritrea-Ethiopia Claims Commission
EFTA	European Free Trade Area
EGC	General Court of the European Court of Justice
ETS	European Treaty Series
EU	European Union
Exch Lett	Exchange of Letters
FCDO	Foreign, Commonwealth & Development Office (UK)
FCN	Freedom, Commerce and Navigation
FET	Fair and Equitable Treatment
FRG	Federal Republic of Germany
FTA	Free Trade Agreement
GC	Grand Chamber (ECtHR)
GC	General Court (ECJ)
GDP	Gross Domestic Product
HC	High Court
HRC	Human Rights Committee
IACHR	Inter-American Commission on Human Rights
IACtHR	Inter-American Court of Human Rights
ICAO	International Civil Aviation Organization
ICC	International Criminal Court
ICJ	International Court of Justice
ICRC	International Committee of the Red Cross
IDI	Institut de droit international

IDP	Internally displaced person
IEC	International Energy Charter Secretariat
IHL	International humanitarian law (*jus in bello*)
ILA	International Law Association
ILC	International Law Commission
ILEP	Institute for Law and Economic Policy
ILO	International Labour Organization
ILO FOAC	ILO Freedom of Association Committee
ISIS	Islamic State of Iraq and Syria
ITLOS	International Tribunal for the Law of the Sea
IUSCT	Iran-US Claims Tribunal
LAS	League of Arab States
LoN	League of Nations
LNTS	League of Nations Treaty Series
MAT	Mixed Arbitral Tribunal
Mem	Memorial
MERCOSUR	Mercado Común del Sur, established under the Treaty establishing a Common Market (Asunción Treaty) between the Argentine Republic, the Federative Republic of Brazil, the Republic of Paraguay and the Eastern Republic of Uruguay (adopted 26 March 1991, entered into force 29 November 1991) (2001) 2140 UNTS 257
MIGA	Multilateral Investment Guarantee Agency
NAM	Non-Aligned Movement
OECD	Organisation for Economic Co-operation and Development, established under the Convention on the Organisation for Economic Co-operation and Development (adopted 14 December 1960, entered into force 30 September 1961) (1973) 888 UNTS 179
OFAC	Office of Foreign Assets Control
OHCHR	United Nations Office of the High Commissioner for Human Rights
OPIC	Overseas Private Investment Corporation
PCA	Permanent Court of Arbitration
PCIJ	Permanent Court of International Justice
PICT	Project on International Courts and Tribunals
POW	Prisoner of war
Rej	Rejoinder
Rep	Reply (in the context of pleadings)
RoP	Rules of Procedure
SADC	Southern African Development Community, established under the SADC Treaty
SADCT	Southern African Development Community Tribunal
SC	Supreme Court
SGCA	Singapore Court of Appeal
SCSA	Small Claims Settlement Agreement
TGI	Tribunal de grande instance (France)
UAE	United Arab Emirates
UK	United Kingdom of Great Britain and Northern Ireland

UKHL	UK House of Lords
UKSC	UK Supreme Court
UN	United Nations
UNCC	United Nations Compensation Commission
UNLS	UN Legislative Series
UNSC	United Nations Security Council
UNSG	Secretary-General of the United Nations
UNTS	United Nations Treaty Series
US	United States
USCA	United States Court of Appeals
USCA, DC Cir	United States Court of Appeals, D.C. Circuit
US Ct Cl	United States Court of Claims
USDOT	United States Department of the Treasury
USSC	United States Supreme Court
WGAD	Working Group on Arbitrary Detention
WTO	World Trade Organization, established under the Marrakesh Agreement establishing the World Trade Organization (adopted 15 April 1994, entered into force 1 January 1995) (1998) 1867 UNTS 154
WWI	First World War
WWII	Second World War

A NOTE ON LUMP SUM SETTLEMENT AGREEMENTS

A number of treaties referred to in this book are reproduced in one of three volumes:

Richard B Lillich and Burns H Weston, *International Claims: Their Settlement By Lump Sum Agreements*, vols 1 and 2 (Virginia UP 1975); and

Burns H Weston, Richard B Lillich, and David J Bederman, *International Claims: Their Settlement By Lump Sum Agreements, 1975–1995* (Transnational Publishers 1999).

In such cases, the relevant treaty is noted by way of referring, in parentheses, to its number in the relevant volume, or in the appendix in which it is located, together with the parties to the agreement.

A NOTE ON OTHER TREATIES

Unless otherwise noted, Bilateral Investment Treaties are available on the UNCTAD website: <http://investmentpolicyhub.unctad.org/IIA>. All BITs are described in the text by reference to the States parties and year of signature.

Other treaties are available in the LNTS or UNTS databases, or elsewhere as indicated.

A NOTE ON TITLES AND ABBREVIATIONS

ILC articles, treaties, statutes, and administrative measures are referred to in the footnotes by way of their abbreviated titles, contained in the table of abbreviations. Lengthy titles for certain authorities have also been shortened in the footnotes, as indicated by an ellipsis (…). Full titles may be found in the bibliography.

COVERAGE

Efforts have been made to ensure information is up to date as at the end of 2022. In some cases, it has been possible to include material through mid-2023.

Introduction

I. States and individuals in international law: growing potential for overlapping claims

Modern public international law was traditionally the domain of States.[1] For the most part, individuals were recognised by international law only as constituent elements of the State of whose population they formed a part: they were, in common parlance, 'objects' rather than 'subjects' of international law.[2] One consequence was that individuals' interests were represented by their States of nationality on the international plane, and claims for violations of international law concerning individuals were made and settled, if at all, between States.[3] An individual aggrieved by another State was obliged to look to their State of nationality to exercise diplomatic protection and claim on their behalf.[4] With doctrines of State immunity overwhelmingly shielding State action from international investigation on the domestic level, individuals were otherwise left largely without the possibility of redress.[5] And even if an individual persuaded their State to claim, there was always a risk that the State would exercise its prerogative under international law to pocket the reparation awarded.[6]

[1] Generally, eg, Kate Parlett, *The Individual in the International Legal System: Continuity and Change in International Law* (CUP 2011) 3, 10–17, 343–44; Anne Peters, *Beyond Human Rights: The Legal Status of the Individual in International Law* (Jonathan Huston tr, CUP 2016) 13–14; ILC, 'Draft Articles on Diplomatic Protection with Commentaries' (2006) 2(2) ILCYB 22, 25 (DADP); Robert McCorquodale, 'The Individual and the International Legal System' in Malcolm Evans (ed), *International Law* (4th edn, OUP 2014) 281–82; Edith Brown Weiss, 'Invoking State Responsibility in the Twenty-First Century' (2002) 96 AJIL 798, 798.

[2] Eg, Robert Jennings and Arthur Watts, *Oppenheim's International Law*, vol 1 (9th edn, Longman 1992) 846–47; Hersch Lauterpacht, *International Law: Being the Collected Papers of Hersch Lauterpacht* (Elihu Lauterpacht ed, CUP 1970) 136–37 ('traditional view'), 141–43; Parlett (n 1) 14–15, 26–30, 36–37, 353–63; also McCorquodale (n 1) 281–82; Peters (n 1) 14, 42–44; Rosalyn Higgins, *Themes and Theories* (OUP 2009) 75; Brigitte Bollecker-Stern, *Le Préjudice Dans La Théorie de La Responsibilité Internationale* (Pedone 1973) 94–95; Nkambo Mugerwa, 'Subjects of International Law' in Max Sørensen (ed), *Manual of Public International Law* (Macmillan 1968) 249, 265–66.

[3] Eg, DADP, 25; James Crawford, *State Responsibility: The General Part* (CUP 2013) 584 (*GP*); Christine Chinkin, *Third Parties in International Law* (OUP 1993) 14; FV Garcia-Amador, 'International Responsibility: Report' (1956) 2 ILCYB 173, 192; McCorquodale (n 1) 280, 288–89; Philip Jessup, *A Modern Law of Nations* (Archon 1968) 8–9; Mugerwa (n 2) 249, 266; Christoph Schreuer, *Decisions of International Institutions Before Domestic Courts* (Oceana 1981) 329; Parlett (n 1) 15–16, 50, 64–65.

[4] DADP, 25; see Ch 2(II), Ch 3(II).

[5] Generally authorities Ch 2, n 86; also Ch 5, nn 291–92; DADP, 26; Crawford, *GP* (n 3) 565.

[6] Authorities Ch 4, n 513. Similarly Christoph Schreuer, *The ICSID Convention: A Commentary* (2nd edn, CUP 2009) 415 ('political risks').

Overlapping Individual and Interstate Claims in International Law. Jessica Howley, Oxford University Press.
 DOI: 10.1093/oso/9780192871466.003.0001

In the last century, however, international law has increasingly evolved to provide individuals with recognition as entities separate from the State, accord them rights and obligations,[7] and, importantly, grant them the ability in certain circumstances to make claims against States for violations of international law, including before international tribunals.[8] Such mechanisms are particularly notable in the human rights and investment law fields, though they encompass other possibilities, including the use of domestic procedures.[9]

These developments are clearly desirable from certain policy perspectives: in line with general cosmopolitan trends,[10] individuals gain autonomy over claims that concern them,[11] relieved of the burden of convincing a State to act.[12] States, too, are freed from expending time, resources, and political capital prosecuting claims for individuals, without abandoning the principle that international law—including rules benefiting their citizens—ought to be respected by other States.[13]

However, the increasing access of individuals to mechanisms for prosecuting violations of international law also gives rise to potential problems. Where once a limited number of States had a more or less orderly system for resolving disputes between themselves, the arena of international dispute settlement is now faced with an influx of new potential claimants vying to have their claims determined before various forums.[14] And, notwithstanding the existence of individual claims mechanisms, States may still be inclined to bring claims concerning their nationals.[15] They may wish to claim for their own injury, additional to that suffered by individual citizens;[16] to add their weight to an individual's claim where, for instance, the claim is considered politically important;[17] to assist individuals who

[7] Eg, Garcia-Amador (n 3) 192; DADP, 25; Parlett (n 1) 3, 27–29, 37–38, 349–51; Peters (n 1) 25–34; McCorquodale (n 1) 284–88; Ch 1, n 127.

[8] Ch 2(I); James Crawford, *The International Law Commission's Articles on State Responsibility: Introduction, Text and Commentaries* (CUP 2002) 210 (*ARSIWA*); Crawford, *GP* (n 3) 584–85; Yuval Shany, *Regulating Jurisdictional Relations Between National and International Courts* (OUP 2007) 10; Weiss (n 1) 809ff; Parlett (n 1) Ch 2, Ch 5.4, 349–50; McCorquodale (n 1) 284, 288–94.

[9] Ch 2(I), particularly authorities nn 10–11.

[10] See Parlett (n 1) 43–44, 369–70.

[11] Similarly Yuval Shany, *The Competing Jurisdictions of International Courts and Tribunals* (OUP 2003) 121, 155; Shany (n 8) 132–33.

[12] Eg, Anthea Roberts, 'Triangular Treaties: The Extent and Limits of Investment Treaty Rights' (2015) 56 Harv ILJ 353, 389–90.

[13] See ibid 390–91; Anthea Roberts, 'State-to-State Investment Treaty Arbitration: A Hybrid Theory of Interdependent Rights and Shared Interpretative Authority' (2014) 55 Harv ILJ 1, 15; *Corn Products v Mexico (Responsibility)* ICSID Case No ARB(AF)/04/01 (15 January 2008) [1] (Sep Op Lowenfeld); Rosalyn Higgins, *Problems and Processes: International Law and How We Use It* (Clarendon 1994) 52 (individual proceedings satisfy State's interest in citizens' treatment); Gabrielle Kaufmann-Kohler and Michele Potestà, 'Investor-State Dispute Settlement and National Courts: Current Framework and Reform Options' [2020] EYBIEL, 17–20; authorities Ch 2, n 97; similarly Chittharanjan Amerasinghe, *Local Remedies in International Law* (2nd edn, CUP 2004) 57.

[14] Generally Shany (n 11), particularly Ch 2.

[15] Similarly Roberts (n 13) 14–15.

[16] Ch 2, nn 108–10 ('mixed' claims); Gerald Fitzmaurice, 'Fourth Report on the Law of Treaties' (1959) 2 ILCYB 37 [161].

[17] Ben Juratowich, 'The Relationship between Diplomatic Protection and Investment Treaties' (2008) 23 ICSID Rev-FILJ 10, 33. Cf Crawford, *GP* (n 3) 586.

might otherwise face difficulties;[18] to resolve a question of principle with wider ramifications than the individual's claim;[19] and/or to efficiently consolidate several claims where the injury is significant or affects numerous nationals,[20] somewhat similarly to 'class actions' under the domestic law of certain States.[21]

Indeed, the continued existence of more traditional routes for the invocation of responsibility by States,[22] when combined with the development and utilisation of individual claims mechanisms, gives rise to actual and potential 'overlap' between individual and interstate claims.[23] By this we mean that both individuals and States may claim for violations of international law arising from the same factual circumstances and against the same respondent State.[24]

The Articles on Responsibility of States for Internationally Wrongful Acts (ARSIWA), finalised by the International Law Commission (ILC) in 2001, contain detailed rules regarding when and how international claims—technically an 'invocation of responsibility'—can be brought.[25] They are widely regarded as reflecting, in major respects, a codification of customary international law.[26] Nonetheless, and despite both the increasing relevance of individual claims, and the overlap—real and potential—with interstate claims, the law of State responsibility reflected in the ARSIWA is designed to operate primarily between States.[27] The ARSIWA do

[18] See Frank Berman, 'The Relevance of the Law on Diplomatic Protection in Investment Arbitration' in Federico Ortino and others (eds), *Investment Treaty Law, Current Issues II* (BIICL 2007) 71–72; Martins Paparinskis, 'Investment Arbitration and the Law of Countermeasures' (2008) 79 BYBIL 264, 291; Roberts (n 13) 14–15.

[19] See Berman (n 18) 72; Roberts (n 12) 395–97; Roberts (n 13) 4, 9–10, 14, 49–50; Fitzmaurice (n 16) [160]; Martins Paparinskis, 'Investment Treaty Arbitration and the (New) Law of State Responsibility' (2013) 24 EJIL 617, 630; Paparinskis, 'Countermeasures' (n 18) 291; also Gabrielle Kaufmann-Kohler, 'Non-Disputing State Submissions in Investment Arbitration: Resurgence of Diplomatic Protection?' in Laurence Boisson de Chazournes, Marcelo Kohen, and Jorge Viñuales (eds), *Diplomatic and Judicial Means of Dispute Settlement* (Martinus Nijhoff 2013) 317; *North American Dredging Company v Mexico* (1926) IV UNRIAA 26 [11]; Ch 2, nn 131–33.

[20] Roberts (n 13) 4, 9–10, 14–15, 29, 67; Roberts (n 12) 395–97; Berman (n 18) 72; Juratowich (n 17) 32–33; also Jessup (n 3) 116–17; Ch 4(V)(B)(ii).

[21] Roberts (n 13) 9, 67, discussed Ch 4, nn 599ff; generally Ch 4(IV)(C),(V)(B)(ii).

[22] See Parlett (n 1) 366; generally Ch 2(III).

[23] Using 'overlap' or 'overlapping' in this context: authorities Ch 2, nn 124, 138, 206, 242, 248; André Nollkaemper, 'Conversations among Courts: Domestic and International Adjudicators' in Cesare Romano, Karen Alter, and Yuval Shany (eds), *The Oxford Handbook of International Adjudication* (OUP 2014) 529; Juratowich (n 17) 34; also James Crawford, 'The ILC's Articles on Diplomatic Protection' (2006) 31 SAYIL 19, 23; n 24; Ch 2, n 164.

[24] Similarly n 28; Roberts (n 12) 383 ('same underlying conduct'); cf Shany (n 11) 21 ('overlap … means … dispute can be addressed by more than one available forum'), 22 ('proceedings … share … sufficient degree of similarity'); Shany (n 8) 2 ('disputes between … same parties … or, closely related … over essentially identical issues'), 23; Hanno Wehland, *The Coordination of Multiple Proceedings in Investment Treaty Arbitration* (OUP 2013) [1.20] ('multiple proceedings'); Kaj Hobér, 'Res Judicata and Lis Pendens in International Arbitration' (2014) 366 RdC 99, 118; Schreuer (n 3) 329; Kaufmann-Kohler and Potestà (n 13) 32; generally Ch 2.

[25] *ARSIWA*, arts 42, 48; Ch 1(II)–(III).

[26] Crawford, *GP* (n 3) 43 ('in whole or … large part an accurate codification'); generally *ARSIWA*, 74 ('codification and progressive development'). Doubt regarding an article's customary status will be noted.

[27] Christian Tams, 'All's Well That Ends Well: Comments on the ILC's Articles on State Responsibility' (2002) 62 ZfaöRV 759, 760–61; Weiss (n 1) 798, 815–16; cf James Crawford, 'The ILC's Articles on

not address the invocation of responsibility by individuals, nor do they govern 'the tricky terrain of the relations between claims of responsibility asserted by States and those, arising from the same conduct, asserted by the actual victims.'[28] Failing to address the impact of international law's evolution towards allowing individuals to claim before an ever-burgeoning number of tribunals risks, however, upending the successful functioning of the field of State responsibility, and of international dispute settlement more broadly.[29]

This book therefore aims to narrow the gap thus left by the ARSIWA. It does so by examining the relationship between interstate and individual invocations of responsibility for violations of international law.[30] More particularly, it asks to what extent the law of State responsibility allows for such overlapping claims, and how far States and individuals can effectively be precluded from bringing claims due to the existence of an overlapping claim belonging to the other, and that other's related conduct.[31]

II. Contributions of the book

In addressing this overarching question, the book undertakes a comprehensive survey of the potential for overlapping individual and interstate claims to emerge, explores how public international law regulates the bringing of such overlapping claims, and proposes a human rights-oriented approach to resolving the complex policy considerations to which such claims give rise. Through a rigorous analysis of the law of State responsibility, it provides clarity in understanding the nature of, and relationship between, individual and interstate claims, including in the

Responsibility of States for Internationally Wrongful Acts: A Retrospect' (2002) 96 AJIL 874, 886–88; also Emmanuel Roucounas, 'Non-State Actors: Areas of International Responsibility in Need of Further Exploration' in Maurizio Ragazzi (ed), *International Responsibility Today: Essays in Memory of Oscar Schachter* (Martinus Nijhoff 2005) 392, 399; Roberts (n 12) 364; Paparinskis, 'Countermeasures' (n 18) 333; Kate Parlett, 'The Application of the Rules on Countermeasures in Investment Claims' in Christine Chinkin and Freya Baetens (eds), *Sovereignty, Statehood and State Responsibility* (CUP 2015) 405.

[28] James Crawford, 'Overview of Part Three of the Articles on State Responsibility' in James Crawford and others (eds), *The Law of International Responsibility* (OUP 2010) 932, referencing *ARSIWA*, art 33(2); similarly Crawford, *GP* (n 3) 549; also André Nollkaemper, *National Courts and the International Rule of Law* (OUP 2011) 98, 170–71; Ch 1, nn 164–71.

[29] See Shany (n 11) 5, 10–11, 80, 114–19, 164, 171.

[30] Similarly: Crawford, *GP* (n 3) 585–93; Roberts (n 13) 3ff; authorities n 31. On 'need[ing] to regulate ... multiple proceedings': Shany (n 8) 17, generally 17–20, 131–32, 155–56; similarly Shany (n 11) 79–82, 110–15, 117–21, 124–25, 154ff; Schreuer (n 3) 328; Burkhard Hess, 'The Private-Public Divide in International Dispute Resolution' (2018) 388 RdC 49, 237–38, 245; Roberts (n 13) 41.

[31] Considering similar situations, particularly Roberts (n 12) 355, 363, 383–86; Annemarieke Vermeer-Künzli, 'Unfinished Business: Concurrence of Claims Presented before a Human Rights Court or Treaty Body and through Diplomatic Protection' (2010) 10 HRLR 269, 270ff; Paparinskis, 'Countermeasures' (n 18), particularly Pts (III)–(V); Paparinskis, 'New' (n 19) 629–35, 640–41, 643–46; generally nn 60–71. On terminology: nn 64, 81–82.

theoretically muddled field of diplomatic protection. And it highlights the under-theorised foundations of topical debates concerning the use of countermeasures and self-defence outside of the interstate arena, essential to understanding how these defences can operate in modern contexts.

The book's foundation lies in the increasing emergence of overlapping individual and interstate claims in recent years.[32] In the human rights field, for example, there have been numerous instances of individual human rights claims overlapping with interstate litigation before the International Court of Justice (ICJ), the European Court of Human Rights (ECtHR), and ad hoc tribunals, including that concerning widescale damage to States' populations. The same is apparent vis-à-vis international investment law, with individual investment claims overlapping with interstate disputes brought before the World Trade Organization (WTO) dispute settlement mechanisms, the ECtHR, and various other tribunals.[33]

The overlap is not, however, limited to international fora.[34] Over time, national courts have become increasingly concerned with questions of international law.[35] 'Jurisdictional interactions between national and international courts' have followed,[36] including 'overlap' between individual and interstate claims for violations of international law before domestic and international tribunals.[37]

Moreover, claims under international law are not brought only before judicial tribunals.[38] In order to provide a comprehensive base for analysing the approach of international law to overlapping individual and interstate claims, this book therefore draws on the practice of claims more generally, including that deriving from settlement agreements.[39]

Conflicting policy interests are discernible in determining whether and to what extent international law should allow for overlapping individual and interstate claims.[40] While this book cannot purport to provide a comprehensive and uncontested list of such considerations, they certainly include those that may be derived from well-established rules of international law relating to multiple claims.[41] On the one hand, for instance, it seems unjust to require a respondent to account

[32] cf Giorgio Gaja, 'The Protection of General Interests in the International Community' (2012) 364 RdC 9, 170 ('unlikely'). Generally: Shany (n 11), particularly Ch 2; Shany (n 8), particularly Chs 1, 4.

[33] Ch 2(III)(A)–(B).

[34] Nollkaemper (n 23) 529; generally Ch 2(III)(C).

[35] Shany (n 8) 8–11, 197; Nollkaemper (n 23) 525; Nollkaemper (n 28) 7–13, 26, 213; Antonios Tzanakopoulos, 'Domestic Courts in International Law: The International Judicial Function of National Courts' (2011) 34 Loy LAI & CLR 133, 133, 136–37.

[36] Shany (n 8) 1, generally Chs 1, 4. Similarly Nollkaemper (n 23) 525–26.

[37] Nollkaemper (n 23) 529; Nollkaemper (n 28) 249, generally 27ff; authorities Ch 2, nn 241–48; Ch 2(III)(C).

[38] Ch 1, nn 104–6.

[39] See particularly Ch 5(III). Cf, eg, Shany (n 11) 13.

[40] Similarly Shany (n 11) Chs 3(4), 4(2).

[41] See, eg, Ch 4(I),(III) (double recovery, *res judicata*), Ch 5(I)(A),(B) (consent/waiver), also Ch 6, nn 33ff, sections (III),(IV)(B)(i) (countermeasures/self-defence and third-party rights); generally Shany (n 11) 23–24, 27–28, Ch 4(2); Shany (n 8) 131.

several times for the same conduct, including to make reparation multiple times over;[42] it is against the public interest to allow litigation to continue indefinitely, inviting inefficiencies and wasted resources;[43] and the existence of multiple related claims raises the risk of inconsistent decisions.[44] On the other hand, to the extent that claims are brought by separate entities, respect for their autonomy would dictate that they should not be bound by another's conduct without their agreement.[45]

These policy considerations are similar to those that arise generally in respect of multiple claims.[46] Nonetheless, they take on a particular flavour vis-à-vis overlapping individual and interstate claims, because of the recognition international law accords to the relationship between a State and its citizens, the character of States as representatives for their populations as a whole, and the interest States retain in claims concerning their nationals.[47] The purpose of providing individuals with their own claims mechanisms would appear defeated if international law allowed States, including the State of nationality, to invariably block such claims in the name of avoiding multiplicity.[48] At the same time, allowing individual claims to take precedence over those of the State may prove equally—if not more—problematic. Particular concerns might arise, for instance, in circumstances such as post-conflict environments, where there are clear benefits in allowing States to settle claims concerning large numbers of affected individuals quickly and on a global basis, and to distribute limited reparations funds in a fair manner.[49]

Overlapping individual and interstate claims may also have broader impacts on State action. Notably, the law of State responsibility provides for various defences to international claims, termed 'circumstances precluding wrongfulness' under the ARSIWA.[50] Certain of these—consent, countermeasures, and self-defence—are said by many to operate as valid defences only to the claims of the entity in response to whose conduct the defence is invoked, and to be unable to impact the rights of third entities under international law.[51] So, to the extent that individuals possess such rights, a State could not agree with another State to revoke those rights, even if they have created them;[52] could not exercise countermeasures in a manner

[42] Ch 4, nn 13, 107–8; Kaufmann-Kohler and Potestà (n 13) 34; Shany (n 11) 27–28, 155, 164–65, 170; Shany (n 8) 155, 160; Roberts (n 13) 41–42.

[43] Kaufmann-Kohler and Potestà (n 13) 34; Shany (n 11) 27–28, 80, 155, 164–65; Shany (n 8) 131, 155; Ch 4, nn 107–8.

[44] Kaufmann-Kohler and Potestà (n 13) 34; Shany (n 11) 23, 80–81, 111–19, 155, 164–65; Shany (n 8) 155; Schreuer (n 6) 421; Roberts (n 13) 41.

[45] Shany (n 11) 23–24, 115, 121, 155; Shany (n 8) 132–33; Ch 4, nn 632–47.

[46] Similarly Shany (n 11) 10, 80, Ch 4(2); Shany (n 8) 155–56.

[47] See nn 2–4, 15–21; Ch 3(II); Ch 4(V)(B)(ii). Generally, eg, Edwin Borchard, *The Diplomatic Protection of Citizens Abroad: Or, the Law of International Claims* (Banks 1915) 351.

[48] cf authorities nn 45, 61. See similarly discussion Roberts (n 13) 49–52.

[49] See authorities Ch 5, nn 49–51. Similarly Peters (n 1) 175.

[50] Ch 1(IV) and see Ch 1, n 148.

[51] See authorities Ch 5, nn 18–21; Ch 6, nn 33–41, 75, 81.

[52] See Ch 5, nn 21, 355–56, 379–82.

affecting those rights, notwithstanding that countermeasures usually impact individuals;[53] and could not violate such rights in exercising self-defence, even though armed conflict almost necessarily impacts civilians.[54] While one can understand the policy basis behind not allowing a respondent to rely on such defences vis-à-vis an 'innocent' party which is not responsible for the behaviour giving rise to the defence,[55] the representative character of the State, and the almost inevitable impact that the exercise of such defences on the interstate level has on individual citizens, must make one query whether the argument holds equally in respect of individuals as in respect of sovereign States.[56] Otherwise, individual claims mechanisms would seem to have a significant potential 'chilling effect'[57] on the traditional capacity of would-be respondent States to exercise their rights, for fear of being forced to make reparation for otherwise defensible interstate conduct on the individual level.[58] In the case of self-defence, moreover, this approach would invariably prevent States from responding to attacks from individual non-State actors—a reality of the modern world—because doing so almost necessarily requires violating another State's rights of territorial sovereignty.[59]

How does public international law address these competing policy positions in situations of multiple claims brought by different entities? This book answers this question by considering two main scenarios.

First, it examines whether rules of international law might operate to prevent *one* of a State or individual from invoking responsibility and claiming reparation in circumstances in which their claims overlap.[60] In particular, it asks whether individuals can prevent States exercising their traditional role of settling disputes concerning their nationals through the existence and utilisation of individual claims mechanisms, or, on the contrary, whether States can override individual claims and continue to exercise that role irrespective of the wishes of the individuals concerned.[61]

Second, it examines circumstances in which a State or individual engages in conduct that would enable a respondent State to invoke a circumstance precluding

[53] See Ch 6, nn 25–41, 89–99.
[54] See Ch 6, nn 54, 79–81.
[55] See Ch 6, nn 39, 378.
[56] See Ch 6(III)(A), (IV).
[57] Terminology borrowed from discussions of investment law's effects on regulatory policies: e.g. Carolina Moehlecke, 'The Chilling Effect of International Investment Disputes: Limited Challenges to State Sovereignty' (2020) 64 ISQ 1. See further Ch 6, n 514.
[58] See Ch 6, nn 513–14.
[59] See Ch 6(IV).
[60] cf authorities nn 65–70; Shany (n 11) 17.
[61] Similarly: Roberts (n 12) 363–64, 383–85, 392–93, 395–99, 403–14; Roberts (n 13) 2, 5–6, 7–8, 49–52, 69–70; Peters (n 1) 169, 175, 212–13, 317; Martins Paparinskis, 'Analogies and Other Regimes of International Law' in Zachary Douglas, Joost Pauwelyn, and Jorge Viñuales (eds), *The Foundations of International Investment Law* (OUP 2014) 104–5; Paparinskis, 'New' (n 19) 643–46; Vermeer-Künzli (n 31) 270–72. Cf nn 3, 22.

wrongfulness, asking whether that conduct might have the effect of precluding not only that entity's claims but also the overlapping claim of an individual or State.[62]

Both scenarios concern whether rules exist under the law of State responsibility that might operate to 'preclude' individual or interstate claims,[63] in circumstances where the application of those rules is not dependent on the conduct of the individual or State bringing the claim—which may have done nothing itself to warrant its claim being barred—but on the conduct of the other entity possessing an overlapping claim.[64]

This book considers six categories of rules fitting this description, and their potential operation in the context of overlapping individual and interstate claims:[65]

(1) the rule on the exhaustion of local remedies, which renders certain interstate claims inadmissible when individuals have failed to bring an overlapping claim on the domestic level;[66]
(2) certain provisions under the Convention on the Settlement of Investment Disputes between States and Nationals of Other States (ICSID) and the Revised Treaty of Chaguaramas Establishing the Caribbean Community (CARICOM Treaty), which are enlivened by the actions of a State or individual in claiming, consenting to claim, or not doing so, and which prevent multiple claims from being made;[67]
(3) *res judicata*, a general principle of international law that operates to render inadmissible a claim brought subsequently to another that, pursuant to criteria to be explained, is similar, as well as certain treaty-based provisions that restrict the bringing of claims that have already been decided, commonly interpreted as reflecting similar elements to *res judicata*;[68]

[62] Similarly: Roberts (n 12) 364, 384–86, 399–402; Paparinskis, 'Countermeasures' (n 18), particularly Pt (V); Paparinskis, 'New' (n 19), particularly 629–35, 639–40, 642–43; Paparinskis, 'Analogies' (n 61) 100–2; Parlett (n 27) 394–405; Ch 1, n 155; Ch 6.

[63] See n 82.

[64] Using the term 'conduct' in this sense: authorities Ch 1, n 150.

[65] Shany considers, vis-à-vis overlapping claims between different tribunals, certain of the same principles, including local remedies: Shany (n 8) 27–33, 178; *res judicata*, waiver-related principles, and abuse of rights: ibid Chs 5–6; Shany (n 11) Chs 5–6; likewise Wehland (n 24), particularly Ch 6 (*res judicata*/*lis pendens*). Matters of discretion, like 'comity', also considered therein (respectively Ch 6(2)(B), Ch 6.1, Ch 7), are not considered here. Cf Shany (n 11) 223, 260–63; Shany (n 8) 172, 176–81; Wehland (n 24) [4.83] (*res judicata* 'non-discretionary'), [4.94]–[4.95]; James Crawford, 'Chance, Order, Change: The Course of International Law' (2013) 365 RdC 9, 221–24; Joost Pauwelyn and Luiz Eduardo Salles, 'Forum Shopping Before International Tribunals: (Real) Concerns, (Im)Possible Solutions' (2009) 42 Corn ILJ 77, 86, 102. Vermeer-Künzli considers admissibility vis-à-vis overlapping human rights/diplomatic protection claims: Vermeer-Künzli (n 31) 270ff.

[66] Similarly: Roberts (n 13) 31 (individual action affecting State claim); Louis Sohn and R Baxter (eds), *Convention on the International Responsibility of States for Injuries to Aliens* (HLS 1961) 51, 201; Ch 3(I)(B).

[67] Ch 3(I)(A).

[68] cf Roberts (n 13) 40, 43; Paparinskis, 'Countermeasures' (n 18) 297–98; Vermeer-Künzli (n 31) 273, 277–79; Peters (n 1) 317; Ch 4, nn 81, 104–16.

(4) the rule precluding double recovery, which prevents a claimant from recovering reparation where damage has already been repaired;[69]

(5) waiver by individuals and States of the claims of the other, querying whether such waivers operate to render those other claims inadmissible;[70] and

(6) consent, countermeasures, and self-defence as circumstances precluding wrongfulness, querying whether they can be invoked by a respondent State to preclude not only the claims of the entity in response to whose conduct they are so invoked, but also the claims of a State or an individual possessing an overlapping claim.[71]

The common features of the rules considered in this book are threefold. First, they relate to secondary rules of State responsibility, rather than primary rules.[72] Second, they have the potential to preclude claim(s) for violation of international law from being brought in circumstances of overlapping individual and interstate claims.[73] Finally, their potential application vis-à-vis an entity's claim is dependent not on that entity's own conduct, but on the conduct of the entity possessing an overlapping claim.

Not all of the rules depend, for their operation, on overlapping claims actually being brought. Some do: *res judicata*, for instance, is only potentially applicable where an earlier claim has been judicially decided, while the rule precluding double recovery operates where reparation has been paid vis-à-vis an earlier claim.[74] However, other rules, such as that requiring exhaustion of local remedies, apply simply where overlapping individual and interstate claims are *available*.[75] For waiver, a given claim could, in theory, be waived without State responsibility having been invoked at all, meaning no overlapping claims would arise.[76]

[69] Similarly: Crawford, *GP* (n 3) 590; Roberts (n 13) 41–42, 50; Wehland (n 24) [1.32]–[1.33]; Paparinskis, 'New' (n 19) 639–40; Shany (n 8) 19; also Andrea Gattini, 'A Trojan Horse for Sudeten Claims? On Some Implications of the Prince of Liechtenstein v Germany' (2002) 13 EJIL 513, 538; Gaja, 'General' (n 22) 169; Vermeer-Künzli (n 31) 288; Kaufmann-Kohler and Potestà (n 13) 34.

[70] Similarly: Paparinskis, 'Analogies' (n 61) 104–5; Paparinskis, 'New' (n 19) 643–46; also Peters (n 1) 175, 212–213; Sohn and Baxter (n 66) 201, 207; Roberts (n 12) 395–99; n 65; Ch 5. While not specifically addressed herein, concepts of acquiescence and estoppel raise similar issues: see Christian Tams, 'Waiver, Acquiescence, and Extinctive Prescription' in Crawford and others, *Responsibility* (n 28) 1043–45, 1048; Ch 5, nn 75ff.

[71] See authorities Ch 5, nn 17–21, section (III)(C)(viii); Ch 6, nn 33ff, section (IV)(B).

[72] For the distinction: *ARSIWA*, 74; also Tams (n 27) 764–65; cf Federica Paddeu, *Justification and Excuse in International Law* (CUP 2018) 53–57. Taking a similar approach: ibid 18. Exceptionally, Chs 5 and 6 discuss some conduct relating to primary norms, but only to demonstrate its bearing on the secondary rules context.

[73] n 82.

[74] Ch 4(I),(III).

[75] Ch 3(I)(A)–(B). Cf Evan Criddle, 'Humanitarian Financial Intervention' (2013) 24 EJIL 583, 597 (fn 68) (vis-à-vis countermeasures).

[76] See Sohn and Baxter (n 66) art 25 ('potential claim'); Ole Spiermann, 'Individual Rights, State Interests and the Power to Waive ICSID Jurisdiction under Bilateral Investment Treaties' (2004) 20 Arb Int 179, 186.

Nonetheless, questions concerning the impact of interstate waivers on individual claims, and vice versa, commonly arise in practice where both States and individuals have endeavoured to claim.[77] Likewise, a circumstance precluding wrongfulness might conceivably be invoked in situations in which only one entity, or indeed neither, has claimed.[78] However, such circumstances have similarly been invoked in practice where overlapping individual and interstate claims are actually brought, in an effort to preclude both of such claims.[79]

The unifying feature of the situations with which this book is concerned is, accordingly, that, *but for* the alleged operation of the rules under consideration, overlapping individual and interstate claims *could* be brought.[80] Thus, 'overlapping claims' is taken to mean that both a State or States and an individual or individuals would, prima facie, and in the absence of rules of preclusion, be able to invoke the responsibility of the same respondent State for violations of international law arising from the same factual circumstances, whether or not they actually make those claims.[81]

The terms 'preclusion' or 'preclude' are taken simply to mean that an entity prima facie possessing an overlapping claim is unable to invoke responsibility successfully.[82] Certain of the rules under consideration, including the local remedies rule, *res judicata* and related provisions and principles, and waiver, might operate to allow one entity's conduct to render the other's claim inadmissible.[83] Other rules, if applicable, relate to breach, with an entity's conduct precluding the other from establishing that international law was violated: as will be seen, this explains certain situations subsumed under the notion of waiver,[84] and how circumstances precluding wrongfulness may operate.[85] Other rules, including that precluding double recovery, might operate to allow one entity's conduct to curtail the other's ability to claim reparation, even if the claim as such might still be brought.[86]

[77] See Ch 5.

[78] cf n 79. Eg, if a circumstance precluding wrongfulness were accepted to apply.

[79] Ch 6, nn 92–93.

[80] For 'but for' language, eg: ILC, 'Draft Articles on the Responsibility of International Organizations, with Commentaries' (2011) 2(2) ILCYB 46, 72.

[81] cf Paddeu (n 72) 102, 109–10, 227 (countermeasures only '*prima facie* … breach'); similarly James Crawford, 'Second Report on State Responsibility' (1999) 2(1) ILCYB 1 [236] (consent); n 24; Ch 1, n 147.

[82] cf Ch 1, n 147 (circumstances precluding wrongfulness) and discussion Crawford, *GP* (n 3) 275 ('true of … armoury of other defensive arguments'); also *ARSIWA*, 266 ('preclude … claim for reparation'); Roberts (n 13) 4, 7, 9, 11, 15, 67; Paparinskis, 'Countermeasures' (n 18) 267; Sohn and Baxter (n 66) 201.

[83] See Ch 3(I)(B); Ch 4(III); Ch 5(I)(B).

[84] Ch 5(II).

[85] Ch 1, n 156.

[86] Ch 4, nn 54–57.

III. Overview of the book

This book will demonstrate that all of these rules have the potential, given certain State or individual conduct, to preclude the overlapping claims of the other, either in totality or in part. It is divided into six chapters.

After this Introduction, Chapter 1 introduces the concepts of State responsibility relevant to, and utilised throughout, the remainder of the book. In particular, it highlights the utility of concepts of *breach* and *damage* to understanding the nature of international claims, the degree of potential overlap between individual and interstate claims, and how rules of preclusion might operate in respect of such claims.[87] Chapter 2 outlines the mechanisms available for individuals to invoke State responsibility for violations of international law, and the potential for resulting overlap with interstate claims. This precedes consideration in the following chapters of the application in practice of the rules and principles identified above to those overlapping claims. The rules are grouped together in Chapters 3–6 according to certain commonalities.

First, the application of certain rules depends expressly on the type of claim at issue. The local remedies rule, and the provisions in ICSID and the CARICOM Treaty, apply only where an overlapping interstate claim is one of diplomatic protection. Chapter 3 addresses the difference between diplomatic protection and other interstate claims in order to appreciate when these rules and provisions will operate.[88]

Second, certain other rules depend on two claims being the 'same' or sufficiently so.[89] *Res judicata* and similar treaty-based exclusions operate where two claims share sufficient 'identities', and the double recovery rule applies where the same damage is alleged.[90] Chapter 4 addresses when overlapping individual and interstate claims are relevantly the same for the purpose of these two rules, arguing that *res judicata* may apply vis-à-vis certain overlapping individual and interstate diplomatic protection or 'mixed' claims, and that double recovery precludes reparation from being awarded in a later claim where individual claims overlap with interstate claims brought consequent on individual injury.

Third, and somewhat relatedly, the application of certain of the rules depends on the issue of third parties and their rights. Thus, because third-party rights cannot be waived, waiver only functions to preclude claims belonging to the same party.[91]

[87] Cf Shany (n 8) 131–44; Shany (n 11) 23–24.

[88] See Ch 3(II). Similarly: Clovis Trevino, 'State-to-State Investment Treaty Arbitration and the Interplay with Investor-State Arbitration Under the Same Treaty' (2014) 5 JIDS 199, 213.

[89] Similarly: Shany (n 11) 23–24 (*electa una via/res judicata/lis pendens*); Shany (n 8) 3, 131, 164; Hobér (n 24) 121. See Ch 4(I), (III).

[90] See Ch 4(I), (III).

[91] Ch 5(I)(B)(ii). See Peters (n 1) 213–16; Parlett (n 1) 93; also Ian Brownlie, *System of the Law of Nations: State Responsibility, Part I* (Clarendon 1983) 58 ('precise identification of the cause of action ... called for'); Hess (n 30) 241.

Similarly, some suggest that respondent States are unable to rely on consent and countermeasures, and possibly self-defence, to preclude the claims of third parties whose conduct did not lead to the exercise of the relevant defence, at least where those third parties claim for a resulting violation of their own rights.[92]

Because of their similarities and the overlap in their application in practice, Chapter 5 addresses both waiver and consent. It considers when overlapping individual and interstate claims may be regarded as involving rights belonging to the same parties, such that these principles might be utilised to preclude one or both such claims. Chapter 6 addresses the remaining circumstances precluding wrongfulness, countermeasures and self-defence, arguing that they can operate, at least in certain circumstances, to preclude both of overlapping individual and interstate claims when invoked by a respondent in response to the conduct of one of those entities.

The Conclusion pulls together the threads of the previous chapters, affirming that overlapping individual and interstate claims may indeed be curtailed by actions of the other entity possessing an overlapping claim that enliven rules under the law of State responsibility relating to admissibility, breach, and reparation. It highlights that how far claims may be thus precluded depends heavily on how far States and individuals, and their rights and claims, are 'identified' with one another.[93] In view of the competing policy positions introduced above, it concludes that at least some of these rules appear to have the potential to operate in a manner that fails to strike an appropriate balance between the interests of applicant and respondent States, and of individuals.[94] It proposes that human rights law provides a foundation for a fitting counterbalance, which should guide State action in addressing the concerns to which overlapping individual and interstate claims give rise.[95]

[92] nn 51–54.

[93] cf on 'identification': Gerald Fitzmaurice, *The Law and Procedure of the International Court of Justice* (Grotius 1986) 24, referencing *Reparation for injuries suffered in the service of the United Nations (Advisory Opinion)* [1949] ICJ Rep 174, 207, 214 (Sep Op Badawi Pasha); similarly Eduardo Jiménez de Aréchaga, 'International Responsibility' in Sørensen (n 2) 573; authorities Conclusion, n 10.

[94] Conclusion, section II.

[95] Conclusion, section III.

1
State Responsibility

I. Introduction to State responsibility

Before examining the existence and potential preclusion of overlapping individual and interstate claims, it is necessary to outline some fundamentals regarding the law of State responsibility. Understanding how rules on State responsibility operate assists in appreciating what 'international claims'[1] are, in what respects they might overlap, and how those claims might be affected by rules of preclusion. This chapter introduces the international framework, taking as its basis the rules reflected in the Articles on Responsibility of States for Internationally Wrongful Acts (ARSIWA) of the International Law Commission (ILC).[2] More specifically, this chapter focuses on the elements of State responsibility that are relevant to:

(a) *for what* a claim is brought; and
(b) the *process* for bringing a claim.

II. For what are claims brought?

In ARSIWA terminology, the making of a claim against a State is called an 'invocation of responsibility'.[3] More precisely, such an invocation is an assertion, through 'measures of a relatively formal character',[4] that, owing to breach of an international obligation, secondary *remedial* obligations must be fulfilled.[5] Invocations of responsibility—the 'claims' that are relevant for this book—are therefore

[1] Generally, those 'based on a rule of international law': André Nollkaemper, *National Courts and the International Rule of Law* (OUP 2011) 9; cf *Illinois Central Railroad v Mexico* (1926) 20 AJIL 794 (US-Mexican Cl Comm) 796–97; Ch 2, nn 64ff.

[2] See Introduction, nn 25–26.

[3] See James Crawford, *The International Law Commission's Articles on State Responsibility: Introduction, Text and Commentaries* (CUP 2002) (*ARSIWA*), arts 42, 48, 256; James Crawford, *State Responsibility: The General Part* (CUP 2013) (*GP*) 541.

[4] *ARSIWA*, 256; also Crawford, *GP* (n 3) 541; Edith Brown Weiss, 'Invoking State Responsibility in the Twenty-First Century' (2002) 96 AJIL 798, 800.

[5] See *ARSIWA*, 254; also Crawford, *GP* (n 3) 554–55; n 12. Cf on 'dispute': Christian Tomuschat, 'Article 36' in Andreas Zimmerman and others (eds), *The Statute of the International Court of Justice: A Commentary* (OUP 2012) 641–43 and authorities.

Overlapping Individual and Interstate Claims in International Law. Jessica Howley, Oxford University Press.
 DOI: 10.1093/oso/9780192871466.003.0002

procedures by which a claimant seeks a remedy for a State having breached its international obligations.

That raises, in turn, questions regarding what amounts to a breach, and what is encapsulated in the notion of a 'remedy'.

As to the former, under the law of State responsibility an 'internationally wrongful act' results from a State breaching its primary international obligations, and 'entails [its] international responsibility'.[6] Breach results from the State acting in a manner 'not in conformity with what is required of it by [an] obligation'.[7] The 'State' is, of course, an abstraction, and must operate through individual persons.[8] Rules of attribution are employed to establish when a given individual's acts are treated as the State's for the purposes of holding the State responsible for a breach of international law.[9] Identifying, in general terms, the actions of individuals or groups acting as the State's *agents* as being those for which the State bears responsibility,[10] the State is thus separated, legally speaking, from its broader population, for whose actions it is not responsible as such.[11] A State therefore breaches international law when one of the individuals for whose actions it is responsible has caused the State to act inconsistently with its obligations.

As to the latter, a remedy does not necessarily mean compensation. Rather, ARSIWA article 28 sets out that a State's 'international responsibility' 'involves

[6] *ARSIWA*, arts 1–2, also 77–85; Julio Barboza, 'Legal Injury: The Tip of the Iceberg in the Law of State Responsibility?' in Maurizio Ragazzi (ed), *International Responsibility Today: Essays in Memory of Oscar Schachter* (Martinus Nijhoff 2005) 8–9; Allain Pellet, 'The Definition of Responsibility in International Law' in James Crawford and others (eds), *The Law of International Responsibility* (OUP 2010) 9; Brigitte Stern, 'The Elements of an Internationally Wrongful Act' in Crawford and others, *Responsibility* (n 6) 194.

[7] *ARSIWA*, art 12.

[8] See Bin Cheng, *General Principles of Law as Applied by International Courts and Tribunals* (Stevens & Sons 1953) 183–84; Robert Jennings and Arthur Watts, *Oppenheim's International Law*, vol 1 (9th edn, Longman 1992) 505–6, 540; Luigi Condorelli and Claus Kress, 'The Rules of Attribution: General Considerations' in Crawford and others, *Responsibility* (n 6) 221; Crawford, *GP* (n 3) 113; Roland Portmann, *Legal Personality in International Law* (CUP 2010) 130; Djamchid Momtaz, 'Attribution of Conduct to the State: State Organs and Entities Empowered to Exercise Elements of Governmental Authority' in Crawford and others, *Responsibility* (n 6) 237; Robert McCorquodale, 'The Individual and the International Legal System' in Malcolm Evans (ed), *International Law* (4th edn, OUP 2014) 283; *ARSIWA*, 94; Stern (n 6) 202.

[9] *ARSIWA*, 91; generally arts 4–11, 91–123; Condorelli and Kress (n 8) 221; Stern (n 6) 202; Cheng (n 8) 180–81; cf Ian Brownlie, *System of the Law of Nations: State Responsibility, Part I* (Clarendon 1983) 36–37.

[10] Momtaz (n 8) 237; *ARSIWA*, 91; James Crawford, *Brownlie's Principles of Public International Law* (8th edn, OUP 2012) 542–43 ('organs or agents', though ARSIWA 'eschew ... terminology of agency'); also Crawford, *GP* (n 3) 125–26; Cheng (n 8) 184; Miles Jackson, *Complicity in International Law* (OUP 2015) 178; cf James Crawford, 'First Report on State Responsibility' (1997) 2(1) ILCYB 1 [158], [162]; Ch 6, nn 16–21.

[11] Cheng (n 8) 181–85; *ARSIWA*, 91; Eduardo Jiménez de Aréchaga, 'International Responsibility' in Max Sørensen (ed), *Manual of Public International Law* (Macmillan 1968) 558–60; also Portmann (n 8) 35–36; John Morss, *International Law as the Law of Collectives* (Ashgate 2013) 131; James Crawford, 'Multilateral Rights and Obligations in International Law' (2006) 319 RdC 325, 459–60; Ch 6, n 21.

[certain] legal consequences' in the form of secondary remedial obligations.[12] These are, relevantly,[13] obligations to:

(1) 'cease [the] act, if it is continuing', and 'offer appropriate assurances and guarantees of non-repetition' (article 30); and
(2) 'make full reparation for the injury caused by the internationally wrongful act' (article 31).[14]

There are thus two distinct categories of remedial obligations. For the second, it will be noted that States are obliged to make reparation for the 'injury' caused by the breach. The concept of 'injury' is, it is suggested, highly significant in understanding the nature and purpose of claims made under international law. The terminology of 'injury' is employed in the ARSIWA both vis-à-vis reparation as a consequence of responsibility, as just noted, but also with respect to invocation of that responsibility, a matter addressed in detail below, with both 'injured' and not 'injured' States entitled to invoke responsibility under ARSIWA articles 42 and 48 respectively.[15] However, despite employing the same terminology, as will be shown, the two notions of 'injury' are distinct.[16] These different conceptions are significant in examining what a given international claim *really* consists of, and, consequently, the potential for, and nature of, overlapping individual and interstate claims. This chapter will therefore consider the notion of 'injury' under international law in some detail.

A. Legal and factual injury

Generally speaking, the term 'injury' can describe two different concepts under international law.[17] Crawford suggests, first, that 'its natural meaning' is 'harm, material or moral, suffered by the victim as obligee or beneficiary of the obligation

12 *ARSIWA*, art 28, 191. Generally Crawford, *GP* (n 3) 459ff, 480ff; Emmanuel Roucounas, 'Non-State Actors: Areas of International Responsibility in Need of Further Exploration' in Ragazzi (n 6) 398–99; Chittharanjan Amerasinghe, *Local Remedies in International Law* (2nd edn, CUP 2004) 103.

13 Similarly: *ARSIWA*, 192; Barboza (n 6) 11. Cf Brigitte Stern, 'A Plea for "Reconstruction" of International Responsibility Based on the Notion of Legal Injury' in Ragazzi (n 6) 97–98, 104 (*inter alia* art 29 continuing performance duty not a consequence).

14 *ARSIWA*, arts 30–31(1), also 201, referencing *Factory at Chórzow (Merits)* [1928] PCIJ Rep Ser A No 17, 47.

15 nn 92, 97, 100.

16 Sections II(A)–(B), III and authorities, particularly Stern (n 13) 102–5; Stern (n 6) 196–200.

17 For the legal/factual distinction made herein, see, eg, Christian Tomuschat, 'Individuals' in Crawford and others, *Responsibility* (n 6) 985 (distinguishing 'harm in fact' and someone 'injured ... in the legal sense'); Martins Paparinskis, 'Investment Treaty Arbitration and the (New) Law of State Responsibility' (2013) 24 EJIL 617, 640 (entities '(factually) injured' in diplomatic protection); F Andrew Hessick, 'Standing, Injury in Fact and Private Rights' (2008) 93 Corn LR 275, 280; FV Garcia-Amador, 'Sixth Report on State Responsibility' (1961) 2 ILCYB 1 [27]–[28]ff, [176]; also nn 18–19, 23; Ch 3, n 52. Generally Crawford, *GP* (n 3) 55, 486–90; Stern (n 13); Stern (n 6) 194–200.

breached',[18] but acknowledges, secondly, that '"injury" involves the concept of *iniuria*—that is, infringement of rights or legally protected interests—whereas the term "damage" refers to material or other loss suffered'.[19]

The first meaning of 'injury', which might be described as 'factual injury',[20] thus refers to *damage*, or the *loss* caused by particular actions.[21] Such damage can be of different kinds in international law:

> Material damage refers to damage to property or other substantive interests of a state and its nationals which is assessable in financial terms. Moral damage encompasses two distinct concepts: moral damage to a state and moral damage to a state's nationals. Moral damage to individuals includes such things as individual pain and suffering, loss of loved ones or the personal affront associated with an intrusion into one's home or private life. Moral damage to a state refers to injury which is not financially assessable but amounts to an affront to the state, for example, a violation of its sovereignty or territorial integrity.[22]

In this book, the terms 'damage' or 'loss' are used to refer to such injury of a 'factual' nature. The identifiers 'material' and 'moral' are employed as necessary to distinguish different types of damage.

The second kind of 'injury' identified above is commonly termed 'legal injury'[23] and is that 'inherent in the violation of [a] right';[24] ie, 'injury arising from the mere fact of the breach of an international obligation'.[25] As Stern suggests, the ARSIWA's structure is both consistent with, and well explained by, recognising legal injury,[26] which assists, as will be shown, in understanding both (1) the consequences of international responsibility; and (2) when that responsibility may be invoked.[27] It is therefore very helpful in elucidating the two issues identified at the outset—*for what* claims are brought, and the *process* for making a claim.

[18] Crawford, *GP* (n 3) 490.

[19] ibid 55. Similarly Brownlie (n 9) 199; also Bernhard Graefrath, 'Responsibility and Damages Caused: Relationship between Responsibility and Damages' (1984) 185 RdC 9, 20, 35, 46–47; ALI, *Restatement of the Law: The Foreign Relations Law of the United States*, vol II (3rd edn, ALI Publishers 1987) §711, 185 ('"injury"... any loss, detriment, or damage to liberty, property, or other interest', including from breach of rules 'protecting [individual] rights or interests'); *Lusitania Cases (US/Germany)* (1923) VII UNRIAA 32, 35; discussion *Aerial Incident of July 27th, 1955 (Israel/US/UK v Bulgaria)* ICJ Pleadings, 533 (Israel).

[20] Hessick (n 17) 280–81; also Tomuschat and Paparinskis, n 17; Paul Craig, *Administrative Law* (8th edn, Sweet & Maxwell 2016) [25-045].

[21] Crawford, *GP* (n 3) 55; *ARSIWA*, art 31(2), 202, 219, referencing *Lusitania* (n 19) 39; text surrounding n 36; also Chester Brown, *A Common Law of International Adjudication* (OUP 2007) 191.

[22] Crawford, *GP* (n 3) 486–87; also *ARSIWA*, 202; *Oppenheim's* (n 8) 528 (fn 2).

[23] Eg, Stern (n 6) 199–200; authorities n 25; Barboza (n 6) 11; Stern (n 13).

[24] Stern (n 6) 199 (emphasis removed); generally Crawford, *GP* (n 3) 489–90 (discussing, *inter alia*, Stern); Graefrath (n 19) 35.

[25] Crawford, *GP* (n 3) 487; also Stern (n 13) 93 ('immaterial injury inherent in breaches of... law'). Similarly Nollkaemper (n 1) 93–95.

[26] See Stern (n 13) 98–99, 101 ('more coherent way of achieving... same objective'), 105–6; Stern (n 6) 197–200.

[27] See discussion Stern (n 13) 95–98, 100–5; Stern (n 6) 198–200.

B. Injury and the consequences of responsibility

As to, first, the consequences of responsibility, recall that responsibility exists where a State has breached its international obligations, resulting in an 'internationally wrongful act'.[28] Importantly, under the ARSIWA, this responsibility arises independently of damage having been caused; claims can thus be brought whether the claimant has suffered damage or not.[29] As Stern observes, the ILC 'eliminated injury [ie, factual injury, or damage] as a condition for responsibility, precisely so as to take account of mere breaches of the law'.[30] Unless the primary rule breached itself incorporates a damage requirement,[31] it therefore suffices that a State has acted inconsistently with its obligations—causing *legal* injury—for it to have committed an 'internationally wrongful act'.[32]

The consequences of responsibility noted above—cessation, assurances, and reparation—flow 'automatically' from such 'an internationally wrongful act'.[33] Nothing more is required for the article 30 remedial consequences: obligations to halt wrongful conduct and give assurances of non-repetition respond to breach and do not depend on whether damage was suffered.[34]

For obligations of *reparation*, article 31 provides that these arise where 'injury' is present,[35] but whether this means legal injury, in that breach would suffice, and/or factual injury, in that damage needs to be shown, is perhaps more complicated than prima facie appears. Article 31 outlines that 'injury', in the reparation context, 'includes any damage, whether material or moral, caused by the internationally wrongful act'.[36] With the use of the word 'includes' being a deliberate choice instead of 'consists of' in order to denote that 'legal wrong[s]' may occur without damage,[37] one might deduce that 'injury' in this context could mean either.[38] Nonetheless, while the existence of responsibility depends only on breach taking place (ie, *legal* injury),[39] reparation is rightly regarded as responding to damage (ie, *factual* injury),[40] even if, as noted below, it may simultaneously remedy

[28] *ARSIWA*, art 2.

[29] *ARSIWA*, 84; Crawford, *GP* (n 3) 49, 57–59; similarly Pellet (n 6) 9; Stern (n 13) 94, 100; Stern (n 6) 194; Barboza (n 6) 7–9; Graefrath (n 19) 35–36; Christian Tams, 'All's Well That Ends Well: Comments on the ILC's Articles on State Responsibility' (2002) 62 ZfaöRV 759, 766.

[30] Stern (n 13) 100; also Stern (n 6) 194 ('legal injury' the 'natural conclusion' of 'responsibility ... aris[ing] as soon as ... international obligation ... breached'), 197.

[31] *ARSIWA*, 84; Pellet (n 6) 9; see Ch 3, n 196.

[32] nn 6–7.

[33] Crawford, *GP* (n 3) 553; *ARSIWA*, 202, also 191–92, 254; de Aréchaga (n 11) 533.

[34] See Stern (n 13) 98, 102, 104–5; Stern (n 6) 199–200; Crawford, *GP* (n 3) 489; *ARSIWA*, 196 (concerns 'restoration and repair of ... legal relationship'); James Crawford, 'Fourth Report on State Responsibility' (2001) 2(1) ILCYB 1 [32]; Paparinskis (n 17) 636–37; also Olivier Corten, 'The Obligation of Cessation' in Crawford and others, *Responsibility* (n 6) 545–46; n 83.

[35] n 14.

[36] *ARSIWA*, art 31(2).

[37] Crawford, *GP* (n 3) 485, citing Crawford, 'FourthRep' (n 34) 9 (see [33]).

[38] cf Crawford, *GP* (n 3) 485–86.

[39] nn 29–32.

[40] See nn 42ff; Graefrath (n 19) 47.

both.[41] This may sound simplistic, or even obvious. However, precision regarding what a claim is responding to is essential to understanding the potential for overlapping claims and the possible application of rules of preclusion.

Turning then to reparation, article 34 of the ARSIWA addresses the matter in greater detail, explaining that '[f]ull reparation for ... injury ... shall take the form of restitution, compensation and satisfaction, either singly or in combination'.[42] Restitution requires 're-establish[ing] the situation which existed before the wrongful act';[43] compensation must be paid 'insofar as such damage is not made good by restitution';[44] and satisfaction repairs 'injury ... [that] cannot be made good by restitution or compensation'.[45] As Crawford suggests, these 'forms of reparation' are for 'material and moral damage',[46] namely types of *factual* injury.

Perhaps most obviously responding to factual injury, compensation is for 'financially assessable damage',[47] the ARSIWA commentary explaining that this 'exclude[s] compensation for ... "moral damage" to a State, i.e., the affront or injury caused by a violation of rights not associated with actual damage to property or persons'.[48] It covers a State's material damage,[49] as well as material damage to individuals,[50] including to their property and person,[51] the latter also encompassing 'non-material losses' like 'pain and suffering'.[52] Compensation is therefore for *material* damage, which is taken to include individuals' moral damage.[53]

Restitution is also a remedy primarily for material damage,[54] as evidenced by compensation usually being an alternative.[55] Restitution can be legal or material,[56] concerning respectively changing 'a legal situation',[57] and acts like returning property or persons.[58] Admittedly, '[t]he result of cessation may be indistinguishable

[41] nn 61, 85.
[42] *ARSIWA*, art 34; Crawford, *GP* (n 3) 507.
[43] *ARSIWA*, art 35.
[44] ibid art 36.
[45] ibid art 37. The types of reparation are addressed in a different order than in the ARSIWA to appreciate their relevance to different types of injury: cf Crawford, *GP* (n 3) 507–10; Brown (n 21) 191.
[46] Crawford, *GP* (n 3) 487; also Barboza (n 6) 9; Stern (n 6) 199.
[47] *ARSIWA*, art 36(2), also 219 ('actual losses incurred').
[48] ibid 218; also Brown (n 21) 191.
[49] *ARSIWA*, 221; also John Barker, 'Compensation' in Crawford and others, *Responsibility* (n 6) 604.
[50] See *ARSIWA*, 220.
[51] ibid 223, 225ff; Barker (n 49) 606–8; generally Brown (n 21) 199–208.
[52] Crawford, *GP* (n 3) 517; also *ARSIWA*, 223; Barker (n 49) 604–5.
[53] See Gateano Arangio-Ruiz, 'Second Report on State Responsibility' (1989) 2(1) ILCYB 1 [4], [7]; Barboza (n 6) 9; FV Garcia-Amador, 'State Responsibility: Some New Problems' (1958) 94 RdC 365, 475–76; Yann Kerbrat, 'Interaction Between the Forms of Reparation' in Crawford and others, *Responsibility* (n 6) 580.
[54] See Garcia-Amador (n 53) 475; Barboza (n 6) 9; Kerbrat (n 53) 580; Barker (n 49) 601.
[55] James Crawford, 'Third Report on State Responsibility' (2000) 2(1) ILCYB 3 [130]; *ARSIWA*, 219, quoting *Chórzow (Merits)* (n 14) 47; Elisabeth Zoller, *Peacetime Unilateral Remedies: An Analysis of Countermeasures* (Transnational 1984) 65.
[56] Christine Gray, 'Restitution' in Crawford and others, *Responsibility* (n 6) 590; Crawford, *GP* (n 3) 511; Graefrath (n 19) 77.
[57] Crawford, *GP* (n 3) 512; *ARSIWA*, 214–15; Gray (n 56) 591.
[58] Crawford, *GP* (n 3) 465, 511; *ARSIWA*, 214–15; also Gray (n 56) 590.

from restitution' in certain cases,[59] notwithstanding the suggestion above that cessation responds to *legal* injury,[60] given that restitution 'necessarily includ[es] a return to legality'.[61] However, while restitution may thus encompass cessation, the two are not the same.[62] Cessation only applies to continuing breaches,[63] while restitution operates even vis-à-vis terminated obligations,[64] and, where 'wrongful conduct produces broader effects, the reversal of those effects falls within the obligation of restitution'.[65] Cessation therefore responds to breach (ie, *legal* injury), while restitution is for material damage (ie, *factual* injury).[66]

Finally, satisfaction:

> is the remedy for those injuries, not financially assessable, which amount to an affront to the State. These injuries are frequently of a symbolic character, arising from the very fact of the breach of the obligation, irrespective of its material consequences.[67]

It therefore remedies a State's *moral* damage.[68] Examples of forms of satisfaction include acknowledgement, apology, and 'symbolic damages'.[69] Declarations may provide satisfaction, but 'are not intrinsically associated with the remedy'.[70]

It is sometimes suggested that satisfaction responds to breach, and can thus repair a State's legal injury.[71] However, as Crawford observes, 'the position taken in

[59] *ARSIWA*, 197; also Crawford, *GP* (n 3) 465; Gray (n 56) 590; Stern (n 13) 104; Barboza (n 6) 13–14; Graefrath (n 19) 84.

[60] n 34.

[61] Stern (n 13) 104, referencing Crawford, 'ThirdRep' (n 55) [131]; see *ARSIWA*, art 35. Similarly Barboza (n 6) 13–15.

[62] See Crawford, *GP* (n 3) 468; cf Barboza (n 6) 13–16; Christine Gray, 'Remedies' in Cesare Romano, Karen Alter, and Yuval Shany (eds), *The Oxford Handbook of International Adjudication* (OUP 2014) 879; Antonios Tzanakopoulos, *Disobeying the Security Council: Countermeasures Against Wrongful Sanctions* (OUP 2011) 143.

[63] Corten (n 34) 547; *Avena and Other Mexican Nationals (Mexico v US) (Judgment)* [2004] ICJ Rep 12 [148], discussed Crawford, *GP* (n 3) 464; also Graefrath (n 19) 73–74.

[64] Crawford, 'ThirdRep' (n 55) [132].

[65] Crawford, *GP* (n 3) 468, citing *Jurisdictional Immunities (Germany v Italy: Greece Intervening) (Judgment)* [2012] ICJ Rep 99 [137], also 465, citing Corten (n 34) 548; Xavier-Baptiste Ruedin, *Exécution Des Arrêts de La Court Européenne Des Droits de l'homme* (Helbing Lichtenhahn 2009) [404]; Graefrath (n 19) 77; cf discussion Barboza (n 6) 13–15.

[66] See nn 34, 54.

[67] *ARSIWA*, 231; also de Aréchaga (n 11) 572.

[68] *ARSIWA*, 218; also Crawford, *GP* (n 3) 527; Garcia-Amador (n 53) 476; de Aréchaga (n 11) 572; Brown (n 21) 192.

[69] *ARSIWA*, 232–33; also Crawford, *GP* (n 3) 527–28; Garcia-Amador (n 53) 476; Eric Wyler and Alain Papaux, 'Satisfaction' in Crawford and others, *Responsibility* (n 6) 630–33.

[70] *ARSIWA*, 233; also Crawford, *GP* (n 3) 529–30. They may repair legal injury: Barboza (n 6) 18–19; discussion Garcia-Amador (n 17) [57]–[61].

[71] See Crawford, *GP* (n 3) 487, citing, *inter alia*, *The Rainbow Warrior Affair* (1990) XX UNRIAA 215 [122], also quoted *ARSIWA*, 232 ('moral or legal damage'); discussion Arangio-Ruiz (n 53) [14], [106], [111], with authorities; Barboza (n 6) 17; Wyler and Papaux (n 69) 626–28, quoting (fn 18) Crawford, 'ThirdRep' (n 55) [181] ('"moral damage" ... the fact of ... breach'); also Garcia-Amador (n 17) [16]–[17], [42]. Cf Graefrath (n 19) 43, 46.

the ARSIWA is clearly that satisfaction is available to make good moral damage and not to remedy the mere breach of an international obligation.'[72] As he notes, satisfaction is described as 'rather exceptional',[73] awarded consequent on, *inter alia*, violating sovereignty, attacking vessels or aircraft, and mistreating officials or embassies.[74] If moral damage resulted from every breach, satisfaction would not be reserved for such violations, nor be 'exceptional'.[75] Rather, moral injury to the State, even if 'arising from the very fact of ... breach', must 'amount to an affront';[76] ie, cause 'offence to [the State's] dignity, honour or prestige'.[77] A State's moral injury, remedied through satisfaction, is therefore factual in nature.[78]

Factual injury (ie, damage) may thus be material or moral, whether suffered by States or individuals. Reparation—restitution, compensation, and satisfaction—is for these kinds of damage.[79] Crawford has suggested that legal injury thus has no place in the ARSIWA,[80] *inter alia* because '[i]t would not be logical [under article 31] to require "full reparation for ... injury" including "legal injury" where none of the available forms of reparation can address that type of damage.'[81] Nonetheless, as noted, article 31 uses the word 'includes', suggesting that legal injury is implicitly acknowledged.[82] As Stern suggests, it is cessation and assurances of non-repetition that respond to such injury.[83] Moreover, even if reparation is strictly for factual injury (damage), such injury presupposes legal injury (breach),[84] and, as already noted vis-à-vis restitution, reparation may simultaneously repair both.[85] Thus, obligations of reparation arise vis-à-vis damage (ie, *factual* injury), even if the ARSIWA recognise breach (or *legal* injury) as enlivening responsibility. The international claims with which this book are concerned thus necessarily respond to breach (*legal* injury) and will seek a remedy for that breach, whether for the legal injury alone (cessation and/or assurances and guarantees of non-repetition) or for the factual injury (damage) which has been suffered (seeking restitution, compensation, and/or satisfaction, as appropriate).[86]

[72] Crawford, *GP* (n 3) 487–88, also 58.
[73] ibid 488, 527; *ARSIWA*, 231.
[74] *ARSIWA*, 232; also Wyler and Papaux (n 69) 625; Garcia-Amador (n 17) [45]ff; Stephan Wittich, 'Direct Injury and the Incidence of the Local Remedies Rule' (2000) 5 Aust Rev I & EL 121, 156–57.
[75] Similarly Barboza (n 6) 17–18; cf Wittich (n 74) 155–57.
[76] n 67; also Crawford, *GP* (n 3) 488.
[77] Arangio-Ruiz (n 53) [14] (though apparently considering offence flows from legal injury; report discussed *RW Affair* (n 71) [122]); also Barboza (n 6) 17–18; Wittich (n 74) 155–56; Wyler and Papaux (n 69) 625 ('classic approach'), cf 626–28.
[78] nn 20–22.
[79] nn 20, 22, 46; also Raphaele Rivier, 'Inter-American Mechanisms' in Crawford and others, *Responsibility* (n 6) 747–48.
[80] See Crawford, *GP* (n 3) 487–91; cf Nollkaemper (n 1) 93.
[81] Crawford, *GP* (n 3) 488. Further n 110. Cf Barboza (n 6) 9.
[82] nn 36–38.
[83] Stern (n 13) 104–5; Stern (n 6) 199–200. Similarly Graefrath (n 19) 47, 72–73; also Crawford, *GP* (n 3) 489.
[84] Stern (n 6) 199; nn 6, 14.
[85] n 61; Barboza (n 6) 18 (reparation also remedies legal injury); similarly Stern (n 6) 199–200.
[86] See nn 139–42.

These conceptions of breach, damage, and reparation assist in understanding a claim's purpose, the consequences that attach to different parts of a claim, and how far separate claims might overlap—whether they respond to the same breach or claim for the same damage, for example. In turn, this assists in determining the operation of rules of preclusion: the rule precluding double recovery is, for instance, concerned with not repairing damage (*factual* injury) twice, while waiver focuses on whose rights are violated by the underlying breach (*legal* injury).[87] Reference to breach (legal injury) and damage (factual injury) as elements of international claims will therefore recur throughout this book.

III. The process for bringing international claims: invocation of responsibility

While obligations to cease conduct, and make assurances and reparation may result 'automatically' from breach,[88] practically speaking, the State's responsibility must be *invoked*.[89] As explained above, an invocation of responsibility is an assertion that a breach must be remedied.[90] This is what takes place when a claim is made.

In terms of process, two key issues arise: *who* may invoke responsibility, and *how* they may do so. As to the first, unless *lex specialis* rules provide otherwise,[91] 'injured' States may, pursuant to ARSIWA article 42, invoke responsibility when they are owed obligations 'individually'.[92] This reflects a bilateral assumption of obligations by one State towards another,[93] akin to under domestic private law.[94] In such cases, the latter State is in possession of a 'right' in the sense famously explained by Hohfeld.[95]

States are also entitled to invoke responsibility vis-à-vis group obligations, in three situations.[96] Pursuant to the rule reflected in ARSIWA article 48, a 'State other than an injured State' may invoke responsibility for breach of (1) obligations

[87] See Chs 4 and 5.
[88] n 33.
[89] Crawford, *GP* (n 3) 553; *ARSIWA*, 254.
[90] nn 4–5.
[91] *ARSIWA*, art 55, 255–56.
[92] ibid art 42, see 257–60. Generally Crawford, *GP* (n 3) 542–46.
[93] Joost Pauwelyn, 'A Typology of Multilateral Treaty Obligations: Are WTO Obligations Bilateral or Collective in Nature?' (2003) 14 EJIL 907, 916.
[94] Crawford, *Brownlie's* (n 10) 16; Anthea Roberts, 'Triangular Treaties: The Extent and Limits of Investment Treaty Rights' (2015) 56 Harv ILJ 353, 374; Pauwelyn (n 93) 909.
[95] ie, A owes B an obligation; B has a corresponding right that A's duty be performed: Wesley Newcomb Hohfeld, *Fundamental Legal Conceptions as Applied in Judicial Reasoning and Other Legal Essays* (Yale UP 1923) 38; authorities n 133; Ch 4, n 150. Similarly Nollkaemper (n 1) 98–99; Tams (n 29) 776; Bruno Simma, 'From Bilateralism to Community Interest in International Law' (1994) 250 RdC 217, 231–32 ('bilateralism').
[96] See Crawford, *GP* (n 3) 546; Pauwelyn (n 93) 917–22 ('collective' obligations); also Tom Ruys, 'Sanctions, Retorsions and Countermeasures: Concepts and International Legal Framework' [2016] <https://papers.ssrn.com/sol3/papers.cfm?abstract_id=2760853>, 14.

'owed to a group', including it, in the 'collective interest' (*erga omnes partes* obligations), or (2) owed to 'the international community as a whole' (*erga omnes* obligations).[97] Article 48 provides 'public interest' rules of standing,[98] vis-à-vis obligations more akin to domestic public law rules.[99] States may also claim (3) as 'injured' under article 42, even where such obligations are concerned, either where breach of an obligation owed to a group 'specially affects' them, or where breach 'radically . . . change[s] the position' of a group of State obligees.[100]

In addition to States, other subjects of international law may invoke responsibility in certain circumstances, including individuals.[101] As Chapter 2 elaborates, individual claims mechanisms are usually treaty-based and appear most prominently, though not exclusively, in the human rights and investment law fields.

As to *how* claims are made, an applicant should give the respondent notice of the claim,[102] and meet any admissibility hurdles, including requirements as to exhaustion of local remedies, discussed in Chapter 3.[103] Importantly, invocation may be undertaken through any 'form[] of lawful dispute settlement',[104] judicial or otherwise.[105] As noted in the Introduction, the claims with which we are concerned are thus not limited to those brought before international tribunals, but include any allegation of breach coupled with seeking of a remedy.[106] This significantly broadens the circumstances in which overlapping individual and interstate claims might arise, providing a wide base of practice on which to draw in analysing the potential operation of rules of preclusion.

[97] *ARSIWA*, art 48, see 277–78. Generally Crawford, *GP* (n 3) 545–53. While art 48(2)(b) was 'progressive development' (*ARSIWA*, 279; Crawford, *GP* (n 3) 555), *erga omnes (partes)* standing is well-established: see ibid 549, 551, referencing *Barcelona Traction, Light and Power Company (Belgium v Spain)* [1970] ICJ Rep 3 [33]–[34] and see Ch 2(III)(B); Weiss (n 4) 803–4. Apparently recognising art 48(2)(b): *Cyprus v Turkey (Just Satisfaction)* ECHR 2014-II 245 (GC) [45]–[46], discussed Ch 4, nn 365, 625–27.

[98] Crawford, *GP* (n 3) 551; also James Crawford, 'Chance, Order, Change: The Course of International Law' (2013) 365 RdC 9, 199; Jost Delbrück, '"Laws in the Public Interest" – Some Observations on the Foundations and Identification of *Erga Omnes* Norms in International Law' in Volkmar Götz, Peter Selmer, and Rüdiger Wolfrum (eds), *Liber amicorum Günther Jaenicke – Zum 85. Geburtstag* (Springer 1998) 17ff; Pauwelyn (n 93) 918–19. Generally Nollkaemper (n 1) 92–93.

[99] See Pauwelyn (n 93) 909 (criminal/constitutional law); Crawford, *GP* (n 3) 551 (domestic analogy); Weiss (n 4) 808–9; Philip Jessup, *A Modern Law of Nations* (Archon 1968) 10–12; Crawford, *Brownlie's* (n 10) 17; generally Mark Elliott and Jason Varuhas, *Administrative Law: Text and Materials* (5th edn, OUP 2017) 545–68; Timothy Endicott, *Administrative Law* (4th edn, OUP 2018) Ch 11; Craig (n 20) [25-009], [25-034]–[25-049]; Hessick (n 17) 293ff; L Neville Brown and John Bell, *French Administrative Law* (5th edn, Clarendon 1998) 166–69, 181; Mahendra Singh, *German Administrative Law in Comparative Perspective* (Springer 2001) 216–18 (UK/India/US), cf 214–16, 218 (Germany).

[100] *ARSIWA*, arts 42(b)(i)–(ii), see 257, 259–60; Pauwelyn (n 93) 919; Ruys (n 96) 14.

[101] See *ARSIWA*, art 33, 209–10; Ch 2(I).

[102] *ARSIWA*, art 43(1), 261–62.

[103] ibid art 44, see Ch 3(I)(B).

[104] ILC, 'Draft Articles on Diplomatic Protection with Commentaries' (2006) 2(2) ILCYB 22 (DADP), 27; also *ARSIWA*, 256; Crawford, *GP* (n 3) 541, 554.

[105] DADP, 27; similarly *ARSIWA*, 256. The reaching of a settlement is taken herein to attest that responsibility has been so invoked: see particularly Ch 5.

[106] cf *ARSIWA*, art 43(2) and 262–63 (no obligation to indicate remedy sought).

A. 'Injury' and the invocation of State responsibility

As with the consequences of State responsibility discussed above, the terminology of 'injury' appears in respect of its invocation: States are able to invoke responsibility when they are 'injured' (under article 42) and, in certain circumstances, when they are not 'injured' (under article 48).[107] Again, the ARSIWA make no distinction here between legal and factual injury.[108] However, unlike vis-à-vis reparation, it is suggested here that States invoking responsibility are responding to breach of an obligation owed to them (ie, *legal* injury), rather than to damage (ie, *factual* injury).[109] Just as in respect of the consequences of responsibility noted above, clarifying what 'injury' means in this context is important in understanding precisely for what a claim is being brought.

It is true, as Crawford suggests, that 'if injury [under the ARSIWA] did include "legal injury" due to the mere fact of breach, then what the ARSIWA define as a "State other than an injured State" [ie, under article 48] would suffer "injury", a terminological inconsistency'.[110] However, such a focus on terminology is misplaced: if damage (factual injury) is not, as noted above, required for international responsibility to arise, then it is possible for both 'injured' States (under article 42) and States other than injured States (under article 48) not to be 'injured' in a factual sense, and yet still meet the requirements of 'injury' for invocation purposes.[111] For example, a State is 'injured' for the purposes of invoking State responsibility pursuant to article 42(a) if a bilateral treaty obligation owed to it is breached; it need not suffer any material damage whatsoever,[112] and moral damage is not, as noted, presumed to result from breach alone.[113] Article 42 'injured' States may well generally suffer, and claim reparation for, some kind of material or moral damage.[114] However, such damage is not essential: they need not necessarily be

[107] nn 92, 97, 100.

[108] cf Pt II(A); Wittich (n 74) 127–28.

[109] nn 111ff; particularly Stern, nn 114, 115, 118; also Nollkaemper (n 1) 93 (States 'invoke responsibility if... legally injured'). Cf, vis-à-vis individuals, Ch 4, n 158; Ch 6, nn 94–97.

[110] Crawford, *GP* (n 3) 488.

[111] Giorgio Gaja, 'The Concept of an Injured State' in Crawford and others, *Responsibility* (n 6) 942; Crawford, *GP* (n 3) 547 (on art 42(b)(ii)); discussion Gateano Arangio-Ruiz, 'Fourth Report on State Responsibility' [1992] 2(1) ILCYB 1 [129]. Stern (n 6) 194 makes a related point (see n 30), but apparently considers that art 42 States must be *factually* injured: ibid 200; similarly Stern (n 13), quoted n 114. See nn 28–32.

[112] See Gaja, 'Concept' (n 111) 942; also n 119; *ARSIWA*, 257. Eg, *Oil Platforms (Iran v USA) (Judgment)* [2003] ICJ Rep 161 [108]–[109], [120] (third-State vessel attacks allegedly violating bilateral treaty obligations), discussed Annemarieke Vermeer-Künzli, 'A Matter of Interest: Diplomatic Protection and State Responsibility *Erga Omnes*' (2007) 56 ICLQ 553, 572; *Case concerning the Air Service Agreement of 27 March 1946 (USA v France)* (1978) XVIII UNRIAA 417 [39] ('vacated' orders '*would* inflict... injury'). Cf Stern (n 6) 196, 200.

[113] nn 71–78; Barboza (n 6) 17–18.

[114] Stern (n 13) 102 (art 42 States 'injured both from ... legal perspective (legal injury) and in other ways (material and/or moral injury)'; art 48 States 'only suffer legal injury'); similarly Stern (n 6) 200; Crawford quoted n 136; also Gaja, 'Concept' (n 111) 942; Wyler and Papaux (n 69) 627.

factually injured to be 'injured' for the purposes of article 42. What 'injured' States *will* necessarily have suffered is *legal* injury: an international obligation owed to them has been breached, and it is this to which the invocation of responsibility responds.[115]

What about States other than injured States (article 48 States)? Such States have not suffered material or moral damage—if they did, they would be specially affected 'injured' States under article 42—and they cannot, therefore, claim reparation for themselves.[116] They can only claim reparation 'in the interest of the injured State or of the beneficiaries of the obligation breached'.[117] Again, as Stern suggests, it is 'legal injury' that explains why States may invoke responsibility under article 48 at all: they too have had an international obligation owed to them breached, and invoke responsibility in response, though they have not incurred factual injury (damage).[118]

There is undoubtedly a distinction in the *kinds* of obligations with which articles 42 and 48 are concerned.[119] Under article 42 the obligation is bilateral, or the injured State is treated as being in that position.[120] Some suggest that under article 48, States have only a 'performance interest' in the relevant obligation,[121] which is owed not to them but to the 'collective'.[122] Accordingly, States would have a purely 'procedural right' to invoke responsibility.[123] By definition, however, obligations *erga omnes (partes)* are owed *to* someone: either the international community or a group of States.[124] As there is no 'legal person, the international community',[125] such obligations are better considered owed to the States *within* the

[115] See Stern (n 13) 96, 102; Stern (n 6) 196–99; also Gaja, 'Concept' (n 111) 942.

[116] See nn 114, 136; Ch 2, n 120; Ch 3, nn 217–18; Wittich (n 74) 128–29; Nollkaemper (n 1) 94; also Amerasinghe (n 12) 418–19; cf Giorgio Gaja, 'States Having an Interest in Compliance with the Obligation Breached' in Crawford and others, *Responsibility* (n 6) 961.

[117] *ARSIWA*, art 48(2)(b); also Stern (n 13) 105; Gaja, 'Concept' (n 111) 942; Crawford, *GP* (n 3) 67; Tams (n 29) 781; Ch 3, n 218, Ch 4, nn 387–88.

[118] Stern (n 6) 196–98; cf Crawford, *GP* (n 3) 490; Stern (n 13) 96, 102; Weiss (n 4) 803; also Gaja, 'Concept' (n 111) 942; Barboza (n 6) 21. Disagreeing with Stern's use of 'legal injury', but accepting that art 48 States 'are legally affected by ... breaches of obligations *erga omnes*': Crawford, *GP* (n 3) 489.

[119] Gaja, 'Concept' (n 111) 942; Wyler and Papaux (n 69) 626 ('injured' State recognised not 'by the nature and ... characteristics of ... damage suffered' but 'characteristics of the obligation breached'); also Tams (n 29) 773. On the public/private rights distinction: Jean Thomas, *Public Rights, Private Relations* (OUP 2015) 114ff; Hessick (n 17) 279–81.

[120] Gaja, 'Compliance' (n 116) 958; James Crawford, *International Law as an Open System* (Cameron May 2002) 337–40, also 317–18; Crawford, 'Multilateral' (n 11) 445–46.

[121] Crawford, 'Multilateral' (n 11) 434, also 446.

[122] Crawford, 'Chance' (n 98) 202; also Crawford, 'Multilateral' (n 11) 432–39, 442–46; Anne Peters, *Beyond Human Rights: The Legal Status of the Individual in International Law* (Jonathan Huston tr, CUP 2016) 475. Cf Crawford, *System* (n 120) 172, 327–29.

[123] Crawford, 'Multilateral' (n 11) 437; Crawford, 'ThirdRep' (n 55) [85].

[124] See *ARSIWA*, art 48(1); Gaja, 'Compliance' (n 116) 957; also Crawford, 'Multilateral' (n 11) 436; Crawford, 'FirstRep' (n 10) [123], [125]; Crawford, *System* (n 120) 331, cf 349.

[125] Crawford, 'Multilateral' (n 11) 447; also Crawford, *System* (n 120) 344–45; Crawford, *Brownlie's* (n 10) 17; Martin Dawidowicz, 'Public Law Enforcement without Public Law Safeguards? ...' (2007) 77 BYBIL 333, 342; Giorgio Gaja, 'The Protection of General Interests in the International Community' (2012) 364 RdC 9, 25–31; Gaja, 'Compliance' (n 116) 958.

relevant group or community,[126] as well as, sometimes, to other entities, including individuals.[127] For instance, while human rights treaties embody obligations *erga omnes partes*,[128] they are nonetheless still treaties, 'creat[ing] rights and obligations between their parties to the effect that any State party is obliged as against any other State party to perform its obligations'.[129] Such treaties do 'not give rise *only* to a set of bilateral obligations',[130] and may even create individual rights.[131] However, as Judge Weeramantry has suggested, '[a]n *erga omnes* right is ... a series of separate rights *erga singulum* ... With the violation by any State of the obligation so lying upon it, the rights enjoyed *erga omnes* become opposable *erga singulum* to the State so acting.'[132] In Hohfeldian terms, a State's right has still been violated by breach of an obligation owed *erga omnes (partes)*.[133]

Rather than considering article 48 States as not injured but nonetheless able to invoke responsibility, they are therefore better considered as 'merely States which are injured differently'.[134] Whenever a State invokes responsibility, under either article 42 or article 48, it does so because it has suffered *legal* injury: an obligation owed to it has been breached.[135] Thus used, 'legal injury' is simply a 'convenient shorthand' describing breach entitling invocation of responsibility.[136] Which entity suffers such injury turns on who holds the 'right' breached.[137]

[126] Gaja, 'Compliance' (n 116) 957–58; similarly Simma (n 95) 310, 314–15, 370; Vermeer-Künzli (n 112) 579; Wittich (n 74) 128; Stern (n 6) 196–99; also Crawford, 'FirstRep' (n 10) [117]; Crawford, *System* (n 120) 338 ('privy'), 349–50; cf Gaja, 'Compliance' (n 116) 25.

[127] See Crawford, *System* (n 120) 349–52 (cf 352), 358, 410–11; Gaja, 'Compliance' (n 116) 24–25; Simma (n 95) 234; Weiss (n 4) 804; Crawford, 'Multilateral' (n 11) 446–47; eg, individuals vis-à-vis human rights: Crawford, *System* (n 120) 333; Gaja, 'Compliance' (n 116) 25; Silvia Borelli and Simon Olleson, 'Obligations Relating to Human Rights and Humanitarian Law' in Crawford and others, *Responsibility* (n 6) 1195; Ch 3, n 78.

[128] Ch 2, n 216.

[129] Simma (n 95) 370, discussion 364–75; similarly Borelli and Olleson (n 126) 1184–85; also Federica Paddeu, *Justification and Excuse in International Law* (CUP 2018) 279 (fn 301); Roucounas (n 12) 398–99; Anthea Roberts, 'State-to-State Investment Treaty Arbitration: A Hybrid Theory of Interdependent Rights and Shared Interpretative Authority' (2014) 55 Harv ILJ 1, 34.

[130] Gaja, 'Compliance' (n 116) 959 (emphasis added).

[131] n 127; Ch 3, n 78; Ch 4, n 156.

[132] *East Timor (Portugal v Australia) (Judgment)* [1995] ICJ Rep 90, 172 (Diss Op Weeramantry), quoted Crawford, *System* (n 120) 325; criticised James Crawford, 'The Relationship between Sanctions and Countermeasures' in Vera Gowlland-Debbas (ed), *United Nations Sanctions and International Law* (Kluwer 2001) 63–64.

[133] n 95; cf Crawford, 'ThirdRep' (n 55) [84].

[134] Stern (n 6) 197, also 196. See Crawford, *GP* (n 3) 489–90 (discussing Stern's approach). Cf Linos-Alexandre Sicilianos, 'Countermeasures in Response to Grave Violations of Obligations Owed to the International Community' in Crawford and others, *Responsibility* (n 6) 1138–39.

[135] Authorities n 115; cf Nollkaemper (n 1) 172–73.

[136] Crawford, *GP* (n 3) 489, see 489–90 ('Although a convenient shorthand ... what is at issue [under art 48] is ... breach of an obligation ... not caus[ing] material or moral damage'). Crawford's concern about revisiting 'the outdated bilateral conception of relations between States' (ibid 490) is overstated: see Stern (n 6) 197–98; Stern (n 13) 100–1. Crawford also objects that using 'injury' legally 'conflicts with its natural meaning' (Crawford, *GP* (n 3) 490), but see n 19.

[137] Nollkaemper (n 1) 93, 98–99; also Peters (n 121) 167–69, 172–73, discussing *ARSIWA*, 209–10, 192–93; Graefrath (n 19) 47; Crawford, *GP* (n 3) 548–49.

Recognising legal injury in this way helpfully[138] shows that States 'can be injured in different ways, material, moral or legal', and that different remedial consequences follow.[139] Article 42 and 48 States may claim cessation and assurances in response to breach of obligations owed to them (legal injury).[140] An 'injured' article 42 State may, if it has suffered damage (factual injury), additionally claim reparation in the form of restitution, compensation, and/or satisfaction, as appropriate.[141] Article 48 States do not suffer such factual injury and may never claim such reparation for themselves; they may claim only, as noted, for the obligation's beneficiaries who have incurred damage.[142]

For individuals, it is possible that they might also incur 'legal injury' through breach of obligations owed to them under international law.[143] However, as later chapters elaborate, significant debate surrounds whether individuals are owed such obligations—and to what extent they are merely granted the procedural possibility to invoke responsibility for breach of interstate obligations.[144] The distinction influences the operation of rules of preclusion, certain of which can only apply where the same rights are invoked in overlapping claims.[145] These matters are addressed in the relevant chapters. The important point here is that it is theoretically possible for individuals to suffer legal injury through breach of an obligation owed to them. It is also undoubtedly possible, as later chapters elucidate, for individuals to suffer factual injury, or damage, resulting from breach, regardless of to whom the relevant obligations are owed.[146]

IV. Circumstances precluding wrongfulness

The final aspect of the law of State responsibility considered here is circumstances precluding wrongfulness. There are six such circumstances contained in the ARSIWA, which, where applicable to a given situation, allow States to raise 'a shield against an otherwise well-founded claim for the breach of an international obligation';[147] in simpler terms, a 'defence' to such a claim.[148]

[138] See Stern (n 13) 105 ('useful'). Ultimately, the outcome under the ARSIWA is unaffected: Stern (n 6) 197–98; also Crawford, *GP* (n 3) 489–90.

[139] Stern (n 6) 198–99; also Stern (n 13) 101–5; Arangio-Ruiz (n 111) 6–7 (cessation/non-repetition protect 'primary legal relationship', other remedies 'erase … injurious consequences … material or moral'). Cf Nollkaemper (n 1) 172–73.

[140] Stern (n 6) 198–200; similarly Stern (n 13) 102; Crawford, *GP* (n 3) 489–90.

[141] Stern (n 6) 199–200; Stern (n 13) 102.

[142] n 117.

[143] Nollkaemper (n 1) 98–99; also Peters (n 122) 167, 172–73, 338, 388; Crawford, *GP* (n 3) 548–49.

[144] Ch 2, n 8; Ch 4, nn 152–58; Ch 6, nn 94–98.

[145] See Chs 4–6 and see Introduction, nn 91–92; generally Paparinskis (n 17); Martins Paparinskis, 'Analogies and Other Regimes of International Law' in Zachary Douglas, Joost Pauwelyn, and Jorge Viñuales (eds), *The Foundations of International Investment Law* (OUP 2014).

[146] See Ch 3, n 152; generally Ch 3(II)(C).

[147] *ARSIWA*, 160.

[148] cf Paddeu (n 129) 7.

Consent, countermeasures, and self-defence provide the focus. Unlike the other circumstances precluding wrongfulness—*force majeure*, distress, and necessity[149]—these circumstances are necessarily invoked in response to an entity's 'conduct'.[150] They cannot be the result of, for instance, natural forces.[151] They are therefore the appropriate focus for a book concerned with the effects of one entity's conduct on another's ability to invoke responsibility.

In theory, circumstances precluding wrongfulness should be invocable vis-à-vis not only interstate claims but also individual claims under international law.[152] States have invoked various such circumstances to defend themselves against claims brought by individuals, and tribunals have examined whether the conditions for their operation were met.[153] However, as will be seen, applying what are traditionally interstate defences in the 'triangular'[154] situation of overlapping individual and interstate claims, involving two States *and* an individual, raises issues regarding how far the claims of one entity can be affected by the conduct of another which has led to the invocation of a defence.[155]

Pursuant to the ARSIWA, while relying on circumstances precluding wrongfulness, States are viewed as not in breach of their obligations at all.[156] Both legal and factual injury are avoided, the consequences of responsibility, including obligations of reparation, do not arise, and no invocation is possible.[157] This approach is, however, somewhat simplistic, unduly discounting scholarly discussion regarding how different circumstances operate, including whether certain circumstances are better conceptualised as 'justifications', where the relevant conduct is considered legal (and therefore not in breach of an obligation), and others as 'excuses', vis-à-vis which certain consequences of responsibility might still follow.[158]

149 Generally *ARSIWA*, arts 23–25.

150 James Crawford, 'Second Report on State Responsibility' (1999) 2(1) ILCYB 1 [278]; also *ARSIWA*, 178; cf Paddeu (n 129) 84–85, 120–22, 125–26.

151 See, eg, Roberto Ago, 'Eighth Report on State Responsibility (Addendum)' (1980) 2(1) ILCYB 13, 44 (fn 143) (necessity vis-à-vis natural phenomena); Ian Brownlie, *International Law and the Use of Force by States* (OUP 1963) 376; also Paddeu (n 129) 85.

152 See Paparinskis (n 17) 629–35; Martins Paparinskis, 'Investment Arbitration and the Law of Countermeasures' (2008) 79 BYBIL 264; cf, eg, Zachary Douglas, 'The Hybrid Foundations of Investment Treaty Arbitration' (2004) 74 BYBIL 151, particularly 184–89.

153 Countermeasures: cases discussed Ch 6, nn 91ff. Necessity: cases discussed Ch 6, n 499. *Force majeure*: *LAFICO v Burundi* (1991) 96 ILR 279 [56], cited *ARSIWA*, 173; *Autopista v Venezuela (Jurisdiction)* (2001) 16 ICSID Rev-FILJ 469 [107]–[129]; *Greentech Energy v Italy (Final Award)* SCC Arbitration V (2015/095) (23 December 2018) [451]; *Güriş and Yamantürk v Syria (Final Award)* ICC Case No 21845/ZF/AYZ (31 August 2020) [315]–[322] all noted Vladislav Djanic, 'Looking Back: High-Profile Tribunal . . .' *IA Rep* (2 September 2021).

154 Terminology borrowed from Roberts (n 94). See also Peters (n 122) 169.

155 Introduction, n 62. Cf Crawford, *GP* (n 3) 319–20, discussing ILC, 'Summary Records of the Meetings of the Fifty-First Session' (1999) 1 ILCYB 1, 174; Paddeu (n 129) 79, 92–93.

156 Sandra Szurek, 'The Notion of Circumstances Precluding Wrongfulness' in Crawford and others, *Responsibility* (n 6) 434; Crawford, *GP* (n 3) 275; Paddeu (n 129) 108, cf 37–52, 61–62 (ILC unclear).

157 See Szurek (n 156) 435–36; also Paddeu (n 129) 64–65, 71–72, 82, 107–10; Crawford, *GP* (n 3) 275.

158 See Crawford, *GP* (n 3) 278–80, 319; and extensive discussion Paddeu (n 129), particularly 11–12, 23, 49–50, 61–66, 77–94, 100–28, generally Chs 1–3 (distinction), Chs 4–7 (different circumstances);

This issue has been extensively considered elsewhere, and therefore is not addressed in depth here.[159] Among the distinction's possible practical implications,[160] only one is particularly relevant: some have suggested that, because for justifications there is no wrongful conduct at all, while for excuses the conduct is still wrongful though excused, there may continue to be an obligation to repair damage in the latter case.[161] The possible implications for overlapping individual and interstate claims are considered in the Conclusion to this book, once the circumstances themselves are addressed in Chapters 5 and 6.

V. Conclusion: overlapping claims and gaps in the State responsibility framework

The foregoing has set out the general framework for State responsibility as relevant to the overlapping claims that are the focus of this book. It has addressed the basis for responsibility, its consequences and invocation, and how circumstances precluding wrongfulness operate. Notably, an interstate invocation of responsibility necessarily responds to a State's alleged legal injury. Whether or not individuals *also* suffer such injury, it is important to realise that obligations are *always* owed on the interstate level.[162] Consequently, whenever an individual can claim, one or more States must also be entitled to invoke responsibility for breach,[163] meaning *every* individual claim gives rise to at least one (and possibly several) overlapping interstate claims. International claims also seek a remedy, whether that be solely for legal injury (cessation and/or assurances of non-repetition) or factual injury in the form of reparation for material or moral damage.

Szurek (n 156) 435–36; Vaughan Lowe, 'Precluding Wrongfulness or Responsibility: A Plea for Excuses' (1999) 10 EJIL 405.

159 Authorities n 158, particularly Paddeu (n 129).

160 Paddeu (n 129) Ch 2; also Lowe (n 158) 410–11.

161 See Lowe (n 158) 406–9; Paddeu (n 129) 77–94.

162 See Amerasinghe (n 12) 47, 152, 164, 308–9; Paparinskis (n 152) 288–91; Hugh Thirlway, *The Law and Procedure of the International Court of Justice: Fifty Years of Jurisprudence* (OUP 2013) 1554; Kate Parlett, *The Individual in the International Legal System: Continuity and Change in International Law* (CUP 2011) 359–65, 370–72, discussing *inter alia* an earlier edition of McCorquodale (n 8) 286, also 292; Nigel White and Ademola Abass, 'Countermeasures and Sanctions' in Evans (n 8) 537; Jessup (n 99) 17; Peters (n 122) 169, cf 475; Roberts (n 129) 34; discussion Ch 3(II)(A).

163 See Peters (n 122) 169 ('dual claim'), 175, 317, 338; Paparinskis (n 152) 288–92; Paparinskis (n 17) 640–41; Roberts (n 129) 16–18, 32, 34–40; Riccardo Pisillo Mazzeschi, 'Impact on the Law of Diplomatic Protection' in Menno Kamminga and Martin Scheinin (eds), *The Impact of Human Rights Law on General International Law* (OUP 2009) 218–19; Paddeu (n 129) 279 (fn 301); McCorquodale (n 8) 285; Gerald Fitzmaurice, *The Law and Procedure of the International Court of Justice* (Grotius 1986) 687; Amerasinghe (n 12) 47, 152, 164, 308–9; Roger O'Keefe, 'Proportionality' in Crawford and others, *Responsibility* (n 6) 1164; Ch 2, nn 116–21.

This framework leaves unanswered several questions.

First, for individuals, no general secondary rules exist for invoking State responsibility.[164] The ARSIWA contain no such rules,[165] and are inapplicable 'to obligations of reparation to the extent that these arise towards or are invoked by' non-States,[166] with article 33(2) providing a 'without prejudice' rule vis-à-vis 'any right, arising from the international responsibility of a State, which may accrue directly to any' non-State.[167] We must therefore look to practice to determine when individuals may invoke responsibility and the consequences of such invocation.

Second, and relatedly, the ARSIWA do not address the relationship between individual and interstate claims.[168] On the interstate level, the ARSIWA largely accept that one incident may cause injury to multiple States, who may each invoke responsibility vis-à-vis the same act; one State's claim does not prevent invocation by others also meeting the necessary conditions.[169] In theory, this should apply equally to the invocation of responsibility by individuals, meaning that a State or individual's invocation of responsibility should not prejudice the ability of the other to claim per se.[170] We must then consider other rules of international law, and State practice, to determine whether and to what extent the potential resulting multiplicity of claims is curtailed, and how far States are hampered from acting under the law of State responsibility more generally.[171]

Filling these gaps are the concern of the remainder of this book. Chapter 2 outlines when individuals may invoke responsibility and the resulting overlap with interstate claims. The remaining chapters then consider whether various rules relating to admissibility, breach, and reparation may operate to preclude one or both of such overlapping claims.

164 See *ADM and Tate & Lyle v Mexico (Award)* ICSID Case No ARB(AF)/04/05 (21 November 2007) [118] (under custom 'only ... States may invoke ... responsibility'), referencing *ARSIWA*, art 33(2); also ibid 209–10; Crawford, *GP* (n 3) 549.

165 *ARSIWA*, 210, 254; Crawford, *GP* (n 3) 541, 549.

166 *ARSIWA*, 193.

167 ibid art 33(2); also Crawford, *GP* (n 3) 548–49; Weiss (n 4) 799; Peters (n 122) 172–73.

168 Introduction, n 28.

169 *ARSIWA* art 46, 270–71 (though referencing double recovery); Ch 4, nn 22–24; similarly Paparinskis (n 152) 289.

170 See Giorgio Gaja, 'The Position of Individuals in International Law: An ILC Perspective' (2010) 21 EJIL 11, 13–14; Bruno Simma and Dirk Pulkowski, '*Leges Speciales* and Self-Contained Regimes' in Crawford and others, *Responsibility* (n 6) 159; Paparinskis (n 152) 289–90, 297. Generally n 162; Ch 2.

171 Similarly Yuval Shany, *The Competing Jurisdictions of International Courts and Tribunals* (OUP 2003); Yuval Shany, *Regulating Jurisdictional Relations Between National and International Courts* (OUP 2007); Introduction, nn 65–71.

2
Overlapping Individual and Interstate Claims

This chapter outlines the circumstances in which overlapping individual and interstate claims may arise.[1] It begins by considering the mechanisms through which individuals may invoke State responsibility, before turning to possible overlaps with the invocation of responsibility on the interstate level. The following chapters then examine rules that may operate to preclude one or both of those overlapping claims.

I. Invocation of responsibility by individuals

When speaking of 'individuals' in the context of individual claims, this book generally means any natural or legal 'non-State actor'[2] whose actions are not attributable to a State.[3] In determining whether a given claim is 'individual'—such as where it is brought by a person who is also a State official—what matters is in which capacity that claim is brought.[4] If the individual is acting *as the State* in claiming, then it is a State claim; if the individual acts in a private capacity, the claim is individual.[5]

[1] Similarly considering overlapping claims before principles precluding multiple claims: Yuval Shany, *Regulating Jurisdictional Relations Between National and International Courts* (OUP 2007) Ch 4; Yuval Shany, *The Competing Jurisdictions of International Courts and Tribunals* (OUP 2003) Pt I, particularly 34–37 (individual/interstate overlap).

[2] As does Robert McCorquodale, 'The Individual and the International Legal System' in Malcolm Evans (ed), *International Law* (4th edn, OUP 2014) 281; similarly Philip Jessup, *A Modern Law of Nations* (Archon 1968) 19–20; cf Kate Parlett, *The Individual in the International Legal System: Continuity and Change in International Law* (CUP 2011) 4–5 (natural persons); Anne Peters, *Beyond Human Rights: The Legal Status of the Individual in International Law* (Jonathan Huston tr, CUP 2016) 9–10.

[3] Similarly Noam Lubell, *Extraterritorial Use of Force Against Non-State Actors* (OUP 2010) 15 ('maintain[s] an identity and existence independent of' State); also Ashley Deeks, '"Unwilling or Unable": Toward a Normative Framework for Extraterritorial Self-Defense' (2012) 52 Virg JIL 483, 494; cf Christine Chinkin, 'Monism and Dualism: The Impact of Private Authority on the Dichotomy Between National and International Law' in Janne Nijman and André Nollkaemper (eds), *New Perspectives on the Divide Between National and International Law* (OUP 2007) 139–42.

[4] See FV Garcia-Amador, 'International Responsibility: Report' (1956) 2 ILCYB 173, 187. Questions of capacity for the purposes of attribution are similar: see James Crawford, *The International Law Commission's Articles on State Responsibility: Introduction, Text and Commentaries* (CUP 2002) (*ARSIWA*) art 4, 94–99. However, questions of representation and attribution are distinct: ibid 164. The former requires considering how the State expresses its will, with 'principles concerning the validity of consent to treaties provid[ing] relevant guidance': ibid.

[5] See Gateano Arangio-Ruiz, 'Second Report on State Responsibility' (1989) 2(1) ILCYB 1, 17 (fn 111) (State agents '[p]rivate parties' where 'privately affected by the internationally wrongful act'); eg

Overlapping Individual and Interstate Claims in International Law. Jessica Howley, Oxford University Press.
 DOI: 10.1093/oso/9780192871466.003.0003

While containing no rules on the invocation of responsibility by individuals, the commentary to the Articles on Responsibility of States for Internationally Wrongful Acts (ARSIWA) nonetheless acknowledges that individuals may sometimes invoke responsibility and claim reparation 'on [their] own account and without the intermediation of any State'.[6] Indeed, such individual claims mechanisms have become relatively commonplace in recent decades.[7]

As Chapter 1 foreshadowed, individuals may potentially either claim through such mechanisms for breach of primary international obligations owed to them, or for the fulfilment of secondary obligations, including of reparation, resulting from breach of obligations owed only at the *interstate* level.[8] Regardless of whose rights are involved, however, individual claims are brought for breach of international law and are thus an invocation of responsibility under the State responsibility framework.[9] The mechanisms through which individuals claim are usually established by treaty and are particularly prevalent in the investment and human rights fields,[10] though other contexts are also relevant.[11] For analytical purposes relating to mapping the landscape here, we will divide the claims into three broad categories based on the norms invoked and relevant fora. However, as will become apparent, these are not mutually exclusive, and their relative importance may shift over time.

A. Investment law

First, in investment law, individual nationals of a State party to an investment treaty are often afforded the possibility to bring claims for breach of obligations

Prince Hans-Adam II of Liechtenstein v Germany ECHR 2001-VIII 7 (officials' private claim). Cf *Certain Property (Liechtenstein v Germany) (Preliminary Objections)* [2005] ICJ Rep 6 (similar facts, State-brought), nn 195–96.

6 *ARSIWA*, 210. Similarly Parlett (n 2) 96, 339; Edith Brown Weiss, 'Invoking State Responsibility in the Twenty-First Century' (2002) 96 AJIL 798, 815; André Nollkaemper, *National Courts and the International Rule of Law* (OUP 2011) 98. See Ch 1, nn 165–67.

7 Authorities Introduction, n 8.

8 See authorities Ch 1, nn 143–44; Ch 4, n 158; Ch 6, nn 94–98; Peters (n 2) 167–73; Emmanuel Roucounas, 'Non-State Actors: Areas of International Responsibility in Need of Further Exploration' in Maurizio Ragazzi (ed), *International Responsibility Today: Essays in Memory of Oscar Schachter* (Martinus Nijhoff 2005) 399; *ARSIWA*, 210.

9 Similarly Anthea Roberts, 'Triangular Treaties: The Extent and Limits of Investment Treaty Rights' (2015) 56 Harv ILJ 353, 372–73; *ARSIWA*, 209–10.

10 James Crawford, 'Overview of Part Three of the Articles on State Responsibility' in James Crawford and others (eds), *The Law of International Responsibility* (OUP 2010) 932; *ARSIWA*, 210; James Crawford, *State Responsibility: The General Part* (CUP 2013) 549 (*GP*); Burkhard Hess, 'The Private-Public Divide in International Dispute Resolution' (2018) 388 RdC 49, 137; Shany, *Competing* (n 1) 74. Cf nn 66ff.

11 Generally Weiss (n 6) 798, 809–14; Christian Tomuschat, 'Individuals' in Crawford and others, *Responsibility* (n 10) 986–90; PICT, *Courts and Tribunals*, <http://www.pict-pcti.org/>; Cesare Romano, Karen Alter, and Yvual Shany, *The Oxford Handbook of International Adjudication* (OUP 2014); also Shany, *Competing* (n 1) 5–7; similarly Jessup (n 2) 18.

thereunder against another State party before an international tribunal.[12] Such mechanisms are commonly found in bilateral investment treaties (BITs),[13] operating within or outside the framework of the Convention on the Settlement of Disputes between States and Nationals of Other States (ICSID),[14] and increasingly also in free trade agreements,[15] such as the North American Free Trade Agreement (NAFTA),[16] and other multilateral agreements, like the Energy Charter Treaty (ECT).[17] Similar mechanisms are found in agreements establishing ad hoc adjudicatory bodies like the Iran–United States Claims Tribunal (IUSCT).[18] These procedures enable individuals to invoke State responsibility for breach of treaty-based standards,[19] and to claim reparation for any resulting damage.[20] They therefore allow for international claims by individuals in the sense explained in Chapter 1.[21]

B. Human rights

Second, individuals may invoke responsibility in the human rights field through three broad kinds of mechanism.[22] First, certain treaties provide individuals with access to a court which will determine allegations of State party violations thereunder, and whether reparation is due.[23] These courts include the European Court of Human Rights (ECtHR),[24] the African Court on Human and Peoples' Rights

[12] Eg, Crawford, *GP* (n 10) 587–88; Weiss (n 6) 812–13; Parlett (n 2) 103–19; Roberts (n 9) 354, 364–65, 382; Christoph Schreuer, 'Investment Arbitration' in Romano, Alter and Shany (n 11) 300–2, 310–11; Peters (n 2) 283–85; McCorquodale (n 2) 291–94.

[13] Eg, Model BITs: UK (2008) art 8; US (2012) art 24; Germany (2008) art 10, reproduced Campbell McLachlan, Laurence Shore, and Matthew Weiniger, *International Investment Arbitration: Substantive Principles* (2nd edn, OUP 2017); Crawford, *GP* (n 10) 589–90; Parlett (n 2) 104.

[14] See ICSID, art 25; generally Schreuer, 'IA' (n 12) 298–99.

[15] Christian Leathley, *International Dispute Resolution in Latin America: An Institutional Overview* (Kluwer 2007) 26–33.

[16] NAFTA arts 1116, 1117; similarly CAFTA, art 10.16. See Schreuer, 'IA' (n 12) 302–4; Carl Baudenbacher and Michael-James Clifton, 'Courts of Regional Economic and Political Integration Agreements' in Romano, Alter, and Shany (n 11) 263–65. NAFTA is considered under section A and not section C as 'not aim[ing] at . . . deep integration': ibid 263. Cf recent NAFTA amendments: Ch 5, n 399.

[17] ECT, art 26; Schreuer, 'IA' (n 12) 304.

[18] CSD, art II(1); Parlett (n 2) 99.

[19] See *ARSIWA*, 210; Schreuer, 'IA' (n 12) 297, 308–9.

[20] Generally Parlett (n 2) 104–5; Schreuer, 'IA' (n 12) 310.

[21] Ch 1(II).

[22] Generally Tomuschat (n 11) 986–88; Crawford, *GP* (n 10) 585–86; Parlett (n 2) 307–37; Weiss (n 6) 809–11; McCorquodale (n 2) 290; Ruth Mackenzie and others, *Manual on International Courts and Tribunals* (OUP 2010) Pt V.

[23] See Solomon Ebobrah, 'International Human Rights Courts' in Romano, Alter, and Shany (n 11) 226, 239.

[24] ECHR, arts 34, 41; discussion Tomuschat (n 11) 986–87; Robert Jennings and Arthur Watts, *Oppenheim's International Law*, vol 1 (9th edn, Longman 1992) 1001; Parlett (n 2) 307–12, 331–35; Steven Greer, 'Europe' in Daniel Moeckli and others (eds), *International Human Rights Law* (3rd edn, OUP 2018) 447–58.

(ACtHPR),[25] and, at least indirectly, the Inter-American Court of Human Rights (IACtHR).[26] Second, both the American Convention on Human Rights (AmCHR) and the African Charter on Human and Peoples' Rights (AfCHPR) additionally establish Commissions to which individuals may complain about violations.[27] These Commissions make recommendations, including regarding reparation.[28] Finally, other mechanisms, including under various global United Nations (UN) human rights treaties, allow bodies to receive petitions from individuals claiming to be victims of a State's violation of its obligations thereunder.[29] These treaty bodies express their views, and/or make recommendations for action.[30] Certain, though not all, bodies also make reparations findings.[31]

These mechanisms have differences, particularly insofar as those in the latter two categories do not result in binding judicial determinations.[32] Nonetheless, State responsibility is invoked when a claim of breach is made, entailing consequent obligations to remedy.[33] All of these mechanisms allow individuals to allege violation of human rights obligations under the respective treaties, and are

[25] AfCHPR Protocol, arts 3, 5(3), 27(1), 34(6); generally Parlett (n 2) 330–31; Christof Heyns and Magnus Killander, 'Africa' in Moeckli and others (n 24) 476–78; Habib Gherari, 'African Mechanisms' in Crawford and others, *Responsibility* (n 10) 781, 788.

[26] Although only accessible to the Commission and States (AmCHR, art 61(1)), in practice individuals 'ha[ve] full standing' after 'case … submitted' (Thomas Antkowiak, 'The Americas' in Moeckli and others (n 24) 432) and are entitled to any compensation: see AmCHR, art 63(1); IACtHR RoP, particularly arts 25(1), 40(2)(d); Tomuschat (n 11) 987; *Oppenheim's* (n 24) 1028–29; Parlett (n 2) 328–30; Ebobrah (n 23) 229, 232, 240; Raphaele Rivier, 'Inter-American Mechanisms' in Crawford and others, *Responsibility* (n 10) 740–60; Weiss (n 6) 810; Leathley (n 15) 70; Antkowiak (n 26) 432–35.

[27] AmCHR arts 44, 50(3), 51(2); see Antkowiak (n 26) 429–30; Leathley (n 15) 62, 65; AfCHPR, arts 55–58; see Heyns and Killander (n 25) 471–74, particularly 472 ('accepts … complaints'); Parlett (n 2) 328–31.

[28] AmCHR, arts 50(3), 51(2); Antkowiak (n 26) 430. While not expressly provided for (see AfCHPR, arts 58(1)–(2)), in practice the ACommHPR issues recommendations, sometimes requesting compensation: Gherari (n 25) 787–88; Heyns and Killander (n 25) 473–74.

[29] ICCPR Protocol, arts 1–2; ICESCR Protocol, arts 1–2; CEDAW Protocol, arts 1–2; UNCAT, art 22(1); CERD, art 14(1); CRPD Protocol, art 1; CRC Protocol, arts 1, 5; ICPMW, art 77(1); CPED, art 31(1); generally *Oppenheim's* (n 24) 1001; Jane Connors, 'United Nations' in Moeckli and others (n 24) 387–88, 393–97; Tomuschat (n 11) 986–88; Crawford, *GP* (n 10) 585–86; Weiss (n 6) 809–10; Parlett (n 2) 312–20.

[30] ICCPR Protocol, art 5(4) ('views'); similarly UNCAT, art 22(7); ICPMW, art 77(7); CPED, art 31(5); ICESCR Protocol, art 9(1) ('views … recommendations'); similarly CEDAW Protocol, arts 7(3)-(4); CRC Protocol, arts 10(5), 11(1); CERD, art 14(7)(b) ('suggestions … recommendations'); similarly CRPD Protocol, art 5. See also Human Rights Council procedures discussed Parlett (n 2) 321–22; Connors (n 29) 377–82.

[31] See Tomuschat (n 11) 987–88 (Human Rights Committee (HRC) reparations findings); Peters (n 2) 176; HRC, 'General Comment No. 33' (2008) UN Doc CCPR/C/GC/33 [12] quoted n 34, also [20]; *Bradshaw*, n 34; generally Connors (n 29) 395.

[32] See Crawford, *GP* (n 10) 586 ('"views" expressed by treaty monitoring bodies … non-binding'); Tomuschat (n 11) 988 ('"views" … not decisions with binding effect'); Parlett (n 2) 316–17, 320; Nollkaemper (n 6) 177–78; Ebobrah (n 23) 228–29 (ACtHPR 'judgments … binding'), 230 (IACtHR '[d]ecisions … binding'), 231 (ECtHR '[j]udgments … binding'), 236–37 (UN bodies 'quasi-judicial'); Rivier (n 26) 749 (IACHR reparation 'rulings … lack binding force'); Gherari (n 25) 788 (ACommHPR 'findings … devoid of any binding force'); Connors (n 29) 393 ('quasi-judicial'), 395 ('not … legally binding'), referencing General Comment 33 (n 31) [11]; Shany, *Competing* (n 1) 16; Chittharanjan Amerasinghe, *Local Remedies in International Law* (2nd edn, CUP 2004) 304; Antkowiak (n 26) 430.

[33] Ch 1(II)–(III).

generally regarded as enabling invocation of State responsibility.[34] They therefore allow for individual claims in the sense relevant herein.

C. Other claims

While investment law and human rights are perhaps the best-known examples, State responsibility may be invoked by individuals in various other fields.[35] For present purposes, three broad categories of claims mechanisms may be noted.[36]

First, tribunals have, at various times, been established to address large numbers of individual claims arising out of international conflicts.[37] Individual claims for reparation were brought, for instance, before post-WWI mixed arbitral tribunals (MATs).[38] While those tribunals' jurisdiction included issues between individuals and within the domain of domestic law,[39] it also covered individual claims against States resulting from violation of international law.[40] And, importantly, the

[34] See *ARSIWA*, 210; similarly Weiss (n 6) 809–11; *Oppenheim's* (n 24) 1001; Crawford, *GP* (n 10) 549; Tomuschat (n 11) 986–87; also General Comment 33 (n 31) [12] ('findings on ... violations alleged ... and ... remedy'); *Bradshaw v Barbados* Comm 489/1992, Doc CCPR/C/51/D/489/1992 (HRC, 29 July 1994) [5.3], cited Ebobrah (n 23) 237; *Musicue and Coicue v Colombia* Case 9853, Rep 4/98 (IACHR, 7 April 1998) [19] ('proceedings ... determination as to State responsibility'); Parlett (n 2) 320. Cf Rivier (n 26) 753–54.

[35] cf Crawford, *GP* (n 10) 592 ('Other fields ... consular relations'); *ARSIWA*, 210.

[36] cf UNCLOS, arts 187, 292 (prompt release/Area-related contractors), discussed Sean Murphy, 'International Judicial Bodies for Resolving Disputes between States' in Romano, Alter, and Shany (n 11) 186–87; also Shany, *Relations* (n 1) 60–63; NAAEC, art 14, discussed Weiss (n 6) 811–12; Shany, *Competing* (n 1) 221–22. These are not specifically considered: UNCLOS, art 292(2) because States must consent to individuals claiming 'on [their] behalf' (ITLOS Rules, art 110), meaning no overlap is possible (Murphy (n 36) 186–87; cf Shany, *Relations* (n 1) 61–63 (domestic); nn 66ff); NAAEC, art 14 because it concerns 'fail[ure] to effectively enforce [domestic] environmental law'.

[37] Generally: Julianne Kokott, 'The Exhaustion of Local Remedies' (2004) 69 ILA Rep Conf 606, 609; Sean Murphy, Won Kidane, and Thomas Snider, *Litigating War: Arbitration of Civil Injury by the Eritrea-Ethiopia Claims Commission* (OUP 2013) 42–49; Howard Holtzmann and Edda Kristjánsdóttir, *International Mass Claims Processes: Legal and Practical Perspectives* (OUP 2007); Hans van Houtte, Bart Delmartino, and Iasson Yi, *Post-War Restoration of Property Rights Under International Law*, vol 1 (CUP 2008), Ch 2; Howard Holtzmann, 'Mass Claims' in Rüdiger Wolfrum (ed), *MPEPIL (Online)* (OUP 2008); Berk Demirkol, 'Does an Investment Treaty Tribunal Need Special Consent for Mass Claims?' (2013) 2 Camb JI & CL 612, 626–27.

[38] Generally Parlett (n 2) 72–73; eg, Treaty of Versailles, art 297(e), quoted Ch 5, n 222; similarly Treaty of St-Germain-en-Laye, art 249(e).

[39] Eg: Treaty of Versailles, art 296, Annex [16], art 304(b) (contract; debts); see generally Parlett (n 2) 72–73; Marta Requejo Isidro and Burkhard Hess, 'The Mixed Arbitral Tribunals in the Peace Treaties of 1919–1922' *MPI for Procedural Law Research Paper Series No 2018(5)*, 6–9, 17.

[40] State responsibility derived from unlawful aggression: see Treaty of Versailles, art 231; similarly Treaty of St-Germain-en-Laye, art 249. Arguging that 'the legal regime of private rights [under these treaties] was conceptually and formally clearly separated from the reparation regime', though noting '[i]n practice, the delineation proved to be difficult': Isidro and Hess (n 39) 7, referencing *Treaty of Neuilly, Article 179, Annex, Paragraph 4 (Interpretation)* [1924] PCIJ Rep, Ser A, No 3. Indeed, the PCIJ held, vis-à-vis wording in provisions relating to individual claims that 'the expression "acts committed" ... contemplates acts contrary to the law of nations and involving an obligation to make reparation', deriving from the part of the treaty on reparations: ibid 8. Regardless, the claims addressed here appear to derive from international law violations. Cf van Houtte, Delmartino, and Yi (n 37) 15–16; *Ethiopia's Claim 4 (Decision 7)* (2007) 135 ILR 251 [22].

claims were considered to belong to those individuals rather than their States of nationality.[41]

Similarly, claims were made before the United Nations Compensation Commission (UNCC) for reparation consequent on the internationally unlawful invasion of Kuwait by Iraq in 1990.[42] While the process before the Commission was essentially 'administrative' in nature,[43] the claims followed findings of a violation of international law by Iraq, and its resulting liability.[44] Many of these claims were likewise 'individual and corporate claims' belonging to those claimants, notwithstanding that they were procedurally filed by governments.[45]

Finally, the Eritrea-Ethiopia Claims Commission (EECC) was given competence to determine

> all claims for loss, damage or injury by one Government against the other, and by nationals (including both natural and juridical persons) of one party against the Government of the other party ... that are (a) related to the conflict [between the States] ... and (b) result from violations of international humanitarian law ... or other violations of international law.[46]

While most of the claims filed before the EECC were interstate in nature,[47] provision was made for certain individual claims, which belonged to those individuals, albeit that they were filed by the two States concerned.[48]

In these examples, where claims were individual in nature and damage was alleged consequent on a breach of international law, they may be regarded as individual invocations of responsibility relevant to the overlapping claims considered herein.

[41] Parlett (n 2) 73; Christoph Schreuer, *Decisions of International Institutions Before Domestic Courts* (Oceana 1981) 329–30; *Ryuichi Shimoda v Japan* (1963) 32 ILR 626 (Tokyo DC) 637–38; Ch 5(III)(C)(i).

[42] Parlett (n 2) 101; Dražen Petrović, 'The UN Compensation Commission' in Crawford and others, *Responsibility* (n 10) 850; Hans van Houtte, Hans Das, and Bart Delmartino, 'The United Nations Compensation Commission' in Pablo de Greiff (ed), *The Handbook of Reparations* (OUP 2006) 324–25, 326, 327; also *Decision 7* (n 40) [30]; Vera Gowlland-Debbas, 'UN Sanctions and International Law: An Overview' in Vera Gowlland-Debbas (ed), *United Nations Sanctions and International Law* (Kluwer 2001) 11.

[43] Petrović (n 42) 850; also Parlett (n 2) 102, referencing 'Report of the Secretary-General Pursuant to Paragraph 19 of Security Council Resolution 687' (1991) UN Doc S/22559 [20] ('essentially fact-finding function', though aspects potentially 'quasi-judicial').

[44] Petrović (n 42) 850; see Security Council Resolution 687 [16] ('liable under international law for any direct loss, damage ... or injury'; also Secretary-General's Report (n 43) [22]: 'procedure foreseen ... relate[s] to liability under international law'.

[45] van Houtte, Delmartino, and Yi (n 37) 62; van Houtte, Das, and Delmartino (n 42) 333; also David Caron, 'International Claims and Compensation Bodies' in Romano, Alter, and Shany (n 11) 293. Cf Parlett (n 2) 102.

[46] EECC Agreement, art 5(1).

[47] *Eritrea's Damages Claims (Final Award)* (2009) XXVI UNRIAA 505 [3] ('almost entirely [State] claims ... rather than claims on behalf of ... nationals'), [25]; van Houtte, Delmartino, and Yi (n 37) 49; Murphy, Kidane, and Snider (n 37) 57; Ch 4, n 452.

[48] Murphy, Kidane, and Snider (n 37) 57 ('claims remained those of ... nationals'); Peters (n 2) 208.

Second, various regional agreements allow for individuals to bring claims alleging violation of those treaties.[49] Perhaps most well-known are individual claims under European Union (EU) law brought for breaches of Member States' treaty obligations,[50] including for human rights violations.[51] The Andean Court also receives individual applications regarding alleged breach of Member State obligations under the Cartagena Agreement.[52] The Caribbean Court of Justice (CCJ) hears certain individual cases concerning 'interpretation and application' of the Revised Treaty of Chaguaramas Establishing the Caribbean Community (CARICOM Treaty).[53] The System of Central American Integration[54] provides individuals with access to the Central American Court of Justice (CACJ) to determine disputes.[55] In Africa, the Common Market for Eastern and Southern Africa (COMESA) Court of Justice hears individual claims, including regarding alleged Member State treaty violations of the COMESA Treaty;[56] the East African Court of Justice (EACJ) hears claims concerning the East African Community Treaty's 'interpretation and application',[57] including individual claims against Member States;[58] and the Economic Community of West African States (ECOWAS) Court of Justice[59] is open to, *inter alia*, individuals alleging human rights violations.[60] Finally, the Southern African Development Community (SADC) has a Tribunal[61] which, until suspension of its operation in 2012,[62] was competent to consider, *inter alia*, individual claims concerning 'interpretation and

[49] Generally Baudenbacher and Clifton (n 16), particularly 251–52, 269, 273; Mackenzie and others (n 22) [9.1.1]–[10.3.14]; Tomuschat (n 11) 989–90; Shany, *Competing* (n 1) 53.

[50] Generally Baudenbacher and Clifton (n 16) 252–55; Bruno Simma and Dirk Pulkowski, '*Leges Speciales* and Self-Contained Regimes' in Crawford and others, *Responsibility* (n 10) 153; Weiss (n 6) 813–14; McCorquodale (n 2) 293; nn 77–78. For space reasons, the BCJ and EFTA Court are omitted: see PICT (n 11); Baudenbacher and Clifton (n 16) 256–60; Mackenzie and others (n 22) [9.2.1]–[9.2.10].

[51] See Ebobrah (n 23) 232–33; Greer (n 24) 461–63, cf 461 ('rare').

[52] Cartagena Protocol, art 25; generally Leathley (n 15) 121–27; Baudenbacher and Clifton (n 16) 260–62. On the Andean Community: Leathley (n 15) 107, 115–20.

[53] CARICOM Treaty, art 211, also art 222. See *TLC v Guyana* [2009] CCJ 1 [18]–[20]; *Time for Action: Report of the West Indian Commission* (West Indian Commission 1992) 500. Generally Baudenbacher and Clifton (n 16) 268–71; Leathley (n 15) 130, 134–35, 142–50.

[54] See Tegucigalpa Protocol, arts 1ff. Generally Leathley (n 15) Ch 9.

[55] See CACJ Statute (interstate disputes (arts 22(a), 23), including consistency with 'Law of Central American Integration' (art 22(c)), open to 'any interested party'); generally ibid 203–9. Claims concerning individuals are allowed in the Mercado Común del Sur (MERCOSUR): Olivos Protocol, art 39; see Leathley (n 15) 172–73, also 151–52, 155, 159–62; Baudenbacher and Clifton (n 16) 265–68. However, they are State-brought: see Ch 3, n 10.

[56] COMESA Treaty, art 26; generally PICT (n 11).

[57] EAC Treaty, art 27. Art 9 establishes the Court.

[58] EAC Treaty, art 30; also arts 34, 44; Heyns and Killander (n 25) 467 (no 'explicit jurisdiction' but addresses 'human rights issues ... constitut[ing] [treaty] violations').

[59] Established by ECOWAS Treaty, art 15.

[60] ECOWAS Protocol, art 4; also art 6; Heyns and Killander (n 25) 467; Ebobrah (n 23) 233–34.

[61] SADC Treaty, arts 9, 16.

[62] See Heyns and Killander (n 25) 467; Ch 5, n 378.

application of the Treaty'.[63] All provide for the invocation of State responsibility by individuals.

Third, while claims before domestic courts would not normally be considered international,[64] tending rather to be for breach of *domestic* law,[65] domestic courts do sometimes 'decide international claims: that is, claims that in whole or in part are based on a rule of international law'.[66] Because of how domestic law incorporates international law,[67] 'the same international legal standards' might be applied domestically as internationally.[68] More generally, 'domestic law may ... coincide, in substance, with international norms'.[69] While perhaps not strictly an invocation of State responsibility,[70] it is important not to ignore such claims entirely, because they may, *substantively speaking*, amount to such an invocation,[71] and may well enliven potential overlap with claims before international courts.[72]

Indeed, domestic court claims may be brought in the fields already considered, including in investment law,[73] and vis-à-vis alleged violations of human rights.[74]

[63] SADC Protocol, arts 14–15.

[64] André Nollkaemper, 'Conversations among Courts: Domestic and International Adjudicators' in Romano, Alter, and Shany (n 11) 524–27; Nollkaemper (n 6) 9. Cf Rosalyn Higgins, *Themes and Theories* (OUP 2009) 80.

[65] See Shany, *Relations* (n 1) 79–80, 142, generally 2–4, 79–86 (dualism); *Chevron and Texaco v Ecuador (Third Interim Award, Jurisdiction/Admissibility)* PCA Case 2009-23 (27 February 2012) [4.76]; cf Antonios Tzanakopoulos, 'Domestic Courts in International Law: The International Judicial Function of National Courts' (2011) 34 Loy LAI & CLR 133, 137–44, 149.

[66] Nollkaemper (n 6) 9, also 44; similarly Nollkaemper (n 64) 526–27; Tzanakopoulos (n 65) 144; also Shany, *Relations* (n 1) 5, 10–13; Weiss (n 6) 811; Gabrielle Kaufmann-Kohler and Michele Potestà, 'Investor–State Dispute Settlement and National Courts: Current Framework and Reform Options' [2020] EYBIEL, 32–34.

[67] See Tzanakopoulos (n 65) 142–43; Nollkaemper (n 6) 12, 44, 69–81, 117–20, 124–29, 232–34; Shany, *Relations* (n 1) 12, 82–85.

[68] Shany, *Relations* (n 1) 13, also 85–86, 93, 104; Nollkaemper (n 64) 528.

[69] Tzanakopoulos (n 65) 143, also 144; Parlett (n 2) 279; Shany, *Relations* (n 1) 86; Nollkaemper (n 64) 527–28.

[70] Similarly Kaufmann-Kohler and Potestà (n 66) 34, also 36–39, 42.

[71] See Nollkaemper (n 6) 7–10, 110–12, 117–18, 131–32, 166–73, 213, 224, 233; Nollkaemper (n 64) 526–28; Shany, *Relations* (n 1) 13, 105, 141–42, 143 ('substance of ... rights and remedies ... not ... source of validity'); McCorquodale (n 2) 293; Peters (n 2) 49–50, 184, 485–88; similarly Tzanakopoulos (n 65) 143–50; Kaufmann-Kohler and Potestà (n 66) 34; n 76.

[72] Shany, *Relations* (n 1) 97, Chs 1, 4; Schreuer, *Decisions* (n 41) 329 ('Identity of Claims'); Nollkaemper (n 64) 527–28; Nollkaemper (n 6) 247–51; Kaufmann-Kohler and Potestà (n 66) 32–34; n 245. Eg, *Dahanayake v Sri Lanka* Comm 1331/2004, Doc CCPR/C/87/D/1331/2004 (HRC, 25 July 2006) [6.5] (constitution ICCPR 'equivalent'); *Tasheku v Nigeria* Case ECW/CCJ/RUL/12/12 (ECOWAS CJ, 12 June 2012) [16] (constitutional rights 'analogous'); *Waste Management v Mexico (Award)* (2000) 121 ILR 29 (ICSID) [28] ('duplication of proceedings'); *Azurix v Argentina (Annulment)* ICSID Case No ARB/01/12 (1 September 2009) [109].

[73] Weiss (n 6) 813; Hess (n 10) 234–37; Tzanakopoulos (n 65) 153 ('"fork in the road" provision[s]'); similarly Schreuer, 'IA' (n 12) 306; Shany, *Relations* (n 1) 36–37, 152–53, 157; Nollkaemper (n 6) 32 (fn 55), 37–38; Parlett (n 2) 100–1, referencing *Dallal v Bank Mellat* (1985) 75 ILR 151 (EWHC), overlapping (see 158–59) with *Dallal v Bank Mellat* (1983) 75 ILR 126 (IUSCT). On local remedies: Tzanakopoulos (n 65) 152; Schreuer, 'IA' (n 12) 305; Nollkaemper (n 64) 529; Shany, *Relations* (n 1) 27–31; Christoph Schreuer, *The ICSID Convention: A Commentary* (2nd edn, CUP 2009) 416; Amerasinghe (n 32) 269–74; Zachary Douglas, *The International Law of Investment Claims* (CUP 2009) 29–30.

[74] Shany, *Relations* (n 1) 10; Parlett (n 2) 279; Nollkaemper (n 6) 29, 36–39, 42, 91, 127–29; cases n 72.

Human rights treaties actually commonly require individuals to have exhausted local remedies before bringing an international claim,[75] meaning that the claim's 'substance' must have been litigated domestically before it is brought before an international tribunal.[76] Many regional treaties also envisage domestic-court claims: claims under European Union (EU) law, for example, invoke State responsibility for treaty breach,[77] even if they are originally filed domestically,[78] while certain other treaties require local remedies to be exhausted.[79] Domestic law claims have also arisen from the same circumstances as individual claims before MATs,[80] the UNCC,[81] and the EECC,[82] while various other violations of international law could also at least potentially give rise to domestic proceedings.[83] Such claims may be brought before the allegedly responsible State's own courts,[84] or sometimes before third-State courts,[85] with 'traditional barriers' like State immunity now often 'removed or considerably relaxed'.[86]

While acknowledging the differences between claims before international and domestic tribunals, this book will, for these reasons, consider individual claims before domestic courts alongside claims before international tribunals where insights may be gleaned from doing so, and especially where there is overlap with interstate claims, to which we now turn.

[75] See ECHR, art 35(1); ICCPR Protocol, arts 2, 5(2)(b); CERD, art 14(7)(a); ICESCR Protocol, art 3(1); CEDAW Protocol, art 4(1); UNCAT, art 22(4)(b); CRC Protocol, art 7(5); ICPMW, art 77(3)(b); CPED, art 31(2)(d); CRPD Protocol, art 2(d); AmCHR, art 46(1)(a); AfCHPR, art 56(5); AfCHPR Protocol, art 6(2). Generally Amerasinghe (n 32) 64–83; also Shany, *Relations* (n 1) 29; Tomuschat (n 11) 986–87; Nollkaemper (n 64) 527, 529; Nollkaemper (n 6) 26–27, 36–37.

[76] *Guzzardi v Italy* (1980) ECHR Ser A, No 39 [71]–[72], cited Shany, *Relations* (n 1) 30, 138; *Vojnović v Croatia* Comm 1510/2006, Doc CCPR/C/95/D/1510/2006 (HRC, 30 March 2009) [7.7]; similarly *Elettronica Sicula SpA (US v Italy) (Judgment)* [1989] ICJ Rep 15 [59]. Generally Amerasinghe (n 32) 319–21; ILC, 'Draft Articles on Diplomatic Protection with Commentaries' (2006) 2(2) ILCYB 22 (DADP), 73; Crawford, *GP* (n 10) 583; Tzanakopoulos (n 65) 153; Ch 3(I)(B).

[77] Weiss (n 6) 813–15; also Friedl Weiss, 'Trade and Investment Law: What Relations?' in Giorgio Sacerdoti and others (eds), *General Interests of Host States in International Investment Law* (CUP 2014) 76.

[78] See Shany, *Relations* (n 1) 11, 16, 33–34, 97, referencing TFEU (now) art 267; also Greer (n 24) 461; Peters (n 2) 483, 489; *Karoussiotis v Portugal* ECHR 2011-II 15 [73]–[74]; similarly Leathley (n 15) 123 (Cartagena Protocol, art 30).

[79] COMESA Treaty, art 26; SADC Protocol, art 15(2).

[80] *Factory at Chórzow (Jurisdiction)* [1927] PCIJ Rep Ser A No 9, 10 (Germano-Polish MAT/Polish courts); *Certain German Interests in Polish Upper Silesia* [1925] PCIJ Rep Ser A No 6, 20, discussed Shany, *Relations* (n 1) 42–43; examples Ch 4, n 140.

[81] See van Houtte, Das, and Delmartino (n 42) 367–68; Shany, *Relations* (n 1) 159; n 245.

[82] *Nemariam v Ethiopia (No 1)* (2003) 135 ILR 671 (USCA, DC), discussed Ch 5(III)(C)(iv); also Murphy, Kidane, and Snider (n 37) 57.

[83] Generally Shany, *Relations* (n 1) Ch 1; Nollkaemper (n 6) 7–9, 27ff and authorities throughout; Tzanakopoulos (n 65) 141–42; n 245.

[84] Nollkaemper (n 6) 15, cf 50–52, 96–97; Rosalyn Higgins, *Problems and Processes: International Law and How We Use It* (Clarendon 1994) 51; Shany, *Relations* (n 1) 13; eg, nn 73–79. Cf Nollkaemper (n 64) 528.

[85] Eg, n 82.

[86] Shany, *Relations* (n 1) 13; similarly Higgins (n 64) 80–81; Hess (n 10) 235. Cf Nollkaemper (n 6) 15.

II. Interstate invocation of responsibility

Particularly as interstate claims commonly 'originate in injuries to private individuals',[87] it is perhaps unsurprising that those claims might overlap with those able to be brought by such individuals themselves.[88] As highlighted in the Introduction, 'overlap' for these purposes signifies that both individuals and States may, prima facie, invoke a given State's responsibility for violations of international law arising from the same factual circumstances.[89]

Chapter 1 outlined that interstate claims are brought pursuant to the rules reflected in ARSIWA article 42 ('injured' States) or article 48 (non-injured States, vis-à-vis *erga omnes* (*partes*) obligations).[90] It is helpful here to further subcategorise these claims, for, as Chapters 3–6 establish, the application of various rules of preclusion often depends on what type of overlap between individual and interstate claims is involved, and this is in turn commonly reflected in the kind of interstate claim that is brought.[91]

Starting with interstate claims brought pursuant to the rule in ARSIWA article 42, these fall into three categories.

First, 'injured' States may exercise 'diplomatic protection',[92] being:

> the invocation by a State, through diplomatic action or other means of peaceful settlement, of the responsibility of another State for an injury caused by an internationally wrongful act of that State to a natural or legal person that is a national of the former State....[93]

Diplomatic protection claims are commonly based on primary rules protecting the 'person or property [of individuals] in accordance with an international minimum standard'.[94] The State makes its claim in respect of injury to an individual person or

[87] Hersch Lauterpacht, *International Law: Being the Collected Papers of Hersch Lauterpacht* (Elihu Lauterpacht ed, CUP 1970) 293–94; also *Mavrommatis Palestine Concessions* [1924] PCIJ Rep Ser A No 2, 12, quoted Ch 3, n 43.

[88] Generally section III; Introduction, nn 23–24; also Jessup (n 2) 137. Because cases under international criminal law do not involve overlapping invocations of State responsibility, the field is largely omitted here (cf Shany, *Relations* (n 1) 10–11, 34–36; Shany, *Competing* (n 1) 9, 39–40; Ch 4, nn 487–94).

[89] Introduction, nn 24, 81.

[90] Ch 1(III).

[91] cf Shany, *Competing* (n 1) 35 (only diplomatic protection overlaps, providing individual–interstate 'competition'), also 37. Similarly authorities nn 147, 157.

[92] *ARSIWA*, 242, referencing *Barcelona Traction, Light and Power Company (Belgium v Spain)* [1970] ICJ Rep 3 [33]; also Giorgio Gaja, 'The Position of Individuals in International Law: An ILC Perspective' (2010) 21 EJIL 11, 13; Giorgio Gaja, 'The Concept of an Injured State' in Crawford and others, *Responsibility* (n 10) 944 ('bilateral obligations'); James Crawford, 'Third Report on State Responsibility' (2000) 2(1) ILCYB 3 [97], [100]; Annemarieke Vermeer-Künzli, 'A Matter of Interest: Diplomatic Protection and State Responsibility *Erga Omnes*' (2007) 56 ICLQ 553, 577; DADP, 26, 87. Cf Crawford, *GP* (n 10) 566.

[93] DADP, art 1; further Ch 3, nn 43–46.

[94] John Dugard, 'Diplomatic Protection' in Crawford and others, *Responsibility* (n 10) 1051; also DADP, 22–23; Crawford, *GP* (n 10) 568; Martins Paparinskis, 'Investment Arbitration and the Law of

corporation who must be the State's national,[95] and who must exhaust any available local remedies before the interstate claim is brought.[96] Conventionally, the State 'assert[s] its own rights—its right to ensure, in the person of its subjects, respect for the rules of international law',[97] and is, pursuant to a 'fiction', 'deemed' to be injured as a result of the injury suffered by the individual national.[98] Diplomatic protection claims are thus considered 'indirect', with the State injured only 'through its national',[99] and with the reparation awarded usually 'consist[ing] in an indemnity corresponding to the damage which the nationals of the injured State have suffered'.[100] The International Law Commission (ILC) has developed Draft Articles on Diplomatic Protection (DADP) outlining the key rules relating to the bringing of such claims.[101]

Second, and by contrast with diplomatic protection claims, States may bring claims for injury to themselves that is 'direct' in nature,[102] 'without the involvement

Countermeasures' (2008) 79 BYBIL 264, 279; Edwin Borchard, *The Diplomatic Protection of Citizens Abroad: Or, the Law of International Claims* (Banks 1915) 349; James Crawford, *Brownlie's Principles of Public International Law* (8th edn, OUP 2012) 613–22; *Oppenheim's* (n 24) 910–22; Ch 3, nn 163ff.

[95] DADP, art 3, 30–31; also *Oppenheim's* (n 24) 512.

[96] DADP, art 14, 70–76; Dugard, 'DP' (n 94) 1061; Shany, *Relations* (n 1) 27–30.

[97] *Mavrommatis* (n 87) 12; also *Barcelona Traction* (n 92) [78],[87]; *Reparation for injuries suffered in the service of the United Nations (Advisory Opinion)* [1949] ICJ Rep 174, 181–82; *Nottebohm Case (Liechtenstein v Guatemala) (Second Phase)* [1955] ICJ Rep 4, 24; Amerasinghe (n 32) 45–47; DADP, 25; Dugard, 'DP' (n 94) 1052; John Dugard, 'First Report on Diplomatic Protection' (2000) 2(1) ILCYB 205 [36], [62]; Borchard (n 94) 18, 353; Peters (n 2) 390–91; Theodor Meron, 'The Incidence of the Rule of Exhaustion of Local Remedies' (1959) 35 BYBIL 83, 88; Tomuschat (n 11) 985; Eduardo Jiménez de Aréchaga, 'International Responsibility' in Max Sørensen (ed), *Manual of Public International Law* (Macmillan 1968) 573; Garcia-Amador (n 4) [98]–[100].

[98] DADP, 25; also Dugard, 'DP' (n 94) 1052; Dugard, 'FirstRep' (n 97) [12], [36], [61], [67]; Annemarieke Vermeer-Künzli, 'As If: The Legal Fiction in Diplomatic Protection' (2007) 18 EJIL 37, 39–40, 60; Chittharanjan Amerasinghe, *Diplomatic Protection* (OUP 2008) 21–23; Ch 3(II)(C).

[99] DADP, 74; also JL Brierly, *Brierly's Law of Nations: An Introduction to the Role of International Law in International Relations* (7th edn, OUP 2012) 269; Stephan Wittich, 'Direct Injury and the Incidence of the Local Remedies Rule' (2000) 5 Aust Rev I & EL 121, 129; Borchard (n 94) 351. See, widely quoted, Emer de Vattel, *The Law of Nations, or, Principles of the Law of Nature Applied to the Conduct and Affairs of Nations and Sovereigns* (T & JW Johnson 1867) 161: '[w]hoever uses a citizen ill, indirectly offends the state', cited, *inter alia*, DADP, 25; Borchard (n 94) 351; Peters (n 2) 390.

[100] *Factory at Chórzow (Merits)* [1928] PCIJ Rep Ser A No 17, 27–28, cited DADP, 97–98; Peters (n 2) 171; also Mohamed Bennouna, 'Preliminary Report on Diplomatic Protection' (1998) 2(1) ILCYB 309 [22]–[23]; Brierly (n 99) 256; ALI, *Restatement of the Law: The Foreign Relations Law of the United States*, vol II (3rd edn, ALI Publishers 1987) 347; de Aréchaga (n 97) 574–75; *Ahmadou Sadio Diallo (Guinea v DRC) (Compensation)* [2012] ICJ Rep 344, 391 (Sep Op Greenwood) (human rights).

[101] DADP, 23.

[102] On direct/indirect claims: ibid 74–76; also Borchard (n 94) 353 (direct 'violation of ... rights affecting the collectivity or people as a whole'; indirect 'violation of [citizens'] rights'), 357, 362, 384; Eric Wyler and Alain Papaux, 'Satisfaction' in Crawford and others, *Responsibility* (n 10) 628. Direct/indirect refers to *who* is affected (Wittich (n 99) 129, citing *inter alia* FV Garcia-Amador, 'Sixth Report on State Responsibility' (1961) 2 ILCYB 1 [30]; also de Aréchaga (n 97) 577; ILC, 'Summary Records of the Meetings of the Fifty-Third Session' (2001) 1 ILCYB 1, 146 (Pellet)), not other potential uses (as to which: Wittich (n 99) 122–29), including vis-à-vis direct/indirect damage, pertaining to causation (see ibid 122–25; de Aréchaga (n 97) 568–69; *ARSIWA*, 204; cf Bernhard Graefrath, 'Responsibility and Damages Caused: Relationship between Responsibility and Damages' (1984) 185 RdC 9, 96).

of one of the victim State's nationals',[103] and without exhausting local remedies.[104] Rather than injury to a national forming the basis of such claims, 'it is State prerogatives that are at stake', with the State 'affect[ed] ... in its status as an independent personality';[105] 'the injured State represents principally its own interests rather than the interests of its nationals'[106] and 'has a distinct reason of its own' to claim.[107]

The third category of interstate claims consists of those described as 'mixed'.[108] This terminology envisages a 'direct' State claim being brought concurrently with a claim of diplomatic protection.[109] In practice, many claims will be of this nature, given that '[a] single set of facts giving rise to international legal proceedings may contain elements of both', and indeed 'most cases of direct injury [also] contain ... elements of diplomatic protection'.[110] Procedurally, the DADP outline that it is where such 'mixed' claims are not 'brought preponderantly on the basis of an injury to a national' that they will be treated as 'direct', with the consequence that no local remedies need be exhausted before the State claims.[111] Albeit 'mixed' in reality, the usual requirements for the claim's diplomatic protection portion need not be fulfilled because the claims are 'regarded as a unity' rather than 'split into [their] constituent elements'.[112]

Article 42 claims may thus be of three kinds. By contrast, as Chapter 1 foreshadowed, claims brought pursuant to the rule reflected in article 48 concern *erga omnes* obligations—those 'owed to the international community as a whole'[113]—and *erga omnes partes* obligations, protecting the 'collective'[114] or 'common' interest of a group of States.[115] Even if such a claim concerns individual persons, it is different to one of diplomatic protection:[116] the capacity of the State to claim

[103] Wittich (n 99) 129. Cf Amerasinghe (n 32) 146; Ch 3(IV)(B).

[104] DADP, art 14(3), 74; Meron (n 97) 84; Wittich (n 99) 121.

[105] *Certain Property (Liechtenstein v Germany)* ICJ Pleadings, Obs Liechtenstein [6.27].

[106] Meron (n 97) 84–85, quoted Amerasinghe (n 32) 160.

[107] DADP, 74. Similarly Meron (n 97) 88.

[108] DADP, 74; Wittich (n 99) 157. Cf de Aréchaga (n 97) 577 ('Composite claims').

[109] See de Aréchaga (n 97) 577 ('state ... claim on its own behalf simultaneously with ... claim on behalf of ... nationals'); DADP, 74; also Hugh Thirlway, *The Law and Procedure of the International Court of Justice: Fifty Years of Jurisprudence* (OUP 2013) 1549, 1554; Wittich (n 99) 170. Cf *Certain Property Pleadings* (n 105) Obs Liechtenstein [6.30] ('same conduct' breaches 'concurrence of different rules').

[110] Meron (n 97) 85–86, quoted Amerasinghe (n 32) 160; similarly DADP, 74; Thirlway (n 109) 1554.

[111] DADP, art 14(3), discussed 74–76; also Meron (n 97) 86; Amerasinghe (n 32) 160, 164; Wittich (n 99) 157, cf 136.

[112] Meron (n 97) 86, quoted Amerasinghe (n 32) 160, also 150; Wittich (n 99) 157, 162, 170; Thirlway (n 109) 1554–55.

[113] *ARSIWA*, art 48(1)(b); also *Barcelona Traction* (n 92) [33].

[114] *ARSIWA*, art 48(1)(a), 276; also Vermeer-Künzli, 'Interest' (n 92) 577–79.

[115] *Questions Relating to the Obligation to Prosecute or Extradite (Belgium v Senegal) (Judgment)* [2012] ICJ Rep 422 [68], [69], discussed James Crawford, 'Chance, Order, Change: The Course of International Law' (2013) 365 RdC 9, 203–4; *Application of the Convention on the Prevention and Punishment of the Crime of Genocide (The Gambia v Myanmar) (Preliminary Objections)* [2022] ICJ Rep 477 [107]–[108].

[116] See Riccardo Pisillo Mazzeschi, 'Impact on the Law of Diplomatic Protection' in Menno Kamminga and Martin Scheinin (eds), *The Impact of Human Rights Law on General International Law*

is not dependent on the victim being that State's national but on the claimant State being part of the international community (for *erga omnes* claims),[117] or the relevant group of States (such as treaty parties)[118] and pursuing the 'collective' interest in making that claim (for *erga omnes partes* claims).[119] Nonetheless, States might be 'injured' under article 42 where they are 'specially affected' by breach of an *erga omnes (partes)* obligation, and this includes if their nationals are victims thereof.[120] In cases concerning their nationals, States therefore have alternative routes for invoking responsibility: pursuant to the rule in article 48 or through diplomatic protection.[121] Which type of claim the State chooses to bring can have potentially important consequences for the application of rules of preclusion considered in later chapters, including vis-à-vis reparation.[122]

III. Overlapping claims

Interstate claims of all of these types may overlap with individual claims in the three broad categories of claims discussed above.[123]

(OUP 2009), 224 (distinguishing 'wide'/'strict' diplomatic protection (emphasis removed)); Vermeer-Künzli, 'Interest' (n 92) 556–61, 564–79; John Dugard, 'Diplomatic Protection' in *MPEPIL* (n 37) (2009) [52]; Giorgio Gaja, 'Is a State Specially Affected When Its Nationals' Human Rights Are Infringed?' in Lal Chand Vohrah and others (eds), *Man's Inhumanity to Man: Essays on International Law in Honour of Antonio Cassese* (Kluwer 2003) 382, 375–76, quoting *Barcelona Traction* (n 92) [33]; Giorgio Gaja, 'The International Court of Justice's Approach to Injuries Suffered by Individuals' (Oxford, 8 May 2014) <https://podcasts.ox.ac.uk/international-court-justices-approach-injuries-suffered-individuals>; ILC, 'Summary Records of the Meetings of the Fifty-Second Session' (2000) 1 ILCYB 1, 43–44 (Gaja); DADP, 87–89; Nobuyuki Kato, 'The Role of Diplomatic Protection in the Implementation Process of Public Interests' in Teruo Komori and Karel Wellens (eds), *Public Interest Rules of International Law: Towards Effective Implementation* (Ashgate 2009) 198, 202–4.

117 Dugard, 'MPEPIL' (n 116) [52]; Vermeer-Künzli, 'Interest' (n 92) 557, 566–67, 576, 578; Gaja, 'Affected' (n 116) 375–76; Mazzeschi (n 116) 230–31.

118 *Armed Activities on the Territory of the Congo (DRC v Uganda) (Judgment)* [2005] ICJ Rep 168 [35]–[37] (Sep Op Simma), discussed Vermeer-Künzli, 'Interest' (n 92) 567–68, 576; *Gambia v Myanmar* (n 115) [109]; Mazzeschi (n 116) 229–30; also Amerasinghe (n 32) 69–70; Lauterpacht (n 87) 299–300.

119 *ARSIWA*, 276; n 213; also *Gambia v Myanmar* (n 115) [109]; Giorgio Gaja, 'States Having an Interest in Compliance with the Obligation Breached' in Crawford and others, *Responsibility* (n 10) 961; Crawford, *GP* (n 10) 551.

120 See Mazzeschi (n 116) 227–31; Gaja, 'Compliance' (n 119) 958; ILC, '52nd' (n 116) 66 (Simma); also Gaja, 'Injuries' (n 116); Christian Tams, *Enforcing Obligations* Erga Omnes *in International Law* (CUP 2005) 134–35; cf Gaja, 'Affected' (n 116) 379–82; generally Ch 1, n 100; *ARSIWA*, art 42(b)(i), cf 279; *Oppenheim's* (n 24) 5; cf *Prosecute/Extradite* (n 115) [70] (left open); Gaja, 'Concept' (n 92) 943–44; also James Crawford, 'Multilateral Rights and Obligations in International Law' (2006) 319 RdC 325, 428 (fn 241).

121 Mazzeschi (n 116) 227–28, 231–32; Crawford, *GP* (n 10) 587; ILC, '52nd' (n 116) 66 (Simma) ('two sets of rules at . . . disposal'); also Vermeer-Künzli, 'Interest' (n 92) 555, 579–81.

122 See Ch 4, nn 624–31.

123 Similarly authorities Introduction, n 23.

A. Investment law

An investor's State of nationality may bring interstate claims for breach of obligations under investment law in the same circumstances as individual investors.[124] There are at least three different ways in which such overlap could arise.

First, States might bring a claim under the same treaty as an investor, with BITs,[125] and multilateral agreements such as NAFTA[126] and the ECT,[127] as well as that establishing the IUSCT,[128] commonly containing provisions for the arbitration of *interstate* disputes concerning their 'interpretation' and/or 'application' in addition to investor–State dispute resolution clauses.[129] Overlapping claims can result: for instance, the Mexico-US *Cross-Border Trucking* claim under NAFTA preceded investor claims against the US concerning the same alleged NAFTA violations.[130]

Other possibilities in terms of overlap are suggested by recent interstate claims concerning matters of interpretation clearly related to individual claims:[131] one claim brought by Peru against Chile aimed to resolve a question of treaty interpretation central to ongoing investor–State proceedings;[132] another was brought

124 Generally Anthea Roberts, 'State-to-State Investment Treaty Arbitration: A Hybrid Theory of Interdependent Rights and Shared Interpretative Authority' (2014) 55 Harv ILJ 1, 7, 67 ('overlap'); Paparinskis, 'Countermeasures' (n 94) section III(B)–(D), 282 ('overlapping claims'), 297–98. On 'parallel' claims: ibid 287, 289, 291–96, 333; similarly Martins Paparinskis, 'Investment Treaty Arbitration and the (New) Law of State Responsibility' (2013) 24 EJIL 617, 620, 640–41; Roberts (n 124) 16–17, 35, 40–41.

125 Eg, Model BITs: UK (2008) art 9; US (2012) art 37(1); Germany (2008) art 9, reproduced McLachlan, Shore, and Weiniger (n 13).

126 NAFTA, art 2004; discussion Baudenbacher and Clifton (n 16) 263–64.

127 ECT, art 27.

128 CSD, art II(3).

129 Roberts (n 124) 6–7; Parlett (n 2) 104; Michele Potestà, 'State-to-State Dispute Settlement Pursuant to Bilateral Investment Treaties: Is There Potential?' in Nerina Boschiero and others (eds), *International Courts and the Development of International Law: Essays in Honour of Tullio Treves* (Asser 2013) 754; Frank Berman, 'The Relevance of the Law on Diplomatic Protection in Investment Arbitration' in Federico Ortino and others (eds), *Investment Treaty Law, Current Issues II* (BIICL 2007) 72; Douglas (n 73) 2–6; Nathalie Bernasconi-Osterwalder, 'State-State Dispute Settlement in Investment Treaties' *IISD Best Practices Series* (October 2014) 3, 7; Clovis Trevino, 'State-to-State Investment Treaty Arbitration and the Interplay with Investor–State Arbitration Under the Same Treaty' (2014) 5 JIDS 199, 199–201; Michele Potestà, 'Towards a Greater Role for State-to-State Arbitration in the Architecture of Investment Treaties?' in Shaheeza Lalani and Rodrigo Polanco Lazo (eds), *The Role of the State in Investor–State Arbitration* (Brill Nijhoff 2015) 250, 253–54; Matilde Recanati, 'Diplomatic Intervention and State-to-State Arbitration as Alternative Means for the Protection of Foreign Investments and Host States' General Interests: The Italian Experience' in Sacerdoti and others (n 77) 425.

130 *Cross-Border Trucking Services* (Ch 20 NAFTA Panel Final Rep) File-USA-MEX-98-2008-01 (6 February 2001), discussed vis-à-vis overlapping claims in Roberts (n 124) 9–10; Bernasconi-Osterwalder (n 129) 15–16, both noting later investor–State proceedings: *CANACAR v US (Notice of Arbitration)*, available: <https://www.italaw.com/cases/3443> (2 April 2009). See Ch 3, nn 341–42; Ch 4, nn 599–602; also Chad MacDonald, 'NAFTA Cross-Border Trucking: Mexico Retaliates After Congress Stops Mexican Trucks at the Border' (2009) 42 VJTL 1631, 1652–55; *Canfor v US (Preliminary Question)* UNCITRAL Tribunal (6 June 2006) [240] (NAFTA investor/interstate claims allowed).

131 Roberts (n 124) 7–9, 58. Cf n 157.

132 See *Empresas Lucchetti v Peru (Award)* (2004) 19 ICSID Rev-FILJ 359 [7],[9], discussed Roberts (n 124) 8, 58; Potestà, 'Potential' (n 129) 754; Bernasconi-Osterwalder (n 129) 10–11; Recanati (n 129) 435.

by Ecuador to clarify the proper interpretation of the Ecuador-US Bilateral Investment Treaty (BIT) subsequent to findings made in an investor–State case with which it disagreed.[133] These interstate claims did not overlap with individual invocations of responsibility.[134] However, their existence demonstrates that future overlap is possible, including where States raise issues of interpretation relevant to investor–State proceedings.[135]

Second, States might claim pursuant to *different* treaties but in circumstances giving rise to overlap: for instance, treaties of friendship, commerce, and navigation (FCN) generally allow for interstate claims regarding obligations akin to those in investment law, enlivening potential overlap with investor–State claims arising from the same circumstances.[136] Interstate World Trade Organization (WTO) proceedings may also concern similar issues to investor–State claims,[137] as evidenced by concurrent WTO and investor–State claims having been brought against Australia concerning tobacco plain packaging requirements,[138] against Mexico in the context of disputes between it and the US regarding Mexico's imposition of corn syrup taxes,[139] against the US in the context of disputes between it and

[133] *Ecuador v US (Award)* PCA Case 2012-5 (29 September 2012) [40]ff, consequent on *Chevron and Texaco v Ecuador (Partial Award)* PCA Case 2007-02 (30 March 2010), discussed Roberts (n 124) 8–9, 58; Bernasconi-Osterwalder (n 129) 11–14; Trevino (n 129) 202–3; Potestà, 'Role' (n 129) 252, 254–55; Recanati (n 129) 435–36.

[134] The claims were both against different States than the investor–State claim; the second arguably never invoked responsibility: see Ch 3, nn 324–30.

[135] Similarly Roberts (n 124) 7–9.

[136] Recanati (n 129) 425–31; Roberts (n 124) 2, 7; Giorgio Sacerdoti, 'Diplomatic Conciliation of Investment Disputes: The Italian-Swiss Controversy on Secondary Residences in Engadine (1990–1992) and Its Lessons' in Marise Cremona and others (eds), *Reflections on the Constitutionalisation of International Economic Law: Liber Amicorum for Ernst-Ulrich Petersmann* (Martinus Nijhoff 2014) 405–8. For FCN cases eg n 150, Ch 6, nn 218–19.

[137] Leathley (n 15) 32; Weiss (n 77) 87–88; Anastasios Gourgourinis, 'Reviewing the Administration of Domestic Regulation in WTO and Investment Law: The International Minimum Standard as "One Standard to Rule Them All"?' in Freya Baetens (ed), *Investment Law Within International Law: Integrationist Perspectives* (CUP 2013) 299–305; Shany, *Competing* (n 1) 8, 49–50; also Shany, *Relations* (n 1) 56–60. While remedies are WTO-specific, State responsibility is usually invoked: Joanna Gomula, 'Responsibility and the World Trade Organization' in Crawford and others, *Responsibility* (n 10), particularly 793–95, 797–801.

[138] Stephanie Hartmann, 'When Two International Regimes Collide: An Analysis of the Tobacco Plain Packaging Disputes and Why Overlapping Jurisdiction of the WTO and Investment Tribunals Does Not Result in Convergence of Norms' (2017) 21 UCLAJILFA 204, particularly 204 ('overlapping disputes'), 224–25, 228–30; Weiss (n 77) 87–88. See *Australia—Certain Measures Concerning Trademarks, Geographical Indications and Other Plain Packaging Requirements Applicable to Tobacco Products and Packaging—Panel Rep* (28 June 2018) WT/DS435/R; WT/DS441/R; WT/DS458/R; WT/DS467/R (WTO); *Philip Morris Asia v Australia (Jurisdiction/Admissibility)* PCA Case 2012-12 (17 December 2015) (investor–State) [5], [178]. Philip Morris reportedly supported interstate claims: McCabe Centre for Law and Cancer, 'Australia's Plain Packaging Laws at the WTO: Progress to Date' <http://untobacco control.org/kh/legal-challenges/australias-plain-packaging-laws-wto/> (3 October 2017).

[139] Michael Ewing-Chow, 'Thesis, Antithesis and Synthesis: Investor Protection in BITs, WTO and FTAs' (2007) 30 UNSWLJ 548, 550–52; Joost Pauwelyn, 'Adding Sweeteners to Softwood Lumber: The WTO-NAFTA "Spaghetti Bowl" Is Cooking' (2006) 9 JIEL 197, 198–201; Junianto Losari and Michael Ewing-Chow, 'A Clash of Treaties: The Lawfulness of Countermeasures in International Trade Law and International Investment Law' (2015) 16 JWIT 274, 285–95; Parlett (n 2) 114–18; Paparinskis, 'Countermeasures' (n 94) 335–36. See *Mexico—Tax Measures on Soft Drinks—Panel Rep* (7 October 2005) WT/DS308/R; *Mexico—Tax Measures on Soft Drinks—AB Rep* (6 March 2006) WT/DS308/AB/R

Canada concerning the softwood lumber trade,[140] and against Saudi Arabia in relation to a dispute concerning treatment accorded to a Qatari media firm.[141] Even treaties far removed from the investment context can be relevant: consequent on an air blockade being imposed by four States on Qatar, overlapping individual and interstate claims arose,[142] with Qatar bringing interstate claims alleging breach of obligations under the Chicago Convention,[143] while State-owned Qatar Airways simultaneously brought proceedings under investment law.[144]

Finally, while individual investors claim pursuant to investment treaties, States might claim in the same circumstances for breach of customary international law obligations regarding the treatment of aliens,[145] which the treaty-based standards invoked by individuals tend substantially to reflect.[146]

Regarding the type of potential overlap,[147] investment law obligations are not owed *erga omnes*,[148] meaning we are within the realm of article 42, rather than article 48, claims. However, in terms of the different types of article 42 claims—diplomatic protection, 'direct' and 'mixed' claims—interstate claims pursuant to 'interpretation' and/or 'application' clauses can, first, encompass diplomatic protection claims.[149] Such claims have been brought under FCN

(WTO); *ADM and Tate & Lyle v Mexico (Award)* ICSID Case No ARB(AF)/04/05 (21 November 2007); *Corn Products v Mexico (Responsibility)* ICSID Case No ARB(AF)/04/01 (15 January 2008); *Cargill v Mexico (Award)* ICSID Case No ARB(AF)/05/2 (18 September 2009) (investor–State); also Crawford, 'Chance' (n 115) 218–20; Shany, *Competing* (n 1) 55; Ch 6, nn 14, 91–97.

140 Pauwelyn (n 139) 198–201. Eg *US—Final Countervailing Duty Determination Certain Softwood Lumber from Canada—AB Rep* (19 January 2004) WT/DS257/AB/R; *US—Final Countervailing Duty Determination Certain Softwood Lumber from Canada—Recourse by Canada to Article 215—AB Rep* (5 December 2005) WT/DS257/AB/RW (WTO, against US); *Canfor* (n 130) [54]ff (investor–State); Shany, *Relations* (n 1) 59; Ch 5(II)(C)(v).

141 See Lisa Bohmer, 'Easing of Qatar-Saudi Arabia Tensions ...' *IA Rep* (14 January 2021); 'Qatar and Saudi Arabia Agree ...' *IA Rep* (10 January 2022); Damien Charlotin, 'Analysis: In WTO Ruling, McRae-Chaired Panel Finds ...' *IA Rep* (3 September 2020); Jarrod Hepburn, 'Saudi Arabia Faces $1 Billion Claim ...' *IA Rep* (1 October 2018); and see *Saudi Arabia—Measures Concerning the Protection of Intellectual Property Rights—Panel Rep* (16 June 2020) WT/DS567/R (WTO); *beIN Corporation v Saudi Arabia* UNCITRAL Arbitration (investor–State).

142 See Bohmer (n 141).

143 See ibid; *Appeal Relating to the Jurisdiction of the ICAO Council under Article 84 of the Convention on International Civil Aviation (Bahrain, Egypt, Saudi Arabia and UAE v Qatar) (Judgment)* [2020] ICJ Rep 81, particularly [21]–[23], [47].

144 See Vladislav Djanic, 'Qatar Airways Lodges Treaty-Based Arbitration ...' *IA Rep* (22 July 2020), referencing <https://www.qatarairways.com/en/press-releases/2020/July/qatarairwaysarbitrations.html?activeTag=Press-releases>.

145 Recanati (n 129) 426, referencing, *inter alia*, *Barcelona Traction* (n 92); generally n 94.

146 Ole Spiermann, 'Individual Rights, State Interests and the Power to Waive ICSID Jurisdiction under Bilateral Investment Treaties' (2004) 20 Arb Int 179, 205.

147 cf n 157, particularly Roberts (n 124) 6–10 ('typology of State-to-State claims').

148 Paparinskis, 'Countermeasures' (n 94) 331; also Paparinskis, 'New' (n 124) 623; Roberts (n 124) 38; Gaja, 'Concept' (n 92) 944; cf Peters (n 2) 319–21.

149 Eg, *LaGrand (Germany v US) (Judgment)* [2001] ICJ Rep 466 [42]; *Mavrommatis* (n 87) 15–16, 29; Roberts (n 124) 7; Parlett (n 2) 104–5; Amerasinghe (n 98) 340; Amerasinghe (n 32) 275; Potestà, 'Potential' (n 129) 756, 758–59; Michele Potestà, 'Republic of Italy v Republic of Cuba' (2012) 106 AJIL 341, 345; Bernasconi-Osterwalder (n 129) 7–10; Potestà, 'Role' (n 129) 256–59, 261–62; Trevino (n 129) 206.

treaties,[150] and pursuant to a BIT in the interstate *Italy v Cuba* case.[151] Those particular claims did not overlap with individual proceedings.[152] However, despite suggestions that diplomatic protection claims cannot be brought where treaties provide for investor–State dispute settlement,[153] the practice and literature convincingly demonstrates that, treaty exclusions aside,[154] that possibility persists.[155] Consequently, there is undoubtedly scope for future overlapping diplomatic protection and investor–State claims, brought under the same treaty or otherwise.[156]

Other interstate claims, not brought by way of diplomatic protection,[157] may also overlap with investor–State proceedings.[158] Thus, Mexico's *Cross-Border Trucking* claim, discussed above and further in Chapters 3–4, did not purport to be one of diplomatic protection, despite overlap with investor–State proceedings.[159] While some argue that WTO claims may amount to diplomatic protection in particular circumstances,[160] they are also generally considered 'direct' in nature, with local remedy exhaustion not required,[161] meaning that overlapping

[150] *ELSI* (n 76) [48]–[52]; *Interhandel (Switzerland v US) (Preliminary Objections* [1959] ICJ Rep 6, 28–29; Roberts (n 124) 7; Paparinskis, 'Countermeasures' (n 94) 290; Recanati (n 129) 425; Potestà, 'Italy/Cuba' (n 149) 345.

[151] *Italy v Cuba (Interim Award)* UNCITRAL Tribunal (15 March 2005) [23]–[25] (diplomatic protection/State's rights), discussed Roberts (n 124) 7; Potestà, 'Italy/Cuba' (n 149) 342; Potestà, 'Potential' (n 129) 754, 758; Bernasconi-Osterwalder (n 129) 9–10; Trevino (n 129) 206; Potestà, 'Role' (n 129) 251, 258–59; Recanati (n 129) 437–40.

[152] Indeed, cf Ch 3, n 389.

[153] See Zachary Douglas, 'The Hybrid Foundations of Investment Treaty Arbitration' (2004) 74 BYBIL 151, 190–91, discussed Paparinskis, 'Countermeasures' (n 94) section III(C); similarly Douglas (n 73) 94–100; also *Ecuador v US (Reisman Expert Opinion)* PCA Case 2012-5 (24 April 2012) [3], [23]–[26], [30], [36]–[38], [57], discussed Roberts (n 124) 10–14; Potestà, 'Role' (n 129) 255–56; authorities Martins Paparinskis and Jessica Howley, 'Article 5: Submission by a Non-Disputing Party to the Treaty' in Dimitrij Euler, Markus Gehring, and Maxi Scherer (eds), *Transparency in International Investment Arbitration* (CUP 2015) 218 (fn 95), including Roberts (n 124) 43, 49, 52; Amerasinghe (n 98) 341.

[154] Ch 3(I)(A); Paparinskis, 'Countermeasures' (n 94) 267.

[155] See *Italy v Cuba* (n 151); Roberts (n 124) 6–20 (cf 47–48); Roberts (n 9) 392–93; Paparinskis, 'Countermeasures' (n 94) 267, sections III(C)–(D); Crawford, *GP* (n 10) 590–91; Paparinskis and Howley (n 153) 218; also *Ecuador v US* (n 85) [204]; Berman (n 129) 72; *Plama Consortium v Bulgaria (Jurisdiction)* ICSID Case No ARB/03/24 (8 February 2005) [150]; *ADM* (n 139) [81] (Sep Op Rovine).

[156] Similarly Potestà, 'Potential' (n 129) 761, cf 766–67; Roberts (n 124) 7.

[157] Distinguishing diplomatic protection/interpretation/'declaratory' claims: Roberts (n 124) 7–10; also Bernasconi-Osterwalder (n 129) 7–8. Distinguishing diplomatic protection/'abstract interpretation' cases: Potestà, 'Potential' (n 129) 755–56, also 761–65; similarly Potestà, 'Role' (n 129) 254–55, 264–71; Trevino (n 129) 204–10, cf 210–11; Paparinskis, 'Countermeasures' (n 94) 313–15; authorities Ch 3, n 307.

[158] Roberts (n 124) 8–10, 58.

[159] n 130; Ch 3, nn 341–42; Ch 4, nn 599–602.

[160] See Giorgio Sacerdoti, 'The Role of Lawyers in the WTO Dispute Settlement System' in Rufus Yerxa and Bruce Wilson (eds), *Key Issues in WTO Dispute Settlement: The first ten years* (CUP 2005) 129; Won-Mog Choi, 'The Present and Future of The Investor–State Dispute Settlement Paradigm' (2007) 10 JIEL 725, 728–29; Weiss (n 77) 87; cf Shany, *Competing* (n 1) 59.

[161] See David Palmeter and Petros Mavroidis, *Dispute Settlement in the World Trade Organization* (CUP 2004) 35; also Shany, *Competing* (n 1) 59; *US—Section 211 Omnibus Appropriations Act—Panel Rep* (6 August 2001) WT/DS176/R [8.95] ('local remedies … not applicable'); cf Choi (n 160) 728–29 (local remedies excluded). Chapter 3 shows that seeking reparation for individual damage is key to diplomatic protection: Ch 3(II)(C). WTO claims do not, however, claim compensation for past losses: see Arie Reich, 'The Effectiveness of the WTO Dispute Settlement System: A Statistical Analysis'

individual investment claims and interstate WTO proceedings are unlikely to involve diplomatic protection. As for interstate claims regarding interpretation, such as those noted above,[162] these may or may not be ones of diplomatic protection, as Chapter 3 elaborates.[163]

The distinction between diplomatic protection and other interstate claims, and the relevance of that distinction to rules potentially precluding overlapping interstate and investor–State claims, is addressed in later chapters. It suffices here to note that investor–State claims may overlap—and have overlapped—with article 42 interstate claims, including diplomatic protection claims.

B. Human rights

Interstate human rights claims may also overlap with those brought by individuals,[164] in at least four possible ways.

First, human rights treaties providing for individual claims tend to also contain interstate dispute resolution mechanisms,[165] allowing State parties either to invoke the responsibility of another State party for violations,[166] and/or to claim regarding the treaty's 'interpretation or application'.[167] Use of both kinds of interstate mechanism has resulted in claims overlapping with those brought by individuals.

Thus, Ireland brought proceedings against the UK before the European Commission on Human Rights (ECommHR) and the EctHR regarding the treatment of prisoners in Northern Ireland in alleged breach of the European Convention on Human Rights (ECHR).[168] Several of the detained individuals themselves likewise brought claims before the EcommHR.[169]

EUI Working Paper LAW 2017/11 <https://cadmus.eui.eu/bitstream/handle/1814/47045/LAW_2017_11.pdf>, 16 and references.

[162] nn 131–33.

[163] Ch 3(IV).

[164] Generally Annemarieke Vermeer-Künzli, 'Unfinished Business: Concurrence of Claims Presented before a Human Rights Court or Treaty Body and through Diplomatic Protection' (2010) 10 HRLR 269, 270, 274–76; ILC, 'Summary Records of the Meetings of the Fiftieth Session' (1998) 1 ILCYB 1, 26–27 (Simma/Economides); Paparinskis, 'Countermeasures' (n 94) 291; Giorgio Gaja, 'The Protection of General Interests in the International Community' (2012) 364 RdC 9, 169 ('parallel claim').

[165] Generally Mackenzie and others (n 22) Chs 11–16; Weiss (n 6) 806; Connors (n 29) 393; Amerasinghe (n 98) 32–33; Roberts (n 124) 32; Frédéric Mégret, 'Nature of Obligations' in Moeckli and others (n 24) 105.

[166] ECHR, art 33; ICCPR, art 41(1); UNCAT, art 21(1); ICESCR Protocol, art 10; CRC Protocol, art 12; ICPMW, art 76; CPED, art 32; CERD, arts 11–13; AmCHR, art 45(1) (IACHR); AfCHPR, arts 47, 49. See Geir Ulfstein and Isabella Risini, 'Inter-State Applications under the European Convention on Human Rights: Strengths and Challenges' *EJIL:Talk!* (24 January 2020).

[167] CERD, art 22; CEDAW, art 29; UNCAT, art 30; ICPMW, art 92; CPED, art 42; AmCHR, art 62(1); AfCHPR Protocol, arts 3(1), 5.

[168] *Ireland v UK (Judgment)* [1978] ECHR Ser A, No 25 [92]–[147].

[169] *Donnelly v UK* (1973) 16 YBkECHR 212, 262–66, discussed Shany, *Competing* (n 1) 36.

The proceedings brought by Belgium against Senegal before the International Court of Justice (ICJ) for violation of obligations under the Convention against Torture (UNCAT) in the *Obligation to Prosecute or Extradite* case were preceded by individual proceedings brought against Senegal before the UNCAT Committee alleging certain of the same breaches.[170]

Cyprus brought claims against Turkey, arising out of activities in northern Cyprus and resulting in a compensation award,[171] in circumstances in which the existence of several 'overlapping' claims brought by affected individuals was acknowledged.[172]

After the 2008 conflict between Georgia and Russia, the former brought claims against the latter for alleged breach of obligations under the Convention on the Elimination of All Forms of Racial Discrimination (CERD),[173] and the ECHR.[174] Thousands of individuals brought claims for alleged violations of the ECHR arising out of the same conflict, against one or both States.[175] And in an earlier interstate claim concerning the alleged arrest, detention, and expulsion of Georgian nationals from Russia, resulting in a compensation award,[176] the ECtHR expressly noted that some of the individual situations referenced to illustrate the existence of the alleged practice were the subject of individual applications.[177]

Finally, various overlapping individual and interstate claims have been instituted in the context of the ongoing conflict between Russia and Ukraine. On the interstate level, Ukraine initially brought proceedings against Russia before the ICJ concerning, *inter alia*, alleged violations of CERD in Crimea,[178] and proceedings alleging breaches of the ECHR in Crimea and Eastern Ukraine.[179] A subsequent

[170] *Prosecute/Extradite* (n 115) [27]; *Guengueng v Senegal* Comm 181/2001, Doc CAT/C/36/D/181/2001 (CAT, 19 May 2006) [3.1]–[3.12].

[171] *Cyprus v Turkey (Just Satisfaction)* ECHR 2014-II 245 (GC) [58].

[172] ibid [14]; see *Varnava and others v Turkey* [2009] ECHR 2009-V 13.

[173] *Application of the International Convention on the Elimination of All Forms of Racial Discrimination (Georgia v Russia) (Preliminary Objections)* [2011] ICJ Rep 70, 77–79, 85.

[174] *Georgia v Russia (II)* App 38263/08 (ECtHR, 13 December 2011) [40]–[47], [56]–[57]; Greer (n 24) 450.

[175] 'Hearing in the Inter-State Case Georgia v. Russia (II) Concerning the 2008 Armed Conflict between the Two Countries' *ECHR Pr Rel* (22 September 2011). As of April 2022, 600 claims were apparently still pending: ECtHR, 'Q&A on Inter-State Cases' (April 2022) <https://echr.coe.int/Documents/Press_Q_A_Inter-State_cases_ENG.pdf>.

[176] *Georgia v Russia (I) (Just satisfaction)*, App 13255/07 (ECtHR, 31 January 2019).

[177] *Georgia v Russia (I)* 2014-IV ECHR 109 [80], generally [3]; see also *Georgia/Russia(I) (Compensation)* (n 176) [66].

[178] *Application of the International Convention for the Suppression of the Financing of Terrorism and of the International Convention on the Elimination of All Forms of Racial Discrimination (Ukraine v Russia) (Provisional Measures)* [2017] ICJ Rep 104 [32]–[34].

[179] 'ECHR Deals with Cases Concerning Crimea and Eastern Ukraine' *ECHR Pr Rel 345/14* (26 November 2014); 'ECHR Communicates to Russia New Inter-State Case Concerning Events in Crimea and Eastern Ukraine' *ECHR Pr Rel 296/15* (1 October 2015); 'ECHR to Adjourn Some Individual Applications on Eastern Ukraine Pending Grand Chamber Judgment in Related Inter-State Case' *ECHR Pr Rel 432* (17 December 2018), noting the five interstate applications pending, including *Ukraine v Russia (re Crimea)*, App 20958/14 and *Ukraine v Russia (re Eastern Ukraine)*, App 8019/16. By 2022, eight interstate applications were pending: see ECtHR, 'Q&A' (n 175). See generally Greer (n 24) 450.

interstate ECHR claim alleging 'mass and gross' violations of human rights was filed after further military action in 2022.[180] For its part, Russia instituted interstate proceedings against Ukraine in 2021 alleging various human rights violations and responsibility for the downing of flight MH-17 over Ukraine due to a failure to close airspace.[181] According to the ECtHR, as of 2022, '[t]here [were] over 8,500 individual applications before the Court which appear to be related to the events in Crimea, Eastern Ukraine and the Sea of Azov'.[182] An interstate ECtHR claim was also brought by the Netherlands against Russia concerning flight MH-17, with individual applications additionally having been lodged by 380 relatives of those killed.[183] The clear possibility for overlap between the interstate and individual cases is demonstrated by Ukraine withdrawing one claim precisely because an individual application 'concerning the same subject matter was pending before the Court',[184] and by the Court deciding, given a key common issue, to adjourn individual cases relating to Eastern Ukraine until judgment in the interstate case was rendered.[185]

While these examples have involved interstate claims focused on a few treaties, the possibility of future overlapping interstate and individual claims under other instruments cannot be excluded.[186] For instance, while interstate treaty-body procedures, including under the International Convention on Civil and Political Rights (ICCPR), are not commonly used,[187] there are examples,[188] and various human rights treaties have been invoked before different fora.[189] The possibility of overlap with individual claims brought under those same treaties is therefore live.

[180] ECtHR, 'Inter-State Case Ukraine v. Russia (X): Receipt of Completed Application Form and Notification to Respondent State' *ECHR Pr Rel 220* (28 June 2022). See Justine Batura and Isabella Risini, 'Of Parties, Third Parties, and Treaty Interpretation: Ukraine v. Russia (X) before the European Court of Human Rights' *EJIL:Talk!* (26 September 2022).

[181] Marko Milanovic, 'Russia Files Interstate Complaint Against Ukraine in Strasbourg' *EJIL:Talk!* (26 July 2021), with references, also noting that 'thousands of individual applications', apparently related, have been instituted against Ukraine. The exact nature of any overlap is difficult to determine.

[182] See ECtHR, 'Q&A' (n 175).

[183] See Isabella Risini and Geir Ulfstein, 'The Netherlands' Inter-State Application against Russia Six Years after MH 17' *EJIL:Talk!* (14 August 2020) (noting '[o]verlapping individual and inter-state applications' and citing ECtHR, 'ECHR Gives Notification to Russia of Cases Brought by Relatives of People Killed in the Downing of Malaysian Airlines Flight MH-17' *ECHR Pr Rel 121* (4 April 2019)); ECtHR, 'Ukraine v Russia (X)' (n 180), citing joined cases *Ukraine and The Netherlands v Russia*, Apps 8019/16, 43800/14 and 28525/20.

[184] 'Decisions of 24 September 2015' *ECHR Pr Rel 286/15* (24 September 2015), referencing *Ukraine v Russia (III)*, App 49537/14 and *Dzhemilov* (App 49522/14).

[185] 'ECHR to Adjourn' (n 179).

[186] Generally Shany, *Competing* (n 1) 34–37, 44–46.

[187] Connors (n 29) 393; Paparinskis, 'Countermeasures' (n 94) 291.

[188] See David Keane, 'ICERD and Palestine's Inter-State Complaint' *EJIL:Talk!* (30 April 2018); David Keane, 'CERD Reaches Historic Decisions in Inter-State Communications' *EJIL:Talk!* (6 September 2019).

[189] Eg *Ahmadou Sadio Diallo (Guinea v DRC) (Merits)* [2010] ICJ Rep 639 [63],[64],[75],[87] (ICCPR); *Armed Activities* (n 118) [190] (ICCPR/AfCHPR/UNCAT); also Shany, *Competing* (n 1) 35, 44–46.

Second, with many human rights obligations existing not only under treaty but also as a matter of customary international law,[190] potential overlap arises between individual treaty claims and interstate claims brought pursuant to those customary rules.[191]

Third, as noted above, rules regarding the treatment of aliens require States to meet an 'international minimum standard'.[192] That standard now 'corresponds largely with the standards expounded in the principal international human rights treaties'.[193] Consequently, individual and interstate claims brought, respectively, for breach of human rights and investment law obligations could overlap.[194] For instance, Liechtenstein brought ICJ proceedings against Germany in the *Certain Property* case, alleging expropriation of an individual national's property,[195] in circumstances in which the relevant individual had earlier instituted ECtHR proceedings for human rights violations.[196] Similarly, in its ECtHR claim concerning activities in Crimea, Ukraine alleged, *inter alia*, expropriation of its citizens' enterprises, and relied, in doing so, on the findings of tribunals in cases brought by individual investors against Russia.[197] As at 2022, ten such publicly known arbitrations had apparently been brought by Ukrainian investors.[198]

Finally, interstate claims in other fields may overlap with individual human rights claims.[199] Thus, Mexico instituted ICJ proceedings against the US in the *Avena* case, concerning the latter's compliance with its obligations under the Vienna Convention on Consular Relations (VCCR) vis-à-vis some fifty Mexican nationals,[200] while individual proceedings, arising from the same circumstances, were initiated for breach of the AmCHR regarding at least eight of those

[190] Eg Crawford, *Brownlie's* (n 94) 642–43.

[191] cf *Diallo (Merits)* (n 189) [87]; Vermeer-Künzli, 'Concurrence' (n 164) 274–75; Amerasinghe (n 98) 33; Shany, *Competing* (n 1) 34–35, 44–46.

[192] n 94.

[193] Dugard, 'MPEPIL' (n 116) [18]; also Tomuschat (n 11) 985; Amerasinghe (n 98) 37–38; Mazzeschi (n 116) 223; Shany, *Competing* (n 1) 8–9; Gaja, 'Affected' (n 116) 373; Jorge Viñuales, 'Sovereignty in Foreign Investment Law' in Zachary Douglas, Joost Pauwelyn, and Jorge Viñuales (eds), *The Foundations of International Investment Law* (OUP 2014) 326; Martins Paparinskis, 'Analogies and Other Regimes of International Law' in Douglas, Pauwelyn, and Viñuales (n 193) 79–80; n 218.

[194] Shany, *Competing* (n 1) 8–9, 67, 84; Ben Juratowich, 'The Relationship between Diplomatic Protection and Investment Treaties' (2008) 23 ICSID Rev-FILJ 10, 34. Cf Judith Levine, 'The Interaction of International Investment Arbitration and the Rights of Indigenous Peoples' in Baetens (n 137) 109 (concurrent individual investment/human rights claims), referencing *Eureko v Slovakia (Jurisdiction, Arbitrability and Suspension)* PCA Case 2008-13 (26 October 2010), particularly [58]; similarly Kaufmann-Kohler and Potestà (n 66) 34–35; Ch 4, n 173.

[195] *Certain Property Pleadings* (n 105), Mem Liechtenstein [5.27]–[5.31].

[196] Shany, *Competing* (n 1) 8, 35, 46, referencing *Prince Hans-Adam* (n 5); *Certain Property* (n 5) [17].

[197] *Ukraine v Russia (re Crimea)* Apps 20958/14 and 38334/18 (ECtHR, 16 December 2020) [29], [136], [341], [484], citing *Everest Estate v Russia* (PCA Case 2015-36) and *Oschadbank v Russia* (PCA Case 2016-14), overlap discussed Jarrod Hepburn, 'Relying on Investment Treaty Case-Law ...' *IA Rep* (1 February 2021).

[198] Hepburn, 'Relying' (n 197).

[199] Generally Shany, *Competing* (n 1) 8–10, 35–37.

[200] *Avena and Other Mexican Nationals (Mexico v US) (Judgment)* [2004] ICJ Rep 12 [15]–[16], discussed DADP, 75; Crawford, *GP* (n 10) 592–93; Parlett (n 2) 94–96.

nationals.[201] The French testing challenged by New Zealand in the ICJ *Nuclear Tests* case was simultaneously the subject of individual proceedings before the ECommHR and the Human Rights Committee (HRC).[202] Individual proceedings were brought for ECHR breach regarding the conduct also alleged to violate international law in the interstate *Legality of Use of Force* cases.[203] In the *Arctic Sunrise* proceedings brought by the Netherlands against Russia under the United Nations Convention on the Law of the Sea (UNCLOS), concerning detention of a vessel and those on board,[204] the relevant individuals had also filed ECtHR claims for human rights violations,[205] the Netherlands acknowledging the consequent 'overlap' in proceedings.[206] Finally, the EECC addressed interstate claims, including under human rights law, arising from the Eritrea/Ethiopia conflict,[207] while an African Commission on Human and Peoples' Rights (ACommHPR) claim, concerning victims of the same conflict, was brought against the two States for breach of individuals' human rights.[208] And, while not an individual claim, it bears mentioning that the restrictions imposed on Qatar that led to interstate WTO and International Civil Aviation Organization proceedings, and an individual investment claim,[209] also led to an interstate claim under CERD, alleging discrimination against Qatari nationals,[210] demonstrating the potential relevance of human rights instruments to multi-faceted disputes.

[201] See *Medellin v US* Case 12644, Rep 90/09 (IACHR, 7 August 2009) (Medellin/Cardenas/Garcia) [65]; *Arias v US* Pet 15-12, Rep 73/12 (IACHR, 17 July 2012) [44]; *Rodriguez v US* Pet 1672-11, Rep 63/12 (IACHR, 29 March 2012) [55]; *Moreno Ramos v US* Pet 4446/02, Rep 61/03 (IACHR, 10 October 2003) [45]–[55]; *Diaz v US* Pet 259-11, Rep 133/11 (IACHR, 19 October 2011) [8]; *Fierro v US* Case 11331, Rep 99/03 (IACHR, 29 December 2003) [52]–[59]. Cf *Avena* (n 200) 24–26 (numbers 31, 36–39, 41–42, 44). Generally Shany, *Relations* (n 1) 48–49. Further: *Right to Information on Consular Assistance in the Framework of the Guarantees of the Due Process of Law (Advisory Opinion)* [1999] IACHR Ser A No 16 [2], [61] (ICJ proceedings not preventing), [49] (no 'rul[ing] on … examples'), referenced Shany, *Competing* (n 1) 35, 46, 241; Shany, *Relations* (n 1) 48.

[202] Shany, *Competing* (n 1) 36, referencing *Examination of the Situation in Accordance with Paragraph 63 of the Court's Judgment of 20 December 1974 in Nuclear Tests (New Zealand v France)* [1995] ICJ Rep 288; *Bordes v France* Comm 645/1995, Doc CCPR/C/57/D/645/1995 (HRC, 22 July 1996); *Tauira v France* (1995) 83 DR 112.

[203] Shany, *Competing* (n 1) 9–10, 40, referencing, *inter alia*, *Legality of Use of Force (Serbia and Montenegro v Belgium) (Preliminary Objections)* [2004] ICJ Rep 279; *Banković v Belgium* ECHR 2001-XII 333.

[204] *Arctic Sunrise Arbitration (Netherlands v Russia) (Merits)* PCA Case 2014-02 (14 August 2015) [140], [144].

[205] ibid [134].

[206] ibid [147]. Cf Shany, *Competing* (n 1) 68.

[207] Generally *Eritrea* (n 47) [3]; nn 46–47.

[208] *Interights v Eritrea and Ethiopia* (2003) AHRLR 74 [40], [49]–[51]; Andres Sotomayer, 'The Rule Against Duplication of Procedures in the Regional Systems of Human Rights Protection' [2009] NDWP 2 <http://www.nd.edu/~ndlaw/cchr/papers/Andres_%20Duplication_Procedures.pdf>, 4; Gherari (n 25) 785; discussion Ch 4, nn 200–5.

[209] nn 142–44.

[210] See *Qatar v Saudi Arabia (Jurisdiction)* Doc CERD/C/99/5 (30 August 2019); *Qatar v Saudi Arabia (Admissibility)* Doc CERD/C/99/6 (30 August 2019); *Qatar v UAE (Jurisdiction)* Doc CERD/C/99/3 (30 August 2019); *Qatar v UAE (Admissibility)* Doc CERD/C/99/4 (30 August 2019). Generally Bohmer (n 141).

Various types of interstate claim could overlap with individual claims in the human rights field.

First, responsibility may be invoked pursuant to the rule in article 48, as *erga omnes* obligations include those 'concerning the basic rights of the human person'.[211] Indeed, if one considers that *erga omnes* obligations are characterised by being non-bilateral,[212] in the sense that they protect a 'collective' interest,[213] rather than that the obligations reach an 'importance' threshold,[214] then arguably *all* customary human rights obligations are owed *erga omnes*.[215] For their part, multilateral human rights treaties undoubtedly contain obligations owed *erga omnes partes*.[216] Interstate human rights claims may thus be brought, under treaty or customary international law, for breach of *erga omnes (partes)* obligations.

However, as foreshadowed above, interstate claims for breach of human rights obligations may also be brought as ones of diplomatic protection.[217] As the ICJ explained in *Diallo*:

[211] *Barcelona Traction* (n 92) [34]; *ARSIWA*, 278.

[212] See Gateano Arangio-Ruiz, 'Fourth Report on State Responsibility' (1992) 2(1) ILCYB 1 [131]–[132], particularly [92], quoted Maurizio Ragazzi, *The Concept of International Obligations* Erga Omnes (Clarendon 1997) 201–2, cf 202–3 (disagreeing); Tams (n 120) 129–31 and authorities, though contesting (ibid 130–36) a 'structural approach' focusing on obligations being 'non-bilateralisable' (ibid 130). He argues that *erga omnes* obligations can be bilateral: ibid 134–36. But strictly, States are 'assimilated to the State to whom a bilateral obligation is due': Gaja, 'Compliance' (n 119) 958, also 959; Linos-Alexandre Sicilianos, 'Countermeasures in Response to Grave Violations of Obligations Owed to the International Community' in Crawford and others, *Responsibility* (n 10) 1139; Martin Dawidowicz, *Third-Party Countermeasures in International Law* (CUP 2017) 91; Paparinskis, 'Countermeasures' (n 94) 330–31; cf James Crawford, 'Responsibility to the International Community as a Whole' (2001) 8 Ind JGLS 303, 321; Ch 1, nn 119–33. Further: Gerald Fitzmaurice, 'Second Report on the Law of Treaties' (1957) 2 ILCYB 16 [125]–[126] (human rights 'absolute rather than … reciprocal'), discussed Tams (n 120) 57, cf 133 (not every absolute obligation *erga omnes*) and Ragazzi (n 212) 200–1, cf 201–3; similarly Mégret (n 165) 89–91. Cf Simma and Pulkowski (n 50) 160–61.

[213] n 119; also Arangio-Ruiz (n 212) [131]; Sicilianos (n 212) 1139 ('extra-State interests'). Obligations are still owed to each State: Ch 1, nn 119–33.

[214] Arangio-Ruiz (n 212) [92]; see Tams (n 120) 136 ('material approach'), generally 136–57; also Ragazzi (n 212) 203 ('intrinsic value'); Vermeer-Künzli, 'Interest' (n 92) 566 ('fundamental'). Nonetheless, it may inhere in 'collective' interests that the obligations are sufficiently important: cf Tams (n 120) 133 ff; also Elisabeth Zoller, *Peacetime Unilateral Remedies: An Analysis of Countermeasures* (Transnational 1984) 90–91.

[215] Similarly Silvia Borelli and Simon Olleson, 'Obligations Relating to Human Rights and Humanitarian Law' in Crawford and others, *Responsibility* (n 10) 1185; see discussion Tams (n 120) 119, referencing, *inter alia*, IDI, 'The Protection of Human Rights and the Principle of Non-Intervention in Internal Affairs of States' (1989) 63(II) IDIA 338, art 1; Mégret (n 165) 89–91, 106; Arangio-Ruiz (n 212) [131], [134]; Gaja, 'Injuries' (n 116); also Gaja, 'Affected' (n 116) 374; ALI (n 100) 179–80. Cf Tams (n 120) 138 (*Barcelona Traction* (n 92) [34] focus is 'basic' human rights); James Crawford, 'First Report on State Responsibility' (1997) 2(1) ILCYB 1 [63].

[216] Crawford, 'ThirdRep' (n 92) [92]; *ARSIWA*, 277; Mégret (n 165) 106, 89–91, referencing, *inter alia*, *Reservations to the Convention on Genocide (Advisory Opinion)* [1951] ICJ Rep 15, 23; *Austria v Italy* (1961) 4 YBkECHR 116, 138–42; *Prosecute/Extradite* (n 115) [69]; Gaja, 'Affected' (n 116) 381; discussion Tams (n 120) 120–21; Rivier (n 26) 756.

[217] nn 120–21; ILC, '50th' (n 164) 22, 26–27 (Hafner/Simma/Economides); Andrea Gattini, 'A Trojan Horse for Sudeten Claims? On Some Implications of the Prince of Liechtenstein v Germany' (2002) 13 EJIL 513, 537.

> Owing to the substantive development of international law over recent decades in respect of the rights it accords to individuals, the scope *ratione materiae* of diplomatic protection, originally limited to alleged violations of the minimum standard of treatment of aliens, has subsequently widened to include, *inter alia*, internationally guaranteed human rights.[218]

Some suggest that this passage simply reiterates that diplomatic protection claims are based on the minimum standard, which is now reflected in human rights norms.[219] Nonetheless, the Court in *Diallo* found that particular human rights treaty provisions had been violated,[220] and therefore apparently regarded 'human rights and the international standard as distinct primary rules that could give rise to diplomatic protection'.[221] The ECtHR in *Cyprus v Turkey* similarly acknowledged that in certain interstate claims, a State:

> denounces violations by another Contracting Party of the basic human rights of its nationals (or other victims). In fact such claims are substantially similar not only to those made in an individual application … but also to claims filed in the context of diplomatic protection ….[222]

The EECC, considering alleged violations of international humanitarian law and human rights obligations,[223] likewise held that 'some of both States' claims [were] made in the exercise of diplomatic protection'.[224] Overlapping individual and interstate diplomatic protection human rights claims are therefore possible.

Other interstate claims overlapping with individual human rights actions may be 'direct' or 'mixed'.[225] The Tribunal in *Arctic Sunrise*, for instance, considered that the Netherlands' claims under UNCLOS were 'direct',[226] while *Avena* is generally considered 'mixed',[227] with Mexico having brought the claim 'in its own right and in the exercise of its right of diplomatic protection'.[228]

The distinction between *erga omnes (partes)*, diplomatic protection, 'direct', and 'mixed' claims is considered further in the following chapters vis-à-vis particular

[218] *Ahmadou Sadio Diallo (Guinea v DRC) (Preliminary Objections)* [2007] ICJ Rep 582 [39].

[219] See Amerasinghe (n 98) 38, 73–74, 76; Brierly (n 99) 259–60; discussion Paparinskis, 'Countermeasures' (n 94) 325–26; Shany, *Relations* (n 1) 27–28.

[220] *Diallo (Merits)* (n 189) [73], [74], [80], [82], [84]–[85], [97]. Cf Brierly (n 99) 259–60.

[221] Paparinskis, 'Countermeasures' (n 94) 327. Similarly Crawford, *GP* (n 10) 587.

[222] *Cyprus v Turkey (Compensation)* (n 171) [45]; see Ch 3, nn 220, 348–49; Ch 4, nn 570–71.

[223] See EECC Agreement, art 5(1); *Eritrea* (n 47) [22]; Nollkaemper (n 6) 106.

[224] *Eritrea* (n 47) [25]; *Ethiopia's Damages Claims (Final Award)* (2009) XXVI UNRIAA 631 [25]; authorities Ch 4, n 454.

[225] Generally nn 102ff.

[226] *Arctic Sunrise (Merits)* (n 204) [173], see Ch 3, n 58. However, see Ch 3, nn 281–82 on whether it is better regarded as 'mixed'. Nonetheless, 'direct' interstate human rights claims are possible: see Ch 3, n 349, generally Ch 3(II)(B)(i).

[227] DADP, 75; Crawford, *GP* (n 10) 584; Thirlway (n 109) 1551.

[228] *Avena* (n 200) [40]. Further Ch 3, nn 59, 376–78.

rules of preclusion. The important point here is that individual human rights claims potentially overlap with all kinds of interstate claims, and across various fields.

C. Other claims

There is also potential overlap with interstate proceedings in other fields in which individuals might invoke State responsibility. The *Chórzow* case, for instance, was brought by Germany against Poland for reparation for its national resulting from treaty violations, and overlapped with a claim brought by that national against Poland, relating to the same conduct, before a MAT.[229] Interstate UNCC claims were brought,[230] giving rise to potential overlap with individual claims before the same body.[231] Further, while most claims brought before the EECC were interstate in nature,[232] as noted above, overlap did arise between those claims and individual human rights actions.[233]

The regional agreements allowing for individual claims discussed above also make provision for interstate dispute settlement.[234] Claims under such interstate procedures, occasionally employed in practice,[235] could potentially overlap with individual proceedings for the same violations.[236] Moreover, with regional agreements often providing human rights[237] and investment protections,[238] individual or interstate claims thereunder could potentially overlap with the investment, WTO, and human rights claims discussed above.[239] For the reasons already noted,

[229] See *Chórzow (Jurisdiction)* (n 80) 5–6, 30, discussed Shany, *Relations* (n 1) 43; *Chórzow (Merits)* (n 100) 27–28. Further: Ch 4, nn 140–41.

[230] See van Houtte, Das, and Delmartino (n 42) 337 (category F). Further: Ch 4, nn 78–79.

[231] Eg, *Seventh Instalment of Individual Claims For Damages up to US$100,000 (Category 'C')* UN Doc S/AC26/1999/11 (UNCC, 24 June 1999), discussed Ch 4, n 79.

[232] n 47.

[233] n 208.

[234] Generally Mackenzie and others (n 22) Chs 9–10; Baudenbacher and Clifton (n 16) 252–62, 265–71; Murphy (n 36) 183; Leathley (n 15) Chs 3, 5–9; also Shany, *Competing* (n 1) 44–45. See (1) EU courts (TFEU, art 259); Greer (n 24) 461; (2) Andean Court (Cartagena Protocol, art 24); (3) CCJ (CARICOM Treaty, art 211); (4) CACJ (CACJ Statute, arts 22(a), 23); (5) COMESA CJ (COMESA Treaty, art 24); (6) EAC CJ (EAC Treaty, arts 27–28); (7) ECOWAS CJ (ECOWAS Treaty, art 76, ECOWAS Protocol, art 3); (8) SADCT (SADC Protocol, art 14). Further on MERCOSUR: Olivos Protocol, arts 1, 6–24, 33.

[235] Eg, *Dispute Between Uruguay and Brazil Concerning Discriminatory and Restrictive Measures to the Commerce of Tobacco and Tobacco Products (Award 08/2005)* MERCOSUR Tribunal (5 August 2005); cf Simma and Pulkowski (n 50) 154 (UK/France EU claim, not pursued); Idriss Jazairy, 'Report of the Special Rapporteur on the Negative Impact of Unilateral Coercive Measures on the Enjoyment of Human Rights' UN Doc A/HRC/33/48 (2 August 2016) [57] (third-State EU claims).

[236] cf Ch 3(I)(A) (CARICOM).

[237] Shany, *Competing* (n 1) 68–71; Ebobrah (n 23) 232–34; Greer (n 24) 461–63; nn 58–60.

[238] Shany, *Competing* (n 1) 67; Mavluda Sattorova, 'Investor Rights under EU Law and International Investment Law' (2016) 17 JWIT 895, 896–913, 917–18, discussing *inter alia Eureko* (n 194), see [58], [247] (BIT/EU 'equivalence'), [249] ('duplication'), [250]–[263]; *Electrabel v Hungary (Jurisdiction, Applicable Law, Liability)* ICSID Case No ARB/07/19 (30 November 2012) [4.177]; Leathley (n 15) 116–20, 134–35, 158–64; Damien Charlotin, 'Twin Arbitrations Started against Spain …' *IA Rep* (24 August 2018) (EU/investment proceedings).

[239] See Shany, *Competing* (n 1) 53, 59 (WTO), 67, 70–72.

interstate claims in these different fields might be diplomatic protection or 'direct' claims, or, for human rights actions, article 48 claims for violation of *erga omnes (partes)* obligations.[240]

Finally, while interstate disputes before domestic courts are unusual,[241] individual claims before domestic courts may concern the conduct also challenged in international interstate proceedings.[242] For example, the ICJ *Immunities Case*, discussed further in Chapters 4–5, concerned agreements between Germany and Italy purporting to settle WWII-related claims, including those of nationals.[243] Italian nationals nonetheless succeeded in bringing claims against Germany domestically, giving rise to complex questions concerning the relationship between those individual and interstate claims.[244] More generally, domestic-level individual claims were brought in many of the situations already noted in which individual and interstate claims overlapped internationally,[245] while the local remedies rule, including as applied vis-à-vis certain interstate human rights claims,[246] raises—for

[240] Sections II, III(A)–(B); further: ALI (n 100) 222 (EU law diplomatic protection); cf Simma and Pulkowski (n 50) 154.

[241] Nollkaemper (n 64) 529; Nollkaemper (n 6) 95–96 (cf exceptions); cf Shany, *Relations* (n 1) 46–48.

[242] See Nollkaemper (n 6) 247, 249 (potential 'overlap' 'in substance'); Shany, *Relations* (n 1) 11–13, 45–63 (with examples); Nollkaemper (n 64) 529–30; Tzanakopoulos (n 65) 141–42, 164; *Distomo Massacre* (2003) 129 ILR 556 (Bundesgerichthof) 567.

[243] Ch 5, nn 105–7.

[244] *Jurisdictional Immunities (Germany v Italy: Greece Intervening) (Judgment)* [2012] ICJ Rep 99 [27]–[36]; also *Sechremelis and others v Greece* Comm 1507/2006, Doc CCPR/C/100/D/1507/2006/Rev.1 (HRC, 25 October 2010); Nollkaemper (n 6) 95–96. Similar issues have arisen vis-à-vis treatment of South Korean so-called 'comfort women' during WWII, with many domestic suits filed against Japan and an interstate settlement ultimately agreed: see summary: Columbia Law School, Centre for Korean Legal Studies, 'Lawsuits Brought against Japan by Former Korean "Comfort Women"' <https://kls.law.columbia.edu/content/lawsuits-brought-against-japan-former-korean-comfort-women.>. South Korean courts have also awarded compensation for WWII-related forced labour, claims Japan maintains were subject to interstate settlement. The claims were against companies, rather than Japan, but overlapping claims against South Korea could have resulted, with interstate arbitration commenced, and threats of investment suits by the relevant companies: see Jarrod Hepburn, 'South Korean Supreme Court Ruling ...' *IA Rep* (31 October 2018). For the interstate settlement: Tong-Hyung Kim and Hyung-Jin Kim, 'South Korean Plan Aims to Heal Forced Labor Feud with Japan' *AP* (6 March 2023) <https://apnews.com/article/south-korea-japan-forced-laborers-colonial-rule-e8e828901148c2f2528ce557f445772b>.

[245] See *Chórzow (Jurisdiction)* (n 80), also n 229; *Nemariam* (n 82); *Danikovic v Netherlands* (2000) Case 759/99 SKG (CA, Amsterdam), discussed Nollkaemper (n 6) 28–29, 249, regarding overlap with *Use of Force* (n 203); US-based litigation concerning the *Avena* (n 200) situation (nn 200–1), discussed Shany, *Relations* (n 1) 1, 48–53; domestic decisions concerning softwood lumber (n 140), discussed ibid 1, 58–59; *Prince Hans-Adam II v Municipality of Cologne* (1999) 149 ILR 1 (Cologne CA); *Re Prince Hans-Adam II of Liechtenstein* (1998) 149 ILR 26 (BVerfG), concerning *Certain Property* (n 5) (nn 195–96); *Habre* (2000) 125 ILR 569 (Senegal Cour Cass), connected with *Prosecute/Extradite* (n 115); UNCC-related UK litigation, discussed in *Fifteenth Instalment of 'E4' Claims* UN Doc S/AC.26/2002/16 (20 June 2002) [57]ff; Hess (n 10) 143.

[246] ICCPR, art 41(1)(c); ICESCR Protocol, art 10(1)(c); UNCAT, art 21(1)(c); CERD, art 11(3); ICPMW, art 76(1)(c); AmCHR, art 46(1)(a); AfCHPR, art 50. Cf, not expressly requiring: ECHR, art 33; CRC Protocol, art 12; CPED, art 32; CERD, art 22; CEDAW, art 29; UNCAT, art 30; ICPMW, art 92; CPED, art 42; but see *Georgia v Russia (II)* (n 174) [84]; *ELSI* (n 76) [50]. Generally Amerasinghe (n 32) 64–83, 305–8; William Dodge, 'National Courts and International Arbitration: Exhaustion of Remedies and Res Judicata Under Chapter Eleven of NAFTA' (2000) 23 Hast I & CLR 357, 365; Nollkaemper (n 64) 527; also Shany, *Relations* (n 1) 162.

the same reasons noted above[247]—an inevitable overlap between those domestic proceedings brought by the affected individual with a view to exhausting local remedies and the later interstate diplomatic protection claim.[248]

IV. Conclusion

This chapter has outlined mechanisms for the invocation of State responsibility by individuals in the investment, human rights, and other fields of law. It has highlighted the possibility for overlap between such proceedings and interstate claims, of varying kinds, arising from the same circumstances. Chapters 3–6 now turn to addressing how the actions of either a State or an individual might, in light of that overlap, affect the ability of the other to successfully invoke responsibility.

[247] n 76.

[248] Nollkaemper (n 6) 247 (diplomatic protection 'in substance ... overlap[s] with claims ... before ... domestic courts'), 27; Shany, *Relations* (n 1) 27–31; 138.

3

The Application of Diplomatic Protection-Based Rules

Nothing in the State responsibility framework per se prevents multiple States, or indeed individuals, from making claims against the same respondent State arising out of the same factual circumstances.[1] Indeed, article 16 of the Draft Articles on Diplomatic Protection (DADP) exemplifies this general position, indicating that the rules leave unaffected the rights of States and of individuals to resort to procedures other than ones of diplomatic protection,[2] with the Special Rapporteur observing that States are not 'obliged to abstain from exercising [diplomatic protection] when the individual enjoys a remedy under a human rights or foreign investment treaty',[3] unless, presumably, there is agreement otherwise.[4]

However, the conduct of States or individuals in circumstances where their claims overlap may engage various principles of international law affecting the other's capacity to claim.[5] Additionally, various of the treaties enabling individuals to invoke State responsibility contain provisions addressing multiple claims,[6] either aiming to avoid such multiplicity, or, in some cases, even requiring it.[7] Because

[1] Ch 1, nn 169–70.

[2] ILC, 'Draft Articles on Diplomatic Protection with Commentaries' (2006) 2(2) ILCYB 22 (DADP), art 16, 87–89; also Giorgio Gaja, 'The Position of Individuals in International Law: An ILC Perspective' (2010) 21 EJIL 11, 13–14; Anthea Roberts, 'State-to-State Investment Treaty Arbitration: A Hybrid Theory of Interdependent Rights and Shared Interpretative Authority' (2014) 55 Harv ILJ 1, 16–17, 35; James Crawford, *State Responsibility: The General Part* (CUP 2013) 586 (*GP*) .

[3] John Dugard, 'First Report on Diplomatic Protection' (2000) 2(1) ILCYB 205 [73]; also Roberts, 'Hybrid' (n 2) 17, 36; Martins Paparinskis, 'Investment Arbitration and the Law of Countermeasures' (2008) 79 BYBIL 264, 293; James Crawford, 'The International Law Commission's Articles on Diplomatic Protection Revisited' in Tiyanjana Maluwa, Max du Plessis, and Dire Tladi (eds), *The Pursuit of a Brave New World in International Law: Essays in Honour of John Dugard* (Brill Nijhoff 2017) 141; Annemarieke Vermeer-Künzli, 'Unfinished Business: Concurrence of Claims Presented before a Human Rights Court or Treaty Body and through Diplomatic Protection' (2010) 10 HRLR 269, 271–72, 276, cf 277; cf Alain Pellet, 'The ILC's Articles on State Responsibility for Internationally Wrongful Acts and Related Texts' in James Crawford and others (eds), *The Law of International Responsibility* (OUP 2010) 90; Andrea Gattini, 'A Trojan Horse for Sudeten Claims? On Some Implications of the Prince of Liechtenstein v Germany' (2002) 13 EJIL 513, 536–37.

[4] See section I(A); Anthea Roberts, 'Triangular Treaties: The Extent and Limits of Investment Treaty Rights' (2015) 56 Harv ILJ 353, 392–93.

[5] Similarly focusing on international rules: Yuval Shany, *Regulating Jurisdictional Relations Between National and International Courts* (OUP 2007) 2, 23.

[6] Section II(A)–(B); Ch 4(III); generally Yuval Shany, *The Competing Jurisdictions of International Courts and Tribunals* (OUP 2003) Ch 5(1)(A)(II), 5(2)(A)–(C).

[7] Similarly Shany (n 5) 89, 128; also Kaj Hobér, 'Res Judicata and Lis Pendens in International Arbitration' (2014) 366 RdC 99, 368.

Overlapping Individual and Interstate Claims in International Law. Jessica Howley, Oxford University Press.
 DOI: 10.1093/oso/9780192871466.003.0004

overlapping individual and interstate claims are most likely to arise where individuals claim under those treaties,[8] these provisions also require examination.

This is the first of four chapters addressing how both international law and such specific treaty provisions approach overlapping individual and interstate claims. This chapter considers regime-specific treaty provisions precluding overlapping individual and interstate claims, and the rule on the exhaustion of local remedies, both of which apply where the interstate claim is one of diplomatic protection. As will be seen, these rules are of limited utility in precluding overlapping claims from arising across the board, but the rigorous analysis taken herein provides essential insights for the consideration of rules in later chapters. Chapters 4 and 5 consider *res judicata* and the principle precluding double recovery, and waiver and consent, respectively, which prove to be far more significant potential means for controlling the pursuit of overlapping claims. Chapter 6 then considers the potential operation of countermeasures and self-defence to preclude not just one but both of overlapping individual and interstate claims.

I. Principles concerning the institution of judicial proceedings

A. Provisions precluding overlapping individual and interstate proceedings

The provisions of certain treaties seek to expressly control the overlapping interstate and individual claims with which this book is concerned.[9] Two such provisions may be noted.[10]

First, under article 222(c) of the Revised Treaty of Chaguaramas Establishing the Caribbean Community (CARICOM Treaty), individuals may bring claims before the Caribbean Court of Justice (CCJ) where, *inter alia*, 'the Contracting Party entitled to espouse the claim ... has (i) omitted or declined to espouse [it], or (ii) expressly agreed that the persons concerned may espouse the claim instead'.[11] The Court understands this provision as a 'means ... to avoid a duplication of suits', 'a

[8] cf domestic law claims: Ch 2(I)(C).

[9] Thus avoiding party identity issues: Shany (n 5) 136 ('individual and ... state exercising diplomatic protection ... same parties for ... applying jurisdiction-regulating rules designed to curb multiple proceedings'). Further Ch 4(IV)(C).

[10] While individual MERCOSUR procedures are only available '[u]nless the claim refers to a matter that has led to a [interstate] Dispute Settlement procedure' (Olivos Protocol, art 41), the State 'espouse[s]' the individual's claim, meaning no individual–interstate overlap results: Christian Leathley, *International Dispute Resolution in Latin America: An Institutional Overview* (Kluwer 2007) 155, also 172–73; Alejandro Perotti, 'Los Particulares y Las Controversias En El Mercosur' (2008) 122 Cuestión Logística 46. My thanks to Gwynn for assistance. However, the Intra-MERCOSUR Investment Protocol does appear to regulate overlapping individual–interstate claims: see arts 23(3)(d), 24(3).

[11] CARICOM Treaty, art 222(c). See *Myrie v Barbados* [2012] CCJ 3 [2]; Carl Baudenbacher and Michael-James Clifton, 'Courts of Regional Economic and Political Integration Agreements' in Cesare

procedural device to avoid a State allegedly in violation being twice vexed, once by an injured private entity and again by the Contracting Party of that private entity'.[12]

Second, article 27(1) of the Convention on the Settlement of Investment Disputes between States and Nationals of Other States (ICSID) provides that:

> No Contracting State shall give diplomatic protection, or bring an international claim, in respect of a dispute which one of its nationals and another Contracting State shall have consented to submit or shall have submitted to arbitration under this Convention ....[13]

According to the *travaux preparatoires*, this provision is likewise concerned with avoiding a 'multiplicity of claims and claimants'.[14]

Both of these provisions allow for individual or State conduct to preclude an overlapping claim from being brought by the other.[15] Under the CARICOM treaty, State conduct, in failing to bring a claim or agreeing that the individual can do so, dictates whether *individuals* can claim, though the CCJ also regards the State as 'surrender[ing] its right to bring its own proceedings' where it consents to the individual acting.[16] Article 27 of ICSID allows the individual's consent to arbitration, or submission of a claim, to prevent their national *State* from bringing a claim,[17] though tribunals have held that individuals must themselves refrain from 'seeking' diplomatic protection where article 27 applies.[18]

These provisions do not, unlike those to be discussed in Chapter 4, expressly reference the 'same' claims,[19] yet similarity between interstate and individual–State claims appears to be presumed, with the exclusions envisaging that 'the claim' or

Romano, Karen Alter, and Yuval Shany (eds), *The Oxford Handbook of International Adjudication* (OUP 2014) 269–70.

[12] *TLC v Guyana* [2009] CCJ 1 [43].

[13] ICSID, art 27(1).

[14] ICSID, *Convention on the Settlement of Investment Disputes between States and Nationals of Other States: Documents Concerning the Origin and the Formulation of the Convention*, vol II (1968) 242, also 273–74, 303, 372; similarly Christoph Schreuer, *The ICSID Convention: A Commentary* (2nd edn, CUP 2009) 419; Roberts, 'Triangular' (n 4) 394; Roberts, 'Hybrid' (n 2) 45–46; Ben Juratowich, 'The Relationship between Diplomatic Protection and Investment Treaties' (2008) 23 ICSID Rev-FILJ 10, 15; also Gabrielle Kaufmann-Kohler, 'Non-Disputing State Submissions in Investment Arbitration: Resurgence of Diplomatic Protection?' in Laurence Boisson de Chazournes, Marcelo Kohen, and Jorge Viñuales (eds), *Diplomatic and Judicial Means of Dispute Settlement* (Martinus Nijhoff 2013) 308 ('duplication'); Paparinskis, 'Countermeasures' (n 3) 283; Shany (n 6) 194.

[15] See ICSID (n 14) 1032; James Crawford, *The International Law Commission's Articles on State Responsibility: Introduction, Text and Commentaries* (CUP 2002) 165 (*ARSIWA*).

[16] *Myrie* (n 11) [25]; also Paparinskis, 'Countermeasures' (n 3) 282; *Hummingbird v Suriname* [2011] CCJ 1 [25], [26].

[17] Schreuer (n 14) 417, discussing *Autopista v Venezuela (Jurisdiction)* (2001) 16 ICSID Rev-FILJ 469 [140].

[18] Under art 26 ('[c]onsent ... to arbitration ... to the exclusion of any other remedy'): *Banro v DRC* (2003) 17 ICSID Rev–FILJ 382 [20], discussed Schreuer (n 14) 418–19; also *Tokios Tokelės v Ukraine (Order No 3)* ICSID Case No ARB/02/18 (18 January 2005) [22].

[19] Ch 4(III).

'a dispute' might be addressed through either individual–State or interstate procedures, but not both.[20] More particularly, both provisions are concerned with individual claims overlapping with the exercise of diplomatic protection.[21] Article 222(c) of the CARICOM treaty focuses on whether the claim has been or will be 'espouse[d]', which the CCJ has confirmed denotes claims by way of diplomatic protection.[22] ICSID's article 27, which prohibits 'giv[ing] diplomatic protection, or bring[ing] an international claim', also precludes concurrent individual and diplomatic protection claims,[23] with the latter phrase interpreted as referring only to diplomatic protection.[24]

B. Multiple claims requirements

Quite differently from provisions aiming to preclude overlapping claims, one common admissibility requirement actually supports multiplicity.[25] The local remedies rule requires that an injured individual exhaust those remedies that are domestically available before a diplomatic protection claim—or one 'preponderantly' of diplomatic protection—may be brought 'in respect of [that individual's] injury'.[26] The rule is one of customary international law,[27] and also applicable under many, particularly human rights, treaties.[28] A claim will be inadmissible if the requirement applies and is unsatisfied.[29]

[20] Cf Shany, n 9. Similarly *Chevron and Texaco v Ecuador (Third Interim Award, Jurisdiction/Admissibility)* PCA Case 2009-23 (27 February 2012) [4.74] ('"the dispute" in [fork-in-the-road] context must mean "the same dispute"... material identity or sameness'); Hobér (n 7) 364; Shany (n 5) 132, 149–50; August Reinisch, 'The Use and Limits of *Res Judicata* and *Lis Pendens* as Procedural Tools to Avoid Conflicting Dispute Settlement Outcomes' (2004) 3 LPICT 37, 67–68; Schreuer (n 14) 421.

[21] See Shany (n 5) 136.

[22] *Myrie* (n 11) [14], [25]–[26]; generally Schreuer (n 14) 415.

[23] Eg, *Banro* (n 18) [15]–[23]; *Autopista* (n 17) [138]; *Tokios (Order)* (n 18) [21]; Schreuer (n 14) 419–22; Hege Elisabeth Kjos, *Applicable Law in Investor-State Arbitration: The Interplay Between National and International Law* (OUP 2013) 92; Anne Peters, *Beyond Human Rights: The Legal Status of the Individual in International Law* (Jonathan Huston tr, CUP 2016) 309.

[24] See Schreuer (n 14) 420–21; Roberts, 'Hybrid' (n 2) 45–47, 59; Paparinskis, 'Countermeasures' (n 3) 313–14; Michele Potestà, 'State-to-State Dispute Settlement Pursuant to Bilateral Investment Treaties: Is There Potential?' in Nerina Boschiero and others (eds), *International Courts and the Development of International Law: Essays in Honour of Tullio Treves* (Asser 2013) 762; nn 305ff. Cf Nathalie Bernasconi-Osterwalder, 'State-State Dispute Settlement in Investment Treaties' *IISD Best Practices Series* (October 2014) 17–18.

[25] Shany (n 5) 89, also 27–30, 128; Chittharanjan Amerasinghe, *Local Remedies in International Law* (2nd edn, CUP 2004) 401; William Dodge, 'National Courts and International Arbitration: Exhaustion of Remedies and Res Judicata Under Chapter Eleven of NAFTA' (2000) 23 Hast I & CLR 357, 360; André Nollkaemper, *National Courts and the International Rule of Law* (OUP 2011) 27; also Gabrielle Kaufmann-Kohler and Michele Potestà, 'Investor-State Dispute Settlement and National Courts: Current Framework and Reform Options' [2020] EYBIEL, 35. The situation differs where individuals are domestically successful: nn 186ff; also Shany (n 5) 28.

[26] DADP, art 14; generally Ch 2, nn 96, 111.

[27] DADP, 71; *ARSIWA*, 265.

[28] Ch 2, n 75.

[29] *ARSIWA*, art 44(b).

Individuals are only required to exhaust domestic remedies, not those potentially available internationally.[30] Nonetheless, as Chapter 2 outlined, individual and State claims brought before, respectively, domestic and international fora, may sometimes overlap.[31] Accordingly, unlike rules to be discussed in Chapter 4, where the bringing of an overlapping claim may render the second such claim inadmissible, for the local remedies rule, a claim in 'essence' the same must have been previously brought, albeit domestically, for the second (interstate) claim to *be admissible*.[32] Because State claims may be precluded if the individual fails to act,[33] the local remedies rule is similar to the other rules considered in this book in operating to preclude the later of two overlapping individual and interstate claims, given certain conduct by the other entity possessing an overlapping claim.

C. Summary

In relation to the local remedies rule and article 27 of ICSID, actions of the individual in either agreeing to, or failing to pursue, certain remedies result in the State's claim being precluded, while under the CARICOM treaty, the State's entitlement to claim prevents the individual from claiming itself unless the State takes or fails to take certain action. Determining when these rules apply depends on accurately identifying diplomatic protection claims. This chapter argues that the notion of *damage* underlies the correct distinction between diplomatic protection and other claims,[34] and demonstrates when these rules accordingly apply.[35] As Chapters 4–6 demonstrate, a proper understanding of the distinction is also essential to appreciating how other rules of preclusion may operate. It is, accordingly, addressed in some detail here.

[30] Paparinskis, 'Countermeasures' (n 3) 301–2 (proposing otherwise *de lege ferenda*); DADP, 88; ILC, 'Diplomatic Protection: Comments and observations received from Governments' (2006) UN Doc A/CN.4/561, 54 (Austria); also William Schabas, *The European Convention on Human Rights: A Commentary* (OUP 2015) 768. Cf Louis Sohn and R Baxter (eds), *Convention on the International Responsibility of States for Injuries to Aliens* (HLS 1961) 165, 202–3.

[31] Ch 2(III)(C).

[32] *Elettronica Sicula SpA (US v Italy) (Judgment)* [1989] ICJ Rep 15 [59], discussed Hugh Thirlway, *The Law and Procedure of the International Court of Justice: Fifty Years of Jurisprudence* (OUP 2013) 620; Nollkaemper (n 25) 260, 247; similarly *X v Austria* (1968) 26 Collection 55, 64 (matter 'substantially raised'), quoted Amerasinghe (n 25) 320; authorities Ch 2, n 76.

[33] Roberts, 'Hybrid' (n 2) 31, and authorities Introduction, n 66; Diana Cucos, 'The Position of the Individual in Post-Codification Diplomatic Protection' (2014) 5 CYBP & PIL 181, 191; Alain Pellet, 'The Second Death of Euripide Mavrommatis? Notes on the International Law Commission's Draft Articles on Diplomatic Protection' (2008) 7 LPICT 33, 37, 54; Zachary Douglas, *The International Law of Investment Claims* (CUP 2009) 29; ALI, *Restatement of the Law: The Foreign Relations Law of the United States*, vol II (3rd edn, ALI Publishers 1987) 347.

[34] Authorities section II(A)–(C).

[35] Section IV.

II. Article 42 claims: diplomatic protection, 'direct', and 'mixed' claims

As Chapter 2 outlined, claims brought under article 42 of the Articles on Responsibility of States for Internationally Wrongful Acts (ARSIWA) can be diplomatic protection, 'direct', or 'mixed', the last incorporating aspects of the first two.[36] How to distinguish between diplomatic protection and 'direct' claims has been the subject of significant debate.[37] The DADP regard the 'principal factors' of relevance as being 'the subject of the dispute, the nature of the claim and the remedy claimed'.[38] The first identifies 'direct' claims through 'categories of acts' tending to cause direct injury, such as vis-à-vis State officials or property,[39] while the claim's nature concerns whether 'the real interests and objects pursued' are the State's or an individual's,[40] a question often elucidated by the reparation requested.[41]

These are useful indicative criteria.[42] However, as will be seen, there is a great deal of conceptual confusion surrounding the nature of diplomatic protection. This chapter endeavours to go beyond guiding factors, instead proposing a rigorous analytical framework for distinguishing diplomatic protection and other claims across the board.

Its starting point is the DADP's definition of diplomatic protection, which focuses on whether the claim is 'for an *injury* caused by an internationally wrongful act ... to ... a [State's] national'.[43] The International Court of Justice (ICJ) considers that definition to be reflective of customary international law,[44] the European

36 Ch 2, nn 92–112; Gerald Fitzmaurice, *The Law and Procedure of the International Court of Justice* (Grotius 1986) 687.

37 On the debate: DADP, 74–76; Stephan Wittich, 'Direct Injury and the Incidence of the Local Remedies Rule' (2000) 5 Aust Rev I & EL 121, 132–37; Theodor Meron, 'The Incidence of the Rule of Exhaustion of Local Remedies' (1959) 35 BYBIL 83, 85–89; Amerasinghe (n 25) 151–68; John Dugard, 'Second Report on Diplomatic Protection' (2001) 2(1) ILCYB 97 [20]–[31]; also Shany (n 5) 140.

38 DADP, 75–76; also Meron (n 37) 86–89, discussed Amerasinghe (n 25) 160–63; Wittich (n 37) 134–35; Dugard, 'SecondRep' (n 37) [24]–[27].

39 Meron (n 37) 87; similarly DADP, 76; Dugard, 'SecondRep' (n 37) [25]; ILC, 'Summary Records of the Meetings of the Fifty-Third Session' (2001) 1 ILCYB 1, 142 (Dugard); FV Garcia-Amador, 'International Responsibility: Report' (1956) 2 ILCYB 173 [41]; Mohamed Bennouna, 'Preliminary Report on Diplomatic Protection' (1998) 2(1) ILCYB 309 [17]; Wittich (n 37) 133–34. See section IV(B)(i).

40 Meron (n 37) 87, discussed Dugard, 'SecondRep' (n 37) [26]; also ILC, '53rd' (n 39) 142 (Dugard).

41 Meron (n 37) 88; Dugard, 'SecondRep' (n 37) [27]; ILC, '53rd' (n 39) 142 (Dugard).

42 See Dugard, 'SecondRep' (n 37) [24]–[27]; Wittich (n 37) 134–37; cf Amerasinghe (n 25) 162–63.

43 DADP, art 1 (emphasis added). Also *Mavrommatis Palestine Concessions* [1924] PCIJ Rep Ser A No 2, 12 (dispute often 'originates in an *injury* to a private interest', State may protect nationals '*injured* by acts contrary to international law' (emphasis added)); Chittharanjan Amerasinghe, *Diplomatic Protection* (OUP 2008) 37 ('injury to person or property'); ALI (n 33) §902(2) ('violations ... resulting in injury to ... nationals'), 347. The definition is consistent with the criteria noted (nn 38–41): see Wittich (n 37) 181–82; DADP, 75–76; similarly Brigitte Bollecker-Stern, *Le Préjudice Dans La Théorie de La Responsibilité Internationale* (Pedone 1973) 100.

44 *Ahmadou Sadio Diallo (Guinea v DRC) (Preliminary Objections)* [2007] ICJ Rep 582 [39]; *Certain Iranian Assets (Iran v USA)* Judgment of 30 March 2023 [61]; also Paparinskis, 'Countermeasures' (n 3) 279.

Court of Human Rights (ECtHR) has confirmed it,[45] and it is reflected in the case law of the Eritrea-Ethiopia Claims Commission (EECC), the Commission observing that ‘some of both States’ claims are made in the exercise of diplomatic protection, *in that they are predicated upon injuries allegedly suffered by numbers of [their] nationals*’.[46] The person who is injured should therefore form the starting point in distinguishing diplomatic protection and ‘direct’ claims.[47] ‘Mixed’ claims, for their part, are treated as ones of diplomatic protection for local remedies purposes when ‘brought preponderantly on the basis of [such] injury’.[48] Focus on the relevant injury thus likewise remains essential in determining when this admissibility rule applies to such claims.[49]

An analytically precise approach begins by recalling that the term ‘injury’ can, somewhat confusingly, refer both to *breach* (legal injury) and *damage* (factual injury).[50] This chapter argues that diplomatic protection claims are brought not for breach of international obligations owed to individuals (their *legal* injury),[51] but for *damage* (or *factual* injury) done to them.[52] The latter is what distinguishes diplomatic protection and ‘direct’ claims.[53]

The argument systematically breaks down the confusion surrounding this distinction in three parts. Section A counters suggestions that the distinction depends on whose rights are breached. Section B refutes arguments distinguishing based on the kind of obligation allegedly violated. Section C shows that the distinction *does* depend on which entity suffers damage. After addressing article 48 claims, the final section elucidates how, given these conclusions, the rules identified above apply

45 *Cyprus v Turkey (Just Satisfaction)* ECHR 2014-II 245 (GC) [45].

46 *Eritrea's Damages Claims (Final Award)* (2009) XXVI UNRIAA 505 [25]; *Ethiopia's Damages Claims (Final Award)* (2009) XXVI UNRIAA 631 [25] (emphasis added).

47 See Ch 2, n102, particularly Wittich (n 37) 129, citing, *inter alia*, FV Garcia-Amador, ‘Sixth Report on State Responsibility’ (1961) 2 ILCYB 1 [30]; also Eduardo Jiménez de Aréchaga, ‘International Responsibility’ in Max Sørensen (ed), *Manual of Public International Law* (Macmillan 1968) 577; ILC, ‘53rd’ (n 39) 146 (Pellet).

48 DADP, art 14(3), also 75; ILC, ‘Summary Records of the Meetings of the Fifty-Fifth Session’ (2003) 1 ILCYB 1, 120 (Kateka); Ch 2, n 111; cf ILC, ‘53rd’ (n 39) 144 (Gaja).

49 See Wittich (n 37) 136 (test requires ‘determination of what distinguishes’ direct/indirect injury).

50 Ch 1(II)(A).

51 Tomuschat, quoted n 52; Wittich (n 37) 131–32, 182; Peters (n 23) 390 (‘traditional view’); Amerasinghe (n 43) 179; Amerasinghe (n 25) 164.

52 Christian Tomuschat, ‘Individuals’ in Crawford and others, *Responsibility* (n 3) 985 (‘despite having suffered harm in fact, a foreigner cannot … be considered an injured person in the legal sense’); Paparinskis, quoted Ch 1, n 17; Bollecker-Stern (n 43) 97, 100–1; Wittich (n 37) 129 (‘“indirect injury” … State commits an internationally wrongful act against [another State's] national … resulting in damage to [them]’); Garcia-Amador, ‘SixthRep’ (n 47) [176]; Bennouna (n 39) [16]; Peters (n 23) 393 (if State rights, ‘individuals … affected only *de facto*, not *de jure*’), 173, cf 171–72; Rosalyn Higgins, *Problems and Processes: International Law and How We Use It* (Clarendon 1994) 51; cf *Aerial Incident of July 27th, 1955 (Israel/US/UK v Bulgaria)* ICJ Pleadings, 531; also Marjorie Whiteman, *Damages in International Law* (US Government 1937) 284; Fitzmaurice (n 36) 25–26; Amerasinghe (n 43) 69. Cf ILC, ‘Summary Records of the Meetings of the Fifty-Second Session’ (2000) 1 ILCYB 1, 63 (Hafner) (‘hesitant to go into … definition of injury’).

53 Section I(C). Similarly Wittich (n 37) 129, cf 137 (‘criterion of the “nature of the injury” is … rather circular’), 150–51 (criticising approach), also 135–36, discussing ideas reproduced Thirlway (n 32) 618.

vis-à-vis overlapping individual and interstate claims, including examples to show the operation of the proposed approach in practice.

A. Diplomatic protection and legal injury

Misunderstandings of diplomatic protection often begin with the notion of 'rights', with various scholars suggesting that in cases of diplomatic protection the rights involved belong to the individual,[54] making particular reference to developments according individuals rights under human rights law.[55] International tribunals have also made reference to individuals' 'rights' when discussing claims of diplomatic protection.[56] Indeed, in certain cases,[57] tribunals have apparently used this notion to distinguish between different types of claims, referring to the 'rights' in question as belonging to the State in concluding that claims were not ones of diplomatic protection to which the local remedies rule applied.[58] The ICJ in *Avena*, for

[54] Eg, DADP, 25–26, 29; discussion Dugard, 'FirstRep' (n 3) [36], [61]–[73]; Bennouna (n 39) [13], [16], [21], [50]–[54]; Crawford, *GP* (n 2) 77, 569; de Aréchaga (n 47) 578; Pellet (n 33) 36–46; Roberts, 'Hybrid' (n 2) 31–34; also Edwin Borchard, *The Diplomatic Protection of Citizens Abroad: Or, the Law of International Claims* (Banks 1915) 13–14, 353; Annemarieke Vermeer-Künzli, 'A Matter of Interest: Diplomatic Protection and State Responsibility *Erga Omnes*' (2007) 56 ICLQ 553, 560–61. Noting this: Peters (n 23) 391; Amerasinghe (n 43) 74; Amerasinghe (n 25) 48; also Roberts, 'Hybrid' (n 2) 33–34.

[55] See Peters (n 23) 391–93; Crawford, *GP* (n 2) 569, 584–85, also quote n 65; Amerasinghe (n 43) 71, 73–74, citing *inter alia*, Bennouna (n 39), see particularly [14], [33]–[37], [50]–[54] and FV Garcia-Amador, 'State Responsibility: Some New Problems' (1958) 94 RdC 365, see 466, 418–22, 462–69; Garcia-Amador, 'Report' (n 39) [111]–[112]; DADP, 25–26; discussion Dugard, 'FirstRep' (n 3) [17]–[32], [36]–[40], [61]–[73]; also Pellet (n 33) 40–42; Hersch Lauterpacht, *International Law: Being the Collected Papers of Hersch Lauterpacht* (Elihu Lauterpacht ed, CUP 1970) 269–99; Roberts, 'Hybrid' (n 2) 31–36; cf Annemarieke Vermeer-Künzli, 'As If: The Legal Fiction in Diplomatic Protection' (2007) 18 EJIL 37, 49, 55–56, 66–67. Generally Orrego Vicuna, 'The Changing Law of Nationality of Claims' (2000) 69 ILA Rep Conf 631, 631–34; John Dugard, 'Diplomatic Protection' in Crawford and others, *Responsibility* (n 3) 1052.

[56] Eg, *Interhandel (Switzerland v US) (Preliminary Objections* [1959] ICJ Rep 6, 27, quoted Dugard, 'FirstRep' (n 3) [64]; de Aréchaga (n 47) 578, also quoting *Factory at Chórzow (Merits)* [1928] PCIJ Rep Ser A No 17, 28; *Barcelona Traction, Light and Power Company (Belgium v Spain)* [1970] ICJ Rep 3 [35], [78]; *ELSI* (n 32) [75] (shareholders' 'rights to control and manage'), [99]; *Arrest Warrant of 11 April 2000 (DRC v Belgium) (Judgment)* [2002] ICJ Rep 3 [40] (not invoking 'personal rights'), quoted Amerasinghe (n 25) 149; *LaGrand (Germany v US) (Judgment)* [2001] ICJ Rep 466 [77]; *Avena and Other Mexican Nationals (Mexico v US) (Judgment)* [2004] ICJ Rep 12 [40] ('individual rights'); *Corn Products v Mexico (Responsibility)* ICSID Case No ARB(AF)/04/01 (15 January 2008) [170].

[57] Discussing many of these: Wittich (n 37) 162–77.

[58] See Crawford, *GP* (n 2) 593 (vis-à-vis *Avena* (n 56)); Wittich (n 37) 164–65 (vis-à-vis *Case concerning the Air Service Agreement of 27 March 1946 (USA v France)* (1978) XVIII UNRIAA 417). See, eg, ibid [30]–[32], particularly [30] (taking account, *inter alia*, of 'the *juridical* character of the *legal relationship* between States'), [31] (treaty rights 'granted by one *government* to the other *government*') (original emphasis), criticised Wittich (n 37) 163–65; also Amerasinghe (n 25) 150 (fn 17), 167 (fn 56); Dugard, 'SecondRep' (n 37) [27]; *Heathrow Airport Usage Charges (US v UK)* (1992) XXIV UNRIAA 3, 60, 68, particularly 60 (treaty 'creates rights and obligations *between the two States*', not 'independent rights' for airlines) (emphasis added), cf 62 (State interest 'predominant'), discussed Wittich (n 37) 168–69; and vis-à-vis UNCLOS: *The M/V 'Saiga' (No 2) Case (Saint Vincent and the Grenadines v Guinea) (Judgment)* [1999] ITLOS Rep 10 [97]–[98], cf [51] (Sep Op Wolfrum), both discussed Wittich (n 37) 172–75; *The*

instance, considered the local remedies requirement inapplicable to a claim concerning alleged violations of consular obligations brought by Mexico 'in its own right and in the exercise of its right of diplomatic protection', because there was an 'interdependence of the *rights of the State* and of *individual rights*' under the relevant provisions.[59] Unable to reach firm conclusions, the DADP 'leave open the question whether the State exercising diplomatic protection does so in its own right or that of its national—or both.'[60]

Careless use of the terminology of 'rights' in this context is, however, apt to cause misunderstanding.[61] When speaking of 'rights' vis-à-vis a claim, we usually mean the rights for breach of which the claim is brought.[62] The right-holder is then the entity to whom the obligation is owed, who suffers legal injury through breach.[63] But in an interstate claim, a State is, by definition, invoking responsibility for breach of international obligations owed to itself: *these* rights undoubtedly belong to the State in a diplomatic protection claim.[64]

When jurists refer more broadly to the 'rights' of individuals in terms of their property or person in diplomatic protection claims,[65] this is understandable, because (and as will become important in Chapters 4–5):

(a) diplomatic protection claims are concerned with individuals and their property;[66]

M/V 'Virginia G' (Panama/Guinea-Bissau) (Judgment) [2014] ITLOS Rep 4 [157] ('principal rights' State's), [156]–[158]; *Arctic Sunrise Arbitration (Netherlands v Russia) (Merits)* PCA Case 2014-02 (14 August 2015) [168], [172]–[173]; *Duzgit Integrity (Malta v São Tomé and Príncipe) (Award)* PCA Case 2014-07 (5 September 2016) [151] ('preponderantly for injury to [Malta's] direct or indirect rights'), cf [155]–[156] (because 'main private entity' settled, no 'remedy', 'direct claims' 'preponderant'); *The M/V 'Norstar' (Panama v Italy) (Preliminary Objections)* [2016] ITLOS Rep 44 [270]–[271].

59 *Avena* (n 56) [40] (emphasis added), discussed, eg, DADP, 75; Crawford, *GP* (n 2) 592–93; Kate Parlett, *The Individual in the International Legal System: Continuity and Change in International Law* (CUP 2011) 94–96, 112; Crawford, 'Revisited' (n 3) 169–70; Roberts, 'Hybrid' (n 2) 40; Amerasinghe (n 43) 33; also Peters (n 23) 391–92 (*LaGrand*). Affirmed: *Iranian Assets* (n 44) [63]–[64].

60 DADP, 26. See discussion Pellet (n 33), 43–45, 51–53.

61 Similarly Rudolf Dolzer, 'The Settlement of War-Related Claims: Does International Law Recognize a Victim's Private Right of Action? Lessons after 1945' (2002) 20 Berk.JIL 296, 303; Thirlway (n 32) 1553–54; Lauterpacht (n 55) 296–97; also Higgins (n 52) 52–53; Robert McCorquodale, 'The Individual and the International Legal System' in Malcolm Evans (ed), *International Law* (4th edn, OUP 2014) 285 (certain individual 'rights ... more ... an immunity ... or a privilege', referencing Hohfeld); also nn 87ff.

62 See Ch 4 (IV)(A).

63 See Ch 1, nn 23–27, 109.

64 DADP, art 1 ('internationally wrongful act'); nn 71, 74; Ch 1(III)(A); Ch 4, n 153; also Wittich (n 37) 165 (criticising *Air Services*); Amerasinghe (n 43) 37, 39; Peters (n 23) 169, 388–91; cf Vermeer-Künzli, 'Fiction' (n 55) 49, 55–56.

65 See Crawford, *GP* (n 2) 584 ('diplomatic protection ... for the protection of individual rights to personal integrity, property and due process'); Borchard (n 54) 12 ('rights ... to personal security ... personal liberty ... private property'), 13–15; Garcia-Amador, 'Problems' (n 55) 441; Garcia-Amador, 'SixthRep' (n 47) 46 (draft art 1); DADP, 26; Bollecker-Stern (n 43) 118–22; nn 54–60.

66 nn 71, 163–64.

(b) legal rights to property, and certain personal rights, are generally established—and *do* belong to individuals—under *domestic* law;[67] and
(c) international claims, such as for expropriation, commonly depend on the existence of such rights, including property rights, within a given domestic system.[68]

That an individual holds domestic law rights does not, however, entail that they also possess 'international rights',[69] and a violation of domestic rights does not necessarily found a claim for breach of international law.[70] At least conventionally, the relevant international rights in diplomatic protection are not the personal and property rights of the individual per se, but the *State's* right to insist upon 'respect [for] the person and property of [its] nationals' to a given standard.[71] In *Barcelona Traction*, for example, the ICJ asked whether 'a right *of Belgium* [was] violated', even though the allegation of breach depended on 'its nationals' having suffered infringement of their rights as shareholders' under *domestic* law.[72] Indeed,

[67] Kjos (n 23) 242; also Borchard (n 54) 13, 15, 18; Peters (n 23) 171, 390; Bennouna (n 39) [50] ('national ... has a legally protected interest at the national level and thus a right'); Garcia-Amador, 'Problems' (n 55) 463 ('original [claim] under municipal law'); ILC, 'Summary Records of the Meetings of the Fiftieth Session' (1998) 1 ILCYB 1, 29 (Hafner); de Aréchaga (n 47) 578–79; also James Crawford, 'Chance, Order, Change: The Course of International Law' (2013) 365 RdC 9, 162; discussion Bollecker-Stern (n 43) 115–21; Douglas (n 33) 41, 52–53, 70–72; Zachary Douglas, 'The Hybrid Foundations of Investment Treaty Arbitration' (2004) 74 BYBIL 151, 155, 194–201, 211, 273–74.

[68] Kjos (n 23) 242, 255; Nollkaemper (n 25) 253, 266 (fn 109), citing Douglas (n 67) 197–99, both cited Peter Tomka, Jessica Howley, and Vincent-Joël Proulx, 'International and Municipal Law before the World Court: One or Two Legal Orders?' (2015) XXXV Pol YBIL 11, 32, also 34–35; Amerasinghe (n 43) 37–38, 63–64; Pellet (n 33) 46–47; Bennouna (n 39) [21]; Peters (n 23) 170–71, 301; Amerasinghe (n 43) 37; cf Thirlway (n 32) 1553–54. Eg, *Chórzow (Merits)* (n 56) 40, 46 (property); *Panevezys-Saldutiskis Railway Case* [1939] PCIJ Rep Ser A/B No 76, 17–18 (property); *Mavrommatis* (n 43) 7 (contracts); *Azinian v Mexico (Award)* ICSID Case No ARB(AF)/97/2 (1 November 1999) [100] (contract), discussed Shany (n 5) 32; Robert Jennings and Arthur Watts, *Oppenheim's International Law*, vol 1 (9th edn, Longman 1992) 916 (contract); *Ryuichi Shimoda v Japan* (1963) 32 ILR 626 (Tokyo DC) 640–41.

[69] *Oppenheim's* (n 68) 16, also 847 (fn 2). Similarly Peters (n 23) 390 ('diplomatic protection relies on [individual's] possibility ... to assert ... own claim under *domestic* law ... traditional view, this has nothing to do with any [individual] rights ... *under international law*' (original emphasis)); Borchard (n 54) 13–14, 18, 27; Arnold McNair, *International Law Opinions*, vol II (OUP 1956) 3.

[70] Amerasinghe (n 43) 38–42 (contract), cf 37 (tort, noting 'standard applied over and above ... national law'); Amerasinghe (n 25) 95–101, 116–26, 130–31, 137–38, 390–91; Wittich (n 37) 139–40; Crawford, 'Revisited' (n 3) 168; Dugard, 'SecondRep' (n 37) [63]–[64], discussed Thirlway (n 32) 1547, also 1553–54; ILC, '52nd' (n 52) 63 (Hafner); ILA, 'Toronto Conference Report: Diplomatic Protection of Persons and Property' (2006) 72 ILA Rep Conf 353 [39]; Bennouna (n 39) [21]; James Crawford, 'The ILC's Articles on Diplomatic Protection' (2006) 31 SAYIL 19, 48; Fitzmaurice (n 36) 697–98; Peters (n 23) 390; *Oppenheim's* (n 68) 927; Garcia-Amador, 'Problems' (n 55) 420; *Spanish Zone of Morocco (UK v Spain)* (1925) II UNRIAA 615, 641; *Azinian* (n 68) [99]–[100], discussed Shany (n 5) 32; generally 162–63; Bollecker-Stern (n 43) 118–21; Philip Jessup, *A Modern Law of Nations* (Archon 1968) 104; *ARSIWA*, 96; Douglas (n 67) 253; *Waste Management v Mexico (Award)* (2000) 121 ILR 29 (ICSID) 45–47; *Impregilo v Argentina (Award)* ICSID Case No ARB/07/17 (21 June 2011) [177] and authorities; cf *Diallo (Objections)* (n 44) [64].

[71] Garcia-Amador, 'Problems' (n 55) 427; also Borchard (n 54) 18; Pellet (n 33) 36; Garcia-Amador, 'SixthRep' (n 47) [42]; Ch 2, n 94; Amerasinghe (n 43) 37, 76; Peters (n 23) 167–68, 390–91, cf 190; *Barcelona Traction* (n 56) [35]; Bollecker-Stern (n 43) 96–97.

[72] *Barcelona Traction* (n 56) [35] (emphasis added), and see [38], [47]; Bennouna (n 39) [21]. Similarly *Diallo (Objections)* (n 44) [64], discussed Rosalyn Higgins, *Themes and Theories* (OUP 2009)

that *international* individual rights are not at issue logically follows from the fact that diplomatic protection emerged when international law only created rights and duties for States.[73] Claims were therefore always brought for breach of the *State's* rights regarding treatment of its nationals,[74] under treaty or customary international law.[75] The relevant international legal rights cannot have belonged to States only in 'direct' claims, as *all* international obligations were, at that time, owed as between States, including those protecting aliens.[76]

It is difficult to agree, as some suggest, that the entire premise of diplomatic protection has changed on account of human rights developments.[77] Individuals are indeed now generally recognised as having certain international human rights,[78] and diplomatic protection claims may be brought for human rights violations.[79] However, even if human rights obligations are also owed to individuals, *interstate* human rights claims are still brought for breach of *interstate* obligations;[80] States

1317; Tomka, Howley, and Proulx (n 68) 33; also DADP, 52–53, 58–59, 66–67; de Aréchaga (n 47) 579–81; Bernhard Graefrath, 'Responsibility and Damages Caused: Relationship between Responsibility and Damages' (1984) 185 RdC 9, 48–49; Bollecker-Stern (n 43) 105.

[73] Peters (n 23) 393; Borchard (n 54) 18; Crawford, *GP* (n 2) 584; DADP, 25; Thirlway (n 32) 1553; Bennouna (n 39) [16]; Garcia-Amador, 'Report' (n 39) [96]; Amerasinghe (n 25) 44–45; Roberts, 'Hybrid' (n 2) 31; Juratowich (n 14) 12.

[74] *Mavrommatis* (n 43) 12; also authorities Ch 2, n 97; Parlett (n 59) 50 ('inter-state rights'), 66–67; Garcia-Amador, 'Problems' (n 55) 462; Wittich (n 37) 131–32, 165; Peters (n 23) 390–91; Amerasinghe (n 25) 45–47, 105, 164 ('injury to ... alien which violates international law ... also a violation of ... state's right'); Riccardo Pisillo Mazzeschi, 'Impact on the Law of Diplomatic Protection' in Menno Kamminga and Martin Scheinin (eds), *The Impact of Human Rights Law on General International Law* (OUP 2009) 211–12; DADP, 22–23, 25; Borchard (n 54) 18, 353, 357. Cf Vermeer-Künzli, 'Fiction' (n 55) 39, 66.

[75] The obligation's source is irrelevant: Amerasinghe (n 25) 47, 155, 162 (criticising Meron (n 37) 87), 158; also Wittich (n 37) 161, 165. Eg, treaty claims: *ELSI* (n 32); *Interhandel* (n 56), referenced Amerasinghe (n 25) 151–53; Wittich (n 37) 135, 161, 165; cf DADP, 74 (*Interhandel* 'mixed': 'direct wrong to [State] arising out of breach of a treaty'); similarly Wittich (n 37) 151–52; Amerasinghe (n 25) 162.

[76] Wittich (n 37) 131–32 also 151, 156, 165; Amerasinghe (n 25) 164; Lauterpacht (n 55) 137; Borchard (n 54) 18; cf Higgins (n 72) 74–77; Thirlway (n 32) 1553; discussion Garcia-Amador, 'Report' (n 39) 192–93, cf 194.

[77] nn 54–55.

[78] Eg, Peters (n 23) 388, 168; Crawford, 'DP' (n 70) 23; *Oppenheim's* (n 68) 847–49, discussed Parlett (n 59) 27–28, also 350; Lauterpacht (n 55) 142; McCorquodale (n 61) 285–86; Roberts, 'Hybrid' (n 2) 32–34; Higgins (n 72) 74, 81ff; DADP, 25–26, 87–89; Garcia-Amador, 'Report' (n 39) 192; also Jessup (n 70) 69–70; Amerasinghe (n 25) 72–73; McCorquodale (n 61) 285–86; Martins Paparinskis, 'Investment Treaty Arbitration and the (New) Law of State Responsibility' (2013) 24 EJIL 617, 623; Eyal Benvenisti, 'Individual Remedies for Victims of Armed Conflicts in the Context of Mass Claims Settlements' in Holger Hestermeyer and others (eds), *Coexistence, Cooperation and Solidarity: Liber Amicorum Rüdiger Wolfrum* (Martinus Nijohoff 2012) 1086; Higgins (n 52) 53–54, 95–96; Ch 1, n 127.

[79] Ch 2, nn 217–24.

[80] Ch 1, nn 124–33; see *Ahmadou Sadio Diallo (Guinea v DRC) (Merits)* [2010] ICJ Rep 639 [63]; similarly *Avena* (n 56), n 59, discussed, eg, Paparinskis, 'Countermeasures' (n 3) 286 (fn 106), also 286–87; Roberts, 'Hybrid' (n 2) 34–36; Crawford, *GP* (n 2) 593; Wittich (n 37) 179; Paparinskis, 'New' (n 78) 640–41; Vermeer-Künzli, 'Interest' (n 54) 571, 575, 579; also Thirlway (n 32) 1554; Amerasinghe (n 25) 47, 164 (quoted n 74), 309; Bruno Simma and Dirk Pulkowski, '*Leges Speciales* and Self-Contained Regimes' in Crawford and others, *Responsibility* (n 3) 160–61; discussion Pellet (n 33) 52; Emmanuel Roucounas, 'Non-State Actors: Areas of International Responsibility in Need of Further Exploration' in Maurizio Ragazzi (ed), *International Responsibility Today: Essays in Memory of Oscar Schachter* (Martinus Nijhoff 2005) 399.

can only invoke responsibility where an obligation owed *to them* is breached.[81] Moreover, not every diplomatic protection claim is brought for human rights violations.[82] Consequently, while a diplomatic protection claim might conceivably concern individuals' international (human) rights, this is not always so and cannot be determinative of the claim's characterisation.[83]

The breach in a diplomatic protection claim is therefore, at least *inter alia*, of obligations owed to the State, and the legal injury done to it; breach of international obligations owed to individuals was not always present and need not be.[84] Indeed, if the DADP's definition of diplomatic protection required "legal injury" to be done to an individual, diplomatic protection would not be 'for an injury *caused* by an internationally wrongful act' to a national,[85] as the 'internationally wrongful act'—the breach—would *be* the injury.[86] When speaking of the 'rights' underlying a given diplomatic protection claim, clarity demands that we mean the State's international rights, for breach of which responsibility is invoked. This does not discount that individual legal 'rights' may be present, domestic or international, but their existence cannot be used to determine the nature of a given claim.

B. The nature of the right

While the rights being invoked in diplomatic protection are thus properly the State's, recent attempts seem to have been made to conceptualise 'rights' as belonging to the individual in an alternative sense, namely that such claims concern the individual's *interests*.[87] Indeed, key literature has, in distinguishing diplomatic protection and 'direct' claims, focused on the 'nature of the injury or right

[81] Ch 1, n 135; *Barcelona Traction* (n 56) [36]; Nollkaemper (n 25) 93, 95; DADP, 26.

[82] See nn 106ff. Observing that rules concerning aliens' treatment are sometimes broader than human rights: ALI (n 33) §711, 187; Peters (n 23) 388; Tomuschat (n 52) 985; Mazzeschi (n 74) 223; Jessup (n 70) 101; also ILC, '52nd' (n 52) 66 (Simma). See Ch 6, nn 248–49.

[83] See DADP, 26 ('inter-State claim, although it *may* result in the assertion of rights enjoyed by the injured national' (emphasis added)); also Thirlway (n 32) 1553–54; Roberts, 'Hybrid' (n 2) 34; Parlett (n 59) 92.

[84] See nn 71–83; cf Parlett (n 59) 92.

[85] DADP, art 1 (emphasis added).

[86] Similarly: *Biwater Gauff v Tanzania (Award)* ICSID Case No ARB/05/22 (24 July 2008) [803] ('"causing *injury*" must mean more than simply the wrongful act itself... otherwise the element of causation would have to be taken as present in every case' (original emphasis)).

[87] Eg, Wittich (n 37) 165, 181–85; Amerasinghe (n 25) 164; Amerasinghe (n 43) 179; nn 89–92; and on the 'interest theory' of rights, eg, Bart Smit Duijzentkunst, 'Of Rights and Powers: Waiving Investment Treaty Protection' *EJIL:Talk!* (9 December 2013); John Morss, *International Law as the Law of Collectives* (Ashgate 2013) 64; generally Matthew Kramer, NE Simmonds, and Hillel Steiner, *A Debate over Rights: Philosophical Enquiries* (OUP 2000); Kenneth Campbell, 'Legal Rights' in Edward Zalta (ed), *The Stanford Encyclopedia of Philosophy* (2017) <https://plato.stanford.edu/archives/win2016/entries/legal-rights/>; Nigel Simmonds, *Central Issues in Jurisprudence* (3rd edn, Sweet & Maxwell 2008) 326–29; similarly discussion Nollkaemper (n 25) 104–6; Parlett (n 59) 362–63. Cf Roland Portmann, *Legal Personality in International Law* (CUP 2010) 130.

violated',[88] and 'the essence of the substantive right violated, as determined by the objects and interests promoted therein'.[89] Amerasinghe thus argues that 'it is really the nature of the "right" violated as being preponderantly one relating to an alien or his property that needs to be considered in determining the indirectness of the injury'.[90] Accordingly:

> [i]f the state's right in its essence has for its object the protection of its nationals as such and if this is the main interest sought from it ... the rule of exhaustion applies to it.... The claim may be for an apology or for an indemnity for damage caused to an alien, or merely damages for the insult to the alien's state, but this would not make a difference if the essence of the substantive right violated is the right to the protection of the alien.[91]

Wittich elaborates, citing '[t]he main focus' as being 'whether the right invoked has for its specific or primary object the *protection of the private individuals involved* as the ultimate beneficiary ... even if the formal holder of the relevant right is the State'.[92]

While initially appealing, however, this approach also seems flawed. The 'right' at issue in a claim depends on what primary obligation has allegedly been breached.[93] And diplomatic protection claims were indeed historically brought for breach of obligations concerning the treatment of aliens, which are clearly focused on protecting individuals.[94] Claims have more recently concerned consular protection and human rights obligations,[95] which still concern individuals' well-being.[96] However, to make good the argument that diplomatic protection and 'direct' claims are distinguishable by the nature of the obligation breached requires establishing that the obligations in diplomatic protection claims *always* concern individual protection, and, conversely, in 'direct' claims, they do not.[97] Neither contention withstands scrutiny.

[88] Amerasinghe (n 25) 163; also discussed Wittich (n 37) 136–37; Dugard, 'SecondRep' (n 37) [26].

[89] Amerasinghe (n 25) 164.

[90] Amerasinghe (n 43) 181.

[91] Amerasinghe (n 25) 164; also Wittich (n 37) 137 ('most suitable criterion'). Similarly Jean Chappez, *La Règle de l'épuisement Des Voies Des Recours Interns* (Pedone 1972) 44; Paparinskis, 'Countermeasures' (n 3) 279–80. Cf Willem Riphagen, 'Third Report on State Responsibility' (1982) ILCYB 22 [96].

[92] Wittich (n 37) 182 (emphasis added), also 181 ('the *substantive right* ... the *interest legally protected* by the relevant *primary norm*' (original emphasis)); Amerasinghe (n 25) 164 ('predominant interest'); Peters (n 23) 173 ('rights ... concerned individuals in substance').

[93] See Wittich (n 37) 181 ('substantive right as embodied in the primary norm'); also Amerasinghe (n 25) 164; generally Ch 1, nn 6, 109.

[94] See sources nn 90ff; Ch 2, n 94; Amerasinghe (n 25) 164–65; similarly Wittich (n 37) 183.

[95] See *LaGrand* (n 56) [75]–[77]; *Avena* (n 56) [40]; ILC, '50th' (n 67) 20 (Bennouna); Crawford, *GP* (n 2) 592–93; ILA (n 70) [28]; Ch 2, nn 217–24; similarly Wittich (n 37) 183.

[96] Wittich (n 37) 166, 183 (human rights); *Avena* (n 56) [47] (consular relations).

[97] See nn 88–92. Cf Wittich (n 37) 184; analysis Nollkaemper (n 25) 104–6.

(i) 'Direct' claims based on rules protecting individuals

On the one hand, 'direct' claims can be based on alleged violations of obligations designed to protect individuals.[98] Thus, the ICJ *Bosnian Genocide*,[99] *Croatian Genocide*,[100] *Georgia v Russia*,[101] and *Ukraine v Russia* cases[102] were not considered diplomatic protection claims subject to the local remedies rule,[103] notwithstanding that the Conventions relevantly invoked are designed to protect individuals and groups from genocide and racial discrimination respectively.[104] The ECtHR also recognises that certain interstate human rights claims can be brought on a "direct" basis, despite human rights obligations being clearly ones for individual protection.[105] Claims concerning obligations centred on individuals are not, consequently, always ones of diplomatic protection.

(ii) Diplomatic protection claims based on rules protecting States

On the other hand, claims that are diplomatic protection, at least in part, may result from violation of obligations primarily for State, rather than individual, protection.[106] First, for instance, claims alleging violation of obligations regulating transboundary harm may contain diplomatic protection aspects,[107] even though such obligations concern not individual protection per se but the preservation of other States' environments.[108] Cases concerning transboundary harm, or environmental pollution more generally, in which clear elements of diplomatic protection are present include the *Aerial Herbicide Spraying*,[109] *Pulp*

[98] Indeed, Amerasinghe suggests that direct claims may result from ECHR violations where the 'injury was in substance an interference with ... [State] functions' (Amerasinghe (n 25) 309), confirming that the *injury* matters, not the rule.

[99] *Application of the Convention on the Prevention and Punishment of the Crime of Genocide (Bosnia and Herzegovina v Serbia and Montenegro) (Judgment)* [2007] ICJ Rep 43.

[100] *Application of the Convention on the Prevention and Punishment of the Crime of Genocide (Croatia v Serbia) (Preliminary Objections)* [2008] ICJ Rep 412.

[101] *Application of the International Convention on the Elimination of All Forms of Racial Discrimination (Georgia v Russia) (Preliminary Objections)* [2011] ICJ Rep 70.

[102] *Application of the International Convention for the Suppression of the Financing of Terrorism and of the International Convention on the Elimination of All Forms of Racial Discrimination (Ukraine v Russia) (Preliminary Objections)* [2019] ICJ Rep 558.

[103] See Gaja, 'Position' (n 2) 12; Christian Tams, *Enforcing Obligations* Erga Omnes *in International Law* (CUP 2005) 135 (fn 81) (*Genocide* cases 'traditional disputes between ... States'); Ch 4(V)(B)(ii). Only the last case considered the local remedies rule, held inapplicable regarding claims alleging CERD breach: *Ukraine v Russia (Objections)* (n 102) [130].

[104] See *Reservations to the Convention on Genocide (Advisory Opinion)* [1951] ICJ Rep 15, 23; *Application of the International Convention on the Elimination of All Forms of Racial Discrimination (Georgia v Russia) (Provisional Measures)* [2008] ICJ Rep 353 [126].

[105] See discussion nn 348ff.

[106] Cf Wittich (n 37) 184 (vis-à-vis UNCLOS); Nollkaemper (n 25) 104–6.

[107] See DADP, 81–82; John Dugard, 'Third Report on Diplomatic Protection' (2002) 2(1) ILCYB 49 [68], [80], [83]; ILC, '50th' (n 67) 14, 17, 19–20 (Hafner/Brownlie); Meron (n 37) 98 (fn 2); also ILC, '53rd' (n 39) 149 (Hafner); nn 109–12.

[108] See *Pulp Mills on the River Uruguay (Argentina v Uruguay)* [2010] ICJ Rep 14 [101]; also Dugard, 'ThirdRep' (n 107) [80].

[109] Claiming for State and individual damage based on, *inter alia*, allegedly wrongful transboundary harm: *Aerial Herbicide Spraying (Ecuador v Colombia)* ICJ Pleadings, Mem Ecuador, Chs VI–IX

Mills,[110] and *Trail Smelter* cases.[111] Indeed, the DADP suggest that, where a person's 'property has suffered environmental harm caused by pollution, radioactive fallout or a fallen space object emanating from [another] State', it is 'unreasonable and unfair to require' exhaustion of local remedies,[112] suggesting that such circumstances *could* involve diplomatic protection, though an exception to the rule may apply.[113] Indeed, diplomatic protection claims could plausibly arise from violations of sovereignty more generally.[114] The EECC, for instance, acknowledged that individual injury, indicative of diplomatic protection,[115] arose not only from violations of international humanitarian law, which consists of rules for individual

(claims); Ch X, particularly [10.29]ff (reparation). While also claiming human rights violations (Ch IX), different violations were not distinguished in claiming for individuals' injury: [10.29]ff, particularly [10.37]. Colombia pointed to 'nationality of claims' requirements (Counter-Mem Colombia [1.25]) and Ecuador confirmed that it 'claim[ed] only *on behalf of its own citizens*', suggesting diplomatic protection: Rep Ecuador [3.152] (emphasis added).

110 Argentina claimed for 'damage ... suffered directly *and through its nationals*' vis-à-vis environmental pollution: *Pulp Mills on the River Uruguay (Argentina v Uruguay)* ICJ Pleadings, Mem Argentina [8.29] (emphasis added); generally Chs V–VII, [8.4], [8.24], [8.30]; *Pulp Mills* (n 108) [170]ff. Uruguay never raised local remedies objections.

111 Concerning damage from cross-border fumes: *Trail Smelter Case (US/Canada)* (1938/1941) III UNRIAA 1905, 1917–31, 1965–66. The Tribunal denied ruling 'upon claims presented by individuals or on [their] behalf' (ibid 1912, 1938); the case was not brought as 'a sum of individual claims for damage to private properties, espoused by the Government, but as a single claim for damage to the national territory': ibid 1961. Nonetheless, it acknowledged that individuals' damage 'may, in part, "afford a convenient scale for the calculation of the reparation due"': ibid 1913, quoting *Chórzow*, n 157, also 1938; Jessup (n 70) 120 ('injury to ... private property'; State claims withdrawn). This suggests diplomatic protection aspects: see DADP, 82; Dugard, 'ThirdRep' (n 107) [75]; ILC, '50th' (n 67) 17 (Hafner); ILC, 'Summary Records of the Meetings of the Fifty-Fourth Session' (2002) 1 ILCYB 1, 34, 41 (Dugard/Brownlie), cf 48–49 (Yamada/Xue); Meron (n 37) 98. Authorities explain the lack of local remedy exhaustion as deriving from the arbitration agreement, the injury being "direct", or the individuals' lack of connection with Canada: DADP, 82; Dugard, 'ThirdRep' (n 107) [75]; also Crawford, 'Revisited' (n 3) 166; ILC, '54th' (n 111) 43 (Opertti Badan); Meron (n 37) 98 (on the 'link'), generally 94–100. The first and third implicitly acknowledge that the claim *was* diplomatic protection (cf ILC, '54th' (n 111) 43 (Opertti Badan)), while the second is consistent with a 'mixed' claim exhibiting 'preponderantly' (DADP, art 14(3)) 'direct' injury: similarly Dugard, 'ThirdRep' (n 107) [84]; ILC, '54th' (n 111) 35 (Dugard).

112 DADP, 81. Similarly Aréchaga, n 382; Crawford, 'Revisited' (n 3) 166–67. The Space Objects Convention excludes the local remedies rule (art XI(1)), suggesting that claims for damage to States' 'natural or juridical persons' (art VIII(1)) could be diplomatic protection-like: see Dugard, 'ThirdRep' (n 107) [80]; ILC, '54th' (n 111) 34 (Dugard). Cf ibid 48 (Tomka) (liability, not responsibility); ILC, '50th' (n 67) 20 (Bennouna). Generally vis-à-vis space-related incidents: ibid 19–20 (Brownlie); Ian Brownlie, *System of the Law of Nations: State Responsibility, Part I* (Clarendon 1983) 237, 239 (direct); discussion Graefrath (n 72) 97.

113 nn 380–81.

114 cf discussion Nollkaemper (n 25) 105–6. See *Heirs of Oswald v Switzerland* (1926) 3 ILR 244; 52 BGE 235 (Swiss FC) (border violation; compensation claim for injured soldier, though apparently partly for State's insurance losses); *Rainbow Warrior (New Zealand v France)* (1985) 74 ILR 241, n 245; *Legality of Use of Force (Serbia and Montenegro v Belgium)* ICJ Pleadings, 351–52 (Mem FRY). Cf *García and Garza v US* (1926) IV UNRIAA 119 (Mexico–US Cl Comm) 120 (whether cross-boundary killing contrary to 'international standard'), discussed Brownlie (n 112) 74–75; Whiteman (n 52) 150.

115 n 46.

protection,[116] but also the *jus ad bellum* (the law relating to the use of force),[117] which does not.[118]

Second, even though immunities for State officials are held for and by States,[119] States may claim not only for their injury through State personnel, but also for individuals' personal damage.[120] The US did so in its 'mixed' claim in *Tehran Hostages*,[121] with reparation found due 'for the injury ... caused'[122] to diplomatic and consular officials through violation of obligations under the Vienna Convention on Consular Relations (VCCR) and Vienna Convention on Diplomatic Relations (VCDR).[123] Similarly, Uganda claimed in *Armed Activities* for injury to persons, including nationals, resulting from VCDR breach, though without having to exhaust local remedies.[124] Notwithstanding that immunities are not for individual protection, claims that are partially ones of diplomatic protection may therefore be brought for individual damage resulting from breach thereof.[125]

[116] Eg, ICRC, 'Introduction', *Customary IHL Database* <https://ihl–databases.icrc.org/customary–ihl/eng/docs/v1_cha_chapterin_in>; Nollkaemper (n 25) 103–4; Parlett (n 59) 350; Peters (n 23) 194; Paparinskis, 'Countermeasures' (n 3) 325.

[117] See *Ethiopia* (n 46) [103], [126], [135], [147], [157]–[158], [161], [180]ff, [199]ff, [214]–[262] (*jus in bello*); [291]–[292], [296], [300], [304]–[305], [332], [356], [386], [391]–[393] (*jus ad bellum*); Sean Murphy, Won Kidane, and Thomas Snider, *Litigating War: Arbitration of Civil Injury by the Eritrea–Ethiopia Claims Commission* (OUP 2013) 133–51, 183–88, 197–202, 219–30, 233–36, 301–3, 347–48, 352–55.

[118] n 132. See *Ethiopia* (n 46) [63] ('illegal use of force ... bearing upon inter-State relations'). Cf *Eritrea* (n 46) [210]–[212].

[119] See *Arrest Warrants* (n 56) [53]; Jessup (n 70) 118–19; Wittich (n 37) 185–86; Amerasinghe (n 25) 308; Jacob Katz Cogan, 'The Regulatory Turn in International Law' (2011) 52 Harv ILJ 321, 323 (fn 1); Garcia-Amador, 'Report' (n 39) [41] Lauterpacht (n 55) 136; Thirlway (n 32) 619 (on *Hostages*, n 121).

[120] Jessup (n 70) 119 ('supplementary claim may lie for ... injury to ... individual as such'), quoted Amerasinghe (n 25) 159, 164, quoted n 125; *ARSIWA*, 223; cf DADP, 28. For examples: Jessup (n 70) 119; Whiteman (n 52) 80–82 (fnn 184–85), 136–42; also Borchard (n 54) 361, cf 352; similarly *Reparation for injuries suffered in the service of the United Nations (Advisory Opinion)* [1949] ICJ Rep 174, 202 (Diss Op Hackworth).

[121] DADP, 74, generally 74–76. The US claimed both for itself and, exercising diplomatic protection, for its nationals taken hostage: *United States Diplomatic and Consular Staff in Tehran (USA v Iran) (Judgment)* [1980] ICJ Rep 3, 7–8 (Mem, sub (c)).

[122] ibid [90].

[123] See ibid [67], [76]–[78]. While a separate bilateral treaty 'ha[d] importance' vis-à-vis 'two private individuals' (ibid [50], also [67], [77]; see Thirlway (n 32) 1555 (fn 674), 619 (fn 327)), only the VCCR and VCDR were apparently relevant for claims concerning hostages with status thereunder (see *Hostages* (n 121) [46], [49]–[50], [22]; cf Thirlway (n 32) 1555 (fn 674)). The diplomatic protection claim for the officials' personal damage therefore rested on breach of obligations for *State* protection. Further: *Certain Property (Liechtenstein v Germany)* ICJ Pleadings, 308 [6.37] (Obs Liechtenstein); Thirlway (n 32) 619.

[124] *Armed Activities on the Territory of the Congo (DRC v Uganda) (Judgment)* [2005] ICJ Rep 168 [331] (in 'substance' part of direct VCDR claim), [338] ('maltreatment ... necessarily consequential' on breach; immaterial whether nationals/officials). Congo considered the claims diplomatic protection: [306], [328]. See Thirlway (n 32) 1554; cf n 369.

[125] See Amerasinghe (n 25) 164 ('right ... violated which has for its object ... carrying on of [State] functions' but claim potentially also 'purport[ing] to recover damages for ... *personal loss* suffered by ... diplomat, an alien'), 308 ('state's interest ... not purely ... protecting ... national ... maintaining its own functions or dignity, which *predominate*' (emphases added)), 370–71; also DADP, 75–76. Cf Thirlway (n 32) 1554–55. Functional protection claims are similar: see Amerasinghe (n 25) 370–71, discussing Fitzmaurice (n 36) 86–87; Garcia-Amador, 'Report' (n 39) [115]–[116]. Organisations claim

Third, various claims arising from damage to vessels beyond State territory suggest that the obligation breached is not decisive.[126] Several States have claimed for, *inter alia*, damage to the person and property of their nationals on board downed civilian aircraft.[127] These were apparently, at least partly, typical diplomatic protection claims.[128] Indeed, the DADP outline that claims concerning persons 'on board an aircraft that is shot down while in overflight of another State's territory' are excused from the local remedies rule because there is no 'connection' between the individual and the respondent State,[129] thus presupposing that they *are* diplomatic protection cases.[130] Yet most States in these claims alleged, at least *inter alia*, violation of the prohibition on using force,[131] which is not an obligation for individual protection.[132]

Cases involving ships include,[133] for instance, the *Costa Rica Packet*, where damages were awarded to the owners, captain and crew of a vessel wrongly detained given the flag State's exclusive jurisdiction,[134] the *I'm Alone Case*, where

for breach of their rights and their officials' personal damage: see Amerasinghe (n 25) 370, discussing Fitzmaurice (n 36) 86–87, in turn discussing *Reparations* (n 120) 181–82, 184; also Bollecker-Stern (n 43) 98. The breach must be identical for each part of the claim: see discussion Fitzmaurice (n 36) 86–87, quoting *Reparations* (n 120) 182, also 180; Amerasinghe (n 25) 370–71; Bollecker-Stern (n 43) 96, 111; Garcia-Amador, 'Problems' (n 55) 442. Generally on separating State/individual damage: Fitzmaurice (n 36) 86–87, 25 (fn 3), 670–71; Amerasinghe (n 25) 164, 371.

126 See DADP, 81 (referencing *Aerial Incident*); Dugard, 'SecondRep' (n 37) [19]; also Meron (n 37) 97.

127 See *Aerial Pleadings* (n 52) 36 (UK App [8](a)), 23 (US App [3]), 29 (Annex 3), 116 (Mem Israel, sub I); *Aerial Incident of 3 July 1988 (Iran v USA)* ICJ Pleadings, vol I, 11 [2] (Mem Iran), 289–91 [5.21]. Generally: DADP, 81; Wittich (n 37) 153–57; Meron (n 37) 92–94.

128 In one case, the US expressly 'espous[ed]' its nationals' claims (*Aerial Pleadings* (n 52) 170 (Mem US), also 167), while Israel claimed for 'the persons *whose cause is being adopted by it*' (ibid 116 (sub II(a) (emphasis added)); see Wittich (n 37) 154; cf Amerasinghe (n 25) 166–67. In another, Iran claimed 'the right to espouse [the victims'] claims': *Iran v USA* (n 127) 304 [5.41]; also Amerasinghe (n 43) 297; Dugard, 'ThirdRep' (n 107) [79].

129 DADP, 81; also Meron (n 37) 98.

130 DADP, art 15(c), 80–83; Meron (n 37) 96; sources nn 380–81. Israel's arguments against the local remedies rule's application—'unity' between the aircraft and persons, violation of its rights, and a lack of 'connection' (*Aerial Pleadings* (n 52) 527–32)—do not undermine that aspects of diplomatic protection were present: see discussion Amerasinghe (n 25) 149, 157–59, 166–67; Wittich (n 37) 153–57; Thirlway (n 32) 619; Meron (n 37) 93–96; n 128; also ILC, '50th' (n 67) 7 (Brownlie); de Aréchaga (n 47) 583; Crawford, 'Revisited' (n 3) 166. Suggesting the case was 'mixed': Dugard, 'SecondRep' (n 37) [19]; Wittich (n 37) 157; n 283. Cf *Aerial Pleadings* (n 52) 531.

131 *Aerial Pleadings* (n 52) 358ff, [66]ff (Mem UK), 84–85, [61]–[62] (Mem Israel); *Iran/USA* (n 127) 12 [3], 155ff (section III). Cf *Aerial Pleadings* (n 52) 213 (Mem US) ('international murder').

132 Oliver Dörr and Albrecht Randelzhofer, 'Article 2(4)' in Bruno Simma and others (eds), *The Charter of the United Nations: A Commentary* (3rd edn, OUP 2012) 213 ('indisputably only protects … States'). Cf Wittich (n 37) 156 (*Aerial Incident* 'concerned with the proper treatment of nationals abroad').

133 Under the DADP, flag States may claim 'on behalf of … crew members, irrespective of their nationality, when … injured in connection with an injury to the vessel': DADP, art 18; generally 91–94, discussing *Saiga* (n 58) [106]; John Dugard, 'Fifth Report on Diplomatic Protection' (2004) 2(1) ILCYB 43 [52]–[66]; similarly *Virginia G* (n 58) [127]; *Arctic Sunrise (Merits)* (n 58) [172]; also Whiteman (n 52) 95. Nationality apart, 'there is … a close resemblance' with diplomatic protection: DADP, 91, also 93–94; generally Dugard, 'FifthRep' (n 133) [44]–[56], [62], [67]; ILC, '54th' (n 111) 6 (Gaja); ILA (n 70) [159].

134 *Costa Rica Packet (UK v Netherlands)* (1897) 5 Moore's 4948, 4953–54.

the Commissioners recommended damages, *inter alia*, 'for the benefit of the captain and members of the crew' after a ship was sunk,[135] and *Wimbledon*, in which Germany had to compensate for damage caused by its unlawfully disallowing a ship canal access.[136] All appear to be classic diplomatic protection cases brought by States on behalf of injured nationals.[137] More recently, at least certain States have brought claims for violations of the United Nations Convention on the Law of the Sea (UNCLOS) expressly as ones of diplomatic protection,[138] with compensation found due for the respective vessels' losses.[139] While no tribunal in an UNCLOS case has required that local remedies be exhausted, the characterisation of these claims by the States themselves, and the tribunals' reasoning, makes clear that elements of diplomatic protection were involved.[140]

In all of these cases involving vessels, then, diplomatic protection was present despite the claims concerning, *inter alia*, violations of rules concerning the use of force,[141] and State jurisdiction,[142] not commonly conceived as for individual protection,[143] and navigation,[144] not always so regarded.[145]

(iii) Conclusion

Both categories of cases discussed—'direct' claims brought based on rules designed for individual protection, and claims brought based on rules *not* concerned primarily with individuals, but clearly containing elements of diplomatic protection—will usually, as elucidated further below, properly be regarded as

[135] *SS 'I'm Alone' (US/Canada)* (1933/1935) III UNRIAA 1609, 1618; also discussed Jessup (n 70) 120, 162; Whiteman (n 52) 150–57; Amerasinghe (n 25) 165–66; DADP, 92.

[136] *The SS 'Wimbledon'* [1923] PCIJ Rep Ser A No 1, 30–33. See *ARSIWA*, 270; Jessup (n 70) 120.

[137] Noting States' 'right ... of protecting and defending [their] nationals abroad ... subjected to ... injuries committed to their prejudice': *Costa Rica Packet* (n 134) 4952. Cf Chappez (n 91) 45. In *I'm Alone*, the claim was brought under a provision for 'claim[s] *by a British vessel* for compensation on the grounds that *it has suffered loss or injury*': art IV, reproduced *I'm Alone* (n 135) 1612 (emphasis added) and see 1616; Whiteman (n 52) 151. In *Wimbledon*, Germany had to 'compensate [France], *acting on behalf of the [national]*': *Wimbledon* (n 136) 30 (emphasis added).

[138] *Virginia G* (n 58) [119]; *Duzgit* (n 58) [146]–[147]. Cf *Norstar* (n 58) [251]; *The 'Enrica Lexie' Incident (Award)* PCA Case 2015-28 (21 May 2020) [1008].

[139] See *Virginia G* (n 58) [446]; *Duzgit* (n 58) [333]; also *Saiga* (n 58) [172], discussed Wittich (n 37) 170–77; Dugard, 'FifthRep' (n 133) [54]–[56]; also Chester Brown, *A Common Law of International Adjudication* (OUP 2007) 206–8.

[140] Finding the State's injury 'preponderant': *Virginia G* (n 58) [157]; *Duzgit* (n 58) [156]. Finding the claim 'direct', but also observing local remedies irrelevant given 'no jurisdictional connection existed': *Saiga* (n 58) [98]–[100]. See Dugard, 'FifthRep' (n 133) [54] (*Saiga* 'also ... diplomatic protection'), [55]–[56]; also DADP, 93; Brown (n 139) 208. Cf cases considered "direct" based on a rights analysis: n 58.

[141] See Jessup (n 70) 162 (*I'm Alone* (n 135)); *Saiga* (n 58) [159], case discussed Wittich (n 37), 170–77.

[142] n 134; *Saiga* (n 58) [130]–[131], [136]; *Duzgit* (n 58) [254]–[261]; *Virginia G* (n 58) [270]–[271].

[143] n 132; *Jurisdictional Immunities (Germany v Italy: Greece Intervening) (Judgment)* [2012] ICJ Rep 99 [57] ('jurisdiction ... flows from' sovereignty); *Virginia G* (n 58) [157] (State rights).

[144] n 136; *Saiga* (n 58).

[145] *Virginia G* (n 58) [157] (State right); similarly *Oppenheim's* (n 68) 614; McCorquodale (n 61) 285; cf *Saiga* (n 58) [53] (Sep Op Wolfrum) (State/individual rights 'interwoven'), discussed Wittich (n 37) 175.

'mixed'.[146] But this necessarily means that both diplomatic protection *and* 'direct' aspects are present.[147] Contrary to academic opinion, a detailed examination of the approaches taken by States and tribunals does not support the nature of the obligation being employed as a tool to distinguish which of such 'mixed' claims are subject to diplomatic protection requirements: rules established for individual protection can found 'direct' claims, while claims of diplomatic protection, at least in part, can be based on rules for State protection.

C. Damage: the correct distinction

The distinction between 'direct' and diplomatic protection claims instead lies in the *injury* caused, taking the term 'injury' to refer to *factual* injury, or damage, and not, as already explained, to *legal* injury, in terms of either the right-holder or the nature of the obligation violated.[148]

As Chapter 1 outlined, reparable damage under international law results from breach of an international obligation.[149] Both States and individuals can suffer such damage.[150] Thus, the Permanent Court of International Justice (PCIJ) outlined in *Chórzow*, a case of diplomatic protection, that 'the reparation of a wrong may consist in an indemnity corresponding to the *damage which the nationals of the injured State have suffered* as a result of the act which is contrary to international law'.[151] It therefore accepted, first, that breaches of international law can cause damage to *individuals*.[152] Second, and significantly, while individuals were later accorded rights under international law,[153] at the time, the rights breached were indisputably the State's.[154] Individual damage can accordingly result even where the rights breached are *not* the individual's—ie where the individual is not *legally* injured.[155] Rather,

[146] Section IV(B)(i). See, eg, on *Trail Smelter*, n 111; on *Tehran Hostages*: DADP, 74; also Crawford, 'Revisited' (n 3) 170; on the UNCLOS cases, n 365.

[147] Ch 2, nn 108–9.

[148] Section II(A)–(C); similarly Sohn and Baxter (n 30) art 14 (defining 'injury'), 46; cf Amerasinghe (n 43) 177.

[149] Ch 1(II)(B).

[150] Ch 1, nn 50–53; Garcia-Amador, 'SixthRep' (n 47) [30]–[31], [176]. Also JL Brierly, *Brierly's Law of Nations: An Introduction to the Role of International Law in International Relations* (7th edn, OUP 2012) 256; Fitzmaurice (n 36) 25–26, 670; Borchard (n 54) 352.

[151] *Chórzow (Merits)* (n 56) 27–28 (emphasis added), discussed authorities n 152; Ch 2, n 100; Ch 4, n 353. See also *Legal Consequences of the Construction of a Wall in the Occupied Palestinian Territory (Advisory Opinion)* [2004] ICJ Rep 136 [152]–[153], cited Diana Contreras Garduño, 'Defining Beneficiaries of Collective Reparations: The Experience of the IACtHR' (2012) 4 Ams LF 40, 42.

[152] Peters (n 23) 170, 357; also Wittich (n 37) 131, 150 ('no identity'); de Aréchaga (n 47) 574–75, 578; Fitzmaurice (n 36) 670–71; Garcia-Amador, 'SixthRep' (n 47) [11], also [30]–[31], [34]–[40], [176].

[153] n 78.

[154] *Chórzow (Merits)* (n 56) 27. See Peters (n 23) 170–71; Parlett (n 59) 70; cf discussion Thirlway (n 32) 1553–54.

[155] n 157. Cf Peters (n 23) 170–71. On individual 'legal injury': Nollkaemper (n 25) 98–99.

which entity suffers damage generally depends on who has experienced the relevant loss.[156] Nonetheless, the PCIJ went on in the same case to suggest that:

> Rights or interests of an individual the violation of which rights causes damage are always in a different plane to rights belonging to a State, which rights may also be infringed by the same act. *The damage suffered by an individual is never therefore identical in kind with that which will be suffered by a State*; it can only afford a convenient scale for the calculation of the reparation due to the State.[157]

The State would thus—contrary to the argument made here—be claiming for *its own* damage when exercising diplomatic protection.[158]

Putting to one side for the moment whether the State might *also* be (factually) injured through injury to its national,[159] in cases of diplomatic protection, the individual is certainly injured in the sense of having suffered damage—this has been recognised in early codifications of diplomatic protection,[160] case law,[161] and academic commentary.[162] Indeed, diplomatic protection is accepted to be exercised vis-à-vis 'personal injury and ... injuries in respect of property',[163] the relevant violations being:

> in respect of the person of the alien, such as arrests, physical injury, torture or improper imprisonment, or ... involv[ing] the property of the alien, when, for

[156] Wittich (n 37) 129 (on direct/indirect injury, discussed Ch 2, n 102); also Garcia-Amador, 'Report' (n 39) [96], [127] ('immediate victim of the injury'); Garcia-Amador, 'Problems' (n 55) 486 ('person who ... directly suffered ... damage'); Harvey McGregor and others, *McGregor on Damages* (19th edn, Sweet & Maxwell 2014) [2-001]; de Aréchaga (n 47) 577, citing *Spanish Zone* (n 70) 730.

[157] *Chórzow (Merits)* (n 56) 28 (emphasis added), discussed authorities n 152; Ch 2, n 100; Ch 4, n 353.

[158] Authorities Ch 2, nn 97–100; Ch 4, nn 136–37, 353–54; cf discussion Frits Kalshoven, 'Expert Opinion' in Hisakazu Fujita, Isomi Suzuki, and Kantaro Nagano (eds), *War and the Rights of Individuals: Renaissance of Individual Compensation* (Nippon Hyoron-sha 1999) 45; Garcia-Amador, 'Problems' (n 55) 482; Fitzmaurice (n 36) 670–71, cf 26.

[159] See section IV(B)(i).

[160] See Garcia-Amador, 'Report' (n 39) 177–80, 192 and reproductions Annexures 1, 3 (see art 1), 5, 9; Dugard, 'FirstRep' (n 3) 215. Cf Meron (n 37) 97.

[161] *ELSI* (n 32) [52] ('alleged *damage* to [nationals]' (emphasis added)), quoted Dugard, 'SecondRep' (n 37) [21]; Wittich (n 37) 161; also *Barcelona Traction* (n 56) [28], [35] ('[shareholders'] *losses*' (emphasis added)); *Chórzow (Merits)* (n 56), quoted n 157; *Reparations* (n 120) 207 (Diss Op Badawi Pasha) ('damage suffered by [national]'); also *Aerial Pleadings* (n 52) 526 (Israel).

[162] Eg, de Aréchaga (n 47) 574; Brierly (n 150) 256; Garcia-Amador, 'Report' (n 39) [17]; Thirlway (n 32) 1551; *Oppenheim's* (n 68) 847 (fn 2); Douglas (n 67) 166; Borchard (n 54) 349; Bollecker-Stern (n 43) 106; Brownlie (n 112) 236, 240; also nn 179–183; Kalshoven (n 158) 45 ('diplomatic protection presupposes ... [nationals'] damage or injury'), 46.

[163] Amerasinghe (n 43) 37. Similarly: Brierly (n 150) 258 ('foreigner (alien) suffers injury in person or property'); de Aréchaga (n 47) 573; Garcia-Amador, 'Problems' (n 55) 462; Crawford, *GP* (n 2) 568; Garcia-Amador, 'Report' (n 39) Annexures 1, 8, 9; also Dugard, 'FirstRep' (n 3) 215; Garcia-Amador, 'SixthRep' (n 47) [34], 46; similarly Dugard, 'SecondRep' (n 37) [39]; ILC, '52nd' (n 52) 35–36, cf 119 (Lukashuk); ILC, '50th' (n 67) 19 (Sepúlveda).

example, the acts cause physical damage to property or in the case of improper deprivation of property.[164]

Such personal and property injury results in damage to the *individual*.[165] This must be so vis-à-vis injury to the person:[166] losses resulting from '[c]ompensable personal injury'—including 'loss of earnings and earning capacity, medical expenses and the like',[167] and 'non-material losses, such as the loss of loved ones and pain and suffering'[168]—are patently suffered by individuals, not the State.[169] Moreover, although a State may be legitimately concerned with the effect of private property damage on its own economy,[170] 'international law does not really treat such assets as being actually the property of the national state'.[171] Rather, damage to private property per se causes the individual owner thereof to suffer loss.[172] Undoubtedly, as Chapter 4 elucidates, States might suffer their own damage as a *consequence* of damage to individuals' person or property.[173] But that does not mean the State has itself suffered the individual's damage; rather, in diplomatic protection a State claims 'over and above any direct injury it may itself have suffered'.[174]

How then do we get to the point of holding that damage to a national's person or property is done to the State? This is the role of the 'fiction' of diplomatic protection,[175] namely '[t]he theory ... that injuries either to private persons or to their property, committed contrary to international law, are injuries against the state

164 Amerasinghe (n 43) 37; also Garcia-Amador, 'SixthRep' (n 47) [31], [34]ff, [119]ff.

165 See Amerasinghe (n 25) 53; *ARSIWA*, 221–25; Garcia-Amador, 'SixthRep' (n 47) [30]–[31], [34]; generally John Barker, 'Compensation' in Crawford and others, *Responsibility* (n 3) 604–8; Brown (n 139) 199–208; n 47.

166 Amerasinghe (n 25) 53; also Borchard (n 54) 362–63. Cf Eric Wyler and Alain Papaux, 'Satisfaction' in Crawford and others, *Responsibility* (n 3) 628.

167 *ARSIWA*, 223.

168 Crawford, *GP* (n 2) 517; also *ARSIWA*, 223; Barker (n 165) 604–5.

169 See Amerasinghe (n 25) 53; Garcia-Amador, 'SixthRep' (n 47) [11], [30]–[31], [34]–[40], [176]; Brown (n 139) 199–208; *ARSIWA*, 223–25; Crawford, *GP* (n 2) 517; Sohn and Baxter (n 30) 46.

170 See Amerasinghe (n 25) 53; Bollecker-Stern (n 43) 100 (quoting Emer de Vattel, *The Law of Nations, or, Principles of the Law of Nature Applied to the Conduct and Affairs of Nations and Sovereigns* (T & JW Johnson 1867) 164, see also 109, 174), also 104–5; Amerasinghe (n 43) 12; Gateano Arangio-Ruiz, 'Second Report on State Responsibility' (1989) 2(1) ILCYB 1, 16 (fn 110) (quoting Reuter); Bennouna (n 39) [17]; Giorgio Gaja, 'The International Court of Justice's Approach to Injuries Suffered by Individuals' (Oxford, 8 May 2014) <https://podcasts.ox.ac.uk/international-court-justices-approach-injuries-suffered-individuals>; Wyler and Papaux (n 166) 628; eg *Military and Paramilitary Activities in and Against Nicaragua (Nicaragua v USA)* ICJ Pleadings, vol V, 306 (Mem Compensation). Further Ch 4, nn 410ff.

171 Amerasinghe (n 25) 53.

172 See *ARSIWA*, 221ff (differentiating State/individual property damage); Borchard (n 54) 362–63; also Bollecker-Stern (n 43) 105, citing *Barcelona Traction* (n 56) 46, also 114–22, 177; similarly de Aréchaga (n 47) 578; Graefrath (n 72) 48–49; Vattel (n 170) 109–10, 174; Brown (n 139) 199–205.

173 See authorities n 256; generally nn 256ff; Ch 4, nn 401ff; eg, *ARSIWA*, 221; Brown (n 139) 200, 206–8; Borchard (n 54) 362; Sohn and Baxter (n 30) 46. Cf Barker (n 165) 604.

174 *ARSIWA*, 223.

175 Generally: Bollecker-Stern (n 43) 95–101; Vermeer-Künzli, 'Fiction' (n 55); Ch 2, n 98.

whose national the individual is'.[176] For the reasons noted,[177] there is no 'fiction' in maintaining that the State is *legally* injured when its rights are breached in circumstances affecting its nationals.[178] What is 'fictional' is to assume that it suffers the resulting damage.[179] As Bennouna observes, 'the fiction resides' in keeping State and individual damage separate, yet 'recognizing that … the damage suffered by an individual … [is] used to calculate the [State's damage] (which remains fictitious)'.[180] Indeed, the State is, through diplomatic protection, able to claim reparation (for damage) for itself.[181] However, as confirmed by the compensation normally reflecting the individual's damage,[182] the relevant damage is, in reality, experienced by the individual.[183] This is why the reparation requested provides insights, for it can indicate that a claim is one of diplomatic protection, being brought, in actuality, for individual damage.[184]

The individual's injury being factual in diplomatic protection is reinforced by the local remedies rule.[185] Implicitly, the rule requires exhaustion of remedies in the sense that the individual has obtained no reparation for the damage caused to them.[186] Thus, the PCIJ described diplomatic protection as 'a State … protect[ing] its subjects, when injured by acts contrary to international law committed by another State, *from whom they have been unable to obtain satisfaction*'.[187] In *ELSI*,

[176] Whiteman (n 52) 82; also Higgins (n 52) 51; Borchard (n 54) 353–54. Famously: Brierly (n 150) 256 ('exaggeration to say … whenever a national is injured … their state as a whole is necessarily injured too'), earlier edition cited DADP, 25; Dugard, 'DP' (n 55) 1052.

[177] nn 73–81.

[178] ILC, '50th' (n 67) 7 (Brownlie), 9 (Simma); ILC, '52nd' (n 52) 66 (Simma) ('nothing fictitious about … diplomatic protection'); Wittich (n 37) 131–32; Douglas (n 67) 166–67; Douglas (n 33) 14; also James Crawford, *Brownlie's Principles of Public International Law* (8th edn, OUP 2012) 607 ('cannot be simply dismissed' as fiction; 'state has a legal interest represented by its citizens'); Brierly, n 286; cf Vermeer-Künzli, 'Fiction' (n 55) 39, 58; Peters (n 23) 390, 393; Pellet (n 33) 36–37; ILC, '53rd' (n 39) 131 (Pellet); Garcia-Amador, 'SixthRep' (n 47) [41].

[179] See ILC, '52nd' (n 52) 49 (Pellet) ('fictional damage'), 50; also ILC, '50th' (n 67) 16 (Hafner) (individual damage 'assumed … caused to the State as if the property of the nationals or perhaps the nationals themselves had been [State] property'); Peters (n 23) 393 ('citizen … as part or "chattel" of … State'); Higgins (n 52) 51–52; cf ILC, '52nd' (n 52) 59 (Candioti); discussion Douglas (n 33) 14.

[180] Bennouna (n 39) [23] (having quoted *Chórzow (Merits)* (n 56) 28), cf [21].

[181] Ch 2, nn 97–100; also Crawford, *GP* (n 2) 76–77.

[182] n 157; Ch 2, n 100; de Aréchaga (n 47) 573–75; Bollecker-Stern (n 43) 97.

[183] Bennouna (n 39) [23]; Amerasinghe (n 25) 53; DADP, 23, 97; similarly Dugard, 'FirstRep' (n 3) [65]; Brierly (n 150) 256; Pellet (n 33) 56; ILC, '50th' (n 67) 9 (Bennouna); Wittich (n 37) 129, quoted n 52; also Peters (n 23) 395; Sohn and Baxter (n 30) 51; Jessup (n 70) 9; *Reparations* (n 120) 207 (Diss Op Badawi Pasha). Further: *US v Germany (Administrative Decision No V)* (1924) VII UNRIAA 119 (US–German Mixed Cl Comm) 153; Garcia-Amador, 'Problems' (n 55) 462, 467.

[184] Authorities n 41, particularly Meron; Wittich (n 37) 170; also DADP, 76.

[185] Similarly Amerasinghe (n 25) 53, 165; also Thirlway (n 32) 618–19; cf Wittich (n 37) 136 (criticising); *Heathrow* (n 58) 60–62, discussed and similarly criticised Wittich (n 37) 169–70. Generally on local remedies demonstrating 'fiction': Dugard, 'FirstRep' (n 3) [19]; Pellet (n 33) 54; also Amerasinghe (n 25) 53.

[186] See Ruth Donner, *The Regulation of Nationality in International Law* (2nd edn, Transnational 1994) 19 ('without satisfaction'); *Fornos Diaz v Guatemala (Admissibility)* (1909) 3 AJIL 737 (CACJ) 743 ('whether … efforts to obtain reparation have failed'), cited Borchard (n 54) 14; Nollkaemper (n 25) 247; also *Waste Management (Award)* (n 70) 66 (Diss Op Highet).

[187] *Mavrommatis* (n 43) 12 (emphasis added); Crawford, *GP* (n 2) 580.

the ICJ held it 'sufficient if the essence of the claim has been ... pursued as far as permitted by local law and procedures, and *without success*'.[188] Given that claims before domestic and international tribunals might differ, with 'different law' applying,[189] local remedies cannot necessarily be pursued for the same *breach* (ie *legal* injury) as that alleged in the later diplomatic protection suit.[190] Rather, the wrongdoing State is allowed 'an opportunity to *redress* [the violation] by its own means' under domestic law,[191] namely, to remedy the individual's *damage* (*factual* injury).[192] And because '[a] State discharges the responsibility incumbent upon it for breach of an international obligation by ... giving reparation for the injury caused',[193] it follows that, at least vis-à-vis purely diplomatic protection claims:[194]

> where local remedies are exhausted and adequate redress is obtained by the injured alien, the delinquent state's responsibility is *completely discharged* and all claims arising from the injury are extinguished. There is no room for a claim of damages for the international injury to the alien's state or for an apology based on the fact that the alien's state also suffered injury.[195]

Individual damage is thus of the essence of a diplomatic protection claim.[196]

188 *ELSI* (n 32) [59] (emphasis added), quoted DADP, 73; Crawford, *GP* (n 2) 583.

189 *ELSI* (n 32) [59]; also DADP, 72, quoting *Ambatielos Claim (Greece/UK)* (1956) XII UNRIAA 83, 120; cf Amerasinghe (n 25) 196.

190 Crawford, *GP* (n 2) 582–83; Shany (n 5) 138; Crawford, 'Revisited' (n 3) 162–63; Nollkaemper (n 25) 260; Thirlway (n 32) 619–20, 1555–56; *Heathrow* (n 58) 60, discussed Wittich (n 37) 169. Cf *Interhandel* (n 56) 28.

191 *Interhandel* (n 56) 27 (emphasis added), quoted DADP, 71; Crawford, *GP* (n 2) 580; also Bennouna (n 39) [10]; Wittich (n 37) 132; DADP, art 15(a) (remedies must 'provide effective redress'), also 78–79; Amerasinghe (n 25) 59–62, 74; de Aréchaga (n 47) 585, 589.

192 See Crawford, *GP* (n 2) 583 (only issue whether remedy obtained); Nollkaemper (n 25) 260–61; also ILC, '52nd' (n 52) 72 (Tomka); *Bissangou v DRC* (2006) AHRLR 80 [55] ('opportunity to compensate ... for [individual's] prejudice'); also *ELSI* (n 32) [56]. Cf Shany (n 5) 30 (need for similar 'substantive contents of ... law and ... remedies').

193 de Aréchaga (n 47) 564.

194 Not so in a 'mixed' claim (n 36) involving additional State injury: ibid 591 ('state may still ... claim for direct injury'); Borchard (n 54) 353 ('affronts to ... nation ... survive [individual] restitution or compensation'); Garcia-Amador, 'SixthRep' (n 47) [176].

195 Amerasinghe (n 25) 165 (emphasis added, though used vis-à-vis argument n 91); similarly 53 ('satisfaction of ... alien's grievance at ... national level ... wipe[s] out [State's] injury'), 103, 397; Borchard (n 54) 353 (where no 'national insult'); ILC, 'Diplomatic Protection' (1997) 2(2) ILCYB 60 [177] (diplomatic protection for 'injury ... not ... redressed through local remedies'), similar quotation ILA (n 70) [26]; also Thirlway (n 32) 618; Meron (n 37) 88, 90, 92, quoting *Interhandel* (n 56) 31 (Decl Basdevant); Wittich (n 37) 149; *Waste Management (Award)* (n 70) 66 (Diss Op Highet); Ch 5, n 84. Cf Nollkaemper (n 25) 250–51.

196 Kalshoven, n 162; Julio Barboza, 'Legal Injury: The Tip of the Iceberg in the Law of State Responsibility?' in Ragazzi (n 80) 8 (fn 6) ('damage ... a condition of responsibility by ... primary norm'); also Raphaele Rivier, 'Inter-American Mechanisms' in Crawford and others, *Responsibility* (n 3) 747–48.

D. Conclusion

In sum, neither the entity to which an obligation is owed nor a given obligation's content can determine whether a claim for breach thereof is diplomatic protection.[197] Both diplomatic protection and 'direct' claims invoke responsibility for violation of obligations owed to the State.[198] Violation of obligations for individual protection or benefit[199] may be *more likely* to give rise to diplomatic protection, but this is because individual *damage* is more likely to result.[200] Diplomatic protection claims can nonetheless arise, as shown, from breach of other obligations, just as 'direct' claims can be brought for violation of obligations for individual protection.[201] Indeed, diplomatic protection claims can be brought for breach of *any* obligation where individual damage results.[202]

Diplomatic protection and 'direct' claims can instead be distinguished as follows. A claim for State injury, legal and/or factual (the latter including material and/or moral damage),[203] with no 'fictional' damage,[204] is direct, because it is not '*for an injury caused* ... to a natural or legal person', but for State injury alone.[205] Regardless of the underlying obligation, when breach is alleged to have caused damage (factual injury) to a national's *person* or *property*,[206] 'as a private individual',[207] and the claim is solely for,[208] or based on,[209] that damage, the claim is one of diplomatic protection.[210] It is for breach of obligations owed to the *State*, but for *individual* damage, done to the State only "fictionally".[211] In the 'mixed' claims in

[197] Cf section II(A)–(B); Wittich (n 37) 173, 165–66 (arguing *Saiga* (n 58) [98] and *Air Services* (n 58) [31] concerned aliens' treatment).

[198] Section II(A).

[199] See Wittich (n 37) 177 (to whom 'provision allocates the benefits of the right'); also Parlett (n 59) 350; Nollkaemper (n 25) 104–6; section II(B).

[200] See Wittich (n 37) 130 (if State 'primary beneficiary' then 'immediate object of the injury'); also Amerasinghe (n 25) 163–65; Riphagen (n 91) [96]; cf Parlett (n 59) 362–63; *Virginia G* (n 58) [16], [22], [24], [27] (using 'rights' and 'injury' interchangeably) (Sep Op Cot/Kelly); discussion *Eritrea* (n 46) [210]–[212], [214], [216].

[201] Section II(A)–(B).

[202] See Crawford, *Brownlie's* (n 178) 607 ('If nationals are subjected to injury or loss by another state, then, whether the harm occurs in the territory of a state, or on the high seas or in outer space, the state of nationality may present a claim on the international plane'); also Meron (n 37) 97; DADP, 81; cf Fitzmaurice (n 36) 86.

[203] See Wittich (n 37) 130; generally Ch 1(II)(A).

[204] nn 175–83; similarly de Aréchaga (n 47) 582; see Brownlie (n 112) 236–40. Further authorities section IV(B).

[205] DADP, art 1. Similarly Sohn and Baxter (n 30) 45–49.

[206] See nn 163ff.

[207] DADP, 76.

[208] ibid art 1; Ch 2, n 93.

[209] DADP, 75–76, art 14(3); n 48 and discussion section IV(B)(i)–(ii).

[210] Similarly DADP, 76; cf Thirlway (n 32) 618; n 196.

[211] n 204. Difficult situations could concern individual interests affected without obvious factual damage, eg, *Biwater* (n 86) [465]–[467] ('economic damage' unnecessary for expropriation), to which Paparinskis pointed me; also James Crawford, 'Fourth Report on State Responsibility' (2001) 2(1) ILCYB 1 [33]; *Eckle v Germany* (1982) 68 ILR 48 (ECtHR) [66] ('absence of prejudice'). Such cases might involve individual (moral) damage: see discussion *ARSIWA*, 31; Crawford, 'FourthRep'

between, the State suffers material and/or moral damage additional to that done to individuals.[212] Whether the local remedies rule applies depends on which part of the injury the suit is 'preponderantly' based, as elaborated further below.[213]

III. Article 48 claims

What about article 48 claims? States claim under article 42 for violation of obligations owed to them, and, usually, for damage,[214] in both 'direct' and diplomatic protection claims (although the damage in the latter case is 'fictional').[215] By contrast, although States claim under the rule in article 48 for breach of obligations *erga omnes (partes)* owed to them,[216] they do not even "fictionally" claim for their own damage.[217] Rather, they claim 'in the interest of' the relevant 'beneficiaries'.[218] Nonetheless, where that beneficiary is an individual, any interstate claim is diplomatic protection-like, being brought for individual damage.[219] The ECtHR recognised this in *Cyprus v Turkey*, where it regarded as 'substantially similar' to diplomatic protection claims in which a State 'denounced violations ... of the basic human rights of its nationals (*or other victims*)',[220] human rights obligations being *erga omnes (partes)* in nature.[221]

Indeed, apparently recognising the potential similarity between diplomatic protection and article 48 claims, ARSIWA article 48(3) outlines that nationality and local remedies requirements also apply to claims brought thereunder.[222] However, as Gaja outlines, this 'is only partly appropriate'.[223] States may clearly bring article

(n 211) [33](b); *Biwater* (n 86) [465], [781]; cf nominal damages: McGregor and others (n 156) [12-001]–[12-003]. But what matters is whether individual damage is *claimed*. Cf nn 41, 329; Paparinskis, 'Countermeasures' (n 3) 314–15; *Plama Consortium v Bulgaria (Jurisdiction)* ICSID Case No ARB/03/24 (8 February 2005) [132]; section IV(B)(ii).

[212] See nn 48, 194, section IV(B)(i); Ch 2, nn 108ff; Gerald Fitzmaurice, 'Fourth Report on the Law of Treaties' (1959) 2 ILCYB 37 [161]; cf Thirlway (n 32) 1554.

[213] n 48. See sections IV(B)(i),(C).

[214] Ch 1, n 114.

[215] nn 175ff.

[216] *ARSIWA*, art 48, 277–78; Ch 1, nn 119–33.

[217] Ch 1, n 142; also Vermeer-Künzli, 'Interest' (n 54) 558–59; Gaja, 'Injuries' (n 170); Giorgio Gaja, 'States Having an Interest in Compliance with the Obligation Breached' in Crawford and others, *Responsibility* (n 3) 961. Claims for breach of *erga omnes (partes)* obligations by 'specially affected' States are art 42 claims: Ch 2, n 120.

[218] *ARSIWA*, art 48(2)(b), generally 209, 279; Ch 1, n 117; Vermeer-Künzli, 'Interest' (n 54) 557–59, 577; Gaja, 'Affected' (n 340) 380, 382; Gaja, 'Compliance' (n 217) 958, 961; Gaja, 'Injuries' (n 170); *Cyprus v Turkey (Compensation)* (n 45) [45]–[46]; also Lauterpacht (n 55) 299–300.

[219] *Cyprus v Turkey (Compensation)* (n 45) [45]. See Ch 2, nn 120–21; also Gaja, 'Position' (n 2) 12–13.

[220] *Cyprus v Turkey (Compensation)* (n 45) [45] (emphasis added), discussed Peters (n 23) 394.

[221] Ch 2, nn 211–16.

[222] *ARSIWA*, art 48(3), 280.

[223] Gaja, 'Compliance' (n 217) 963. Cf Enrico Milano, 'Diplomatic Protection and Human Rights before the International Court of Justice: Re-Fashioning Tradition' (2004) 35 Neth YBIL 85, 105–8.

48 claims concerning individuals other than their nationals, as they assert the 'collective interest' rather than one reflected in nationality.[224] In terms of local remedies, however, while some suggest that article 48 claims are also not subject to this rule,[225] there would appear to be no reason not to apply that requirement to such claims seeking reparation for individual damage,[226] giving the wrongdoing State an opportunity to remedy that damage.[227] Indeed, a requirement to exhaust local remedies is common under many human rights treaties,[228] even though they embody *erga omnes partes* obligations.[229] In this book, claims for breach of obligations *erga omnes (partes)* will, bar nationality requirements and insofar as they are based on individual damage, therefore be treated similarly to diplomatic protection claims.[230]

IV. The application of rules based on the nature of the claim

Based on the foregoing distinction between 'direct', diplomatic protection, and article 48 claims, the rules identified at the outset—the local remedies rule, and those contained in the ICSID and CARICOM treaties—rules which apply only where the interstate claim is, or would be, one of diplomatic protection, will operate where a claim is brought for damage to an individual's person or property, arising from breach of an international obligation owed, at least *inter alia*, to the State of nationality. Distinguishing diplomatic protection from 'direct' claims can be complex;[231] however, adopting the correct analytical framework makes addressing controversial circumstances more straightforward. This will be demonstrated here by addressing two situations in which the distinction between diplomatic protection and other claims has proved problematic in practice.[232] These are situations where claims are said to be 'direct':

[224] Gaja, 'Compliance' (n 217) 963; also *Application of the Convention on the Prevention and Punishment of the Crime of Genocide (The Gambia v Myanmar) (Preliminary Objections)* [2022] ICJ Rep 477 [107]–[108]; Vermeer-Künzli, 'Interest' (n 54) 557; n 220; Ch 2, nn 114–19; Nobuyuki Kato, 'The Role of Diplomatic Protection in the Implementation Process of Public Interests' in Teruo Komori and Karel Wellens (eds), *Public Interest Rules of International Law: Towards Effective Implementation* (Ashgate 2009) 202–4.

[225] See DADP, 87; Crawford, *GP* (n 2) 587, 597; Vermeer-Künzli, 'Interest' (n 54) 555, 579.

[226] Gaja, 'Compliance' (n 217) 963; *Armed Activities* (n 124) 347–48 (Sep Op Simma); ILC, 'Draft Articles on the Responsibility of International Organizations, with Commentaries' (2011) 2(2) ILCYB 46, 86; Amerasinghe (n 25) 303–8, cf 66–68.

[227] Authorities nn 191–92. See *Austria v Italy* (1961) 4 YBkECHR 116, section II(A) (rule applicable vis-à-vis non-national claims), discussed Amerasinghe (n 25) 80.

[228] Ch 2, n 75.

[229] Ch 1, n 128.

[230] Similarly: Amerasinghe (n 25) 308.

[231] Wittich (n 37) 132, 152–53, DADP, 74; nn 37–41.

[232] See authorities nn 37–38; section IV(A)–(C); similarly Paparinskis, 'Countermeasures' (n 3) 314–15; DADP, 74–76.

(1) because of allegations of breach; and
(2) despite individuals being 'involved' in the factual matrix underlying the claim.[233]

A. Allegations of breach

As to the first, States have sometimes suggested that claims are not diplomatic protection claims because obligations owed to them have been violated: the US argued, in *ELSI*, that it was unnecessary to exhaust local remedies because it was claiming for breach of treaty obligations,[234] and Switzerland did likewise in *Interhandel*.[235] However, as noted above, *every* interstate claim is brought for breach of obligations owed to the State.[236] This is therefore immaterial in distinguishing diplomatic protection from 'direct' claims.[237] The ICJ thus rightly rejected the argument in *ELSI*, observing that the national's damage 'pervade[d]' its claim,[238] while the local remedies rule applied in *Interhandel*, discussed further below.[239] Breach alone does not equate to moral damage to the State.[240] These were, accordingly, cases of diplomatic protection in which no *State damage* was alleged at all, except that done "fictionally".[241]

B. 'Direct' claims despite individual involvement

The second category of difficult cases concerns situations in which State damage *is* present. It is certainly possible to imagine 'direct' claims in which *only* State damage is alleged,[242] including to a State's territory,[243] or its property.[244] An example may

233 n 251.
234 *ELSI* (n 32) [51], discussed Wittich (n 37) 135, 160–62; DADP, 75; Amerasinghe (n 25) 152–53.
235 *Interhandel* (n 56) 28, discussed Wittich (n 37) 143–47; Amerasinghe (n 25) 149–52.
236 Generally section II(A); Ch 1(III)(A).
237 See Amerasinghe (n 25) 152–64; Wittich (n 37) 151, 156, 165; also Borchard (n 54) 353–54; generally section II(A), particularly nn 74–76.
238 *ELSI* (n 32) [52], discussed Amerasinghe (n 25) 152–53; Amerasinghe (n 43) 175; Wittich (n 37) 135, 161; Thirlway (n 32) 617–18.
239 *Interhandel* (n 56) 28–29, discussed Amerasinghe (n 25) 152; Amerasinghe (n 43) 175, 178–79; Fitzmaurice (n 36) 688–89; cf DADP, 74 (n 75); Wittich (n 37) 151–52. See nn 316ff.
240 Ch 1, nn 71–77.
241 cf nn 75, 175ff.
242 Similarly Brownlie (n 112) 31–32 ('direct injury' claims possible), disagreeing with, *inter alia*, Clive Parry, 'Of Treaties' in Peter Feuerstein and Clive Parry (eds), *Multum non Multa: Festschrift für Kurt Lipstein* (CF Müller 1980) 238 (no 'exclusively' State compensation claims); also Amerasinghe (n 25) 146–51; Lauterpacht (n 55) 687.
243 See *Oppenheim's* (n 68) 511–12; Brown (n 139) 199; Brownlie (n 112) 29; Bennouna (n 39) [17]; Graefrath (n 72) 47; *ARSIWA*, 174–75 (distress); *Aerial Incident of 7 October 1952 (USA v USSR)* ICJ Pleadings, 15 (App US).
244 See Borchard (n 54) 352, 362; Whiteman (n 52) 80–81; Garcia-Amador, 'Report' (n 39) [41]; *ARSIWA*, 221; Murphy, Kidane, and Snider (n 117) 34; Brown (n 139) 199; *Oppenheim's* (n 68) 511 ('naval vessels'); similarly Amerasinghe (n 25) 159; Meron (n 37) 86, 87 (fn 3), referencing *Corfu Channel* discussed nn 257ff. Eg, *Treatment in Hungary of Aircraft and Crew of USA (USA v Hungary;*

be *Rainbow Warrior*, in which New Zealand claimed compensation for material damage caused by the sinking of a vessel, and moral damage for violation of its sovereignty,[245] with no exercise of diplomatic protection because the only individuals harmed were non-nationals.[246] However, such 'exclusively' State injury[247] is likely to be rare,[248] given that States 'act through and are comprised of individuals'.[249] The question which causes perhaps the most difficulty in distinguishing 'direct' and diplomatic protection claims is what to do when both State and individual damage is present.[250]

As will be shown, there are three circumstances in which an interstate claim might remain 'direct' notwithstanding the presence of individual injury:

(1) State damage has resulted from circumstances in which individuals are 'involved',[251] but the claim either:
  (a) concerns only the former;[252] or
  (b) is 'mixed' but brought preponderantly for the State's damage;[253] or
(2) the State claims for breach alone.[254]

Using the framework outlined above, the following will first address (1), explaining how a 'direct' or 'mixed' claim can result even from circumstances concerning individuals. It then explains, vis-à-vis (2), how a claim for breach alone might be brought despite individual damage being present.

(i) 'Direct' and 'mixed' claims

As Chapter 4 elaborates, damage that is properly regarded as State damage can be a consequence of—yet analytically distinct from—damage done to individuals.[255]

USA v USSR) ICJ Pleadings, 18–19, 37–38, 51, 58–59 (Apps US); *Aerial Incident of 10 March 1953 (USA v Czechoslovakia)* ICJ Pleadings, 25 (App US); *Aerial Incident (US/USSR 1952)* (n 243) 26; vis-à-vis immunities: *Immunities* (n 143) [35], [118]–[120], [139]; *The 'ARA Libertad' Case (Argentina v Ghana) (Provisional Measures)* [2012] ITLOS Rep 332 [1], [40], [93]–[95].

[245] *Rainbow Warrior* (n 114) 267, generally 256–59, 271 (costs for clearing, police enquiries, trials and detention).

[246] *Oppenheim's* (n 68) 513 (fn 7) (no 'standing to ... claim on behalf of non-national interests'; also *Rainbow Warrior* (n 114) 259; ILC, '50th' (n 67) 19 (Brownlie).

[247] Fitzmaurice (n 36) 687; Parry, quoted n 242.

[248] See n 43; Ch 2, n 87; similarly Whiteman (n 52) 94; Meron (n 37) 86 (underlying 'almost every international claim ... interests of individuals'); Sohn and Baxter (n 30) 50.

[249] Lauterpacht (n 55) 34; also McCorquodale (n 61) 283; *ARSIWA*, 94; Crawford, *GP* (n 2) 113; *Oppenheim's* (n 68) 540; *Air Services* (n 58) 431; Ch 1 nn 8–11.

[250] Cf DADP, 74; also Jessup (n 70) 120; generally nn 37ff, 231.

[251] Amerasinghe (n 25) 146; *Certain Property Pleadings* (n 123), Obs Liechtenstein [6.37]; cf Ch 2, n 103; Brownlie (n 112) 236–38, 240.

[252] See section IV(B)(i); Ch 4(V)(B).

[253] Generally nn 48, 194, sections IV(B)(i), (C)(i); Ch 2, nn 108ff.

[254] See section IV(B)(ii) and authorities.

[255] See Ch 4, nn 400ff; nn 256ff and authorities.

Material State damage might, for instance, result from individuals' personal injury.[256] Thus, the *Corfu Channel* case concerned damage to State warships and associated injury to navy personnel.[257] However, the UK actually claimed for 'the cost of pensions and other grants made by it to victims or their dependants, and for costs of administration, medical treatment, etc'.[258] The claim, commonly considered 'direct',[259] was therefore for State costs resulting from individual injury, not for that individual injury per se.[260] Practice suggests that similar State losses may both result and be claimed even where private individuals are concerned.[261]

Likewise, while claims for personal property damage are normally diplomatic protection claims,[262] Chapter 4 outlines that material damage to *the State* might result from such losses.[263] For example, if a State guarantees its nationals' investments, and compensates any losses they suffer through host State action,[264] the former State might claim against the latter for its *own* ensuing material damage.[265] The *travaux préparatoires* to ICSID's article 27, one of the rules of present concern, suggests that such claims were not perceived to be ones of diplomatic protection.[266] Chapter 4 outlines further examples from practice in which State damage derives from harm to individual property.[267] The point here is that, where a State alleges only material damage to itself, even if consequent on individual injury, the claim is 'direct'.[268] Where, however, such damage is alleged together with that to

[256] The following is particularly informed by Bollecker-Stern (n 43) 101ff, particularly 101 (public social insurance may remove fiction); Arangio-Ruiz (n 170) 16 (fn 110) (quoting Reuter) (taxation/healthcare); Sohn and Baxter (n 30) 46; also *ARSIWA*, 221; similarly *Nicaragua's Pleadings* (n 170) 306; Gaja, 'Injuries' (n 170) and discussion and authorities Ch 4, nn 400ff. Generally Whiteman (n 52) 275.

[257] *Corfu Channel (UK v Albania) (Merits)* [1949] ICJ Rep 4, 10–11.

[258] *Corfu Channel (UK v Albania) (Compensation)* [1949] ICJ Rep 244, 249; also *Corfu Channel (UK v Albania)* ICJ Pleadings, 25, 52; *ARSIWA*, 221; Arangio-Ruiz (n 170) [57]; Barker (n 165) 604; Brown (n 139) 200.

[259] See Brownlie (n 112) 32; DADP, 76; Barker (n 165) 604; Meron (n 37) 87.

[260] See *ARSIWA*, 221; DADP, 100, and see art 1. Cf Meron (n 37) 86. Generally Sohn and Baxter (n 30) 46.

[261] See n 256 and, eg, *Eritrea* (n 46) [290] (post-expulsion), [307] (payments; 'social services'), [308] ('expenses'); *Ethiopia* (n 46) [143] ('public expenditure'), [471] (IDP care), [156], [159] (medical treatment), Ch XI(O) (civilian assistance/reconstruction); *Aerial Pleadings* (n 52) 112 ('accelerated pensions payable'); *Aerial Incident of 7 November 1954 (US v USSR)* ICJ Pleadings, 28; *Texas v American Tobacco* 14 F Supp 2d 956 (1997) 968; *Seventh Instalment of Individual Claims For Damages up to US$100,000 (Category 'C')* UN Doc S/AC26/1999/11 (UNCC, 24 June 1999) [78]–[83]; cf *Hunt v Severs* [1994] 2 AC 350, 361 (State-funded hospital costs not recoverable), referenced McGregor and others (n 156) [9–111].

[262] nn 163ff.

[263] Ch 4, nn 400ff.

[264] See Garcia-Amador, 'Problems' (n 55) 472–73; Bollecker-Stern (n 43) 101–3; generally ALI (n 33) §713, 226–27 (OPIC; proposed MIGA).

[265] Garcia-Amador, 'Problems' (n 55) 473 (State claiming '"in its *own* name and behalf", because ... asserting interests or rights ... acquired from ... national'), generally 472–73; further n 290; Bollecker-Stern (n 43) 101–3; Schreuer (n 14) 422.

[266] See ICSID (n 14) 61, 63, 65, 275, 348, 503 ('successor of ... private national'), 528, 959; authorities Ch 4, n 344.

[267] Ch 4, nn 410ff.

[268] nn 256, 259, 266. Similarly Sohn and Baxter (n 30) 46, 49.

individuals' person or property, the claim is 'mixed',[269] with important implications for the local remedies rule.[270]

The foregoing concerned *material* damage, but *moral* damage to the State may also result from actions affecting individuals.[271] For instance, damage done to State officials may cause moral damage to their State.[272] Thus, in the *Arrest Warrants* case, concerning a Minister's immunity,[273] the ICJ observed that the local remedies rules was inapplicable, as Congo was 'not acting in the context of protection of one of its nationals' by invoking his '*personal* rights'.[274] Despite the ever-misleading 'rights' terminology, the case was rightly considered 'direct' because the only claim concerned the individual as a State agent,[275] and was made for the State's consequent moral damage,[276] not for personal damage to the individual.[277] By contrast, claims are 'mixed' where claims for damage to the State, through its officials, are combined with claims for damage to individuals' person or property, as in the *Tehran Hostages* and *Armed Activities* cases.[278]

Violations of international law vis-à-vis ships and aircraft are also, as Chapter 1 noted, commonly regarded as causing the State moral damage.[279] Rather than trying to determine whose 'rights' are involved,[280] the tribunals in the various cases concerned with whether claims under UNCLOS were 'direct' should have acknowledged that they were 'mixed' because the States' allegations included moral damage claims.[281] Indeed, in every case concerned with the distinction,

[269] See nn 48, 163ff, 194, 296, discussing *Bosnian Genocide* (n 99) 64; *Croatian Genocide* (n 100) [20]; *Nicaragua's Pleadings* (n 170) Chs 5–6; Ch 2, nn 108–12. Further: *Treatment in Hungary* (n 244) 38, 59; *Aerial Incident (US/Czechoslovakia)* (n 244) 25; *Aerial Incident (US/USSR 1952)* (n 243) 26; cf Brownlie (n 112) 236–40.

[270] Section IV(C)(i).

[271] Similarly Wyler and Papaux (n 166) 628; also Sohn and Baxter (n 30) 47–49; Higgins (n 52) 52.

[272] Ch 1, n 74; see Sohn and Baxter (n 30) 48.

[273] See *Arrest Warrants* (n 56) [11]–[12], [17].

[274] ibid [40] (emphasis added); also Amerasinghe (n 25) 149, 151, 167–68; Amerasinghe (n 43) 174–75, 180–81; Crawford, 'Revisited' (n 3) 138.

[275] See Thirlway (n 32) 1552; similarly *Armed Activities* (n 124) [330]; Amerasinghe (n 25) 80, 161, 308; also DADP, 28, 69. Cf ibid 74–75, considering the case 'mixed'. Generally on officials' 'representative character': Jessup (n 70) 119, cited Amerasinghe (n 43) 177; also Lauterpacht (n 55) 136; cf McCorquodale (n 61) 294.

[276] Congo sought declaratory relief as satisfaction for 'moral injury': *Arrest Warrants* (n 56) 8.

[277] cf n 120; Amerasinghe (n 25) 164 (n 125), cf 168 (*Arrest Warrants* focuses on 'the "essence" of... right violated'); Thirlway (n 32) 1551–52.

[278] nn 121–24. Similarly Sohn and Baxter (n 30) 48, 163.

[279] Ch 1, n 74; Wittich (n 37) 155–57, 168–69, 185; similarly Amerasinghe (n 25) 167; Meron (n 37) 84; Barboza (n 196) 18 (fn 43); Garcia-Amador, 'SixthRep' (n 47) [48]; *Aerial Pleadings* (n 52) 33 (App US); also ILC, '53rd' (n 39) 149 (Hafner); cf *Heathrow* (n 58) 53, 60; *Certain Property Pleadings* (n 123) Obs Leichtenstein [6.38]–[6.43].

[280] See nn 54–60.

[281] Similarly Fitzmaurice (n 212) [161]; Fitzmaurice (n 36) 687. Some cases have apparently been considered 'mixed', but rarely because of the presence of moral damage (cf Wittich (n 37) 155–57 vis-à-vis *Aerial Incident*): eg, on *Saiga* (n 58): Wittich (n 37) 172–73; Dugard, n 140; *Saiga* (n 58) 107–11 (Sep Op Wolfrum), 129–30 (Sep Op Rao); on *Virginia G* (n 58): n 140; on *Norstar* (n 58): 115 [8] (Dec Cot), 136–37 [48]–[50] (Sep Op Wolfrum/Attard), 234–35 [19]–[20] (Diss Op Treves); on *Arctic Sunrise (Merits)* (n 58) [373] (explicit satisfaction request); on *Duzgit* (n 58) [154]–[156]. Further: *I'm Alone* (n 135) 1618 (apology and damages 'material amend'); see Whiteman (n 52) 154; also Jessup (n 70) 120. Cf

declarations provided satisfaction for such moral damage.[282] Similar observations apply to the cases concerning aircraft, in which State moral (and sometimes also material) damage was alleged.[283] Violations of sovereignty also undoubtedly cause moral damage,[284] explaining why cases concerned with States' environments or territory should be regarded as 'mixed', irrespective of whether *material* damage to the State is alleged.[285]

More generally, Borchard outlines that States exercising diplomatic protection are 'presumed to avenge and seek compensation for the injury to [their] national welfare and dignity, an injury quite independent of that sustained by [the] citizen'.[286] As Chapter 1 outlined, injury to a State's 'dignity' amounts to moral damage, repaired through satisfaction.[287] While breach does not cause such damage per se,[288] it may do so where 'the particular acts complained of are so flagrant as obviously to be intended as an affront'.[289] Thus, as Garcia-Amador convincingly argues:

> where an injury is caused to the person or property of an alien, the consequence of the wrongful act or omission may, owing to their gravity or to their frequency or because they show a manifestly hostile attitude towards the foreigner, extend beyond the specific, personal injury. When such is the case a distinction can be drawn between two different categories of interests, the purely private and exclusive interest of the alien and the 'general interest' of the State . . . .[290]

Dugard similarly contends that certain human rights breaches 'engage the interests of the national State', including 'where the violations are systematic and

de Aréchaga (n 47) 571. Based on 'injury to . . . flag' (Amerasinghe (n 25) 165), this was apparently 'satisfaction': Crawford, *GP* (n 2) 528–29; also Barboza (n 196) 18 (fn 43); Arangio-Ruiz (n 170) [15]; Sohn and Baxter (n 30) 48.

282 *Virginia G* (n 58) [447]–[448]; *Arctic Sunrise (Merits)* (n 58) [380]; *Duzgit* (n 58) [332]; *Saiga* (n 58) [176]; also Amerasinghe (n 43) 297. Further: *Enrica Lexie* (n 138), clearly distinguishing satisfaction and compensation: [1086]–[1088]; Ch 1, n 70.

283 See Dugard, 'SecondRep' (n 37) [19] ('mixed'); also Wittich (n 37) 157; Amerasinghe (n 25) 166–67; nn 126–32. For moral damage: Wittich (n 37) 155–57, fn 112, discussing *Aerial Pleadings* (n 52) 246, 248 (Mem US), also quoted *Nicaragua's Pleadings* (n 170) 259–60. For material damage: *Iran v USA* (n 127) vol I, 289–91 [5.21] (Mem Iran).

284 Ch 1, n 74.

285 See nn 107ff.

286 Borchard (n 54) 352; cf JL Brierly, 'The Theory of Implied State Complicity in International Claims' (1928) 9 BYBIL 42, 48, discussed Garcia-Amador, 'Report' (n 39) [101]–[102]; Dugard, 'FirstRep' (n 3) [63]; ILC, '50th' (n 67) 12 (Addo, referencing different publication); also Vattel (n 170) 148.

287 Ch 1, n 77. Cf Bollecker-Stern (n 43) 97.

288 Ch 1, nn 71–78. Cf Wyler and Papaux (n 166) 628 (State moral damage from nationals' harm; reparation as satisfaction); Yann Kerbrat, 'Interaction Between the Forms of Reparation' in Crawford and others, *Responsibility* (n 3) 581.

289 Borchard (n 54) 363, also 353. Similarly Sohn and Baxter (n 30) 47–49; also Roger O'Keefe, 'Proportionality' in Crawford and others, *Responsibility* (n 3) 1163.

290 Garcia-Amador, 'Problems' (n 55) 474; similarly, quoting ibid 422: Dugard, 'FirstRep' (n 3) [72] (fn 125); also Garcia-Amador, 'Report' (n 39) [112] (difficulty distinguishing individual/State interest); Jessup (n 70) 98, 120.

demonstrate a policy ... to discriminate against all nationals'.[291] Thus, while damage is solely fictional where 'the State intervenes to protect an isolated individual or small group of individuals', in other cases States are 'in fact injured as the conduct ... constitutes an affront',[292] a descriptor of *moral* damage.[293] The State then 'act[s] in its own name and on its own behalf, since it [is] asserting an interest of a rather general or collective character'.[294]

This understanding of moral damage helps us to appreciate one reason why the four cases discussed at the outset, relating to genocide and racial discrimination,[295] were 'mixed', with the States alleging mass injury to their respective populations.[296] It would, moreover, appear to be the only justification for regarding *Avena*, concerned with persistent alleged violations concerning multiple nationals,[297] as 'mixed',[298] and not, as the ICJ suggested, that Mexico's 'rights' were at issue,[299] which they would be in *any* diplomatic protection suit.[300]

In sum, 'direct' claims, concerning a State's material or moral damage, may result from individual damage. Where a claim encompasses both State and individual damage, one must consider the rules for 'mixed' cases, addressed below. First, however, the next section considers whether claims are 'direct' when, despite individual damage, the State purports to claim only for breach.

(ii) Claims for breach alone

Given the focus here on damage as distinguishing diplomatic protection and 'direct' claims, it is tempting to also focus on reparation, and to conclude that claims cannot

[291] Dugard, 'FirstRep' (n 3) [19], referencing *inter alia*, Brierly, n 286; similarly ILC, '52nd' (n 52) 37 (Dugard); Gaja, 'Injuries' (n 170); Jan Paulsson, *Denial of Justice in International Law* (CUP 2005) 213; also James Crawford, *International Law as an Open System* (Cameron May 2002) 332.

[292] Dugard, 'FirstRep' (n 3) [72], summarising Garcia-Amador, 'Problems' (n 55) 422; similarly ibid 473–74, discussed nn 265, 290; Ch 4, n 522.

[293] Ch 1, n 67; Wyler and Papaux (n 166) 629 (moral damage where citizens used to harm State; gravity, discrimination relevant); Wittich (n 37) 133 (discussing Chappez (n 91) 44 including 'injury to [State's] prestige' through 'flagrant violation'), 156 (moral damages for violation's gravity/severity), 185. Cf Garcia-Amador, 'SixthRep' (n 47) [73].

[294] Garcia-Amador, 'Problems' (n 55) 474; also Dugard, n 291; Cucos (n 33), 189. Cf Sohn and Baxter (n 30) 47 ("direct" where 'injuries to nationals ... inflicted on so wide a scale that they evince ... general disregard for international obligations'; States 'make a blanket claim'); Borchard, Ch 2, n 102.

[295] nn 99–104.

[296] *Bosnian Genocide* (n 99) 64 ('persons and property ... economy and environment'), also 72 (State 'expenditures'); *Croatian Genocide* (n 100) [20]; *Georgia v Russia* (n 101) 79 ('all injuries'); cf *Application of the International Convention on the Elimination of All Forms of Racial Discrimination (Georgia v Russia)* ICJ Pleadings, Mem Georgia [11.21]; discussion Ch 4(V)(B)(ii).

[297] *Avena* (n 56) [12] (fifty-four nationals; 'pattern ... of violations'), [13] ('regular ... continuing violations').

[298] Ch 2, nn 227–28. Cf Roberts, 'Hybrid' (n 2) 42.

[299] cf n 59.

[300] Similarly *Avena* (n 56) 89–90 (Sep Op Parra-Aranguren); also section II(A) and authorities; nn 178, 236–37. Explaining *Avena* as involving 'inextricably linked' individual and State rights, violation of one 'entail[ing]' violation of the other: *Iranian Assets* (n 44) [64]. However, this is unpersuasive: it would hold true in *any* diplomatic protection claim where the individual holds the same rights, including human rights: see Ch 2, nn 217–24; similarly Roberts, 'Hybrid' (n 2) 40; cf Parlett (n 59) 112.

be ones of diplomatic protection if only declaratory relief is sought.[301] That, however, is not the accepted approach,[302] for 'otherwise it would be too easy to evade the local remedy rule by promoting declaratory judgments which could ... acquire force of *res judicata* with respect to international proceedings for reparation'.[303]

Nonetheless, there is a recognised distinction between the exercise of diplomatic protection and the seeking of declarations regarding a given treaty's interpretation.[304] Indeed, the *travaux préparatoires* to ICSID's article 27 demonstrate that, despite prohibiting States from resorting to diplomatic protection in certain circumstances, the possibility of States bringing interpretative claims was presumed to continue to exist.[305] Later practice has affirmed this.[306] There is, however, a fine line between claims concerning interpretation (not ones of diplomatic protection) and application (potentially ones of diplomatic protection).[307] A claim regarding

[301] See Dugard, 'SecondRep' (n 37) [27], [29]; DADP, 76; also Amerasinghe (n 43) 169; Amerasinghe (n 25) 265–67; Thirlway (n 32) 615; Meron (n 37) 86.

[302] See DADP, art 14(3), 76, following *Interhandel/ELSI*, nn 238–39; de Aréchaga (n 47) 582; also Amerasinghe (n 43) 179 ('avoid giving ... claimant's formulation ... too much weight'); Meron (n 37) 87; Amerasinghe (n 25) 152. Vis-à-vis allegedly contrary authorities (DADP, 76), *Applicability of the Obligation to Arbitrate under Section 21 of the United Nations Headquarters Agreement of 26 June 1947 (Advisory Opinion)* [1988] ICJ Rep 12 [41] does not support (see Amerasinghe (n 25) 37, 255; cf Thirlway (n 32) 615; Wittich (n 37) 157–59); and *Air Services* (n 58) is 'mixed': see n 283. A potentially problematic counter-example is *Certain German Interests in Polish Upper Silesia* [1925] PCIJ Rep Ser A No 6, 20, discussed Amerasinghe (n 43) 169. However, the PCIJ addressed *litispendence*, not local remedies: 19–21; Ch 4, n 140.

[303] de Aréchaga (n 47) 582; similarly Dugard, 'SecondRep' (n 37) [29]–[30]; ILC, '53rd' (n 39) 144 (Gaja); Meron (n 37) 88–89; Wittich (n 37) 146–47, discussing *Interhandel* (n 56) 29; Thirlway (n 32) 615–18; DADP, 76.

[304] See authorities Ch 2, n 157; Paparinskis, 'Countermeasures' (n 3) 313–15; Martins Paparinskis and Jessica Howley, 'Article 5: Submission by a Non-Disputing Party to the Treaty' in Dimitrij Euler, Markus Gehring, and Maxi Scherer (eds), *Transparency in International Investment Arbitration* (CUP 2015) 219–20; Kaufmann-Kohler (n 14) 321–22; Anthea Roberts, 'Power and Persuasion in Investment Treaty Interpretation: The Dual Role of States' (2010) 104 AJIL 179, 218–20.

[305] ICSID (n 14) 63, 66 ('abstract questions of interpretation'), 274, 350, 438–41, 527–28, 576–77, 906; Paparinskis, 'Countermeasures' (n 3) 313–14; Schreuer (n 14) 420–22; also Roberts, 'Hybrid' (n 2) 15, 59.

[306] See *Pac Rim Cayman v El Salvador (Respondent's Jurisdiction Reply)* ICSID Case No ARB/09/12 [171]–[172]; *Pac Rim Cayman v El Salvador (Claimant's Jurisdiction Rejoinder)* ICSID Case No ARB/09/12 [207]–[208]; *Pac Rim Cayman v El Salvador (Costa Rica Non-Disputing Party Submission)* ICSID Case No ARB/09/12 [5]; n 311. Similarly Paparinskis and Howley (n 304) 214–15, 219–20 (Mauritius Convention, art 5(2)); n 328; Paparinskis, 'Countermeasures' (n 3) 313. Cf concerns regarding States' interpretative discussions during individual-State proceedings: Roberts, 'Power' (n 304) 179–80; Roberts, 'Hybrid' (n 2) 9, 53; Paparinskis and Howley (n 304) 225 and authorities (fn 123); cases Ch 5(III)(C)(viii). Generally on treaty parties' interpretative powers: Roberts, 'Power' (n 304) 198–202, 215–24; Paparinskis and Howley (n 304) 207, 209–12, 222–23; Roberts, 'Hybrid' (n 2) 18, 22, 28, 52ff; Kaufmann-Kohler (n 14) 314–17; Martins Paparinskis, 'Analogies and Other Regimes of International Law' in Zachary Douglas, Joost Pauwelyn, and Jorge Viñuales (eds), *The Foundations of International Investment Law* (OUP 2014) 88–90; Michele Potestà, 'Towards a Greater Role for State-to-State Arbitration in the Architecture of Investment Treaties?' in Shaheeza Lalani and Rodrigo Polanco Lazo (eds), *The Role of the State in Investor-State Arbitration* (Brill Nijhoff 2015) 267–68, 272–73; also ICSID (n 14) 275, 350, 438–41.

[307] Paparinskis and Howley (n 304) 220, 222, 204, referencing Frank Berman, 'International Treaties and British Statutes' (2005) 26 Stat L Rev 1, 10; similarly Anastasios Gourgourinis, 'The Distinction Between Interpretation and Application of Norms in International Adjudication' (2011) 2 JIDS 31, 31, generally 43–48; James Harrison, 'The Life and Death of BITs: Legal Issues Concerning Survival Clauses and the Termination of Investment Treaties' (2012) 13 JWIT 928, 949; also Antonios Tzanakopoulos,

the latter usually presupposes a claim regarding the former,[308] and questions of interpretation can undoubtedly influence a dispute's outcome on the facts.[309]

It is often suggested that the distinction lies between 'abstract' and detailed factual submissions.[310] The *Aguas del Tunari* Tribunal was clear, for instance, in requesting information from the State of nationality, that given ICSID's article 27, it only wished to receive 'information supporting interpretative positions of general application rather than ones related to a specific case'.[311]

However, comparing the *Ambatielos* and *Interhandel* cases suggests a more accurate distinction.[312] In the former, even if the underlying dispute concerned a diplomatic protection claim,[313] the ICJ only had jurisdiction to determine the question raised whether that claim had to be submitted to arbitration.[314] Thus limited, no local remedy exhaustion was necessary.[315] By contrast, Switzerland had, in *Interhandel*, alleged that the US must return its nationals' assets.[316] While framed in declaratory terms,[317] and albeit coupled with a similar interpretative question,[318] the difference is that any obligation to make restitution can only arise from a breach of international law causing damage.[319] Switzerland had thus necessarily invoked responsibility for damage to its national, even if it only sought declaratory relief.[320] Given that obligations of reparation flow 'automatically' from breach,[321] we may conclude that if the finding of breach sought would suffice to establish that reparation is due for personal or property damage done to the claimant State's nationals,[322] then the claim is one of

'Domestic Courts in International Law: The International Judicial Function of National Courts' (2011) 34 Loy LAI & CLR 133, 134–35; cf Roberts, 'Hybrid' (n 2) 6.

[308] See Gourgourinis (n 307) 46–47; Roberts, 'Hybrid' (n 2) 18, 52; Roberts, 'Power' (n 304) 179, 189.

[309] Paparinskis and Howley (n 304) 204, 220; also ICSID (n 14) 281; n 333.

[310] Paparinskis and Howley (n 304) 219–20, 222; similarly Kaufmann-Kohler (n 14) 321–24; also Roberts, 'Power' (n 304) 219–20; ICSID (n 14) 66; authorities nn 305, 311, Ch 2, n 157; cf Roberts, 'Hybrid' (n 2) 8–9, 54–59.

[311] *Aguas del Tunari v Bolivia (Jurisdiction)* ICSID Case No ARB/02/3 (21 October 2005) [258]; also Kaufmann-Kohler (n 14) 316.

[312] As done in Wittich (n 37) 151–52; Amerasinghe (n 43) 167; Amerasinghe (n 25) 255–56. Further n 329.

[313] See *Ambatielos Claim* (n 189) 103.

[314] *Ambatielos Case (Greece v UK) (Merits)* [1953] ICJ Rep 10, 12, 14–16.

[315] ibid 23, discussed Wittich (n 37) 151. Cf *Ambatielos Claim* (n 189) 103, 118–23.

[316] *Interhandel* (n 56) 9, 28. See Wittich (n 37) 145.

[317] *Interhandel* (n 56) 9.

[318] See ibid 9–10, 13; discussion Wittich (n 37) 151–52.

[319] Ch 1(II)(B). Cf Wittich (n 37) 151–52.

[320] See *Interhandel* (n 56) 18, 24–25, 28–29; Amerasinghe (n 43) 167 (no local remedies where 'not relate[d] to material compensation ... restitution'), 169 (distinguishing 'cases ... merely declaring ... violation ... and [those] in which ... remedial right is asserted'); Amerasinghe (n 25) 256, 266; also Thirlway (n 32) 616; Dugard, 'SecondRep' (n 37) [29]; Meron (n 37) 90, 92. Cf Amerasinghe (n 25) 163.

[321] Crawford, *GP* (n 2) 553; *ARSIWA*, 202; Ch 1, n 33.

[322] Similarly Paparinskis, 'Countermeasures' (n 3) 315 (non-diplomatic protection where 'no material damage'; concerns 'obligations to cease and appropriately confirm non-repetition [which] automatically follow from ... breach'). See nn 148, 163ff.

diplomatic protection, and it is immaterial whether that reparation is actually claimed.[323]

By contrast, in some cases, there will be no claim for breach at all, whereas diplomatic protection claims must involve an invocation of State responsibility,[324] in order 'to secure the performance of the obligations of cessation and reparation'.[325] States might, for instance, bring claims concerning interpretation of the rules on the treatment of aliens, but without any allegation of damage.[326] Thus, while finding no dispute *in casu*,[327] the *Ecuador v US* Tribunal, in considering a claim regarding a BIT's interpretation, accepted that a 'tribunal could answer an abstract question of interpretation … if properly put before it'.[328] Such interpretative claims are not ones of diplomatic protection, not only because no individual has allegedly experienced *any* injury,[329] but also because no responsibility for breach is invoked.[330]

Indeed, article 27 of ICSID recognises that 'informal diplomatic exchanges for the sole purpose of facilitating a settlement of the dispute' are allowed.[331] Such 'informal requests for corrective action' are not diplomatic protection precisely because they do not 'involve the invocation of the legal responsibility of another State'.[332] The case law provides examples of allowed action,[333] while a 'formal' assertion that measures violated a national's rights under domestic law and international judicial orders would cross the line into diplomatic protection.[334]

323 Similarly Dugard, 'SecondRep' (n 37) [29], [30] (claim not determinative); nn 302–3. Cf *Avena* (n 56) 82 (Sep Op Vereshchetin).

324 See DADP, 27; Ch 2, n 93. Similarly *Pac Rim Cayman v El Salvador (Jurisdiction)* ICSID Case No ARB 09/12 (1 June 2012) [4.87]. Cf Crawford, *GP* (n 2) 566, 572.

325 *ARSIWA*, 254.

326 See discussion Paparinskis, 'Countermeasures' (n 3) 313–15; Roberts, 'Hybrid' (n 2) 54–56, 58–59, cf 66–68.

327 *Ecuador v US (Award)* PCA Case 2012-5 (29 September 2012) [228].

328 ibid [196], also [204]–[205] (apparently distinguishing diplomatic protection), [207], discussion [76]–[115] (Diss Op Vinuesa); case discussed Roberts, 'Hybrid' (n 2) 8–9, 54–55.

329 See Paparinskis, 'Countermeasures' (n 3) 314–15; *Ambatielos* (n 314) 22–23, discussed Wittich (n 37) 151 and nn 312ff; ILC, '52nd' (n 52) 71 (Tomka); similarly *Oppenheim's* (n 68) 523 (fn 3); ILC, '50th' (n 67) 16, 29 (Hafner); ILC, '53rd' (n 39) 143 (Lukashuk), discussing Dugard, 'SecondRep' (n 37) [29]; Sohn and Baxter (n 30) 48; also Crawford, *Brownlie's* (n 178) 548. Naturally, damage can be claimed and unproved: eg, *The Jessie (UK v US)* (1922) 16 AJIL 114, 115, cited DADP, 82; discussion Garcia-Amador, 'SixthRep' (n 47) [58]. Cf *Ambatielos* (n 314) 17–18; Vermeer-Künzli, 'Fiction' (n 55) 51; also n 211.

330 See Potestà, 'Role' (n 306) 254, discussing *Ecuador v US* (n 327). Further: cases discussed Damien Charlotin, Facundo Perez Aznar, and Luke Eric Peterson, 'Looking Back: Long-Confidential Benhamou v. Uruguay Award …' *IA Rep* (2 April 2018). Generally Ch 1(III)(A).

331 ICSID, art 27; also ICSID (n 14) 764–67, 1031–32; Schreuer (n 14) 427–28.

332 DADP, 27; also *ARSIWA*, 256 (referencing ICSID, art 27); Crawford, 'ThirdRep' (n 144) [105]; ICSID (n 14) 765; Paparinskis and Howley (n 304) 219.

333 *Kılıç v Turkmenistan (Award)* ICSID Case No ARB/10/1 (2 July 2013) [1.2.39]–[1.2.41] (officials' presence); *Autopista* (n 17) [73] (exchanges, 'no … formal protest'), [139]; Schreuer (n 14) 428. Cf *Myrie* (n 11) [26] (State's intervention not diplomatic protection, because must 'accept the case as it is at the time of intervention'). This seems questionable insofar as intervention would invoke responsibility: see Paparinskis and Howley (n 304) 211–12 and authorities; and on interventions amounting to diplomatic protection: ibid 216–22 and authorities; Roberts, 'Power' (n 304) 219–20; Kaufmann-Kohler (n 14) 309; 314, 320–22, 324; cf ibid 314–15; Paparinskis and Howley (n 304) 204–5; Douglas (n 67) 170.

334 *Tokios (Order)* (n 18) [21] ('formal diplomatic interventions'), see [19]–[22]. Cf *Banro* (n 18) [18] (unclear); *PacRim Rejoinder* (n 306) [203]. Considering that denial of benefit consultations envisaged

Particular difficulty nonetheless arises vis-à-vis what Roberts terms 'declaratory relief' claims, which arise out of (usually significant-scale) damage to individuals, but where the State neither claims compensation nor identifies the individuals affected.[335] As Chapter 4 elucidates, claims may be regarded as diplomatic protection (in part) where, as in 'class actions' under domestic law, reparation is claimed on behalf of a class, even if not every individual constituting that class is identified.[336] However, where no such reparation is claimed, the principles outlined above suggest that whether a claim is *really* one for breach alone, or is one of diplomatic protection, depends on whether reparation would be due for individual damage if the allegations were proved.[337]

In some such situations, the claim appears to be for breach alone, without any implied obligation to repair individual damage. For instance, the ECtHR may consider allegations of breach arising from a law's existence 'in abstracto', without elaboration on its application 'in concreto', at least where the law 'is couched in terms sufficiently clear and precise to make the breach immediately apparent'.[338] The Inter-American Court of Human Rights (IACtHR) is likewise prepared to entertain, at least in interstate applications, 'not only situations that have affected individual or identifiable victims but also generalized situations of widespread or systematic violation of human rights',[339] with no 'need to individually identify each possible victim'.[340] Similarly, in one of its claims in the *Cross-Border Trucking* case, Mexico had alleged that the US had violated the North American Free Trade Agreement (NAFTA) by maintaining a moratorium on certain investments.[341] The

under CAFTA were not an invocation of responsibility within the DADP's definition: *PacRim* (n 324) [4.87]–[4.89], see [4.27]–[4.29], [4.45]–[4.47]; similarly *PacRim (Resp Rep)* (n 306) [171]–[172]. The decision was hypothetical, and the claimant's contention that certain consultations might involve diplomatic protection is plausible: see *PacRim Rejoinder* (n 306) [204]–[208]. Cf *PacRim (CR)* (n 306) [5] (consultations 'aimed at elucidating Treaty interpretation and application'). Further: *Duke Energy v Peru (Jurisdiction)* ICSID Case No ARB/03/28 (1 February 2006) [15]–[18] (apparent argument that considering revoking ATPA benefits violated art 27), discussed *Pac Rim Cayman v El Salvador (Claimant's Post-Hearing Jurisdiction Submission)* ICSID Case No ARB/09/12 [58] (fn 94); see ATPA, s 3202(c). Cf *ARSIWA*, 256 (countermeasures invoke responsibility); Paparinskis, 'Countermeasures' (n 3) 279–80, 306–9; *European Communities–Measures Affecting Trade in Commercial Vessels–Panel Rep* (22 April 2005) WT/DS301/R [7.197] (internal compensation not concerning interstate relations).

335 Roberts, 'Hybrid' (n 2) 67, generally 9–10, 66–68.

336 See ibid 67, also 9 ('resembling representative and class actions'); Frank Berman, 'The Relevance of the Law on Diplomatic Protection in Investment Arbitration' in Federico Ortino and others (eds), *Investment Treaty Law, Current Issues II* (BIICL 2007) 72; and see Ch 4(V)(B), and authorities therein. Cf *Cyprus v Turkey (Compensation)* (n 45) 302–4 (Diss Op Karakaş); Paparinskis and Howley (n 304) 221.

337 Authorities nn 321–23.

338 *Ireland v UK (Judgment)* [1978] ECHR Ser A, No 25 [240], discussed Schabas (n 30) 727; also Leo Zwaak (revisor), 'The Procedure Before the European Court of Human Rights' in Pieter van Dijk and others (eds), *Theory and Practice of the European Convention on Human Rights* (4th edn, Intersentia 2006) 128 (local remedies inapplicable where 'State brings up ... legislation or administrative practice' and not 'related to ... concrete persons').

339 *Nicaragua v Costa Rica* Pet 1/06, Rep 11/07 (IACHR, 8 March 2007) [195].

340 ibid [196].

341 *Cross-Border Trucking Services* (Ch 20 NAFTA Panel Final Rep) File-USA-MEX-98-2008-01 (6 February 2001) [279], discussed Roberts, 'Hybrid' (n 2) 9, 67.

panel considered that there was a '*prima facie* case of inconsistency with NAFTA' on the face of US law, 'even if Mexico [could not] identify a particular Mexican national or nationals' actually affected.[342] Where there are no 'identifiable individual victim[s]'[343] at all, it is difficult to regard such claims as ones of diplomatic protection.[344] Indeed, if no individual is actually alleged to have suffered damage, there could be no consequential obligation to make reparation for it upon proof of breach, whether reparation is claimed or not.[345] There is simply nothing on which the 'fiction' can operate.[346]

By contrast, there may be interstate cases where, even if the claim is for declaratory relief, individuals who have suffered damage are identified, or at least 'identifiable'.[347] The ECtHR's reasoning in *Cyprus v Turkey* is helpful in this respect, where it distinguished between claims 'substantially similar' to those of diplomatic protection, in which the State 'denounces violations ... of the basic human rights of its nationals (or other victims)', and where reparation may be awarded 'for the benefit of [those] individual victims',[348] and claims 'about general issues (systemic problems and shortcomings, administrative practices, etc.)' where the applicant's 'primary goal' is to 'vindicat[e] the public order' and in which reparation awards may be inappropriate.[349] Notwithstanding that the claim at issue concerned large numbers of individuals, not all of whom were named,[350] the Court considered it to fall within the former category, awarding reparation in respect of 'two sufficiently precise and objectively *identifiable* groups of people'.[351] The Court summarised its approach in *Georgia v Russia (I)*, indicating that whether compensation should be awarded in an interstate case depended on 'the type of complaint made', 'whether the victims could be identified' and 'the main purpose of bringing the proceeding'.[352]

Cyprus v Turkey did not involve a claim for declaratory relief alone; on the contrary, compensation was expressly sought. However, the reasoning in respect of 'identifiable' victims helpfully elucidates a distinction between diplomatic protection and 'direct' claims, which can apply even where no reparation is claimed. For instance, in *Ireland v UK*, claims were made regarding the alleged mistreatment of prisoners without any claim for reparation.[353] This case involved an alleged 'administrative

342 *Cross-Border* (n 341) [283], [292], discussed Roberts, 'Hybrid' (n 2) 9, 67.

343 Schabas (n 30) 727. See also Rivier (n 196) 747–48; Ch 4(V)(B).

344 Similarly Paparinskis, 'Countermeasures' (n 3) 314–15; also Schabas (n 30) 766 (local remedies inapplicable where 'legislative or administrative practice ... challenged'); Amerasinghe (n 25) 342–43; Douglas (n 67) 189; Paparinskis and Howley (n 304) 221. Cf Wittich (n 37) 142.

345 See similarly *Cyprus v Turkey (Compensation)* (n 45) 302–6 (Diss Op Karakaş); also Ch 1(II)(B).

346 See n 175. Cf Bollecker-Stern (n 43) 32–33; de Aréchaga (n 47) 546.

347 Cf n 351; also *Cyprus v Turkey (Compensation)* (n 45) 303 (Diss Op Karakaş) (cases 'on behalf of certain identifiable individuals').

348 *Cyprus v Turkey (Compensation)* (n 45) [45]–[46].

349 ibid [44].

350 Relatives of 1,456 named missing persons and non-identified residents of a particular area: see ibid [58], 296–97 (Sep Op Casadevall), 304–9 (Diss Op Karakaş).

351 ibid [47] (emphasis added).

352 *Georgia v Russia (I) (Just satisfaction)* App 13255/07 (ECtHR, 31 January 2019) [22].

353 *Ireland v UK* (n 338) [244]–[246].

practice', that is, 'an accumulation of identical or analogous breaches which are sufficiently numerous and inter-connected not to amount to merely isolated incidents or exceptions but to a pattern or system' subject to 'official tolerance'.[354] Although such administrative practices were among the 'general issues' that the Court in *Cyprus v Turkey* considered could form the basis of a non-diplomatic protection-like inter-state claim,[355] that elements of diplomatic protection are present in cases like *Ireland v UK* is indicated by breach vis-à-vis at least certain identified individuals being elaborated,[356] for which reparation would be due under international law, even if not claimed.[357] Indeed, in *Georgia v Russia (I)*, the ECtHR awarded reparation, even though the case similarly concerned an administrative practice, for a 'sufficiently precise and objectively identifiable' group.[358] Cases involving such administrative practices *can* therefore be akin to diplomatic protection claims, even though there are broader 'general issues' at stake, as long as the individuals concerned are identifiable.[359] The true distinction between diplomatic protection and 'direct' claims thus lies not in the nature of the underlying obligations but in whether a claim is made that identifiable individuals have suffered reparable harm.

Admittedly, local remedies need not be exhausted where States have 'the aim of preventing [the] continuation or recurrence' of an administrative practice, without seeking 'a decision on each of the cases put forward as proof or illustrations' thereof.[360] But, as seen below, the inapplicability of the local remedies rule does not mean that such cases contain no elements of diplomatic protection.[361] Rather, as Qatar rightly argued in its case concerning the Convention on the Elimination of All Forms of Racial Discrimination (CERD), cases consisting of 'a systematic, generalized policy and practice' that causes 'widespread violations' are 'mixed' in nature.[362] Moral injury to the State is present due to the violation's scale and seriousness,[363] but so is individual damage. As long as the individuals are either identified or identifiable, the case remains diplomatic protection in part. The tests for 'mixed' cases outlined below dictate how the rules of present concern apply in such situations.

[354] *Georgia v Russia (I)* 2014–IV ECHR 109 [123]–[124], citing, *inter alia*, *Ireland v UK* (n 338) [159]; *Cyprus v Turkey (Judgment)* ECHR 2001-IV 1 [99], [115]; generally Schabas (n 30) 728; Zwaak (n 338) 128–29; Amerasinghe (n 25) 343; Wittich (n 37) 178.

[355] n 349.

[356] Eg, *Ireland v UK* (n 338) [165]–[185], generally [93]–[143]. Cf *Cyprus v Turkey (Compensation)* (n 45) 303–4 (Diss Op Karakaş).

[357] See *Ireland v UK* (n 338) [244]–[246] (no compensation claimed). Cf n 323.

[358] *Georgia v Russia (I) (Compensation)* (n 352) [71].

[359] n 349.

[360] *Georgia v Russia (I)* (n 354) [125], citing *Ireland v UK* (n 338) [159]; also Schabas (n 30) 728; Zwaak, n 338. Apparently similarly *Ukraine v Russia (Objections)* (n 102) [130] (not requiring local remedy exhaustion where 'alleged pattern of conduct'; 'individual instances' used 'as illustrations').

[361] nn 371ff.

[362] *Qatar v UAE (Admissibility)* Doc CERD/C/99/4 (CERD, 30 August 2019) [25] and see discussion David Keane, 'CERD Reaches Historic Decisions in Inter-State Communications' *EJIL:Talk!* (6 September 2019).

[363] nn 286ff.

C. Conclusion on the rules' applicability

Having outlined how diplomatic protection, 'mixed', and 'direct' claims should be characterised, conclusions may be reached regarding the applicability of the rules under consideration, and thus when the actions of a State or individual may impact the ability of the other to bring an overlapping claim due to the operation of these rules.

(i) Local remedies

As to the application, first, of the local remedies rule:

(1) A claim is one of diplomatic protection when responsibility is invoked for violation of obligations owed to the State, but the only damage claimed, material or moral, is to an individual's person or property. Reparation for such damage may be claimed expressly. It may also be claimed implicitly where reparation would be due for damage done to an identified or identifiable individual if the alleged breach is proved. Local remedies must be exhausted in such cases.

(2) A claim is 'direct' either where only a claim for breach is made, or the only damage alleged is to the State (consequent on individual damage or otherwise). In neither case is reparation claimed for damage to identifiable individuals, expressly or by implication. In such cases, the local remedies rule is inapplicable.

(3) A claim is 'mixed' where it alleges, expressly or by implication, damage to both a State and to identifiable individuals. State damage may be material or moral, the latter potentially resulting from violations regarding State representatives, vessels, or affecting many nationals.

The DADP's approach, vis-à-vis the third category, is to require local remedy exhaustion where claims are 'preponderantly' brought for individual injury.[364] However, as has been remarked, particularly vis-à-vis claims concerning ships, few cases suggest that individual damage would be considered so 'preponderant' in truly 'mixed' claims.[365] Indeed, in almost all of the 'mixed' cases considered above, including those concerning ships, the environment, human rights,

[364] n 48. See also *Iranian Assets* (n 44) [66]–[67] (not explicitly endorsing).

[365] See *Norstar* (n 58) 115 [5] (Dec Cot), 137 [50] (Sep Op Wolfrum/Attard), 235 [20] (Diss Op Treves); *Virginia G* (n 58) 169 (Sep Op Cot/Kelly), 367 (Diss Op Servulo Correia); similarly Wittich (n 37) 156–57 (moral damage), 170, cf 162. Cf, regarding 'mixed' cases as diplomatic protection: *Avena* (n 56) 82 (Sep Op Vereshchetin) ('preponderantly'), 91 (Sep Op Parra-Aranguren), 95–97 (Sep Op Tomka); *Saiga* (n 58) 110–11 (Sep Op Wolfrum), 130 (Sep Op Rao); *Virginia G* (n 58) 168–69 (Sep Op Cot/Kelly), 215–16 (Joint Diss Op), 284 (Diss Op Ndiaye), 353–56 (Diss Op Jesus), 364–69 (Diss Op Servulo Correia); also *Norstar* (n 58) 115–16 [4]–[9] (Dec Cot), 235 [20] (Diss Op Treves); Amerasinghe (n 25) 165–67 (*I'm Alone/Aerial Incident*). Similarly Sohn and Baxter (n 30) 50.

consular notification, and immunities, tribunals have not required local remedy exhaustion.[366]

By way of apparent exception, the ICJ in *Armed Activities* refused to hear the diplomatic protection part of a claim otherwise involving State damage for failure to exhaust local remedies.[367] It understandably did not require the *State* to exhaust local remedies, for '[S]tates are not subject to the jurisdiction of foreign courts',[368] but it did apparently consider that the 'direct' and diplomatic protection parts of the claim were insufficiently connected to warrant their being brought together without meeting the requirements apposite to diplomatic protection.[369]

Moreover, the foregoing has demonstrated how moral damage results from serious or widespread violations vis-à-vis a State's nationals.[370] Nonetheless, neither the ECtHR nor IACtHR apparently accepts that injury to numerous nationals alone suffices to render local remedies irrelevant.[371] They require, respectively, an 'administrative practice',[372] and a 'generalized practice of acts ... shown to be officially tolerated'.[373] The requirement to exhaust local remedies is inapplicable, vis-à-vis the latter, 'because it is reasonable to presume that no adequate or effective remedies exist to remedy a generalized situation'.[374] The ECtHR's approach is probably best explained on the same basis.[375] The 'mixed' claim in *Avena*[376] should likewise be regarded as determined based on an absence of effective remedies,[377] which was

[366] See discussion sections II(A), (B)(i)–(ii). If moral damage, including via damage to ships, always renders the State's injury "preponderant", however, the local remedies rule in UNCLOS seems superfluous: cf Wittich (n 37) 166–67 ('hardly any' UNCLOS obligations 'genuine rules on the treatment of aliens'; UNCLOS 'nevertheless explicitly provides for the local remedies rule'), 173, 184–86. Tribunals should therefore be more exacting in employing the preponderance test, particularly as regards moral damage.

[367] *Armed Activities* (n 124) [333]; Thirlway (n 32) 1554.

[368] de Aréchaga (n 47) 582; also Meron (n 37) 85, discussed Amerasinghe (n 25) 160; Schabas (n 30) 766.

[369] See Thirlway (n 32) 1554 (diplomatic protection cannot always 'ride on ... back of ... direct claim'), referencing *Armed Activities* (n 124) [333]; Wittich (n 37) 162 ('divisibility of ... claims'), also 152, cf 170; Ch 2, n 112.

[370] nn 286ff.

[371] See *Cyprus v Turkey (Judgment)* (n 354) [90]–[91] and [20], [28], [34], [49] (alleged victims); *Nicaragua v Costa Rica* (n 339) [256], [257]–[306] and [49] (individuals; 'Nicaraguan migrant population'); nn 360–63.

[372] n 354; *Cyprus v Turkey (Judgment)* (n 354) [99].

[373] *Nicaragua v Costa Rica* (n 339) [257]. See also *Qatar v UAE* (n 362) [40] (exhaustion unnecessary 'where a "generalized policy and practice" has been authorized').

[374] *Nicaragua v Costa Rica* (n 339) [257]; also Amerasinghe (n 25) 327.

[375] See Amerasinghe (n 25) 342–44, 213–14; also Crawford, *GP* (n 2) 587; *Cyprus v Turkey (Judgment)* (n 354) [99]; *Georgia v Russia (I)* (n 354) [125], cf [126] ('effectiveness and accessibility of domestic remedies ... *additional evidence* of whether or not such a practice exists' (emphasis added)); Zwaak (n 338) 130–32. Cf Wittich (n 37) 178–79 (non-exhaustion 'pragmatic'; 'no ... victim'; in addition 'tests of availability and effectiveness of domestic remedies ... likely render the local remedies rule inoperable to such complaints concerning a prevailing practice'); Sohn and Baxter (n 30) 47 ('not necessarily ... ineffectual' in widescale claims); *Application of the International Convention on the Elimination of All Forms of Racial Discrimination (Qatar v UAE) (Provisional Measures)* [2018] ICJ Rep 406 [42].

[376] nn 298–300.

[377] See *Avena* (n 56) 96–97 (Sep Op Tomka), 108–9 (Sep Op Sepulveda), cf 82–83 (Sep Op Vereshchetin).

indeed Mexico's argument against the rule's application.[378] As the DADP recognise, a lack of effective remedies constitutes an *exception* to the local remedies rule,[379] suggesting that the existence of material and/or moral State damage in these cases does not, in and of itself, render local remedies inapplicable.

Nonetheless, and relatedly, even if the local remedies rule might apply to certain 'mixed' claims, most will likely be covered by an exception:[380] in addition to cases concerning an absence of remedies already considered, the DADP recognise an exception where the individuals affected have 'no relevant connection' with the responsible State.[381] Many 'mixed' cases not requiring exhaustion are explicable on this basis.[382]

It is therefore unlikely—though not impossible—that local remedies will need to be exhausted in cases properly described as 'mixed'.[383] However, undertaking the analysis above is essential to determining why this is so in particular factual circumstances.[384]

(ii) The treaty-based provisions

As to article 27 of ICSID and article 222(c) of the CARICOM treaty, it would appear sufficient, for their application, that the claim be *in part* one of diplomatic protection.[385] The purpose of these rules is to avoid States facing both diplomatic protection and individual claims.[386] 'Mixed' claims consist, by definition, of diplomatic protection and 'direct' claims brought together.[387] To allow such claims concurrently with individual claims would therefore violate these rules' purpose.[388] Indeed, the *Italy v Cuba* Tribunal suggested that a rule akin to article 27 would have applied had both individuals and the State claimed, notwithstanding that Italy claimed for both individual damage and moral damage to itself.[389] Accordingly, these rules would seem to apply unless a State brings a purely 'direct' claim.

[378] ibid [39]. Similarly Thirlway (n 32) 1556 (*LaGrand*).

[379] DADP, art 15(a) ('no reasonably available local remedies to provide effective redress'), 77–79; also de Aréchaga (n 47) 588–90; Amerasinghe (n 43) 151–57; Amerasinghe (n 25) 189–92, 203–10, 325–39.

[380] Generally on exceptions: DADP, art 15, 74–86; Amerasinghe (n 43) 149–61, 181–87; Amerasinghe (n 25) 168–78, 189–92, 203–14, 325–45.

[381] DADP, art 15(c), 80–83; Amerasinghe (n 43) 181–87; Amerasinghe (n 25) 168–78; Meron (n 37) 94–100.

[382] See discussion nn 111–12, 130; de Aréchaga (n 47) 583 ('person injured ... [*inter alia*] by ... space object, or ... fishing vessel damaged on ... high seas ... not supposed to exhaust remedies'). On ships and aircraft: n 140 (*Saiga*); Amerasinghe (n 25) 165–66 (*I'm Alone* (n 135)), 168; n 130 (*Aerial Incident*).

[383] Similarly nn 366, 374–82; Thirlway (n 32) 1554.

[384] cf Wittich (n 37) 136, 142.

[385] Similarly Paparinskis, 'Countermeasures' (n 3) 313–14.

[386] nn 12–14.

[387] n 36.

[388] nn 385–86. Cf n 286.

[389] *Italy v Cuba (Interim Award)* UNCITRAL Tribunal (15 March 2005) [34], [65]; see Ch 4, n 327; generally Michele Potestà, 'Republic of Italy v Republic of Cuba' (2012) 106 AJIL 341, 342; Roberts, 'Hybrid' (n 2) 40.

V. Conclusion

This chapter has outlined how to distinguish diplomatic protection, 'mixed', and 'direct' claims. The rules considered—the local remedies requirement, and those contained in article 27 of ICSID and article 222(c) of the CARICOM treaty—apply to diplomatic protection claims, but not to 'direct' claims, properly so-called. This is understandable, given their purposes. The local remedies rule encourages the bringing of domestic proceedings in order to allow the respondent State to remedy an individual's injury and avert the bringing of overlapping interstate proceedings.[390] But that rule serves no purpose vis-à-vis 'direct' interstate claims alleging only State damage, which generally cannot and should not be brought domestically.[391] For their part, the ICSID and CARICOM rules are designed to avoid overlapping individual and interstate proceedings. But the practice makes clear that only claims of diplomatic protection are sufficiently similar to individual claims to warrant their application.[392]

As to 'mixed' claims, the purpose of all these rules would arguably be undermined if they were inapplicable to such claims in principle. This is more obviously so vis-à-vis the ICSID and CARICOM rules, where to allow both individual and interstate diplomatic protection claims based on the same injury (even as part of a 'mixed' claim) would be to allow the very multiplicity the rules are intended to avoid.[393] The purpose of the local remedies rule—to allow the respondent State to remedy the wrong domestically—is also defeated if 'mixed' claims can be brought. However, the practice suggests that interests of efficiency in avoiding an applicant State having to bring the diplomatic protection and 'direct' portions of its claims separately may outweigh this purpose, at least where the 'mixed' parts of the claim are sufficiently connected.[394]

In totality, these rules may be of limited significance in addressing the concerns relating to overlapping individual and interstate claims identified at the outset.[395] With similar provisions existing in only some BITs, ICSID's article 27 is unlikely to codify customary international law.[396] This means its application may be avoided as long as the State exercising diplomatic protection is not an ICSID party.[397] The CARICOM rule is equally regime-specific. Nonetheless, these rules demonstrate

[390] n 191; Amerasinghe (n 25) 59–62, 74.
[391] nn 368–69.
[392] Similarly Ch 4, nn 372–93.
[393] Section I(A).
[394] See Thirlway, n 369, generally Amerasinghe (n 25) 56–64, also 61 (interests in 'efficient justice').
[395] Introduction, nn 40–59.
[396] See Paparinskis, 'Countermeasures' (n 3) 282–85; Juratowich (n 14) 16–17, 19–21; Potestà, 'Italy/Cuba' (n 389) 346; also Roberts, 'Hybrid' (n 2) 46–47.
[397] Schreuer (n 14) 418; Paparinskis, 'Countermeasures' (n 3) 317 and see *Autopista* (n 17) [135]–[140]. Cf *Italy v Cuba*, n 389.

that there is a real concern regarding such overlap, and provide insights into how it might be addressed.

For its part, the local remedies rule only prevents overlap insofar as an overlapping interstate claim is rendered unnecessary if domestic redress is considered satisfactory; the State's claim is otherwise merely delayed.[398] However, it does demonstrate the relevance of considerations of reparation and efficiency in addressing overlapping claims. As later chapters demonstrate, the detailed consideration of the rule's application undertaken here also provides insights into the nature of international claims that are critical to appreciating when other rules of preclusion might operate.

[398] Amerasinghe (n 25) 61.

4

Res Judicata, Double Recovery, and Related Provisions and Principles

This chapter is the first addressing rules relevant to admissibility, breach, and reparation that might operate to preclude overlapping claims, but whose application is not, unlike those considered in Chapter 3, dependent on the type of interstate claim brought, but instead on claims, or the rights underlying them, being in some broader sense the 'same'.[1] Drawing extensively on the analysis of injury developed in Chapter 3, this chapter addresses *res judicata*, treaty provisions with similar effect, and the rule precluding double recovery, while Chapter 5 considers waiver and consent.

Given the more limited requirements for its application, this chapter begins by outlining when the rule precluding double recovery applies, followed by case law demonstrating its almost certain operation to preclude reparation being awarded in the second of two overlapping individual and interstate claims, where the latter seeks reparation for the individual's damage.

It then considers the requirements for *res judicata* and treaty-based provisions reflecting its elements to apply, noting the prima facie difficulties in demonstrating the required 'identity' as between overlapping individual and interstate claims.[2] However, drawing out principles from the case law, the chapter suggests that a pragmatic approach to the application of *res judicata* is consistent with international law and with policy considerations.[3] Alternatively, tribunals may prevent overlapping individual and interstate claims through the application of principles including abuse of process,[4] where the operation of *res judicata* as such is avoided.[5]

[1] Introduction, nn 89–92. Contribution to injury, including by 'any person or entity in relation to whom reparation is sought' (James Crawford, *The International Law Commission's Articles on State Responsibility: Introduction, Text and Commentaries* (CUP 2002) art 39 (*ARSIWA*)) could also operate to (partially) preclude overlapping claims, for instance where individual conduct contributing to that individual's injury affects a State's diplomatic protection claim: see ibid 241. However, as the rule reflects issues largely of causation (see ibid 240), it is not considered further herein.

[2] n 113.

[3] Sections IV–V and authorities, see particularly nn 143–44, 167, 260–61, 386; Shany, nn 612, 648.

[4] Generally Yuval Shany, *Regulating Jurisdictional Relations Between National and International Courts* (OUP 2007) 192 (abuse of rights general principle/custom, preventing 'abuse of process'); also Yuval Shany, *The Competing Jurisdictions of International Courts and Tribunals* (OUP 2003) 256–59; *Waste Management v Mexico (Preliminary Objection)* (2004) 6 ICSID Rep 549 [49]–[50].

[5] Suggesting this approach: Shany, *Relations* (n 4) 192–94; Shany, *Competing* (n 4) 258–59, 287; Hanno Wehland, *The Coordination of Multiple Proceedings in Investment Treaty Arbitration* (OUP 2013) [7.29]–[7.52]; Emmanuel Gaillard, 'Abuse of Process in International Arbitration' (2017) 32 ICSID Rev-FILJ 17, 22–26, 32–37. Also *Dallal v Bank Mellat* (1985) 75 ILR 151 (EWHC) 162–63, discussed Kate

Overlapping Individual and Interstate Claims in International Law. Jessica Howley, Oxford University Press.
 DOI: 10.1093/oso/9780192871466.003.0005

The final section outlines, utilising the categorisation of interstate claims from earlier chapters (diplomatic protection, 'mixed', and 'direct' claims), those circumstances of overlap with individual claims that are likely to give rise to the application of both rules. It concludes that, with the exception of 'direct' claims properly so-called, interstate claims are necessarily brought at least partially for individual damage, meaning that the double recovery rule will operate as between them and individual claims for the same damage.[6] It also argues that there is good reason for *res judicata* to operate in circumstances in which individual claims and interstate diplomatic protection claims overlap.[7] In elaborating the position vis-à-vis 'mixed' claims, this chapter teases out a distinction between individual and 'collective' claims, arguing that interstate claims are sometimes a compilation of individual claims—sharing an identity with claims brought by the affected individuals themselves—and are sometimes more 'general' or 'collective' in nature.[8] Both rules may potentially operate as between claims in the first category overlapping with individual claims. Finally, while *res judicata* does not operate vis-à-vis overlapping individual and interstate 'direct' claims properly so-called, even some of these claims may be caught by the double recovery rule.[9]

I. Double recovery

International claims seek a remedy, which may include reparation for damage.[10] In this context, it is apt to consider the possible application of the principle precluding double recovery to overlapping individual and interstate claims.[11]

Double recovery commonly refers to 'recovery by the injured party of more than its assessed damage or injury'.[12] The rule precluding double recovery is designed to prevent a party from being unjustly enriched through a 'double claim',[13] including where multiple claims are made before different tribunals,[14] where reparation is

Parlett, *The Individual in the International Legal System: Continuity and Change in International Law* (CUP 2011) 100–1; *Caratube International Oil v Kazakhstan (Award)* ICSID Case No ARB/13/13 (27 September 2017) [498]. See nn 125–26.

[6] Sections V(A)–(B); similarly James Crawford, *State Responsibility: The General Part* (CUP 2013) 590 (*GP*); Anthea Roberts, 'State-to-State Investment Treaty Arbitration: A Hybrid Theory of Interdependent Rights and Shared Interpretative Authority' (2014) 55 Harv ILJ 1, 50 (fn 228).

[7] Section V(A)(ii).

[8] Section V(B)(ii).

[9] Section V(B).

[10] Ch 1, nn 5ff.

[11] Introduction, n 69.

[12] James Crawford, 'Third Report on State Responsibility' (2000) 2(1) ILCYB 3 [248].

[13] *Gold Looted from the Netherlands* (1963) 44 ILR 448 (Italy-Netherlands Conc Comm) 471.

[14] See *Chevron and Texaco v Ecuador (Partial Award)* PCA Case 2007-02 (30 March 2010) [517], [557] (domestic actions); similarly *Occidental v Ecuador (Award)* (2004) 12 ICSID Rep 59 [209]; *Hochtief v Argentina (Jurisdiction)* ICSID Case No ARB/07/31 (24 October 2011) [121]–[122]; *Waste Management v Mexico (Award)* (2000) 121 ILR 29 (ICSID) [27] (waiver avoids); *International Thunderbird Gaming v*

claimed from several different respondents,[15] or where loss resulting from distinct breaches is claimed multiple times.[16]

The rule precluding double recovery can operate as an aspect of *res judicata*, which bars, as seen below, a claim for both breach and reparation.[17] However, a distinct equitable rule prevents duplication of relief, regardless of whether *res judicata* operates,[18] including when *res judicata* would be inapplicable because the claims involve different parties.[19] Significantly, the rule can therefore operate when 'different persons or entities are entitled to bring what is effectively the same claim before different forums'.[20]

This latter, equitable, aspect of the principle, which is the focus here, is well-recognised in international law.[21] Thus, the International Court of Justice (ICJ) in the *Reparations Case* held that, while no rule prioritised between diplomatic and functional protection claims arising from an individual's injury,[22] '[i]nternational tribunals are already familiar with the problem of a claim in which two or more national States are interested, and they know how to protect the defendant State'.[23] The commentary to article 46 of the Articles on Responsibility of States

Mexico (Award) UNCITRAL Tribunal (26 January 2006) [118]; *Renco v Peru (Jurisdiction)* UNCITRAL Tribunal (15 July 2016) [84]–[88].

15 *ARSIWA*, 275 (vis-à-vis art 47); *Netherlands Gold* (n 13) 471; also *Eritrea's Damages Claims (Final Award)* (2009) XXVI UNRIAA 505 [46] (no damages 'reflecting … donations or payments not required or expected to be repaid').

16 *SD Myers v Canada (Partial Award)* (2000) 8 ICSID Rep 18 [316]; *Ethiopia's Damages Claims (Final Award)* (2009) XXVI UNRIAA 631 [329], [366]; *Duke Energy v Ecuador (Award)* ICSID Case No ARB/04/19 (12 August 2008) [476]; *Total SA v Argentina (Liability)* ICSID Case No ARB/04/1 (21 December 2010) [198]; generally Sergey Ripinsky and Kevin Williams, *Damages in International Investment Law* (BIICL 2008) 101; KR Handley, *Spencer Bower and Handley: Res Judicata* (4th edn, LexisNexis 2009) [21.04]; Crawford, 'ThirdRep' (n 12) [248]; similarly Stephan Wittich, 'Compensation' in Rüdiger Wolfrum (ed), *MPEPIL (Online)* (OUP 2012) [34]; *ARSIWA*, 230.

17 See Handley (n 16) [1.04], [19.01]–[19.02] (*transit in res judicatum*), [27.03]; Peter Barnett, *Res Judicata, Estoppel, and Foreign Judgments* (OUP 2001) [1.37], [1.41]–[1.42]; Luiz Eduardo Salles, *Forum Shopping in International Adjudication: The Role of Preliminary Objections* (CUP 2014) 268; *Hochtief Aktiengesellschaft v Argentina (Liability)* ICSID Case No ARB/07/31 (29 December 2014) [180]; section III.

18 Barnett (n 17) [1.45] ('double satisfaction'), referencing *Kohnke v Karger* [1951] 2 KB 670, 675–76; *Cuttel v Bentz* [1985] 6 WWR 193 (BCCA), 198, referenced Donald Lange, *The Doctrine of Res Judicata in Canada* (Butterworths 2000) 132; ILA, 'Interim Report on *Res Judicata* and Arbitration' (2004) 25 Arb Int 35, 43 (distinguishing 'former recovery'/'equitable … double satisfaction'); Crawford, 'ThirdRep' (n 12) [249] ('principle … subsumed in general principle of full (equitable) reparation'); also *Nagel v Czech Republic (Final Award)* (2003) 13 ICSID Rep 30 (SCC) [239]; nn 54–57.

19 See *Kohnke* (n 18) 675–76; *Netherlands Gold* (n 13) 471; *Burlington Resources v Ecuador (Counterclaims)* ICSID Case No ARB/08/5 (7 February 2017) [1080]–[1086]; nn 20–30. It may be sufficient that an order for reparation has been made, regardless of whether it has (yet) been paid: see discussion *Marryshow v McBurnie*, GDAHCV2011/0189 (February 2016) (ECSC) [22]–[26], but see *ConocoPhillips v Venezuela (Award)* ICSID Case No ARB/07/30 (8 March 2019) [963] (only issue at enforcement stage). Cf nn 112–16.

20 Crawford, 'ThirdRep' (n 12) [248].

21 Similarly *Burlington (Counterclaims)* (n 19) [1083].

22 *Reparation for injuries suffered in the service of the United Nations (Advisory Opinion)* [1949] ICJ Rep 174, 185.

23 ibid 186. Cf *Barcelona Traction, Light and Power Company (Belgium v Spain)* [1970] ICJ Rep 3 [53], [98].

for Internationally Wrongful Acts (ARSIWA), addressing multiple injured States, quotes this as evidencing that States 'claiming in respect of the same wrongful act' should 'coordinate their claims so as to avoid double recovery'.[24]

Similarly, because investment treaties commonly protect both companies and their shareholders,[25] separate entities affected by given conduct may bring a claim against the same State.[26] Tribunals have allowed shareholder claims in such circumstances, including over respondent State objections concerning double recovery.[27] Nonetheless, aside from when the risk of double recovery is considered 'hypothetical',[28] tribunals have recognised that it must be prevented, by: (i) suggesting that there are 'pragmatic ways' of addressing such situations;[29] (ii) asserting, *Reparations*-style, that international law has 'mechanisms' for avoiding double recovery;[30] (iii) emphasising that compensation awarded to one entity would be accounted for in the other's claim;[31] or (iv) actually making orders to ensure no double recovery results.[32] In the infamous *Lauder* case, for example,

[24] *ARSIWA*, 271; also Elizabeth Wu, 'Addressing Multiplicity of Shareholder Claims in ICSID Arbitrations Under Bilateral Investment Treaties: A "Tiered Approach" to Prioritising Claims?' (2010) 6 AIAJ 134, 151; Martins Paparinskis, 'Investment Arbitration and the Law of Countermeasures' (2008) 79 BYBIL 264, 300.

[25] Ripinsky and Williams (n 16) 150–54; Paparinskis (n 24) 316; Gabriel Bottini, 'Indirect Shareholder Claims' in Meg Kinnear and others (eds), *Building International Investment Law: The First 50 Years of ICSID* (Kluwer 2016) 203ff.

[26] Zachary Douglas, 'The Hybrid Foundations of Investment Treaty Arbitration' (2004) 74 BYBIL 151, 173–75; Wu (n 24) 134–35, 137–39; Kaj Hobér, 'Res Judicata and Lis Pendens in International Arbitration' (2014) 366 RdC 99, 343; Salles (n 17) 275; James Crawford, 'The International Law Commission's Articles on Diplomatic Protection Revisited' in Tiyanjana Maluwa, Max du Plessis, and Dire Tladi (eds), *The Pursuit of a Brave New World in International Law: Essays in Honour of John Dugard* (Brill Nijhoff 2017) 157–58; generally Zachary Douglas, *The International Law of Investment Claims* (CUP 2009) Ch 11. Cf *Barcelona Traction* (n 23) [90], [96].

[27] Generally Wu (n 24) 153; also Wehland (n 5) [1.32]–[1.34]; Bottini (n 25) 216–18; eg, *Enron v Argentina (Annulment)* ICSID Case No ARB/01/3 (30 July 2010) [123]–[124]; *Azurix v Argentina (Annulment)* ICSID Case No ARB/01/12 (1 September 2009) [113]–[130]; *Suez v Argentina (Jurisdiction)* ICSID Case No ARB/03/17 (16 May 2006) [51].

[28] *Azurix (Annulment)* (n 27) [114]; also *Impregilo v Argentina (Jurisdiction)* ICSID Case No ARB/15/39 (23 February 2018) [148]; *Murphy Exploration v Ecuador (Partial Final Award)* Case No 2012-16 UNCITRAL Tribunal (6 May 2016) [381] (no risk). Cf *Pan American Energy v Argentina (Preliminary Objections)* ICSID Case Nos ARB/03/13, ARB/04/8 (27 July 2006) [219] ('danger … real').

[29] *Enron* (n 27) [124].

[30] Wu (n 24) 153; eg *Azurix (Annulment)* (n 27) [116], referencing *Camuzzi v Argentina (Jurisdiction)* ICSID Case No ARB/03/2 (11 May 2005) [91] and *Bayindir v Pakistan (Jurisdiction)* ICSID Case No ARB/03/29 (14 November 2005) [270]; *Chevron/Ecuador (PA)* (n 14) [557]; also *Perenco v Ecuador (Counterclaims Dismissal)* ICSID Case No ARB/08/6 (18 August 2017) [52]; *Suez (Jurisdiction)* (n 27) [51]; *Burlington (Counterclaims)* (n 19) [1086]; Douglas, *Investment* (n 26) 457.

[31] *Impregilo v Argentina (Award)* ICSID Case No ARB/07/17 (21 June 2011) [139]; *Azurix (Annulment)* (n 27) [117]; *Urbaser v Argentina (Jurisdiction)* ICSID Case No ARB/07/26 (19 December 2012) [253]; *Hochtief (Liability)* (n 17) [180]; *Suez v Argentina (Award)* ICSID Case No ARB/03/19 (9 April 2015) [38]–[40]; n 34; also *Union Fenosa v Egypt (Award)* ICSID Case No ARB/4/4 (31 August 2018) [11.33]; *Lion Mexico v Mexico (Award)* ICSID Case No ARB(AF)/15/2 (20 September 2021) [798] (local courts to address), see Lisa Bohmer, 'Tribunal in Lion Mexico v. Mexico Finds …' *IA Rep* (24 September 2021); *Gosling v Mauritius (Award)* ICSID Case No ARB/16/32 (18 February 2020) [164], see Lisa Bohmer, 'Analysis: In Gosling v. Mauritius …' *IA Rep* (24 February 2020).

[32] *Railroad Development v Guatemala (Award)* ICSID Case No ARB/07/23 (29 June 2012) [265]; also *Venezuela Holdings v Venezuela (Award)* ICSID Case No ARB/07/27 (9 October 2014) [378]–[381]; *ADM and Tate & Lyle v Mexico (Correction/Interpretation)* ICSID Case No ARB(AF)/04/05 (10 July

involving separate proceedings by a company and its owner before different fora, the tribunal refused to bar one of the claims, given that the parties and claims were different.[33] Nonetheless, the tribunal noted the 'risk':

> that damages be concurrently granted by more than one court or arbitral tribunal, in which case the … second deciding court or arbitral tribunal could take this fact into consideration when assessing the final damage.[34]

Similarly, the *Micula* tribunal, to avoid double recovery,[35] allocated damages in a way that 'dispose[d] of the total amount that [the respondent State] has to pay fully to discharge its obligations' without 'deal[ing] with the specific entitlement of each Claimant individually'.[36]

Regarding human rights, the European Court of Human Rights (ECtHR), in *Petroiu*, found a compensable unlawful taking of property where domestic courts had already held the applicant entitled to possession.[37] The Court held that it could not sanction the unjust enrichment that would result:

> si la requérante devait obtenir en plus de la mise en possession de l'immeuble, ultérieurement, une somme au titre de la satisfaction équitable pour préjudice matériel, calculée sur la base de la valeur de cet immeuble: en effet, la requérante obtiendrait alors deux fois la valeur dudit bien ….[38]

Implicitly recognising the double recovery principle, the Court considered the application an abuse of process,[39] as it did in another case concerning multiple requests for compensation for the same damage,[40] and as the European Commission on Human Rights (ECommHR) indicated it would vis-à-vis a claim where compensation received through 'friendly settlement' had provided 'complete redress'.[41]

2008) [21]–[24]; *Occidental* (n 14) [209]; *Deutsche Telekom v India (Final Award)* PCA Case 2014–10 (27 May 2020) [357](e) (undertaking); similarly *ConocoPhillips* (n 19) [965], [1010](5); Johanna Braun, 'Analysis: On Quantum, Deutsche Telekom v. India Tribunal …' *IA Rep* (23 April 2021); Lisa Bohmer, 'Analysis: In Previously Unseen Turkey-Syria BIT Award …' *IA Rep* (31 November 2020) (share transfer); nn 35–36.

[33] *Lauder v Czech Republic* (2001) 9 ICSID Rep 66 [171] (*lis pendens*); further nn 147, 281.

[34] ibid [172]; also Shany, *Relations* (n 4) 135; Roberts (n 6) 42; Paparinskis (n 24) 300; *British Caribbean Bank v Belize (Award)* PCA Case 2010–18 (19 December 2014) [190].

[35] *Micula v Romania (Award)* ICSID Case No ARB/05/20 (11 December 2013) [1246].

[36] ibid [1247].

[37] *Petroiu v Romania (Revision)* App 33055/09 (ECtHR, 7 February 2017) [20]–[21].

[38] ibid [25].

[39] ibid [26], [30]. Similarly *Vidu v Romania (Revision)* App 9835/02 (ECtHR, 17 January 2017) [17]–[30].

[40] *Migliore v Italy* App 58511/13 (ECtHR, 12 November 2013) [39]–[40]. Similarly *Alves v Portugal* App 56297/11 (ECtHR, 21 January 2014) [14]–[15], [17].

[41] *Andronicou and Constantinou v Cyprus* (1995) 82A DR 102, 113 (also discussing victim status), referencing *Inze v Austria* (1987) ECHR Ser A No 126 [32].

The Inter-American Court of Human Rights (IACtHR) has also recognised the rule against double recovery,[42] while other treaty bodies cease to regard individuals as 'victims' once settlement is reached.[43] Even the Human Rights Committee (HRC), which is not prevented from considering a claim previously heard elsewhere,[44] considered that an applicant awarded reparation by the ECtHR was not a 'victim', and held their claim inadmissible.[45]

As to other international tribunals, the United Nations Compensation Commission (UNCC) expressly recognised that double recovery must be avoided,[46] as did the Eritrea-Ethiopia Claims Commission (EECC),[47] while the Caribbean Court of Justice (CCJ) has declared double recovery 'contrary to elementary judicial principles'.[48] The *Arctic Sunrise* Tribunal awarded the Netherlands compensation for 'non-material damages in relation to the arrest, detention, and prosecution of [persons] on board' the vessel.[49] With claims by the relevant individuals themselves still pending before the ECtHR, the Tribunal considered that it was unnecessary to 'consider the possibility of double compensation', but it thereby implicitly recognised the principle.[50] The International Criminal Court (ICC) also recognises that victims should not be 'over-compensated for the harm they have suffered' in situations involving multiple perpetrators.[51]

International tribunals thus recognise that international law prevents double recovery from materialising, including, importantly, where it would result from claims brought by multiple claimants against a single defendant.[52] Its application encompasses claims for which reparation has been paid both consequent on adjudication by a tribunal and through other means of settlement.[53]

[42] *Mapiripán Massacre (Merits)* (2005) IACHR Ser C No 134 [214] (domestic damages), [287]; *La Cantuta and Muñoz Sánchez v Peru (Merits)* (2006) IACHR Ser C No 162 [210], both discussed in *Fujimori*, File-AV/19-2001 (SC Peru, 7 April 2009) [780], in turn discussed in André Nollkaemper, *National Courts and the International Rule of Law* (OUP 2011) 209.

[43] Eg, *X v Austria* Doc CEDAW/C/64/D/67/2014 (CEDAW, 11 July 2016) [6.7]; *Dahanayake v Sri Lanka* Doc CCPR/C/87/D/1331/2004 (HRC, 25 July 2006) [6.5]; Ch 5, n 38. Generally Tom Zwart, *The Admissibility of Human Rights Petitions* (Martinus Nijhoff 1994) 62–69; Nollkaemper (n 42) 262.

[44] nn 92, 122.

[45] *Smirnova v Russia* Doc CCPR/C/81/D/712/1996 (HRC, 5 July 2004) [9.3]–[9.4].

[46] *Category 'C' Claims against Iraq* (1994) 109 ILR 205 (UNCC) 267; *First Instalment of 'E3' Claims* UN Doc S/AC26/1998/13 (UNCC, 17 December 1998) [434]; n 79; generally Hans van Houtte, Hans Das, and Bart Delmartino, 'The United Nations Compensation Commission' in Pablo de Greiff (ed), *The Handbook of Reparations* (OUP 2006) 367–68, 374–75; Shany, *Competing* (n 4) 225.

[47] *Ethiopia* (n 16) [329], [366].

[48] *British Caribbean Bank v Belize* [2013] CCJ 4 [47]. Further: *Headstart Class F Holdings v Y2K Finance* (2008) Case BVIHCV2007/0278 (ECSC) [67]–[69].

[49] *Arctic Sunrise Arbitration (Netherlands v Russia) (Compensation)* PCA Case 2014-02 (10 July 2017) [85].

[50] ibid [86]. See *Bryan and others v Russia*, App 22515/14.

[51] *Prosecutor v Bosco Ntaganda (Reparations Order)* Case ICC-01/04-02/06 (8 March 2021) [100]. See Marina Lostal, 'The Ntaganda Reparations Order: A Marked Step towards a Victim-Centred Reparations Legal Framework at the ICC' *EJIL:Talk!* (24 May 2021).

[52] nn 22–23, 29–36, 50. Cf Roberts (n 6) 42 ('discretionary').

[53] Annemarieke Vermeer-Künzli, 'Unfinished Business: Concurrence of Claims Presented before a Human Rights Court or Treaty Body and through Diplomatic Protection' (2010) 10 HRLR 269, 276; Ch 1, nn 104–5; Paparinskis (n 24) 282. Cf *res judicata* n 112.

In terms of how the rule precluding double recovery actually operates, it may apparently do so either to bar a later claim entirely, or to reduce the compensation that might be awarded, depending on circumstances.[54] Thus, while one tribunal considered that where damage is 'fully repaired', a later claim 'may become inadmissible',[55] another suggested that—unless formulated as a *res judicata* objection—double recovery instead concerns how reparation is calculated.[56] The two approaches are logically distinct: if the claim is inadmissible, then responsibility cannot be invoked at all for either legal or factual injury; otherwise it instead impacts the amount of reparation awarded for demonstrated factual injury.[57]

In either case, the rule operates where there would otherwise be double compensation for the 'same loss'.[58] As an example of what this means in practice where multiple parties are involved, shareholders are commonly awarded damages in their claims pursuant to bilateral investment treaties (BITs) for losses in dividends and share value.[59] However, such losses are generally 'derivative'[60] or 'reflective'[61] of those suffered by the company. Insofar as the loss ceases to exist once the company is compensated, the shareholder cannot obtain separate reparation for that loss.[62] Similarly, in *Chórzow*, the 'interests' of two German companies were 'interdependent and complementary',[63] ultimately dependent on the same undertaking's value, meaning that both could not be separately compensated.[64] Nonetheless, not

[54] Crawford, 'ThirdRep' (n 12) [248]; nn 55–56. See also *Police Cooperation Credit Union v Alleyne* SKBHCV2013/0122 (23 February 2016) (ECSC) [40]–[42] (partial satisfaction from multiple defendants). On difficulties where claimed 'remedies diverge': Paparinskis (n 24) 300; also Roberts (n 6) 67; Edwin Borchard, *The Diplomatic Protection of Citizens Abroad: Or, the Law of International Claims* (Banks 1915) 370.

[55] *Orascom v Algeria (Award)* ICSID Case No ARB/12/35 (31 May 2017) [495], also [496]–[518]. Cf [488] ('dispute ... effectively one and the same'); Ian Brownlie, *Principles of Public International Law* (7th edn, OUP 2008) 51; also n 45.

[56] *Hochtief (Liability)* (n 17) [180]; also *Azurix v Argentina (Jurisdiction)* (2003) 10 ICSID Rep 416 [101] (merits); *Sempra v Argentina (Annulment)* ICSID Case No ARB/02/16 (10 June 2010) [104].

[57] Ch 1(II)–(III).

[58] Eg *Burlington (Counterclaims)* (n 19) [1081]; *Venezuela Holdings* (n 32) [378]; *ADM (Correction/Interpretation)* (n 32) [21]; *Cuttel* (n 18) 205.

[59] Ripinsky and Williams (n 16) 157–61; also n 62.

[60] Eg *Inmaris Perestroika v Ukraine (Jurisdiction)* ICSID Case No ARB/08/8 (8 March 2010) [112]; generally Robert Wisner, 'Derivative Actions and Indirect Claims' in Federico Ortino and others (eds), *Investment Treaty Law: Current Issues II* (BIICL 2007) 74–76; n 62.

[61] Eg Douglas, *Investment* (n 26) 416, 418–20; *Johnson v Gore Wood* [2002] 2 AC 1, 66; n 62.

[62] See *Johnson* (n 61) 35–37, 62 (dividend loss/share value diminution reflecting company's loss); *Orascom* (n 55) [498]ff; also *Ahmadou Sadio Diallo (Guinea v DRC) (Compensation)* [2012] ICJ Rep 344 (Sep Op Greenwood) [2] (share value diminution 'in substance ... same' as company's claim); similarly n 31; *Headstart* (n 48) [67]–[69]; Wu (n 24) 141–42; generally Thomas Wälde and Borzu Sabahi, 'Compensation, Damages, and Valuation' in Peter Muchlinski, Federico Ortino, and Christoph Schreuer (eds), *The Oxford Handbook of International Investment Law* (OUP 2008) 1101–3; Robert Jennings and Arthur Watts, *Oppenheim's International Law*, vol 1 (9th edn, Longman 1992) 520 ('loss indirectly'); Crawford, 'Revisited' (n 26) 158 ('derivative claims' for 'reflective loss'), cf 160 ('not ... derivative'); Theodor Meron, 'The Insurer and the Insured under International Claims Law' (1974) 68 AJIL 628, 641; *Twenty-Second Instalment of 'E3' Claims* UN Doc S/AC26/2002/32 (UNCC, 12 December 2002) 132 (Annex, Summary ('contractual chain')).

[63] *Factory at Chórzow (Merits)* [1928] PCIJ Rep Ser A No 17, 48.

[64] ibid 48–49, also 55–56; Crawford, 'ThirdRep' (n 12) [248]; Wu (n 24) 151.

all shareholder losses are necessarily identical with those of the company; personal damage additional to losses in share value may, for instance, be separate.[65] As will be seen, the difficulty in determining the potential operation of the rule precluding double recovery vis-à-vis overlapping individual and interstate claims lies in distinguishing individual and interstate losses that are the same from those that are not.

II. Double recovery and overlapping individual and interstate claims

Turning to overlapping individual and interstate claims specifically, case law relevant to the preclusion of double recovery reveals that, on the one hand, reparation awarded to a State may preclude later individual claims for compensation.[66] Thus, as just noted, the *Arctic Sunrise* tribunal appeared to acknowledge that the double recovery rule could operate to preclude individual human rights claims where these overlapped with interstate proceedings under the United Nations Convention on the Law of the Sea (UNCLOS).[67] Similarly, in the *Pad* case, the applicants alleged various violations of the European Convention on Human Rights (ECHR) by Turkey resulting from the killing of their Iranian relatives.[68] After Iran's diplomatic intervention, Turkey agreed to pay the State compensation, for the families, in 'final settlement'.[69] Iran ultimately determined to transfer to the victims less than half of that money.[70] While ultimately declaring the case inadmissible on other grounds,[71] the ECtHR considered that, given the interstate payment, Turkey 'could be deemed to have fulfilled [its] duty to make reparation for the alleged wrong' and that further proceedings might, consequently, be unwarranted.[72]

On the other hand, the granting of reparation to an individual would appear to affect an overlapping interstate reparation claim. Thus, the Special Rapporteur on State Responsibility of the International Law Commission (ILC), observing

[65] *Johnson* (n 61) 35–36; Douglas, *Investment* (n 26) 417; also Wu (n 24) 143; *Chórzow (Merits)* (n 63) 48–49, 55–56.

[66] Similarly Borchard (n 54) 368 ('settlement of a claim by agreement of ... two governments ... estops the claimant from ... again demand[ing] any redress').

[67] n 50.

[68] *Pad v Turkey (Admissibility)* App 60167/00 (ECtHR, 28 June 2007) [39]–[47], discussed Vermeer-Künzli (n 53) 284–85 (vis-à-vis overlapping individual/interstate claims).

[69] *Pad v Turkey* (n 68) [31] (Turkish-Iranian Protocol).

[70] ibid [31], [33].

[71] ibid [71]–[72].

[72] ibid [65] (under art 37(1)(c)); also Martins Paparinskis, 'Investment Treaty Arbitration and the (New) Law of State Responsibility' (2013) 24 EJIL 617, 639–40. Further: *Association SOS Attentats and De Boëry v France* ECHR 2006-XIV 375 [38]–[39] (compensation agreement resulting from diplomatic intervention 'in line with ... interests'; claim struck out), discussed Vermeer-Künzli (n 53) 282–84; Ruth Mackenzie and others, *Manual on International Courts and Tribunals* (OUP 2010) [11.20]; Ch 5(III)(C)(iii).

that the *Chórzow* case concerned proceedings brought both by affected German companies before Mixed Arbitral Tribunals (MATs), and by Germany before the Permanent Court of International Justice (PCIJ), concluded that 'it is quite clear that any compensation payable to the companies would have been taken into account in assessing the amount of compensation payable to Germany.'[73] Indeed, as Chapter 3 highlighted, even where individuals are compensated by *domestic* courts in the process of exhausting local remedies, States are precluded from bringing diplomatic protection claims for their injury.[74] The Franco-Italian Commission, for instance, considered that obligations at issue in interstate proceedings concerning the restitution of nationals' property could have been 'discharged' had the individual—claiming before domestic courts—had their property restored.[75] Consistent with this position, Cyprus withdrew from its interstate reparation case against Turkey claims concerning persons already compensated through individual applications.[76] Similarly, in *Georgia v Russia (I)*, the ECtHR, in calculating interstate reparation for an administrative practice of detention and forcible expulsion, removed from consideration any individual who had lodged their own application.[77] The UNCC, having categorised its claims into six groups,[78] also recognised the application of the double recovery rule in overlapping individual and interstate claims, observing:

> While the potential for duplicate recovery is more subtle and not as directly ascertainable between individuals in category "C" and the corporations, Governments or international organizations who may have compensated them for the same losses they claim in their individual capacities, ... it certainly does exist.
>
> This duplicate recovery potential has most relevance when the corporation, Government or international organization is also claiming for losses that are essentially the same but viewed from another perspective, e.g., amounts paid by these entities to reimburse individuals for costs related to departure, relocation,

[73] Crawford, 'ThirdRep' (n 12) [248], referencing *Chórzow (Merits)* (n 63); also Shany, *Relations* (n 4) 43.

[74] Ch 3, nn 185–95. Even concerning different defendants: *The Neptune* (1797) 3 Moore's 3076, 3088 (Pinkney); *CME v Czech Republic (Partial Award)* (2001) 9 ICSID Rep 121 [304], [410] (may influence quantum); and vis-à-vis the opposite: *Fujimori* (n 42) [780]–[781], cited Nollkaemper (n 42) 209 (no double recovery; IACtHR already compensated); also *Georgia v Russia (I) (Just satisfaction)*, App 13255/07 (ECtHR, 31 January 2019) [70] (individuals removed from consideration, where 'successfully used available remedies').

[75] *Ottoz (France v Italy)* (1950) 18 ILR 435 (Franco-Italian Cl Comm) 439. See Brownlie (n 55) 51.

[76] *Cyprus v Turkey (Just Satisfaction)* ECHR 2014-II 245 (GC) [48].

[77] *Georgia/Russia(I) (Compensation)* (n 74) [70], see generally [48]–[49].

[78] Hans van Houtte, Bart Delmartino, and Iasson Yi, *Post-War Restoration of Property Rights Under International Law*, vol 1 (CUP 2008) 57–58 (individual departures (A); personal injury (B); individual damage under/over $100,000 (C/D); corporations' claims (E); State/organisational claims (evacuation/relief/State property/environmental) (F)); also Sean Murphy, Won Kidane, and Thomas Snider, *Litigating War: Arbitration of Civil Injury by the Eritrea-Ethiopia Claims Commission* (OUP 2013) 48; van Houtte, Das, and Delmartino (n 46) 335–38.

> personal property, real property or employment losses, in addition to relief, injury and death benefits....
>
> ... the Panel therefore urges that all attempts reasonably possible be made to minimize the risks of double recovery ....[79]

These authorities demonstrate that the principle precluding double recovery does indeed operate vis-à-vis overlapping individual and interstate claims when the respondent State has repaired the relevant damage, regardless of which entity invoked that State's responsibility first.[80]

III. *Res judicata* and provisions precluding multiple claims

The second principle considered here that could be relevant to the regulation of overlapping individual and interstate claims is *res judicata*. Before turning to the general principle, however, various of the treaties enabling individuals to invoke State responsibility also contain provisions addressing multiple claims.[81] Because overlapping individual and interstate claims are most likely to arise where individuals claim pursuant to those treaty-based mechanisms,[82] and because, as will be seen, these provisions reflect, in terms or application, generally applicable principles of international law, including *res judicata*, it is fitting to begin by examining them.

Thus, certain treaties allowing for individual claims, particularly in the human rights field, contain provisions rendering multiple claims inadmissible.[83] Article

[79] *Seventh Instalment of Individual Claims For Damages up to US$100,000 (Category 'C')* UN Doc S/AC26/1999/11 (UNCC, 24 June 1999) [75]–[77].

[80] See Paparinskis (n 24) 297–300; *Pad v Turkey* (n 68), n 72; similarly Paparinskis (n 72) 639–40; also Eduardo Jiménez de Aréchaga, 'International Responsibility' in Max Sørensen (ed), *Manual of Public International Law* (Macmillan 1968) 564; n 20. I thank Paparinskis for discussion. Double recovery issues could arise under international criminal law if a perpetrator paid reparations and a State were also responsible for that conduct: see *Prosecutor v Ruto and Sang (Decisions on the Requests regarding Reparations)* Case ICC-01/09/11-2038 (1 July 2016) [4] (questions regarding State's obligations for officials' actions), discussed Miriam Cohen, 'The Politics of Reparations at the International Criminal Court' in Holly Cullen, Philipp Kastner, and Sean Richmond (eds), *The Politics of International Criminal Law* (Brill Nijhoff 2020) 271; see also Christine Evans, *The Right to Reparation in International Law for Victims of Armed Conflict* (CUP 2012) 100–1; *Armed Activities on the Territory of the Congo (DRC v Uganda) (Reparations)* ICJ Judgment of 9 February 2022 [123] (noting ICC reparations award 'concern[ing] acts ... in the course of the same armed conflict', but apparently unconcerned about double recovery).

[81] Generally Shany, *Competing* (n 4) Chs 5(1)(A)(II), 5(2)(A)–(C).

[82] Generally Ch 2, cf Ch 2, nn 241–48.

[83] Generally: Andres Sotomayer, 'The Rule Against Duplication of Procedures in the Regional Systems of Human Rights Protection' [2009] NDWP 2 <http://www.nd.edu/~ndlaw/cchr/papers/Andres_%20Duplication_Procedures.pdf>; Jane Connors, 'United Nations' in Daniel Moeckli and others (eds), *International Human Rights Law* (3rd edn, OUP 2018) 394–95; Thomas Antkowiak, 'The Americas' in Moeckli and others (n 83) 429; Steven Greer, 'Europe' in Moeckli and others (n 83) 454; Christof Heyns and Magnus Killander, 'Africa' in Moeckli and others (n 83) 472; Shany, *Competing* (n 4) 213ff. Cf *Le Bridge v Moldova* App 48027/10 (ECtHR, 27 March 2018) [25] (jurisdictional), [26] (admissibility).

35(2)(b) of the ECHR, for instance, precludes the ECtHR from hearing an individual application that is:

> substantially the same as a matter that has already been examined by the Court or has already been submitted to another procedure of international investigation or settlement and contains no relevant new information.[84]

The Court has found matters 'substantially the same' where they concern 'substantially the same person, facts and complaints',[85] or sometimes, apparently more stringently, 'where the parties, the complaints and the facts are identical'.[86]

Under the American Convention on Human Rights (AmCHR), Commission communications are inadmissible where their 'subject' is 'pending in another international proceeding for settlement'[87] or they are 'substantially the same as one previously studied by the Commission or by another international organization'.[88] The IACtHR, like its European counterpart, regards these provisions as applicable when 'identity between the cases' exists, in the sense that 'the parties are the same, that the object of the action is the same, and that the legal grounds are identical'.[89]

For their part, certain United Nations (UN) human rights treaties preclude individual communications from being brought where '[t]he same matter has already been examined by the Committee or has been or is being examined under another procedure of international investigation or settlement';[90] 'unless ... [t]he same matter has not been, and is not being, [so] examined';[91] or 'unless ... [t]he same matter is not being [so] examined', the last thereby limiting the restriction to cases *simultaneously* under examination before the relevant Committee or elsewhere.[92] In the jurisprudence of these treaty bodies, such exclusions apply where 'the same

[84] ECHR, art 35(2)(b).

[85] *Pauger v Austria* (1995) 80-A DR 170, 174; similarly *Harkins v UK* App No 71537/14 (ECtHR, 15 June 2017) [42]; *Vojnović v Croatia* App 4819/10 (ECtHR, 26 June 2012) [28] ('essentially'); *Yukos v Russia* (2012) 54 EHRR 19 [520]–[522]. Generally Zwart (n 43) 181. Cf *Kafkaris v Cyprus* App 9644/09 (ECtHR, 21 June 2011) [68] ('same factual basis').

[86] *Khadzhimuradov v Russia* App 21194/90 (ECtHR, 10 October 2017) [80]; cf Shany, *Competing* (n 4) 218–19. See nn 167ff, 260ff.

[87] AmCHR, art 46(1)(c), read with art 47(a).

[88] AmCHR, art 47(d).

[89] *Saramaka People v Suriname* (2007) IACHR Ser C No 172 [48], quoting *Baena Ricardo v Panama* (1999) IACHR Ser C No 61 [53]; also *Shaw v Jamaica* Case 12018, Rep 25/99 (IACHR, 9 March 1999) [25] ('same rights, facts, persons and issues'); generally Shany, *Competing* (n 4) 223–24; nn 177–78.

[90] ICESCR Protocol, art 3(2)(c); CEDAW Protocol, art 4(2)(a); CRC Protocol, art 7(4); CRPD Protocol, art 2(c).

[91] UNCAT, art 22(4)(a); ICPMW, art 77(3)(a). Cf *Koptova v Slovakia* Doc CERD/C/57/D/13/1998 (CERD, 8 August 2000) [6.3] (no rule), but see Shany, *Competing* (n 4) 61, 216 (reservations); Mackenzie and others (n 72) [14.14]; Connors (n 83) 394.

[92] ICCPR Protocol, art 5(2)(a); similarly CPED, arts 31(2)(c), 30(2)(e); see Shany, *Competing* (n 4) 60. Reservations extend the restrictions to previously determined matters: ibid 60–61, 215–16; Zwart (n 43) 178; eg, *Fanali v Italy* (1983) 78 ILR 54 (HRC) [5.1].

parties, the same facts and the same substantive rights' are at issue,[93] or similar tests are met.[94]

Human rights applications to the Court of the Economic Community of West African States (ECOWAS) are similarly disallowed 'whilst the same matter has been instituted before another International Court for adjudication',[95] the Court observing that 'the same case' should not be 'brought before several international bodies'.[96] The African Commission on Human and Peoples' Rights (ACommHPR) can only consider non-State communications which '[d]o not deal with cases which have been settled by those States involved'.[97] This provision aims, according to the Commission, to avoid 'faulting member states twice for the same alleged violations of human rights',[98] indicating that 'for a matter to fall within [that provision's] scope... it should have involved the same parties, [and] the same issues'.[99] Any such settlement is also 'tak[en] into account' in determining whether individual applications to the African Court on Human and Peoples' Rights (ACtHPR) are admissible.[100] Finally, a claim before the Andean Court 'excludes the possibility of simultaneous recourse for the same purpose' to national courts,[101] while the Rules of the Southern African Development Community Tribunal (SADCT) allow a stay of proceedings if 'a national court is already [seized] of the matter and the same relief is sought'.[102]

Provisions such as these are designed 'to avoid a plurality of international proceedings relating to the same cases',[103] and bear a similarity—as tribunals have sometimes expressly acknowledged[104]—to principles of *res judicata* and/or *lis pendens*.[105] The *res judicata* principle precludes a party from relitigating a claim

[93] *S v Sweden* Doc CAT/C/59/D/691/2015 (CAT, 27 January 2017) [7.3].

[94] Eg, *Sierra v Spain* Doc E/C12/59/D/4/2014 (CESCR, 29 September 2016) [6.4]; *Vojnović v Croatia* Doc CCPR/C/112/D/2068/2011 (HRC, 30 October 2014) [6.2]. Cf Shany, *Competing* (n 4) 218–19, citing *i.a.* HRC, 'General Comment No. 24' (1994) UN Doc CCPR/C/21/Rev.1/Add.6 [14] ('legal right and... subject matter... identical'); nn 174ff.

[95] ECOWAS Protocol, art 4.

[96] *Koraou v Niger* (2008) AHRLR 182 (ECOWAS CJ) [51].

[97] AfCHPR, art 56(7). Generally Shany, *Competing* (n 4) 225; nn 313–17.

[98] *Okiring v Uganda* Comm 339/2007 (ACommHPR, August 2017) [66].

[99] *Gunme v Cameroon* (2009) AHRLR 9 (ACommHPR) [86]; also *Spilg v Botswana* (2011) AHRLR 3 (ACommHPR) [110].

[100] AfCHPR Protocol, art 6(2); Habib Gherari, 'African Mechanisms' in James Crawford and others (eds), *The Law of International Responsibility* (OUP 2010) 786.

[101] Cartagena Protocol, art 25, also art 31.

[102] SADCT Rules, r 60 (original apparently containing error ('ceased')).

[103] *Yukos* (n 85) [520]; *Karoussiotis v Portugal* ECHR 2011-II 15 [62]; similarly *Celniku v Greece* App 21449/04 (ECtHR, 5 July 2007) [39]; *Koraou* (n 96) [50]–[51]; *Kethusegile-Juru v SADC Parliamentary Forum* [2010] SADCT 2 [10]; also *Harkins* (n 85) [41]; *Kafkaris* (n 85) [67] ('ensure[s] ... finality'); Shany, *Competing* (n 4) 212.

[104] *Res judicata*: *Saramaka* (n 89) [56]; *Shaw* (n 89) [22], [37], [45]; *SINTRAOFAN v Colombia* Pet 1470-05, Rep 140/09 (IACHR, 30 December 2009) [75]; *Spilg* (n 99) [110]; *Sudan HRO v Sudan* (2009) AHRLR 153 (ACommHPR) [104]; *Okiring* (n 98) [65]. *Lis pendens*: *Garcia Fajardo v Nicaragua* Case 11381, Rep 14/97 (IACHR, 12 March 1997) [42]. Also *Koraou* (n 96) [52] (both); *VØ v Norway* Doc CCPR/C/25/D/168/1984 (HRC, 17 July 1985) [4.1] (*non bis in idem*).

[105] Gherari (n 100) 784 (AfCHPR provision 'stems from ... principle of *res judicata* ... found in other regional systems', referencing ECHR/AmCHR); Wehland (n 5) [6.47]; Zwart (n 43) 183; Fatsah

already judicially decided, other than through the mechanism of appeal.[106] It is premised on the desirability of finality in litigation,[107] in the interests of both the public and the defendant, with justice requiring that persons not be subjected to recurring claims.[108] The related *lis pendens* doctrine precludes multiple claims from being brought in parallel.[109]

Res judicata is recognised across domestic legal systems,[110] and as a general principle of international law.[111] It operates where a judicial tribunal has rendered a final decision on the merits of a claim,[112] and the second claim that follows shares three 'identities' with the first: identity of (i) cause of action; (ii) subject-matter or object; and (iii) parties.[113] The first and second require that the legal grounds, or rights, and claimed relief in each of the proceedings be the same.[114] The third requires that the same legal persons be a party to each of the claims.[115] Where the

Ouguergouz, *The African Charter on Human and Peoples' Rights* (Martinus Nijhoff 2003) 613–19; Shany, *Competing* (n 4) 212ff, 218 (ICCPR *lis pendens*), 223–25 (AmCHR/AfCHPR *res judicata*-like), cf 60, 213–16 (ECHR/UNCAT/CEDAW/ICPMW *electa una via*); similarly Shany, *Relations* (n 4) 156; Salles (n 17) 251 (fork-in-the-road), cf 252. Cf *X v Belgium* (1956) 24 ILR 391 (ECommHR) 392 (decisions not *res judicata*).

[106] Handley (n 16) [1.01]; ILA, 'InterimRep' (n 18) 36.

[107] Eg Shany, *Competing* (n 4) 22, 165, 223; Handley (n 16) [1.10]; Wehland (n 5) [4.56]; cf n103.

[108] Handley (n 16) [1.10]; Barnett (n 17) [1.13]; ILA, 'InterimRep' (n 18) 36; Lange (n 18) 4; Paul McDermott, *Res Judicata and Double Jeopardy* (Butterworths 1999) [3.01]–[3.09]; Shany, *Relations* (n 4) 160; August Reinisch, 'The Use and Limits of *Res Judicata* and *Lis Pendens* as Procedural Tools to Avoid Conflicting Dispute Settlement Outcomes' (2004) 3 LPICT 37, 43; Shany, *Competing* (n 4) 165; Hobér (n 26) 120; Wehland (n 5) [4.55]–[4.56]; Salles (n 17) 268; *Dallal* (n 5) 162.

[109] Shany, *Competing* (n 4) 22; Charles Brower and Paula Henin, 'Res Judicata' in Kinnear and others (n 25) 56.

[110] See ILA, 'InterimRep' (n 18) 36, 41–54; Hobér (n 26) Ch II; Barnett (n 17) [1.12] ('ancient precedents'); Reinisch (n 108) 43; *Delimitation of the Continental Shelf between Nicaragua and Colombia beyond 200 nautical miles from the Nicaraguan Coast (Nicaragua v Colombia) (Preliminary Objections)* [2016] ICJ Rep 100, 142–43 (Joint Diss Op); *Sooknanan v Medical Council Guyana* [2014] CCJ 18 [5] ('ancient legal principle').

[111] *Nicaragua v Colombia* (n 110) [58]; Bin Cheng, *General Principles of Law as Applied by International Courts and Tribunals* (Stevens & Sons 1953) 336; ILA, 'InterimRep' (n 18) 55–57; Vaughan Lowe, '*Res Judicata* and the Rule of Law in International Arbitration' (1996) 8 AfJICL 38, 39; Reinisch (n 108) 44–48; Chester Brown, *A Common Law of International Adjudication* (OUP 2007) 155; Shany, *Competing* (n 4) 245–46 (alternatively custom); Shany, *Relations* (n 4) 159–60; *Waste Management (Objection)* (n 4) [39]; *Apotex Holdings v US (Award)* ICSID Case No ARB(AF)/12/1 (25 August 2014) [7.11]. Cf *India–Measures Affecting the Automotive Sector–Panel Rep* (21 December 2001) WT/DS146/R; WT/DS175/R [7.55]–[7.103]; also *Iberdrola v Guatemala (Final Award)* PCA Case 2017–41 (24 August 2020) [256], discussed Damien Charlotin, 'Iberdrola Tribunal Applies Res Judicata ...' *IA Rep* (2 September 2020).

[112] Handley (n 16) [1.02]; Barnett (n 17) [1.18]–[1.34]; Shany, *Competing* (n 4) 22–23, 165.

[113] ILA, 'InterimRep' (n 18) 36; ILA, 'Final Report on Res Judicata and Arbitration' (2009) 25 Arb Int 67 [29]; *Nicaragua v Colombia* (n 110) [55] (parties, object, 'legal ground'), 143 (Joint Diss Op); Lowe (n 111) 40; Wehland (n 5) [6.52]; Joost Pauwelyn and Luiz Eduardo Salles, 'Forum Shopping Before International Tribunals: (Real) Concerns, (Im)Possible Solutions' (2009) 42 Corn ILJ 77, 103; Cheng (n 111) 339–40, 343–46 (doubting cause/object distinction); similarly *Apotex* (n 111) [7.13]–[7.16]; Shany, *Relations* (n 4) 133, 138; Shany, *Competing* (n 4) 24; Salles (n 17) 271–72; also *Iberdrola* (n 111) [256], [272]. Cf *Automotive* (n 516) [7.66].

[114] Reinisch (n 108) 62; also *Nicaragua v Colombia* (n 110) [55]; Shany, *Competing* (n 4) 25; Shany, *Relations* (n 4) 138–44.

[115] ILA, 'InterimRep' (n 18) 44; Wehland (n 5) [6.53]–[6.56]; Handley (n 16) [1.02]; also Shany, *Relations* (n 4) 133–35.

conditions are satisfied, the later claim is inadmissible.[116] Because *lis pendens* is of less clear status internationally,[117] but in any event requires the same identities,[118] the focus in this book is on *res judicata*.[119]

As foreshadowed, there are similarities between the requirements for *res judicata* (and/or *lis pendens*) to operate and those of the treaty-based provisions discussed above, with the application of each depending on the presence of comparable claim "identities".[120] Where the treaty-based provisions apply, it would likely therefore be unnecessary to consider whether *res judicata* might also operate.[121] However, not every treaty enabling individual claims contains such provisions, and, as noted, some such provisions only exclude simultaneous proceedings from being brought, and not consecutive claims.[122] Moreover, apart from the provisions of the AmCHR, the provisions outlined above prima facie restrict only claims brought by individuals, and not those brought on an interstate basis.[123]

Potential scope therefore remains for *res judicata* to operate as between overlapping individual and interstate claims, either as such[124] or, as certain bodies have recognised, as founding an abuse of process objection,[125] an objection explicitly provided for in several of the treaties establishing individual claims mechanisms.[126] This remains true in respect of those regimes discussed in Chapter 3 that expressly address overlapping individual and interstate claims.[127] Article 27 of the Convention on the Settlement of Investment Disputes between States and Nationals of Other States (ICSID), for instance, is unlikely to reflect custom,[128] and

[116] *Nicaragua v Colombia* (n 110) [48]; also *Iberdrola* (n 111) [245].

[117] Hobér (n 26) 325, 330–31; James Crawford, 'Chance, Order, Change: The Course of International Law' (2013) 365 RdC 9, 224; Wehland (n 5) [6.95]–[6.99]; Shany, *Relations* (n 4) 158–59; Salles (n 17) 277–81; cf Shany, *Competing* (n 4) 244.

[118] Salles (n 17) 277; Wehland (n 5) [4.82]; *Chevron and Texaco v Ecuador (Third Interim Award, Jurisdiction/Admissibility)* PCA Case 2009-23 (27 February 2012) [4.77].

[119] Additionally, as *lis pendens* operates only during the first proceedings, only *res judicata* permanently precludes a later claim: Vermeer-Künzli (n 53) 274; Shany, *Competing* (n 4) 212.

[120] nn 85–86, 89, 93–94, 99, 113–15; also Wehland (n 5) [6.52].

[121] cf Shany, *Competing* (n 4) 223.

[122] See Connors (n 83) 394; Shany, *Competing* (n 4) 218 (HRC); Salles (n 17) 252; eg, n 92.

[123] See Shany, *Competing* (n 4) 224; *Georgia v Russia (II)* App 38263/08 (ECtHR, 13 December 2011) [79]; cf *Cyprus v Turkey* (1996) 86A DR 104, 135.

[124] Similarly Salles (n 17) 267; Shany, *Competing* (n 4) 254; cf *Cyprus v Turkey (ECommHR)* (n 123) 134 (provision 'reflects ... basic legal principle'); *Durand and Ugarte v Peru* (1999) IACHR Ser C No 50 [45]–[49] (referencing *res judicata*, not art 47(d)).

[125] *Conde v Spain* Doc CCPR/C/92/D/1527/2006 (HRC, 1 April 2008) [4.2] (communication 'based on exactly the same facts' abusive); also *Hylton v Jamaica* Doc CCPR/C/57/D/600/1994 (HRC, 16 July 1996) [6.3]; *Agiza v Sweden* Doc CAT/C/34/D/233/2003 (CAT, 20 May 2005) [4.4], [9.2]; *Kethusegile-Juru* (n 103) [10] ('abuse of remedies through concurrent proceedings'). Generally Shany, *Relations* (n 4) 192–93; Shany, *Competing* (n 4) 258–59; Zwart (n 43) 164–68; Wehland (n 5) [7.29]–[7.52]; nn 4–5, 273, 289, 612–13. Cf *SPP v Egypt* (1985) 106 ILR 501 (ICSID) [63].

[126] See ECHR, art 35(3)(a); ICCPR Protocol, art 3; ICESCR Protocol, art 3(2)(f); CEDAW Protocol, art 4(2)(d); UNCAT, art 22(2); CRC Protocol, art 7(3); ICPMW, art 77(2); CPED, art 31(2)(b); CRPD Protocol, art 2(b); also AmCHR, art 47(c) ('out of order').

[127] Similarly Salles (n 17) 267.

[128] Ch 3, n 396.

in any event operates 'only from the moment that the consent' of the individual and State to have their claims determined before an international tribunal 'becomes mutual'.[129] Diplomatic protection might have already been commenced *before* this time, meaning the possibility of overlap would persist.[130]

IV. *Res judicata* and overlapping individual and interstate claims

An obvious question, however, is how the provisions discussed, or the principle of *res judicata*, even potentially operate to render the later of two overlapping individual or interstate claims inadmissible where there will, at the very least, be no identity of parties across those claims.[131] Indeed, the very inclusion of provisions like ICSID's article 27, expressly addressing overlapping interstate and individual claims,[132] might suggest that *res judicata* was not otherwise expected to operate,[133] except perhaps in the very particular circumstances addressed below.[134]

Even in diplomatic protection claims, which arise out of injury done to an individual,[135] as Chapter 3 outlined, a State is considered to institute proceedings in defence of its own rights, on a cause of action peculiar to it,[136] and for its own reparation.[137] This view, accepted 'for centuries',[138] gives diplomatic protection

[129] Paparinskis (n 24) 281, also 305–6, 312–13. Generally Christoph Schreuer, *The ICSID Convention: A Commentary* (2nd edn, CUP 2009) 424–25.

[130] Schreuer, *ICSID* (n 129) 425; Roberts (n 6) 44–45; Paparinskis (n 24) 312–15; Clovis Trevino, 'State-to-State Investment Treaty Arbitration and the Interplay with Investor-State Arbitration Under the Same Treaty' (2014) 5 JIDS 199, 214; Ben Juratowich, 'The Relationship between Diplomatic Protection and Investment Treaties' (2008) 23 ICSID Rev-FILJ 10, 21; ICSID, *Convention on the Settlement of Investment Disputes between States and Nationals of Other States: Documents Concerning the Origin and the Formulation of the Convention*, vol II (1968) 350.

[131] See Shany, *Relations* (n 4) 134; Roberts (n 6) 40; Paparinskis (n 24) 297, cf 298; Michael Ewing-Chow, 'Thesis, Antithesis and Synthesis: Investor Protection in BITs, WTO and FTAs' (2007) 30 UNSWLJ 548, 552; Joost Pauwelyn, 'Adding Sweeteners to Softwood Lumber: The WTO-NAFTA "Spaghetti Bowl" Is Cooking' (2006) 9 JIEL 197, 200–1; Hobér (n 26) 376; Brown (n 111) 155; Michele Potestà, 'Towards a Greater Role for State-to-State Arbitration in the Architecture of Investment Treaties?' in Shaheeza Lalani and Rodrigo Polanco Lazo (eds), *The Role of the State in Investor-State Arbitration* (Brill Nijhoff 2015) 264; Brownlie (n 55) 51; cf Nollkaemper (n 42) 251.

[132] Ch 3(I)(A).

[133] cf *Argentina—Definitive Anti-Dumping Duties on Poultry from Brazil—Panel Rep* (22 April 2003) WT/DS241R [7.38], cited Shany, *Relations* (n 4) 156; Salles (n 17) 259; cf Wehland (n 5) [6.49] (ICCPR); Shany, *Competing* (n 4) 254; Schreuer, *ICSID* (n 129) 421 (interstate/investor–State parties separate). Further: Shany, quoted Ch 3, n 9.

[134] n 344 (subrogation).

[135] Ch 3, nn 43ff.

[136] Shany, *Competing* (n 4) 36, citing *Mavrommatis* (n 313) 11; also Shany, *Relations* (n 4) 136, 140–41; Borchard (n 54) 799; Vermeer-Künzli (n 53) 277–78; *Barcelona Traction* (n 23) [79]; Ch 3, nn 71–86.

[137] Ch 3, nn 157–58; *Chórzow (Merits)* (n 63) 28, discussed Anne Peters, *Beyond Human Rights: The Legal Status of the Individual in International Law* (Jonathan Huston tr, CUP 2016) 171; Chittharanjan Amerasinghe, *Diplomatic Protection* (OUP 2008) 67 (*DP*), also 22; Chittharanjan Amerasinghe, *Local Remedies in International Law* (2nd edn, CUP 2004) 49 (*LR*); ILC, 'Draft Articles on Diplomatic Protection with Commentaries' (2006) 2(2) ILCYB 22 (DADP), 97–98.

[138] John Dugard, 'First Report on Diplomatic Protection' (2000) 2(1) ILCYB 205 [62].

claims a 'qualitatively different character' to individual claims arising from the same circumstances.[139] Accordingly, the PCIJ considered that an individual's restitution claim before the German-Polish MAT, and an interstate diplomatic protection claim concerning a convention's 'interpretation and application', were neither 'identical actions', nor brought by the same parties, for *lis pendens* purposes,[140] despite concerning, in part, the same property.[141] As Brownlie notes, albeit vis-à-vis domestic and international proceedings, 'although the subject-matter may be substantially the same, the parties will not be, and the issues will have a very different aspect'.[142] Nonetheless, this chapter argues that the three *res judicata* 'identities' may be applied adaptably,[143] such that the principle *might* operate vis-à-vis at least certain overlapping interstate diplomatic protection and individual claims.[144] In the following sections, each 'identity' is considered in turn to draw out principles suggestive of this more adaptable approach, which is then applied to overlapping individual and interstate claims.

A. Cause of action

Cause of action identity requires that the rights allegedly breached in two claims be the same.[145] The rights breached in overlapping individual and interstate claims may indeed be indistinguishable.[146] However, at least strictly speaking, this requires two elements to be present. First, the relevant obligations must have the same basis, for claims brought under different treaties, or treaty and custom respectively, do not share grounds.[147] The individual claims with which this book is

[139] Shany, *Competing* (n 4) 36; also Shany, *Relations* (n 4) 42–43, 136, 140–41.

[140] *Certain German Interests in Polish Upper Silesia* [1925] PCIJ Rep Ser A No 6, 20 (additionally 'not courts of the same character'), also 19; Shany, *Competing* (n 4) 26, 231–32, 239–40; Shany, *Relations* (n 4) 42–43; Hobér (n 26) 325. Similarly *The 'Camouco' (Panama v France) (Prompt Release)* [2000] ITLOS Rep 10 [55]–[58], discussed Shany, *Relations* (n 4) 62–63; Nollkaemper (n 42) 34; *Bužau-Nehoiași (Allemagne c Roumanie)* (1939) III UNRIAA 1827, 1836, cited Cheng (n 111) 337; Christoph Schreuer, *Decisions of International Institutions Before Domestic Courts* (Oceana 1981) 330 and authorities (*lis pendens* inapplicability between MATs and domestic courts); *Chemins de Fer du Nord* (1929) 5 AD 498 (Franco-German MAT) 499; Shany, *Competing* (n 4) 242.

[141] *Silesia* (n 140) 19; *Chórzow (Merits)* (n 63) 26–28; Amerasinghe, *DP* (n 137) 17; cf Shany, *Competing* (n 4) 231–32.

[142] Brownlie (n 55) 51; also André Nollkaemper, 'Conversations among Courts: Domestic and International Adjudicators' in Cesare Romano, Karen Alter, and Yuval Shany (eds), *The Oxford Handbook of International Adjudication* (OUP 2014) 529–30.

[143] Similarly Salles (n 17) 246–47 ('substantive'/'formal'/'strict' identity options), 271–77 (*res judicata* depends on 'identity' elasticity); Shany, *Relations* (n 4) 133–44, 160; Reinisch (n 108) 55–72; cf Shany, *Competing* (n 4) 24–26.

[144] Section V(A)–(B); similarly Vermeer-Künzli (n 53) 277.

[145] nn 113–14.

[146] See nn 151–59. Cf Shany, *Relations* (n 4) 136; Salles (n 17) 273–74 (unlikely); also Dugard (n 138) [69], n 152.

[147] Reinisch (n 108) 64–65, 68–70, discussing *Mox Plant Case (Ireland v UK) (Provisional Measures)* [2001] ITLOS Rep 95 [50]–[51], also Shany, *Relations* (n 4) 7–8, 111; Hobér (n 26) 305–11, 344–55, discussing *CME v Czech Republic (Final Award)* (2003) 9 ICSID Rep 264 [432]–[433] and *Lauder* (n

concerned are treaty or domestic law-based.[148] As interstate domestic law claims are unusual,[149] identity as between the rights invoked in overlapping individual and interstate claims is only therefore likely where States invoke responsibility under the same treaties as individuals.

Second, the term 'right' denotes a duty, owed to the holder, not to violate it.[150] Cause of action identity requires that two claims concern the same entity's rights, as causes differ where they allege breach of rights held by distinct persons.[151] Although not addressing *res judicata* as such, the ILC's Special Rapporteur on Diplomatic Protection noted, vis-à-vis overlapping claims, that:

> If the holder of the right is the State, it may enforce its right irrespective of whether the individual himself has a remedy before an international forum. If . . . the individual is the holder of the right, it becomes possible to argue that the State's right is purely residual and procedural, that is, a right that may only be exercised in the absence of a remedy pertaining to the individual.[152]

While one can understand the policy basis behind such a suggestion, as Chapters 1 and 3 demonstrated, in all interstate claims, including diplomatic protection and human rights claims, a State invokes breach of obligations owed to itself.[153] States never, therefore, exercise merely 'procedural' rights to enforce obligations owed to individuals, but always claim for breach of their own rights.[154] Whether or not

33) [165], [171], [177]; Salles (n 17) 246, 273–75; Wehland (n 5) [6.124], [6.127]; Roberts (n 6) 40; Shany, *Competing* (n 4) 27; ILA, 'InterimRep' (n 18) 57–58; Pauwelyn and Salles (n 113) 103–4.

[148] Ch 2(I).

[149] Ch 2, n 241.

[150] See Wesley Newcomb Hohfeld, *Fundamental Legal Conceptions as Applied in Judicial Reasoning and Other Legal Essays* (Yale UP 1923) 38; Ch 1, n 95, discussed, eg, Robert McCorquodale, 'The Individual and the International Legal System' in Malcolm Evans (ed), *International Law* (4th edn, OUP 2014) 285; Jason Varuhas, *Damages and Human Rights* (Hart 2016) 16–17; Bart Smit Duijzentkunst, 'Of Rights and Powers: Waiving Investment Treaty Protection' *EJIL:Talk!* (9 December 2013); Federica Paddeu, *Justification and Excuse in International Law* (CUP 2018) 103–5; generally Matthew Kramer, NE Simmonds and Hillel Steiner, *A Debate over Rights: Philosophical Enquiries* (OUP 2000), eg, 245–47, cf 9; Jean Thomas, *Public Rights, Private Relations* (OUP 2015) 82, 88–91; Nollkaemper (n 42) 95, 98–99; Peters (n 137) 167–69, 172–73, discussing *ARSIWA*, 209–10, 192–93; Bernhard Graefrath, 'Responsibility and Damages Caused: Relationship between Responsibility and Damages' (1984) 185 RdC 9, 47; cf Crawford, 'ThirdRep' (n 12) [84]–[85]; James Crawford, 'Multilateral Rights and Obligations in International Law' (2006) 319 RdC 325, 436–37.

[151] See n 136; Roberts (n 6) 40; cf n 377; Douglas, 'Hybrid' (n 26) 182; also Vermeer-Künzli (n 53) 277–78; discussion nn 559ff; *Caratube* (n 5) [495]. Cf Paparinskis (n 24) 297–98 (same primary rule breached).

[152] Dugard (n 138) [69], referenced Crawford, 'Revisited' (n 26) 141; Diana Cucos, 'The Position of the Individual in Post-Codification Diplomatic Protection' (2014) 5 CYBP & PIL 181, 185.

[153] Ch 1(III)(A); Ch 3(II)(A)–(B),(III) and authorities, particularly *ARSIWA*, arts 42, 48; Giorgio Gaja, 'States Having an Interest in Compliance with the Obligation Breached' in Crawford and others, *Responsibility* (n 100) 957–58; Nollkaemper (n 42) 95; Bruno Simma and Dirk Pulkowski, '*Leges Speciales* and Self-Contained Regimes' in Crawford and others, *Responsibility* (n 100) 160–61; Annemarieke Vermeer-Künzli, 'A Matter of Interest: Diplomatic Protection and State Responsibility *Erga Omnes*' (2007) 56 ICLQ 553, 571, 579–80.

[154] See Paparinskis (n 72) 640–41; Dugard (n 138) [73] ('codifie[d] ... in its traditional form'), cf [65]–[66]; cf Crawford, 'ThirdRep' (n 12) [85]; Roberts (n 6) 33–34; Mohamed Bennouna, 'Preliminary

the rights—and alleged breach—in overlapping individual and interstate claims are the same therefore turns on whether the individual is invoking its own or the State's rights.[155] Human rights, for instance, are held by individuals,[156] meaning that interstate claims for their breach necessarily invoke rights that have a 'parallel' existence to, but are not the same as, those invoked in individual claims.[157] In other claims, an individual may likewise conceivably claim for breach of its own rights (so-called 'direct' claims), or alternatively may invoke responsibility for breach of obligations owed to the State alone (so-called 'derivative' claims).[158] Only in the latter case would the breach alleged by individuals and States be precisely the same.[159]

The question of whose rights are being invoked in overlapping claims may be of importance for *res judicata* purposes. Thus, considering whether two individual claims were 'substantially the same' as the interstate *Avena* proceedings, the Inter-American Commission on Human Rights (IACHR) observed that:

> the jurisdiction of the ICJ differs from that of the IACHR in significant respects, particularly insofar as the ICJ deals with interstate litigation whereas the Commission deals with petitions brought by individuals against states, *and insofar as the rights at issue and the remedies provided by the Commission correspond directly to the individual presumably concerned.*[160]

Report on Diplomatic Protection' (1998) 2(1) ILCYB 309 [49]; Peters (n 137) 389; Nobuyuki Kato, 'The Role of Diplomatic Protection in the Implementation Process of Public Interests' in Teruo Komori and Karel Wellens (eds), *Public Interest Rules of International Law: Towards Effective Implementation* (Ashgate 2009) 192–93.

[155] cf Roberts (n 6) 40, 43; Nollkaemper (n 42) 98–99. See n 158.

[156] Eg Nollkaemper (n 42) 100; Roberts (n 6) 32; DADP, 25–26; Ch 3, n 78.

[157] Peters (n 137) 169; ILC, 'Summary Records of the Meetings of the Fiftieth Session' (1998) 1 ILCYB 1, 27 (Brownlie); similarly ILC, 'Summary Records of the Meetings of the Fifty-Third Session' (2001) 1 ILCYB 1, 131 (Crawford); Roberts (n 6) 33–35; Simma and Pulkowski (n 153) 159. Cf Paparinskis (n 24) 287, 295; Parlett (n 5) 112; Ch 1, nn 130–33, 162–63.

[158] See Douglas, 'Hybrid' (n 26) 163–64 ('derivative' approach), 183–84 ('direct'); Douglas, *Investment* (n 26) 11–17, 32–38; Paparinskis (n 24) 288–92, 334–35; Paparinskis (n 72) 622–27; Parlett (n 5) 108–12; Peters (n 137) 284–317 ('procedural'/'substantive'/'direct'/'derivative' rights), particularly 301–15 and authorities; Roberts (n 6) 36–39; Anthea Roberts, 'Triangular Treaties: The Extent and Limits of Investment Treaty Rights' (2015) 56 Harv ILJ 353, 355–56; Smit Duijzentkunst (n 150); Hege Elisabeth Kjos, *Applicable Law in Investor-State Arbitration: The Interplay Between National and International Law* (OUP 2013) 92, 225; cf Ole Spiermann, 'Individual Rights, State Interests and the Power to Waive ICSID Jurisdiction under Bilateral Investment Treaties' (2004) 20 Arb Int 179, 185, referencing James Crawford, 'The ILC's Articles on Responsibility of States for Internationally Wrongful Acts: A Retrospect' (2002) 96 AJIL 874, 888 (regardless of substantive BIT rights, 'investor ... opts in ... as a secondary right holder'). The issue is generally regarded as turning on treaty interpretation: eg ibid 887–88; Douglas, *Investment* (n 26) 34–35; Kjos (n 158) 225; Nollkaemper (n 42) 98–106; Peters (n 137) 315–17; Parlett (n 5) 108–9, 112–13; Paparinskis (n 72) 626. Further Ch 6, nn 92–97.

[159] cf Douglas, 'Hybrid' (n 26) 182; Roberts (n 6) 40, 42 ('interdependent'); Paparinskis (n 24) 297, 312.

[160] *Rodriguez v US* Pet 1672-11, Rep 63/12 (IACHR, 29 March 2012) [55] (emphasis added), also quoted *Arias v US* Pet 15-12, Rep 73/12 (IACHR, 17 July 2012) [44]. Generally Ch 2, nn 200–1.

Nonetheless, complete cause of action identity may be unnecessary for *res judicata*, and provisions reflecting its elements, to apply.[161] Thus, while 'cause of action' can be narrowly defined as turning on a given legal provision or basis, it may also refer broadly to the facts giving rise to relief.[162] It thus often suffices for *res judicata* to operate—at least under common law—if claims are the same in essentials, even if they could be brought under separate legal heads.[163] Indeed, parties are precluded, through 'issue estoppel' (sometimes also called 'collateral estoppel' in the literature),[164] from re-litigating essential factual or legal *issues* 'distinctly raised and finally decided in earlier proceedings'.[165] This minimises the necessity that the causes of action be identical across two claims.[166]

Certain international case law reflects this non-formalistic approach.[167] One tribunal considering alleged violations of UNCLOS determined, for instance, that it would be 'artificial' to treat disputes under two separate treaty regimes as 'distinct'.[168] Human rights tribunals also overwhelmingly accept that provisions precluding multiple claims can apply when separate decisions are rendered

[161] Shany, *Competing* (n 4) 26 ('degree of flexibility'), 133; Reinisch (n 108) 68; Lowe (n 111) 41; Shany, *Relations* (n 4) 141–42, 160; Burkhard Hess, 'The Private-Public Divide in International Dispute Resolution' (2018) 388 RdC 49, 245; *Vivendi v Argentina (Jurisdiction)* ICSID Case No ARB/97/3 (14 November 2005) [74]; Wehland (n 5) [6.87]–[6.88]; Salles (n 17) 273–74; Crawford, 'Chance' (n 117) 224; cf Roberts (n 6) 40, 43.

[162] See discussion Hobér (n 26) 276; Wehland (n 5) [1.16]–[1.18], [6.85]–[6.87], [6.122]–[6.130]; also Shany, *Competing* (n 4) 25–26; Barnett (n 17) [4.86]ff and authorities; McDermott (n 108) [6.21] ff; Reinisch (n 108) 70; *Trawl Industries v Effem Foods* (1992) 36 FCR 406, 418; Alexander Layton and others, *European Civil Practice*, vol 1 (2nd edn, Sweet & Maxwell 2004) [22.008], cf [22.011], referencing *The Tatry* [1994] ECR I-5460 [38]–[39]; *Iberdrola* (n 111) [283]–[285].

[163] Handley (n 16) [7.05]–[7.06], citing *Trawl* (n 162) 422 (statutory/tortious claims same in 'substance'); Lange (n 18) 124–25; Barnett (n 17) [4.86]ff; *Garraway v Williams* [2011] CCJ 12 [14] ('essentially the same'). Cf McDermott (n 108) [6.04]–[6.07], [6.14]–[6.15], [6.32].

[164] Strictly, this is a different US doctrine disregarding party identity in certain cases: Barnett (n 17) [5.92]–[5.98]; ILA, 'FinalRep' (n 113) [59]. However, the two are sometimes used interchangeably: *Apotex* (n 111) [7.18]; eg Roberts (n 6) 43; William Dodge, 'National Courts and International Arbitration: Exhaustion of Remedies and Res Judicata Under Chapter Eleven of NAFTA' (2000) 23 Hast I & CLR 357, 366–67; ILA, 'InterimRep' (n 18) 46, 48; Salles (n 17) 272–73; Shany, *Competing* (n 4) 165.

[165] ILA, 'InterimRep' (n 18) 42, also 47, cf 50, 63; see *Apotex* (n 111) [7.17]–[7.23]; *Tokios Tokelės v Ukraine (Award)* ICSID Case No ARB/02/18 (29 June 2007) [98]; *RSM Production v Grenada (Award)* ICSID Case No ARB/10/6 (10 December 2010) [7.1.1]–[7.1.2]; *Caratube* (n 5) [460]–[465]; generally Handley (n 16) Ch 8; Barnett (n 17) Ch 5; Shany, *Competing* (n 4) 23, 28, 165; Brower and Henin (n 109) 56; Wehland (n 5) [6.73], [6.116], [6.121].

[166] Barnett (n 17) [5.05]; Lange (n 18) 29–30; Salles (n 17) 273; Lowe (n 111) 41–42. Generally on both reasoning and *dispositif* being *res judicata*: Lowe (n 111) 39–40; Cheng (n 111) 348–50; ILA, 'InterimRep' (n 18) 51–52, 59–60, discussing *Delimitation of the Continental Shelf (UK v France)* (1978) XVIII UNRIAA 271 [28], and *Pious Fund (US v Mexico)* (1902) IX UNRIAA 1; *CME v Czech Republic (Schreuer and Reinisch Expert Opinion on Quantum)* UNCITRAL (20 June 2002) [67]–[70]; *Apotex* (n 111) [7.23]–[7.32].

[167] See Reinisch (n 108) 68, 71; Salles (n 17) 247; Shany, *Competing* (n 4) 26; Shany, *Relations* (n 4) 114–16, cf 7, 111–14, 139–44; *Libananco Holdings v Turkey (Award)* ICSID Case No ARB/06/8 (31 August 2011) [548] ('strict'); Roberts (n 6) 40.

[168] *Southern Bluefin Tuna Case (Australia/NZ v Japan) (Jurisdiction/Admissibility)* (2000) 39 ILM 1359 [54], discussed, eg, Reinisch (n 108) 66; *Schreuer/Reinisch Opinion* (n 166) [52]–[55]; ILA, 'InterimRep' (n 18) 57; Shany, *Relations* (n 4) 8, 119; Shany, *Competing* (n 4) 236–37; Salles (n 17) 261–62. Cf *Caratube* (n 5) [497] ('not artificial').

pursuant to different treaties.[169] For the ECtHR, for instance, a 'complaint is characterised by the facts alleged in it and not merely by the legal grounds or arguments relied on'.[170] Article 35(2)(b) of the ECHR, preventing reconsideration of matters 'substantially the same',[171] was therefore engaged where complaints were previously brought before various other fora,[172] including before tribunals considering BIT claims.[173] Similarly, various UN treaty bodies, which are precluded from rehearing the '*same* matter',[174] have accepted that ECtHR decisions can render claims inadmissible as concerning 'the same substantive rights',[175] as can Inter-American procedures.[176] The IACtHR likewise considers that it is 'the behavior or the event that is a violation of some human right' that is relevant.[177] It has accepted that previous consideration by different bodies under different treaties may render applications inadmissible,[178] while the ACommHPR has acknowledged the preclusive effect of UN treaty body decisions.[179]

Issue estoppel has also gained acceptance in international law, one investment tribunal observing that '[i]t is clear that past international tribunals have applied forms of issue estoppel, without necessarily using the term'.[180] That tribunal rejected, as *res judicata*, an attempt by the claimants to relitigate issues previously decided, though the claims related to similar, though not identical, alleged

[169] *Schreuer/Reinisch Opinion* (n 166) [51], [59]–[62], [73]; Reinisch (n 108) 70–72; cf n 175.

[170] *Khadzhimuradov* (n 86) [80]; similarly *Previti v Italy*, App 45291/06 (ECtHR, 8 December 2009) [293]; also Reinisch (n 108) 71.

[171] nn 84–86. Noting the treaty already references matters '*substantially* the same': Shany, *Competing* (n 4) 26 (emphasis added). But cf n 174.

[172] Generally Shany, *Competing* (n 4) 25–26, 214; Reinisch (n 108) 71–72; eg *Vojnović* (ECHR) (n 85) [31]–[32] (HRC 'essentially the same complaints'); similarly *Pauger* (n 85) 174; *Peraldi v France* App 2096/05 (ECtHR, 7 April 2009) 11–13 (WGAD); *FHSESB v Greece* App 72808/10 (ECtHR, 6 December 2011) [41]–[44] (ILO FOAC); also *Karoussiotis* (n 103) [64] (EC), cf [76].

[173] *LeBridge* (n 83) [26] (ECHR/BIT proceedings 'same in substance'), discussed Jarrod Hepburn, 'European Court of Human Rights Dismisses Investor Claim …' *IA Rep* (30 April 2018); also *Yukos* (n 85) [524] ('similarities in … subject-matters'), cf [524]–[526] (parties different).

[174] nn 90–92 (emphasis added); see Salles (n 17) 253–57 (similar standards to ECtHR despite textual differences). Cf n 171.

[175] *NB v Russia* Doc CAT/C/56/D/577/2013 (CAT, 25 November 2015) [8.2]; similarly *Vojnović (HRC)* (n 94) [6.2]; *Crippa v France* Doc CCPR/C/85/D/993-995/2001 (HRC, 28 October 2005) [6.6] (no 'substantial difference', 'provisions … sufficiently close'); *Kollar v Austria* (2003) 8 Sel Dec HRC 21 [8.6] ('content and scope … largely converge'). Cf *Lederbauer v Austria* Doc CCPR/C/90/D/1454/2006 (HRC, 13 July 2007) [7.3] ('differ in substance'); generally Shany, *Competing* (n 4) 27, 216, cf 216–19; Salles (n 17) 254–57. However, the HRC—which is only barred from hearing the same matter *simultaneously* as another body (n 92)—sometimes admits cases previously considered elsewhere: see Shany, *Competing* (n 4) 61, 254 (undermining *res judicata*); cf Wehland (n 5) [6.47]–[6.49]; Zwart (n 43) 177–78; *Smirnova* (n 45) [9.2]; *Prince v South Africa* Doc CCPR/C/91/D/1474/2006 (HRC, 31 October 2007) [6.2] ('clear wording' of art 5(2)(a) 'militates against' broader application).

[176] *Acuna v Venezuela* Doc CCPR/C/65/D/739/1997 (HRC, 25 March 1999) [5.2]; *X v Canada* Doc CAT/C/15/D/26/1995 (CAT, 20 November 1995) [3].

[177] *Ricardo* (n 89) [55] (though vis-à-vis 'object'), referencing *Durand* (n 124) [43].

[178] Eg, *Shaw* (n 89) [37]–[46] (HRC). Cf *Ricardo* (n 89) [56] (ILO/IACHR different 'legal grounds').

[179] *Gabre-Salassie v Ethiopia* Comm 301/2005 (ACommHPR, 2011) [114]–[116].

[180] *Apotex* (n 111) [7.18], referencing *inter alia RSM* (n 165), see [7.1.2] (parties had 'not disputed that the doctrine of collateral estoppel is now well established as a general principle of law applicable in the international courts and tribunals').

'investments'.[181] It observed that *res judicata*—and the consequent bringing to an end of litigation, minimising the time and cost involved—would be rendered 'meaningless' if claimants could 'simply reformulat[e] their claims and arguments' in a new case.[182]

Indeed, although having distinct legal bases, some tribunals have considered claims the same across the international-domestic divide.[183] At least one tribunal did so vis-à-vis cases brought before a national court and an MAT.[184] Similarly, while most investment tribunals have regarded contractually and treaty-based claims as different for fork-in-the-road clause purposes,[185] one tribunal considered such claims, brought before domestic and international tribunals respectively, as the same, with the 'claimed entitlements hav[ing] the same normative source'[186] and 'fundamental basis'.[187] Another tribunal has more recently taken the same approach.[188] More generally, as one tribunal observed, '[investment] tribunals do not reopen the municipal law decisions of competent *fora*, absent a denial of justice'.[189] As international claims may depend on the existence of domestic rights,[190] such acceptance of other tribunals' determinations on domestic law can dispose of later treaty-based claims.[191] Finally, the ECOWAS Court has accepted the *res judicata*

[181] *Apotex* (n 111) [7.59]–[7.61].
[182] ibid [7.59].
[183] cf nn 140–42; also *Iberdrola* (n 111) [282]–[283] (grounds relied on, not tribunal's characterisation).
[184] *Banque Meyer* (1923) 3 TAM 639 (Franco-German MAT) 642, cited Cheng (n 111) 337. Similarly *Popanastassoglou v Bulgaria* (1924) 2 ILR 376 (Greco-Bulgarian MAT) 377; also *Waste Management (Award)* (n 14) [29] ('identical subjects').
[185] Generally Christoph Schreuer, 'Interaction of International Tribunals and Domestic Courts in Investment Law' in Arthur Rovine (ed), *Contemporary Issues in International Arbitration and Mediation* (Martinus Nijhoff 2011) 78–79; Hobér (n 26) 384–88; Wehland (n 5) [3.140]; eg, *Toto Costruzioni v Lebanon (Jurisdiction)* ICSID Case No ARB/07/12 (8 September 2009) [211]; *CMS Gas v Argentina (Jurisdiction)* (2003) 7 ICSID Rep 494 [80]; *Desert Line Projects v Yemen (Award)* ICSID Case No ARB/05/17 (6 February 2008) [136]–[138]; also *Helnan International Hotels v Egypt (Award)* ICSID Case No ARB/05/19 (7 June 2008) [124]–[125]; *Fraport v Philippines (Order No 1)* ICSID Case No ARB/11/12 (17 May 2012) [81]–[84]; *Caratube* (n 5) [495]; *SGS v Pakistan (Jurisdiction)* (2003) 18 ICSID Rev-FILJ 307 [182] Cf authorities Ch 5, n 73; and, accepting contractual *res judicata*: *Desert Line* (n 185) [204]; *Ampal-American Israel v Egypt (Liability and Loss)* ICSID Case No ARB/12/11 (21 February 2017) [259]; *Hochtief* (n 14) [9] (Op Thomas); *Occidental* (n 14) [51]–[63]; generally Brower and Henin (n 109) 59.
[186] *Pantechniki v Albania (Award)* ICSID Case No ARB/07/21 (28 July 2009) [62].
[187] ibid [67], discussed, eg, Salles (n 17) 249–50; Wehland (n 5) [3.126]; Lee Steven and Nicole Thornton, 'Two Roads-Two Tribunals: Recent "Fork-in-the-Road" Interpretations' *Kluwer Arbitration Blog* (16 December 2009); similarly *Malicorp v Egypt (Award)* ICSID Case No ARB/08/18 (31 January 2011) [103]; also *Vivendi v Argentina (Award)* ICSID Case No ARB/97/3 (21 November 2000) [78], discussed Shany, *Relations* (n 4) 64–66; Kjos (n 158) 110–11. Cf *Chevron (TIA)* (n 118) [4.76] ('unlikely ... triple identity test will be satisfied' vis-à-vis national/international claims), [4.77]; *Libananco* (n 167) [548].
[188] *Supervisíon y Control v Costa Rica (Award)* ICSID Case No ARB/12/4 (18 January 2017) [308]–[310], also [315]–[318].
[189] *RSM* (n 165) [7.1.11].
[190] Ch 3, nn 65–68.
[191] As in *RSM* (n 165): see [7.2.1], [7.2.2]–[7.2.25], also [7.1.12]–[7.1.13] discussing *Helnan* (n 185) [163].

effect of domestic decisions vis-à-vis claims under the ECOWAS treaty where the protected rights in the two claims are 'analogous' and the cases 'essentially the same'.[192]

Good reasons exist, even putting aside questions of identity, to be wary of *res judicata* operating as between domestic and international courts, including because a State's organs should not be able to conclusively determine that State's compliance with international law.[193] Indeed, the international/domestic distinction explains, in part, the PCIJ's decision, noted above, that *lis pendens* was inapplicable as between individual and interstate claims.[194] Nonetheless, the cases suggest that—at least where party identity is present—international tribunals are prepared to compare causes of action, domestic and international, in a 'substantive' rather than strict sense.[195]

Most importantly for present purposes, the same approach to the identity of causes of action appears applicable vis-à-vis overlapping individual and interstate claims. Thus, the IACHR, in two individual claims, accepted that 'the basis for the claim before the Commission is essentially the same, and concerns the same alleged victim' as in the interstate *Avena* case,[196] suggesting that cause of action identity could subsist even where claims are brought by different persons under different treaties in different fields of law.[197] In three other cases, the Commission determined that claims concerned 'substantive issues that are distinct',[198] but this was apparently because *Avena* concerned obligations under the Vienna Convention on Consular Relations (VCCR), while the individual claims alleged violations of 'due process' and 'fair trial' rights.[199]

Similarly, Ethiopia and Eritrea objected, under the relevant provision of the African Charter on Human and Peoples' Rights (AfCHPR), to an individual application before the ACommHPR, arguing that they had agreed to settle the conflict-related claims between themselves before the EECC.[200] The Commission observed

[192] *Tasheku v Nigeria* Case ECW/CCJ/RUL/12/12 (ECOWAS CJ, 12 June 2012) [13]–[16], [18]–[19]; similarly *Umar v Nigeria* Case ECW/CCJ/JUD/17/12 (ECOWAS CJ, 14 December 2012) [19]. Cf Antonios Tzanakopoulos, 'Domestic Courts in International Law: The International Judicial Function of National Courts' (2011) 34 Loy LAI & CLR 133, 143–44, 149; Nollkaemper (n 42) 9, 44, 247–49.

[193] See Dodge (n 164) 368–70; Reinisch (n 108) 51; Shany, *Relations* (n 4) 2–5, 32–33, 79–94, 162–63; Nollkaemper (n 42) 34, 47, 245, 255; *Chevron and Texaco v Ecuador (Decision on Track IB)* PCA Case 2009-23 (12 March 2015) [144], quoting *Fraport v Philippines (Annulment)* ICSID Case No ARB/03/25 (23 December 2010) [242]; *Inceysa Vallisoletane v El Salvador (Award)* ICSID Case No ARB/03/26 (2 August 2006) [213]; *Indústria Nacional de Alimentos v Peru (Annulment)* ICSID Case No ARB/03/4 (13 August 2007) [87]; also *Waste Management (Award)* (n 14) 66 (Diss Op Highet).

[194] n 140, discussed Shany, *Competing* (n 4) 26, 232; Shany, *Relations* (n 4) 42–44.

[195] Eg n175; generally nn 163ff; Wehland (n 5) [6.130]; also Shany, *Relations* (n 4) 160–61.

[196] *Rodriguez* (n 160) [55], also quoted *Arias* (n 160) [44].

[197] See Ch 2, nn 200–1.

[198] *Fierro v US* Case 11331 Rep 99/03 (IACHR, 29 December 2003) [57]; *Medellin v US* Case 12644, Rep 90/09 (IACHR, 7 August 2009) [104]; *Moreno Ramos v US* Pet 4446/02, Rep 61/03 (IACHR, 10 October 2003) [53]. Also Shany, *Relations* (n 4) 139.

[199] *Fierro* (n 198) [57]–[58]; *Medellin* (n 198) [104]–[105]; *Ramos* (n 198) [53]–[54].

[200] *Interights v Eritrea and Ethiopia* (2003) AHRLR 74 [40], [49]–[51]. See Ch 2, n 208.

'that the matters brought before it, are matters that have been placed before the [EECC] which can therefore adequately deal with [them]'.[201] As the EECC would address 'all the issues before the African Commission',[202] it suspended the case, only to 'reopen the matter' if the EECC failed to 'fully address the human rights violations contained herein'.[203] The ACommHPR thus apparently accepted that the EECC claims, which were overwhelmingly interstate, not individual,[204] and largely addressed violations of international humanitarian law, rather than human rights, nonetheless concerned the same subject-matter as human rights actions brought on behalf of individuals.[205]

Finally, the CCJ declared, in a case concerned with potential overlap between individual claims and the State of nationality's intervention, that it:

> does not consider that the nature of a claim alters radically dependent upon whether it is brought by a national herself or by her State on her behalf. The character of the remedies sought from or given by the Court may vary but irrespective of which entity institutes proceedings the inquiry of the Court remains, at least in part, focused on whether alleged conduct . . . constitutes a violation of the Revised Treaty.[206]

In sum, while the cause of action identity requirement is more obviously satisfied where the parties are relying on exactly the same rights in making their claims,[207] it may suffice that those rights, and the underlying facts, are substantially similar.[208] As will be shown, the overlap is most likely to be apparent between individual and interstate diplomatic protection claims.[209]

B. Object

Turning to the 'object' identity requirement, while claims for the same reparation prima facie evidence a common object,[210] identity may also be present even if two

[201] ibid [57].
[202] ibid [60].
[203] ibid [61]; also Gherari (n 100) 785.
[204] Ch 2, n 47.
[205] While the EECC also considered human rights violations (*Eritrea* (n 15) [22]), EECC claims were not regarded as brought for breach of the AfCHPR; rather Eritrea 'made claims' which '*also* constitute' such violations, and Ethiopia ones which presumably could fall thereunder: see *Interights* (n 200) [49]–[50] (emphasis added). Consistently: *Ethiopia's Claim 5 (Partial Award)* (2004) XXVI UNRIAA 249 [27] (no 'particular reliance' on AfCHPR); also Murphy, Kidane, and Snider (n 78) 310; Sotomayer (n 83) 4.
[206] *Myrie v Barbados* [2012] CCJ 3 [23]. Cf n151.
[207] nn 146ff.
[208] nn 161ff. Cf *Rosneft v Council* Case T-715/14 (13 September 2018) (EUGC) [95]–[99] (differing procedural contexts).
[209] Section (V)(A) and authorities; similarly Nollkaemper, n 384; Shany, quoted Ch 3, n 9.
[210] See Hobér (n 26) 272–73, 303; Wehland (n 5) [6.65], [6.68]; Salles (n 17) 275; Reinisch (n 108) 62; *Trawl* (n 162) 422, cited Handley (n 16) [7.06].

claims are for relief of a different form or scope.[211] Thus, in the widely cited *Machado* case, the Umpire held a claim for restitution of a house, rent, and compensation inadmissible, being the same as a previous claim for the value of the seized house, loss of debts, and seizure of livestock.[212] Identity did 'not depend on whether the items included be the same in both cases' but on 'whether both claims are founded on the same injury'.[213] The house's seizure being the common injury, the later claim was struck out.[214] Similarly, in *Delgado*, where a claim had been brought for lost property and income consequent on an estate's seizure, a second claim for the seized land's value was dismissed: no 'new rights' were asserted, the injury was the same, and all relief should have been claimed upfront.[215] More recently, as noted, one investment tribunal considered claims barred by *res judicata*, although the second claim related to slightly different investments, and was thus necessarily for different relief.[216] In two ECOWAS cases, receiving reparation under domestic law for 'essentially the same' violations sufficed for *res judicata* to bar later international claims.[217]

By contrast, tribunals have, in overlapping individual and interstate claims, tended to emphasise the distinct objects involved. Thus, the individual applications in *Varnava*, which concerned alleged disappearances consequent on Turkish military activities in Northern Cyprus,[218] were instituted after the interstate proceedings in *Cyprus v Turkey*, in which, the ECtHR acknowledged, 'findings of violations ... concerning missing Greek Cypriots and their families' were made.[219] In determining not to strike out the individual applications,[220] the Court emphasised, *inter alia*, that compensation might be awarded for the individuals' damage, potentially resulting in different outcomes to those in the interstate case.[221] Similarly, in *Donnelly*, the applicants complained of mistreatment in custody in circumstances in which Ireland had also instituted proceedings against the UK.[222] The ECommHR, holding that the interstate claim had not yet been 'examined', also remarked that the parties and claims were 'different'.[223] Importantly, although the

[211] See *Schreuer/Reinisch Opinion* (n 166) [45]–[46]; Reinisch (n 108) 62–63; Dodge (n 164) 366; Hobér (n 26) 303; also Cheng (n 111) 343–46; Shany, *Relations* (n 4) 139–44, referencing (at 139) *Gubisch Maschinenfabrik v Palumbo* [1987] ECR 4871 [16]–[17]; cf Salles (n 17) 275.

[212] *Machado* (1880) 3 Moore's 2193 (US-Spanish Cl Comm) 2193–94, discussed, together with *Delgado*, vis-à-vis *res judicata*: Cheng (n 111) 343–46; *Schreuer/Reinisch Opinion* (n 166) [47]–[48]; Reinisch (n 108) 63–64; also Dodge (n 164) 366.

[213] *Machado* (n 212) 2194.

[214] ibid.

[215] *Delgado* (1881) 3 Moore's 2196 (US-Spanish Cl Comm) 2199, cf 2200, also cited Shany, *Relations* (n 4) 139; Salles (n 17) 270; authorities n 212.

[216] *Apotex* (n 111) [7.59]–[7.61].

[217] *Tasheku* (n 192) [18]–[19]; *Umar* (n 192) [19]–[21].

[218] See *Varnava and others v Turkey* [2009] ECHR 2009-V 13 [3], [20]–[65].

[219] ibid [118].

[220] cf n320 (on art 35(2)(b)).

[221] *Varnava* (n 218) [119]; nn 322–24. Interstate compensation was, however, ultimately awarded: n 585.

[222] *Donnelly v UK* (1973) 16 YBk ECHR 212, 262–66.

[223] ibid 266, discussed Shany, *Competing* (n 4) 36.

interstate claim drew on certain individual applicants' situations as examples,[224] it alleged the existence of an 'administrative practice' without claiming reparation for any individual,[225] while the individuals necessarily claimed as *victims*, for breach of their rights, and their own relief.[226] The IACHR similarly emphasised, as noted above, that, unlike Mexico's interstate restitution claim in *Avena*,[227] the Commission's 'remedies ... correspond directly to the individual presumably concerned'.[228]

More broadly, the IACtHR considers that proceedings concerning 'the general human rights situation in [a] country' have a different 'object and purpose' from procedures 'for the adjudication of certain rights'.[229] The HRC has likewise indicated that '[t]he study of human rights problems of a more global character, although it might refer to or draw on information concerning individuals' is not 'the same matter as the examination of individual cases'.[230] Rather, in determining whether procedures are covered by *res judicata*-like treaty provisions, human rights institutions consistently examine whether reparation can and will be afforded to the individuals affected.[231]

The situation differs, however, where a more general interstate claim encompasses a claim for reparation for individual damage. Thus, *Georgia v Russia (I)* concerned an alleged 'administrative practice of arresting, detaining and collectively expelling Georgian nationals from [Russia]'.[232] The ECtHR considered Georgia's claims, despite several individual applications relating to the same events having been made.[233] However, as already noted, when addressing interstate reparation, the Court removed from consideration any person in respect of whom an individual decision had been rendered, whether a violation was found or not.[234] The

224 *Donnelly* (n 222) 266.

225 ibid 260.

226 ibid. Similarly *Sequeira v Uruguay* (1980) 1 Sel Dec HRC 52 [7], [9](a), [11] (brief reference to applicant among hundreds not same as individual application); Zwart (n 43) 175; Shany, *Competing* (n 4) 36, 63. Cf Ch 3, nn 338ff.

227 *Avena and Other Mexican Nationals (Mexico v US) (Judgment)* [2004] ICJ Rep 12 [12]–[13].

228 n 160.

229 *Saramaka* (n 89) [51], also [54]. Similarly *Bustamante v Peru* Case 11756, Rep 54/9 (IACHR, December 1998) [16] (not inadmissible where 'limited to an examination of the general situation' and 'no decision on the specific facts that are the subject of the petition, or when it will not lead to an effective settlement of the violation denounced'); *Menendez and others v Argentina* Case 11670, Rep 3/01 (IACHR, 19 January 2001) [64] (Rules, art 39(2)); Shany, *Competing* (n 4) 65; Sotomayer (n 83) 6–8.

230 *SID v Bulgaria* Doc CCPR/C/111/D/1926/2010 (HRC, 21 July 2014) [8.3]; similarly *Bashasha v Libya* Doc CCPR/C/100/D/1776/2008 (HRC, 20 October 2010) [6.2]. Generally Shany, *Competing* (n 4) 63; Zwart (n 43) 174.

231 *SHRO* (n 104) [105] ('capable of granting [victims] declaratory or compensatory relief'); *Musicue and Coicue v Colombia* Case 9853, Rep 4/98 (IACHR, 7 April 1998) [19] ('effective remedy'); similarly *SINTRAOFAN* (n 104) [75]; *Gabre-Salassie* (n 179) [117]; *Karoussiotis* (n 103) [74]–[75] (not 'similar'; *inter alia* no 'individual reparation'); also *Garzón Guzmán v Ecuador* Pet 11-587, Rep 70/10 (IACHR, 12 July 2010) [38]; *Celniku* (n 103) [40].

232 *Georgia v Russia (I)* 2014-IV ECHR 109 [3].

233 ibid [80], 174–76.

234 *Georgia v Russia (I) (Compensation)* (n 74) [70] (not 'victims').

Court did not apply *res judicata* to bar the interstate claim, whose merits had indeed already been determined by the compensation stage.[235] However, once findings were reached in individual cases, the Court deferred to those findings. Unlike in *Donnelly* or *Varnava*, the State was, just like the individual applicants, claiming for damage to individuals,[236] suggesting that the individual and interstate claims shared an object.[237] Interstate reparation could not therefore be considered when it had already been determined, vis-à-vis the same person, in an individual case.

The case law thus provides clues for when object identity is likely to subsist, namely where findings are made vis-à-vis particular individuals, and their injury remedied.[238] Given that: (i) diplomatic protection claims are based on individual injury,[239] thus sharing a common 'injury' with overlapping individual claims;[240] and (ii) reparation is usually sought, in such claims, to remedy the individual's damage,[241] the necessary object identity may be present across such claims.[242] Indeed, as noted, the ACommHPR was prepared to bar an individual claim in light of interstate EECC proceedings which were diplomatic protection in part,[243] envisaging that both tribunals would look to award compensation, but that the EECC would be better placed to do so,[244] while the ECtHR was prepared to defer to individual findings in an interstate human rights case insofar as it concerned those same individuals.[245] Consistent with the conclusions already reached vis-à-vis double recovery, individual and interstate claims may thus have similar objects.

C. Parties

Notwithstanding the foregoing conclusions, party identity remains an obvious obstacle for applying *res judicata*—and treaty provisions embodying its requirements—vis-à-vis overlapping individual and interstate claims.[246] Even so,

[235] Cf n 112. Art 35(2)(b) applies only to individual applications: nn 84, 123.

[236] See *Georgia v Russia (I) (Compensation)* (n 74) [26]. Cf nn 221, 226.

[237] Cf nn 218–26.

[238] nn 218ff; also Nollkaemper (n 42) 251.

[239] Ch 3(II), particularly nn 43ff.

[240] Cf nn 213ff, 579.

[241] See DADP, 23 ('designed to secure reparation for [national's] injury'); similarly *US v Germany (Administrative Decision No V)* (1924) VII UNRIAA 119 (US–German Mixed Cl Comm) 153; FV Garcia-Amador, 'State Responsibility: Some New Problems' (1958) 94 RdC 365, 462, 467; Ch 3, nn 181–84.

[242] Similarly Theodor Meron, 'The Incidence of the Rule of Exhaustion of Local Remedies' (1959) 35 BYBIL 83, 90 (*Interhandel* claims 'same object'); Hugh Thirlway, *The Law and Procedure of the International Court of Justice: Fifty Years of Jurisprudence* (OUP 2013) 616; Paparinskis (n 24) 297, cf 300, discussed n 54; Garcia-Amador, 'Problems' (n 241) 462; n 379.

[243] nn 200ff. On being diplomatic protection: Ch 3, n 46.

[244] *Interights* (n 200) [55], [59]. Also Sotomayer (n 83) 4.

[245] n 234.

[246] Authorities n 131; cf Nollkaemper (n 142) 529.

the case law of various tribunals accepts some leniency regarding this requirement where two parties are 'closely related'.[247] Under common law, for example, in an approach that has, as will be seen, gained some traction before international tribunals,[248] *res judicata* operates vis-à-vis 'privies in interest', non-parties with such a 'legal or beneficial' interest in earlier proceedings that binding them to the outcome is fair.[249] A privy has been described as one who 'claims a title or right under, through, or on behalf of, a party bound'.[250] Privies include trustees and beneficiaries,[251] ships and their owners,[252] an insured and insurer subrogated to the insured's rights,[253] and, in some cases, corporations and shareholders.[254] The matter depends, substantively, on the parties' 'degree of identification',[255] and whether their interests are the same.[256] Additionally, domestic systems widely recognise class or representative actions,[257] in which members of the relevant class (named or otherwise) are bound by *res judicata*,[258] because their interests are represented in the action brought on behalf of the class of which they form a part.[259]

While certain international tribunals have interpreted party identity stringently,[260] others have similarly recognised that *res judicata* may apply despite its 'formal' absence.[261] The general approach, divided into three categories, will be

[247] ILA, 'InterimRep' (n 18) 39 (privies); see nn 249ff; also Shany, *Relations* (n 4) 36, 134, 136 (vis-à-vis diplomatic protection); Hobér (n 26) 297. Cf n 260.

[248] nn 265, 280–82, 290.

[249] Barnett (n 17) [3.21]–[3.22]; also Handley (n 16) [9.45]; ILA, 'InterimRep' (n 18) 45; Shany, *Competing* (n 4) 24, 155; Shany, *Relations* (n 4) 137, citing *Gleeson v Wippell* [1977] 1 WLR 510, 515.

[250] Barnett (n 17) [3.20]; similarly Handley (n 16) [9.45]; Hobér (n 26) 156.

[251] Handley (n 16) [9.44]; Barnett (n 17) [3.23]; ILA, 'InterimRep' (n 18) 44; *Gleeson* (n 249) 515; also *Kinnear v Falconfilms* [1994] ILPr 731 [26], cited Peter Kaye, *European Case Law on the Judgements Convention* (Wiley & Sons 1998) 297–98; Layton and others (n 162) [22.014] 785 (claims for another's benefit).

[252] *India v India Steamship (No 2)* [1998] AC 878, 896, 909–13, discussed Barnett (n 17) [3.50]–[3.63].

[253] *Drouot Assurances v CMI* [1998] ECR I-3075 [19]–[20] (where interests same), cited Shany, *Competing* (n 4) 25; Handley (n 16) [9.23]; n 344.

[254] Handley (n 16) [9.47]; *Johnson* (n 61) 32; *Berkeley Administration v McClelland* [1995] ILPr 201 [30] ('wholly owned subsidiary'), cited Layton and others (n 162) [22.014].

[255] *Gleeson* (n 249) 515, referenced Handley (n 16) [9.45]; Barnett (n 17) [3.22]; Shany, *Relations* (n 4) 137.

[256] *Drouot* (n 253) [25] ('identical … and indissociable'), quoted Handley (n 16) [9.23]; also Shany, *Relations* (n 4) 133–37.

[257] See Omar Shah (ed), *Class Actions: A Global Guide from Practical Law* (Thomson Reuters 2015); Peter Cashman, *Class Action Law and Practice* (Federation Press 2007), particularly Ch 10; *Abaclat v Argentina (Jurisdiction/Admissibility)* ICSID Case No ARB/07/5 (4 August 2011) [483]–[484] ('collective proceedings'). Cf nn 499, 569, 580, 599. While often associated with common law, civil law systems also recognise class actions: see Deborah Hensler, 'The Globalization of Class Actions: An Overview' (2009) 662 Annals AAPSS 7.

[258] Handley (n 16) [9.20]; Barnett (n 17) [3.32]; McDermott (n 108) [5.09]; authorities nn 606, 646.

[259] n 646.

[260] Shany, *Competing* (n 4) 24–25; Shany, *Relations* (n 4) 135; Zwart (n 43) 173, 176–77, 180–81; Wehland (n 5) [6.59]–[6.62]; Vermeer-Künzli (n 53) 280–81 (*Unn/Folgero* litigation), see *Folgero v Norway* App 15472/02 (ECtHR, 14 February 2006) §'The Law'(2)(B); *Unn v Norway* (2004) 8 Sel Dec HRC 385 [13.3]; *Fanali* (n 92) [7.2].

[261] Shany, *Relations* (n 4) 135 ('formal'/'informal' methodologies); also Salles (n 17) 275–76; ILA, 'InterimRep' (n 18) 58–59; n 386.

considered first, before outlining how the same conclusions may apply vis-à-vis overlapping individual and interstate claims.

First, cases have acknowledged that one party may represent another, the HRC observing, for instance, that the 'same matter' 'must be understood as referring to one and the same claim concerning the same individual, as submitted by that individual, *or by some other person empowered to act on his behalf*.'[262] The ECtHR has likewise considered complaints 'essentially the same' where the first was lodged 'on behalf of' one of the later applicants.[263] One investment tribunal considered that the acts of a given entity being attributable to the State—and thus undertaken on the State's behalf[264]—was indicative of 'privity' between it and the State for *res judicata* purposes.[265] Another has recognised 'representative actions' under BITs, allowing thousands of individuals to consent to another 'represent[ing] their interests' and deciding 'on their behalf'.[266] By contrast, human rights tribunals have considered treaty provisions inapplicable where an earlier claim, even regarding the same individual, was submitted by an *unauthorised* third party.[267]

Second, tribunals may be more lenient where the same person is the *subject* of the claim in both cases, if not the claimant.[268] Thus, even while requiring that parties be 'identical',[269] the ECtHR accepted that article 35(2)(b) of the ECHR was engaged where previous proceedings examined a particular individual's situation, despite being brought by another applicant.[270] The IACHR similarly declared a complaint inadmissible on the basis that it had earlier considered the violations alleged vis-à-vis a particular individual, despite that earlier petition's having been brought without the surviving relatives' consent.[271] The ECommHR declared an application substantially the same as an earlier claim before the

[262] *Unn* (n 260) [13.3] (emphasis added); similarly *Fanali* (n 92) [7.2], cited Shany, *Relations* (n 4) 135; Shany, *Competing* (n 4) 24; generally Zwart (n 43) 175–77, 71–80; affirmed *Kayhan v Turkey* Doc CEDAW/C/34/D/8/2005 (CEDAW, 27 January 2006) [7.3].

[263] *Vojnović (ECHR)* (n 85) [31]. Cf *Peltonen v Finland* (1995) 80 DR 38, 43 (brother).

[264] Ch 1, nn 9–11; generally *ARSIWA*, 94; Crawford, *GP* (n 6) 115ff.

[265] *Ampal-American* (n 185) [269]–[270]; also *Helnan* (n 185) [127].

[266] *Abaclat* (n 257) [487], cf [486] (not class action), discussed SI Strong, *Class, Mass, and Collective Arbitration in National and International Law* (OUP 2013) [2.123]–[2.143]. Cf the ECtHR's 'pilot judgment' procedure, with class action-like effects: Tatiana Sainati, 'Human Rights Class Actions: Rethinking the Pilot-Judgment Procedure at the European Court of Human Rights' (2015) 56 HILJ 147, 151; Parlett (n 5) 333; eg *Broniowski v Poland* ECHR 2004-V 1 [2].

[267] *Estrella v Uruguay* (1983) 2 Sel Dec HRC 93 [4.3] ('unrelated third party, acting without [victim's] knowledge and consent'); *de Casariego v Uruguay* Comm 56/1979, Doc CCPR/C/OP/1 (HRC, 29 July 1981) [5], both cited Shany, *Competing* (n 4) 25, 63; Shany, *Relations* (n 4) 135; also Zwart (n 43) 177; *Akwanga v Cameroon* Doc CCPR/C/101/D/1813/2008 (HRC, 22 March 2011) [6.2]; *Celniku* (n 103) [40]; *Domingues v US* Case 12285, Rep 62/02 (IACHR, October 2002) [35] ('no mandate'); Wehland (n 5) [6.61].

[268] Similarly Zwart (n 43) 165; n 384.

[269] *Peraldi* (n 172) 10.

[270] ibid 10–11 (brother).

[271] *Martín de Mejía v Peru* [1996] IAYBkHR 1120, 1134, 1144–48, cited Shany, *Competing* (n 4) 25; Sotomayer (n 83) 5–6.

Freedom of Association Committee (FOAC) of the International Labour Organization (ILO), notwithstanding the applicants being 'formally' different, where the ILO proceedings 'precisely concerned the dismissal of the ... applicants' and 'the complaint was, in substance, submitted by the same complainants': the individual workers on the one hand, and the trade union representing them on the other.[272] Finally, the ECtHR considered two distinct complaints, concerning civil proceedings to which the complainants were joined, 'essentially the same'.[273] The Court reasoned that no additional damages could be awarded in the second case, given that, *inter alia*, the complainants were 'parties to the same domestic proceedings' and the second complaint's 'subject matter' was therefore 'the same' as that of the first.[274]

By contrast, the ECtHR declined in another case to consider individual workers the same as an organisation 'protect[ing] employers' interests', considering it 'of importance' that the earlier claim 'was of a general character' while the later concerned 'the specific situation of the ... individual applicants'.[275] The IACtHR has likewise emphasised that 'the concept of "persons" is related to the active and passive subjects of the violation and mainly to the latter, that is, the victims',[276] finding party identity missing where one case referenced 'workers and trade union leaders who were dismissed in general, without individualizing them specifically' while the second 'individualize[d] 270 alleged victims'.[277]

Finally, as under domestic law, tribunals take account of whether the parties' interests are the same across claims.[278] Thus, a 'successor-in-interest' was held bound by the outcome of earlier proceedings in an investment case.[279] Additionally, some international tribunals acknowledge the concept of 'privity' discussed earlier.[280] Accordingly, although shareholder-company privity is not commonly recognised in investment law,[281] one tribunal applied the doctrine where shareholders claimed 'for damage they allege they have suffered indirectly',

[272] *Martin v Spain* (1992) 73 DR 120, 134–35, also 132–33, cited Shany, *Competing* (n 4) 24 ('*alter ego*'), 65; Shany, *Relations* (n 4) 135; Zwart (n 43) 182 (noting earlier contrary decision: *CCSU v UK* [1987] ECHR 34); Wehland (n 5) [6.58], [6.60]; Reinisch (n 108) 61.

[273] *Alves* (n 40) [14], see [2]–[5], [12]–[13]. Admittedly, based on abuse of process: ibid [8]–[10], [17].

[274] *Alves* (n 40) [15]. Cf *Nobili Massuero v Italy* App 58587/00 (ECtHR, 1 April 2004) 3.

[275] *Evaldsson v Sweden* App 75252/01 (ECtHR, 28 March 2006) 10. Cf *Fajardo* (n 104) [38]–[42]; Shany, *Competing* (n 4) 65.

[276] *Ricardo* (n 89) [54], referencing *Durand* (n 124) [43], discussed Sotomayer (n 83) 8–9.

[277] *Ricardo* (n 89) [54].

[278] cf nn 247–59.

[279] *Vivendi (Jurisdiction)* (n 161) [73], also [82]–[87].

[280] *Garraway* (n 163) [14]; also *Katabazi v Secretary-General EAC* (EACJ, 1 November 2007) [37] ('parties ... litigating under the same title'); *Fenosa* (n 31) [11.32]; authorities nn 265, 282ff.

[281] Wehland (n 5) [6.117] ('formally identical' parties), discussion [6.114]–[6.119]; cf Brower and Henin (n 109) 58 ('inconsistent'). Eg *CME (Final)* (n 147) and *Lauder* (n 33), n 147; *Fraport (Order)* (n 185) [82] (no 'privity'); *Yukos* (n 85) [524]–[525] (shareholders/company different); generally ILA, 'InterimRep' (n 18) 58–59; cf Reinisch (n 108) 55–61; *Schreuer/Reinisch Opinion* (n 166) [21]–[37]; also *Perenco* (n 30) [11], [37]–[39], [43]–[52] (consortium).

via the company.[282] The tribunal explained that where shareholders claim based on 'their indirect interest in corporate assets, they must be subject to defences that would be available against the corporation—including collateral estoppel'.[283] The ECtHR also recently accepted that a company bringing ECHR proceedings and a sole shareholder claiming under a BIT were 'in substance ... the same'.[284] Noting its case law allowing 'piercing of the "corporate veil"' where a shareholder 'complain[s] of acts directly affecting the company', it observed that the shareholder was 'directly involved' in the company's claim, and the two did not 'disassociate' themselves from one another.[285] An investment tribunal recently held that such an approach is not limited to companies that are 'wholly-owned',[286] but applies where shareholder claims 'exist only through [the company]', and vis-à-vis the company's rights, as 'reflected in [a] claim for damages' for share value diminution.[287] The bringing of proceedings by different parties 'for recovery of the same sum'[288] and 'in respect of the same interest' was also considered 'an abuse of process for in substance the same claim is to be pursued on the merits before two tribunals'.[289] A final tribunal similarly held a company bound as a 'privy' where its claim was dependent on the rights of another company it owned,[290] the former having only an 'indirect interest'.[291]

However, in an employment case, the ECtHR considered the parties different where earlier proceedings before the ILO FOAC had been instituted by an organisation with which the later applicant was affiliated and on its behalf, but where the applicant was not joined, and the *interests* of the two did not necessarily correspond.[292] In addition, and by contrast with those decisions binding shareholders to the outcome of the company's previous claims where the former hold only an indirect interest,[293] an investment tribunal denied that an award rendered vis-à-vis a majority shareholder was *res judicata* for the company where the shareholder did not represent the company's interests and had 'no intention ... of channelling compensation through [the company]'.[294] Interestingly, decisions of the ECommHR

[282] *RSM* (n 165) [7.1.5]–[7.1.6]; see Hobér (n 26) 297–98; Wehland (n 5) [6.116]. Approving: *Eskosol v Italy (Rule 41(5) Application)* ICSID Case No ARB/15/50 (20 March 2017) [167] (where 'interests represented'); also *Orascom* (n 55) [488]; *Amoco International Finance v Iran* (1987) 83 ILR 500 (IUSCT) [16]–[18] ('indirect claim' with *res judicata* effect), cited Wehland (n 5) [6.58].

[283] *RSM* (n 165) [7.1.7]. See Salles (n 17) 272–73, 276.

[284] *LeBridge* (n 83) [33], discussed Hepburn (n 173), contrasting *Arif v Moldova (Award)* ICSID Case No ARB/11/23 (8 April 2013) [14] (ECtHR proceedings not 'substantially similar ... relate to different claimants, different scope of claims and different relief').

[285] *LeBridge* (n 83) [29]–[32].

[286] *Ampal-American* (n 185) [267].

[287] ibid [268], cited *Perenco* (n 30) [11]. Cf nn 59ff.

[288] *Ampal-American Israel v Egypt (Jurisdiction)* ICSID Case No ARB/12/11 (1 February 2016) [330].

[289] ibid [331], discussed Gaillard (n 5) 25. Similarly *Orascom* (n 55) [542]–[545]. Cf *Fenosa* (n 31) [6.81].

[290] *Apotex* (n 111) [7.39]–[7.40], see [1.2].

[291] ibid [7.60].

[292] *Eğitim ve Bilim Emekçileri Sendikası v Turkey* ECHR 2012-III 483 [38]–[39].

[293] nn 282–91.

[294] *Eskosol* (n 282) [168]. Cf Shany, *Relations* (n 4) 137; Wehland (n 5) [6.118], [7.48]–[7.50].

have made a similar distinction, with claims concerning a single victim's situation found to be 'substantially the same' where an 'indirect victim' claims after the *actual* victim,[295] but not, conversely, where the actual victim files after an 'indirect victim', as the actual victim is taken to have a 'specific personal interest' in proceeding 'in his own name'.[296]

The case law thus suggests that party identity may exist across claims where one party represents another,[297] where the same party's situation has already been examined,[298] and where the parties' interests are consistent.[299] Importantly, the same concepts run through the case law concerning overlapping individual and interstate claims.

First, relating to the notion of representation, the UNCC *Well Blowout Control Claim*, brought by the State-owned Kuwait Oil Company, concerned damaged oil fields.[300] The Commission having queried whether the claim was interstate,[301] the company, a separate entity,[302] clarified that it was not claiming on the State's behalf.[303] Nonetheless, the Commission, taking account of the company's being State-funded,[304] the risk of double recovery, and that in its activities the company 'appear[ed] … to act[], in effect, on behalf of the Ministry of Oil',[305] concluded that the company claimed 'on behalf of Kuwait's public oil sector as a whole'.[306] Consequently, the State was 'bound by the decision' and 'estopped from bringing the same claim'.[307]

In other cases, individuals have run into issues by apparently having accepted State representation.[308] Thus, one tribunal declined jurisdiction over an individual claim, on 'international public policy' grounds, where an investor had earlier sought diplomatic protection from its owner's State of nationality.[309] A French court held, in another case, that an interstate settlement of claims through diplomatic protection was *res judicata* vis-à-vis a later individual claim, the individual having 'at least … tacitly accepted' it.[310] By contrast, in holding that an individual claim and the interstate *Avena* proceedings were not the same, the IACHR

[295] Zwart (n 43) 165, referencing *X c Allemagne* (1959) 2 YBkECHR 397, 399.
[296] Zwart (n 43) 165, referencing *X v Germany* (1980) 22 DR 236, 237.
[297] nn 262–67.
[298] nn 268–77; also Nollkaemper (n 42) 251.
[299] nn 278ff.
[300] *Well Blowout Control Claim* (1996) 109 ILR 479 (UNCC) [1], [28].
[301] ibid [48].
[302] ibid [28], also [30].
[303] ibid [57].
[304] ibid [41], [55].
[305] ibid [60].
[306] ibid [61].
[307] ibid.
[308] cf nn 383, 385–86.
[309] *Banro v DRC* (2003) 17 ICSID Rev-FILJ 382 [24]–[26], discussed Schreuer, *ICSID* (n 129) 419. Cf *Tokios Tokelės v Ukraine (Order No 3)* ICSID Case No ARB/02/18 (18 January 2005) [22]–[23].
[310] *Yugoslavia v SEEE* (1970) 65 ILR 46 (TGI Paris) 49, cf 50 (on appeal, diplomatic protection not considered to 'deprive' individual of contractual 'legal remedies').

observed, *inter alia*, that 'Mexico has no mandate from [the individual] and has brought its claim ... in its own right'.[311]

As to the second theme, regarding subject-matter, the ACommHPR, in the case against Ethiopia and Eritrea noted above, appeared unconcerned that the claimants were different from those in the interstate EECC proceedings.[312] Admittedly, article 56(7) of the AfCHPR bars consideration of cases 'settled by these States involved',[313] a rule that could be taken as applying to individual claims even without party identity.[314] Yet the French text does not mention *interstate* settlement,[315] and the Commission has interpreted the provision as requiring that 'the same parties' be involved in the respective claims,[316] while also referring to *res judicata* as meaning that 'a final judgment of a competent court or tribunal is conclusive *on the parties* in any subsequent litigation involving the same cause of action'.[317] The Commission nonetheless accepted the preclusive effect of interstate EECC claims on a claim before it where both claims concerned compensation for alleged violations of international law vis-à-vis the victims of the conflict.[318] Similar reasoning can be detected, with opposite results, in *Donnelly* and *Varnava*: in both cases, the distinct objects in the overlapping claims were emphasised, with individuals claiming compensation for individual injury, and the State on a more general basis.[319] Admittedly, the ECtHR did, in *Varnava*, hold that article 35(2)(b) of the ECHR required that 'complaints ... be introduced by the same persons', concluding that States could not 'by introducing an inter-State application ... thereby depriv[e] individual applicants of the possibility of introducing, or pursuing, their own claims'.[320] Nonetheless, despite apparently thus requiring party identity, the Court proceeded to discuss potential strike-out under article 37(1)(c), a broader provision applicable where 'for any other reason ... it is no longer justified to continue the examination'.[321] The Court refused, holding that the interstate judgment 'did not specify in respect of which individual missing persons [findings] were made', could not thus 'be regarded as determining the issues and claims' in question, and that different remedies might be awarded.[322] Accordingly, 'the individual

[311] *Ramos* (n 198) [50] and see [49]–[55].

[312] nn 200ff.

[313] AfCHPR, art 56(7).

[314] Shany, *Competing* (n 4) 225.

[315] Ouguergouz (n 105) 613; also Shany, *Competing* (n 4) 225.

[316] *Gunme* (n 99) [86]; *Okiring* (n 98) [68].

[317] *Spilg* (n 99) [110] (emphasis added); similarly *SHRO* (n 104) [104], though cf [106] ('the content of the current complaints were not submitted to any such bodies, by the Complainants, *or any other individual or institution*' (emphasis added)); similarly *Gabre-Salassie* (n 179) [117]; Gherari (n 100) 783; Shany, *Competing* (n 4) 64.

[318] nn 200–5. Compare *Interights* (n 200) [2]–[9] and nn 574–75.

[319] nn 218–26.

[320] *Varnava* (n 218) [118]. Cf *Arctic Sunrise Arbitration (Netherlands v Russia) (Merits)* PCA Case 2014-02 (14 August 2015) [148].

[321] *Varnava* (n 218) [119].

[322] ibid; n 221. Also *Varnava and others v Turkey* (1998) 73 DR 5, 13 (not deciding if 'precluded ... from examining in the context of an individual application a "matter" ... examined in an inter-State case').

applicants' interests' had not 'been subsumed by the judgment in [the interstate] case'.[323] The ECtHR thus appeared willing to control overlapping individual and interstate claims, albeit not through the *res judicata*-like provision of the ECHR, only where the same individual injury had been considered and remedied.[324] And it did just that in *Georgia v Russia (I)* by omitting from the interstate claim for reparation the circumstances of individuals whose individual claims had already been determined.[325]

Turning to investment law, Italy's proceedings against Cuba were brought both to protect its own rights and as an exercise of diplomatic protection.[326] Despite being a non-ICSID arbitration, the Tribunal considered that ICSID's article 27 could be applied 'par analogie', meaning that diplomatic protection was only available in the absence of investor consent to arbitration.[327] For reasons already noted, this is unlikely to be an application of custom.[328] Nor were *res judicata* or *lis pendens* expressly referenced. However, the case demonstrates a preparedness to prevent overlapping individual and interstate diplomatic protection claims involving a given 'dispute',[329] regardless of party identity.[330] Although achieved through treaty language, the Brazilian model Cooperation and Investment Facilitation Agreement similarly appears to treat individual investor claims, including before domestic courts, as having *res judicata* effect vis-à-vis, and therefore being preclusive of, interstate claims concerning the same investor.[331]

In terms of other cases concerning diplomatic protection, the Umpire in *Fabiani* concluded that an individual's denial of justice claim was barred by an earlier claim brought and resolved by France, his State of nationality.[332] This was so

[323] *Varnava* (n 218) [119].

[324] Similarly nn 218–31. Cf Leo Zwaak (revisor), 'The Procedure Before the European Court of Human Rights' in Pieter van Dijk and others (eds), *Theory and Practice of the European Convention on Human Rights* (4th edn, Intersentia 2006) 179; n 268.

[325] *Georgia v Russia (I) (Compensation)* (n 74) [70]. See n 234.

[326] Roberts (n 6) 7, 17; Ch 3, n 389.

[327] *Italy v Cuba (Interim Award)* UNCITRAL Tribunal (15 March 2005) [65], discussed Michele Potestà, 'Republic of Italy v Republic of Cuba' (2012) 106 AJIL 341, 342; Michele Potestà, 'State-to-State Dispute Settlement Pursuant to Bilateral Investment Treaties: Is There Potential?' in Nerina Boschiero and others (eds), *International Courts and the Development of International Law: Essays in Honour of Tullio Treves* (Asser 2013) 765; Potestà, 'Role' (n 131) 259; Matilde Recanati, 'Diplomatic Intervention and State-to-State Arbitration as Alternative Means for the Protection of Foreign Investments and Host States' General Interests: The Italian Experience' in Giorgio Sacerdoti and others (eds), *General Interests of Host States in International Investment Law* (CUP 2014) 439; Roberts (n 6) 47.

[328] Potestà, 'Italy/Cuba' (n 327) 346; Paparinskis (n 72) 643; Crawford, *GP* (n 6) 591; Ch 3, n 396.

[329] Cf ICSID, art 27, Ch 3, n 20. Similarly Potestà, 'Role' (n 131) 271.

[330] See Ch 3, n 9; similarly Roberts (n 6) 47 and, supporting approach: ibid 48–49; Juratowich (n 130) 22, 32, 34–35; Wehland (n 5) [1.57]; Amerasinghe, *DP* (n 137) 341; Potestà, 'Role' (n 131) 271; cf Paparinskis (n 24) 281; Shany, *Competing* (n 4) 195.

[331] Gabrielle Kaufmann-Kohler and Michele Potestà, 'Investor-State Dispute Settlement and National Courts: Current Framework and Reform Options' [2020] EYBIEL, 96, citing CIFA, art 24(13)(b) (interstate dispute settlement provision not applicable 'to a dispute concerning a particular investor which has been previously resolved and where protection of res judicata applies').

[332] *Antoine Fabiani Case* (1905) X UNRIAA 83 (French-Venezuelan Cl Comm) 139, discussed Parlett (n 5) 59–60; Cheng (n 111) 337, 344.

notwithstanding that Fabiani's claim was apparently brought in his own right,[333] with the Umpire considering that the 'individual and private claims ... became national' upon France's intervention.[334] *Apostolidis* similarly concerned 'independent' individual and interstate compensation claims against Germany.[335] Nonetheless, upon Greece's making a claim, the individual's claim was considered to have lost 'any significance of its own', being 'completely absorbed by' that of the State.[336] In *Houard*, the Tribunal considered that 'questions ... disposed of' between States 'should [not] be reopened' by an individual claimant.[337] Finally, in *Newchang*, Britain exercised diplomatic protection following a domestic court decision concerning an injured British corporation and the US.[338] Faced with a *res judicata* contention, the Tribunal noted the requirements of identity of parties and questions.[339] Interestingly, it did not deny that they *could* have been met, but regarded the question in the previous case as distinct.[340] While caution is required vis-à-vis early cases, given that what appear to be individual claims were sometimes actually State-brought,[341] these authorities all appear to have concerned individual claims as such,[342] and their potential preclusion consequent on, or preclusive effect vis-à-vis, interstate diplomatic protection claims, including on *res judicata* grounds.

As to the third feature of the party identity cases, relating to shared interests, the drafters of ICSID accepted that *res judicata* would, as under domestic common law,[343] bar claims brought subsequent to investor–State proceedings by a State subrogated to the investor's rights.[344] Moreover, in three of the cases overlapping with *Avena*, the IACHR observed that the individuals were, in the interstate proceedings, without 'independent standing to make submissions ... or to request relief',[345] and in two cases that there was no 'requirement or certainty that Mexico will represent [the individuals'] interests'.[346] Such reasoning suggests a concern

[333] The Protocol, art 1, provided for 'Frenchmen' to claim: *Fabiani* (n 332) 120. While France presented the initial claim, the second was 'wholly the work of an individual': ibid 130.

[334] *Fabiani* (n 332) 127. Similarly Parlett (n 5) 59.

[335] *Greece (on behalf of Apostolidis) v Germany* (1960) 34 ILR 219 (Arbitral Commission) 228, cited *Oppenheim's* (n 62) 512.

[336] *Apostolidis* (n 335) 229. Cf *Decision No V* (n 241) 153.

[337] *Houard* (1880) 3 Moore's 2428 (US–Spanish Cl Comm) 2429, cited Borchard (n 54) 368. Cf Parlett (n 5) Appendix II (18) (State-controlled claims).

[338] *Matter of the SS Newchang* (1922) 16 AJIL 323, 323–24, discussed Cheng (n 111) 339–40, 346.

[339] *Newchang* (n 338) 324.

[340] ibid.

[341] See Parlett (n 5) section II(2). Cf interstate settlement affecting apparently State-brought claims concerning individuals: *Chase v Panama* (1933) VI UNRIAA 352, 357; *McLeod* (1855) Hornsby's 428 (British–US Cl Comm) 446, both cited Cheng (n 111) 337.

[342] See nn 333, 335, 338; cf n 337.

[343] n 253.

[344] See ICSID (n 130) 275, also 503 (no greater rights than subrogor). Generally Juratowich (n 130) 24–27; Peters (n 137) 313–14.

[345] *Ramos* (n 198) [52]; *Fierro* (n 198) [56]; *Medellin* (n 198) [103]. Also Shany, *Relations* (n 4) 141.

[346] *Ramos* (n 198) [52]; *Fierro* (n 198) [56].

less with party identity per se and more with whether the individuals' interests are represented.[347] The notion, discussed above, that the 'direct' victim has a greater interest in their own proceedings than an 'indirect' victim—meaning the latter is more likely to be barred than the former[348]—is also reflected in cases concerning overlapping claims: as already noted, in *Georgia v Russia (I)*, the ECtHR omitted from the interstate reparation claim the cases of individuals with their own claims already considered, but refused to do so vice versa, allowing individual applications to proceed in *Varnava* despite ongoing interstate proceedings.[349]

Overall, these cases suggest, in line with the case law more generally, that party identity may not necessarily be an obstacle to the preclusion of overlapping individual and interstate claims.

V. *Res judicata*, double recovery, and the different categories of interstate claim

Having reviewed the case law relating to double recovery and *res judicata*, we may reach certain conclusions at this point. First, the double recovery rule can clearly operate to preclude reparation being awarded in the later of two overlapping individual and interstate claims. As to which claims may be so affected, individuals claim reparation, pursuant to the mechanisms discussed in Chapter 2, for damage suffered by them.[350] It follows that the rule should operate insofar as a State claims for the same damage suffered by that individual.

For *res judicata*, the case law does not conclusively determine that the principle applies vis-à-vis overlapping individual and interstate claims.[351] Yet the authorities suggest that there is potential for *res judicata*, provisions with similar effect, or other principles such as abuse of process, to operate to render inadmissible the later of at least certain such overlapping claims.[352]

In determining the precise potential for the operation of each of these rules, it is helpful to examine the different categories of interstate claim introduced in Chapters 2–3, considering diplomatic protection, followed by 'mixed' and 'direct' claims.

[347] Further: *Sayadi v Belgium* Doc CCPR/C/94/D/1472/2006 (HRC, 29 December 2008) [7.3] (UNSC sanctions de-listing proceedings and individual proceedings alleging ICCPR violations resulting from listing different, as brought by separate parties (individuals and national State)). While the individuals had *also* sought their de-listing (see ibid [2.3], [4.3]), their ICCPR claim alleged violations by the very State instituting de-listing procedures (ibid [5.3]), meaning there was no shared interest: cf nn 278ff.

[348] nn 282, 291, 295–96.

[349] nn 323–25.

[350] n 579; generally Ch 2(I); *ARSIWA*, 209–10; Crawford, *GP* (n 6) 585–88.

[351] Similarly Vermeer-Künzli (n 53) 277; Shany, *Relations* (n 4) 136 (law 'unsettled'); Salles (n 17) 276–77. *Res judicata* objections are not often made.

[352] nn 3–5, 289–90, 307, 309–10, 318, 327–40, 344.

A. Diplomatic protection

(i) Double recovery

As Chapter 3 highlighted, the PCIJ considered, in diplomatic protection claims, that 'the damage suffered by an individual is never ... identical in kind with that which will be suffered by a State; it can only afford a convenient scale for the calculation of the reparation due'.[353] Accordingly, States theoretically claim for *their own* damage when bringing diplomatic protection suits.[354] Nonetheless, Chapter 3 outlined that diplomatic protection claims are in reality based on damage suffered by an individual,[355] the State's damage being purely 'fictional' in nature.[356] Indeed, the Draft Articles on Diplomatic Protection (DADP) observe that defendant State objections regarding the bringing of diplomatic protection claims by multiple States with respect to injury suffered by dual nationals, particularly where one State has already been compensated, 'should be dealt with in accordance with the general principles of law ... governing the satisfaction of *joint claims*'.[357] In *Reparations*, the ICJ likewise noted that, although diplomatic protection claims and functional protection claims brought by international organisations on behalf of their officials are different, a defendant State could not 'be compelled to pay the reparation due in respect of *the damage* twice over'.[358] Both assume, contrary to the premise of diplomatic protection, that the claims are for the same damage in each case, namely that done to the individual.[359]

The authorities discussed above bear out the same understanding. They establish that, whatever the forum, the principle precluding double recovery operates vis-à-vis overlapping individual claims and such cases of diplomatic protection,[360] including the diplomatic protection aspect of 'mixed' claims,[361] to avoid a respondent

[353] *Chórzow (Merits)* (n 63) 28 (emphasis added), discussed Stephan Wittich, 'Direct Injury and the Incidence of the Local Remedies Rule' (2000) 5 Aust Rev I & EL 121, 150 ('no identity'); de Aréchaga (n 80) 574–75; Peters (n 137) 170; FV Garcia-Amador, 'Sixth Report on State Responsibility' (1961) 2 ILCYB 1 [11]; Gerald Fitzmaurice, *The Law and Procedure of the International Court of Justice* (Grotius 1986) 670–71; Frits Kalshoven, 'Expert Opinion' in Hisakazu Fujita, Isomi Suzuki, and Kantaro Nagano (eds), *War and the Rights of Individuals: Renaissance of Individual Compensation* (Nippon Hyoron-sha 1999) 45–46; Ch 3, n 157.

[354] Ch 3, n 158.

[355] Ch 3(II)(C) and authorities.

[356] Ch 3, nn 175ff.

[357] DADP, 43 (emphasis added). Cf Amerasinghe, *LR* (n 137) 50–51.

[358] *Reparations* (n 22) 186 (emphasis added). Similarly *Barcelona Traction* (n 23) 130–31 (Sep Op Tanaka) (where one 'claim ... realized', the other is 'extinguished'), 200 (Sep Op Jessup); ALI, *Restatement of the Law: The Foreign Relations Law of the United States* (2nd edn, ALI Publishers 1965) 609; authorities nn 22–24.

[359] Similarly Amerasinghe, *LR* (n 137) 50.

[360] See *Chórzow (Merits)* (n 63), discussed n 73; local remedy compensation: nn 74–75; also *Cyprus v Turkey (Compensation)* (n 76) (diplomatic protection: see Ch 3, nn 348–51). Further Paparinskis (n 24) 300.

[361] *Arctic Sunrise (Compensation)* (n 49), n 50. Ch 3 explained why this claim is 'mixed': Ch 3, n 281.

State compensating an individual's damage twice, even if one claim concerns "fictionally" distinct State damage.[362]

What is true for diplomatic protection is even more so where article 48 human rights claims are brought,[363] because such claims are not made by 'injured' States for their own damage and reparation, but in the affected individual's interest.[364] The ECtHR has thus emphasised that 'it is the individual, and not the State, who is directly or indirectly harmed and primarily "injured" by a violation' and who should therefore receive any reparation.[365] And the authorities confirm, consistently with human rights claims being premised on individual damage, that the double recovery principle precludes reparation being awarded in the later of two overlapping individual and interstate human rights claims.[366]

As Chapter 3 outlined, individual damage, for these purposes, means 'personal injury and … injuries in respect of property',[367] with the resulting losses suffered by the individual, not the State.[368] Any interstate claim brought for such damage is 'indirect', with the damage experienced by the State only via the individual,[369] and is thus 'derivative' in nature and brought for the same loss for which the individual can claim themselves.[370] Where interstate diplomatic protection and human rights claims are thus made seeking reparation for the same damage for which an individual claims, those claims will be caught by the double recovery rule, with the later claim for reparation precluded.[371]

(ii) *Res judicata*

In all cases where tribunals were prepared to hold an overlapping individual or interstate claim precluded, on *res judicata* or similar grounds, the interstate claim was one of diplomatic protection, at least in part.[372] This makes intuitive sense, for three reasons.[373] First, diplomatic protection claims are commonly, though not

362 nn 355–59.

363 See Ch 2, nn 211–16.

364 nn 387–88.

365 *Cyprus v Turkey (Compensation)* (n 76) [46]; see Peters (n 137) 394–96 (secondary rights individual); Vermeer-Künzli (n 153) 557–58.

366 *Pad v Turkey* (n 68), nn 68ff; also *Cyprus v Turkey (Compensation)* (n 76).

367 Amerasinghe, *DP* (n 137) 37. See Ch 3, nn 163–64.

368 See authorities Ch 3, nn 163ff; generally Garcia-Amador, 'SixthRep' (n 353) [11], [30]–[31], [34]–[40], [176]; Brown (n 109) 199–208; *ARSIWA*, 222–25; Crawford, *GP* (n 6) 517.

369 Ch 2, n 99.

370 ALI, *Restatement of the Law: The Foreign Relations Law of the United States*, vol II (3rd edn, ALI Publishers 1987) 217; similarly *Heathrow Airport Usage Charges (US v UK)* (1992) XXIV UNRIAA 3, 51, 53. Cf nn 60–62 (shareholders). Generally Ch 3(IV)(B)(i).

371 See section I.

372 See *Banro* (n 309); *SEEE* (n 310); *Interights* (n 200) (nn 312–18) and *Eritrea* (n 15) [25] quoted n 454; *Fabiani* (n 332); *Apostolidis* (n 335); *Italy v Cuba* (n 327). Cf Vermeer-Künzli (n 53) 273–79 (*res judicata* vis-à-vis diplomatic protection/individual human rights claims); *Sayadi* (n 347) and *Ayadi v Council* [2006] II-ECR 2148 [141], [149] (de-listing suit as diplomatic protection), cited Riccardo Pisillo Mazzeschi, 'Impact on the Law of Diplomatic Protection' in Menno Kamminga and Martin Scheinin (eds), *The Impact of Human Rights Law on General International Law* (OUP 2009) 226.

373 Similarly authorities nn 384–86; Paparinskis (n 24) 297–98; Vermeer-Künzli (n 53) 276.

always, brought for breach of rules established for the protection of individuals.[374] An overlapping individual claim, brought for the individuals' own protection,[375] will likely therefore have a similar cause of action to that of the State's claim.[376] This is particularly so where the individual makes a claim, outside of the human rights context, based on breach of rights belonging to a State—precisely the same rights for breach of which that State might claim itself.[377]

Second, while tribunals have emphasised that cases not examining nor obtaining remedies for violations in individual situations have different objects from individual claims,[378] diplomatic protection claims are brought based on, and generally seek reparation for, individual injury.[379] Put another way, such claims have the same object—of repairing the injury caused to the individual.[380] Indeed, as noted, the ECtHR's refusal to consider any interstate reparation claim in *Georgia v Russia (I)* where a decision had already been rendered in an individual case apparently recognised the similarity in object between those claims.[381] In other cases, the similarity in damage or the possibility of double recovery has swayed tribunals in finding the later of two claims inadmissible on *res judicata* or similar grounds, even where the parties were not the same.[382]

Third, party identity may be more leniently interpreted where overlapping diplomatic protection and individual claims are concerned, because: (i) the State is actually acting on the individual's behalf;[383] (ii) the claims concern the same individual's injury;[384] and/or (iii) the State is representing the individual's interest (common in diplomatic protection)[385] meaning that the relevant individuals are the 'true beneficiaries' of the claim, and reference to the parties' 'formal identity' to deny the applicability of *res judicata* is not 'satisfactory'.[386] Indeed, where States bring *erga omnes*-type claims, including human rights claims, pursuant to article

[374] See discussion Amerasinghe, *LR* (n 137) 163–65; Wittich (n 353) 136–37, 181–82; Ch 3(II)(B).

[375] See n 579.

[376] See section IV(A). Similarly Paparinskis (n 24) 297; Peters (n 137) 173; Roberts, n 377.

[377] nn 155ff. Cf Roberts (n 6) 43 (*res judicata* where State/individual rights 'interdependent').

[378] nn 218–31, 275–77.

[379] nn 238–44. Similarly Paparinskis (n 24) 298; JL Brierly, *Brierly's Law of Nations: An Introduction to the Role of International Law in International Relations* (7th edn, OUP 2012) 256; Vermeer-Künzli (n 53) 276–77.

[380] See nn 213–15.

[381] n 325.

[382] Eg nn 274, 282, 288–89, 305–7.

[383] Eg, DADP, 99, discussing *Decision No V* (n 241) 152 ('Ordinarily a nation will not espouse a claim on behalf of its national against another nation unless requested so to do by such national'); cf Garcia-Amador, 'Problems' (n 241) 472 ('representative'). See *Banro* (n 309) (protection sought); cf *Ramos* (n 198), discussed n 311 ('no mandate'); nn 262–67.

[384] nn 268ff; similarly Nollkaemper (n 142) 529 (party identity 'closer' where 'international proceedings ... based on diplomatic protection and related to ... same individuals'); Nollkaemper (n 42) 251.

[385] Shany, *Relations* (n 4) 133–35; also Amerasinghe, *DP* (n 137) 69, 76; Roberts (n 6) 7–8 (*Italy v Cuba*), cf 49–50; cf Fitzmaurice (n 353) 670–71; nn 640–45.

[386] Schreuer, *Decisions* (n 140) 331–32, discussed Shany, *Relations* (n 4) 134–35, also 136–37. Cf Vermeer-Künzli (n 53) 276–78.

48, they *must* seek reparation in the beneficiary's interest,[387] ie, the relevant individuals.[388] The ECtHR accordingly requires that interstate reparation be distributed to the relevant victims.[389]

For these reasons, there is a good argument that *res judicata*—or provisions embodying its requirements—should apply as between overlapping individual and interstate diplomatic protection claims, to avoid respondents being faced with two essentially identical actions.[390] The case law suggests that the argument is particularly strong when the State is claiming *after* the individual concerned has already claimed for the same injury: in such circumstances, allowing the State's derivative, 'indirect', claim has little justification.[391] The argument may be less obviously tenable in the opposite direction, where the individual who is the 'direct' victim of the internationally wrongful act attempts to claim after the State.[392] However, the case law suggests that, where the individual's interests are protected, including where any reparation awarded is provided to that individual, the application of *res judicata* may nonetheless be justified.[393]

B. 'Direct' and 'mixed' claims

While the application of the double recovery rule is relatively straightforward as between overlapping individual and interstate diplomatic protection claims, how it applies when the overlapping interstate claim is 'direct' or 'mixed' is not so immediately clear. For *res judicata*, whose application is already less certain vis-à-vis the former, the situation is even more complicated for the other categories. Nonetheless, this section argues that the double recovery rule may apply even vis-à-vis certain 'direct' claims, and both rules may operate as between overlapping individual and interstate 'mixed' claims insofar as the damage suffered derives from individual injury.

[387] *ARSIWA*, art 48(2)(b); generally Vermeer-Künzli (n 153) 557–59; Hersch Lauterpacht, *International Law: Being the Collected Papers of Hersch Lauterpacht* (Elihu Lauterpacht ed, CUP 1970) 299–300; Giorgio Gaja, 'Is a State Specially Affected When Its Nationals' Human Rights Are Infringed?' in Lal Chand Vohrah and others (eds), *Man's Inhumanity to Man: Essays on International Law in Honour of Antonio Cassese* (Kluwer 2003) 382; Ch 1, nn 96–99, 116–17; Ch 3, n 218.

[388] See *ARSIWA*, 209, 279; Gaja, 'Position' (n 455) 12; Gaja, 'Affected' (n 387) 380, 382; Gaja, 'Compliance' (n 153) 958, 961; Giorgio Gaja, 'The International Court of Justice's Approach to Injuries Suffered by Individuals' (Oxford, 8 May 2014)' <https://podcasts.ox.ac.uk/international-court-justices-approach-injuries-suffered-individuals>; Vermeer-Künzli (n 153) 577; Linos-Alexandre Sicilianos, 'Countermeasures in Response to Grave Violations of Obligations Owed to the International Community' in Crawford and others, *Responsibility* (n 100) 1144; Simma and Pulkowski (n 153) 160. Cf Shany, *Competing* (n 4) 171–73 (rejecting special human rights considerations).

[389] *Cyprus v Turkey (Compensation)* (n 76) 272; *Georgia v Russia (I) (Compensation)* (n 74), *dispositif* [2](c).

[390] cf nn 167ff, 377, generally nn 3–5; similarly Vermeer-Künzli (n 53) 278.

[391] nn 282, 291, 295–96, 348–49. Cf Peters (n 137) 175.

[392] nn 294–96; Peters (n 137) 175.

[393] nn 231, 279ff, 343ff.

(i) Double recovery

(a) 'Direct' claims

The interstate diplomatic protection and human rights claims which engage the double recovery rule vis-à-vis overlapping individual claims are brought for personal or property damage suffered by individuals, while 'direct' claims are not.[394] Indeed, insofar as such 'direct' claims are brought for damage peculiar to the State—to State-owned property, for instance,[395] or for 'security and defence costs',[396] which can be appreciated as 'public' in nature[397]—the double recovery rule seems unlikely to be engaged even if an overlapping individual claim is brought, as the individual claims for its damage alone.[398] The individual and State damage is, in such cases, distinct, and the rule has no scope for operation.[399]

However, States may bring claims that are 'direct' but still 'derivative' of individual injury in a sense different to that occurring in diplomatic protection claims, namely in the same way that heirs, dependents, and insurers[400] may claim for their *own* loss resulting from damage done to others.[401] Borchard, for instance, foresaw such losses being suffered by the State if 'the citizen has been rendered unable to perform his duties toward [that] state, *e.g.*, his duties of loyalty, the performance of military service, or the payment of taxes'.[402] More generally, individuals who have suffered personal injury may, for example, be entitled to State-funded medical care, or social benefits, meaning the State bears certain costs resulting from that

[394] Ch 3, nn 203–11.

[395] Ch 3, n 244 and, eg, *Ethiopia* (n 16) [53] ('public property'), [143]ff, [162]ff, [357]ff, [410]ff, [436] (government property), Ch X(C) (diplomatic property), Ch XI(M) ('State-owned' ([449]) airline); *Eritrea* (n 15) [101]–[103], [108], [111], [114]–[133], [136], [142], [157]–[172], [179], [186], [188], Ch VII(J) (diplomatic); *Armed Activities (Reparations)* (n 80) [230] ('civilian infrastructure'), [254]–[256] (public electricity provider/military property).

[396] *Military and Paramilitary Activities in and Against Nicaragua (Nicaragua v USA)* ICJ Pleadings, 273, Ch 4.

[397] Robert Weinstock, 'The Lorax State: Parens Patriae and the Provision of Public Goods' (2009) 109 Colum LR 798, 831 ('public good ... national defense'); *Lusitania Cases (US/Germany)* (1923) VII UNRIAA 32, 42 ('cost to [US] in prosecuting the war'), 43 ('cost... falls on all American taxpayers'). Cf *Ethiopia* (n 16) [286].

[398] See analysis in Note, 'State Protection of Its Economy and Environment: Parens Patriae Suits for Damages' (1970) 6 Colum JL & Soc Probs 411, 414–18, 424. Cf n 419 (separate State/individual damage), n 579.

[399] See section I.

[400] See Borchard (n 54) 627 ('Derivative Claimants', namely 'successors in interest'); *Wyoming v Oklahoma* 502 US 437 (1992) 476 (Diss Op Thomas) (tax loss 'derivative injury'); *Texas v American Tobacco* 14 F Supp 2d 956 (1997) 965 (argument State healthcare costs 'derivative'), discussed Jack Ratliff, '*Parens Patriae:* An Overview' (2000) 74 Tul LR 1847, 1853–54; Meron (n 62), particularly 641, 643, 646; cf *US v Germany (Administrative Decision No VI)* (1925) VII UNRIAA 155 (US–German Mixed Cl Comm) 165 (survivors' claims 'not derivative').

[401] Similarly: Louis Sohn and R Baxter (eds), *Convention on the International Responsibility of States for Injuries to Aliens* (HLS 1961) 46 and nn 402–3. Cf 'indirect' human rights victims: Zwart (n 43) 69–71, 80–84; n 65 (shareholders). Generally on 'consequential losses': de Aréchaga (n 80) 568–69; also *Eritrea* (n 15) [203] (no 'separate category of compensable "consequential damages"' under international law); Wittich (n 353) 122–25; *ARSIWA*, 203–5 (causation).

[402] Borchard (n 54) 362. See also Fitzmaurice (n 353) 26.

injury.[403] Chapter 3 outlined how, in *Corfu Channel*, such damage was properly regarded as *State* damage, with the State having incurred costs for pensions and medical treatment consequent on the personal injury suffered by its personnel.[404] State practice gives other examples of similar claims: the UNCC compensated States for relief payments made to their citizens;[405] in the *Bosnian Genocide* case, Bosnia claimed for its own 'expenditures' in 'remedy[ing] or mitigat[ing] damage' separately from its claims for damage to persons and property;[406] and both Ethiopia and Eritrea claimed before the EECC for public spending consequent on individual injury.[407]

The above extract from the UNCC suggests that the principle precluding double recovery will operate to preclude the latter of such interstate claims and overlapping individual claims where the State costs were themselves incurred to compensate the relevant individual's damage.[408] Indeed, a case brought under the US law of *parens patriae*, discussed in greater detail below, provides a useful example of how this might play out in practice: where Guatemala brought a claim against tobacco companies for additional healthcare costs it had incurred for its citizens occasioned by tobacco use, a US court concluded that the State was claiming for 'identical injuries' to those suffered by the individual smokers themselves, in the form of medical expenses resulting from personal injury.[409] Whether costs resulting from personal injury are incurred by the individual, or paid out of State coffers, the damage is the same, and the double recovery rule prevents multiple claims to repair it.

[403] See Brigitte Bollecker-Stern, *Le Préjudice Dans La Théorie de La Responsibilité Internationale* (Pedone 1973) 101ff, particularly 101 (public social insurance may remove fiction); Gateano Arangio-Ruiz, 'Second Report on State Responsibility' (1989) 2(1) ILCYB 1, 16 (fn 110) (quoting Reuter) (taxation/healthcare); *ARSIWA*, 221 (officials' 'pensions and medical expenses' State damage); Sohn and Baxter (n 401) 46 (hospital expenses/benefits/travel/repatriation/legal costs); similarly *Reparations* (n 22) 181, 197 (Diss Op Hackworth), 215–16 (Diss Op Badawi Pasha), 217 (Diss Op Krylov).

[404] Ch 3, nn 257ff.

[405] van Houtte, Delmartino, and Yi (n 78) 58.

[406] *Application of the Convention on the Prevention and Punishment of the Crime of Genocide (Bosnia and Herzegovina v Serbia and Montenegro) (Judgment)* [2007] ICJ Rep 43, 72.

[407] *Eritrea* (n 15) [290] (post-expulsion), [307]–[308] ('cash subsidy', 'provision of social services', 'expenses ... in receiving, caring for and resettling rural Ethiopian nationals'); *Ethiopia* (n 16) [143] ('public expenditure'), [156], [159] (civilians' medical treatment), [471] (IDP care), Ch XI(O) (civilian assistance/reconstruction). Generally Murphy, Kidane, and Snider (n 78) 140, 143–52, 199, 201.

[408] See *Seventh Instalment* (n 79). Generally Note (n 398) 414ff.

[409] *In Re Tobacco/Governmental Healthcare Costs Litigation* 83 F Supp 2d 125 (1999) 131 (while 'pursuing the recoupment of ... medical expenses under different legal theories than would individual smokers, [Guatemala] ... seeks damages for identical injuries'), 132; generally Sean Murphy, 'Liability and the WHO Framework Convention on Tobacco Control' (2003) 5 Int L Forum 62, 63; cf Note (n 398) 417–18, 428 ('effects on ... individual[s] ... indirect'). Cf *American Tobacco* (n 400) 960–63, discussed Ratliff (n 400) 1853–54; Benjamin E Metz, 'Reconstitutionalizing *Parens Patriae*: How Federal *Parens Patriae* Doctrine Appropriately Permits State Damages Suits Aggregating Private Tort Claims' <http://www.law.columbia.edu/sites/default/files/microsites/career-services/Reconstitutionalizing%20Parens%20Patriae.pdf>, 1.

Similarly, it is not uncommon for States to claim for damage to their economy,[410] representing, as discussed in greater detail below vis-à-vis *res judicata*, the State's own interest in doing so.[411] Nicaragua, for instance, claimed against the US for losses resulting from trade embargoes[412] and to its 'development potential',[413] the latter including GDP and 'social losses' vis-à-vis health, education, housing, and infrastructure,[414] calculated respectively based on import and export figures, and welfare expenditure combined with more general overall effect estimates.[415] In *Armed Activities*, the DRC likewise claimed for 'macroeconomic damage' resulting from Uganda's use of force, in the form of 'considerable [economic] slowdown'.[416]

As Chapter 3 outlined, however, it is only 'by a fiction' that 'the economic assets of an individual' are 'regarded as part of the wealth of his national state'.[417] A case brought under the US *parens patriae* doctrine again provides a useful elucidation of the factual issues that arise in this context:[418] there, the US Supreme Court noted 'the problems of double recovery inherent in allowing damages for harm both to the economic interests of individuals and for the quasi-sovereign interests of the State' given that:

> [a] large and ultimately indeterminable part of the injury to the "general economy", as it is measured by economists, is no more than a reflection of injuries to the "business or property" of consumers, for which they may recover themselves ....[419]

410 See cases n 524; *Ethiopia* (n 16) Ch XI(N) (tourism/aid/investment), particularly [468] (economy); *Nicaragua's Pleadings* (n 396) 307–8; also Murphy (n 409) 202 (WTO).

411 nn 526, 544.

412 *Nicaragua's Pleadings* (n 396) Ch 5.

413 ibid Ch 6.

414 ibid 298.

415 See ibid 313–17; also *Guyana v Suriname (Award)* PCA Case 2002-4 (17 September 2007) [266].

416 *Armed Activities (Reparations)* (n 80) [368]–[369].

417 Amerasinghe, *LR* (n 137) 53. Similarly Eric Wyler and Alain Papaux, 'Satisfaction' in Crawford and others, *Responsibility* (n 100) 628; authorities Ch 3, nn 170–71.

418 On individual/*parens patriae* double recovery risks: n 419; Note (n 398) 414, 417; Metz (n 409) 4, 22–24. Cf Lisa Moscati Hawkes, '*Parens Patriae* and the Union Carbide Case: The Disaster at Bhopal Continues' (1988) 21 Corn ILJ 181, 184, 190, 192, 194; Russell L Caplan, 'Parens Patriae Antitrust Suits by Foreign Nations' (1977) 6 Denv J Intl L & Pol 705, 744–45; Gabrielle Hanna, 'The Helicopter State: Misuse of Parens Patriae Unconstitutionality Precludes Individual and Class Claims' (2017) 92 Wash LR 1955, 1985–86.

419 *Hawaii v Standard Oil* 405 US 251 (1972) 264; cf 276–77 (Diss Op Brennan) (State claim independent, 'excluded from its recovery any monetary damages that might be claimed by its citizens individually or as part of a properly constituted class'), 269 (Diss Op Douglas) ('Injury to ... collective will commonly include injury to members of the collective'), cf 269–70 (possible distinctions), case discussed Hawkes (n 418) 191–92; Caplan (n 418) 710–11, 728–29, 744; Metz (n 409) 15; George Curtis, 'The Checkered Career of *Parens Patriae*: The State as Parent or Tyrant?' (1976) 25 Depaul LR 895, 912–13.

Being such a 'reflection' of individual injury, this suggests that—even if economic loss may indeed amount to State damage[420]—it is often, as in the shareholder claims discussed above, 'reflective' or 'derivative' loss,[421] which cannot be claimed both by the State (as economic loss) and by the nationals individually affected.[422] Indeed, in the *Armed Activities* case, Uganda objected to the DRC's claim 'under the guise of macroeconomic damage' on the basis, *inter alia*, that it would grant the latter double recovery vis-à-vis amounts claimed pursuant to other heads of damage.[423]

The same applies for tax revenue losses which, again, while amounting to damage to the State,[424] are often consequent on individual economic losses.[425] A loss of State services may also be claimed as State damage,[426] but with the losses ultimately harming individuals, one might expect an overlap in the damage suffered.[427] Indeed, as Chapter 3 noted, even environmental damage, often claimed by States,[428] and which may indeed amount to State damage under international law,[429] may

[420] See nn 410–11; *New York v Seneci* 817 F 2d 1015 (1987) 1017, quoted Metz (n 409) 15 (fn 61). Cf Bollecker-Stern (n 403) 100–5.

[421] nn 60–62, 400, 425. Similarly *Ethiopia* (n 16) [468], discussed Murphy, Kidane, and Snider (n 78) 150; also *Nicaragua's Pleadings* (n 396) 277 ('direct repercussions upon … economy'), 306 (and authorities), 311–12. Cf Anastasios Gourgourinis, 'Reviewing the Administration of Domestic Regulation in WTO and Investment Law: The International Minimum Standard as "One Standard to Rule Them All"?' in Freya Baetens (ed), *Investment Law Within International Law: Integrationist Perspectives* (CUP 2013) 301 (WTO 'beneficiaries … private parties').

[422] n 419. Cf *Eritrea* (n 15) [195]ff (individual 'consequential damages'); Murphy, Kidane, and Snider (n 78) 221–23.

[423] *Armed Activities (Reparations)* (n 80) [379]. See *Armed Activities on the Territory of the Congo (DRC v Uganda)* ICJ Pleadings, Counter-Mem Uganda (reparations) [9.35].

[424] See *Wyoming v Oklahoma* (n 400) 448, also 449, 451, discussed John E Nowak and Ronald D Rotunda, *Constitutional Law* (6th edn, West 2000) 102; *Standard Oil* (n 419) 274 (Sep Op Brennan) ('additional payments from … public purse … or the failure to generate additional wealth' represent 'harm to … economic wellbeing'); Curtis (n 419) 914 (fn 83); *Eritrea* (n 15) [174] ('direct claim for lost tax revenue'), discussed Murphy, Kidane, and Snider (n 78) 224; also *The M/V "Saiga" (No 2) Case (Saint Vincent and the Grenadines v Guinea) (Judgment)* [1999] ITLOS Rep 10 [135] (State's 'interest in maximizing … tax revenue'); Note (n 398) 414–17.

[425] *Wyoming v Oklahoma* (n 400) 476 (Diss Op Thomas) ('derivative injury'); Ioannis Dimitrakopoulos, *Individual Rights and Liberties Under the U.S. Constitution: The Case Law of the U.S. Supreme Court* (Martinus Nijhoff 2007) 19 (fn 89) ('consequential loss'); nn 400–2. Cf Note (n 398) 415–17.

[426] See nn 414, 526–27; *Eritrea* (n 15) [125]–[128], [208] (hospital costs), [136], [183] (schools).

[427] Cf nn 409, 414–15, 465, 527; *Standard Oil* (n 419) 262–63 (fn 14) ('[State] injury … affects the citizens' similarly to *parens patriae* injury. 'Each … increas[es] taxes, or reduc[es] government services, or both'); *Eritrea* (n 15) [195]–[196] and following ('consequential damages' for individuals injured through damage to 'educational facilities', 'telecommunications and other infrastructure', 'devastation of the local economy' and 'loss of access to healthcare'); also Note (n 398) 428 ('compensation, in … form of increased governmental services or lowered taxes'); cf *Eritrea* (n 15) [21] (significant compensation risks 'diversions of national resources from … paying country—and … citizens needing health care, education … other public services'), 630 (award 'to provide relief to [States'] civilian populations'); discussed Crawford, *GP* (n 6) 483–84.

[428] Cases nn 528–29; *Ethiopia* (n 16) Ch XI(H) (environment), [421]–[422]; *Nuclear Tests (Australia v France; New Zealand v France)* ICJ Pleadings, vol I, 14; vol II, 8, discussed Ian Brownlie, *System of the Law of Nations: State Responsibility, Part I* (Clarendon 1983) 68–69, also 237 (*Cosmos* incident).

[429] *ARSIWA*, 223; John Barker, 'Compensation' in Crawford and others, *Responsibility* (n 100) 604; van Houtte, Delmartino, and Yi (n 78) 58 (UNCC State category); further Allan Kanner, 'The Public

in some circumstances actually reflect individual damage, where the reparation sought is quantified based on losses suffered vis-à-vis private property.[430] In *Trail Smelter*, for instance, interstate compensation was ultimately provided to the private landowners affected.[431] For its part, in awarding the DRC reparation for 'the looting, plundering and exploitation of natural resources', the ICJ did not distinguish between public and private losses,[432] though double recovery concerns could have arisen had both the State and private entities claimed.[433]

Unless claims like these—for public spending, or economic or environmental damage—are in fact brought for individual damage and thus in reality diplomatic protection claims, they remain properly regarded as 'direct' claims for State damage under international law.[434] Nonetheless, the double recovery rule will still operate to preclude reparation being awarded in the latter of two overlapping individual and 'direct' interstate claims where the latter, State, claim is one for damage *reflecting* that suffered by the individual.

(b) 'Mixed' claims

Previous chapters outlined that 'mixed' claims combine the diplomatic protection and 'direct' claims just discussed.[435] Accordingly, a State claims both for damage done to an individual (which is 'fictionally' done to it), and for damage (material or moral) *actually* suffered by the State.[436] Given the conclusions already reached, the application of the double recovery rule in 'mixed' claims appears unproblematic in principle: the rule would only preclude overlapping individual and interstate claims for reparation insofar as the claim for State damage reflects individual losses for which reparation is also claimed on the individual level, and not separately quantified State damage. For instance, if a State-owned aircraft were shot down, a 'mixed' claim could be separated into that for material damage to the aircraft (State damage) and that for personal injury to those on board (individual damage), with the double recovery rule only

Trust Doctrine, *Parens Patriae*, and the Attorney General as the Guardian of the State's Natural Resources' (2005) 16 Duke Env L & Pol For 57, 61–90, 94, 100–12, discussing authorities; Note (n 398) 417–18 ('public injury'), 421.

[430] See *Trail Smelter Case (US/Canada)* (1938/1941) III UNRIAA 1905, discussed nn 589–90; Philip Jessup, *A Modern Law of Nations* (Archon 1968) 120; also Kanner (n 429) 99.

[431] David Caron, 'The Place of the Environment in International Tribunals' in Jay Austin and Carl Bruch (eds), *The Environmental Consequences of War: Legal, Economic, and Scientific Perspectives* (CUP 2000) 254; Bollecker-Stern (n 403) 109.

[432] *Armed Activities (Reparations)* (n 80) [366].

[433] Certain resources were apparently subject to private concessions: see *Armed Activities Pleadings* (n 423) Mem DRC (reparations) [5.22], [5.65]–[5.67], [5.176] (diamonds, gold, coffee, timber). Cf 'public' resources, such as national park fauna: ibid [351].

[434] See Ch 3(IV)(B)(i).

[435] Ch 2, nn 108–9.

[436] Ch 3(IV)(B)(i).

precluding overlapping individual and interstate claims to repair the latter, individual, damage.[437]

More complicated 'mixed' claims scenarios may, however, be envisioned, where the distinction between State and individual damage is less obvious. In order to tease out how the rule precluding double recovery functions, this section examines one such situation, arising commonly in practice and involving States bringing 'mass claims'[438] for damage to their populations. Despite the complexity of such claims and the blurring of lines between State and individual damage, we will see that the element of individual injury subsists in such an interstate claim—and together with it, the possibility for the double recovery rule to operate vis-à-vis an overlapping individual claim—even if claims are not individually addressed, nor the full loss repaired.[439]

As previous chapters have foreshadowed, extensive or serious violations vis-à-vis individuals may entail moral damage to those individuals' State of nationality.[440] Often, the voluminous claims thereby arising are settled on the interstate level through lump-sum settlements,[441] settlements that commonly involve no effort 'to adjudicate each claim or to allocate any specified amount to any designated claim'.[442]

Nonetheless, the case law suggests that the individual element, while obscured, remains present. For instance, as Chapter 3 discussed, in *Cyprus v Turkey*, the ECtHR, having distinguished diplomatic protection and other interstate claims,[443] considered that claims brought 'for the benefit of individual victims' vis-à-vis 'two sufficiently precise and objectively identifiable groups of people' were diplomatic

[437] cf aircraft cases Ch 3, nn 127–28, 283; *Corfu Channel*, Ch 3, n 257. On satisfaction for moral damage: Ch 3, nn 279–85.

[438] Generally Howard Holtzmann and Edda Kristjánsdóttir, *International Mass Claims Processes: Legal and Practical Perspectives* (OUP 2007); Murphy, Kidane, and Snider (n 78) 45–49, also 32–45; van Houtte, Delmartino, and Yi (n 78) Ch 2; Howard Holtzmann, 'Mass Claims' in *MPEPIL* (n 16) (2008); Berk Demirkol, 'Does an Investment Treaty Tribunal Need Special Consent for Mass Claims?' (2013) 2 Camb JI & CL 612, 616, 626–28; Christine Gray, 'Remedies' in Romano, Alter and Shany (n 142) 887–90; Hans Das and Hans van Houtte, *Post-War Restoration of Property Rights under International Law*, vol 2 (CUP 2008), particularly 24–25 (defined vis-à-vis 'high number of claims' being 'sufficiently similar').

[439] See nn 441ff; Holtzmann (n 438) [2] (States may exercise diplomatic protection); Kalshoven (n 353) 46, cf 46–47 (where 'lump-sum' interstate settlement 'does not ... meet the actual damage ... difficult to maintain that ... in [*sic*] behalf of ... victims'; 'cannot ... depriv[e] individual victims of ... right to press ... own claims for damage'). Cf Demirkol (n 438) 627 ('international mass claims processes ... not collective'; 'fast but individualised proceeding'); n 580.

[440] See n 522.

[441] See Gaja, 'Injuries' (n 388); *Decision No V* (n 241) 152, quoted DADP, 99; Eyal Benvenisti, 'Individual Remedies for Victims of Armed Conflicts in the Context of Mass Claims Settlements' in Holger Hestermeyer and others (eds), *Coexistence, Cooperation and Solidarity: Liber Amicorum Rüdiger Wolfrum* (Martinus Nijohoff 2012) 1095; Murphy, Kidane, and Snider (n 78) 32–34. Generally Ch 5, nn 48–52.

[442] *Decision No V* (n 241) 152, quoted DADP, 99; also *Oppenheim's* (n 62) 538; cf Murphy, Kidane, and Snider (n 78) 33–35.

[443] *Cyprus v Turkey (Compensation)* (n 76) [44]–[45], cf 302–3 (Diss Op Karakaş).

protection-like, notwithstanding that the individuals numbered over a thousand,[444] that the State was ultimately awarded sizeable 'aggregate sums',[445] and that one group was 'defined in an abstract manner'.[446] Cyprus was left to locate, and distribute sums to, the individual victims.[447] Similarly, in *Georgia v Russia (I)*, the Court held that reparation could be awarded in respect of 'a "sufficiently precise and objectively identifiable" group of at least 1,500 Georgian nationals' who were victims of the relevant violations,[448] leaving Georgia to distribute the lump-sum amounts.[449] In these cases, amounts are awarded to repair individual damage, even though the award is an overall lump-sum one, and the precise individuals are not identified but defined as members of a group.[450] And the individual element persists notwithstanding that these States would, given the nature and scale of the violations, have their own potential claims for moral damage.[451]

A similar approach may be seen in interstate claims concerning mass post-conflict damage. For its part, while the EECC acknowledged that it was mainly addressing interstate, not individual, claims per se,[452] and 'mass claims' mechanisms were not used,[453] it nonetheless observed that 'some of both States' claims are made in the exercise of diplomatic protection, *in that they are predicated upon injuries allegedly suffered by numbers of [their] nationals*'.[454] For instance, Ethiopia claimed 'fixed-sum[s] ... multiplied by the number of victims' in its 'claims for deaths and injuries, for certain property losses, for moral damages, and for injuries to prisoners of war'.[455] The EECC raised concerns, including that 'claimant classes' were 'abstract',[456] but ultimately awarded lump-sums for '*jus in bello* violations ... involving death, physical injury, disappearance, forced labor and conscription of civilians',[457] individual property damage,[458] and civilian injuries in Eritrea.[459] It also held Eritrea responsible for

444 ibid [47].
445 ibid [58]. Cf [3]–[6] (Op Casadevall).
446 ibid [4] (Op Casadevall), 306 (Diss Op Karakaş).
447 ibid 272.
448 *Georgia v Russia(I) (Compensation)* (n 74) [71]
449 ibid [79].
450 Cf on a 'class': nn 257–58.
451 See Ch 3, nn 289–96; also Andrea Gattini, 'A Trojan Horse for Sudeten Claims? On Some Implications of the Prince of Liechtenstein v Germany' (2002) 13 EJIL 513, 537.
452 *Eritrea* (n 15) [3], Ch 2, n 47; also [25], [229] (POWs); Murphy, Kidane, and Snider (n 78) 57 ('largely ... traditional interstate claims, albeit ... often [seeking] recovery for loss, damage, or injury to thousands of people'), 301–3; van Houtte, Delmartino, and Yi (n 78) 49, 99.
453 Murphy, Kidane, and Snider (n 78) 57, also 60–62; *Eritrea* (n 15) [38] ('State claims, not mass claims'), [53] (not 'mass claims on behalf of individuals'), [65]; David Caron, 'International Claims and Compensation Bodies' in Romano, Alter, and Shany (n 142) 293.
454 *Eritrea* (n 15) [25]; *Ethiopia* (n 428) [25] (emphasis added); also Murphy, Kidane, and Snider (n 78) 57 ('espousing' claims), 68–70 (nationality). Generally on the damages awards: ibid 137–51, 183–88, 197–202, 219–28, 230–36, 301–3, 383–93. Cf Demirkol (n 438) 627.
455 *Ethiopia* (n 16) [68], generally [71]–[78].
456 ibid [84], further concerns [84]–[92]. Discussion Murphy, Kidane, and Snider (n 78) 185.
457 *Ethiopia* (n 16) [103], also [157]–[158], [161]. Discussion Murphy, Kidane, and Snider (n 78) 187.
458 Eg *Ethiopia* (n 16) [126], [135], [147], [180]ff, [199]ff.
459 ibid [214]–[262] (numbers often unclear).

personal and property damage arising from *jus ad bellum* violations,[460] awarding lump-sum compensation.[461] In Eritrea's case, in addition to awards for identified individuals,[462] the EECC made, for instance, lump-sum awards for losses of persons' 'residential and business property'[463] based on population estimates and likely damage incidence and severity,[464] for civilian injury regarding 'loss of access to medical care',[465] expulsion of residents,[466] deprivation of nationality concerning an 'unknown, but apparently small, number of dual nationals',[467] and detention of some thousand civilians.[468] In both cases, awards were made 'for failing to prevent the rape of known and unknown victims'[469] and for prisoners' personal injury, taking account, *inter alia*, of 'the total numbers of probable victims', and 'the extent of the injury or damage'.[470] Such claims appear to be, in the EECC's words, 'predicated' on individual injury, and thus diplomatic protection,[471] notwithstanding that the awards are lump-sum in nature and generally not made for identified individuals, and that significant material and moral State damage was also alleged.[472]

The ICJ took a similar approach in its reparation award in the *Armed Activities* case,[473] noting that in post-conflict cases involving large numbers of victims, global awards are commonly made, reflecting the evidence available, with 'less rigorous standards of proof' required and sums reduced accordingly.[474] It awarded such 'a global sum' for damage to persons, including for loss of life, injuries and mutilations, sexual violence, and displacement, and relating to child soldiers, admitting that it could not determine, even approximately, the number of victims, but basing itself on a 'range of possibilities indicated by the evidence'.[475] It also made awards for damage to property including to 'private dwellings',[476] on the same global basis.[477] The claim was, unsurprisingly, not brought as diplomatic protection per se, given the extensive damage alleged to the DRC itself,[478] but there are

460 ibid [292], [296], [300], [304]–[305], [391]. See Murphy, Kidane, and Snider (n 78) 133–36; Ch 3, n 117.

461 *Ethiopia* (n 16) [332], [349], [356], [393]. See Murphy, Kidane, and Snider (n 78) 137–47.

462 See *Eritrea* (n 15) [393]ff ('Individual Claims').

463 ibid [76].

464 ibid [72]–[76]; also [99]ff (building claims, some private), [331]–[340], [344]–[365] (property). Discussion Murphy, Kidane, and Snider (n 78) 199.

465 *Eritrea* (n 15) [216].

466 ibid [244]–[246]. See Murphy, Kidane, and Snider (n 78) 236.

467 *Eritrea* (n 15) [267].

468 ibid [374]–[376].

469 ibid [239]; *Ethiopia* (n 16) [110].

470 *Eritrea* (n 15) [229]; *Ethiopia* (n 16) [209].

471 n 454; also Caron (n 453) 293 (EECC 'state espousal'); cf Juratowich (n 130) 28–29.

472 See *Ethiopia* (n 16) [54]–[65] (moral damage); nn 395, 407 (State damage).

473 See *Armed Activities (Reparations)* (n 80) [108].

474 ibid [107].

475 ibid [166], [181], [193], [206], [225].

476 ibid [230]–[232].

477 ibid [258].

478 Eg ibid [231], [254]–[256], [260]ff, [367], [385] (public property, resources, economic/moral damage). Cf Ch 3, nn 295–96.

clearly elements of diplomatic protection here, with various claims being made for damage to private persons and property.[479] Indeed, the Court itself acknowledged that reparation for damage to persons and property 'reflects the harm suffered by individuals and communities',[480] and that the 'reparation is intended, as far as possible, to benefit all those who suffered injury',[481] welcoming the DRC's undertaking to 'fairly and effectively' distribute compensation 'to victims of the harm'.[482] Despite being awarded as global sums, on the basis of damage suffered by often unidentified persons, and intended to encompass the State's moral damage,[483] the compensation still therefore repaired individual injury.

The claims brought against the US in the *Nicaragua* case reflect comparable reasoning. Nicaragua engaged in diplomatic protection,[484] providing detailed evidence of personal injury to thousands of individuals, and significant property losses.[485] Even so, 'because of the difficulties both moral and economic of calculating damages for persons killed, wounded and missing on a case-by-case basis', it ultimately claimed 'a lump-sum award of reparation for all the injuries to persons'.[486]

Indeed, though taking place in the separate field of international criminal law, ICC reparations also provide a useful analogy, with awards on a 'collective' basis also designed to compensate for injuries suffered by individual victims.[487] Such 'collective' awards may be made, in place of individual awards, 'where the number of the victims and the scope, forms and modalities of reparations makes [this] more appropriate'.[488] In *Lubanga*, the Appeals Chamber noted that reparations could only be awarded to victims 'who suffered harm as a result of the commission of the [relevant] crimes'.[489] Where a crime affects 'a community as a whole', supposing 'a sufficient causal link', it might be 'appropriate to award collective reparations to that community', but this must be 'understood as a group of victims',[490] meaning a

479 See Ch 3, nn 163–64; cf Ch 3, nn 367–69 (inadmissible claim).

480 *Armed Activities (Reparations)* (n 80) [408].

481 ibid [102].

482 ibid [408].

483 See ibid [392] (DRC's US$100 million 'non-material harm' claim 'included in the global sums awarded . . . for various heads of damage').

484 *Certain Property (Liechtenstein v Germany)* ICJ Pleadings, Obs Liechtenstein [6.37].

485 *Nicaragua's Pleadings* (n 396) vol V, 263–68.

486 ibid 268.

487 On 'collective' reparations generally: Cohen (n 80), particularly 264–70; Diana Contreras Garduño, 'Collective Reparations: Tensions and Dilemmas Between Collective Reparations and the Individual Right to Receive Reparations' (2018) Utrecht University Human Rights Research Series, vol 84 <https://dspace.library.uu.nl/handle/1874/369720>. Cf understanding 'collective' reparations as addressing group harm: Diana Contreras Garduño, 'Defining Beneficiaries of Collective Reparations: The Experience of the IACtHR' (2012) 4 Ams LF 40, 46–47; n 494.

488 ICC, RoPE (2019), r 98; also r 97 (reparations 'on an individualized basis, or . . . collective basis or both').

489 *Prosecutor v Lubanga (Judgment on the appeals against the "Decision establishing the principles and procedures to be applied to reparations" of 7 August 2012)* Case ICC-01/04-01/06AA2A3 (3 March 2015) [211].

490 ibid [212].

'group of people sharing a certain characteristic'.[491] Thus, in the case of an award 'to the benefit of a community, only members of the community meeting the relevant criteria are eligible'.[492] Again, then, even if awarded on a group basis, with actual identification of victims left to a later stage,[493] reparation responds to individual injury. Of course, 'collective' reparations designed to compensate a group *qua* group, rather than the individual members thereof, and thus to benefit an entire community, are also possible.[494] But the point is that an award of lump-sum reparation can still respond to individual injury, even if calculated on an all-inclusive basis, and even if the individuals affected are not identified.

Other practice confirms that limiting the reparation awarded does not detract from the individual nature of a claim. Thus, the numerous 'individual and corporate claims' for injury before the UNCC belonged to those claimants, notwithstanding their filing by governments,[495] and irrespective of certain compensation amounts being capped.[496] The ECtHR has likewise adopted 'fixed-rate sums' of reparation when addressing thousands of similar applications, but it remains reparation for individual injury.[497]

Taken holistically, these cases suggest—as the ECtHR made particularly clear—that, although it is relevant 'whether the victims of violations can be identified',[498] a claim can still be one made for individual damage, notwithstanding that a group of persons is identified in an 'abstract' way.[499] The EECC and *Armed Activities* cases bear this out particularly clearly, with both tribunals having to estimate, sometimes very roughly, the populations affected.[500] Moreover, claims can still

[491] ibid [210].

[492] ibid [211].

[493] ibid [167]. Cf *Armed Activities (Reparations)* (n 80) [408] (encouraging consideration of sums to individual victims and 'the possibility of adopting measures for the benefit of the affected communities as a whole').

[494] Eg IACtHR case law: *Sanchez Massacre v Guatemala (Reparations)* (2004) IACHR Ser C No 116 [86] (reparation for 'members of the community as a whole'), [93] ('public repercussions'), [94]–[111] (investigations, acknowledgement, publicisation, collective memory, housing, medical and development programmes). However, calling community compensation 'exceptional': *Aloeboetoe v Suriname (Reparations)* (1993) IACHR Ser C No 15 [83]. Generally Contreras Garduño, 'Defining' (n 487); n 500. Cf *Lubanga* (n 489) [214]–[215] ('community-based' activities through Trust Fund assistance).

[495] van Houtte, Delmartino, and Yi (n 78) 62 and authorities Ch 2, n 45.

[496] See van Houtte, Delmartino, and Yi (n 78) 63, 309; Caron (n 453) 290; van Houtte, Das, and Delmartino (n 46) 359, generally 341–44, 348–51, 353–66.

[497] *Burmych v Ukraine* App 46852/13 (ECtHR, 12 October 2017) [32] and see [8], [13], [43]–[44]. See also *Georgia v Russia (I) (Compensation)* (n 74) [77]. Generally Demirkol (n 438) 627; n 266.

[498] *Cyprus v Turkey (Compensation)* (n 76) [43]; similarly nn 604, 635; also *Decision No V* (n 241) 152 ('where a demand is made on behalf of a *designated national* ... and payment is made on that *specific demand*, the fund so paid is not a national fund' (emphasis added)), quoted DADP, 99; also Borchard (n 54) 353, 357; cf Note (n 398) 425 ('unknown plaintiffs').

[499] nn 446, 456; also *Eritrea* (n 15) [38]; Rachael Mulheron, *The Class Action in Common Law Legal Systems: A Comparative Perspective* (Hart 2004) Ch 9(B) (on class definition).

[500] nn 464, 474–77; similarly Murphy, Kidane, and Snider (n 78) 138; also Gray (n 438) 888–89. Cf Laurence Burgorgue-Larsen and Amaya Úbeda de Torres, *The Inter-American Court of Human Rights: Case Law and Commentary* (Rosalind Greenstein tr, OUP 2011) 227 (IACtHR awards group reparation 'even if ... impossible to define ... precise contour of the group').

be for individual damage even if lump-sums are awarded,[501] or compensation is capped.[502] Because such claims are nonetheless brought for individual damage,[503] the double recovery rule should continue to operate as between any interstate claim for such damage and individual claims for the same damage, precluding recovery of reparation in whichever claim is brought second.[504]

Indeed, although not described in such terms, that was precisely the outcome in *Georgia v Russia (I)*, where the State could not recover reparation for damage caused to any individual whose application had already been considered.[505] More generally, the sense of such an outcome lingers in the ICJ judgment in the *Immunities Case*, addressing circumstances in which Germany had agreed with Italy to settle 'all outstanding claims on the part of [Italy] or Italian natural or legal persons' arising from WWII, paying sums in 'final settlement' 'for the benefit of' the latter's persecuted nationals.[506] Although the case primarily concerned State immunity, the ICJ considered that the consistent post-war practice of concluding 'lump-sum settlements'—or otherwise not requiring reparation—evidenced the absence of any *jus cogens* rule 'requiring the payment of full compensation to each and every individual victim'.[507] The Court expressly did not rule on whether individuals have 'directly enforceable' international rights to compensation for violations of international humanitarian law.[508] Nonetheless, it appeared to assume that States can settle claims for such violations, thereby displacing any obligation to compensate affected individuals, observing:

> Where the State receiving funds as part of what was intended as a comprehensive settlement in the aftermath of an armed conflict has elected to use those funds to rebuild its national economy and infrastructure, rather than distributing them to individual victims amongst its nationals, it is difficult to see why the fact that those individuals had not received a share in the money should be a reason for entitling them to claim against the State that had transferred money to their State of nationality.[509]

While the primary point is that the rules on State immunity cannot be relaxed merely because individuals have not received compensation,[510] the tenor of the

[501] Eg vis-à-vis quantification problems: nn 474–75, 486; *Eritrea* (n 15) [38] ('compensation levels ... reduced, balancing the uncertainties flowing from the lower standard of proof'); Gray (n 438) 888–89; generally Caron (n 453) 290; Kalshoven (n 353) 46.
[502] nn 496–97. Cf Note (n 398) 425.
[503] cf authorities Ch 3, nn 208–10; generally Ch 3(II).
[504] cf Kalshoven, n 439.
[505] n 325.
[506] See *Jurisdictional Immunities (Germany v Italy: Greece Intervening) (Judgment)* [2012] ICJ Rep 99 [24]–[25].
[507] ibid [94]. Further: Peters (n 137) 209.
[508] *Immunities* (n 506) [108]; generally Ch 5, nn 105–9, 210.
[509] *Immunities* (n 506) [102]. I thank Paparinskis for discussion.
[510] ibid [101]–[102].

judgment suggests that States may preclude later individual compensation claims by accepting reparation, even where it is lump sum and the compensation is not spent, at least directly, on those affected.[511]

The ECtHR in *Pad* likewise appeared to envisage individual claims being precluded even where, as discussed above, the national State was only prepared to distribute a portion of the compensation intended for the victims.[512] Indeed, how the compensation received in an interstate claim is *actually* spent is, in the traditional law of diplomatic protection, immaterial, the State having complete discretion in this respect.[513]

The practice therefore suggests that interstate claims can be brought for individual damage, at least in part, even if: (i) there is significant State damage as well; (ii) the individuals affected are classified into 'abstract' groups, or otherwise unidentified; (iii) lump-sum reparation is awarded; and (iv) individuals in fact receive limited or no compensation.[514] While mass claims are likely to be 'mixed', owing to the presence of a State's moral or material damage,[515] the diplomatic protection element therefore remains present and, with it, the claim for reparation for individual damage that is the same as that in an overlapping individual claim.[516] The rule against double recovery will, accordingly, be engaged, and preclude the later of those claims for reparation.

(ii) *Res judicata*: distinguishing the 'general interest' from diplomatic protection

The application of *res judicata* in 'mixed' claims is more complicated. For diplomatic protection claims there is, as suggested above, a good argument for applying *res judicata* vis-à-vis an overlapping individual claim given that the State is claiming for individual injury and often representing the individual's interest.[517] By contrast, in 'direct' claims, the State 'represents principally its own interests rather than the interests of its nationals'.[518] Accordingly, the *res judicata* effect of a claim that is truly 'direct' is unlikely, as shown below, to bar an individual claim.[519] However, in many interstate 'mixed' claims, combining these diplomatic protection and 'direct'

[511] cf Note (n 398) 428–29; Hanna (n 418) 1985–86 (*parens patriae*); Christian Tomuschat, 'Individuals' in Crawford and others, *Responsibility* (n 100) 988–89; *Jurisdictional Immunities (Germany v Italy: Greece Intervening)* ICJ Pleadings, Rep Germany [46]; n 631.

[512] nn 68–72; Vermeer-Künzli (n 53) 284, 288.

[513] See DADP, 97–100, 29, quoting *Barcelona Traction* (n 23) [78]–[79]; Borchard (n 54) 29, 353, 357–58, 366–68; Vermeer-Künzli (n 53) 276–78; Mazzeschi (n 372) 211; Fitzmaurice (n 353) 26; de Aréchaga (n 80) 575; Bollecker-Stern (n 403) 107–9; Amerasinghe, *DP* (n 137) 22, 67; Marjorie Whiteman, *Damages in International Law* (US Government 1937) 275, 282–83; Douglas, 'Hybrid' (n 26) 169; Roberts (n 6) 30, 35–36; *Decision 8 (Relief to War Victims)* (2007) XXVI UNRIAA 21 [3]. Cf Hanna (n 418) 1967 (similar *parens patriae* concerns).

[514] Section V(B)(i)(b).

[515] n 522.

[516] Section V(A)(i). Generally Ch 3(II).

[517] Section V(A)(ii).

[518] Meron (n 242) 84–85, quoted Amerasinghe, *LR* (n 137) 160.

[519] nn 559ff; also ICSID (n 130) 66, 274.

aspects, State and individual interests are intermingled.[520] The question is whether the argument for *res judicata's* operation extends to such 'mixed' claims.[521]

Building on what has been said regarding double recovery, this section will focus on two situations drawn from State practice to elucidate when *res judicata* may operate to preclude an individual claim from being brought given previous consideration of an overlapping 'mixed' interstate claim, and vice versa.

First, as Chapter 3 discussed, a State's 'general interest' is enlivened and moral injury caused where extensive or serious violations affect its nationals,[522] including in situations involving alleged widespread human rights abuses.[523] For instance, despite the *Nicaragua*, *Bosnian Genocide* and *Croatian Genocide* cases concerning claims for individual personal and property damage on a large scale, they were brought not as diplomatic protection claims but in the respective States' 'own right and as *parens patriae* for [their] citizens'.[524] The question considered here is whether the State's 'general interest' in such situations obviates the potential application of *res judicata* as between the State's claim and any claim brought by the individuals affected, or whether *res judicata* could still operate, providing the State scope to take over the claim entirely and bar the bringing of its citizens' claims with a single proceeding.[525]

Second, States' interests include the economy and environment, as well as their population's safety.[526] As discussed above regarding double recovery, individuals

[520] nn 522ff; Ch 2, 108ff. Cf Roland Portmann, *Legal Personality in International Law* (CUP 2010) 130 (State/individual interests aligned).

[521] Cf Roberts (n 6) 10 and discussion nn 569, 580, 599ff.

[522] Garcia-Amador, 'Problems' (n 241) 474, also 485–86, 422, discussed Dugard (n 138) [72]; Jessup (n 430) 98; generally Ch 3, nn 286–94 and authorities.

[523] Ch 3, n 291.

[524] *Application of the Convention on the Prevention and Punishment of the Crime of Genocide (Croatia v Serbia) (Preliminary Objections)* [2008] ICJ Rep 412 [20] ('damages to persons and property ... economy and environment'); similarly *Bosnian Genocide* (n 406) 64; *Military and Paramilitary Activities in and against Nicaragua (Nicaragua v US) (Merits)* [1986] ICJ Rep 14 [15]; also *Application of the International Convention on the Elimination of All Forms of Racial Discrimination (Georgia v Russia) (Preliminary Objections)* [2011] ICJ Rep 70, 77–78. See Giorgio Gaja, 'The Position of Individuals in International Law: An ILC Perspective' (2010) 21 EJIL 11, 12; Christian Tams, *Enforcing Obligations* Erga Omnes *in International Law* (CUP 2005) 135; Julianne Kokott, 'The Exhaustion of Local Remedies' (2004) 69 ILA Rep Conf 606, 608; cf ILA, 'Toronto Conference Report: Diplomatic Protection of Persons and Property' (2006) 72 ILA Rep Conf 353 [28]; Ch 3, nn 99–104, 269.

[525] Similarly Roberts (n 6) 4, 9–10, 29, 67 (vis-à-vis 'class'); Kalshoven (n 353) 46–47; Gattini (n 451) 537 ('state ... might use diplomatic protection without consulting the individual concerned, especially where disputes concerning a large number of individuals are involved'); n 580. Struggling with a similar distinction, see Sohn and Baxter (n 401) 47 (when 'claims must begin to be treated on ... wholesale basis ... left to ... particular cases'); authorities nn 599, 648.

[526] The law of necessity recognises a State's 'essential interest' (*ARSIWA*, art 25) in such matters: see Roberto Ago, 'Eighth Report on State Responsibility (Addendum)' (1980) 2(1) ILCYB 13, 14; Sarah Heathcote, 'Necessity' in Crawford and others, *Responsibility* (n 100) 495–96; *ARSIWA*, 183; Crawford, *GP* (n 6) 308; Paddeu (n 150) 389–413; *Impregilo (Award)* (n 31) [346] (including 'fundamental needs of ... population'); *Continental Casualty v Argentina (Award)* ICSID Case No ARB/03/9 (5 September 2008) [177]–[180]; n 542. Similarly Robert Sloane, 'On the Use and Abuse of Necessity in the Law of State Responsibility' (2012) 106 AJIL 447, 454 ('state security, fiscal crises ... ecological harms'), cf 460ff. Cf Paparinskis (n 72) 634; nn 535–36.

may have a shared interest in such issues, the protection of which ultimately contributes to their welfare.[527] Indeed, in some interstate claims to defend such interests, large numbers of individuals are also affected by the conduct at issue: take the environmental claims in *Trail Smelter*,[528] and *Aerial Herbicide Spraying*,[529] or economic claims such as those made in the *Nicaragua* and *Genocide* cases.[530] As in respect of claims for widescale human rights abuses, States often likewise purport to bring such environmental or economic claims 'as *parens patriae* for [their] citizens'.[531] The question considered here is whether *res judicata* has any potential relevance in such circumstances, as between interstate claims and those that might be brought by the affected individuals themselves.

In answering these questions, analytical insights may be gleaned by comparing common law, as interpreted by US courts, concerning *parens patriae* claims.[532] Although States have employed this *parens patriae* terminology in interstate claims where significant individual injury has occurred alongside injury to State interests, and it is therefore appealing to compare domestic law in considering what was thereby intended,[533] this aspect of US law is not being employed here as a potential source of international law. Rather, the operation of the *parens patriae* doctrine under US law is being considered primarily because, with the benefit of a wealth of case law, it provides a helpful comparative framework in the endeavour to distinguish general State interests from those reflected in individual claims, including for considering when *res judicata* might operate between interstate and individual claims in these kinds of circumstances.[534]

US courts relevantly distinguish two kinds of claims: first, there are *parens patriae* claims proper, brought for a US state's 'quasi-sovereign interest'[535] in 'the health and well-being—both physical and economic—of [its] residents in

[527] See Margaret Lemos, 'Aggregate Litigation Goes Public: Representative Suits by State Attorneys General' (2012) 126 Harv LR 486, 494 ('state's interest in [residents'] well-being ... might overlap with the [residents'] personal interests'); Sloane (n 526) 504 ('for ... sake of ... state's constituents'); Portmann (n 520) 130. Also FV Garcia-Amador, 'International Responsibility: Report' (1956) 2 ILCYB 173 [112].

[528] *Trail Smelter* (n 430) 1917, 1920, 1924–31, 1965–66, discussed DADP, 82 and other authorities Ch 3, n 111.

[529] *Aerial Herbicide Spraying (Ecuador v Colombia)* ICJ Pleadings, Mem Ecuador, Chs VI–IX (claims), Ch X, particularly [10.29]ff (reparation); Rep Ecuador [3.152] ('claims ... on behalf of ... citizens'); Ch 3, n 109.

[530] n 524. Also nn 410ff.

[531] n 524.

[532] Explaining differences with common law: *Alfred Snapp & Son v Puerto Rico* 458 US 592 (1982) 600; Ratliff (n 400) 1850–51; Curtis (n 419) 895–98, 907–8; Hawkes (n 418) 186–87.

[533] n 524. Cf James Crawford, *International Law as an Open System* (Cameron May 2002) 352; James Crawford, 'Responsibility to the International Community as a Whole' (2001) 8 Ind JGLS 303, 315; David Sloss, 'Using International Court of Justice Advisory Opinions to Adjudicate Secessionist Claims' (2001) 42 SCLR 357, 375–78.

[534] See nn 535ff. On the US law 'analogy', cf Demirkol (n 438) 624; authorities n 542.

[535] *Snapp* (n 532) 601–2; also Laurence H Tribe, *American Constitutional Law*, vol 1 (3rd edn, Foundation Press 2000) 453; Curtis (n 419) 895, 908; Hawkes (n 418) 187; Ratliff (n 400) 1851–53; Metz (n 409) 6–7.

general'.[536] Second, there are claims which, even if asserting such interests,[537] cannot be brought by the individual US States under US law,[538] because the States are actually 'pursu[ing] the interests of a private party ... only for the sake of the real party in interest'[539] and do not 'articulate an interest apart from the interests of particular private parties'.[540] The latter have been held by US courts to be akin to diplomatic protection claims under international law.[541]

Importantly, reflecting the same State interests recognised under international law,[542] *parens patriae* suits can concern environmental damage and other 'public nuisances',[543] as well as economic damage,[544] where the State acts as 'representative of the public' in subjects 'of grave public concern'[545] 'affect[ing] [its] citizens at large'.[546] However, not all claims involving such interests are properly regarded as *parens patriae* claims:[547] claims based on the economy are not considered *parens patriae* in nature when they are really brought on behalf of particular individuals,[548]

536 *Snapp* (n 532) 607, quoted Tribe (n 535) 453; also Ratliff (n 400) 1853; Hawkes (n 418) 187–89; *Kansas v Colorado* 206 US 46 (1907) 99 ('general welfare'); Caplan (n 418) 724–25.

537 See nn 547ff.

538 See Metz (n 409) 13–19, discussing US Constitution, art III, Eleventh Amendment; *Snapp* (n 532) 611 (Sep Op Brennan).

539 *Snapp* (n 532) 602; also Tribe (n 535) 453, 452 (cannot be 'conduit for [citizens'] claims'); Ratliff (n 400) 1851; Hawkes (n 418) 188–90; Jay L Himes, 'State *Parens Patriae* Authority: The Evolution of the State Attorney General's Authority' (ILEP Symposium: Protecting the Public: The Role of Private and Public Attorneys' General, Miami, 23–24 April 2004) 4; Metz (n 409) 6, 15.

540 *Snapp* (n 532) 607; also Ratliff (n 400) 1852–53; Himes (n 539) 7; Hawkes (n 418) 190, 193–94; Bryan A Garner, *Black's Law Dictionary* (10th edn, Thomson Reuters 2014) 1287. Cf *Impregilo (Award)* (n 31) [354].

541 See *North Dakota v Minnesota* 263 US 365 (1923) 376 (*parens patriae* 'differentiated from [state's] lost power ... to present and enforce individual [citizens'] claims'); discussion Nowak and Rotunda (n 424) 102; Margaret Thomas, 'Parens Patriae and The States' Historic Police Power' (2016) 69 SMULR 759, 788; cf Himes (n 539) 3–4.

542 n 526; also Thomas (n 541) 790, 802 (*parens patriae* based on 'police power'), 791 ('general welfare'); similarly Borchard (n 54) 31; Garcia-Amador, 'Problems' (n 241) 427; Caplan (n 418) 719, 724; and on 'analogy to independent countries': *Snapp* (n 532) 603, referencing (at 603–4) *Missouri v Illinois & Sanitary District of Chicago* 180 US 208 (1901) 241; also *Trail Smelter* (n 430) 1964.

543 Hawkes (n 418) 188, also 193; *Snapp* (n 532) 603–5, discussing cases; similarly Tribe (n 535) 454–55; Nowak and Rotunda (n 424) 102; Curtis (n 419) 908–9; Himes (n 539) 3–4, 10–11, 20–22; Metz (n 409) 6; Ratliff (n 400) 1852, 1856; Note (n 398) 412–13. Eg, *Missouri v Illinois* (n 542) 211–14, 241–43 (sewerage); *Georgia v Tennessee Copper Co* 206 US 230 (1907) 238–39 (fumes); *Kansas v Colorado* (n 536) 98–100 (water diversion); *ND v Minnesota* (n 541) 371–72 (flooding). Further Paul Craig, *Administrative Law* (8th edn, Sweet & Maxwell 2016) [25-009].

544 Generally Hawkes (n 418) 188–89, cf 191–92; Himes (n 539) 11–12; Curtis (n 419) 909; Ratliff (n 400) 1852, 1855. Eg, *Pennsylvania v West Virginia* 262 US 553 (1923) 591–98 (gas restrictions); *Maryland v Louisiana* 451 US 725 (1981) 734–38 (tax affecting consumers), discussed Himes (n 539) 8–9; *Louisiana v Texas* 176 US 1 (1900) 19 (quarantine restrictions), discussed Hawkes (n 418) 186–87 (fn 41).

545 *Pennsylvania v WV* (n 544) 592; *Georgia v Pennsylvania Railroad* 324 US 439 (1945) 451, both quoted *Snapp* (n 532) 605–6. Also Tribe (n 535) 455.

546 *Louisiana v Texas* (n 544) 19, quoted *Snapp* (n 532) 603.

547 On difficulties differentiating: Caplan (n 418) 723–24; Note (n 398) 414–18; Hanna (n 418) 1961–64, 1973; Hawkes (n 418) 191–94; also Metz (n 409) 18; Ratliff (n 400) 1857–58; authorities nn 418ff (damages).

548 See *New Hampshire v Louisiana* 108 US 76 (1883), particularly 89 (assigned debts claim 'by and for [citizens]'), discussed Himes (n 539) 4–5; Metz (n 409) 16–18; *Maryland v Louisiana* (n 544) 767–68 (Diss Op Rehnquist); also *Kansas v Colorado* (n 536) 99; similarly Note (n 398) 412–13.

or a category thereof,[549] or are in reality 'nothing more than a collectivity of private suits';[550] and an environmental case regarding flooding of State territory was not a *parens patriae* claim where damages were claimed 'for the benefit of' affected farmers.[551] Importantly, at least under federal US common law, when States make claims akin to class actions, alleging and claiming compensation for mass injury to the state's citizens, they are not acting as *parens patriae* and in the general interest within the traditional meaning of the doctrine.[552] A case brought simply to recover for losses suffered by individuals, even where those individuals are numerous, does not concern State damage.[553]

The difference is critical for *res judicata* purposes because members of class actions—which are recognised across legal systems—are bound by the suit's outcome.[554] The same is true vis-à-vis the relevant individuals where, pursuant to dedicated legislation overcoming the common law bar,[555] US States are in fact able to bring 'aggregated private claims'[556] as *parens patriae*.[557] In such cases, as has been explained in a domestic context, States are 'represent[ing] unknown but real individuals' and their 'claims are not severable from the legitimate claims of their individual inhabitants'.[558] By contrast, *res judicata* does not bar individuals from bringing their own claims where *parens patriae* suits concerning 'public' interests have already been brought, except insofar as those individuals are 'privies' because they seek compensation for damage arising from violation of the same 'public' rights.[559]

549 *Oklahoma v Atchison, Topeka & Sante Fe Railway* 220 US 277 (1911) 286, 289 (shippers), discussed Hawkes (n 418) 188–92.

550 *Pennsylvania v New Jersey* 426 US 660 (1976) 666, discussed Himes (n 539) 5; Metz (n 409) 16.

551 *ND v Minnesota* (n 541) 374–75, discussed Metz (n 409) 16; *Maryland v Louisiana* (n 544) 768 (Diss Op Rehnquist).

552 Note (n 398) 418, 423–24, 426–28; also Hawkes (n 418) 191, 193–94, 198–99, discussing *Pfizer v Lord* 522 F 2d 612 (1975) 617–18 (class action alternatives); Curtis (n 419) 912–14; Caplan (n 418) 736–37; *California v Frito-Lay* 474 F 2d 774 (1973) 775–77 and *Seneci* (n 420) 1017–18, both discussed Metz (n 409) 7–9, cf 15, 18; also Enrique Schaerer, 'A Rose by Any Other Name: Why a Parens Patriae Action Can Be a Mass Action under the Class Action Fairness Act' (2013) 16 NYUJ Legis & Pub Pol 39, 76 ('where a State seeks monetary relief for discrete group of its citizens' they 'are real parties in interest'); see nn 419, 553. Cf Ratliff (n 400) 1854, 1856; Lemos (n 527) 494–95; Hanna (n 418) 1967 ('minority' approach); Tribe (n 535) 454; Himes (n 539) 9; Thomas (n 541) 762–63, 798–99.

553 n 552; *Seneci* (n 420) 1017 (no separate State damage '[w]here … only seeks to recover money damages for injuries suffered by individuals'); also *Frito-Lay* (n 552) 775–76, both discussed Metz (n 409) 7–9, see 9 (State damages suit 'only insofar as the damages it seeks are discrete from those potentially recoverable by individuals'), 24.

554 nn 257–58.

555 On such claims being normally statutorily-based: Prentiss Cox, 'Public Enforcement Compensation and Private Rights' (2016) 100 Minn LR 2313, 2322–31; Hanna (n 418) 1967–68; Lemos (n 527) 493, 495–98; Thomas (n 541) 762, 799; also Metz (n 409) 8.

556 Metz (n 409) 8 and authorities, particularly fnn 42–43; also Thomas (n 541) 762, 796–99; Himes (n 539) 12–14; Ratliff (n 400) 1847, 1854.

557 Lemos (n 527) 500; Metz (n 409) 22–24; Schaerer (n 552) 76; Hanna (n 418) 1966. Cf Cox (n 555) 2336–39 ('public compensation' not precluding), cf 2340 ('class actions'), 2346–49 (depends on claim's statutory basis); n 558.

558 Note (n 398) 426.

559 *Alaska Sport Fishing Association v Exxon* 34 F 3d 769 (1994) [12]–[19] (damages for lost use resulting from oil spill settled by government), discussed Hanna (n 418) 1978–80; Metz (n 409) 23–24; also Lemos (n 527) 532–35; Cox (n 555) 2342–44; similarly Handley (n 16) [9.13].

The Tribunal in the *Chevron v Ecuador* investment arbitration drew the same distinction between public and individual claims, albeit under Ecuadorian law,[560] in determining whether mass environmental litigation by citizens was barred by a settlement agreement entered into by the State.[561] It held that the settlement agreement would be *res judicata* regarding environmental claims brought in the relevant community's 'diffuse' or 'collective' interest,[562] but would not prevent individuals bringing 'separate and different claim[s] for personal harm' resulting from the alleged pollution of the environment,[563] the latter including a class action for thousands of named and unnamed persons.[564]

This case law suggests two important points of relevance here. First, there is a distinction between a State's 'public' claims and claims more akin to class action suits where mass individual injury is alleged.[565] While *res judicata* is unlikely to operate to preclude the later of a State's 'public' claim and individual claims for their own private damage, it would appear possible for the doctrine to operate as between such individual claims and a State claim that is more like a class action, brought in respect of numerous individuals including the individual claimant.[566] Second, claims may be akin to class actions even where broader State interests are involved, including those deriving from significant impacts on that State's citizens.[567]

Again, without suggesting that US law has any status as a *source* of international law on this point, it is suggested that this analysis can nonetheless be helpful[568] because—as introduced in Chapter 3 and discussed above in respect of double recovery—international law recognises a similar distinction between interstate claims in the 'general interest', akin to *parens patriae* suits proper, and claims, more like class actions, where States bring suits concerning numerous individuals.[569]

Thus, the ECtHR distinguished, in the *Cyprus v Turkey* case, interstate claims 'substantially similar' to diplomatic protection[570] from claims 'about general issues (systemic problems and shortcomings, administrative practices, etc.)' where 'the primary goal … is that of vindicating the public order'.[571] As noted above

560 And although in turn referencing US law: *Chevron (Track IB)* (n 193) [176]–[180].

561 ibid [150]ff.

562 See *Chevron and Texaco v Ecuador (First Partial Award, Track I)* PCA Case 2009-23 (17 September 2013) [96], [108]; cf *Chevron (Track IB)* (n 193) [186] (not on facts).

563 *Chevron (FPA (Track I))* (n 562) [108]. See also [45].

564 *Chevron (Track IB)* (n 193) [147]–[149], also [159]ff.

565 nn 542–64.

566 nn 554–59.

567 nn 548–52. Cf nn 522ff.

568 cf Fitzmaurice (n 353) 11; *Trail Smelter* (n 430) 1964; Peters (n 137) 47 and see nn 534, 542.

569 cf Frank Berman, 'The Relevance of the Law on Diplomatic Protection in Investment Arbitration' in Ortino and others (n 60) 72 ('generic situation' regarding 'class'); Roberts (n 6) 4, 9, 14–15, 29, 67 (class action); Juratowich (n 130) 32–33; Borchard (n 54) 353; Kalshoven (n 353) 46; generally nn 394ff, 439ff, 580ff, 593ff; section V(B)(i); Ch 3(IV)(B)(i)–(ii). Cf Edwin Borchard, 'Protection of Citizens Abroad and Change of Original Nationality' (1934) 20 YLJ 359, 363 (diplomatic protection as *parens patriae*); *Certain Property Pleadings* (n 484), Obs Liechtenstein [6.37].

570 *Cyprus v Turkey (Compensation)* (n 76) [45], discussed Peters (n 137) 394.

571 *Cyprus v Turkey (Compensation)* (n 76) [44].

vis-à-vis double recovery, a claim could be of the former type where large numbers of nationals are impacted, notwithstanding that such situations also implicate State interests.[572] Indeed, as Chapter 3 explained, the ECtHR in *Georgia v Russia (I)* considered that even an administrative practice claim could be diplomatic protection-like when it sought compensation for the individuals affected.[573] The EECC likewise acknowledged the individual basis partially underlying interstate claims between Ethiopia and Eritrea concerning hundreds of thousands of persons,[574] notwithstanding the alleged material and consequent moral State damage.[575]

Comparing the *parens patriae* case law, it would appear that diplomatic protection-like claims where reparation is sought for damage suffered by large numbers of individuals could be considered something like an international law version of a domestic class action, albeit that the State may have its own interests underlying the claim as well—economic, environmental, or more generally arising from widescale effects on its citizens.[576] By contrast, States may bring claims that are truly 'public'[577] in nature, which do not seek reparation for damage suffered by particular individuals.[578] Given that individual claims under international law generally seek reparation for the claimants' own damage, rather than to defend the 'public' interest,[579] it would only be where interstate claims are likewise seeking reparation for individual damage—even if State interests are also involved—that one can see the possibility of the principle of *res judicata* being engaged vis-à-vis these overlapping claims.[580]

There is no precedent for the principle of *res judicata* being applied as such by international courts and tribunals to preclude one of two overlapping individual and 'mixed' interstate claims, where the latter is brought for widescale personal and property damage. However, the approach taken by various tribunals suggests that the operation of *res judicata*, not only vis-à-vis overlapping individual and diplomatic protection claims, but also such 'mixed' claims, is not out of the question. Thus, the ACommHPR was prepared to suspend a claim brought regarding individuals affected by the same conflict at issue in the interstate EECC claim,[581]

[572] See nn 440ff. Also Gattini (n 451) 537.

[573] *Georgia v Russia (I) (Compensation)* (n 74) [26]; see Ch 3, n 358.

[574] See *Eritrea* (n 15) [197], [205]–[206]; *Ethiopia* (n 16) [55].

[575] See n 472; also *Nicaragua v Costa Rica* Pet 1/06, Rep 11/07 (IACHR, 8 March 2007) [195], discussed Ch 3, nn 339–40.

[576] nn 522ff.

[577] cf *Cyprus v Turkey (Compensation)* (n 76), n 571; n 397.

[578] cf nn 593ff.

[579] Douglas, *Investment* (n 26) 31; also *Picq v France* Doc CCPR/C/94/D/1632/2007 (HRC, 17 August 2009) [6.3] (no *actio popularis*); *Nicaragua v Costa Rica* (n 575) [189]–[193]; generally Zwart (n 43) 50ff; Connors (n 83) 394. Cf nn 306–7, 317, 559; Crawford, *GP* (n 6) 374; Peters (n 137) 291–93, 303, 472ff; Shany, *Competing* (n 4) 64.

[580] See section V(A); nn 554ff. Cf Rosalyn Higgins, *Problems and Processes: International Law and How We Use It* (Clarendon 1994) 52, Introduction, n 13; Roberts (n 158) 395–96 (States may 'settle . . . class action diplomatic protection claim'); similarly nn 601, 648.

[581] nn 200–5, 243–44, 312–18.

while the *Italy v Cuba* Tribunal considered that overlapping diplomatic protection and individual claims were to be prevented,[582] notwithstanding that the interstate claim was arguably 'mixed', with multiple individuals affected, and Italy making a satisfaction claim for consequent moral damage.[583] Admittedly, the ECtHR did not consider that the bringing of an interstate claim in the *Cyprus v Turkey* case precluded some of the individuals affected from bringing their own claims.[584] However, it reached that conclusion five years before deciding—in the context of an interstate claim being brought for *reparation* for damage caused to individual victims—that the interstate claim was in the nature of diplomatic protection.[585] As noted above, the Court had apparently not been satisfied at the earlier stage that the same individuals' claims would be determined and remedied during the interstate proceedings.[586] However when, in the *Georgia v Russia (I)* case, individual cases had already been determined *before* the interstate claim, the Court deferred to those findings.[587]

Other cases did not consider the possible preclusion of one or the other of overlapping individual and interstate claims, but one can detect the same presence of diplomatic protection elements alongside claims defending State interests, meaning that *res judicata* is of potential application vis-à-vis the former part of the claim.[588] The *Trail Smelter* case was, for instance, arguably more an exercise of diplomatic protection vis-à-vis numerous individuals affected by sulphur fumes than a 'direct' claim, even if State interests in the environment were also present.[589] Indeed, a US court concluded, in strikingly similar circumstances, that a claim was not one brought *parens patriae*, but in reality on behalf of the affected individuals.[590] Moreover, that a class action was lodged by individuals arising from the same circumstances as the *Aerial Herbicide Spraying* case, albeit under domestic law,[591] suggests that the interstate claim may also have been—at least in part—brought for individual injury.[592]

Such cases may be contrasted with truly "public" cases brought in the State's interest and *without* a claim for reparation for damage suffered by individuals.[593] Some examples were given in Chapter 3's elucidation of 'direct' claims: claims

582 nn 327–30.

583 *Italy v Cuba* (n 327) [34], discussed Potestà, 'Italy/Cuba' (n 327) 342; Potestà, 'Potential' (n 327) 758. See Ch 2, n 151.

584 nn 221, 320.

585 n 570, cf *Varnava* (n 218); n 76. Further: Roberts (n 6) 48.

586 n 322.

587 n 234.

588 cf nn 526ff.

589 Ch 3, n 111; see *Trail Smelter* (n 430) 1964 ('quasi-sovereign').

590 n 551.

591 *Arias v Dyncorp* 752 F.3d 1011 (2014) 1013; Defendant's Dismissal Motion (26 June 2009) <http://www.expose-the-war-profiteers.org/archive/legal/2009-1/20090624.pdf>, 3.

592 See n 529.

593 cf nn 526, 569; Ch 3(II)(C), (IV)(B); also *Ecuador v US (Award)* PCA Case 2012-5 (29 September 2012) [203]–[204].

in which the only damage alleged is that to the State,[594] and claims for breach alone, without any corresponding allegation of damage to identifiable individuals.[595] These kind of 'direct' claims are not brought for individual damage and do not share an object with an overlapping individual claim for *res judicata* purposes.[596]

Just as distinguishing between diplomatic protection and 'direct' claims is not always easy,[597] distinguishing interstate claims that may or may not be preclusive of an overlapping individual claim is also complicated, particularly when 'general' State interests coincide with damage to individual citizens—as indeed the *parens patriae* case law attests.[598] For instance, Roberts has suggested that States could bring claims for declaratory relief on an interstate basis 'in a manner resembling representative and class actions' and that collateral estoppel could then bind individuals vis-à-vis liability findings in such claims, citing the *Cross-Border Trucking* case as an example.[599] One can certainly see the appeal of such an approach: as Roberts outlines, allowing interstate claims to definitively determine at least certain issues where several individuals are affected avoids multiplicity and potential inconsistencies across different claims and may encourage the reaching of a 'global settlement' on the interstate level.[600] However, it will be recalled that Mexico's claim under NAFTA neither sought reparation for, nor identified, any affected individuals.[601] It is not therefore rightly regarded as a case of diplomatic protection.[602] Even assuming that a tribunal would accept the operation of the doctrine of collateral—or issue—estoppel,[603] the case law discussed above demonstrates that decisions examining circumstances in general are not the same, for *res judicata* and related purposes, as those concerning, and repairing violations vis-à-vis, particular individuals, even if individual examples are given.[604] Rather, it is diplomatic protection claims made for reparation that provide the potential for *res judicata* to operate vis-à-vis individual claims.[605] Therefore, only where 'mixed' claims are made for reparation for damage concerning large numbers of individuals is the claim more like a domestic class action, where 'unnamed' individuals may form

[594] Ch 3(IV)(B)(i).

[595] Ch 3(IV)(B)(ii).

[596] Even a diplomatic protection claim may not share an individual claim's object if reparation is not sought: see Ch 3(IV)(B)(ii) and section (IV)(B).

[597] Ch 3, n 231.

[598] nn 535ff.

[599] Roberts (n 6) 67.

[600] ibid 67–68. See Ch 5, nn 48–52.

[601] *Cross-Border Trucking Services (Ch 20 NAFTA Panel Final Rep)* File-USA-MEX-98-2008-01 (6 February 2001) [281]–[283], [292], [298]; Roberts (n 6) 67; Ch 3, nn 341–42.

[602] Ch 3, nn 341–46.

[603] nn 164, 180, 283.

[604] nn 218–31, 275–77, 322; similarly *Right to Information on Consular Assistance in the Framework of the Guarantees of the Due Process of Law (Advisory Opinion)* [1999] IACHR Ser A No 16; Ch 2, n 201; cf nn 535–52.

[605] Section V(A)–(B). Similarly Juratowich (n 130) 32 (estoppel).

part of the 'abstract class' bound by the outcome.[606] The next chapter will consider alternative means of avoiding overlapping claims in circumstances in which *res judicata* does not apply.

VI. Conclusion

This chapter has confirmed Chapter 3's finding that diplomatic protection claims are premised on individual damage. The consequence is that the rule precluding double recovery will almost certainly operate to preclude reparation being awarded in both such a claim—including the diplomatic protection parts of 'mixed' claims—and an overlapping individual claim, whether the damage is repaired on the State or individual level. Moreover, as discussed above, even certain 'direct' claims for damage suffered by the State may be sufficiently derived from individual damage for the purposes of the rule's application.[607]

For *res judicata*, the limited case law does not demonstrate that the principle would certainly bar the second of two overlapping individual and interstate claims.[608] It seems particularly unlikely to do so vis-à-vis 'direct' interstate claims that do not address, nor award remedies for, individual injury. However, there is good reason for tribunals faced with individual claims overlapping with a diplomatic protection action, or a similar article 48 human rights claim, even if as part of a 'mixed' claim, to seriously consider invoking the doctrine, or treaty provisions with similar effect, to preclude one or the other of those claims.[609] The purpose of the *res judicata* doctrine—to protect respondents and the dispute settlement system from the same claim being brought multiple times—is arguably thwarted if multiple claims are brought seeking reparation for the same injury, even if the claimants are different.[610] The case law suggests ways to avoid this outcome, focusing on the parties' degree of closeness: ie, to what extent one represents the other; the claims' subject-matters are the same; and the parties' interests align.[611] As they suggest, a 'liberal construction' of *res judicata* may be justified, in some circumstances, to avoid abuse of process,[612] which may also provide an alternative basis for addressing the same situations.[613]

[606] Demirkol (n 438) 624 and authorities; n 258. Cf nn 499, 558; Kalshoven (n 353) 46 (if individuals 'failed without … fault to join the group … requesting diplomatic protection … right to claim compensation … remains intact').

[607] Section V(B)(i)(a).

[608] cf authorities nn 143, 351, 644. Similarly Vermeer-Künzli (n 53) 277.

[609] nn 108, 167ff, 352, 390, 580. Similarly Vermeer-Künzli (n 53) 278.

[610] See nn 107–8, 249, 261ff, 278ff, 386, 390; similarly Shany, *Relations* (n 4) 137; Shany, *Competing* (n 4) 259.

[611] Section IV(C). Similarly Shany, *Relations* (n 4) 114, 125, 131–35; Shany, *Competing* (n 4) 23–27, 155; also Nollkaemper (n 42) 251.

[612] Shany, *Competing* (n 4) 259, also 270–71; Shany, *Relations* (n 4) 135, 137.

[613] nn 4–5, 125, 273, 289.

Having said that, the operation of both doctrines in circumstances of overlapping individual and interstate claims runs the risk of causing either State or individual prejudice.[614]

For the State, if an individual were to claim and receive reparation for damage they have suffered, a State would not, by virtue of the double recovery rule, be able to seek reparation for that same damage, whether through diplomatic protection or a broader 'mixed' suit.[615] A tribunal might also consider such a claim barred by *res judicata*, or related principles.[616] Indeed, given that interstate diplomatic protection claims are 'indirect',[617] the jurisprudence suggests that there may be greater justification for the 'direct' individual's claim to bar that of the State than the contrary.[618] The consequent prejudice to the State appears minimal, however. While the State's traditional freedoms under the law of diplomatic protection to utilise its nationals' claims and any remedies awarded in its discretion would be impaired,[619] at least where the claims relate to a small number of individuals, this appears to be no cause for concern: there is no reason the State should be allowed to make a second claim, for damage it has suffered indirectly, when the 'direct' victim has already done so.[620] That would be the outcome anyway if the individual's damage is repaired while exhausting local remedies.[621] And the State can, of course, still pursue any claim for its own damage.

Where this scenario becomes problematic is where substantial numbers of individuals are affected. As noted in the Introduction, States have traditionally played important roles in settling such disputes, including in post-conflict scenarios, where it may be both easier and fairer to have the State claim, similarly to a 'class action', and use the reparations funds for the benefit of all, than to have thousands of individual claimants jockeying for relief.[622] The State's ability to fulfil that role may be impeded if large numbers of individuals file—or threaten to file—their own claims, and there is uncertainty regarding the application of *res judicata* in particular.[623] What, if anything, the State might do in such a situation will be considered in the Conclusion to this book.

[614] Similarly Vermeer-Künzli (n 53) 285–86; also Shany, *Competing* (n 4) 23–24, 115, 121, 155.

[615] Section V(A)(i),(B)(i).

[616] Section V(A)–(B). Similarly Juratowich (n 130) 32 (estoppel).

[617] Ch 2, nn 99, 102.

[618] See cases nn 282–91, 294-296. Cf Roberts (n 6) 47; Vermeer-Künzli (n 53) 277, 288; Paparinskis (n 24) 298.

[619] Authorities n 513.

[620] Potentially, a State could make payments to its national, who then also recovers for the damage suffered. Double recovery would prevent the State claiming its costs from the respondent: see *Seventh Instalment* (n 79); n 62 (loss disappearing once primary entity compensated). However, the State would presumably have domestic law mechanisms to recover overpayments to individuals. Cf Ch 5(III).

[621] Ch 3, nn 185–95.

[622] Introduction, nn 20–21, 49. See Ch 5, nn 48–51.

[623] Cf Roberts (n 158) 396.

For the individual, the prejudice is perhaps more immediately apparent. Given that, as just mentioned, the funds received in a diplomatic protection suit belong to the State, there is every risk that an individual bringing a claim after its State's claim—diplomatic protection, 'mixed', or even possibly 'direct'—would end up both unable to recover reparation, on double recovery grounds, and unable to access that already obtained.[624] The DADP do recommend that compensation from diplomatic protection claims be given to the injured individual.[625] It is also true that tribunals have suggested that compensation payments made in human rights cases 'substantially similar' to diplomatic protection 'should always be done for the benefit of individual victims',[626] and are 'intended to provide reparation for the [individual's] injury',[627] consistent with the injunction under article 48(2)(b) that reparation be sought in those individuals' interest.[628] Nonetheless, with the exception perhaps of mass interstate claims brought under the ECHR regime, in which the Court has ordered payment to be distributed to victims under the supervision of the Committee of Ministers,[629] there is no guarantee that money will be paid to the relevant individuals.[630] On the contrary, the case law suggests that, even in human rights cases, payment to the State may preclude later individual compensation claims, including where those individuals have received nothing.[631]

The protections for the individual may be broader in respect of the potential application of *res judicata*, with the party identity requirement designed specifically to recognise the injustice of binding an entity to the outcome of litigation over which it has no control.[632] This may explain why the IACHR was reluctant to allow Mexico's *Avena* claim to preclude the individual claims overlapping with it.[633] The 'mixed' interstate claim, both diplomatic protection and 'in [Mexico's] own right',[634] would prima facie appear to be akin to those just discussed in which *res judicata* might potentially operate vis-à-vis an overlapping individual claim.[635]

[624] n 513.

[625] DADP, art 19(c), quoted *Cyprus v Turkey (Compensation)* (n 76) [46]. Generally Roberts (n 6) 50–51; Mazzeschi (n 372) 221; Francis Vallat, *International Law and the Practitioner* (Manchester UP 1966) 39–41; Parlett (n 5) 89–90; Roberts (n 158) 397–98.

[626] *Cyprus v Turkey (Compensation)* (n 76) [45]–[46].

[627] ibid [46], quoting *Diallo (Compensation)* (n 62) [57], also 391 (Sep Op Greenwood); Peters (n 137) 395–96.

[628] nn 363–64. Also *Pad v Turkey* (n 68) [65]; n72.

[629] *Cyprus v Turkey (Compensation)* (n 76) 272; *Georgia v Russia (I) (Compensation)* (n 74), *dispositif*.

[630] See n 513. Cf n 482.

[631] See Vermeer-Künzli (n 53) 285 (interstate settlement possibly denying 'effective remedy'); Roberts (n 158) 395; n 512.

[632] *Gleeson* (n 249) 516; also Cheng (n 111) 341–43 (*audi alteram partem*); Shany, *Relations* (n 4) 132–33, 137; Shany, *Competing* (n 4) 23–24, 155; Wehland (n 5) [7.47]–[7.51]; also Roberts (n 6) 10.

[633] nn 311, 345–46.

[634] Ch 2, nn 227–28.

[635] Section (V)(B); see *Avena* (n 227) (Sep Op Vereshchetin) [8] ('specific individuals', 'specific injuries' suggests diplomatic protection); also Berman (n 569) 72; Nollkaemper (n 142) 529–30; Nollkaemper (n 42) 251 (potential identity vis-à-vis similar cases). Cf n 377.

Nonetheless, the IACHR expressed concern in certain cases that Mexico had no 'mandate' from the individuals, and did not have to act in their interests.[636]

It is difficult to say in the abstract when a tribunal addressing overlapping individual and interstate claims might be prepared to bind a non-party,[637] though we can appreciate factors that might play into the decision. Certainly, it appears unproblematic to bind individuals where they have sought, or consented to, diplomatic protection,[638] as indeed the IACHR's decision, by noting the absence of 'mandate', implicitly suggests.[639] More generally, article 19 of the DADP recommends that States '[t]ake into account, wherever feasible, the views of injured persons with regard to resort to diplomatic protection and the reparation … sought',[640] which would require consultation.[641] Insofar as article 48 claims are at issue, as noted above, States are obliged to act 'in the interest of' the 'beneficiaries',[642] the same phrase used vis-à-vis countermeasures envisaging action requested by, and 'on behalf of', another.[643] Where individuals are similarly involved in the prosecution of a diplomatic protection suit, this would appear to mitigate concerns regarding *res judicata* or provisions with similar effect barring those individuals' claims.[644] Where they are not so involved, it may be less likely—albeit not impossible—that *res judicata* will operate, though the rule precluding double recovery will still apply.[645]

As to broader 'mixed' claims akin to class actions, under domestic systems such actions tend to be binding on members of the class only provided the representative actually represents the class's interests,[646] with individuals normally obtaining notice and the possibility to decline their inclusion in the class.[647] The question that tribunals will have to consider, in an appropriate case, is how far it can be assumed

[636] nn 311, 345–46. Cf *Nicaragua v Costa Rica* (n 575) [183].

[637] Similarly Wehland (n 5) [7.33]; Salles (n 17) 247 ('case-by-case'); Shany, *Competing* (n 4) 155 ('overly broad … bar' unduly limits 'party autonomy'); Shany, *Relations* (n 4) 133.

[638] See, eg, *Banro* (n 309); also *SEEE* (n 310); *Chagos Islanders v UK* (2012) 162 ILR 318 (ECtHR) [79]–[81] (individual settlements; 'proceedings … widely known'). Similarly Borchard (n 54) 357; Peters (n 137) 175, 212–13. Generally nn 383–88.

[639] n 311.

[640] DADP, art 19(b).

[641] ibid 97; similarly *Mexican Union Railway* (1930) 5 ILR 207 (UK–Mexican Cl Comm) 209. Cf Christian Tams, 'All's Well That Ends Well: Comments on the ILC's Articles on State Responsibility' (2002) 62 ZfaöRV 759, 782; Gattini (n 451) 537.

[642] *ARSIWA*, art 48(2)(b); see n 387.

[643] *ARSIWA*, 305 (vis-à-vis ARSIWA, art 54), citing *Nicaragua (Merits)* (n 524) [199]; similarly Crawford, 'Community' (n 533) 321.

[644] cf Vermeer-Künzli (n 53) 276; Shany, *Competing* (n 4) 36; Wehland (n 5) [7.47] (inconsistent interests); Roberts (n 6) 29, 51, 67, 69 (possibility of intervention by individuals).

[645] Section V(A).

[646] See discussion Mulheron (n 499) 276, 289–303; Hanna (n 418) 1975, 1978; Lemos (n 527) 501–3; *Hansberry v Lee* 311 US 32 (1940) 42 ('due process' breached if not 'fairly insur[ing] the protection of the interests of absent parties'), cited Richard Nagareda, *The Law of Class Actions and Other Aggregate Litigation* (Foundation 2009) 45, generally 76ff; Metz (n 409) 20–21; Handley (n 16) [9.20]; Barnett (n 17) [3.26].

[647] Mulheron (n 499) 337–59; Barnett (n 17) [3.32]; Hanna (n 418) 1975, cf 1967, 1976–80 (*parens patriae* concerns); Lemos (n 527) 507, cf 508–10.

that States represent their citizens, and thus how far *res judicata* should operate to bar their individual claims.[648] For, as the Introduction outlined, it may sometimes be important that States are able to settle claims on their population's behalf.[649]

Whether an individual can overcome prejudice occasioned through the application of *res judicata* and/or the double recovery rule vis-à-vis their overlapping claim, and how individual and State interests may be balanced in this respect, will be considered further in the Conclusion to this book.

648 Raising the same concerns vis-à-vis *parens patriae* claims: Hanna (n 418) 1958–59, 1964–67, 1974–83; Lemos (n 527) 503–9, 511ff, 531–42; discussion Metz (n 409) 20–24; Hawkes (n 418) 196–98, cf 199; Ratliff (n 400) 1857–58; also Note (n 398) 428–32; Caplan (n 418) 737–39 and see authorities n 644. Cf Kalshoven (n 353) 46–47, nn 439, 606; Tams (n 640) 782; *Decision No V* (n 241) 152; *Nemariam v Ethiopia (No 1)* (2003) 135 ILR 671 (USCA, DC) 677–78; Portmann (n 520) 130; also Shany, *Relations* (n 4) 133 ('[p]olicy choices ... flexible reading of ... sameness standards'), 136–37. Suggesting States might settle without individuals' consent: Roberts (n 6) 49, 69, also 8, 10 ('weigh[ing] ... interests' of individuals/States); see also Gattini, n 525.

649 Introduction, n 49; Peters (n 137) 175, 212–13; also Roberts (n 6) 49; Metz (n 409) 23–24.

5
Consent and Waiver

This chapter focuses on consent as a means of addressing overlapping claims. It considers both the consent of a State or an individual as a means of precluding the wrongfulness of conduct otherwise in breach of an obligation owed to the other, and the consensual waiver by a State or an individual of the claims of that other, as mechanisms through which an entity may purport to preclude that other's overlapping claim. As will be seen, each has significant scope to preclude overlapping claims, either impacting the claims directly or, in the case of State consent, by preventing claims from being brought altogether through alteration of individual claims mechanisms.

I. Consent and waiver

A. Consent

Reflecting a rule of custom,[1] the Articles on the Responsibility of States for Internationally Wrongful Acts (ARSIWA) provide that a State's 'valid consent to the commission of an act by another State precludes the wrongfulness of that act'.[2] As the commentary explains:

> States have the right to dispense with the performance of an obligation owed to them individually, or generally to permit conduct to occur which (absent such permission) would be unlawful so far as they are concerned.[3]

Consent is given before, or at most while, the relevant act is being undertaken.[4] It 'displace[s]' the obligation for the time being, and there cannot therefore be any breach of that obligation resulting from the conduct consented to.[5] Waiver, on the

[1] Affef Ben Mansour, 'Consent' in James Crawford and others (eds), *The Law of International Responsibility* (OUP 2010) 439.
[2] James Crawford, *The International Law Commission's Articles on State Responsibility: Introduction, Text and Commentaries* (CUP 2002) art 20, 163 (*ARSIWA*).
[3] ibid 163.
[4] ibid 163; also Mansour (n 1) 441–44.
[5] *ARSIWA*, 163. See also Mansour (n 1) 445; Christian Tams, 'Waiver, Acquiescence, and Extinctive Prescription' in Crawford and others, *Responsibility* (n 1) 1041.

Overlapping Individual and Interstate Claims in International Law. Jessica Howley, Oxford University Press.
 DOI: 10.1093/oso/9780192871466.003.0006

other hand, is consent given after the conduct takes place.[6] The breach has still occurred but, as will be seen, the right to invoke responsibility is lost.[7]

The ARSIWA are only concerned with consent given by States.[8] Whether individuals can consent and thereby preclude the wrongfulness of State action is more difficult to establish.[9] Certainly, as the ARSIWA acknowledge, primary obligations may themselves already incorporate the possibility for consent, including by individuals, to impact their operation.[10] For instance, as the ARSIWA note, the International Covenant on Civil and Political Rights (ICCPR) prohibits States from *compelling* individuals to testify against themselves or admit guilt, but they can freely agree to do so.[11] Individual consent, such as that expressed through contract, may also be relevant in determining whether investment law is violated.[12] These are not, however, the kind of situations envisaged by consent as a circumstance precluding wrongfulness, which operates vis-à-vis conduct 'otherwise in breach of an international obligation'.[13] If the obligation makes the absence of consent a necessary element of breach, there could not—even prima facie—be a breach where that consent is present.[14] It is difficult in practice to distinguish between consent operating as part of a primary rule and as a circumstance precluding wrongfulness.[15] Nonetheless, given that international law pays *some* regard to individual consent in its application in respect of the former, it is at least possible that individuals could consent in a way that would preclude wrongfulness.[16]

Even so, whether individuals could consent to precluding the wrongfulness of an act vis-à-vis both themselves *and* a State, and vice versa whether States could consent to action to preclude breach *also* vis-à-vis an individual, thereby also precluding any overlapping claims otherwise arising,[17] raises the sticking point

[6] *ARSIWA*, 163; also Mansour (n 1) 444; Tams (n 5) 1036.

[7] *ARSIWA*, 163; Tams (n 5) 1041; Martins Paparinskis, 'Investment Treaty Arbitration and the (New) Law of State Responsibility' (2013) 24 EJIL 617, 629 (fn 70); Eduardo Jiménez de Aréchaga, 'International Responsibility' in Max Sørensen (ed), *Manual of Public International Law* (Macmillan 1968) 541.

[8] *ARSIWA*, 165. Cf James Crawford, 'Second Report on State Responsibility' (1999) 2(1) ILCYB 1 [242](c). In reality, individual State representatives will give this consent: see Ch 2, nn 4–5; also Mansour (n 1) 441–43; Tams (n 5) 1041; Crawford, 'SecondRep' (n 8) [237].

[9] Generally Paparinskis, 'New' (n 7) 629–30; Martins Paparinskis, 'Analogies and Other Regimes of International Law' in Zachary Douglas, Joost Pauwelyn, and Jorge Viñuales (eds), *The Foundations of International Investment Law* (OUP 2014) 100–1.

[10] See *ARSIWA*, 165; Crawford, 'SecondRep' (n 8) [242]; Paparinskis, 'New' (n 7) 629–30; Paparinskis, 'Analogies' (n 9) 100.

[11] ICCPR, art 14(3)(g), example cited *ARSIWA*, 165 (although as art 14(1)(g)); Crawford, 'SecondRep' (n 8) [242](c).

[12] See Paparinskis, 'New' (n 7) 629–30; Paparinskis, 'Analogies' (n 9) 100; cf nn 70ff.

[13] *ARSIWA*, 165.

[14] See *ARSIWA*, 165; Crawford, 'SecondRep' (n 8) [238].

[15] See, eg, ibid [238]–[240]; Mansour (n 1) 440–41, 445. Indeed, doubting the circumstance's operation in practice: Crawford, 'SecondRep' (n 8) [240].

[16] See discussion Paparinskis, 'Analogies' (n 9) 100–1; Paparinskis, 'New' (n 7) 629–30.

[17] Similarly Paparinskis, 'New' (n 7) 629–31; Paparinskis, 'Analogies' (n 9) 100–1.

of third-party rights.[18] As the ARSIWA commentary explains, 'the consent of one State will not preclude wrongfulness in relation to another',[19] meaning that the other State could still invoke responsibility for breach arising from the same circumstances.[20] Logically, the same should apply to States and individuals; that is, if a State owes those entities separate obligations, the consent of one could not preclude a breach of obligations owed to the other, nor any resulting claims.[21]

B. Waiver

Waiver refers broadly to conduct by which a person relinquishes a given right.[22] Pursuant to ARSIWA article 45, injured States may lose the right to invoke responsibility through waiver,[23] where the renunciation of their claim is 'unequivocal'.[24] Any waived claim is rendered inadmissible, meaning that responsibility cannot be invoked and no claim made for any remedy otherwise due.[25]

(i) Waiver by individuals

The ARSIWA only address waiver by States.[26] However, individuals may also waive their right to invoke responsibility pursuant to the procedures discussed in Chapter 2.[27] In investment law, for instance, the premise of 'fork-in-the-road' clauses found in many bilateral investment treaties (BITs) is that individual investors may elect—election between alternative rights being one form of waiver[28]—to

[18] See Paparinskis, 'Analogies' (n 9) 101; Paparinskis, 'New' (n 7) 630–31.

[19] *ARSIWA*, 165.

[20] Mansour (n 1) 446.

[21] See Paparinskis, 'Analogies' (n 9) 101; Paparinskis, 'New' (n 7) 630–31.

[22] Sean Wilken and Karim Ghaly, *The Law of Waiver, Variation, and Estoppel* (3rd edn, OUP 2012) [3.14], [4.01]; Tams (n 5) 1036; *Waste Management v Mexico (Award)* (2000) 121 ILR 29 (ICSID) [18]. Cf Yuval Shany, *The Competing Jurisdictions of International Courts and Tribunals* (OUP 2003) 23 (*electa una via*).

[23] *ARSIWA*, art 45.

[24] ibid 267; Tams (n 5) 1038; James Crawford, *State Responsibility: The General Part* (CUP 2013) 71 (*GP*); *Armed Activities on the Territory of the Congo (DRC v Uganda) (Judgment)* [2005] ICJ Rep 168 [293], cited Isabel Feichtner, 'Waiver' in Rüdiger Wolfrum (ed), *MPEPIL (Online)* (OUP 2012) [8].

[25] *ARSIWA*, art 45, 266–67; *Armed Activities* (n 24) [292]–[293]; Tams (n 5) 1036.

[26] Individuals of course act *for* the State: see Ch 2, n 4.

[27] Generally Ole Spiermann, 'Individual Rights, State Interests and the Power to Waive ICSID Jurisdiction under Bilateral Investment Treaties' (2004) 20 Arb Int 179, 204, 207; Hanno Wehland, *The Coordination of Multiple Proceedings in Investment Treaty Arbitration* (OUP 2013) [3.101]; Louis Sohn and R Baxter (eds), *Convention on the International Responsibility of States for Injuries to Aliens* (HLS 1961) art 22(4); also *Impregilo v Argentina (Jurisdiction)* ICSID Case No ARB/15/39 (23 February 2018) [87]; *ADM and Tate & Lyle v Mexico (Award)* ICSID Case No ARB(AF)/04/05 (21 November 2007) [174]. It must likewise be 'unequivocal': eg *Barbera v Spain* (1989) 11 EHRR 360 [82]; *Association SOS Attentats and De Boëry v France* ECHR 2006-XIV 375 [30]; also *Waste Management (Award)* (n 22) 41 ('clear, explicit . . . categorical'); Kate Parlett, *The Individual in the International Legal System: Continuity and Change in International Law* (CUP 2011) 93, 311.

[28] Wilken and Ghaly (n 22) [3.14], [3.08]; *TANESCO v Independent Power Tanzania (Preliminary Issues)* ICSID Case No ARB/98/8 (22 June 2001) [101]. Cf Shany (n 22) 23.

claim before either international or domestic tribunals.[29] Indeed, certain treaties expressly require investors to waive alternative procedures,[30] with tribunals otherwise refusing to hear claims.[31] Moreover, while contractually agreed exclusive jurisdiction clauses are not generally regarded as waiving the individual signatory's access to arbitration for *treaty* claims,[32] tribunals have considered whether individual investors have waived international claims through other means,[33] and have accepted individuals' settlement and withdrawal of such claims.[34] The implication is that investors can waive—expressly, through settlement, or by proceeding elsewhere—investment treaty claims.[35]

[29] Zachary Douglas, 'The Hybrid Foundations of Investment Treaty Arbitration' (2004) 74 BYBIL 151, 176–77; Zachary Douglas, *The International Law of Investment Claims* (CUP 2009) 27; Wehland (n 27) [3.102]. Generally on *electa una via*: Shany (n 22) 23, 213–17; Yuval Shany, *Regulating Jurisdictional Relations Between National and International Courts* (OUP 2007) 36–37, 156–57. Eg *CMS Gas v Argentina (Jurisdiction)* (2003) 7 ICSID Rep 494 [81]; *Banque Meyer* (1923) 3 TAM 639 (Franco-German MAT) 640, cited Bin Cheng, *General Principles of Law as Applied by International Courts and Tribunals* (Stevens & Sons 1953) 337; *SB v Prussian Treasury* (1924) 2 ILR 377 (Reichsgericht) 378. Cf *Roy* (1931) 6 ILR 421 (UK–Mexican Cl Comm) 422–23.

[30] NAFTA, art 1121; CAFTA, art 10.18(2); Shany (n 22) 209; Luiz Eduardo Salles, *Forum Shopping in International Adjudication: The Role of Preliminary Objections* (CUP 2014) 251; discussion *Ethyl v Canada (Jurisdiction)* (1998) 7 ICSID Rep 12 [90].

[31] Eg *Waste Management (Award)* (n 22) 49; *Pac Rim Cayman v El Salvador (Reisman Expert Opinion on Waiver)* ICSID Case No ARB/09/12 (22 March 2010) [36]; *Railroad Development v Guatemala (Jurisdiction)* ICSID Case No ARB/07/23 (17 November 2008) [75]–[76], discussed *Railroad Development v Guatemala (Clarification)* ICSID Case No ARB/07/23 (13 January 2009) [12]–[13]; *San Sebastian v El Salvador (Award)* ICSID Case No ARB/09/17 (14 March 2011) [114]–[116]; *Detroit International Bridge v Canada (Jurisdiction)* PCA Case 2012-25 (2 April 2015) [320], [336]–[337]; *Supervision y Control v Costa Rica (Award)* ICSID Case No ARB/12/4 (18 January 2017) [330]–[331]; *Renco v Peru (Jurisdiction)* UNCITRAL Tribunal (15 July 2016) [189]; also *EAIB v Slovakia (Second Jurisdictional Award)* PCA Case 2010-17 (4 June 2014) [264].

[32] See Wehland (n 27) [3.109]–[3.116]; Anne Peters, *Beyond Human Rights: The Legal Status of the Individual in International Law* (Jonathan Huston tr, CUP 2016) 325; Christoph Schreuer, 'Investment Arbitration' in Cesare Romano, Karen Alter, and Yvual Shany (eds), *The Oxford Handbook of International Adjudication* (OUP 2014) 307–8; Spiermann (n 27) 190–203, 207–9; Shany (n 29) 63–77, 80, discussing, eg, *Vivendi v Argentina (Annulment)* (2004) 6 ICSID Rep 340 [76], [96], [98]–[102]. Cf Douglas, *Investment* (n 29) Ch 10; n 73; Ch 4, nn 185–88.

[33] Eg, *Duke Energy v Ecuador (Award)* ICSID Case No ARB/04/19 (12 August 2008) [159]; *Burlington Resources v Ecuador (Jurisdiction)* ICSID Case No ARB/08/5 (2 June 2010) [117]–[120]; *Lemire v Ukraine (Award)* ICSID Case No ARB/06/18 (28 March 2011) [85]–[91]; *Eureko v Poland (Partial Award)* UNCITRAL Tribunal (19 August 2005) [168]–[184]; *Aguas del Tunari v Bolivia (Jurisdiction)* ICSID Case No ARB/02/3 (21 October 2005) [118]; also *ADM* (n 27) [174]; *Occidental v Ecuador (Jurisdiction)* ICSID Case No ARB/06/11 (9 September 2008) [70]–[74], [76]–[81], [85], [88]; generally *PacRim (Opinion)* (n 31) [35]–[42]; Wehland (n 27) [3.113].

[34] Wehland (n 27) [3.102]; Douglas, *Investment* (n 29) 36; Paparinskis, 'New' (n 7) 644. Eg, *Note of Settlement of Proceedings (SGS v Pakistan)* (2004) 8 ICSID Rep 451; *Lemire* (n 33) [85]–[91]; *Azpetrol International v Azerbaijan (Award)* ICSID Case No ARB/06/15 (8 September 2009) [105] (settlement; no 'dispute'); *EVN AG v Macedonia (Award)* ICSID Case No ARB/09/10 (2 September 2011) [15]; *Orascom v Algeria (Award)* ICSID Case No ARB/12/35 (31 May 2017) [524]; *Abaclat v Argentina (Consent Award)* ICSID Case No ARB/07/05 (29 December 2016).

[35] Similarly Douglas, *Investment* (n 29) 36; Patrick Juillard, 'Calvo Doctrine/Calvo Clause' in *MPEPIL* (n 24) (2007) [26]; also *Hochtief Aktiengesellschaft v Argentina (Liability)* ICSID Case No ARB/07/31 (29 December 2014) [165]–[166]. On settlement as waiver: James Crawford, 'Third Report on State Responsibility' (2000) 2(1) ILCYB 3 [261]; cf Andrea Gattini, 'A Trojan Horse for Sudeten Claims? On Some Implications of the Prince of Liechtenstein v Germany' (2002) 13 EJIL 513, 540.

As to other fields, while there may be limits regarding how far human rights can be waived when considerations of public interest arise,[36] human rights tribunals have nonetheless allowed certain waivers of individual claims,[37] and accepted settlements thereof.[38] For its part, the Caribbean Court of Justice (CCJ) has also given consideration to waivers of claims by individuals.[39]

(ii) Waiver and third parties

While both States and individuals may therefore waive claims, similarly to consent, waiver by one party to an obligation cannot preclude invocation of responsibility by another to whom that obligation is also owed: States cannot, for instance, waive the rights of third States.[40] Other entities can likewise only waive their own rights.[41] As elaborated below, whether individuals and States can waive the claims of the other in situations of overlapping claims, thereby providing a mechanism for avoiding multiple claims against the same State, revolves ultimately around the application of this principle, which has given rise to interesting questions in practice, both where individuals have purported to waive interstate claims and vice versa.[42]

C. Summary

In sum, three broad principles relating to consent and waiver may be noted:

(1) both principles preclude a claim from being made: consent precludes a claim for breach, while waiver renders that claim inadmissible; and

[36] See *Trymbach v Ukraine* App 44385/02 (ECtHR, 12 January 2012) [61], [65] (waive treaty rights within limits); *Neumeister Case* (1974) 57 ILR 180 (ECtHR) [33]; *Oršuš v Croatia* App 15766/03 (ECtHR, 16 March 2010) [178]–[179] (discrimination); *Deweer v Belgium* [1980] ECHR 1 [49] (court access); J Merrills, *The Development of International Law by the European Court of Human Rights* (2nd edn, Manchester UP 1993) 60–63 (public interest cases sometimes continue), 177–85; *ARSIWA*, 165 (rights unwaivable); Spiermann (n 27) 181, 186; Parlett (n 27) 93, 311–12. Similarly *MNSS v Montenegro (Award)* ICSID Case No ARB(AF)/12/8 (4 May 2016) [163]–[164].

[37] *Zu Leiningen v Germany* ECHR 2005-XIII 187, 194 (generally 'free to renounce' claim's pursuit); *Association SOS* (n 27) [30]; *Kimel v Argentina (Merits)* (2008) IACHR Ser C No 177 [26]–[27]; *Garrido and Baigorria v Argentina (Reparation)* (1998) IACHR Ser C No 39 [72]; *Barrios Altos v Peru (Reparation)* (2001) IACHR Ser C No 87 [33], [38]–[39]; also *Durand and Ugarte v Peru (Reparations)* [2001] IACHR 19 [28]–[32]; Parlett (n 27) 93, 311–12.

[38] *Kezer v Turkey* App 58058/00 (ECtHR, 5 October 2004) 3-4 ('friendly settlement' 'express[] waiver'); *Chagos Islanders v UK* (2012) 162 ILR 318 (ECtHR) [81]; *Calvelli v Italy (Merits)* ECHR 2002-I 3 (GC) [54]–[55] (settlement, not 'victim'); also Paparinskis, 'New' (n 7) 644.

[39] Eg, *Hummingbird Rice v Suriname* [2012] CCJ 1 [23]; *Bain v Trinidad and Tobago* [2019] CCJ 3 [6]–[7].

[40] Tams (n 5) 1039; Crawford, *GP* (n 24) 71, 563–64; also *ARSIWA*, 165. On individuals: *Jurisdictional Immunities (Germany v Italy: Greece Intervening) (Counterclaims)* [2010] ICJ Rep 310, 373, 396 (Diss Op Cancado).

[41] Feichtner (n 24) [13]; Wehland (n 27) [3.94]; also Tams (n 5) 1039; Crawford, *GP* (n 24) 565. Cf *Orascom* (n 34) [524]–[525] (company's settlement bound shareholder).

[42] Feichtner (n 24) [13]–[14]; authorities sections II–III.

(2) both States and individuals can, within certain limits, consent to conduct so as to avoid a breach of international law taking place, and waive their rights to bring claims thereunder; but
(3) they cannot consent to a breach of rights, nor waive rights to claim, that belong to another.[43]

The third factor provides the unifying link with the principles of *res judicata* and double recovery considered in the previous chapter, for the rights in the relevant overlapping claims must be the 'same', in the sense of belonging to the same entity, for these principles to operate.[44] Notwithstanding that the overlapping claims introduced in Chapter 2 appear, prima facie, to belong to States and individuals respectively,[45] both States and individuals have purported to waive the claims of the other in international practice.[46] Individual waivers are commonly relevant where interstate claims are brought for individual injury, raising questions regarding how far individuals can influence claims concerning them.[47] Interstate waivers are commonly employed where States and their nationals are affected by violations of international law causing extensive damage, such as in a post-conflict or post-nationalisation environment.[48] It is understandable that States may wish to settle all claims thereby arising on a global, lump-sum, basis: it may be infeasible to attempt to process individual claims numbering in the tens or hundreds of thousands;[49] such holistic settlements may be easier to reach, allowing peace after conflict to be realised more quickly;[50] and interstate payment may facilitate a fair

[43] nn 23–41.
[44] cf Ch 4, n 151.
[45] Ch 2(I)–(II); section I(B)(i); similarly Parlett (n 27) 93, 311–12.
[46] Sections II–III.
[47] Section II. Similarly Edwin Borchard, *The Diplomatic Protection of Citizens Abroad: Or, the Law of International Claims* (Banks 1915) 372.
[48] Generally section III; Gattini, 'Trojan' (n 35) 541; Christian Tomuschat, 'Individuals' in Crawford and others, *Responsibility* (n 1) 988–89; Robert Jennings and Arthur Watts, *Oppenheim's International Law*, vol 1 (9th edn, Longman 1992) 537–38; Francis Vallat, *International Law and the Practitioner* (Manchester UP 1966) 41; de Aréchaga (n 7) 575; cf Sean Murphy, Won Kidane, and Thomas Snider, *Litigating War: Arbitration of Civil Injury by the Eritrea-Ethiopia Claims Commission* (OUP 2013) 45.
[49] See Tomuschat (n 48) 988; *Decision 8 (Relief to War Victims)* (2007) XXVI UNRIAA 21 (EECC) [5]; also *Jurisdictional Immunities (Germany v Italy: Greece Intervening)* ICJ Pleadings, Rep Germany [53]; Eyal Benvenisti, 'Individual Remedies for Victims of Armed Conflicts in the Context of Mass Claims Settlements' in Holger Hestermeyer and others (eds), *Coexistence, Cooperation and Solidarity: Liber Amicorum Rüdiger Wolfrum* (Martinus Nijohoff 2012) 1087–88; *Oppenheim's* (n 48) 538; Vallat (n 48) 42. Cf David Caron, 'International Claims and Compensation Bodies' in Romano, Alter, and Shany (n 32) 282–87, 290; Hans van Houtte, Bart Delmartino, and Iasson Yi, *Post-War Restoration of Property Rights Under International Law*, vol 1 (CUP 2008) 43–45; Murphy, Kidane, and Snider (n 48) 40–50.
[50] Tomuschat (n 48) 988 (*inter alia* 'individualization of the settlement of consequences of ... armed conflict would block ... re-establishment of peace'); *Immunities Pleadings* (n 49), Rep Germany [46]; Andrea Gattini, 'To What Extent Are Immunity and Non-Justiciability Major Hurdles to Individuals' Claims for War Damages?' (2003) 1 JICJ 348, 364–65; Richard Lillich and Burns Weston, *International Claims: Their Settlement By Lump Sum Agreements*, vol I (Virginia UP 1975) 13; Rudolf Dolzer, 'The Settlement of War-Related Claims: Does International Law Recognize a Victim's Private Right of Action? Lessons after 1945' (2002) 20 Berk JIL 296, 300–1, 340; Peters (n 32) 487; *X1 v Nishimatsu Construction* Case 2004 (Ju) No 1658, ILDC 1812 (JP 2007) (Japan SC, 27 April 2007) §II[2]; *Dames and*

distribution of limited funds available to repair widescale damage.[51] The question, addressed here, is whether States can continue to engage in such settlements in the face of individual claims mechanisms.[52]

There are no apparent cases of consent being employed by a State or individual as a circumstance precluding wrongfulness to preclude the overlapping claim of the other. However, examining the practice relating to waiver demonstrates that consent plays an important role in controlling overlapping individual and interstate claims. While taking place under the law of treaties,[53] because the principles underlying consent are similar under the law of State responsibility—notably vis-à-vis the incapacity to consent to the modification of third parties' rights[54]—insights may be gleaned from this practice also for our current purposes.

This chapter begins by considering the effect of individual waivers on interstate claims, before turning to interstate waivers of individual claims. The practice confirms that both categories of claim belong to the respective entities, for an individual cannot waive a State's claims as such, and nor is an interstate waiver of nationals' claims properly to be regarded as a waiver. However, an individual waiver, or the consent of that individual, can affect the existence of breach or damage on which an interstate claim depends, while an interstate waiver may nonetheless effectively preclude certain individual claims.[55] In addition, there continues to be significant scope for States to preclude individuals' international claims through consent to the alteration of claims mechanisms.[56]

II. Individual waivers of interstate claims

The effect of individual waivers on interstate claims has historically arisen in various situations. Perhaps the most well-known concern the use of 'Calvo' clauses in contracts between States and aliens in the early twentieth century, in which the

Moore v Regan (1981) 453 US 654 (USSC) 683; *In re World War II Era Japanese Forced Labor Litigation* (2000) 14 F Supp 2d 939 (DC ND Cal) 946; also *Ethiopia's Damages Claims (Final Award)* (2009) XXVI UNRIAA 631 [315]; Vallat (n 48) 43; Murphy, Kidane, and Snider (n 48) 35, 43; Benvenisti (n 49) 1087–90, 1095. Cf Caron (n 49) 284–85; Conclusion, n 71.

[51] Tomuschat (n 48) 988–89; Benvenisti (n 49) 1088, 1090; also van Houtte, Delmartino, and Yi (n 49) 305; *Ethiopia* (n 50) [22]; *Forced Labor* (n 50) 946–47; Peters (n 32) 212; Anthea Roberts, 'State-to-State Investment Treaty Arbitration: A Hybrid Theory of Interdependent Rights and Shared Interpretative Authority' (2014) 55 Harv ILJ 1, 49. Generally Cheng (n 29) 48; Dolzer (n 50) 314–16, 320, 340; Rainer Hofman and Frank Riemann, 'ILA Committee on Compensation for Victims of War: Background Report' (2004) 37.

[52] Similarly authorities Introduction, nn 61, 70; Roberts, 'Hybrid' (n 51) 49–50.

[53] Consent in State responsibility is premised on the obligation continuing, not having been terminated under treaty law: *ARSIWA*, 164; Mansour (n 1) 445–46.

[54] nn 18–21, 40–41, 382.

[55] Sections II–III.

[56] Section III(C)(viii).

latter purport to waive international remedies, including diplomatic protection by their State of nationality.[57] It is generally accepted, however, that such clauses cannot actually preclude States from exercising diplomatic protection.[58] The individual simply 'has no right . . . to waive a right that belongs to the State'.[59]

More recently, the *Duzgit Integrity* tribunal considered the effect of a settlement agreement reached between the respondent State and 'the main private entity' involved in a dispute,[60] in which the latter waived any further claims and reparation.[61] The Tribunal affirmed that the settlement 'ha[d] no bearing on [the State of nationality's] entitlement to bring claims' under the United Nations Convention on the Law of the Sea (UNCLOS),[62] claims which were, in part, diplomatic protection claims.[63] This makes sense, for as Chapter 3 highlighted, diplomatic protection claims are brought for breach of interstate obligations.[64] Individuals cannot waive a State's right to the performance of such interstate obligations, even if they benefit from their application.[65]

Individual waivers can nonetheless *affect* interstate claims.[66] To understand such effects, we must recall from Chapter 1 that *breach* (legal injury) is essential for

[57] John Dugard, 'Third Report on Diplomatic Protection' (2002) 2(1) ILCYB 49 [119], [122]; Juillard (n 35) [5]; Chittharanjan Amerasinghe, *Diplomatic Protection* (OUP 2008) 192–93; FV Garcia-Amador, 'International Responsibility: Report' (1956) 2 ILCYB 173 [178]; generally Borchard (n 47) 792–810; Parlett (n 27) 79.

[58] See Amerasinghe (n 57) 201–10; Parlett (n 27) 80; Juillard (n 35) [9]; Borchard (n 47) 797–99, 809–10, cf 800–8 (inconsistent cases); Dugard (n 57), particularly [139], [146]–[149]; Paul Weis, *Nationality and Statelessness in International Law* (2nd edn, Sijthoff & Noordhoff 1979) 38; Douglas, *Investment* (n 29) 26–27, 366; James Crawford, 'The International Law Commission's Articles on Diplomatic Protection Revisited' in Tiyanjana Maluwa, Max du Plessis, and Dire Tladi (eds), *The Pursuit of a Brave New World in International Law: Essays in Honour of John Dugard* (Brill Nijhoff 2017) 168; also Shany (n 29) 40–42.

[59] ILC, 'Draft Articles on Diplomatic Protection with Commentaries' (2006) 2(2) ILCYB 22 (DADP), 73, also 74; also Borchard (n 47) 372, 798–99, 810; ALI, *Restatement of the Law: The Foreign Relations Law of the United States*, vol II (3rd edn, ALI Publishers 1987) §713(g); Feichtner (n 24) [13]; Juillard (n 35) [9], [26]; Amerasinghe (n 57) 202, 206, 209; Weis (n 58) 34, 38; Crawford, *GP* (n 24) 565; Tams (n 5) 1039; Peters (n 32) 393–94. See *North American Dredging Company v Mexico* (1926) IV UNRIAA 26 [11], [15], [22], [24]; *Mexican Union Railway* (1930) 5 ILR 207 (UK–Mexican Cl Comm) 209–10; *Woodruff Case* (1903) IX UNRIAA 213 (US–Venezuelan Cl Comm) 222; *Martini Case* (1903) X UNRIAA 644 (Italy–Venezuela Cl Comm) 663; *Rudloff Case* (1903) IX UNRIAA 244 (US-Venezuelan Cl Comm) 247–48; *AES v Argentina (Jurisdiction)* (2005) 12 ICSID Rep 308 [98]. Discussing case law: references n 73. Cf Garcia-Amador (n 57) [182].

[60] *Duzgit Integrity (Malta v São Tomé and Príncipe) (Award)* PCA Case 2014-07 (5 September 2016) [155].

[61] ibid [180], [118], also [265].

[62] ibid [181].

[63] ibid [146]–[147], also [181] ('claims settled ... distinct from [State's]'). Similarly *Schneider (for Walter Bau) v Thailand (Award)* UNCITRAL Tribunal (1 July 2009) [8.8], [8.17], [12.23], [13.1](b)–(d).

[64] Ch 3(II)(A).

[65] See Gerald Fitzmaurice, 'Fourth Report on the Law of Treaties' (1959) 2 ILCYB 37 [160]; *ADM* (n 27) [174] (treaty 'obligations . . . cannot be waived'); *SGS v Philippines (Jurisdiction)* (2004) 8 ICSID Rep 518 [154]; generally Spiermann (n 27) 199–200, cf 206; Arnold McNair, *International Law Opinions*, vol II (OUP 1956) 60–61, 63; Arnold McNair, *The Law of Treaties: British Practice and Opinions* (Clarendon 1938) 333–34. Cf Paparinskis, 'Analogies' (n 9) 104; Peters (n 32) 326–28.

[66] Accepting individual waiver: Sohn and Baxter (n 27) art 24; ALI (n 59) §713(g); ALI, *Restatement of the Law: The Foreign Relations Law of the United States* (2nd edn, ALI Publishers 1965) 605; Vallat (n 48) 32 (fn 1); also Borchard (n 47) 799.

responsibility to be invoked, while *damage* (factual injury) is necessary for obligations of reparation to arise.[67]

An individual's actions may affect the existence of *breach* in two ways. The first relates to circumstances where the primary obligation gives effect to such waivers: individuals may waive, for instance, and within limits, certain human rights relating to fair trial and court access.[68] However, despite terminology, and as noted above, this is really a question of *consent* as an allowance built into the primary obligation itself.[69]

Second, as Chapter 3 highlighted, diplomatic protection claims often presuppose the existence of certain individual *domestic* law rights, including those concerning property and contract.[70] Such rights *are* usually within the relevant individual's control under domestic law.[71] Accordingly, while denying that Calvo clauses impacted the State's ability to exercise diplomatic protection for breach of international law,[72] tribunals historically did often accept that such clauses would preclude interstate claims from being brought for breach of *contract*.[73]

[67] Ch 1(II)–(III).

[68] See *Meftah v France* ECHR 2002-VII (GC) [46]–[47]; *Estevill v Spain* Doc CCPR/C/77/D/1004/2001 (HRC, 25 March 2003) [6.2]; *Perterer v Austria* Doc CCPR/C/81/D/1015/2001 (HRC, 20 July 2004) [9.3]; *Hermi v Italy* (2008) 46 EHRR 46 [73], [102]–[103]; *Kimel* (n 37) [22], [26]; *Paulo v Tanzania*, App 020/2016 (ACommHPR, 21 September 2018) [81]; Merrills (n 36) 180–85; *ARSIWA*, 165; Crawford, 'SecondRep' (n 8) [242].

[69] Paparinskis, 'New' (n 7) 630; Crawford, 'SecondRep' (n 8) [241]–[242]; Paparinskis, 'Analogies' (n 9) 100; also Spiermann (n 27) 181.

[70] Ch 3, nn 65–68; generally Douglas, *Investment* (n 29) 370ff.

[71] Eg, Peters (n 32) 325; *Lemire* (n 33) [33] (Diss Op Voss); de Aréchaga (n 7) 591; Crawford, 'Revisited' (n 58) 167–68; authorities nn 73, 86; Ch 3, n 67; Sohn and Baxter (n 27) 51; also *Geschäftshaus-GmbH v Schweizerische Rückversicherungs* (1930) 5 ILR 378 (Reichsgericht) 378 (State to '*advise* ... creditors ... to waive ... right to repayment' (emphasis added)). Cf Garcia-Amador (n 57) [182]; DADP, 74 (Calvo clause's acceptability if individual rights); Philip Jessup, *A Modern Law of Nations* (Archon 1968) 111; Parlett (n 27) 93, 111.

[72] nn 58–59.

[73] See, discussing various cases addressed herein: Borchard (n 47) 800–10, also referencing Jackson Ralston, *International Arbitral Law and Procedure* (Ginn 1910), see 34–44; Dugard (n 57) [146]–[149]; Amerasinghe (n 57) 194–95, 201–5; Shany (n 29) 40–42, 147; de Aréchaga (n 7) 591–92. Eg, *Dredging* (n 59) [14]–[15], [20], [22]–[25]; *Woodruff* (n 59) 222 ('source of ... rights and duties'), 223; *Orinoco Steamship* (1903) IX UNRIAA 180 (US–Venezuelan Cl Comm) 199–200; *Day and Garrison* (1885) 4 Moore's 3548 (US–Venezuela Cl Comm) 3562–64; *Flannagan* (1885) 4 Moore's 3564 (US–Venezuelan Cl Comm) 3565–66; *North and South American Construction v Chile* (1892) 3 Moore's 2318 (US–Chile Cl Comm) 2320; *Tehuantepec Ship Canal* (1873) 3 Moore's 3132 (US–Mexican Cl Comm) 3132–33; *Turnbull* (1903) IX UNRIAA 261 (US–Venezuelan Cl Comm) 305. Cf *Rudloff* (n 59) 249–50, 254–55; *Martini* (n 59) 663–64; *Azurix v Argentina (Jurisdiction)* (2003) 10 ICSID Rep 416 [84]–[85]; *SGS v Philippines* (n 65) [149]–[154]; *Aguaytia Energy v Peru (Award)* ICSID Case No ARB/06/13 (28 November 2008) [69]–[70]; *MNSS* (n 36) [159], [308]. Further: Sohn and Baxter (n 27) art 22(5); ALI (n 59) §713(g); contractual choice-of-forum cases: Juillard (n 35) [25], [22], citing *Azurix (Jurisdiction)* [83]; also *SGS v Philippines* (n 65) [154]–[155], [169], [176]; *Occidental v Ecuador (Award)* (2004) 12 ICSID Rep 59 [51]–[63]; *Aguas* (n 33) [119]; *Malicorp v Egypt (Award)* ICSID Case No ARB/08/18 (31 January 2011) [103]; Crawford, 'Revisited' (n 58) 167–68; Douglas, *Investment* (n 29) 367–71, 378ff; Douglas, 'Hybrid' (n 29) 242ff; Peters (n 32) 394, generally 293–301, 324–27, 334–36; authorities n 32. Cf *AES* (n 59) [97]–[99]; *SGS v Paraguay (Jurisdiction)* ICSID Case No ARB/07/29 (12 February 2010) [177]–[185].

Similarly, the interstate *Serbian Loans* case, one of diplomatic protection,[74] concerned the modalities of payment under certain agreements between French nationals and the respondent State.[75] The latter invoked the individuals' acceptance of a particular method of payment as estopping arguments for an alternative claimed method in the interstate claim.[76] The Permanent Court of International Justice (PCIJ) did not deny that estoppel *could* have operated 'to establish a loss of right' under the contracts, though it did not in the circumstances.[77] At least where the interstate dispute was 'fundamentally identical' to that between the State and the individual nationals,[78] and 'exclusively concerned with relations between [them] ... within the domain of municipal law',[79] the PCIJ thus envisaged that individual actions could affect an interstate diplomatic protection claim.[80]

There is no difficulty with such conclusions insofar as they imply that an individual's waiver of, or consent to changes of, domestic rights can preclude interstate claims relying on those rights.[81] As Weis argues in respect of waiver:

> the right of protection and the right of the individual are on different planes: the former is a right under international law, the latter a right under municipal law. The effect of renunciation of a claim depends on the nature of the right of the national. If this may be renounced according to municipal law, as, for instance, a claim for damages under civil law, no diplomatic action can be taken after the national's renunciation. This, however, is not because the renunciation is binding upon the State, but because, in view of renunciation, the right whose infringement has been complained of has been destroyed or extinguished and there is thus no longer any violation of a right which would warrant diplomatic action—provided, of course, that the renunciation was made in full freedom without any pressure ....[82]

[74] *Payment of Various Serbian Loans Issued in France* [1929] PCIJ Rep Ser A No 20, 17; Gerald Sander, 'Brazilian Loans Case and Serbian Loans Case' in *MPEPIL* (n 24) (2014) [5].

[75] *Serbian Loans* (n 74) 6, discussed vis-à-vis estoppel in Marjorie Whiteman, *Damages in International Law* (US Government 1937) 188.

[76] *Serbian Loans* (n 74) 38.

[77] ibid 39.

[78] ibid 18.

[79] ibid. See Peter Tomka, Jessica Howley, and Vincent-Joël Proulx, 'International and Municipal Law before the World Court: One or Two Legal Orders?' (2015) XXXV Pol YBIL 11, 34, with authorities; Parlett (n 27) 66–67.

[80] See *Serbian Loans* (n 74) 17 (diplomatic protection); also Whiteman (n 75) 188.

[81] See nn 70–71; also Vallat (n 48) 32 (fn 1).

[82] Weis (n 58) 38. On forced settlement: *Desert Line Projects v Yemen (Award)* ICSID Case No ARB/05/17 (6 February 2008) [148]–[195], discussed Hege Elisabeth Kjos, *Applicable Law in Investor-State Arbitration: The Interplay Between National and International Law* (OUP 2013) 289–90; *Howard* (1931) 6 ILR 233 (UK–Mexican Cl Comm).

An individual's waiver of domestic rights may, in certain circumstances, therefore prevent breach under international law from being established and, consequently, undermine the basis for an interstate claim.[83]

An individual's waiver might, alternatively, affect the existence of *damage*, and the consequent reparation due on the interstate level.[84] Albeit concerning only individual claims, the *Toto* tribunal's holding demonstrates the point that a waiver of damage may preclude reparation even for a distinct breach: there, a contractual waiver did not preclude treaty claims, but where both claims concerned 'the same damage', 'compensation that a Claimant has waived under the Contract cannot be recovered under the Treaty'.[85] *Interstate* reparation claims have similarly been precluded when individuals have renounced contractual losses,[86] while individual waivers of reparation for personal injury have likewise barred interstate claims based on the same damage.[87] Indeed, the *Duzgit Integrity* tribunal acknowledged that the waiver given by a national discussed above—while not affecting the State's ability to claim vis-à-vis that national's injury[88]—could impact the quantum of reparation ultimately awarded to the State.[89] Likewise, in another early case concerned with treatment of a vessel, the owners had waived all claims 'before any court or tribunal' arising out of the ship's detention, including vis-à-vis damage caused.[90]

[83] See *Del Genovese* (1903) IX UNRIAA 236 (US–Venezuelan Cl Comm) 238–39 (no breach given waiver), cited Borchard (n 47) 808; also *Martini* (n 59) 661 (contractual claim 'satisfied'); *Orinoco* (n 73) 199; *Re Governments of Norway and US* (1959) 28 ILR 611 (US Ct Cl) 617, 621 (contractual settlement binding).

[84] See ALI (n 66) §203, 605 (where individual 'freely accepted whatever reparation ... deem[ed] satisfactory ... no remaining obligation to make reparation on which ... state ... can base ... claim'); also FV Garcia-Amador, 'Sixth Report on State Responsibility' (1961) 2 ILCYB 1, 48, 53 (draft art 19(3)); *Eureko* (n 33) [174]–[175]; Whiteman (n 75) 179–80, 187; also Merrills (n 36) 179. On individual settlements: *Desert Line* (n 82) [179]; *Toto Costruzioni v Lebanon (Award)* ICSID Case No ARB/07/12 (30 May 2012) [84]–[85]. Cf Borchard (n 47) 370; individual waivers not precluding later treaty claims: *La Houve* (1927) 8 TAM 100 (Franco-German MAT) 103; *Marqua* (1921) 1 TAM 104 (Franco-German MAT) 104–5 (both cited Whiteman (n 75) 179 (fn 425)); *In re Roy* (1931) 6 ILR 421 (British–Mexican Cl Comm) 422–23; *Wollemborg Claim* (1956) 24 ILR 654 (Italian–US Conc Comm) 662–63. Similarly Ch 3, nn 193–95.

[85] *Toto* (n 84) [85].

[86] *Norway/US* (n 83) 617, 621; *Campbell Claim (UK v Portugal)* (1931) 7 ILR 261, 262–63 (concession); *de Chambo* (1915) Shoenrich's Rep 45 (Spanish–Nicaraguan Cl Comm), discussed Whiteman (n 75) 187; also *French Claims Against Peru* (1922) 16 AJIL 480 (PCA) 481–82, discussed Whiteman (n 75) 193; similarly *Turnbull* (n 73) 305 (no damages without competent court breach decision).

[87] *Jencken (UK/Spain)* (1870–71) 62 BFSP 985, 1004 (State 'not ... justified in pressing ... claim' for damages 'voluntarily waived'), discussed Weis (n 58) 38; Whiteman (n 75) 184–85; Borchard (n 47) 372. *Magee (UK/Guatemala)* (1874) 65 BFSP 875 is cited in opposition: see ibid 889, 897–1, 908, 911–12, 921 (compensation despite individual renunciation), discussed Whiteman (n 75) 184; Borchard (n 47) 372. But *Magee* concerned a Vice-Consul, the claim reflecting 'grave ... indignity to ... nation': *Magee* (n 89) 901, also 920. Compensation thus apparently satisfied the *State's* moral damage, which the individual could not waive: see ALI, n 103; Ch 3, nn 272–76. Cf *Jarr and Hurst v Mexico* (1868) 3 Moore's 2707 (US–Mexican Cl Comm) 2707–8, 2713, discussed Borchard (n 47) 372 ('private waiver ... bar[ring] ... international reclamation'). But there, a US official had agreed: *Jarr* (n 87) 2707–8; Borchard (n 47) 800.

[88] nn 60–63.

[89] *Duzgit* (n 60) [183], also [33] (Diss Op Kateka).

[90] *The Tattler* (1920) VI UNRIAA 48, 49. Case discussed: Weis (n 58) 37–38; Ian Brownlie, *Principles of Public International Law* (4th edn, OUP 1990) 506; Whiteman (n 75) 182–84; de Aréchaga (n 7) 591.

The tribunal held that 'the only right' that the State was 'supporting [was] that of its national' and it could 'rely on no legal ground other than those which would have been open to its national'; consequently it dismissed the claim concerning detention.[91] Considered controversial for apparently allowing an individual waiver to preclude an interstate claim,[92] the case is better viewed, despite the ever-misleading 'rights' terminology,[93] as confirming that an individual's waiver of *damage* precludes a successful interstate reparation claim for that damage.[94]

Individual waivers do not therefore actually *waive* States' claims: individuals cannot waive such rights to claim belonging to another.[95] Rather, an individual 'waiver' may constitute conduct that would preclude *breach* from being established, either because the primary obligation so allows, or because a waiver of domestic law rights undermines the claim's basis.[96] An individual's waiver of *damage* also precludes an interstate reparation claim for that damage.[97] Chapter 3 outlined that it is diplomatic protection claims that are brought for alleged damage to individuals, and that may depend on the relevant individual's domestic law entitlements.[98] It is therefore these claims which may be impacted by the latter two classes of waiver.[99] Similarly, in respect of article 48 claims, States claiming reparation for breach of *erga omnes (partes)* human rights obligations may only do so in the individual's interest.[100] It is difficult to see how a State could continue to claim such reparation where that individual has waived it.[101] However, in a 'direct' claim, the State has suffered its own damage,[102] the claim for which would subsist regardless of any individual waiver.[103]

III. Interstate waiver of individual claims

Perhaps more prevalent than waivers of interstate claims by individuals is the converse practice, in which States have purported to waive or settle the claims of

[91] *Tattler* (n 90) 49.
[92] Brownlie (n 90) 506 (fn 76) (*Tattler* 'in error'); cf ALI (n 66) 607.
[93] cf Ch 3, n 61.
[94] Similarly ALI (n 66) 607; Weis (n 58) 38, quoted n 82 (vis-à-vis *Tattler*); also n 84.
[95] nn 41, 59, 65.
[96] nn 70ff.
[97] nn 84ff.
[98] Ch 3(II), particularly nn 65–68.
[99] See nn 82ff.
[100] Ch 1, n 117.
[101] cf *Cyprus v Turkey (Just Satisfaction)* ECHR 2014-II 245 (GC) [10] (Sep Op Albuquerque/Vučinić), n 349. On waivers' relevance to reparation: *Neumeister* (n 36) [33]; *Eckle v Germany* (1982) 68 ILR 48 (ECtHR) [66].
[102] Ch 3(IV)(B).
[103] de Aréchaga (n 7) 591; ALI (n 66) 606, discussing *Magee*, n 87; Sohn and Baxter (n 27) 207; Ch 3, nn 193–95.

individual nationals.[104] For instance, the *Immunities* case concerned, *inter alia*, the 1947 Peace Treaty between Italy and the Allied Powers, article 77 of which provides that 'Italy waives on its own behalf *and on behalf of Italian nationals* all claims against Germany and German nationals outstanding on May 8, 1945' including 'all claims for loss or damage arising during the war'.[105] Under further supplementary treaties Germany paid sums to Italy in 'final settlement' of certain claims,[106] while other 'outstanding claims' of Italy and its nationals were 'settled'.[107] The International Court of Justice (ICJ) did not determine the effect of such waivers under international law, despite acknowledging that the issue was not 'unimportant'.[108] However, as Chapter 4 highlighted, it did express apparent approval of such use of lump-sum agreements to settle war-related claims affecting numerous individuals.[109]

The treaties in the *Immunities* case are not anomalous. States often conclude treaties in which they purport, in varying language, to waive not only their own claims, but also those of their nationals.[110] An express waiver on behalf of both the State and nationals is particularly common in peace treaties like that considered in *Immunities*,[111] but also in treaties settling, on a lump-sum basis, significant economic claims affecting many individuals.[112] There is further, extensive, practice in which other language is employed with apparent intent to effect a similar result.[113] Thus, States have 'renounc[ed]' reparations claims in their own and nationals' names,[114] rendered individual claims that had been settled in various spheres

[104] See Tams (n 5) 1037, 1039; *Oppenheim's* (n 48) 538; Crawford, *GP* (n 24) 571–72; Lillich and Weston (n 50) 108–9; Vallat (n 48) 32, 44–45; Feichtner (n 24) [14].

[105] Art 77(4), cited *Jurisdictional Immunities (Germany v Italy: Greece Intervening) (Judgment)* [2012] ICJ Rep 99 [22] (emphasis added).

[106] ibid [24].

[107] ibid [25]. Treating both as waiver: n 113.

[108] ibid [108].

[109] ibid [102], discussed Ch 4, nn 506ff.

[110] Generally Tams (n 5) 1039; Crawford, *GP* (n 24) 571–72; Feichtner (n 24) [14]; Lillich and Weston (n 50) 108–9; Peters (n 32) 214. Cf Lillich and Weston (n 50) App B, Belgium–Germany, art 3 (nationals' claims excluded).

[111] Eg, post-WWII: Japan PT, arts 14(b), 19; Austria PT, arts 23(3), 24; Hungary PT, arts 30(4), 32(1); Finland PT, art 29; Romania PT, arts 28(4), 30; Bulgaria PT, arts 26(4), 28; Burma PT, arts V, VIII; US–Austria, art III(1); Japan–Czechoslovakia, art 4; UK–Austria, art 8; Canada–Japan, art 2; Greece–Japan, art 2; US–Japan (Awa Maru), art I; US–Japan (Amami Islands), art IV; Richard Lillich and Burns Weston, *International Claims: Their Settlement By Lump Sum Agreements*, vol II (Virginia UP 1975): (42) Greece–Rumania, arts 3(2)-(3); (49) Indonesia–Japan, arts 4(2), 5(1); also (73) UK–Japan, art 3. Post-WWI: Treaty of Versailles, art 137, also art 244 (Annex III(8)–(9)); Hague Agreement, art III; Rapallo Agreement, arts 1–2. Generally Tomuschat (n 48) 988; André Nollkaemper, *National Courts and the International Rule of Law* (OUP 2011) 31; Crawford, *GP* (n 24) 571; Caron (n 49) 282; Dolzer (n 50) 311–12, 319, 322, 326; Feichtner (n 24) [14].

[112] Eg, Lillich and Weston (n 111): (6) UK–Yugoslavia, arts 3(a),(b) (nationalisation); US–Iceland, art 4 (occupation); similarly US–Germany Settlement, art II; UK/France/US/Italy/Germany, art I(c); Thailand–Japan Settlement, art III.

[113] Eg, treating settlement provisions as waiver: *Immunities Pleadings* (n 49), Mem Germany [11]; Rep Germany [30]–[31]; Rej Italy [3.18].

[114] See Lillich and Weston (n 111): (1) UAR–Italy, arts 3, 8. Similarly: Treaty of Paris, art VII ('relinquish'), discussed Coleman Phillipson, *Termination of War and Treaties of Peace* (Unwin 1916) 331; Murphy, Kidane, and Snider (n 48) 32.

'void',[115] or 'expired',[116] and provided that such claims are otherwise unable to be asserted.[117] In other agreements, the responsible State is released from,[118] held free from,[119] 'exonerated of',[120] or 'relieved of',[121] responsibility towards the receiving State and its nationals, with many treaties referring to settlement with 'liberating effect'.[122] Lump-sum settlements commonly contain words to the effect that compensation is paid in 'full and final settlement'[123] or 'full settlement and discharge'[124] of the claims of both the State and its nationals, or provide more generally that nationals' claims, and/or liabilities thereby arising, are settled,[125] satisfied,[126] discharged,[127] cancelled,[128] or extinguished.[129]

Although some suggest that States may waive their nationals' claims in the exercise of their personal sovereign jurisdiction over such nationals under international law,[130] this assertion deserves some analysis. In particular, the effective scope of such waivers must be examined to establish how far States endeavour to, and succeed in, precluding their nationals' claims, for interstate waivers could

115 See Lillich and Weston (n 111): (5) Switzerland–Yugoslavia, art 3.

116 See ibid: (48) Bulgaria–USSR, art 2; (50) Hungary–USSR, art 2.

117 Eg, ibid: (5) Switzerland–Yugoslavia, art 3 ('any claims whatsoever'); (14) Switzerland–Hungary, art 3; (24) Denmark–Poland, art 2; (28) Yugoslavia–Italy, art 12; (37) Czechoslovakia–Yugoslavia, art 5; (106) Netherlands–Hungary, art 3(2)(a); also (102) Hungary–Austria, art 4 (claims transferred); similarly (22) Belgium/Luxembourg–Czechoslovakia, art 3; Burns Weston, Richard Lillich, and David Bederman, *International Claims: Their Settlement By Lump Sum Agreements, 1975–1995* (Transnational Publishers 1999): (42) Switzerland–Zaire, art 7.

118 Lillich and Weston (n 111): (6) UK–Yugoslavia, art 2(b); (24) Denmark–Poland, art 2; (56) France–Rumania, arts 2–3; (61) Greece–Yugoslavia, art 2; (77) Netherlands–Bulgaria, art 3(1); Weston, Lillich, and Bederman (n 117): (47) Italy–Morocco, art 3.

119 Lillich and Weston (n 111): (12) France–Czechoslovakia, art 3; (21) Canada–Italy, art 1; Weston, Lillich, and Bederman (n 117): (29) Austria–Czechoslovakia, art 5.

120 Lillich and Weston (n 111): (58) Finland–USSR, art 1; similarly (22) Belgium/Luxembourg–Czechoslovakia, art 3.

121 ibid: (47) Brazil–Italy [5].

122 Eg, ibid: (19) Switzerland–Rumania, art 3; (31) Belgium/Luxembourg–Hungary, art 6; (35) Norway–Bulgaria, art 3; (41) Turkey–Yugoslavia, art 3.

123 Eg, ibid: (46) Sweden–Japan, art 4; (66) Norway–USSR, art 3; (109) Canada–Bulgaria, art 1; (112) Netherlands–Indonesia, art 3(1); similarly (76) Japan–US; (126) Austria–Poland, art 1; Weston, Lillich, and Bederman (n 117): (40) US–China, art 2(a); (49) UK–Mauritius, art 1.

124 Eg, Lillich and Weston (n 111): (4) US–Yugoslavia, art 1(a); similarly (6) Great Britain–Yugoslavia, art 2(a); (44) Spain–Japan [3]; (57) Great Britain–UAR, art 4(5); Weston, Lillich, and Bederman (n 117): (34) US–Egypt, art 1(1); also (12) Italy–Romania, arts 1, 4 ('global ... definitive settlement'; 'discharging effect'); (43) Canada–Cuba, art 3 ('discharge ... completely settled'); (67) US–Vietnam, art 3(1).

125 Eg, Lillich and Weston (n 111): (3) France–Poland, art 4; (53) Netherlands–Yugoslavia, art 2; (68) Denmark–Rumania, arts 1, 4; Weston, Lillich, and Bederman (n 117): (17) Austria–Italy, art 2(1).

126 Lillich and Weston (n 111): (39) Yugoslavia–Hungary, art 1(1).

127 ibid: (13) France–Hungary, art 4; (97) Netherlands–Czechoslovakia, art 4(1); (111) Greece–Rumania, art 2; Weston, Lillich, and Bederman (n 117): (37) France–Guinea, §1(3), 2(2); (44) Canada–China, art 4.

128 Weston, Lillich, and Bederman (n 117): (27) US–Peru, art 4.

129 Italy PT, art 76(2); Lillich and Weston (n 111): (84) Austria–Bulgaria, art 2; (98) Greece–Bulgaria, art 2; (101) Hungary–Austria, art 2; Weston, Lillich, and Bederman (n 117): (15) Denmark–Hungary, art 3; (16) Canada–Romania, art 4(1); (52) Finland–GDR, art 6.

130 Feichtner (n 24) [14] and authorities section III(B), particularly n 168.

potentially be intending to encapsulate one or more of the different types of claim discussed in previous chapters:

(1) diplomatic protection claims;
(2) the claims of nationals under municipal law before domestic courts; and
(3) the claims of nationals under international law before international tribunals.[131]

Each type of claim is considered in turn to determine whether interstate waivers do indeed cover, and operate to preclude, such claims.

A. Preclusion of diplomatic protection claims

As Chapter 3 outlined, in diplomatic protection claims, a State claims for damage suffered by its national consequent on violation of international law.[132] Because a State exercising diplomatic protection is espousing its national's cause,[133] a waiver of nationals' claims could potentially be read as referring to diplomatic protection claims.[134] However, even if brought for individual *damage*,[135] the premise of diplomatic protection is that the State 'assert[s] its own rights'.[136] The claim is the State's, and is therefore waivable by it in its own right.[137]

Consequently, as the Tokyo District Court rightly concluded in interpreting the waiver clause in the post-WWII Peace Treaty with Japan, a waiver of the State's claims incorporates diplomatic protection claims; a waiver of its nationals' claims must therefore envisage something else.[138] A similar approach is suggested by certain settlement agreements which treat the diplomatic protection claims of States as distinct from claims belonging to nationals.[139] Moreover, where tribunals have

[131] Similarly Gattini, 'Trojan' (n 35) 539 (fn 102); Gattini, 'Hurdles' (n 50) 364, 366; Dolzer (n 50) 303 (need to distinguish private/State; national/international claims), 305–6; Nollkaemper (n 111) 31; also Caron (n 49) 282; Crawford, *GP* (n 24) 571; Peters (n 32) 204–8, 216–20.

[132] Ch 3(II).

[133] Ch 3, nn 22, 111, 128.

[134] As Japan argued: *Ryuichi Shimoda v Japan* (1963) 32 ILR 626 (Tokyo DC) 640.

[135] Ch 3(II)(C).

[136] *Mavrommatis Palestine Concessions* [1924] PCIJ Rep Ser A No 2, 12, quoted Ch 2, n 97, with other authorities.

[137] Tams (n 5) 1039; Crawford, *GP* (n 24) 565; Garcia-Amador (n 57) [174]–[175]; also *Avena and Other Mexican Nationals (Mexico v US) (Judgment)* [2004] ICJ Rep 12 [44]; Sohn and Baxter (n 27) art 25, 209–11; *Park v Mitsubishi* Da-22549, ILDC 1909 (KR 2012) (SC Korea, 24 May 2012) [60]; *Kandyrine v France* Recueil Lebon 303678, ILDC 2734 (FR 2011) (Cons d'Etat, 23 December 2011) [23]; nn 58–65. Cf *Oppenheim's* (n 48) 527; DADP, art 19(a). For individual involvement in settlements: *Red Crusader* (1962) 35 ILR 485 (Denmark–UK Comm) 500; Whiteman (n 75) 180–81.

[138] *Shimoda* (n 134) 640. Treating diplomatic protection as potentially included within interstate waiver: eg US–UK Interpretation, 368–70; US–Norway, art III(B)(4); Weston, Lillich, and Bederman (n 117): (55) US–Ethiopia, art 5(3).

[139] See Lillich and Weston (n 111): (22) Belgium/Luxembourg–Czechoslovakia, art 3 ('undertakes… not to support… espouse'); similarly (61) Greece–Yugoslavia, art 3; (77) Netherlands–Bulgaria,

found that treaty language constituted a waiver of diplomatic protection, this language generally concerned *State* action, and did not consist in a waiver of nationals' claims.[140] While a waiver of diplomatic protection may, practically speaking, relieve individuals of any means of obtaining recourse for a violation of international law, particularly if there is no other tribunal, international or domestic, available to hear the claims,[141] it remains a waiver of the State's own claims, much as a waiver of other States' rights or claims, such as those concerning officials' immunity,[142] remains a State waiver, even if the circumstances might have serious consequences for particular individuals.[143] The question is what States *do* intend by agreeing waiver clauses referring specifically to their nationals' claims.

B. Preclusion of claims before the parties' courts

For starters, as this section demonstrates, States almost certainly intend to preclude the institution or continuance of individual claims under municipal law before their own domestic authorities.[144] Some agreements make this express, precluding claims from being brought in the State receiving funds for its nationals' injury,[145] in the compensating State,[146] or both.[147] More generally, clauses waiving nationals'

art 3(4); (98) Greece–Bulgaria, art 2; Weston, Lillich, and Bederman (n 117): (55) US–Ethiopia, art 5(3); (64) US–Germany, art 2(6); Lillich and Weston (n 50): App B, Belgium/Luxembourg–Bulgaria, art 5; Belgium–Morocco, art 8; Belgium–Tunisia, art 6; US–UK Settlement, 434–38.

[140] *German Assets in Switzerland Case* (1957) 24 ILR 542 (BVerfG) 546 (State's non-objection to liquidations diplomatic protection waiver); similarly *Togen Akiyama v State* (1963) 32 ILR 233 (Tokyo DC) 235; cf *Kandyrine* (n 137) [23]; also Gattini, 'Trojan' (n 35) 539.

[141] Crawford, *GP* (n 24) 565; also Borchard (n 47) 370; Vallat (n 48) 39, 45; Whiteman (n 75) 186–87; van Houtte, Delmartino, and Yi (n 49) 304; Sohn and Baxter (n 27) 202–03, 209–10; *Dames* (n 50) 679–80; *US v Germany (Administrative Decision No V)* (1924) VII UNRIAA 119 (US-German Mixed Cl Comm) 152; *Russian Indemnity Case (Award)* PCA Case (11 November 1912) <https://pcacases.com/web/sendAttach/643> 4, 15–16; ICSID, *Convention on the Settlement of Investment Disputes between States and Nationals of Other States: Documents Concerning the Origin and the Formulation of the Convention*, vol II (1968) 496. Cf nn 291–292.

[142] Eg *Arrest Warrant of 11 April 2000 (DRC v Belgium) (Judgment)* [2002] ICJ Rep 3 [61]; VCDR, art 32.

[143] Fitzmaurice (n 65) [159]; eg, *Doe v US* (1988) 121 ILR 567 (USCA 2nd Cir) 572–73.

[144] Generally nn 145ff; eg, Lillich and Weston (n 50) 6; Nollkaemper (n 111) 31, with references; Caron (n 49) 282; McNair, *Treaties* (n 65) 336; Arnold McNair, *Legal Effects of War* (4th edn, CUP 1966) 417–18; Gattini, 'Trojan' (n 35) 539; Vallat (n 48) 38–39, 45; Andrea Gattini, 'Compensation to Victims' in Antonio Cassese (ed), *The Oxford Companion to International Criminal Justice* (OUP 2009) 277. On certain cases discussed herein: Tams (n 5) 1039; *Oppenheim's* (n 48) 538–39; Crawford, *GP* (n 24) 571–72; ICRC, 'Practice Relating to Rule 150: Reparation', *Customary IHL Database* <https://ihl-databases.icrc.org/customary-ihl/eng/docs/v2_rul_rule150>; McNair, *War (4th)* (n 144) 418; van Houtte, Delmartino, and Yi (n 49) 23–24; Peters (n 32) 204–6, 215; Hofman and Riemann (n 51) 19–27.

[145] Lillich and Weston (n 111): (10) Switzerland–Czechoslovakia, art 2 ('no longer ... raise claims in Switzerland').

[146] ibid: (122) FRG–Italy, art 3(2) (Italian petitions transferred to Germany).

[147] ibid: (51) Czechoslovakia–Poland, art 8(1) ('entitled to refuse to consider [settled] claims'); US–France, art V.

claims have unfailingly been held to encompass claims before municipal courts.[148] Thus, the Tokyo District Court considered that it was:

> natural to interpret the term "claims of Japanese nationals" waived by Article 19 (*a*) [of the Japanese Peace Treaty] as including the claims of Japanese nationals against the Allied Powers and their nationals under the municipal laws of Japan and of the Allied Powers.[149]

In addition to the Japanese courts, treaty-based waiver clauses have similarly been held to bar domestic law claims by courts in Austria,[150] Germany,[151] Italy,[152] Singapore,[153] the UK,[154] and the US.[155]

To understand how such preclusion might be brought about, one must appreciate the two potential bases of jurisdiction States possess to thus affect their nationals' claims. First, States exercise jurisdiction over their territory.[156] This encapsulates the capacity to control which claims are brought before their courts.[157] Indeed, States commonly, for instance, recognise State immunity as precluding certain claims from being brought under domestic law.[158] Both a waiving State and a State benefiting from a waiver may prevent claims proceeding before their own judicial organs by, for example, using legislative or executive power to preclude,[159]

[148] See cases nn 149ff; also Weston, Lillich, and Bederman (n 117): (4) FRG–Italy, Exchange of Letters [1(a)], discussed *Immunities Pleadings* (n 49) Counter-Mem Italy [5.56].

[149] *Shimoda* (n 134) 641. Further: *Inao Horimoto v Japan* (1954) 32 ILR 161 (Tokyo HC) 164, n 189; *Nishimatsu* (n 50) §II[2]–[3]; Dolzer (n 50) 312–13.

[150] *Austrian State Treaty Case* (1961) 40 ILR 184 (SC Austria) 184–85; *S v Austria* 1Ob149/02, ILDC 1618 (AT 2002) (30 September 2002) (SC Austria) [1.7], [2] (Russian law).

[151] *German External Debts Agreement Case* (1955) 22 ILR 611 (BGH) 613–14, cf 614 ('precise legal effect' undecided); *Austrian Citizen's Entitlement to Compensation Case* (1960) 32 ILR 153 (BGH) 157; *Shareholders of the ZAG v A Bank* (1965) 45 ILR 436 (CA, Berlin) 438–45; *Restitution of Household Effects Belonging to Jews Deported from Hungary* (1965) 44 ILR 301 (CA, Berlin) 307–8, 315–16 (right's 'complete extinction'); *Aktiengesellschaft C v Firma S and L* (1930) 5 ILR 22 (Reichsgericht) 23; *Immunities Pleadings* (n 49), Rep Germany [25].

[152] *Ditta Pomante v Germany* (1960) 40 ILR 64 (L'Aquila Civ Ct) 71–73; also *External Debts* (n 151) 613; *Immunities Pleadings* (n 49), Rep Germany [25].

[153] Albeit *obiter dicta*: *Public Trustee v Chartered Bank of India, Australia and China* (1956) 23 ILR 687 (Singapore) 699 ('by implication, adverse to ... claim').

[154] *The Bellaman and the Agostino Bertani* (1948) 16 ILR 560 (EWHC) 560–61, 564.

[155] *Ozanic v USA (The Petar)* (1949) 16 ILR 176 (USCA, 2nd Cir) 179 (waiver enlivened immunity); *Neri v US* (1951) 20 ILR 223 (USCA, 2nd Cir) 224–25; *Pauly v US* (1961) 32 ILR 585 (US Ct Cl) 587–88; *Hwang Geum Joo v Japan* (2003) 332 F 3d 679 (USCA) 684–85, also *Hwang Geum Joo v Japan* (2005) 413 F 3d 45 (USCA) 50–53, citing *Forced Labor* (n 50) 944–48; similarly *Hee Nam You v Japan* (2015) US Dist LEXIS 149104 (DC ND Cal) (tort claims 'extinguished'); cf *Haas v Humphrey* (1957) 24 ILR 316 (USCA) 318; also *Tag v Rogers* (1959) 28 ILR 467 (USCA DC) 470 (property interests 'extinguished'). Generally, eg, Hofman and Riemann (n 51) 23–27.

[156] Generally *Oppenheim's* (n 48) §137.

[157] Eg, *Dames* (n 50) 684–85; Gattini, 'Trojan' (n 35) 539 (fn 102) (waiver 'procedural bar'); nn 164, 294. On domestic limitations: n 164; Conclusion, nn 52ff.

[158] *Dames* (n 50) 684–85; Vallat (n 48) 39 (immunity prevents claims 'in practice'); Caron (n 49) 283; *Shimoda* (n 134) 638–40; Nollkaemper (n 111) 22.

[159] Eg, EO 13477 (31 October 2008), ss 1(a)(i),(b)(i); EO12283 (19 January 1981), cited *Persinger v Iran* (1982) 72 ILR 132 (USCA DC) 135, ss 1-101(a),(b); also *External Debts* (n 151) 613–14; similarly

terminate,[160] or suspend[161] claims. However, as the Iran-US Claims Tribunal (IUSCT) observed:

> Termination of municipal litigation … cannot be mistaken for, or identified with, a waiver of any claims. The claims continue to exist, although the nationals no longer have at their disposal any domestic court procedures to pursue their claims. Closing the road to municipal courts cannot, in itself, amount to a waiver.[162]

The Japanese Supreme Court likewise concluded that a waiver of individuals' claims 'does not mean to effectively extinguish claims but … to have the competency of these claims in litigations lost'.[163] Such an exercise of jurisdiction as a means for controlling nationals' claims is thus not, strictly, a waiver, even if it has the same desired effect.[164]

Indeed, given territorial-based limits on the jurisdictional competence of States, the Japanese Supreme Court was understandably hesitant about the effectiveness of a waiver where the State was not in control of the relevant territory at the time.[165] Another interstate settlement agreement explained a requirement that a State free another from claims by its nationals as merely requiring that State to 'take all the measures *in its power* to ensure' that the other would not be 'held liable for any charge or obligation' except as contained in the settlement.[166] The existence of jurisdictional limitations suggests that, insofar as the effect of a waiver clause is merely to control access to certain domestic courts, it cannot be understood as a universal waiver of claims.[167]

ZAG Shareholders (n 151) 438; *Ditta* (n 152) 70–71; *Whitley v Aitchison* (1958) 26 ILR 196 (Cour Cass, France) 198.

[160] Eg, EO 13477, ss 1(a)(ii),(b)(ii); EO 12283, s 1-101(1)(c); *Persinger* (n 159) 150 ('extinguished … claims'). Cf n 162.

[161] See *Dames* (n 50) 684 (effect of EO 12294 (24 February 1981), barring US court claims for IUSCT); similarly Crawford, *GP* (n 24) 571–72; nn 290–92. For the distinction between suspension and termination: *Iran v US (Cases A/15 (IV) and A/24)* (1998) 34 Iran–USCTR 105 [92]–[99].

[162] *Iran v US (A15/24)* (n 161) [85]; cf n 294. Generally Caron (n 49) 282–83; Nollkaemper (n 111) 31.

[163] *Nishimatsu* (n 50) §II[2](3). Cf *Household Effects* (n 151) 315–16.

[164] Similarly nn 162, 290–92. Cf *Lectures on International Law and the United Nations* (Univ Mich 1957) 193 (Cardozo), on agreements for States to settle own nationals' claims: 'We did not say … claims were waived or cancelled, because it seemed … questionable whether the Executive … could constitutionally cut off … right of a … national to sue … like taking private property without just compensation'. Nonetheless, US courts interpreted clauses as impeding claims: ibid 193–94, referencing *Etlimar v US* (1952) 19 ILR 454 (US Ct Cl). Other treaties did use such terminology: nn 110ff, also n 155. On constitutional issues: Conclusion, nn 54ff.

[165] *Nishimatsu* (n 50) §II [3](2)–(3). Further: McNair, *Treaties* (n 65) 336; n175.

[166] Lillich and Weston (n 111): (12) France–Czechoslovakia, Annex 1 (emphasis added); similarly (22) Belgium/Luxembourg–Czechoslovakia, Protocol, Annex, ad art 3; also *Diverted Cargoes (Greece v UK)* (1955) 22 ILR 820, 822.

[167] Similarly *Prince Hans-Adam II v Municipality of Cologne* (1999) 149 ILR 1 (Cologne CA) 13 (German court jurisdiction barred, 'not … foreign or international'); nn 162–64.

The second basis on which States might affect the claims of their nationals is through exercising the personal jurisdiction a State possesses over its citizens, even outside its territory.[168] A State may thus 'under its municipal law', either 'forbid the submission of a claim by its national or nationalize the claim'.[169] As to the first, certain States have prohibited their nationals from bringing claims—following an interstate lump-sum agreement—not only before their own courts, but in any forum.[170] As to the second, a State might extinguish the private rights of its nationals underlying a given claim insofar as these rights are established in the State's own domestic law,[171] such as rights to property and other personal rights, wherever these rights are located.[172] While not apparently the intent behind all waiver clauses,[173] many interstate lump-sum settlement agreements thus envisage, for example, that title to property belonging to individual nationals will be transferred to the settling State as part of the settlement.[174]

However, again, to characterise such actions as effecting a *waiver* of claims is problematic, given that a State's exercise of personal jurisdiction is limited by the territorial rights of other States.[175] Anti-suit injunctions—prohibitions on bringing claims in another forum—are, for instance, not always given effect by courts located elsewhere, including by international tribunals.[176] A State might, under its

[168] *Austrian Citizen's* (n 151) 156; *ZAG Shareholders* (n 151) 439; see *Oppenheim's* (n 48) §138; n 130.

[169] Sohn and Baxter (n 27) 211.

[170] Eg, EO 13477, s 1(a)(i), cf s 1(b)(i), (iii) (vis-à-vis foreign nationals); EO 12283, s 1-101(a), cf s 101-1(b); also *Iran v US (A15/24)* (n 161) [143], [145].

[171] See Arnold McNair, *Legal Effects of War* (3rd edn, CUP 1948) 395–96 (State 'can bind itself by treaty to affect … rights of its nationals, both proprietary and personal, in whatever way a State can affect … persons and things subject to its sovereignty'), 391, citing *The Blonde* [1922] 1AC 313, 335 (waiver effected property transfer); similarly McNair, *Treaties* (n 65) 335–36; Louis Henkin, *Foreign Affairs and the United States Constitution* (2nd edn, Clarendon 1996) 300 (settlements 'wipe out … underlying private debt, terminating … recourse under domestic law'), cited *Asociacion de Reclamantes v Mexico* (1984) 84 ILR 87 (USCA, DC) 93 (treaty 'extinguished' 'property claims'); Gattini, 'Trojan' (n 35) 539 (fn 102); nn 129, 200, 419. Cf Paparinskis, 'New' (n 7) 645.

[172] McNair, *War (3rd)* (n 171) 392–93; also *Shimoda* (n 134) 641; *Germany v Milde* (2009) 92 RDI 618; ILDC 1224 (IT 2009) (Cour Cass, Italy) [8] (property rights); similarly *De Guglielmi v Germany* ILDC 1784 (IT 2010) 46 RDIP & P 1006 (CFI Italy) [4.1] (waiver non-tortious); *Immunities (Counterclaims)* (n 40) 369–70 (Diss Op Cancado); *Oppenheim's* (n 48) 915 (fn 8) (extra-territorial nationalisation).

[173] See Yoshida-Stikker Protocol, quoted ICRC (n 144), s B(I) (Japan not considering Netherlands 'expropriated … private claims of its nationals' making them 'non-existent'). Similarly US Dept of State, *Conference for the Conclusion and Signature of the Treaty of Peace with Japan: Record of Proceedings* (US Govt 1951) 197 (no expropriation; legal 'limitations'), volume cited Dolzer (n 50) 302 (fn 15). Further: Vallat (n 48) 38–39, 45.

[174] Eg, Lillich and Weston (n 111): (8) UK–Czechoslovakia, art 5(c); (88) Belgium/Luxembourg–Poland, art 8; (106) Netherlands–Hungary, art 3(2)(b); Weston, Lillich, and Bederman (n 117): (35) France–Brazil [9]; (34) US–Egypt, arts 6(3), 5(2) (State subrogated); Lillich and Weston (n 50), App B, Belgium/Luxembourg–Bulgaria, art 5; Belgium–Morocco, art 8; Belgium–Tunisia, art 6; Canada–Hungary, art 6(3); Canada–Poland, art 7. Generally Vallat (n 48) 46–47.

[175] *Oppenheim's* (n 48) §138; McNair, *Treaties* (n 65) 336; Omer Elagab, *The Legality of Non-Forcible Counter-Measures in International Law* (Clarendon 1988) 129–32; Tom Ruys, 'Sanctions, Retorsions and Countermeasures: Concepts and International Legal Framework' [2016] <https://papers.ssrn.com/sol3/papers.cfm?abstract_id=2760853>, 9. Also *ZAG Shareholders* (n 151) 439; n167.

[176] See *Phillip Alexander Securities and Futures Ltd v Bamberger* [1997] ILPr 73 [4]–[6] (English anti-suit injunction rejected in Germany); *British Caribbean Bank v Belize (Award)* PCA Case 2010-18 (19

rules of private international law, likewise refuse to recognise the efficacy of measures taken by another State—even where it has waived the right to object to them—if, for example, an attempt is made to affect property rights outside the territory where the property is situated.[177] Accordingly, another State might continue to recognise the existence of a claim under its own law that an individual was, through action by its State of nationality under a waiver clause, purportedly prevented from pursuing.[178]

States are evidently aware of these limitations on their capacity to effectively waive individual claims under the municipal law of other States, and are not necessarily content to rely on sovereign immunity to protect themselves.[179] States sometimes in settlement agreements therefore require that the State receiving compensation obtain waivers of claims from the affected individuals themselves,[180] or make partaking in the lump-sum distribution conditional on the individual accepting the terms of settlement.[181] This was generally the approach taken, for instance, vis-à-vis more recent compensation programmes for victims of Nazi persecution.[182] In other settlement agreements, the State receiving funds 'guarantees' that the compensating State will not have to pay anything further, presumably guarding against additional individual claims.[183] Certain interstate agreements even expressly contemplate that individuals may successfully bring further claims,

December 2014) [112], [114]–[115]; *SGS v Pakistan (Jurisdiction)* (2003) 18 ICSID Rev-FILJ 307 [39], [186]–[189]; discussion Shany (n 29) 18; Shany (n 22) 160–61.

177 *Assignment of Confiscated Debt Case* (1957) 24 ILR 31 (BGH) 34. Similarly *Koh-i-Noor, Hardtmuth v Koh-i-Noor, Tuzkaárna Hardtmuth* (1958) 26 ILR 40 (SC Austria) 41–42; *ZAG Shareholders* (n 151) 439; also McNair, *Treaties* (n 65) 336–37; McNair, *War (4th)* (n 144) 428–38. Cf McNair, *War (3rd)* (n 171) 393; *Hans-Adam* (n 167) 16ff (foreign law deferral). See discussion Gattini, 'Trojan' (n 35) 524–25.

178 See *Abel v Reich* (1960) 32 ILR 151 (Restitution SC) 152–53 ('doubtful' Austrian waiver covered German-law claims); *ZAG Shareholders* (n 151) 439 (State might not recognise); *Trampler v High Court Zürich* (1925) 3 ILR 351 (Swiss Federal Tribunal) (ineffective vis-à-vis Swiss jurisdiction), cited McNair, *War (3rd)* (n 171) 396; *Distomo Massacre* (2003) 129 ILR 556 (BGH) 564 (unclear 'how Greece can validly renounce individual claims'). Cf *Austrian Citizen's* (n 151) 156–58; *Household Effects* (n 151) 307–8.

179 cf n 158; Ch 2, nn 85–86. *Immunities* (n 105) demonstrates that, even with waivers, immunity is not always recognised: n 113; Ch 2, n 244.

180 Eg, Lillich and Weston (n 111): (8) Great Britain–Czechoslovakia, art 5(b) (where title unavailable); (88) Belgium/Luxembourg–Poland, art 8; (106) Netherlands–Hungary, art 3(3); Weston, Lillich, and Bederman (n 117): (35) France–Brazil [4], [6], [9]; (49) UK–Mauritius, art 4 ('best endeavours to procure'); (55) US–Ethiopia, Agreed Minutes; (69) US–FRG, art 4(3); also (34) US–Egypt, art 5(2) (State subrogated); Lillich and Weston (n 50) App B: Belgium/Luxembourg–Bulgaria, art 5; Belgium–Tunisia, art 6; Canada–Hungary, art 6(2); Canada–Rumania, art 7; Canada–France [4]. See Vallat (n 48) 46; Caron (n 49) 282.

181 Eg, Lillich and Weston (n 111): (20) France–Poland, art 3; (54) France–Yugoslavia, art 7; (82) Sweden–Yugoslavia, art 5; Weston, Lillich, and Bederman (n 117): (64) US–Germany, art 3 (election). See Vallat (n 48) 46–47; Lillich and Weston (n 50) 6.

182 See Germany–US, Annex A [14], arts 1–2; Austria–US, Annex A [9]. Cf Germany–Netherlands, arts 2, 15; also Dolzer (n 50) 324–28, 334–35; Burkhard Hess, 'The Private–Public Divide in International Dispute Resolution' (2018) 388 RdC 49, 145–46.

183 Eg, Lillich and Weston (n 111): (9) Sweden–Poland, art 2; (45) Norway–Hungary, art 4; similarly (16) Sweden–Hungary, art 3; also *Lectures* (n 164) 193.

notwithstanding the purported settlement, with provision made for set-off of compensation,[184] indemnification,[185] referral to the State of nationality,[186] and the supply of information regarding claims in third-country fora.[187] Such provisions appear to acknowledge that a State's waiver of its nationals' claims may not always be effective, raising doubts as to its nature as a true waiver.[188] Indeed, the Tokyo High Court in the *Horimoto Case* explained a waiver clause as being:

> related to the rights and obligations of States as subjects of international law, ... (As is contended on behalf of the respondent, the private claims of nationals as individuals are not rights of the State in its own name, and cannot be waived by the State in a treaty.) Thus the net result of this article amounts to a pledge by Japan to the Allied Powers that she will acquiesce in the eventual denial by these Powers of claims of Japanese nationals against Allied nationals which might otherwise be enforceable under the municipal law of any of the Allied Powers or of Japan. Consequently, by virtue of these provisions, the Allied Powers are entitled as against Japan to deny, without being in breach of the rules of international law, claims of Japanese nationals against the Allied Powers or their nationals which, in the absence of these provisions, would have been recognised in their municipal law.[189]

On this reasoning, an interstate waiver of nationals' claims operates under international law as a defence, vis-à-vis the waiving State, to the nullification of individuals' domestic law claims by the beneficiary State.[190] This would actually therefore appear to be treaty-based *consent* to the breach that would otherwise result when such claims are denied under the domestic law of the State benefiting from the waiver. The *effect* of such a waiver clause may be that individuals are precluded from claiming before the domestic courts of the wrongdoing State.[191] However, individuals might still pursue those claims under other States' municipal law.[192] Interstate waiver clauses do not therefore effectively *waive* these individuals' claims, even under domestic law.[193]

[184] Lillich and Weston (n 111): (16) Sweden–Hungary, art 3; Weston, Lillich, and Bederman (n 117): (64) US–Germany, arts 2(5)–(8).

[185] Lillich and Weston (n 111): (55) Demark–Czechoslovakia, Art 4; Weston, Lillich, and Bederman (n 117): (49) UK–Mauritius, art 5(1).

[186] Weston, Lillich, and Bederman (n 117): (27) US–Peru, art 7; (34) US–Egypt, art 5(3); (40) US–China, art 5; (45) UK–Czechoslovakia, art 8(3); Lillich and Weston (n 50) App B, US–Hungary, art 6(3).

[187] See Lillich and Weston (n 111): (4) US–Yugoslavia, art 9(b); (10) Switzerland–Czechoslovakia, art 9. Cf Vallat (n 48) 39 ('unlikely').

[188] See *Mantelli v Germany* (2008) 168 ILR 477 (Cour Cass, Italy) 481 (holding State 'harmless' inexplicable if waiver deprived courts' jurisdiction).

[189] *Horimoto* (n 149) 163–64.

[190] Similarly Hans Kelsen, 'Opinion Concerning the Claims of the Italian Owners of the Ship "Fausto"' (1986) 37 ÖZ 1, 14, cited n 200.

[191] Section III(B).

[192] nn 175–88.

[193] nn 188–89; Peters (n 32) 215.

C. Preclusion of individuals' international claims

The foregoing has established that interstate waivers of nationals' claims are, though perhaps more by way of consent, intended to prevent those individuals from bringing claims under municipal law.[194] As Chapter 2 outlined, certain individual domestic court claims may invoke State responsibility under international law.[195] Insofar as such individual claims are caught by an interstate waiver clause, they may indeed be precluded by State action.

If this were the limit of the effect of waiver clauses, then they would not appear to prevent individuals from bringing claims before *international* courts.[196] Continued access to individual claims mechanisms would, however, limit the power of States to fully settle and dispose of claims.[197] What, then, is the effect—if any—of a waiver by a State of its nationals' claims on those individuals' *international* claims?[198]

On the one hand, if a State uses language whereby it purports to waive 'all claims'—or similar phrasing—a literal interpretation would demand that it be 'understood in the widest sense'.[199] In addition, certain authorities suggest that a waiver completely and directly extinguishes the individual's claim, regardless of its basis.[200]

On the other hand, these authorities were not directly concerned with individual claims under international law.[201] Moreover, although scholars have asserted that States can waive their nationals' claims, this is apparently premised on those nationals having no rights distinct from the State.[202] The previous section

[194] Section III(B).

[195] Ch 2, nn 64–86.

[196] Even State attempts to prevent individuals claiming before international courts through domestic anti-suit injunctions do not always succeed: see *British Caribbean Bank v Belize* [2013] CCJ 4; *Balkan Energy v Ghana (Interim Award)* PCA Case 2010-7 (22 December 2010) [190]–[193].

[197] Similarly Roberts, 'Hybrid' (n 51) 49–52.

[198] Cf Dolzer (n 50) 303–6; n 131; Ch 1, n 1.

[199] *Ditta* (n 152) 71; similarly *ZAG Shareholders* (n 151) 439; *Forced Labor* (n 50) 945 ('waiver . . . strikingly broad'); *Immunities Pleadings* (n 49), Rep Germany [23]–[24]. Cf *Sch v Germany* (1932) 6 ILR 62 (German SC) 63 ('all claims' not including 'claims of private creditors').

[200] See *Household Effects* (n 151) 309 (rights on 'any legal basis' waived), 315–16 (rights' 'complete extinction'); Hess (n 182) 136. Considering waiver 'abolishes the rights . . . the basis of [the relevant] claims': Kelsen (n 190) 14, cited Gattini, 'Trojan' (n 35) 539 (fn 103); generally Humphrey Waldock, 'Third Report on the Law of Treaties' (1964) 2 ILCYB 5, 24; *Immunities Pleadings* (n 49), Rep Germany [21]. The PCIJ considered treaties could create individual rights enforceable domestically absent incorporating legislation: *Jurisdiction of the Courts of Danzig* [1928] PCIJ Rep Ser B No 15, 17–18, discussed Parlett (n 27) 17–26; Peters (n 32) 29–31. Treaties could conceivably similarly extinguish international rights, but cases focus on domestic law: eg, *AdR* (n 171) 93; *Household Effects* (n 151) 308; also Kelsen (n 190) 15; cf nn 82, 129, 155, 200. Cf *Abel* (n 178) 152–53; Vallat (n 48) 38–39.

[201] See *Household Effects* (n 151) 308; *Ditta* (n 152) 64, 70–72; *ZAG Shareholders* (n 151) 438; *Forced Labor* (n 50) 944. The headnote in *Austrian Citizen's* (n 151) references waiving claims 'vested by treaty or . . . municipal law' (155). However, the actual decision references 'private legal relations' (156); also Peters (n 32) 204–7.

[202] See Henkin (n 171) 299 ('individual and . . . debt . . . no independent existence'); McNair, *Treaties* (n 65) 336 (waiver prevents nationals' municipal actions, *State's* international actions); ALI (n 66) 608; also *Distomo Massacre* (n 178) 565–66.

has established that such separate rights to claim might exist, beyond the national State's reach, albeit under a third State's municipal law.[203] The question is whether such separate rights to claim similarly exist under international law.[204]

Only a few decisions appear to have directly addressed the issue. In *Park*, the Korean Supreme Court considered that States cannot waive international claims belonging to individuals without their consent.[205] The Tokyo District Court in *Shimoda* suggested, likewise, that a waiver clause would not affect nationals' international claims.[206] It recognised, however, that treaty-based claims procedures for individuals were rare,[207] and indeed, much of the practice concerning waiver clauses stems from before many of the individual procedural mechanisms discussed in Chapter 2 existed.[208]

This book mainly focuses on individuals' international claims brought pursuant to such treaty-based mechanisms. It is possible that individuals might possess claims under customary international law that cannot be waived:[209] Italy argued, for instance, in the *Immunities* case, that its nationals' reparations claims for violations of international humanitarian law were not 'at [its] disposal', and thus not waivable through interstate agreement.[210] However, as Chapter 2 outlined, individuals in practice invoke State responsibility under treaty-based mechanisms and, to a lesser extent, before domestic courts.[211] Claims pursuant to the former are, by and large, restricted to alleged violations of the relevant treaty, meaning that there is little scope for tribunals deciding such claims to consider claims under custom, and potential waiver thereof.[212] As to domestic courts, certain municipal laws,

[203] nn 167, 175–89, 204. Cf Lillich and Weston (n 50) 6.

[204] Cf *Rudloff* (n 59) 248 (international claims 'outside the legislative jurisdiction of any one nation'). For a waiver distinguishing domestic and international claims: *Gassner Claim (The MY Gerry)* (1954) 22 ILR 972 (UK–Italy Conc Comm) 975.

[205] *Park* (n 137) [60]; similarly *Yeo v Nippon Steel* Na 44947, ILDC 2104 (KR 2013) (HC Korea, 10 July 2013) [4]. See Jarrod Hepburn, 'South Korean Supreme Court Ruling . . .' *IA Rep* (31 October 2018).

[206] *Shimoda* (n 134) 641.

[207] ibid 637–38, 641–42.

[208] Cf ibid 637–38, 641–42 (earlier mechanisms).

[209] Generally, eg, Peters (n 32) 184–89, 196–203, 210–16; Nollkaemper (n 111) 183–84; Benvenisti (n 49) 1086–101; Gattini, 'Hurdles' (n 50) 366–67.

[210] *Immunities Pleadings* (n 49), Counter-Mem Italy [5.48]; see n 108 (not decided). Similarly Jean de Preux, 'Article 91—Responsibility' in Yves Sandoz, Christophe Swinarski, and Bruno Zimmerman (eds), *Commentary on the Additional Protocols* (ICRC, Martinus Nijhoff 1987) [3651] (States can settle war damages, not 'deny [victims] compensation'); Gattini, 'Compensation' (n 144) 276–77; Frits Kalshoven, 'Expert Opinion' in Hisakazu Fujita, Isomi Suzuki, and Kantaro Nagano (eds), *War and the Rights of Individuals: Renaissance of Individual Compensation* (Nippon Hyoron-sha 1999) 44. Cf Tomuschat (n 48) 988; Peters (n 32) 204–10, 213–16. Cf Ch 4, n 508.

[211] Ch 2(I)(A)–(C).

[212] See Ch 2(I)(A)–(B); Clara Reinder and Christoph Schreuer, 'Human Rights and International Investment Arbitration' in Pierre-Marie Dupuy, Ernst-Ulrich Petersmann, and Francesco Francioni (eds), *Human Rights in International Investment Law and Arbitration* (OUP 2009) 82–85, 88, particularly 83–84, discussing *Biloune v Ghana* (1989) 95 ILR 183 (UNCITRAL) 203 (no jurisdiction over alleged human rights violations 'as . . . independent cause of action'); Annemarieke Vermeer-Künzli, 'Unfinished Business: Concurrence of Claims Presented before a Human Rights Court or Treaty Body and through Diplomatic Protection' (2010) 10 HRLR 269, 275. Exceptionally, the EECC had

such as the US Alien Tort Statute, make an individual's claim dependent on international law having been violated,[213] and questions concerning the impact of an interstate waiver on such claims could theoretically arise.[214] However, cases before domestic courts overwhelmingly determine the effects of waiver clauses on individual claims as a matter of domestic law.[215] And, whether or not individuals have unwaivable claims under customary international law, States undoubtedly retain the capacity to restrict access to their domestic courts, as discussed above.[216] Thus, the 2010 US–Iraq lump-sum settlement agreement aimed 'to settle and extinguish all U.S. national claims wherever asserted', under both domestic and international law.[217] However, in return for payment, the US' undertaking was to preclude and terminate claims before its courts, and to substitute itself vis-à-vis claims 'presented directly to Iraq'.[218] Notwithstanding that the settlement agreement referred to individual claims under international law, then, the agreement took an approach akin to that normally taken in such settlements, namely that the claims were precluded domestically. And, like other agreements, the settlement agreement envisaged that claims might, despite being 'settle[d] and extinguish[ed]', nonetheless be brought elsewhere, suggesting that the settlement did not operate as a blanket extinguishment of individual claims, but only to preclude claims within the jurisdictional reach of the parties.[219]

More useful, then, is to consider the impact of interstate waivers on claims brought pursuant to treaty-based mechanisms, an issue which has arisen in several historical examples.[220] If States routinely attempt to waive their nationals' claims before international fora, this would suggest an entitlement to engage in waiver properly so-called, meaning that these claims, despite apparently belonging to those individuals, are in reality subject to State control.[221] However, as the following section demonstrates, notwithstanding some divergences, overall the

jurisdiction over alleged violations of both human rights and international humanitarian law: Ch 2, n 46; Nollkaemper (n 111) 106; Shany (n 22) 102.

213 28 USC §1350 (jurisdiction over torts, *inter alia*, 'in violation of the law of nations'); see *Sosa v Alvarez-Machain* 542 US 692 (2004) 724 (common law action for certain 'international law violations'), discussion Beth Stephens, 'The Curious History of the Alien Tort Statute' (2014) 89 NDLR 1467, particularly 1495–512; Tomuschat (n 48) 990; Parlett (n 27) 325–26; Nollkaemper (n 111) 193; Peters (n 32) 479.

214 cf n 215 (referencing *Hwang*).

215 See section III(B); eg *Hwang* (n 155) 681 (invoking ATS), 686–87 (immunity precludes). Concerning whether international law claims existed, but not vis-à-vis waiver: *ANRP v Germany* App 45563/04 (ECtHR, 4 September 2007) 13–17, discussed *Immunities Pleadings* (n 49), Rep Germany [40]; also cases Peters (n 32) 204–7.

216 Section III(B).

217 US–Iraq, art II(1), referenced Anthea Roberts, 'Triangular Treaties: The Extent and Limits of Investment Treaty Rights' (2015) 56 Harv ILJ 353, 413.

218 US–Iraq, art V.

219 cf nn 175–93.

220 See authorities section (C)(i)–(vii).

221 Because third-party rights are unwaivable: nn 40–41.

practice suggests that States do not consider themselves able to *waive* such claims per se. Yet they do employ other mechanisms for controlling their pursuit, notably through the medium of consent.

(i) Post-WWI Mixed Arbitral Tribunals

The first example from State practice relates to claims before the post-WWI Mixed Arbitral Tribunals (MATs). Pursuant to article 297(e) of the Treaty of Versailles:

> The nationals of Allied and Associated Powers shall be entitled to compensation in respect of damage or injury inflicted upon their property, rights or interests ... The claims made in this respect by such nationals shall be investigated, and the total of the compensation shall be determined by the Mixed Arbitral Tribunal ... or by an Arbitrator appointed by that Tribunal.[222]

Similar treaty-based mechanisms for making claims before international tribunals against Germany were established under other treaties.[223] Importantly, MATs generally recognised claims under such provisions as having been brought by individuals themselves, rather than by States in the exercise of diplomatic protection, even if the States played an administrative role in the claims.[224]

Nonetheless, developments took place with respect to the reparations regime as a result of Germany's inability to meet its payment obligations,[225] with various States endeavouring to alter the framework for individual claims.[226] Certain authors have suggested that States, in reaching settlements vis-à-vis those individual claims, engaged in a waiver thereof, implying that those claims were not truly

222 Treaty of Versailles, art 297(e).

223 Treaty of St-Germain-en-Laye, art 249(e); Treaty of Trianon, art 232(e); Treaty of Neuilly-sur-Seine, art 177(e). See Parlett (n 27) 72; *Shimoda* (n 134) 637; Ch 2, nn 38–41.

224 See Parlett (n 27) 73, referencing *Sigwald Charles v Germany* (1926) 3 ILR 337; 6 TAM 888 (French-German MAT); *Lederer v Germany* (1924) 3 TAM 762 (Anglo-German MAT) 768; Norbert Wühler, 'Mixed Arbitral Tribunals' in Rudolf Bernhardt (ed), *Encyclopedia of Public International Law* (Elsevier 1997) 433–34; *Morgenstern v Germany* (1926) 7 TAM 713 (Germano-Polish MAT) 722, cited Hess (n 182) 135; *Shimoda* (n 134) 637; Jessup (n 71) 18; Peters (n 32) 207; Hersch Lauterpacht, *International Law: Being the Collected Papers of Hersch Lauterpacht* (Elihu Lauterpacht ed, CUP 1970) 145–46; n 366; Ch 2, n 41; also *Societe Petrol Block v Germany* (1928) 4 ILR 261 (Germano-Roumanian MAT) (individual claimant unaffected by national State retaining claimed property). The report notes (ibid 261) that this is explicable by the 'Tribunal attach[ing] decisive importance to the purely private nature of the claim', though noting the view that claims were State-controlled, given, *inter alia*, States' 'right to dispose of the claim altogether in subsequent treaties without the consent of the interested parties', referencing Schmid, 'Anmerkung: Societe Petrol Block' (1929) I ZfaöRV 102; cf Rudolf Blühdorn, 'Le Fonctionnement et La Jurisprudence Des Tribunaux Arbitraux Mixtes Créés Par Les Traités de Paris' (1932) 41 RdC 137, 144–45, 174. Further n 244.

225 Generally Waldo Stephens, *Revisions of the Treaty of Versailles* (Columbia UP 1939) Ch X; *Greece v FRG* (1972) 47 ILR 418 (External Debts Tribunal) 418–20; Dolzer (n 50) 310; Wühler (n 224) 436; *Execution of German-Portuguese Arbitral Award* (1933) III UNARIAA 1371, 1378–384.

226 See Wühler (n 224) 436; Marta Requejo Isidro and Burkhard Hess, 'The Mixed Arbitral Tribunals in the Peace Treaties of 1919–1922' *MPI for Procedural Law Research Paper Series No 2018(5)*, 13–14. On altering rights to seize German nationals' property: Stephens (n 225) 243–44. Cf reasons for the Trianon Settlement Treaty: András Jakab, 'Trianon Peace Treaty (1920)' in *MPEPIL* (n 24) (2015) [16]–[17].

individual in nature but rather State-owned.[227] However, as shown below, this appears to be too simplistic an interpretation of the practice. That practice is both complex and sometimes inconsistent, but can, it is suggested, best be understood according to three propositions: first, States generally (though not always) considered that individual claims could not be *waived* as such; second, States could nonetheless freely alter the procedural mechanisms under which those individual claims were brought; and third, States could reach settlements regarding the post-decision award payments.[228]

As to the first, in an Exchange of Notes between Japan and Germany regarding the settlement of claims under article 297, Japan observed that, at least 'within the ambit of the existing provisions' of the Treaty of Versailles, an agreement 'cannot be forced upon the nationals of either State'.[229] The obtaining of a waiver by the individuals concerned, and the withdrawal of their own MAT claims, was therefore the preferable mechanism for settlement.[230] Similarly, when the UK and Germany settled certain claims under the Treaty of Versailles, they acknowledged that an MAT might nonetheless 'decid[e] that any item of a claim included in this "forfait" falls within the provision of Article 297' or other relevant articles and might therefore 'mak[e] an award in favour of any firm or person in respect of such item of their claims'.[231] Apparently envisaging that individual claims might continue notwithstanding their settlement, the agreement provided for the return of interstate settlement funds of the same value in such a case.[232] Both instances of practice suggest that these States considered themselves unable to waive individual claims brought before the MATs. Less conclusive but also worth mentioning is that Germany and Romania, for their part, in 'mutually renounc[ing] all action before the [MAT]', clarified that this only applied to interstate claims.[233]

In the *Railways* case, concerned with a waiver of nationals' claims contained in a post-WWI reparations restructure treaty,[234] the tribunal held that the waiver had not resulted in the loss of an individual's right of petition.[235] An earlier League of Nations legal opinion on the same issue[236] had emphasised that rights that were 'internationally guaranteed' and 'not exercised' by individuals '*qua* … national'

[227] Isidro and Hess (n 226) 13–14 (espousal), referencing Hess (n 182) 135; similarly n 224, particularly Schmid (n 224) 103 (settlements demonstrate claims were those of States).

[228] See authorities nn 229ff; also Paparinskis, 'New' (n 7) 645.

[229] Sequestration Removal Agreement (SRA), 33.

[230] SRA, 35–37. Claimants usually presented claims: see RoP, art 3, reproduced Martens, vol XVII, 714, cited JHW Verzijl, *International Law in Historical Perspective*, vol VIII (AW Sijthoff 1976) 247.

[231] UK–Germany [5].

[232] ibid.

[233] Germany–Romania, art IV read with Final Protocol [4].

[234] Hague Agreement, art III, cited *In re Zeltweg-Wolfsberg and Unterdrauburg-Woellan Railways* (1934) 7 ILR 484; LON OJ 1005 (Doc C2111934VIII) (LoN Special Tribunal) 484–85.

[235] ibid 1005–7, particularly 1006–7 (no 'new right' but merely 'procedure to enable [individuals] to 'avail themselves of [contractual] rights'; claim therefore not 'under' treaty and not waived). For the right of petition: Treaty of St-Germain-en-Laye, art 320.

[236] Opinion referenced ibid 487 (ILR version).

were unwaivable by the individual's State of nationality.[237] Moreover, a 'right to arbitration as such' could not 'be regarded as a claim'.[238] This case was concerned with a peculiar claims mechanism, and the reasoning is not directly translatable to mechanisms like that under article 297; indeed some of the reasoning could suggest that waiving nationals' claims under such provisions might be possible.[239] On the other hand, at least some of the reasoning appears relevant to individual MAT claims more generally, and to suggest that waiver may not be so straightforward.[240] For instance, the League Opinion made reference to the States' closure of the MAT consequent on the waiver provision, querying why this was necessary if the claims had in fact disappeared[241]—a point to which we will return below.

Admittedly, there is some apparently contrary practice. Thus, Italy and Hungary agreed that, upon abolition of the Italian-Hungarian MAT, '[a]ctions pending' were 'deemed to be withdrawn',[242] and 'settled' through lump-sum payment.[243] This might, however, be explicable by noting that Italy apparently had the power, before that MAT, to withdraw its nationals' claims.[244] More difficult is the Germano-Polish Agreement, in which Poland recognised the Young Plan,[245] and undertook 'a complete and final renunciation' of 'financial claims or claims relating to property ... arising out of the war or the Treaty of Peace', including of 'its nationals'.[246] A Protocol outlined that this included the article 297 claims of Polish nationals 'already brought ... and those which might be brought'.[247] This purported waiver is surprising, given that the Germano-Polish MAT had earlier recognised that individual rights under article 297 were 'direct[s] et indépendant[s]' and unaffected by provisions of the Treaty of Versailles concerning interstate relations.[248] Nonetheless, Poland and Germany acknowledged, in a later agreement regarding the closure of the Germano-Polish MAT, that claims would still be pending or '*sub*

[237] Permanent Legal Committee, Communications and Transit Organisation, 'Petition of the Radkersburg-Luettenberg Railway' (LON Doc CCT/CJ/28) (1934) [37], also [32] (provision also applicable to disputes between an individual and their own State).

[238] ibid [47], also [39] (waiver vis-à-vis 'claims of ... financial nature'), cf 23–24 (Diss Op Soubbotitch).

[239] ibid [37] ('the right arising out of Article 320 cannot be regarded as the right of an Austrian national which the Austrian State could have waived reciprocally').

[240] Indeed, see ibid 24 (Diss Op Soubbotitch) (art 320 like MAT mechanisms). On individuals claiming against own State: *Steiner and Gross v Poland* (1928) 4 ILR 291 (Upper Silesia Arbitral Tribunal) 292, discussed Parlett (n 27) 75–76.

[241] 'Petition' (n 237) [48], cf 24–25 (Diss Op Soubbotitch).

[242] Hungary–Italy (1932), art 1.

[243] Hungary–Italy (1932), art 2, also Protocol [(a)].

[244] This assumption underlies Hungary–Italy (1927), art 2 (agent withdraws); also Italy–Germany, Annex 3, art 2 (agent 'discontinue[s]'). On agents' roles: Blühdorn (n 224) 144–45; Isidro and Hess (n 226) 12–13. Cf n 289.

[245] This reduced Germany's reparations: Stephens (n 225) 236, generally 233–47; sources nn 225–26.

[246] Germany–Poland (1929), art II.

[247] ibid Protocol [2]. Not apparently concerned with presently relevant claims, see: Belgium–Austria, art 6; Belgium–Germany, art 2.

[248] *Morgenstern* (n 224) 722, see n 224. States had extensive participatory powers, but claimants were not necessarily State-represented: RoP, arts 8–9, 11 reproduced Martens, vol XVII, 752, cited Verzijl (n 230) 247.

judice' at the date of termination.[249] It is difficult to see how claims could still be pending if all claims of the State and its nationals had been waived, actually and effectively, by the earlier agreement, nor why—akin to the point made in the League Opinion above—closure of the MAT would, in that case, be necessary.[250]

Taken as a whole, therefore, the practice suggests that States doubted their ability to waive the MAT claims of individuals, even when it was desirable, given changing circumstances, that all claims be finally settled. States did, however, envisage *other* means for controlling such claims. Japan and Germany, for instance, while denying that they could affect existing claims under the Treaty of Versailles,[251] contemplated that a 'new treaty' could render 'a settlement binding on the nationals of either State'.[252] For their part, Germany and France agreed that 'pleas', encompassing those under article 297, submitted to the MAT more than three months after the date of their agreement were to 'be rejected as invalid'.[253] A similar approach was taken in settling nationals' claims against Bulgaria, with '[n]o private claims' to 'be received' by the MAT after the agreement's entry into force.[254] These approaches do not involve waiver; instead the States appear to contemplate modifying, by consent, the treaty regime pursuant to which individual claims are brought.[255] The Franco-German MAT appeared to endorse such an approach in *Sigwald*, a case concerned with an argument that the two States had, by signing a subsequent treaty, settled their nationals' claims under article 297.[256] The MAT held:

> il faut admettre que, dans l'hypothèse où les signataires du Traité de paix auraient, en concluant la Convention de Baden-Baden, voulu exclure les Alsaciens-Lorraines, en tant qu'il s'agit de mesure d'un caractère politique, du droit individuel résultant de l'art. 297 *e*, ils auraient dû le stipuler par une dérogation expresse aux dispositions du Traité ....[257]

The Tribunal appears, in this passage, to accept that an individual claims mechanism *could* be modified by a later treaty between the relevant States, though this would need to be done expressly.[258] The parties to the Treaty of Trianon likewise

[249] Germany–Poland (1931), art II. The termination date was 31 January 1932; the earlier agreement (n246) was dated 31 October 1929, and ratifications were exchanged 21 April 1931, ie, pre-termination.

[250] Similarly n 241; cf nn 246–47.

[251] nn 229–30.

[252] SRA (n 229) 33. However, this posed 'considerable difficulties': ibid.

[253] Germany–France, art 12(1). Similarly Belgium–Germany, art 4.

[254] Bulgarian Settlement [10]. Further: Germany–France, art 12(4); Anglo-Austrian (1930) 404, 407; cf Anglo-Austrian (1931) (terminating MAT when claims exhausted); Anglo-German (1932) 100–1; Anglo-Bulgarian, art I.

[255] cf n366; section (C)(viii) and authorities.

[256] *Sigwald* (n 224) 890–91.

[257] ibid 891. Also Isidro and Hess (n 226) 14.

[258] Indeed, they later excluded these claims prospectively: n 253. Further: *Bank of Egypt v Austro-Hungarian Bank* (1923) 2 ILR 23 (Anglo-Austrian MAT) 25 (nationality deprivation, consequent claim loss, required '[v]ery clear language'), cited Lauterpacht (n 224) 292.

altered the bases for certain MAT claims,[259] including vis-à-vis 'pending' legal proceedings.[260] When decisions enforcing limitations under the new treaties were appealed to the PCIJ, that Court did not question the efficacy of these measures.[261] The League Opinion discussed above, in referencing the closure of the MATs, similarly implies that the mechanism available to individuals to bring claims before those tribunals could be ended, even where claims were 'pending',[262] and even if not automatically resulting from waiver.[263]

A final category of State practice from this period concerns award payments. As Blühdorn noted in his 1932 Hague lectures, whatever the nature of the rights under article 297, if payment was not made on a claim, the individuals concerned could only have recourse to their State of nationality.[264] Indeed, awards were often paid by the State of nationality itself from confiscation funds.[265] Practice reflects this State control over payment. Thus, the Anglo-Austrian settlement left unaffected MAT procedures but provided that 'no claim for payment shall be made' vis-à-vis future awards.[266] In another agreement, lump-sum amounts were paid to settle outstanding MAT awards.[267] And Greece and Germany had a long-running dispute regarding whether payments due to Greek nationals under MAT awards had been waived.[268] An arbitral decision concluded that they had not.[269] The matter, treated as one of diplomatic protection,[270] was finally settled by an interstate lump-sum agreement.[271]

The post-WWI practice is complex. Overall, however, it suggests that—with some exceptions—States did not purport to waive, or succeed in waiving, their nationals' claims, but had no difficulty with altering, by way of treaty-based consent,

[259] Trianon Settlement Treaty (TST), Agreement II Concerning the settlement of questions relating to the agrarian reforms and Mixed Arbitral Tribunals, particularly art VII ('Tribunals shall deliver and frame their judgments solely upon the basis of the present Agreement'), art XIII ('claims out of time ... inadmissible'); see *Case concerning Pajzs, Csáky, Esterházy* (1936) PCIJ Rep Ser A/B No 68, 49, 57–59; generally Jakab (n 226) [15]–[20]; Isidro and Hess (n 226) 14.

[260] TST, Agreement II, Preamble (nonetheless, not 'surrender[ing] of the rights which ... nationals derive directly from the Treaty of Trianon' concerning questions not settled); *Pajzs* (n 259) 59–60.

[261] *Pajzs* (n 259) 57–60, 63–65; see Jakab (n 226) [20].

[262] 'Petition' (n 237) 25 (Diss Op Soubbotitch).

[263] n 241, particularly ibid [48] (no automatic abolition, else subsequent agreement unnecessary).

[264] Blühdorn (n 224) 145.

[265] Wühler (n 224) 435. See, eg, arrangements in Anglo-Austrian (1920) [2].

[266] Anglo-Austrian (1930), art 11, referencing Hague Agreement, art IIII. Cf Anglo-German (1929) art 11; Australia-Germany, art 8.

[267] Anglo-Turkish [1]–[2].

[268] See *Greece v FRG* (n 225) 418–21, 424–25, 428, 429 (claimants' 'vested right'), cf 430–31 ('intergovernmental debt'), 432–37. The original claims were under the Treaty of Versailles, art 298: ibid 424.

[269] *Greece v FRG* (n 225) 456–57, 460–62. Cf *German-Portuguese Award* (n 225) 1385–86 (interstate debt covered).

[270] *Greece v FRG* (n 225) 437; also Weston, Lillich, and Bederman (n 117): (28) FRG–Greece, art 1(1) ('pending between ... Governments').

[271] Weston, Lillich, and Bederman (n 117): (28) FRG–Greece, art 1(2) (payment 'completely and finally release[s] ... claims arising out of [Graeco-German MAT] decisions'). Cf Lillich and Weston (n 50), App B, Canada–Hungary, art 1(5) (including claims under art 232 of the Treaty of Trianon); Parlett (n 27) 51.

the procedural mechanisms pursuant to which those claims were brought, even where they remained pending.[272] They also in some cases interfered with, or settled, payments owing under various awards, but in a manner suggesting that, even if the original claim was an individual's, the obligation to make payment was owed—and could be settled—on the interstate level.[273]

(ii) Iran–US Claims Tribunal Small Claims

The second historical example that appears, on its face, to reflect an interstate settlement of individual claims arises from the IUSCT, established by treaty in 1981.[274] In 1990, Iran and the US settled all remaining claims for less than $250,000 between US nationals and Iran through a lump-sum Small Claims Settlement Agreement (SCSA).[275] Certain authors have suggested that this did not settle individual claims, because, pursuant to the Claims Settlement Declaration establishing the Tribunal, such claims were to 'be presented to the Tribunal ... by the [individual's] government', not the individuals themselves.[276] Nonetheless, the Tribunal did not regard these claims as ones of diplomatic protection belonging to the State:

> In [the] typical case, the State espouses the claims of its nationals, and the injuries for which it claims redress are deemed to be injuries to itself; here the Government of the United States is not a party to the arbitration of claims of United States nationals, not even in the small claims where it acts as counsel for those nationals.[277]

Whether or not one agrees,[278] the SCSA was reached *after* the Tribunal had, on multiple occasions, confirmed this position.[279] The States must therefore have been aware that they were, at least arguably, settling individual claims under international law. Indeed, under the SCSA, the US was '*deemed* to have espoused' the relevant claims, not to actually have done so,[280] suggesting some doubt as to whether they were actually diplomatic protection claims.

[272] nn 252ff.
[273] nn 268–71. Cf Schmid (n 224) 103, n 224.
[274] Ch 2, nn 18, 128.
[275] Weston, Lillich, and Bederman (n 117): (63) US–Iran, arts 2, 3; reproduced *US v Iran (Claims of less than $250,000)* (1990) 25 Iran-USCTR 327, 331–38 (*Iran/US Settlement*). See Parlett (n 27) 100.
[276] Parlett (n 27) 99, citing CSD, art III(3).
[277] *Esphahanian v Bank Tejarat* (1983) 2 Iran-USCTR 157, 165; discussed Parlett (n 27) 99; Douglas, *Investment* (n 29) 15–16. Also *Iran v US (Case A/18)* (1984) 5 Iran-USCTR 251, 261, cf 294, 297–98 (Diss Op); *Iran v US (Case A/21)* (1987) 14 Iran-USCTR 324, 330; *Iran v US (A15/24)* (n 161) [141], all referenced Parlett (n 27) 99.
[278] Cf Parlett (n 27) 99–00; Hess (n 182) 140; *Lord v IHSRC* (1988) 18 Iran-USCTR 377, 382–90 (Sep Op Khalilian), referenced *Iran/US Settlement* (n 275) 328.
[279] n 277. Indeed, an individual's small claim was earlier settled, though via a US-requested agreed award: *Lord* (n 278) 377–82.
[280] *Iran/US Settlement* (n 275) art III (emphasis added). Cf 328 (fn 2) (Sep Op Khalilian), asserting consistency with *Lord* (n 278).

Having said that, a closer examination of the SCSA suggests that the States may not have *waived* individual claims per se. Payment under the SCSA was '[i]n consideration of complete, full, final and definitive settlement, liquidation, discharge and satisfaction' of the claims.[281] The US was to 'cause' proceedings against Iran 'to be definitively and with prejudice dismissed, withdrawn and terminated', with the US 'barred from instituting or continuing with any such proceedings'[282] and to 'release and forever and definitively discharge [Iran] ... from any and all claims'.[283] The 'Claimants' tangible and intangible assets, rights, properties and real estate' in Iran, insofar as 'asserted in the [relevant] [c]laims', were 'quitclaimed and transferred' to Iran,[284] while 'the interested parties' might 'reach agreements' regarding the transfer of US-based property.[285]

Two points of interest may be noted. First, with the exception of a point relating to costs, the agreement does not, unlike other settlement agreements, employ the language of 'waiver'.[286] Second, although the agreement apparently acknowledges that individuals were the actual claimants,[287] as noted above, only the US could actually present those claims to the Tribunal.[288] The two States were therefore the parties to any arbitration regarding those claims, with the power, under the Rules of Procedure, to settle.[289] With all domestic litigation already suspended,[290] the US barring itself from bringing further proceedings removed the only available avenue for hearing these claims.[291] It thus had much the same effect as a State's termination of municipal litigation where no international tribunal exists.[292] Indeed, the references to property transfers resemble the provisions of other lump-sum settlement agreements discussed above.[293] This suggests that the SCSA was not envisaged to be that different from agreements settling claims through termination of domestic claims procedures, notwithstanding the presence of individuals' international claims.[294] The US did not, therefore, apparently *waive* claims

[281] ibid art III.
[282] ibid art V.
[283] ibid art VI.
[284] ibid art VII.
[285] ibid art X.
[286] ibid art VIII. Neither, admittedly, do certain individual-Iran settlements: eg, *Amoco Iran Oil v Iran (Agreed Award)* (1990) 25 Iran-USCTR 301, 305–13.
[287] See *Iran/US Settlement* (n 275) art I(B).
[288] n 276.
[289] IUSCT, RoP, art 34; *Iran/US Settlement* (n 275) 328, 330. Similarly *Greece v FRG* (n 225) 425. In issuing an agreed award (*Iran/US Settlement* (n 275)), the Tribunal apparently concurred. Cf Parlett (n 27) 100.
[290] As required by General Declaration [11], see n 161. Generally Caron (n 49) 282–83; Parlett (n 27) 100; Roberts, 'Triangular' (n 217) 384.
[291] nn 162, 282; similarly Caron (n 49) 283 ('claims outside both US and IUSCT jurisdiction ... effectively denying their viability').
[292] See section III(B); similarly Vallat (n 48) 39 (post-settlement 'for all practical purposes ... claim will disappear'), 45 ('claimant ... effectively deprived of any process'). Cf Gut Dam Agreement (claims US-presented (art VIII(2)), but waivers individual (art II(4))).
[293] See n 174.
[294] Indeed, discussing domestic litigation termination, the tribunal noted no individual claims were waived, except under General Declaration [11] (*Iran/US (A15/24)* (n 161) [84]–[86]). However, even

belonging to its nationals, nor dispense in any way with international claims not belonging to it. It rather terminated access to available fora, as it was empowered to do, and ensured transfer of the relevant underlying domestic rights.[295] This approach does, nonetheless, suggest that States may exercise powers available to them under treaties establishing international tribunals to preclude individual claims.[296]

(iii) Flight UTA 772

The third example arises out of the destruction of Flight UTA 772, with many French citizens onboard, in 1989.[297] Certain Libyan nationals were convicted before French courts *in absentia*, though rules of immunity barred a suit against Colonel Gaddafi, Libya's Head of State.[298] Negotiations took place between the French and Libyan governments regarding payment of compensation to the victims' families.[299] The agreement ultimately reached between the Gaddafi International Foundation and the French victims' associations required those receiving compensation to 'waive the right to bring any kind of civil or criminal proceedings', before both French and international courts.[300] When certain victims claimed that France had, by according immunity to Colonel Gaddafi, denied them their right to court access,[301] the European Court of Human Rights (ECtHR)—while acknowledging that the dispute was different from those to which the waiver clause applied[302]—accepted that the conclusion of the agreement, 'in line with the [victims'] interests', taken together with other factors, warranted the proceedings' being struck out.[303]

This was not a case in which a State waived its nationals' claims, with France not even party to the settlement agreement.[304] But this is what makes it

here the US does not "waive"; it merely agrees to 'bar and preclude' certain nationals' claims against Iran. This cannot be waiver, as the US also does so vis-à-vis non-national claims: General Declaration [11]; cf nn 156–74.

295 cf nn 162–64, 174.
296 cf authorities section III(C)(viii).
297 *Association SOS* (n 27) [9], discussed Vermeer-Künzli (n 212) 282–84; Ch 4, n 72.
298 *Association SOS* (n 27) [9], [13], [15], [38].
299 See ibid [14] (citing Agreement, Preamble), [17], [38].
300 ibid [14] (citing Agreement, art 1), also [17], [28].
301 ibid [15].
302 ibid [34]. Not deciding whether waiver could have encompassed ECtHR proceedings: ibid [30].
303 ibid [38]–[39] (when taken with judgment *in absentia*). On US claimants' domestic claims: Vibeke Venema, 'The Sahara Memorial Seen From Space' *BBC World Service* (22 January 2014) <https://www.bbc.com/news/magazine-25643103>; *Pugh v Libya* (2008) 530 F Supp 2d 216 (USDC, DC), 219–20; discussion *Alimanestianu v US* (2018) 888 F 3d 1374, 1377–78. These were settled by lump-sum agreement, the US terminating domestic litigation and recognising Libya's immunity: US–Libya, art III(1)–(2); EO 13477; discussion *Alimanestianu* (n 303) 1378–79; Kristina Daugirdas and Julian Mortenson (eds), 'Contemporary Practice of the United States Relating to International Law' (2016) 110 AJIL 789, 831–32.
304 *Association SOS* (n 27) [34].

interesting: despite government involvement in the settlement negotiations,[305] where the waiver referred explicitly to claims before both French and international courts, its form was individual in nature.[306] While hardly conclusive, this might suggest that individual waiver is the preferred method for finalising such claims.

(iv) The EECC

A fourth example comes from the Eritrea-Ethiopia Claims Commission (EECC), which was 'to decide ... all claims for loss, damage or injury ... related to the [Ethiopia/Eritrea] conflict' and which 'result[ed] from violations ... of international law'.[307] Pursuant to article 5(8) of the EECC Agreement, the States accepted that the EECC was the only forum for such claims (unless those claims had already been filed previously) and that claims not filed within a year would 'be extinguished'.[308] One may query whether that extinguishment was intended to cover individual claims.

Chapter 2 outlined that claims overlapping with the interstate EECC proceedings were indeed brought by individuals before both the African Commission on Human and Peoples' Rights (ACommHPR) and domestic courts.[309] They were filed prior to the deadline date,[310] and no overlapping individual claims were apparently brought thereafter. Consequently, the effect of article 5(8) on such claims remains unknown.[311] However, it is interesting to note that the interstate agreement did not—unlike certain of the claims settlement agreements discussed above[312]—purport to settle individual claims already filed prior to the Agreement's effective date.[313] This may have been an oversight. More plausibly, perhaps, it may have stemmed from a recognition that those claims were effectively beyond the control of the States—having been brought before an international tribunal and third-State courts respectively—and thus be taken as providing some support for recognition of States' inability to waive individual claims outside of their territory.[314]

305 n 299.

306 n 300.

307 EECC Agreement, art 5(1).

308 ibid art 5(8).

309 Ch 2, n 208.

310 One year after the 'effective date of [the] agreement' (art 5(8)). It was signed on 12 December 2000. For the filing dates of claims, see: *Interights v Eritrea and Ethiopia* (2003) AHRLR 74 [11] (5 October 1999); *Nemariam v Ethiopia (No 1)* (2003) 135 ILR 671 (USCA, DC) 672 (June 2000).

311 Both cases referenced art 5(8), but without discussing currently relevant aspects: see *Interights* (n 310) [47]; *Nemariam* (n 310) 674.

312 See nn 243, 247, 274–85, 290, 303 (MAT/IUSCT/US-Libya).

313 See *Nemariam v Ethiopia* (2005) 400 F Supp 2d 76 (USDC, DC), 80 ('Agreement specifically provided for ... continuance of claims ... filed in another forum before [12 December 2000]').

314 cf nn 203–4.

(v) The Softwood Lumber dispute

Fifth, a long-running dispute between Canada and the US regarding softwood lumber was ultimately settled between the two countries in 2006.[315] Critically, as discussed in Chapter 2, certain individual investors involved in the dispute had previously brought claims before investment tribunals under the North American Free Trade Agreement (NAFTA), and before domestic courts.[316]

There are two important facets to the settlement agreement. First, it would not enter into force until waivers had been obtained from those engaged in litigation,[317] including certain NAFTA claimants.[318] The individuals were to 'irrevocably consent to the termination' of their claims.[319] Second, the US and Canada suspended the operation of NAFTA's investor–State dispute settlement provisions in the following terms:

> The operation and application of Section B of Chapter Eleven of the NAFTA is hereby suspended with respect to any matter arising under [this agreement] and any measure taken by a Party that is necessary to give effect to or implement [this agreement]. Consequently, no claim under Section B of Chapter Eleven of the NAFTA may be made against a Party by investors of the United States or Canada in respect of any such matter or measure . . . .[320]

The two States did not themselves waive claims that had already been filed, whether before domestic or international tribunals, preferring to leave this to the individual claimants.[321] However, they clearly considered themselves capable of modifying the NAFTA treaty regime going forward.[322] Indeed, the US and Canada took a similar approach in 2009 in suspending, *inter se*, the operation of article 1709(10)(f) of NAFTA in order to implement a World Trade Organization (WTO) Decision on Compulsory Licensing.[323]

[315] See Softwood Lumber Agreement (SLA); generally Matthew Simpson, 'Chopping Away at Chapter 11: The Softwood Lumber Agreement's Effect on the NAFTA Investor-State Dispute Resolution Mechanism' (2007) 22 AUILR 479, particularly 481–83, 491–93; Paparinskis, 'New' (n 7) 631, 645; Ch 2, n 140.

[316] See the list: SLA, Annex 2A(1); also Ch 2, n 140.

[317] SLA, art II(1)(a).

[318] See ibid Annex 2A(1); generally Simpson (n 315) 482.

[319] SLA, Annex 2A(2). Similarly Weston, Lillich, and Bederman (n 117): (55) US–Ethiopia, Agreed Minutes.

[320] SLA, art XI(2); see Simpson (n 315) 482–83, 498ff; Paparinskis, 'Analogies' (n 9) 97–98, 105; Paparinskis, 'New' (n 7) 631, 645.

[321] nn 317–19, 409.

[322] Similarly *ADM* (n 27) [164]. Cf Simpson (n 315) 498ff (doubts). On recent NAFTA amendments: n 399.

[323] See Access Agreement, 1. Mendenhall alerted me to this. Although affecting substantive NAFTA provisions, this has flow-on effects for investors' Ch 11 claims, as granting compulsory licences consistent with Ch 17 is not expropriation (NAFTA, art 1110(7)).

(vi) Claims under intra-EU BITs

A sixth example emerges from the interplay between investment and European Union (EU) law. In 2018, the European Court of Justice (ECJ) held, in the now infamous *Achmea* judgment, that provisions for investor–State dispute settlement in BITs between EU Member States were incompatible with EU law.[324] With tribunals nonetheless continuing to take jurisdiction over investor–State cases under intra-EU BITs,[325] EU Member States were left to determine how to prevent such cases, and to settle those already brought.[326]

The approach taken was to sign, in 2020, an intra-EU Termination Agreement, which terminated all intra-EU BITs between the parties thereto, including all mechanisms for investor–State dispute settlement, as of the date when the last party to a BIT became an EU member, and with immediate effect upon entry into force.[327] The Termination Agreement divides investor–State cases into three classes: (1) concluded proceedings, being those finalised prior to 6 March 2018 (the date of *Achmea*), with 'no challenge, review, set-aside, annulment, enforcement, revision or other similar proceedings' still ongoing, or vis-à-vis which 'the award was set aside or annulled' before the Agreement's entry into force; (2) pending proceedings, being those initiated before 6 March 2018 and not finalised so as to amount to a concluded proceeding; and (3) new proceedings, being those initiated after 6 March 2018.[328]

Concluded proceedings remain untouched by the Agreement.[329] For new proceedings, the Agreement provides that State parties must inform tribunals of their

[324] *Slovak Republic v Achmea* Case C-284/16 (6 March 2018) (ECJ, GC) [60]. Generally: Alexander Reuter, 'Taking Investors' Rights Seriously: The Achmea and CETA Rulings of the European Court of Justice Do Not Bar Intra-EU Investment Arbitration' (2021) 36 ICSID Rev-FILJ 33.

[325] See, eg, *Sevilla Beheer v Spain (Jurisdiction, Liability and Quantum)* ICISD Case No ARB/16/27 (11 February 2022) [613]–[678]; *InfraRed Environmental Infrastructure v Spain (Annulment)* ICSID Case No ARB/14/12 (10 June 2022) [443]–[506].

[326] See Achmea Declaration, 1 (no 'valid offer to arbitrate' under intra-EU BIT), 3 (addressing pending and new proceedings). For the history: Reuter (n 324) 36–38.

[327] Termination Agreement, arts 2 and 4. See generally Lisa Bohmer, 'Breaking: EU Member States Sign Plurilateral Treaty ...' *IA Rep* (6 May 2020); Johannes Tropper and August Reinisch, 'The 2020 Termination Agreement of Intra-EU BITs and Its Effect on Investment Arbitration in the EU: A Public International Law Analysis of the Termination Agreement' (2022) 16 Aust YBIA 301; Dimitry Vladimirovich Kochenov and Nikos Lavranos, 'Achmea versus the Rule of Law: CJEU's Dogmatic Dismissal of Investors' Rights in Backsliding Member States of the European Union' (2021) 14 Hague JRL 195. On the background to the Agreement: Joel Dahlquist and Luke Eric Peterson, 'European Commission's Infringement Arguments Come into Focus ...' *IA Rep* (10 September 2015); Joel Dahlquist, 'Investigation: European Commission's Push for Termination of Intra-EU Investment Treaties ...' *IA Rep* (15 November 2018). Further: Tania Voon and Andrew Mitchell, 'Denunciation, Termination and Survival: The Interplay of Treaty Law and Investment Law' (2016) 31 ICSID Rev-FILJ 413, 428–29.

[328] Termination Agreement, art 1. Generally Devin Bray and Surya Kapoor, 'Agreement on the Termination of Intra-EU BITs: Sunset in Stone?' *Kluwer Arbitration Blog* (4 November 2020); also Debevoise & Plimpton, '23 EU Member States Sign Treaty to Terminate Intra-EU Bilateral Investment Treaties' *Debevoise In Depth* (11 May 2020) <https://www.debevoise.com/-/media/files/insights/publications/2020/05/2020051123-eu-member-states-sign-treaty-to-termina.pdf>; Tropper and Reinisch (n 327) 306–11.

[329] Termination Agreement, art 6.

common understanding that clauses for investor–State dispute settlement in covered BITs are inapplicable and 'cannot serve as a legal basis for' arbitration, and ask national courts to set side, annul, or otherwise not recognise or enforce any award issued on the basis of such a BIT.[330]

For pending proceedings, the Termination Agreement additionally sets up a 'structured dialogue' procedure for settlement.[331] The procedure may, by consent of the investor and State, be commenced within six months of the relevant BIT's termination,[332] where there is a potential violation of EU law by the State,[333] with deference to national or EU court proceedings.[334] The Agreement provides a detailed procedure for supporting the parties in reaching an amicable settlement on certain conditions.[335] Notably, the procedure may be commenced only if the investor has suspended its pending arbitration proceedings, and undertaken to suspend or otherwise not to begin proceedings for recognition, execution, enforcement or payment.[336] Settlement is conditional on the investor binding itself 'to withdraw the arbitration claim or renounce execution of an award already issued', to avoid double compensation vis-à-vis any amounts already paid, and to refrain from commencing new proceedings.[337] The settlement may also 'include a waiver of all other rights and claims relating to the [relevant] measure'.[338] Investors with pending proceedings also have expanded access to national courts where no settlement is reached,[339] but such access is conditional: the investor must withdraw its proceedings, 'waive[] all rights and claims' under the relevant BIT, 'renounce[] execution of an award already issued' and undertake not to institute new proceedings.[340]

This again then is a situation in which States, faced with individual claims mechanisms that they regard as problematic, do not attempt to themselves waive individual claims; this is left to the individual investors themselves, with beneficial access to alternative fora conditional on those claims being renounced. However, as discussed further below, the States do appear to be comfortable altering the procedural regime pursuant to which those individual claims were originally brought, including retroactively with respect to ongoing claims.[341]

330 ibid art 9, Annex C.
331 ibid art 9.
332 ibid art 9(2). Parties can also agree to 'any other appropriate resolution': art 8(4).
333 ibid art 9(6).
334 ibid arts 9(3)–(5).
335 ibid arts 9(7)–(13).
336 ibid art 9(1).
337 ibid art 9(14)(a).
338 ibid art 9(14)(b).
339 ibid art 10(1).
340 ibid.
341 See Tropper and Reinisch (n 327) 307, 326; Krzysztof Wierzbowski and Aleksander Szostak, 'Extinguishing Intra-EU Bilateral Investment Treaties: Recent Developments' *CPR Speaks* (19 January 2021) <https://blog.cpradr.org/2021/01/19/exinguishing-intra-eu-bilateral-investment-treaties-recent-developments/>; Alexander Yanos and Carlos Ramos-Mrosovsky, 'Intra-EU Investment Treaty Disputes in US Courts: Achmea, Micula and Beyond' *GAR* (12 August 2021).

(vii) Human rights procedures

Having considered waiver of various of the individual claims introduced in Chapter 2, we now turn to human rights mechanisms.[342] Chapter 2 argued that human rights obligations are owed *erga omnes (partes)*.[343] Given that such obligations protect the 'collective interest' of a group or the international community,[344] it would follow that States are able to waive claims arising from their breach only insofar as they pertain to themselves.[345] Thus, the ARSIWA commentary provides:

> Since such a breach engages the interest of the international community as a whole, even the consent or acquiescence of the injured State does not preclude that interest from being expressed in order to ensure a settlement in conformity with international law.[346]

Of particular importance for present purposes is authority suggesting that this extends to procedural mechanisms: the Inter-American Court of Human Rights (IACtHR) held, for example, that States cannot waive procedures before the Commission in favour of a direct decision by the Court,[347] because the Commission procedures, accessible as they are to individuals, were not 'created for the sole benefit of the States, but also . . . for the exercise of important individual rights'.[348]

By parity of reasoning, any interstate waiver of individual claims under human rights instruments would be ineffective: the individual claims mechanisms are not established in the interests of any given State,[349] and States' reparations claims are made 'in the interest of' the relevant individuals.[350] Indeed, in the *Pad* case, discussed in Chapter 4, the ECtHR did not regard an agreement between Iran and Turkey in 'final settlement' of a dispute arising from the deaths of certain Iranian citizens as, in and of itself, precluding family members bringing claims against Turkey,[351] suggesting that States cannot, through settlement, simply terminate

[342] See, eg, Tams (n 5) 1039; ALI (n 59) §703, n 2.

[343] Ch 2, nn 211–16.

[344] *ARSIWA*, art 48(1)(a); see Ch 2, n 114.

[345] Feichtner (n 24) [15]; ALI (n 59) §703, n 2; §902(i); Martin Dawidowicz, *Third-Party Countermeasures in International Law* (CUP 2017) 304. Contending that injured States can 'extinguish all claims that "other interested States" have under article 48': Tams (n 5) 1041. But, at least vis-à-vis non-reparation claims, this is doubtful: see Crawford, *GP* (n 24) 564–65; ILC, 'State Responsibility: Comments and observations received from Governments' (2001) UN Doc A/CN.4/515, 78–79 (Netherlands/Korea).

[346] *ARSIWA*, 266–67; also Tams (n 5) 1040.

[347] *Gallardo v Costa Rica* (1981) 21 ILM 1424 (IACtHR) [25], also [21]; see Tams (n 5) 1039.

[348] *Gallardo* (n 347) [25].

[349] Also *Cyprus v Turkey (Compensation)* (n 101) [10] (Sep Op Albuquerque/Vučinić) (State cannot 'waive the rights of the individual victims they represent without the latter's consent'). Cf nn 344–45.

[350] *ARSIWA*, art 48(2)(b); Ch 1, n 117.

[351] *Pad v Turkey (Admissibility)* App 60167/00 (ECtHR, 28 June 2007) [31], [65] (cf reparation possibly justifying discontinuance: Ch 4, nn 68–72 and authorities). Further: *Denmark v Turkey (Friendly Settlement)* ECHR 2000-IV 1 (concerning, *inter alia*, individual citizen: ibid [2], [14]–[20] and

their nationals' claims. Nonetheless, as elucidated below, States may circumvent these limitations through the consensual suspension of human rights claims mechanisms.[352]

(viii) International claims: conclusion

Taking the practice holistically, it appears that—whatever language might be employed—States generally do not purport to *waive* the claims of their nationals brought pursuant to international treaty-based mechanisms. Consistently with the position of various tribunals in allowing individuals to waive such claims themselves,[353] the practice suggests that States consider those claims as belonging to the relevant individuals and thus as unwaivable on the interstate plane.[354]

Nonetheless, States do sometimes employ other mechanisms, primarily through the medium of *consent*, to control treaty-based individual claims. This should be unsurprising, for those rights were initially granted by States,[355] and their very existence is therefore subject to State consent.[356]

In some cases, States utilise powers already available under the relevant treaty: the US, for instance, leveraged its being able to present, and settle, its nationals' small claims before the IUSCT to remove the access of those individuals to the only remaining forum available for them to be heard.[357] This cannot be objectionable in principle, for, if States grant individuals rights under treaties, they can define the scope of those rights.[358] And this may include a capacity to block those claims: States had, for instance, a mechanism built into the 1907 International Prize Court Convention, allowing them to veto their nationals' access to the Court.[359] Similarly, as Chapter 4 outlined, individuals cannot, under article 56(7) of the African Charter on Human and Peoples' Rights (AfCHPR), present claims that have already been 'settled' to the ACommHPR.[360] For reasons already outlined,

Court-approved settlement: [21], [25]). However, the individual instituted no proceedings. Both discussed Vermeer-Künzli (n 212) 284–85.

352 nn 377–78.
353 nn 27–38.
354 Similarly Tomuschat (n 48) 986; Parlett (n 27) 106–8; Peters (n 32) 215.
355 Parlett (n 27) 360, also 350, 353, 367.
356 ibid 359–63. Similarly Roberts, 'Triangular' (n 217) 368–69; Roberts, 'Hybrid' (n 51) 19, 24, 39; Lauterpacht (n 224) 288. Cf Peters (n 32) 417–18.
357 Section III(C)(ii).
358 ILC, 'Summary Records of the Meetings of the Fiftieth Session' (1998) 1 ILCYB 1, 13 (Pambou-Tchivounda) (use 'within ... limits of those procedures'); Roberts, 'Triangular' (n 217) 370–73; Roberts, 'Hybrid' (n 51) 19; Anthea Roberts, 'Power and Persuasion in Investment Treaty Interpretation: The Dual Role of States' (2010) 104 AJIL 179, 208; cf VCLT, art 36(2) (third-State rights exercisable according to conditions); *Prosecutor v Katanga (Admissibility)* Case ICC-01/04-01/07 (16 June 2009) [88] (admissibility within State's power); Giorgio Gaja, 'The Protection of General Interests in the International Community' (2012) 364 RdC 9, 167.
359 Prize Court Convention, art 4(2); see Parlett (n 27) 60; Lauterpacht (n 224) 287. Similarly MTA, art 6.
360 AfCHPR, art 56(7), Ch 4, nn 97, 312–18.

that Commission was not, when faced with claims overlapping with those before the EECC, concerned with whether those claims had been 'extinguished' by the EECC Agreement.[361] It did, however, consider that article 56(7) prevented the institution of Commission proceedings for claims already being addressed by the EECC,[362] utilising the condition already contained in the treaty establishing the individual claims mechanism. Similarly, at least some investment tribunals have held that States may invoke 'denial of benefits' clauses, allowing protections to be denied to a given investor, even after that investor has filed claims.[363] As one tribunal explained, the States' consent to arbitration contains 'an express prior reservation of the right to deny ... benefits',[364] and 'investors are aware of the possibility of such a denial, such that no legitimate expectations are frustrated by [it]'.[365]

In other cases, States purport to modify the existing procedural scheme. This was the approach taken by various States vis-à-vis claims before the post-WWI MATs,[366] by the US and Canada for NAFTA claims consequent on the Softwood Lumber Agreement,[367] by EU Member States in terminating intra-EU BITs,[368] and, as outlined below, by Member States of the Southern African Development Community (SADC) in altering provisions allowing for individual claims.[369] Treaty law allows States to so modify their agreements by consent, as long as other parties' rights are unaffected and it is not contrary to the treaty's object and purpose.[370] They may also denounce treaties that expressly or implicitly so allow,[371] suspend their operation,[372] and terminate treaties by 'conclud[ing] a later treaty relating to

[361] Section III(C)(iv).

[362] *Interights* (n 310) [57]–[60], discussed Ch 4, nn 200–5.

[363] See Douglas, *Investment* (n 29) 468–72; also Martins Paparinskis, 'Investment Arbitration and the Law of Countermeasures' (2008) 79 BYBIL 264, 343; eg *Guaracachi America v Bolivia (Award)* PCA Case 2011-17 (31 January 2014) [371]–[384]; *Ulysseas v Ecuador (Interim Award)* UNCITRAL Tribunal (28 September 2010) [173], discussed Luke Eric Peterson, 'UNCITRAL Claim by U.S. Hedge Fund ...' *IA Rep* (16 December 2010). *Plama Consortium v Bulgaria (Jurisdiction)* ICSID Case No ARB/03/24 (8 February 2005) [161]–[162] appears incorrect: Douglas, *Investment* (n 29) 470–72. Similarly Peters (n 32) 314–15 (tax). Cf *Liman Caspian Oil v Kazakhstan (Award (excerpts))* ICSID Case No ARB/07/14 (22 June 2010) [224]–[227] (denials must usually be prospective); *Pac Rim Cayman v El Salvador (Jurisdiction)* ICSID Case No ARB 09/12 (1 June 2012) [4.83] ('potential unfairness of a State ... thwart[ing]' arbitration, but ultimately allowed: [4.92]). Further: Lisa Bohmer, 'Breaking: Parties Reach Agreement in Principle ...' *IA Rep* (24 June 2022) and 'Decision of the Energy Charter Conference' (24 June 2022) 5, <https://www.energycharter.org/fileadmin/DocumentsMedia/CCDECS/2022/CCDEC202210.pdf> (making explicit that can deny benefits after arbitration commenced).

[364] *Guaracachi* (n 363) [373], also [375].

[365] ibid [372]. Similarly Paparinskis, 'Countermeasures' (n 363) 343, 335 (fn 392).

[366] Section III(C)(i); see Lauterpacht (n 224) 287 (MATs 'creation of Governments ... relevant provisions could be and eventually were terminated by States, but so long as they existed ... individual could enforce his right independently'); Hess (n 182) 135 ('claims ... dependent on ... home States').

[367] Section III(C)(v).

[368] Section III(C)(vi).

[369] n 378.

[370] VCLT, arts 39–41 (multilateral treaties); Roberts, 'Triangular' (n 217) 386, 404.

[371] VCLT, art 56; Voon and Mitchell (n 327) 415–16; Paparinskis, 'Countermeasures' (n 363) 342.

[372] VCLT, arts 57–58.

the same subject-matter'.[373] This applies equally to human rights, investment and other treaties creating individual claims mechanisms, which commonly contain denunciation and/or amendment provisions.[374] Even though human rights treaty obligations are owed *erga omnes partes*,[375] with modifications therefore necessarily affecting the other parties' rights,[376] nothing prevents the States parties' acting 'collectively' to alter their terms:[377] the SADC Member States recently appear to have done just that by suspending the capacity of individuals to bring claims before the Tribunal of the Southern African Development Community (SADCT) for alleged human rights violations.[378]

[373] VCLT, art 59; Voon and Mitchell (n 327) 426; also authorities nn 391, 431.

[374] Eg, AmCHR, arts 76–78; ICCPR Protocol, arts 11–12; also *Cifuentes Elgueta v Chile*, Doc CCPR/C/96/D/1536/2006 (HRC, 28 July 2009) [8.2] ('declaration' limiting ICCPR Protocol consent), cf [5]–[8] (Ind Op Keller/Salvioli) (contrary to object/purpose); ECHR, art 58; NAFTA, arts 2202, 2205; ECT, arts 42, 47; TEU, arts 48–50; CARICOM Treaty, art 236; *ADM* (n 27) [50]–[52] (Sep Op Rovine); Voon and Mitchell (n 327) 416; Roberts, 'Hybrid' (n 51) 22; Roberts, 'Power' (n 358) 210; nn 387–389. Exceptionally, the ICCPR, which contains no denunciation clause, was held not denounceable: HRC, 'General Comment No. 26: Continuity of Obligations' UN Doc CCPR/C/21/Rev.1/Add.8/Rev.1 (8 December 1997); generally Frédéric Mégret, 'Nature of Obligations' in Daniel Moeckli and others (eds), *International Human Rights Law* (3rd edn, OUP 2018) 106–8; Roberts, 'Triangular' (n 217) 405–6; Peters (n 32) 418. This is unusual, while the UN Secretary-General opined, vis-à-vis a purported denunciation, that withdrawal 'would not appear possible *unless all States Parties to the Covenant agree*' ('Notification by the Democratic People's Republic of Korea', Communication from the Secretary-General of the UN, C.N.467.1997.TREATIES-10 (Depository Notification), <https://treaties.un.org/doc/Publication/CN/1997/CN.467.1997-Eng.pdf>, p 1, emphasis added), implying that consensual action was possible: cf VCLT, art 54.

[375] Ch 2, n 216.

[376] See nn 345ff.

[377] Paparinskis, 'Analogies' (n 9) 97, also 97–98, discussing (vis-à-vis art 103, UN Charter): *R (Al-Jedda) v Secretary of State for Defence* [2007] UKHL 58, particularly [26]–[39]; also *Ahmed v HM Treasury* [2010] UKSC 2 [74], [203]. Cf *Kadi v Council and Commission* [2005] ECR II-3469 [231]–[232] (*jus cogens* human rights review); *Kadi and Al Barakaat v Council and Commission* [2008] ECR I-6351 (GC) [316]; Antonios Tzanakopoulos, 'Domestic Courts in International Law: The International Judicial Function of National Courts' (2011) 34 Loy LAI & CLR 133, 161, 165; Roberts, 'Triangular' (n 217) 386. Similarly *International Status of South West Africa (Advisory Opinion)* [1950] ICJ Rep 128, 167 (Sep Op Read). I thank Paparinskis and Spagnolo for discussion.

[378] See Erika de Wet, 'Reactions to the Backlash: Trying to Revive the SADC Tribunal through Litigation' *EJIL:Talk!* (5 August 2016); Karen Alter, James Gathii, and Laurence Helfer, 'Backlash against International Courts in West, East and Southern Africa: Causes and Consequences' (2016) 27 EJIL 293, 312–14; cf Paparinskis, 'Analogies' (n 9) 97 ('clear legal evaluation ... complicated'). The suspension took place in stages: 2010–11 (decisions to stop appointing judges and halt the Tribunal's deciding cases (see particularly Communique, Extraordinary Summit Heads of State and Government (20 May 2011) <http://www.swradioafrica.com/Documents/SADCSummit240511.pdf>)); 2012 (new Protocol would limit Tribunal's jurisdiction to interstate disputes (see Final Communique of the 32nd Summit of SADC Heads of State and Government (18 August 2012) <https://www.afdb.org/fileadmin/uploads/afdb/Documents/Generic-Documents/Communique_32nd_Summit_of_Heads_of_States.pdf>)); 2014 (new Protocol adopted): see Dire Tladi, 'The Constitutional Court's Judgment in the SADC Tribunal Case: International Law Continues to Befuddle' (2020) 10 CCR 129, 132; Laurie Nathan, 'The Disbanding of the SADC Tribunal: A Cautionary Tale' (2013) 35 HRQ 870, 877–78; Frederick Cowell, 'The Death of the Southern African Development Community Tribunal's Human Rights Jurisdiction' (2013) 13 HRLR 1. The Protocol has not entered into force: see Jarrod Hepburn, 'South African Court Finds Fault ...' *IA Rep* (2 March 2018). Nonetheless, the parties' intent was to alter the existing Protocol, including its individual claims mechanism.

Nonetheless, a tension arises when individuals anticipate that procedures will continue to exist and States wish to alter the regimes which they have established,[379] a tension that has emerged most recently vis-à-vis actual and proposed investment treaty reforms.[380] Given that rights to claim under treaty-based mechanisms do appear to belong to individuals,[381] one might be tempted to compare them with the rights of third States to treaties, rights which 'may not be revoked or modified by the parties if it is established that the right was intended not to be revocable or subject to modification without the consent of the third State'.[382] However, while this is the position for *States*, State practice, including that considered above, does not generally suggest that States consider that the consent of *individuals* is necessary before modifying treaty regimes enabling individual claims.[383] This is demonstrated by examining potential modification at three time periods.[384]

First, concerning modification *before* claims are brought, one might consider that fairness would require that individuals be given notice of any modification of claims mechanisms,[385] much as the ICJ held, in *Nicaragua*, that the US was obliged to wait 'a reasonable time' before withdrawing its consent to the Court's jurisdiction vis-à-vis other States.[386]

Unilateral denunciations are indeed commonly subject to a notice period,[387] and may be ineffective for longer where treaties contain 'survival' clauses, which

[379] Eg, *Fábrica de Vidrios v Venezuela (Award)* ICSID Case No ARB/12/21 (13 November 2017) [286], [289]; Roberts, 'Triangular' (n 217) 406–11, 387–88, 370–74 (necessary focus *State* intent); Voon and Mitchell (n 327) 433; James Harrison, 'The Life and Death of BITs: Legal Issues Concerning Survival Clauses and the Termination of Investment Treaties' (2012) 13 JWIT 928, 931–33, 943–46; Peters (n 32) 323–24. Similarly Roberts, 'Power' (n 358) 183–85, 207, 212–14.

[380] Harrison (n 379) 929–30, 950; Voon and Mitchell (n 327), particularly 414–15, 424–26, 433; Catharine Titi, 'Most-Favoured-Nation Treatment: Survival Clauses and Reform of International Investment Law' (2016) 33 JIA 425, 425–28, 435–40, all cited Paula Henin and others, 'Innovating International Investment Agreements: A Proposed Green Investment Protocol for Climate Change Mitigation and Adaptation' (2019) 36 Arb Int 37, 46; Roberts, 'Triangular' (n 217) 387, 404–5; Peters (n 32) 323; authorities nn 385ff.

[381] Section III(C).

[382] VCLT, art 37(2); see Paparinskis, 'Analogies' (n 9) 82, 98 generally 79–84 ('direct'/third-party/'delegated' rights perspectives); similarly Paparinskis, 'New' (n 7) 622–26, 645; Harrison (n 379) 943–45; Roberts, 'Triangular' (n 217) 370–73; Roberts, 'Power' (n 358) 211; Peters (n 32) 312.

[383] cf Harrison (n 379) 946–47. Also Junianto Losari and Michael Ewing-Chow, 'A Clash of Treaties: The Lawfulness of Countermeasures in International Trade Law and International Investment Law' (2015) 16 JWIT 274, 299–302. See section III(C)(i),(ii),(v),(vi), nn 384ff.

[384] Considering same three time periods vis-à-vis interpretation awards: Roberts, 'Hybrid' (n 51) 58–66; similarly Michele Potestà, 'Towards a Greater Role for State-to-State Arbitration in the Architecture of Investment Treaties?' in Shaheeza Lalani and Rodrigo Polanco Lazo (eds), *The Role of the State in Investor-State Arbitration* (Brill Nijhoff 2015) 265–68; also Roberts, 'Triangular' (n 217) 387, 409–12; Roberts, 'Power' (n 358) 212. Cf Paparinskis, 'Analogies' (n 9) 87.

[385] Similarly Harrison (n 379) 946; Roberts, 'Triangular' (n 217) 388, cf 407–11; Peters (n 32) 323; relatedly *Fedax v Venezuela (Jurisdiction)* (1998) 37 ILM 1378 (ICSID) [33] (art 25(4) 'put[s] investors on notice'). Cf *HICEE v Slovakia (Partial Award)* PCA Case 2009-11 (23 May 2011) [140]; Paparinskis, 'Analogies' (n 9) 92–94, 96, 99.

[386] *Military and Paramilitary Activities in and against Nicaragua (Nicaragua v USA) (Jurisdiction/Admissibility)* [1984] ICJ Rep 392, 420; also Cheng (n 29) 119; Luke Eric Peterson, 'Arbitrators Hold State Liable ...' *IA Rep* (14 July 2016). Cf *Vidrios* (n 379) [287].

[387] Eg, ICSID, art 71 (6 months); ECHR, art 58 (6 months); generally VCLT, art 56 (12 months); Voon and Mitchell (n 327) 415–16, 421, 423–24; Roberts, 'Triangular' (n 217) 403.

extend the obligations of parties beyond the date of termination, and which are particularly common in investment law.[388] Nonetheless, the effectiveness of denunciations after any required notice period, including those that remove individual claims mechanisms, is not generally doubted.[389]

So much for unilateral denunciation, but there are other ways to modify and terminate treaties. Indeed, unlike unilateral denunciation notice periods, treaty law generally provides no limitations on termination by *consent*,[390] with scholarly authority suggesting that treaties, including those containing 'survival' clauses, may be terminated immediately by the joint action of the State parties.[391] State practice appears to align with this view, with Argentina, Australia, Austria, the Czech Republic, Denmark, Estonia, Indonesia, Italy, Malta, Mexico, Slovakia, Slovenia, Peru, and Viet Nam having agreed to terminate various BITs and in the process either eliminate or alter survival clauses.[392] Additionally, as noted above, the intra-EU Termination Agreement terminates all intra-EU BITs between the Parties, and this includes all survival provisions (called 'sunset provisions' therein).[393] A draft Protocol on Investment to the Agreement Establishing the African Continental Free Trade Area, being negotiated by African Union members, likewise contains a provision which would terminate existing BITs between the parties, including any survival clauses.[394] Such practice, stemming from a broad spectrum

[388] See Voon and Mitchell (n 327) 421–22, 429–30; Harrison (n 379) 935–41; Titi (n 380) 435–39; Peters (n 32) 323; Paparinskis, 'Countermeasures' (n 363) 386–87; Campbell McLachlan, Laurence Shore, and Matthew Weiniger, *International Investment Arbitration: Substantive Principles* (2nd edn, OUP 2017) [2.38]; eg Model BITs: UK (2008), art 15; Germany (2008), art 13(3), reproduced ibid.

[389] See discussion Christoph Schreuer, *The ICSID Convention: A Commentary* (2nd edn, CUP 2009) 1279–81; Voon and Mitchell (n 327) 417–19; also Parlett (n 27) 106; cf Peters (n 32) 323–24. Tribunals disagree on whether individuals can consent during an ICSID denunciation notice period, however generally agree that denunciation is effective thereafter: see discussion Luke Eric Peterson, 'Analysis: What Have We Learned ...?' *IA Rep* (30 November 2017); Voon and Mitchell (n 327) 417–19; eg, *Venoklim Holding v Venezuela (Award)* ICSID Case No ARB/12/22 (3 April 2015) [59]–[66]; *Tenaris and Talta v Venezuela (Award)* ICSID Case No ARB/12/23 (12 November 2016) [62]–[65]; *Blue Bank v Venezuela (Award)* ICSID Case No ARB/12/20 (26 April 2017) [119]–[120]; cf [45]–[56] (Sep Op Söderlund); *Vidrios* (n 379) [250]–[304], particularly [286]–[296]. For BIT denunciations: Voon and Mitchell (n 327) 416–17 (Bolivia/Ecuador/Venezuela), 424–25 (South Africa/Indonesia); Titi (n 380) 435–36; Harrison (n 379) 930–31.

[390] See VCLT, art 54(b) (termination/withdrawal 'at any time by consent of all'); Voon and Mitchell (n 327) 426; Roberts, 'Triangular' (n 217) 386, 404; Harrison (n 379) 941–43; Tropper and Reinisch (n 327) 313–14.

[391] M Sornarajah, *The International Law on Foreign Investment* (4th edn, CUP 2017) 276–77 (noting (fn 221) that views expressed in *Eastern Sugar v Czech Republic (Partial Award)* SCC Case 088/2004 (27 March 2007) [175] are 'unsound'); Voon and Mitchell (n 327) 430–32; Roberts, 'Triangular' (n 217) 404, 411–14; Titi (n 380) 437–40; also Paparinskis, 'Analogies' (n 9) 96. Cf Harrison (n 379) 942–47; Peters (n 32) 324; *Oostergetel v Slovakia (Jurisdiction)* UNCITRAL Tribunal (30 April 2010) [95]–[97].

[392] For outline and discussion of practice: Voon and Mitchell (n 327) 427, 430–31; also Luke Eric Peterson, 'Czech Republic Terminates ...' *IA Rep* (1 February 2011); Luke Eric Peterson, 'Indonesia Ramps up Termination of BITs ...' (20 November 2015); Jarrod Hepburn, 'Investor-State Arbitration Opt-Outs Proliferate ...' *IA Rep* (8 March 2018); Paparinskis, 'Analogies' (n 9) 97; Roberts, 'Triangular' (n 217) 387; Titi (n 380) 437–38; Tropper and Reinisch (n 327) 333.

[393] Termination Agreement, art 2. See generally Bohmer, 'Plurilateral' (n 327); Debevoise (n 328) 3; Wierzbowski and Szostak (n 341); Tropper and Reinisch (n 327) 315–21.

[394] Draft Protocol on Investment to the Agreement Establishing the African Continental Free Trade Area (zero draft, November 2021, <https://www.isds.bilaterals.org/IMG/pdf/afcfta_protocol_on_inv

of States, suggests that the termination even of such survival clauses is considered unproblematic under treaty law.[395] Indeed, at least one domestic court has upheld the effectiveness of the immediate sunset clause termination in the intra-EU Termination Agreement.[396]

Practice also suggests that termination by consent can include individual–State dispute settlement mechanisms: States terminated mechanisms for the hearing of post-WWI claims before the MATs;[397] NAFTA Parties have previously suspended individual claims mechanisms,[398] and have more recently amended NAFTA significantly, eliminating investor–State dispute settlement altogether for Canada and otherwise restricting its availability;[399] the SADC Member States signed an agreement to remove individual access to the SADCT;[400] the intra-EU Termination Agreement terminates investor-State claims mechanisms;[401] and agreement has been reached in principle on modernising the ECT, an instrument with a significant number of parties,[402] including to eliminate intra-EU investor–State dispute settlement.[403]

At least insofar as that termination would operate to affect prospective *future* claims, there cannot be any real doubts as to its effectiveness.[404] While not yet tested before an international tribunal,[405] it would be surprising if recognition were not

estment_first_draft.pdf)>, art 5, discussed Erik Brouwer, 'Analysis: Investment Protocol to the African Continental Free Trade Area Agreement . . .' *IA Rep* (25 May 2023).

[395] Agreeing, see Tropper and Reinisch (n 327) 318, citing *UP and CD Holding v Hungary (Award)* ICSID Case No ARB/13/35 (9 October 2018) [265] in support, and see particularly 322–23 (investors should not be equated to third parties under treaty law in this analysis). Cf 323–26 (possible application of estoppel/legitimate expectations/acquired rights). Doubting, see Kochenov and Lavranos (n 327) 203–4; Bray and Kapoor (n 328); also UNCTAD, 'UNCTAD's Reform Package for the International Investment Regime' (2017) 84 (suggesting two cases brought despite joint termination). However, one termination was 'subject to' a survival clause: *Gavazzi v Romania (Jurisdiction, Admissibility, Liability)* ICSID Case No ARB/12/25 (21 April 2015) (fn 1). No public information seems to be available on the other: *Impresa Grassetto v Slovenia* ICSID Case No ARB/13/10. Further: *Magyar Farming Company Ltd, Kintyre Kft and Inicia Zrt v Hungary (Award)* ICSID Case No ARB/17/27 (13 November 2019) [222]–[223], discussed Tropper and Reinisch (n 327) 322 (sunset clause reflecting private party rights); Sornarajah (n 391) 276–77.

[396] Lisa Bohmer, 'Vilnius Court Decides . . .' *IA Rep* (14 February 2022).

[397] nn 252ff.

[398] n 320.

[399] See USMCA, Annexures 14-C, 14-D, 14-E. Generally Luke Eric Peterson, 'NAFTA Parties Unveil Text . . .' *IA Rep* (1 October 2018).

[400] n 378.

[401] Termination Agreement, art 4.

[402] See <https://www.energycharter.org/process/energy-charter-treaty–1994/energy-charter-treaty/signatories-contracting-parties/>.

[403] See 'Public Communication explaining the main changes contained in the agreement in principle' (24 June 2022) <energycharter.org/fileadmin/DocumentsMedia/CCDECS/2022/CCDEC202210.pdf>, [6], discussed Bohmer, 'Modernizing' (n 363). More recently: Erik Brouwer, 'Planned Vote on Modernised ECT . . .' *IA Rep* (28 April 2023).

[404] See Yanos and Ramos-Mrosovsky (n 341) ('right of states to terminate treaties is beyond serious question', but querying retroactive aspects, discussed below); Tropper and Reinisch (n 327) 314–15. Cf, more doubtful: Bray and Kapoor (n 328) (referring, *inter alia*, to art 70 VCLT).

[405] But see request for arbitration made under a terminated BIT after the Agreement's entry into force for those parties: *Plaza Centers NV v Romania* (ICSID Case No ARB/22/15). See '[Updated] Dutch Real

given to the Parties' ability to terminate an agreement, consistently with the law of treaties, even where that agreement provides for individual claims.[406] Nothing in the practice suggests that States consider individual rights to claim granted by them irrevocable without the relevant individuals' consent.[407]

The question arises, second, whether this position differs where States attempt to modify procedural mechanisms while proceedings are afoot.[408] Practice suggests that States are more wary of interfering at this stage: in suspending softwood lumber-related NAFTA claims, the US and Canada obtained the claimants' consent to termination,[409] while the EECC Agreement left existing claims untouched.[410] When modifying NAFTA more broadly in 2018, the parties allowed claims to continue under the original regime for three years, with ongoing proceedings unaffected.[411] In other cases, though, States are more cavalier: in the post-WWI practice, States altered procedural mechanisms even where claims were pending;[412] the operation of the SADCT was suspended while individual claims were afoot;[413] the intra-EU Agreement discussed above affects not only future, but also existing proceedings, in a retroactive manner;[414] and the US–Iran settlement, albeit premised on US control of the proceedings, likewise affected ongoing cases.[415]

Some treaties providing for individual claims mechanisms, such as the Convention on the Settlement of Investment Disputes between States and Nationals of Other States (ICSID), prevent States unilaterally withdrawing their consent to arbitrate.[416] Where a joint termination purports to have that effect in

Estate Investor …' *IA Rep* (5 June 2022); similarly Debevoise & Plimpton, 'The Future of Investment Law in the EU: A Practical Perspective' *Debevoise Update* (8 December 2021) <https://www.debevoise.com/-/media/files/insights/publications/2021/12/20211208-the-future-of-investment-law-in-the-eu.pdf>, 2 (intra-EU proceedings both pending and continue to be brought); Yanos and Ramos-Mrosovsky (n 341).

406 Indeed, tribunals have suggested parties *should* follow treaty law procedures to do away with obligations: see Tropper and Reinisch (n 327) 312–13, referencing, eg, *Marfin Investment Group Holdings v Cyprus (Award)* ICSID Case No ARB/13/27 (26 July 2018) [594]; *Fynderdale Holdings v Czech Republic (Award)* PCA Case 2018-18 (29 April 2021) [292], also [294] (Termination Agreement effect upon entry into force).

407 Cf n 382.

408 Roberts, 'Triangular' (n 217) 411–14. Generally authorities n 384.

409 SLA, Annex 2A; see Paparinskis, 'New' (n 7) 631, 645. Cf Luke Eric Peterson, 'U.S. Financial Firm Discontinues Argentine Claim …' *IA Rep* (2 April 2009).

410 Section III(C)(iv). Similarly Losari and Ewing-Chow (n 383) 299–300 (Mauritius Convention).

411 See USMCA, Annex 14-C, particularly [3]–[5]. See generally Peterson, 'Unveil' (n 399).

412 Section III(C)(i), particularly nn 260–62.

413 See Luke Eric Peterson, 'INVESTIGATION: Lesotho Is Held Liable …' *IA Rep* (14 July 2016); Luke Eric Peterson, 'Multilateral Investment Treaty's Exhaustion …' *IA Rep* (14 July 2016) ('small docket of cases').

414 Tropper and Reinisch (n 327) 326–27; Wierzbowski and Szostak (n 341); Yanos and Ramos-Mrosovsky (n 341).

415 Section III(C)(ii).

416 ICSID, art 25; discussion Schreuer (n 389) 254ff, 1280 (on art 72); ICSID (n 141) 1009–10 (subsists notwithstanding ICSID denunciation); Bray and Kapoor (n 328). Also *ADM* (n 27) [174] ('irrevocable offer'); Peters (n 32) 286, 288; Roberts, 'Triangular' (n 217) 396.

cases covered by such treaties—such as the intra-EU Agreement insofar as it affects ICSID proceedings—one might doubt whether a tribunal would accept that outcome.[417] Indeed, various ICSID tribunals have rejected the possibility of any withdrawal of consent deriving from EU law having retroactive effect.[418]

But what about where there is no such bar at play? On the one hand, Roberts makes a convincing argument from the perspective of domestic public law that the State of nationality can, together with other treaty parties, jointly modify existing claims.[419] The argument goes that a State retains the power domestically to expropriate property rights in the public interest, and there is no reason that two sovereigns should not be able to so act also on the international plane vis-à-vis an individual's legal claim.[420] This protects the ability of States to jointly act to settle individual claims where the public interest so demands.[421]

That this should be possible is supported by the law of treaties allowing for treaties to function retroactively, provided that the parties so intend.[422] In addition, the very inclusion of provisions preventing unilateral withdrawal, as under ICSID, suggests that the situation may otherwise be more flexible.[423] One might also note that even where investment tribunals have been faced with joint treaty interpretations midway through a case, they have generally given these effect,[424] notwithstanding that the interpretation may be detrimental to the investor's case.[425]

[417] Bray and Kapoor (n 328) ('untenable'). See also Debevoise (n 328) 3–5; Yanos and Ramos-Mrosovsky (n 341); Lisa Bohmer, 'In Now-Public Decision ...' *IA Rep* (11 November 2018) (EU-law effect to terminate arbitration offer).

[418] See Tropper and Reinisch (n 327) 330, referencing *Eskosol v Italy (Termination and Intra-EU Objection)* ICSID Case No ARB/15/50 (7 May 2019) [199]–[226]; *ESPF Beteiligungs and others v Italy (Award)* ICSID Case No ARB/16/5 (14 September 2020) [303]–[327]; *Magyar* (n 395) [213]–[214]. See also Kochenov and Lavranos (n 327) 209, discussing *UP* (n 395), see particularly [221].

[419] Roberts, 'Triangular' (n 217) 409–14.

[420] ibid 412–13.

[421] ibid.

[422] VLCT, art 29. See Tropper and Reinisch (n 327) 327; also Roberts, 'Triangular' (n 217) 407–8.

[423] See discussion Schreuer (n 389) 1280, cf 254.

[424] *ADF v US* (2003) ICSID Rev-FILJ 195 [175]–[178]; *Pope & Talbot v Canada (Damages)* UNCITRAL (31 May 2002) [51] (NAFTA, art 1131 mandating, even where impact on award would be retrospective), cf [47] (were determination necessary, would be amendment); *Methanex v US (Award)* UNCITRAL (3 August 2005), Pt IV(C) [17]–[22]; all discussed Roberts, 'Power' (n 358) 180–81, 194; Gabrielle Kaufmann-Kohler, 'Non-Disputing State Submissions in Investment Arbitration: Resurgence of Diplomatic Protection?' in Laurence Boisson de Chazournes, Marcelo Kohen, and Jorge Viñuales (eds), *Diplomatic and Judicial Means of Dispute Settlement* (Martinus Nijhoff 2013) 316–17, referencing *CME v Czech Republic (Final Award)* (2003) 9 ICSID Rep 264 [437], [504]; also Michele Potestà, 'State-to-State Dispute Settlement Pursuant to Bilateral Investment Treaties: Is There Potential?' in Nerina Boschiero and others (eds), *International Courts and the Development of International Law: Essays in Honour of Tullio Treves* (Asser 2013) 763; generally Roberts, 'Hybrid' (n 51) 53; Ch 3, n 306. Further: *HICEE* (n 385) [139]–[140].

[425] The NAFTA interpretation limited the minimum standard of treatment to the customary standard: see *ADF* (n 424) [178] (investor failing to prove breached ([187]–[192])); *Pope* (n 424) [55] (not affecting the outcome: [65]–[66]); *Methanex* (n 424) [18] (not affecting outcome: [19]–[27]). The common position in *CME* was argued, *inter alia*, to 'limit the claims that [could] be pursued': *CME (Final)* (n 424) [220].

Although interpretation may be different from amendment or termination,[426] at the very least, this suggests an openness to States using treaty powers to affect ongoing claims.[427] And as just noted, a variety of States have, recently and over previous decades, endeavoured to do just that.[428]

On the other hand, the trend of the jurisprudence suggests that tribunals are unlikely to accept State action under treaty law impacting individual claims already afoot.[429] Tropper and Reinisch highlight, for instance, that a tribunal's jurisdiction is generally assessed at the time proceedings are filed.[430] Even outside of the ICSID context, tribunals have looked unfavourably on arguments made in many intra-EU cases that EU law has led to the retraction of consent to arbitration, even if that were possible under treaty law.[431] In another case concerned with the SADCT's suspension, a tribunal held that Lesotho's consent to SADCT jurisdiction was irrevocable once proceedings had begun.[432] Lesotho had therefore breached the SADC Protocol by (with the other Member States) allowing the SADCT to be suspended, providing no alternative forum, and thus preventing an individual from continuing its claim.[433] It may be noted that for all practical purposes, the States *did* succeed in preventing claims from being brought before the SADCT, this finding having been made not by the SADCT but by a tribunal whose jurisdiction was based on a *different* instrument.[434] Such success may be easier to achieve in practice with standing courts more obviously under those States' control—like the

[426] Considering the interpretation more an amendment: *Pope* (n 424) [47]. Cf *ADF* (n 424) [177]. Generally Roberts, 'Power' (n 358) 200–01, 210–11; also *Eskosol (Objection)* (n 418) [225] (reservation rather than interpretation).

[427] Particularly *ADF* (n 424) [177]; *Methanex* (n 424) [20]–[22]; also *Pope* (n 424) [51]. Admittedly, NAFTA rendered joint interpretations binding (art 1131). But *CME (Final)* (n 424) also concerned deference to a parties' joint position midway through a case based on a provision for 'consultations' to resolve issues: [87]–[89], [217]. This is consistent with treaty parties' power to interpret their treaties: see Roberts, 'Power' (n 358), particularly 199–202, 208, 216.

[428] nn 408–15.

[429] See generally Tropper and Reinisch (n 327) 327–32.

[430] ibid 328; also Roberts, 'Triangular' (n 217) 411–13; eg, *Alleged Violations of Sovereign Rights and Maritime Spaces in the Caribbean Sea (Nicaragua v Colombia) (Preliminary Objections)* [2016] ICJ Rep 3 [33]–[34].

[431] Tropper and Reinisch (n 327) 330–31, referencing *AMF Aircraft Leasing Meier & Fischer v Czech Republic (Final Award)* PCA Case 2017-15 (11 May 2020) [338] (acquired rights); *Muszynianka Spółka z Ograniczoną Odpowiedzialnością v Slovak Republic (Award)* PCA Case 2017-8 (7 October 2020) [262]–[265] (jurisdiction evaluated on institution); also *Wirtgen v Czech Republic (Final Award)* PCA Case 2014-03 (11 October 2017) [253] (VCLT requirements unmet); *Eastern Sugar* (n 391) [158]–[176] and *Oostergetel* (n 391) [72]–[98], referenced therein (suggesting not possible); discussion Voon and Mitchell (n 327) 432 and Sornarajah, n 391. Further: Debevoise (n 405) 2; Wierzbowski and Szostak (n 341); Kochenov and Lavranos (n 327) 211 and referencing *Addiko Bank v Croatia (Croatia's Jurisdictional Objection)* ICSID Case No ARB/17/37 (12 June 2020), particularly [277]–[280] (referencing VCLT, arts 46 and 69), [289]–[290] (critical date for jurisdiction).

[432] Peterson, 'Denial' (n 386) (decision unreported).

[433] ibid.

[434] Indeed domestic courts set the award aside for lack of jurisdiction: Luke Eric Peterson, 'Singapore Judge Sees Investors …' *IA Rep* (17 August 2017), affirmed on appeal: Damien Charlotin, 'Singapore Appeal Court Grapples …' *IA Rep* (29 November 2018), referencing *Swissbourgh v Lesotho* [2018] SGCA 81.

SADCT, or even the MATs discussed above[435]—than ad hoc tribunals.[436] Indeed, the case law discussed above suggests that such ad hoc tribunals may disregard attempts at curtailing ongoing proceedings, and simply continue to act.[437] And even if tribunals were to decline jurisdiction, the action of treaty parties in preventing the continuation of pending claims may be challenged on *different* grounds, as indeed the case concerning Lesotho and the SADCT suggests.[438] The question of what recourse individuals may have where their claims are thus interfered with is addressed in the Conclusion to this book.

Third, States might attempt to settle a claim already adjudicated. At this stage, the individual procedural mechanism has been exhausted and the respondent State is obliged to pay any reparation awarded.[439] However, the individual will usually—in the absence of voluntary payment—be obliged to turn either to its State of nationality,[440] or to domestic courts, to enforce any award.[441] This State of affairs may explain why States felt able to settle claims for amounts owing under post-WWI MAT awards.[442] For, whatever the source of the original debt, States undoubtedly have the power, as discussed above, to control both their own claims, and claims before their municipal courts.[443] The intra-EU Agreement does not encompass already adjudicated claims,[444] but does target the point of enforcement for pending claims, as noted above.[445] Although the claims may still be brought,[446] such action may well be effective in precluding reparation from being obtained, at least in EU Member States.[447] Again, however, as discussed above, this may have limited effects in third-State courts.[448]

[435] Section III(C)(i).

[436] Blocking of WTO Appellate Body's functioning demonstrates the power of even one State if the constituent rules so allow: see Simon Lester, 'Ending the WTO Dispute Settlement Crisis: Where to from Here?' *IISD Policy Analysis* (2 March 2022).

[437] Roberts, 'Power' (n 358) 213–15.

[438] See, eg, Bray and Kapoor (n 328). Generally Conclusion, nn 52ff.

[439] Victorino Tejera Perez, 'Diplomatic Protection Revival for Failure to Comply with Investment Arbitration Awards' (2012) 3 JIDS 445, 447–48; eg, concerning enforcement of *res judicata* individual–State award: *The 'Société Commercial de Belgique'* [1939] PCIJ Rep Ser A/B No 78, 175–76; also *Pious Fund (US v Mexico)* (1902) IX UNRIAA 1, 13.

[440] Eg, ICSID, art 27(1) (diplomatic protection for enforcement); discussion Schreuer (n 389) 426–27; Paparinskis, 'Countermeasures' (n 363) 309–11; Perez (n 439) 446, 455ff. Cf n 264.

[441] See ICSID, art 54; Schreuer (n 389) 1118; Douglas, 'Hybrid' (n 29) 226–36; Douglas, *Investment* (n 29) 31–32 (NY Convention); Perez (n 439) 451–52; Robert McCorquodale, 'The Individual and the International Legal System' in Malcolm Evans (ed), *International Law* (4th edn, OUP 2014) 292; Tzanakopoulos (n 377) 145; Nollkaemper (n 111) 3, 9, 177.

[442] nn 264–71.

[443] Section III(A)–(B).

[444] Termination Agreement, art 6.

[445] ibid art 7(b).

[446] Indeed, potential enforcement problems leave tribunals' jurisdiction unaffected: see discussion Kochenov and Lavranos (n 327), fn 38; also Wierzbowski and Szostak (n 341).

[447] Tropper and Reinisch (n 327) 334–36; also Wierzbowski and Szostak (n 341) (noting potential conflicts with ICSID obligations).

[448] See Bray and Kapoor (n 328); Yanos and Ramos-Mrosovsky (n 341); Debevoise (n 405) 2–3 (enforcement of intra-EU arbitral awards in non-EU States); also Wierzbowski and Szostak (n 341); Tropper and Reinisch (n 327) 336; Kochenov and Lavranos (n 327) 212.

IV. Conclusion

The foregoing has suggested that both individuals and States have the capacity, through waiver and consent, to affect claims belonging to the other. Individual waivers may affect a State's ability to establish breach or damage in a later claim. Where States waive their nationals' claims, usually as part of a settlement, the practice suggests that they intend to prevent claims before domestic courts, measures which can control overlapping claims at least to a limited extent. States generally acknowledge, however, an inability to control actions in third-State courts. Additionally, it appears that they do not generally intend—nor have the capacity—to waive their nationals' *international* claims. What States *can* do is withdraw from, or consensually modify the operation of, the treaties establishing individual claims mechanisms, and in practice this provides a significant means for States to control overlapping claims. Such actions are not without risk, however. The Conclusion to this book will consider the possibility of affected individuals bringing actions against the interfering State pursuant to human rights, investment, or domestic law, and where an appropriate balance between State and individual interests may lie.

6

Countermeasures and Self-Defence

I. Introduction

Like previous chapters, this chapter considers situations in which, but for the operation of rules related to the law of State responsibility, States and individuals could bring overlapping claims against the same respondent State, and asks how far an individual or State can have their claims thwarted due to conduct that is not their own.[1] In this chapter, the relevant conduct is that which enables two circumstances precluding wrongfulness—countermeasures and self-defence—to be invoked by a respondent State. The chapter considers how far these defences may be so invoked to preclude *both* the claim of an entity that has itself engaged in the conduct giving rise to the defence, *and* that of the entity possessing an overlapping claim.[2] It thus considers to what extent respondent States can invoke countermeasures and self-defence to preclude the successful raising of claims by:

(1) *individuals*, but where the conduct relied upon in invoking the defence is that of *another State*; and
(2) *a State*, but where the conduct relied upon in invoking the defence is that of *an individual.*

As noted in the Introduction, these two defences are being considered together because, as will be seen, it is often assumed that they cannot be exercised in a way that would impact third-party rights, meaning their application in circumstances of overlapping claims is questionable.[3] This chapter will show, however, that there is at least an argument to be made that these defences can be employed to preclude overlapping individual or interstate claims *even if* third-party rights would thereby be affected.[4] In doing so, it draws on a wealth of recent practice: for countermeasures, that in which States impose asset freezes on individuals as part of a 'sanctions' regime in response to the allegedly wrongful conduct of a State; for self-defence, that in which States exercise self-defence against non-State actors.[5] The chapter begins

[1] See Introduction, nn 60–71.
[2] Except consent, previously considered rules concerned the potential preclusion of only *one* overlapping claim: see Introduction, nn 60–62, 65–70.
[3] Introduction, n 92.
[4] Authorities sections III–IV.
[5] Sections III(A), IV(B)(ii).

Overlapping Individual and Interstate Claims in International Law. Jessica Howley, Oxford University Press.
 DOI: 10.1093/oso/9780192871466.003.0007

by providing an overview of these two circumstances, before detailing their potential and actual operation vis-à-vis overlapping individual and interstate claims.

II. Countermeasures, self-defence, and overlapping claims

A. Countermeasures

Pursuant to the Articles on Responsibility of States for Internationally Wrongful Acts (ARSIWA), countermeasures are actions, otherwise internationally wrongful,[6] that are justified where taken 'against a State which is responsible for an internationally wrongful act' and 'in order to induce that State to comply with its obligations'.[7] They are a 'self-help' mechanism, utilised by States to enforce obligations owed to them in the decentralised international legal system.[8] Countermeasures must be 'limited to the non-performance for the time being of international obligations of the State taking the measures towards the responsible State',[9] and 'commensurate with the injury suffered'.[10]

The ARSIWA outline that certain obligations, including those regulating the use of force, 'for the protection of fundamental human rights', 'of a humanitarian

[6] James Crawford, *The International Law Commission's Articles on State Responsibility: Introduction, Text and Commentaries* (CUP 2002) art 22, 168 (*ARSIWA*); Martin Dawidowicz, *Third-Party Countermeasures in International Law* (CUP 2017) 19; Denis Alland, 'The Definition of Countermeasures' in James Crawford and others (eds), *The Law of International Responsibility* (OUP 2010) 1132.

[7] *ARSIWA*, art 49(1), 284–85, also referencing *Gabčíkovo-Nagymaros Project (Hungary/Slovakia) (Judgment)* [1997] ICJ Rep 7 [83]; similarly Alland (n 6) 1135; Dawidowicz (n 6) 19; Omer Elagab, *The Legality of Non-Forcible Counter-Measures in International Law* (Clarendon 1988) 44–51, 62; Nigel White and Ademola Abass, 'Countermeasures and Sanctions' in Malcolm Evans (ed), *International Law* (4th edn, OUP 2014) 540. The ARSIWA are relevantly assumed to reflect custom: see James Crawford, *State Responsibility: The General Part* (CUP 2013) 293–94 (*GP*); *Corn Products v Mexico (Responsibility)* ICSID Case No ARB(AF)/04/01 (15 January 2008) [145]; *ADM and Tate & Lyle v Mexico (Award)* ICSID Case No ARB(AF)/04/05 (21 November 2007) [125], cf [2] (Op Rovine); Hubert Lesaffre, 'Countermeasures' in Crawford and others, *Responsibility* (n 6) 472–73, cf 470. Cf White and Abass (n 7) 540; *Cargill v Mexico (Award)* ICSID Case No ARB(AF)/05/2 (18 September 2009) [381]; also Tom Ruys, 'Sanctions, Retorsions and Countermeasures: Concepts and International Legal Framework' [2016] <https://papers.ssrn.com/sol3/papers.cfm?abstract_id=2760853>, 4.

[8] Martins Paparinskis, 'Investment Arbitration and the Law of Countermeasures' (2008) 79 BYBIL 264, 269; Douglas Guilfoyle, 'Interdicting Vessels to Enforce the Common Interest: Maritime Countermeasures and the Use of Force' (2007) 56 ICLQ 69, 69; Evan Criddle, 'Humanitarian Financial Intervention' (2013) 24 EJIL 583, 596; also Christian Tams, 'The Use of Force against Terrorists' (2009) 20 EJIL 359, 372; Federica Paddeu, *Justification and Excuse in International Law* (CUP 2018) 225–26, 247–51, 268–69; Kate Parlett, 'The Application of the Rules on Countermeasures in Investment Claims' in Christine Chinkin and Freya Baetens (eds), *Sovereignty, Statehood and State Responsibility* (CUP 2015) 395; Anne van Aaken, 'International Investment Law and Decentralized Targeted Sanctions: An Uneasy Relationship' (2016) 164 Columbia FDI Perspectives < https://academiccommons.columbia.edu/doi/10.7916/D8ZG6SF5>, 1.

[9] *ARSIWA*, art 49(2).

[10] ibid art 51; also *Case concerning the Air Service Agreement of 27 March 1946 (USA v France)* (1978) XVIII UNRIAA 417, 443; Roger O'Keefe, 'Proportionality' in Crawford and others, *Responsibility* (n 6) 1157ff.

character prohibiting reprisals', and of *jus cogens*, are not subject to countermeasures.[11] Any other international obligation is in theory so subject,[12] including those found in investment law.[13] And in practice, Mexico defended both an interstate World Trade Organization (WTO) claim brought by the US and claims brought against it by investors under the North American Free Trade Agreement (NAFTA) by arguing that its actions were legitimate countermeasures taken against the US, the investors' State of nationality.[14] Mexico thus defended an alleged breach of international law underlying an *individual* claim under investment law by pointing to *State* conduct which, it said, justified its response.

Countermeasures cannot operate in the opposite direction: they cannot be invoked by a State in response to *individual* conduct because a lawful countermeasure must respond to a breach of interstate obligations (*legal* injury) committed by another State.[15] Of course, as Chapter 1 noted, States act *through* individuals, and rules on attribution determine when the State is responsible for wrongful conduct ultimately undertaken by such individuals.[16] Those rules generally identify individuals or entities who are *agents* for the State,[17] primarily its organs, or those acting with government authority, or under the State's direction or control.[18] The conduct of such individuals is treated as that of the State,[19] where it is 'official' in nature.[20] Private conduct is not, conversely, attributable to the State without more.[21] Countermeasures can only therefore respond to individual conduct where those individuals act *as* the State.[22] Accordingly, when considering possible impacts

[11] *ARSIWA*, art 50; further n 351.

[12] Paddeu, *Justification* (n 8) 264; Elisabeth Zoller, *Peacetime Unilateral Remedies: An Analysis of Countermeasures* (Transnational 1984) 42–43; Dawidowicz (n 6) 307. Cf O'Keefe (n 10) 1158–59.

[13] Paparinskis, 'Countermeasures' (n 8) 270, 317, 351–52; see nn 91ff.

[14] See authorities nn 91–93.

[15] n 7; see Paparinskis, 'Countermeasures' (n 8) 332–34; *Corn Products* (n 7) [146]; Ruys (n 7) 13; cf Alain Pellet and Alina Miron, 'Sanctions' in Rüdiger Wolfrum (ed), *MPEPIL (Online)* (OUP 2013) [22] (UNSC). Vis-à-vis art 48 States, see n 122.

[16] Ch 1, nn 8–11.

[17] Authorities Ch 1, n 10.

[18] *ARSIWA*, arts 4–11, 94-123; Crawford, *GP* (n 7) 115, generally 113ff; Luigi Condorelli and Claus Kress, 'The Rules of Attribution: General Considerations' in Crawford and others, *Responsibility* (n 6) 229–31.

[19] Condorelli and Kress (n 18) 221.

[20] *ARSIWA*, 96; Crawford, *GP* (n 7) 117; Bin Cheng, *General Principles of Law as Applied by International Courts and Tribunals* (Stevens & Sons 1953) 210; Brigitte Stern, 'The Elements of an Internationally Wrongful Act' in Crawford and others, *Responsibility* (n 6) 203.

[21] *ARSIWA*, 110, also 38–39; Cheng (n 20) 184, 208–10; Tom Ruys, *'Armed Attack' and Article 51 of the UN Charter* (CUP 2010) 409; Christine Chinkin, 'A Critique of the Public/Private Dimension' (1999) 10 EJIL 387, 387–88; Emer de Vattel, *The Law of Nations, or, Principles of the Law of Nature Applied to the Conduct and Affairs of Nations and Sovereigns* (T&JW Johnson 1867) 161.

[22] n 15; eg, Philip Jessup, *A Modern Law of Nations* (Archon 1968) 181 (boycotts); similarly Zoller (n 12) 103–4; cf Eduardo Jiménez de Aréchaga, 'International Responsibility' in Max Sørensen (ed), *Manual of Public International Law* (Macmillan 1968) 562. Cf States failing in 'preventive and remedial obligations' vis-à-vis private individuals: Robert Jennings and Arthur Watts, *Oppenheim's International Law*, vol 1 (9th edn, Longman 1992) 502, also 549 ('due diligence'); similarly Jessup (n 22) 104, 107–8; Ruys (n 21) 375; de Aréchaga (n 22) 536, 560–61; Ian Brownlie, *System of the Law of Nations: State*

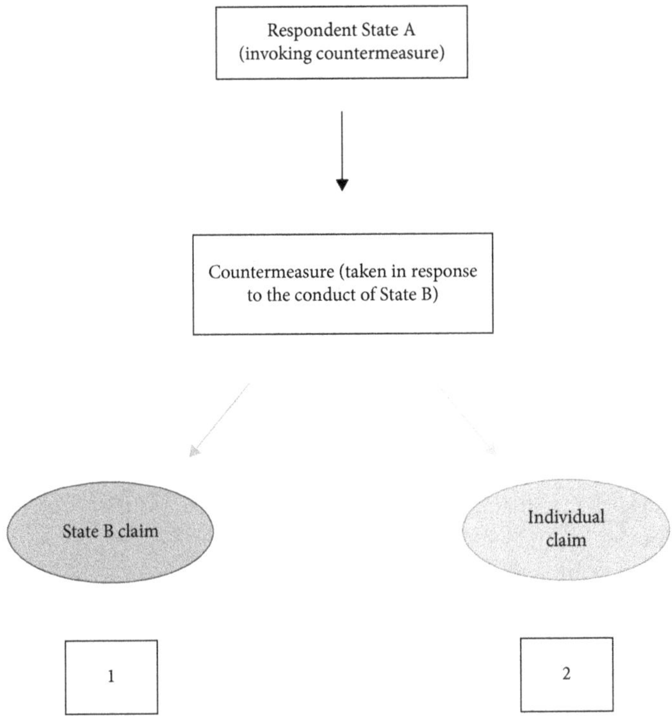

Figure 6.1 Potential overlapping individual and interstate claims resulting from a purported countermeasure

of countermeasures on overlapping claims, we are concerned with situations in which *State* conduct gives rise to the countermeasure, but the countermeasure is argued to be a good defence to overlapping *individual* claims as well, as shown in Figure 6.1.

Thus, State A takes action that would, if not justifiable as a countermeasure in response to State B's wrongful act, be itself internationally wrongful. Both State B and an individual bring claims alleging breach and seeking reparation. While State A can defend its actions as a valid countermeasure responding to State B's conduct vis-à-vis the claim of State B in scenario (1), the situation is less clear in scenario (2), where the respondent also seeks to defend an overlapping individual claim. Because individual claims necessarily invoke breach of obligations simultaneously owed by the respondent to at least one other State,[23] whenever a countermeasure

Responsibility, Part I (Clarendon 1983) 36; Stern (n 20) 208–9; FV Garcia-Amador, 'International Responsibility: Report' (1956) 2 ILCYB 173, 187.

[23] Ch 1, nn 162–63.

is invoked to defend an individual claim, the question will arise whether an overlapping interstate claim is also precluded.

Historically, it was clear that countermeasures could *affect* individuals, and indeed reprisals (as they used to be known[24]) were commonly directed at individuals and their property precisely as a retaliation for the actions of their State of nationality.[25] While reprisals have since been supplanted by non-forcible countermeasures,[26] and diplomatic protection,[27] one tribunal recently mused 'that countermeasures directed at an offending State will in many, if not most, circumstances have its [*sic*] intended effect on the offending State through its impact on nationals of that offending State.'[28] In *Air Services*, for instance, the US took action vis-à-vis a French carrier in response to France's refusal to allow a US airline to undertake certain flights.[29] The Tribunal accepted this as a proportionate countermeasure, considering, *inter alia*, 'the injuries suffered by the companies concerned' and their respective 'losses'.[30] 'Injury' to the companies in this context apparently means *factual* injury (ie, damage), the Tribunal determining that it was the State's rights that had been breached (and which therefore suffered the *legal* injury).[31] Consequently, it appears that States may legitimately, through countermeasures, cause *damage* to the nationals of another State acting wrongfully.[32]

However, as individual claims mechanisms have emerged on the international plane, a familiar doubt arises regarding whether countermeasures can continue

[24] Paparinskis, 'Countermeasures' (n 8) 268–69; Paddeu, *Justification* (n 8) 226, 228, 250.

[25] See Paddeu, *Justification* (n 8) 228–29, generally 230–35; Roberto Ago, 'Eighth Report on State Responsibility' (1979) 2(1) ILCYB 3, 42; Paparinskis, 'Countermeasures' (n 8) 266, quoting Lassa Oppenheim, *International Law: A Treatise*, vol 2 (Longmans 1905) 38 (reprisals vis-à-vis 'everything that belongs ... to the delinquent State *or its citizens*' (emphasis added)), also 277–78, 324; de Aréchaga (n 22) 553 (sovereign sanctioned a citizen 'to retrieve ... his property or the equivalent of the same, from the subjects of the prince who had denied him justice'); Jessup (n 22) 174–75; Chittharanjan Amerasinghe, *Local Remedies in International Law* (2nd edn, CUP 2004) 25. Generally Zoller (n 12) 36–37; Elagab (n 7) 7–9, 12, 17–23, 29–30, 36; Edwin Borchard, *The Diplomatic Protection of Citizens Abroad: Or, the Law of International Claims* (Banks 1915) 453.

[26] See Alland (n 6) 1130; Ruys (n 7) 12; Paparinskis, 'Countermeasures' (n 8) 268–69; Parlett (n 8) 395; also Paddeu, *Justification* (n 8) 229.

[27] de Aréchaga (n 22) 555; Kate Parlett, *The Individual in the International Legal System: Continuity and Change in International Law* (CUP 2011) 49; Amerasinghe (n 25) 27, 86.

[28] *Cargill* (n 7) [421]; also Parlett (n 8) 404; Anne Peters, *Beyond Human Rights: The Legal Status of the Individual in International Law* (Jonathan Huston tr, CUP 2016) 329–30; Zoller (n 12) 101; Junianto Losari and Michael Ewing-Chow, 'A Clash of Treaties: The Lawfulness of Countermeasures in International Trade Law and International Investment Law' (2015) 16 JWIT 274, 283–84, 294.

[29] *Air Services* (n 10) 420–21, 426; discussion *ARSIWA*, 294–95.

[30] ibid 443–44; also *ARSIWA*, 294–95; White and Abass (n 7) 540–41; Dawidowicz (n 6) 349–51.

[31] See Ch 3, n 58; Ch 1, nn 20ff; also *Corn Products* (n 7) [177]–[178]; Paparinskis, 'Countermeasures' (n 8) 349.

[32] Eg Paparinskis, 'Countermeasures' (n 8) 266, 307, 322–24, 329, 336–37; Martin Dawidowicz, 'Public Law Enforcement without Public Law Safeguards? ...' (2007) 77 BYBIL 333, 365–67, 369, 374–75, 377–79, 393; Dawidowicz (n 6) 129–43, 153–58, 186–91 (fishing/airlines); Losari and Ewing-Chow (n 28) 281–84 (WTO); *Brazil–Export Financing Programme for Aircraft–Arbitrators* (28 August 2000) WT/DS46/ARB [IV.114] (concession suspension countermeasure); *Heathrow Airport Usage Charges (US v UK)* (1992) XXIV UNRIAA 3, 55 ('retaliatory ... charges'); *Guyana v Suriname (Award)* PCA Case 2002-4 (17 September 2007) [446] (against licensee).

to be employed in this way, at least where individual rights would thereby be breached.[33] The starting point for this argument is that countermeasures '"must be directed against" a State which has committed an internationally wrongful act'[34] and 'may only be adopted against a State which is the author of [that] act.'[35] Consequently, countermeasures cannot preclude the wrongfulness of actions taken against *other* States.[36] The ARSIWA commentary acknowledges that countermeasures might 'incidentally affect the position of third States or indeed other third parties', and '[i]f they have no individual rights in the matter they cannot complain.'[37] However:

> where a third State is owed an international obligation by the State taking countermeasures and that obligation is breached by the countermeasure, the wrongfulness of the measure is not precluded as against the third State. In that sense the effect of countermeasures in precluding wrongfulness is relative.[38]

The policy basis is understandable: an 'innocent' State should not be held responsible for wrongful conduct in which it has not engaged.[39] States accept that countermeasures cannot, therefore, infringe the rights of third States.[40] The question here is whether individual nationals of a wrongdoing State are to be treated like such third States, meaning that countermeasures cannot cause legal injury in breach of obligations owed to those individuals, nor preclude their claims for that injury.[41]

33 Authorities n 90.

34 *ARSIWA*, 285, quoting *Gabcikovo* (n 7) [83], also 169; Parlett (n 8) 396.

35 *ARSIWA*, 285; also Martins Paparinskis, 'Investment Treaty Arbitration and the (New) Law of State Responsibility' (2013) 24 EJIL 617, 632; Paparinskis, 'Countermeasures' (n 8) 332; *Corn Products* (n 7) [148].

36 *ARSIWA*, 169, 285; Ago (n 25) [96]–[98]; Dawidowicz (n 6) 288–90.

37 *ARSIWA*, 285; also Parlett (n 8) 397. Different to "third parties" vis-à-vis treaties (see Ch 5, n 382): Paparinskis, 'Countermeasures' (n 8) 333–34; André Nollkaemper, *National Courts and the International Rule of Law* (OUP 2011) 98.

38 *ARSIWA*, 285, also 169. Similarly Parlett (n 8) 396; Elagab (n 7) 34, 111–12; Zoller (n 12) 98; *ADM* (n 7) [4], [7] (Op Rovine); *Corn Products* (n 7) [163]–[164]; *Cargill* (n 7) [422].

39 See *ARSIWA*, 169, referencing *Cysne (Portugal v Germany)* (1930) II UNRIAA 1035, 1056–57, also 190 (art 27(b)), discussed Conclusion, n 96. 'Innocent' terminology is more commonly used vis-à-vis self-defence: see n 378.

40 Zoller (n 12) 99 ('[b]eyond doubt'), 99–102; eg ILC, 'State Responsibility: Comments and observations received from Governments' (1998) UN Doc A/CN.4/488; Add.1–3, 155 (Nordic States/Ireland), 154 (Singapore), referencing ILC, 'Report of the ILC on the Work of Its Thirty-First Session' (1979) 2 ILCYB 1, 120; ILC, 'State Responsibility: Comments and observations received from Governments' (2001) UN Doc A/CN.4/515, 55, 57 (UK/Japan); generally James Crawford, 'Second Report on State Responsibility' (1999) 2(1) ILCYB 1 [381]; cf Elagab (n 7) 111–13.

41 Similarly Peters (n 28) 329, cf 330–31; Paparinskis, 'Countermeasures' (n 8) 332, 336–37; Martins Paparinskis, 'Analogies and Other Regimes of International Law' in Zachary Douglas, Joost Pauwelyn, and Jorge Viñuales (eds), *The Foundations of International Investment Law* (OUP 2014) 102 ('analogized to third states'); van Aaken (n 8) 2, cf *Cargill* (n 7) [422] (effects of countermeasures on nationals not necessarily implying 'legal effects on ... obligations owed directly to [them]'); Comments (n 40) 155 (Ireland: organisations); authorities nn 90ff.

B. Self-defence

As a circumstance precluding wrongfulness, self-defence adopts the definition in article 51 of the UN Charter,[42] which recognises a State's 'inherent right of individual or collective self-defence if an armed attack occurs against [it]'.[43] Self-defence thus responds to an 'armed attack'—a use of armed force of a sufficiently grave nature[44]—with actions taken in self-defence needing to be both necessary and proportionate.[45] Like countermeasures, self-defence accordingly responds to conduct[46] and is a 'self-help' mechanism.[47]

Much discussion of self-defence focuses on its operation vis-à-vis the prohibition on the use of force contained in article 2(4) of the UN Charter,[48] with actions taken in self-defence 'not, even potentially, in breach of [that] Article'.[49] Additionally, however, under ARSIWA article 21, '[s]elf-defence may justify non-performance of certain [other] obligations ... provided that such non-performance is related to the breach of [article 2(4)]'.[50] As Paddeu highlights, it is vis-à-vis claims for breach of these other obligations that self-defence as a circumstance precluding wrongfulness may be invoked.[51] Interstate claims potentially precluded because otherwise wrongful actions are taken in self-defence include those for breach of obligations concerning territorial sovereignty or non-intervention, the law of the sea, and trade and commerce.[52]

[42] *ARSIWA*, 166–67; Crawford, *GP* (n 7) 289.

[43] UN Charter, art 51.

[44] See *Oil Platforms (Iran v USA) (Judgment)* [2003] ICJ Rep 161 [64], [72]; *Military and Paramilitary Activities in and against Nicaragua (Nicaragua v US) (Merits)* [1986] ICJ Rep 14 [191]; discussion Christine Gray, *International Law and the Use of Force* (4th edn, OUP 2018) 150–57; Tams, 'Terrorists' (n 8) 369–70; Christopher Greenwood, 'Self-Defence' in *MPEPIL* (n 15) (2011) [12]; Olivier Corten, *The Law against War: The Prohibition on the Use of Force in Contemporary International Law* (Christopher Sutcliffe tr, Hart 2010) 403.

[45] *Nicaragua (Merits)* (n 44) [176]; Greenwood, 'Self-Defence' (n 44) [8], [25]–[29]; Gray (n 44) 157–64.

[46] Ch 1, n 150; Alland (n 6) 1132. Cf *Oppenheim's* (n 22) 417–18 (fn 3) ('wider sense' against natural forces).

[47] Yoram Dinstein, *War, Aggression and Self-Defence* (6th edn, CUP 2017) [534]–[535]; also DW Bowett, *Self-Defence in International Law* (MUP 1958) 3–4, cf 11; cf Zoller (n 12) 40–41; Tams, 'Terrorists' (n 8) 372.

[48] Eg, Noam Lubell, *Extraterritorial Use of Force Against Non-State Actors* (OUP 2010) 25–26; Greenwood, 'Self-Defence' (n 44) [4]; Tams, 'Terrorists' (n 8) 360–62; Bowett (n 47) 22–24; generally nn 362–79, 386; similarly Paddeu, *Justification* (n 8) 176, 187–89. See UN Charter, art 2(4) (States to 'refrain in their international relations from the threat or use of force against the territorial integrity or political independence of any state ...').

[49] *ARSIWA*, 166; similarly Greenwood, 'Self-Defence' (n 44) [4]; Federica Paddeu, 'Use of Force against Non-State Actors and the Circumstance Precluding Wrongfulness of Self-Defence' (2017) 30 Leid JIL 93, 99–102; Paddeu, *Justification* (n 8) 177–78, 189, 194–97; Bowett (n 47) 185–86; Corten, *War* (n 44) 402; Crawford, *GP* (n 7) 290.

[50] *ARSIWA*, 166; see Paddeu, *Justification* (n 8) 175, 192, 197–205; Paddeu, 'Force' (n 49) 102–4.

[51] Paddeu, *Justification* (n 8) 175–205; Paddeu, 'Force' (n 49) 102–4. Cf Greenwood, 'Self-Defence' (n 44) [4].

[52] Paddeu, *Justification* (n 8) 176–77, 182–83, 197–205 (with references); Crawford, *GP* (n 7) 290; eg *Oil Platforms* (n 44) [25]–[26], [37], [43]–[44], [77]–[79]; *Nicaragua (Merits)* (n 44) [221]–[224]. See nn 386ff, section IV(B)(ii)

Regarding *individual* claims, no reported claim under international law appears to have yet been held precluded on self-defence grounds, though the success of one such claim depended on the legality of action purportedly taken in self-defence.[53] Nonetheless, self-defence could well become relevant in individual claims, given that States exercising self-defence will commonly harm individuals,[54] and individuals have made claims for violations of international law arising from States' exercises of force.[55]

More particularly, self-defence could be relevant to individual claims under both human rights and investment law.

First, human rights obligations and those under international humanitarian law apply in armed conflict.[56] Human rights norms protect individuals from arbitrary deprivation of life,[57] though such deprivation will not be arbitrary if it is in compliance with international humanitarian law.[58] Self-defence cannot, in any event, excuse violations of human rights norms nor of those under international humanitarian law.[59] However, it could nonetheless be relevant to a claim for breach of such obligations: the Human Rights Committee (HRC) has recently outlined that 'acts of aggression as defined in international law, resulting in deprivation of life, violate ipso facto article 6 of the [International Covenant on Civil and Political Rights (ICCPR)]', on the right to life, implying that a deprivation will be considered arbitrary, and thus in breach of human rights norms, if the requirements of the *jus ad bellum* are unmet—ie, where force has been unlawfully used.[60] With States relying

[53] *Coenca Brothers v Germany* (1927) 7 TAM 683 (Greco-German MAT) 686–88, cited Cheng (n 20) 88; also Timothy Guideu, 'Defending America's Cambodian Incursion' (1994) 11 Ariz JICL 215, 223–24.

[54] See *Chemical Weapons Deployment* (1987) 106 ILR 389 (BVerfG) 395–96; Jessup (n 22) 211–12; Dinstein (n 47) [478]; eg Gray (n 44) 213; discussion Christoph Schreuer, 'The Protection of Investments in Armed Conflict' in Freya Baetens (ed), *Investment Law within International Law: Integrationist Perspectives* (CUP 2013) 13–16 Indeed, international humanitarian law dictates when individuals cannot be harmed: eg, ICRC, 'Introduction', *Customary IHL Database* <https://ihl-databases.icrc.org/customary-ihl/eng/docs/v1_cha_chapterin_in>; Philip Alston, 'Study on Targeted Killings' UN Doc A/HRC/124/24/Add.6 (28 May 2010) [30], [57]–[67].

[55] Eg, Ch 2, nn 175, 182–83, 207–8; Schreuer (n 54) 6–10, 15–16; Sean Murphy, Won Kidane, and Thomas Snider, *Litigating War: Arbitration of Civil Injury by the Eritrea-Ethiopia Claims Commission* (OUP 2013) 39; Nollkaemper (n 37) 12.

[56] *ARSIWA*, 166; also ILC, 'Draft Articles on the Effects of Armed Conflicts on Treaties, with Commentaries' (2011) 2(2) ILCYB 108 (DAEAC), Ann (f), 126–27.

[57] ICCPR, art 6; AmCHR, art 4; AfCHPR, art 4; also ECHR, art 2 ('force . . . absolutely necessary'); eg, *Giuliani and Gaggio v Italy* ECHR 2011-II 275 (GC) [298] ('general legal prohibition of arbitrary killing').

[58] *Legality of the Threat or Use of Nuclear Weapons* [1996] ICJ Rep 226 [25]; also *Legal Consequences of the Construction of a Wall in the Occupied Palestinian Territory (Advisory Opinion)* [2004] ICJ Rep 136 [105]–[106]; Parlett (n 27) 194–95; Hans van Houtte, Bart Delmartino, and Iasson Yi, *Post-War Restoration of Property Rights Under International Law*, vol 1 (CUP 2008) 247–49.

[59] *ARSIWA*, 166; Paddeu, *Justification* (n 8) 175–76, 198–99; Paddeu, 'Force' (n 49) 104.

[60] HRC, 'General Comment No. 36' UN Doc CCPR/C/GC/36 (3 September 2019) [70], see generally [64], [67], [69]. Further: State practice and authorities in support reproduced Ka Lok Yip, 'Written Contribution to the General Discussion' (14 July 2015) <https://www.ohchr.org/Documents/HRBodies/CCPR/Discussion/2015/KaLokYip.doc> [11]–[13], particularly Derek Jinks, 'International Human Rights Law in Time of Armed Conflict' in Andrew Clapham and Paola Gaeta (eds), *The Oxford Handbook of International Law in Armed Conflict* (OUP 2014) 668; also Marko Milanovic and Sangeeta

on self-defence in situations giving rise to individual human rights claims,[61] whether actions are indeed undertaken in self-defence could become relevant to whether force was lawfully used, and thus to such claims' success.[62]

Second, investment treaties are presumed to remain in force during armed conflicts.[63] Cases before investment tribunals have concerned alleged bilateral investment treaty (BIT) breaches resulting from State action during civil war,[64] and relating to the Russia/Ukraine conflict.[65] It is certainly foreseeable that a State might argue that BIT violations resulted from actions taken in self-defence within its territory:[66] for instance, as justifying failure to protect an investment from violence in breach of a 'full protection and security' provision,[67] or as justifying requisition of property in breach of obligations not to expropriate.[68] Self-defence

Shah, 'Ukraine and the Netherlands v. Russia (Nos 8019/16, 43800/14, 28525/20, 11055/22): Amicus Curiae Brief' (2023) <https://papers.ssrn.com/sol3/papers.cfm?abstract_id=4427214> [28] (with authorities, disagreeing with approach). Self-defence might also be invoked where international humanitarian law is inapplicable: see Marko Milanovic, 'More on Drones, Self-Defense, and the Alston Report on Targeted Killings' *EJIL:Talk!* (5 June 2010); Alston (n 54) [28]–[33], [44], [50], [56], [86]; also Claus Kress, 'Some Reflections on the International Legal Framework Governing Transnational Armed Conflicts' (2010) 15 JC & SL 245, 259–64; Gray (n 44) 233–37.

61 See, vis-à-vis Ethiopia/Eritrea: *Jus Ad Bellum–Ethiopia's Claims 1–8 (Partial Award)* (2005) XXVI UNRIAA 457 [11]–[12], [14], [17], [19]; Russia/Georgia: *Application of the International Convention on the Elimination of All Forms of Racial Discrimination (Georgia v Russia) (Preliminary Objections)* [2011] ICJ Rep 70 [108]; Gray (n 44) 168–69; generally Corten, *War* (n 44) 465; Russia/Ukraine: Daniel Wisehart, 'The Crisis in Ukraine and the Prohibition of the Use of Force: A Legal Basis for Russia's Intervention?' *EJIL:Talk!* (4 March 2014).

62 See Marko Milanovic, 'The European Court's Admissibility Decision in Ukraine and the Netherlands v Russia: The Good, the Bad and the Ugly—Part II' *EJIL:Talk!* (26 January 2023) (whether aggression 'should matter in the human rights justifiability analysis'). Cf *R (Gentle and Clarke) v Prime Minister* (2006) 132 ILR 721 (EWCA) [41]–[51] (right to life does not imply obligation to ensure legality of military operations).

63 See Schreuer (n 54) 4–5, referencing DAEAC, see arts 5–7, Ann (e), also 124–26. Similarly Gleider Hernández, 'The Interaction between Investment Law and the Law of Armed Conflict in the Interpretation of Full Protection and Security Clauses' in Baetens (n 54) 31–32; Paddeu, 'Force' (n 49) 99; Paddeu, *Justification* (n 8) 181–82.

64 *AAPL v Sri Lanka (Award)* (1991) 6 ICSID Rev-FILJ 526 [8], [62], [79]–[86], see [63]–[64] (considering necessity), discussed Schreuer (n 54) 8–11, 14–15; Hernández (n 63) 36–37.

65 See G Matteo Vaccaro-Incisa, 'Crimea Investment Disputes: Are Jurisdictional Hurdles Being Overcome Too Easily?' *EJIL:Talk!* (9 May 2018); Jarrod Hepburn and Ridhi Kabra, 'Investigation: Further Russia Investment Treaty Decisions Uncovered …' *IA Rep* (17 November 2017); Ch 2, n 198.

66 BITs are usually territorially limited (n 224), and self-defence may require action within the host State's territory: Bowett (n 47) 23–24; Ruys (n 21) 185–87; also Cheng (n 20) 87; n 68.

67 On such clauses and conflict: Schreuer (n 54) 6–10; Hernández (n 63) 33–43; *AAPL* (n 64) [7], [43], [46]ff; also Pierre-Emmanuel Dupont, 'The Arbitration of Disputes Related to Foreign Investments Affected by Unilateral Sanctions' in Ali Marossi and Marisa Bassett (eds), *Economic Sanctions under International Law: Unilateralism, Multilateralism, Legitimacy and Consequences* (Asser 2015) 205; Caroline Henckels, 'Investment Treaty Security Exceptions, Necessity and Self-Defence in the Context of Armed Conflict' (2018) <https://papers.ssrn.com/sol3/papers.cfm?abstract_id=3136191>, 10–11.

68 Considering self-defence vis-à-vis requisition: Bowett (n 47) 23–24; cf Cheng (n 20) 40–49; Paddeu, *Justification* (n 8) 184; similarly Arnold McNair, *International Law Opinions*, vol II (OUP 1956) 231–32 (necessity); Dawidowicz (n 32) 372–73, 407 (self-defence asset freeze); generally Ruys (n 7) 12 ('economic sanctions' self-defence); cf Federica Paddeu, 'Self-Defence as a Circumstance Precluding Wrongfulness: Understanding Article 21 of the Articles on State Responsibility' (2015) 85 BYBIL

might, therefore, be invoked to preclude individual claims under investment law.[69]

So much for the interstate and individual claims vis-à-vis which a respondent State *might* invoke self-defence. Turning to the question of to *whose* conduct self-defence responds, like countermeasures, self-defence is a concept that has commonly been of relevance between States.[70] States can thus clearly invoke self-defence in response to armed attacks by *States* (including those undertaken by individuals whose conduct is attributable to the attacking State), and to defend any resulting claims by those States.[71] What is less clear is whether, like countermeasures, self-defence can *only* be exercised against (ie, in response to an attack by) States: as elaborated below, debates continue regarding whether States can respond to attacks emanating from individual non-State actors.[72] *If*, however, States can respond in self-defence to attacks initiated by individuals, then the practice vis-à-vis

90, section III(A)(1); and on 'war clauses': Schreuer (n 54) 13–16; similarly Noradele Radjai, Laura Halonen, and Panagiotis Kyriakou, 'An Analysis of the Compensation Regime Applicable to Claims Arising from Armed Conflicts Affecting Investments in MENA' (2016) 3 BCDRIAR 219, 231ff; Criddle (n 8) 600. On expropriation, section III(A)(ii)(b); vis-à-vis conflict: eg: *Ports—Ethiopia's Claim 6* (2005) XXVI UNRIAA 489 [10], [27]; *Partial Award: Civilian Claims—Eritrea's Claims 15, 16, 23 and 27–32* (2004) XXVI UNRIAA 195 [124]–[125], [152]. International humanitarian law allows requisition in some circumstances: ICRC, 'Rule 51: Public and Private Property in Occupied Territory', *Customary IHL Database* (n 54); *Ports* (n 68) [23]–[31]; *Ethiopia's Damages Claims (Final Award)* (2009) XXVI UNRIAA 631 [455]; *Eritrea (Civilian)* (n 68) [123]–[129], [146], [151]–[152]; discussion Murphy, Kidane, and Snider (n 55) 345ff; Criddle (n 8) 599–601; also Borchard (n 25) 109–15, 246–55, 262–70. However, self-defence remains potentially relevant: (1) international humanitarian law may not apply: cf n 60; (2) the relationship with investment law might be unclear: Radjai, Halonen, and Kyriakou (n 68) 225; cf Hernández (n 63) 25–29 (*lex specialis*); Schreuer (n 54) 14; cf n 60; (3) investment law may impact reparation: van Houtte, Delmartino, and Yi (n 58) 225; also Schreuer (n 54) 14; Radjai, Halonen, and Kyriakou (n 68) 225–29, 233–34; Paparinskis, 'New' (n 35) 632–33; cf n 78.

[69] On self-defence and exception clauses: *Oil Platforms* (n 44) [40]–[43]; *Nicaragua (Merits)* (n 44) [224]; generally Henckels (n 67), particularly 7–10; Schreuer (n 54) 16–18. Discussing the custom/exception clause relationship: eg Peter Tomka, 'Defences Based on Necessity under Customary International Law and on Emergency Clauses in Bilateral Investment Treaties' in Meg Kinnear and others (eds), *Building International Investment Law: The First 50 Years of ICSID* (Kluwer 2016) 485–87 and authorities; Henckels (n 67) 3–12.

[70] See Ian Brownlie, *International Law and the Use of Force by States* (OUP 1963) 375, 278–79; Paddeu, 'Force' (n 49) 94; Lindsay Moir, 'Action Against Host States of Terrorist Groups' in Marc Weller (ed), *The Oxford Handbook of the Use of Force in International Law* (OUP 2015) 720; Corten, *War* (n 44) 126, 172–74; Christopher Greenwood, 'International Law and the Pre-Emptive Use of Force: Afghanistan, Al-Qaida, and Iraq' (2003) 4 SDILJ 7, 16; Greenwood, 'Self-Defence' (n 44) [17]; Gray (n 44) 134–35, 207; James Crawford, 'The Relationship between Sanctions and Countermeasures' in Vera Gowlland-Debbas (ed), *United Nations Sanctions and International Law* (Kluwer 2001) 67.

[71] See, eg, Greenwood, 'Self-Defence' (n 44) [16]; Kimberley Trapp, 'Can Non-State Actors Mount an Armed Attack?' in Weller (n 70) 680; Ruys (n 21) 371–72, 408; Lubell (n 48) 38, also 26; generally nn480ff.

[72] See authorities section IV; generally Lubell (n 48) 25–36; Corten, *War* (n 44) 405–6; Miles Jackson, *Complicity in International Law* (OUP 2015) Ch 8.3; Christian Tams, 'The Use of Force against Terrorists: A Rejoinder to Federico Sperotto and Kimberley N. Trapp' (2009) 20 EJIL 1057, 1059; Paddeu, 'Force' (n 49) 95–97; Greenwood, 'Self-Defence' (n 44) [15]ff; Daniel Bethlehem, 'Self-Defense Against an Imminent or Actual Armed Attack by Nonstate Actors' (2012) 106 AJIL 769, 773; Ashley Deeks, '"Unwilling or Unable": Toward a Normative Framework for Extraterritorial Self-Defense' (2012) 52 Virg JIL 483, 492–93.

other circumstances precluding wrongfulness would suggest that States could defend claims brought by those individuals on this basis.[73]

But what about overlapping claims? Could a respondent State argue that self-defence in response to an attack by an individual (if possible at all) is a good defence also to an *interstate* claim, and that self-defence in response to an attack by a State is a good defence also to an *individual* claim?[74]

For the former, the answer will apparently depend, as Paddeu sets out, on whether self-defence can, *unlike* countermeasures, justify violations of third-party rights (in this case, the rights of the State).[75] While countermeasures and self-defence are outwardly similar in nature, in that both respond to a "wrong",[76] this chapter argues that the two do indeed operate differently in this respect, with implications for their operation vis-à-vis overlapping claims.[77]

For the latter, it certainly appears that a State responding in self-defence to an attack by another State will not be responsible to that State for *damage* thereby caused to its nationals.[78] It should follow that, as for countermeasures, individuals' claims could be precluded insofar as they are not brought for those individuals' own legal injury but invoke obligations owed only between the relevant States.[79] However, should individuals make claims invoking their own rights under international law,[80] then—as in the countermeasures context—the question will arise whether self-defence can justify third-party rights violations (in this case, the rights of the individual).[81]

In sum, unlike countermeasures which are only potentially relevant to overlapping claims on one level—being invoked in response to *State* action—the possibility of self-defence responding to attacks by individuals means it is at least potentially relevant on *two* levels—being invoked in response to both State and individual action to preclude overlapping claims. We are thus concerned with *four* potential overlapping claims scenarios in which self-defence might potentially

[73] See n 499.

[74] As for countermeasures, because individual claims necessarily overlap with at least one interstate claim, the question of overlapping interstate preclusion will *always* arise: text surrounding n 23.

[75] See Paddeu, 'Force' (n 49) 100, 105–6, 110–15 and discussion nn 89ff, section IV(B).

[76] nn 7–8, 43–47, 402; Alland (n 6) 1132.

[77] nn 402ff.

[78] Eg the EECC held that Eritrea had breached art 2(4) and that Ethiopia had acted in self-defence: *Claims 1–8* (n 61) [14]–[19]. Eritrea was subsequently held liable for all damage 'proximately caused' thereby (*Ethiopia* (n 68) [291]), including partially consequent on *Ethiopia's* conduct (ibid [293]–[296], [299], [303]–[305]), and by actions not violating international humanitarian law: ibid [311]. Apparently, Ethiopia (acting in self-defence) was not responsible for damage it had caused. Further: Murphy, Kidane, and Snider (n 55) 115–19, 133–51; van Houtte, Delmartino, and Yi (n 58) 237–38. Suggesting no compensation is due to nationals of neutrals during war: *Eastern Extension, Australasia and China Telegraph* (1923) 2 ILR 415 (UK–US Claims Tribunal) 417–18; Alexander Orakhelashvili, 'Overlap and Convergence: The Interaction between Jus Ad Bellum and Jus in Bello' (2007) 12 JC & SL 157, 186–87 and authorities.

[79] cf nn 25ff.

[80] nn 90ff.

[81] See Paparinskis, 'Countermeasures' (n 8) 342; section IV and authorities; cf nn 94–99.

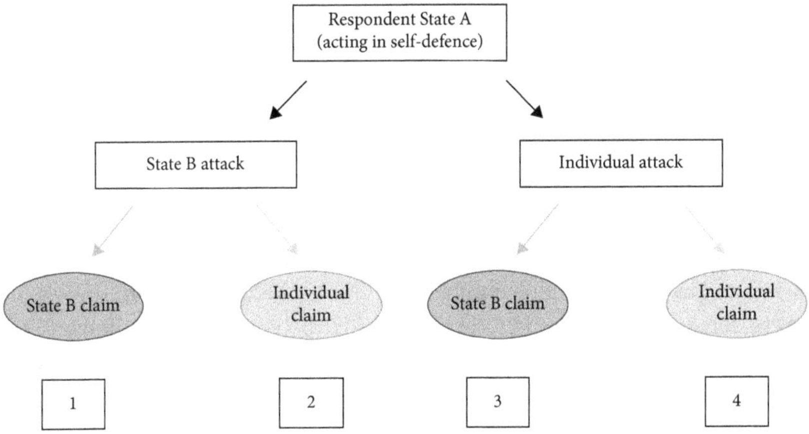

Figure 6.2 Potential overlapping individual and interstate claims resulting from a purported exercise of self-defence in response to an attack by either a State or an individual non-State actor

operate, two vis-à-vis attacks by individuals and two vis-à-vis attacks by States, as Figure 6.2 shows.

Self-defence can clearly operate in scenario (1) and allow a State to defend itself against a claim by another, attacking, State. Questions surround the other three.[82] Scenario (2) represents an overlapping claim made by an individual, non-attacking, entity. Insofar as individuals invoke their own rights under international law in making such claims, they could apparently only be precluded if self-defence can justify third-party rights violations.[83] Self-defence's operation with respect to individual claims in scenario (4) depends on whether States can invoke self-defence in response to attacks by individuals to preclude those individuals' claims.[84] And the outcome in scenario (3) depends on the answer to both of these questions—whether a respondent can invoke self-defence in response to individual attacks, *and* in a way that would preclude the claim of a third-party State invoking its own rights under international law.

C. Summary

For both countermeasures and self-defence, limitations on their potential operation in the overlapping claims context appear to derive largely from the contention

[82] cf Brownlie (n 70) 375.
[83] n 81.
[84] See section IV.

that these defences can only preclude the wrongfulness of legal injury vis-à-vis the entity whose conduct has given rise to the operation of the relevant defence, ie the entity in breach of its obligations (countermeasures), or undertaking an 'armed attack' (self-defence).[85] This chapter now examines whether, and to what extent, such limitations are reflected in practice. It also addresses whether self-defence can respond to attacks by individuals. However, as will be seen, this issue boils down largely to a question of third-party rights as well.[86]

Given that individuals sometimes 'pose an equal or greater threat to public order' than States,[87] this chapter argues that we should hesitate in limiting the use of these defences to States, and rather be open to their exercise in response to certain individual actions, and to preclude certain individual claims, including where those individuals are implicated in the relevant wrongful conduct.[88] Each defence is now considered in turn.

III. Countermeasures and third parties

Addressing the question of countermeasures and individual claims, scholars overwhelmingly take what might be described as a 'third-party rights approach',[89] considering that countermeasures may preclude wrongfulness vis-à-vis individuals and their claims where the allegedly wrongdoing State's rights alone are violated, but not if those individuals invoke their own 'individual rights' under international law.[90] They often point to three investment tribunal decisions which accepted that interstate countermeasures cannot affect individuals' rights under BITs.[91] These cases concerned Mexican allegations that a corn syrup tax

[85] nn 75, 81.

[86] nn 374ff.

[87] Jacob Katz Cogan, 'The Regulatory Turn in International Law' (2011) 52 Harv ILJ 321, 330, also 344–45; authorities n 359.

[88] Sections III–IV and authorities therein.

[89] For 'third parties' language: n 37; also Paparinskis, 'Countermeasures' (n 8) 332–33, 344 ('quasi-third party' more accurate) and referencing, *inter alia*, Christine Chinkin, *Third Parties in International Law* (OUP 1993) 13–14; Paddeu, *Justification* (n 8) 278–79. Cf Criddle's 'intermediate approach', n 108; Peters, n 107; n 287; 'rights-based' terminology, used in human rights: eg, OHCHR, *Frequently Asked Questions on a Human Rights-Based Approach to Development Cooperation* (UN 2006).

[90] Parlett (n 8) 397 (emphasis removed, discussing *ARSIWA*, 285), also 398–403; Parlett (n 27) 110–11, 116; Paparinskis, 'Countermeasures' (n 8) 268, 332, 336–37; Paparinskis, 'New' (n 35) 632; van Aaken (n 8) 2; Ruys (n 7) 13; Criddle (n 8) 598; Dupont, 'Investments' (n 67) 210–11; also Paddeu, *Justification* (n 8) 278–79; n 96; cf Anthea Roberts, 'Triangular Treaties: The Extent and Limits of Investment Treaty Rights' (2015) 56 Harv ILJ 353, 356, 357 ('more nuanced'), 400–2; Losari and Ewing-Chow (n 28) 296, 302–3; Peters, n 107.

[91] Eg Parlett (n 8) 397–404; Parlett (n 27) 116–18; Paparinskis, 'New' (n 35) 632; Paparinskis, 'Countermeasures' (n 8) 335–36; van Aaken (n 8) 2; Dupont, 'Investments' (n 67) 210–11; Peters (n 28) 329. See *Corn Products* (n 7) [162], [165], [176]; *ADM* (n 7) [127], [180]; also [5]–[15], [80], [82]–[83] (Op Rovine); *Cargill* (n 7) [424]–[429], [553], also [387].

was a valid countermeasure against the US, responding to its wrongful conduct in, *inter alia*, refusing Mexican sugar producers market access.[92] As noted above, when claims relating to the tax were brought against Mexico by US investors, Mexico alleged that its actions *also* constituted a valid countermeasure vis-à-vis those individuals, precluding the successful bringing of their claims under NAFTA.[93]

Engaging in the debate introduced in Chapter 4 regarding whether rights under investment treaties are 'direct' (owed to individuals as such), or 'derivative' (owed to the State and only enforced by individuals),[94] two tribunals held that rights under NAFTA were owed directly to individuals, and thus not subject to interstate countermeasures.[95] The other tribunal held that those rights were interstate only, and so in theory subject to countermeasures.[96] Each tribunal accepted, however, that *if* individuals held rights under BITs, countermeasures could not be used to preclude breach thereof, and any consequent individual claim.[97] By parity of reasoning, countermeasures could not be used to preclude the wrongfulness of human rights violations, with those rights belonging to individuals.[98] Thus, while countermeasures can be taken against States in a manner causing individual *damage*,[99] they cannot preclude individual claims, on this approach, insofar as individuals' own rights under international law are violated.

Human rights treaties give rise to particular considerations, and are examined separately below.[100] For investment law, notwithstanding the position taken in the literature and the majority of these NAFTA cases, Chapter 5 outlined that States appear overwhelmingly *not* to accept that individuals are 'third parties' under the law of treaties in this field, with a large cross-section of such States prepared to

[92] *ADM* (n 7) [4], [88]–[89], [106], [110]; *Corn Products* (n 7) [150]; *Mexico–Tax Measures on Soft Drinks–Panel Rep* (7 October 2005) WT/DS308/R [8.162], [8.176]–[8.180], [8.186]–[8.190] (defending WTO claim); Parlett (n 8) 397; Joost Pauwelyn, 'Adding Sweeteners to Softwood Lumber: The WTO-NAFTA "Spaghetti Bowl" Is Cooking' (2006) 9 JIEL 197, 199.

[93] *ADM* (n 7) [4], [106], [110], [127]; *Corn Products* (n 7) [151]; see Roberts (n 90) 386; Paparinskis, 'Countermeasures' (n 8) 276; Losari and Ewing-Chow (n 28) 287–94.

[94] Ch 4, n 158. See *ADM* (n 7) [161]–[180]; *Corn Products* (n 7) [153]–[176]; *Cargill* (n 7) [415]–[416], [424]–[426]; Paparinskis, 'Countermeasures' (n 8) 336–37; Losari and Ewing-Chow (n 28) 288–91; Parlett (n 8) 398–404. Suggesting 'substantive'/'procedural' rights indistinguishable: *ADM* (n 7) [47]–[49] (Op Rovine); also *Cargill* (n 7) [426]. Cf *ADM* (n 7) [179]–[180]; Ch 1(III).

[95] *Corn Products* (n 7) [161], [167] ('substantive rights separate and distinct from ... State'), [174], [176]; *Cargill* (n 7) [424]–[429]; discussion Paparinskis, 'Countermeasures' (n 8) 275, 335–36; Parlett (n 8) 399–404; also *ADM* (n 7) [12] (Op Rovine), quoting *ARSIWA*, 210.

[96] *ADM* (n 7) [171] (no 'individual rights'), [180] (nonetheless countermeasure 'not ... valid'), cf [5], [43]ff, [77]–[80], [82]–[83] (Op Rovine); discussion Paparinskis, 'Countermeasures' (n 8) 275, 335–36; Parlett (n 8) 398–99.

[97] n 91.

[98] Paparinskis, 'Countermeasures' (n 8) 329, 332–34; van Aaken (n 8) 2; also *ADM* (n 7) [170]–[171]; cf section III(A)(ii)(a).

[99] nn 25ff.

[100] nn 351–56.

modify and revoke rights under investment treaties, both substantive and concerning the capacity to claim, without the consent of the individual beneficiaries thereof.[101] If correct, it would appear unlikely that individuals do indeed possess their own rights thereunder.[102]

Countermeasures properly taken against a State of nationality would, accordingly, be equally effective against individual nationals and their claims brought pursuant to such treaties.[103] There is, however, a paucity of practice specifically relating to countermeasures and individual claims, including under investment law. There has, however, in recent decades and particularly in recent years, been an explosion of practice relating to 'sanctions' in which States take actions which, as will be seen below, may plausibly be regarded as countermeasures, and which may plausibly breach investment law.[104] This book looks to this practice as an indirect indication of whether States do indeed regard individuals as 'third parties' under such treaties for the purposes of the customary international law of countermeasures, or at least as an indication of the direction in which custom may be developing in this respect.[105]

As will be seen, this practice suggests that States regard at least certain countermeasures responding to a State's conduct as effective to also preclude the claims of that State's nationals under investment law. This could be, consistently with the findings of Chapter 5, because those States simply do not regard investment treaties as creating individual rights which are immune from otherwise legitimate countermeasures against the State of nationality.[106] Given, however, that the majority of investment tribunals faced with this question—albeit only three to date—have not shared that view, it may leave States open, as shown below, to claims for violations of investment law.

Consequently, it is suggested that a second, narrower, argument might also be derived from the practice, namely that *even if* individuals possess their own rights under investment treaties, the third-party rights approach goes too far in assuming that *all* individuals really are 'third parties' vis-à-vis States for countermeasures purposes and that such measures cannot, consequently, affect their rights.[107] The argument builds on an observation made by Criddle in the context of asset freezes:

[101] Ch 5, nn 382ff.
[102] As explained Ch 5, nn 381ff.
[103] See n 25ff.
[104] Section III(A).
[105] See nn 107–10ff, 287.
[106] cf nn 94–99.
[107] nn 37–41; similarly nn 108–10, 287, 322, 514; cf Peters (n 28) 330 ('investors ... sometimes ... at fault for breaches of international law'; '"third parties" ... should only include uninvolved third parties, such as ... nationals of third-party States'; 'not all kinds of rights should enjoy equal protection'), 331 ('intermediate solution'; compensation payable), 312; also Roberts (n 90) 356, 399–402.

> that an intermediate approach may be emerging in state practice. Even if states generally may not target private foreign assets when imposing countermeasures, the intermediate approach suggests that states may freeze the private assets of foreign officials who bear direct responsibility for a target state's internationally wrongful conduct.[108]

Referring to certain measures directed at government regimes, but targeting 'public officials who directed or carried out [human rights] abuses',[109] he argues:

> In effect, these countermeasures struck a compromise between the derivative-rights theory and the direct-rights theory: they preserved direct-rights style investment protection for ordinary foreign investors, while treating the private property of regime leaders as constructively 'public assets' that were valid targets for interstate countermeasures. Further study will be necessary to confirm whether this growing body of state practice meets the generality and *opinio juris* requirements for customary international law. Nonetheless, the early returns suggest that the law of countermeasures may be evolving to permit host states to freeze not only the public assets of rights-abusing states but also, at a minimum, the private assets of public officials who orchestrate or carry out a target state's internationally wrongful conduct.[110]

This chapter argues that practice does seem to suggest that at least certain individuals might be treated as akin to the State for countermeasures purposes. If practice continues in this vein, there would be a good argument that where the State has acted in breach of international law resulting in the application of countermeasures against it, those countermeasures could *also* be employed to preclude certain individual treaty-based claims *even if* the relevant individuals possess rights under those treaties.[111]

A. Countermeasures: an alternative to the third-party rights approach?

Difficulties in evaluating State practice in the countermeasures context are plentiful because, *inter alia*, States seldom actually characterise their actions as

[108] Criddle (n 8) 598.
[109] ibid.
[110] ibid 598–99, also 609–10.
[111] Cf nn 351–56 (human rights).

countermeasures,[112] and not all States employ such practices.[113] Nonetheless, this section examines actions that:

(i) purport to respond to a State's internationally wrongful conduct; and
(ii) would, but for being defensible, arguably themselves be unlawful,

and could potentially therefore be characterised as countermeasures.[114] Like Criddle, this section concentrates on asset freezes because, as elucidated below, they appear most likely to violate obligations under the international investment law treaties said to establish individual rights.[115] Moreover, with custom established by practice that is 'sufficiently widespread and representative, as well as consistent',[116] together with the requisite *opinio juris*,[117] the focus is on measures taken by multiple States.[118] In particular, consideration is given to 'sanctions'[119] insofar as that term refers to measures taken outside of the United

[112] Dawidowicz (n 6) 14, 112, 251, referencing Antonios Tzanakopoulos, *Disobeying the Security Council: Countermeasures Against Wrongful Sanctions* (OUP 2011) 188–89; Dawidowicz (n 32) 349–50, 407, 412–15; Ruys (n 7) 24. My thanks here to Franchini. For exceptions: n 93; *Application of the Interim Accord of 13 September 1995 (Macedonia v Greece)* [2011] ICJ Rep 644 [114], [120]–[122]; *Gabcikovo* (n 7) [69], [82]–[83]; *Guyana v Suriname* (n 32) [270], [446]. Procedurally, while *ARSIWA*, art 52(1) requires that the acting State call upon the other to fulfil its obligations, notify it of countermeasures, and offer to negotiate, these requirements are met through the adoption of the legal acts discussed below and associated diplomatic efforts, without needing to actually call those acts countermeasures: see Dawidowicz (n 6) 377–79; Tzanakopoulos (n 112) 188. In any event, asset freezes could be regarded as 'urgent countermeasures' under art 52(3), not subject to notification requirements: Dawidowicz (n 6) 379; *ARSIWA*, 298–99. Cf Pierre-Emmanuel Dupont, 'Countermeasures and Collective Security: The Case of the EU Sanctions Against Iran' (2012) 17 JC & SL 301, 324–25, 331–32.

[113] Dawidowicz (n 32) 409–12; cf n 337.

[114] Similarly ibid 349–50; Dawidowicz (n 6) 111–231, 253, 263–68, 287–88; Criddle (n 8) 595–99, cf 584, 599–603 (other asset freeze justifications); Ruys (n 7) 5, 24; Pierre-Emmanuel Dupont, 'Unilateral European Sanctions as Countermeasures: The Case of the EU Measures Against Iran' in Matthew Happold and Paul Eden (eds), *Economic Sanctions and International Law* (Hart 2016) 40–41, 51–63; also Alland (n 6) 1131–32; White and Abass (n 7) 540; Frédéric Dopagne, 'Sanctions and Countermeasures by International Organizations: Diverging Lessons for the Idea of Autonomy' in Richard Collins and Nigel White (eds), *International Organizations and the Idea of Autonomy* (Routledge 2011) 180; Lesaffre (n 7) 469, 471; Linos-Alexandre Sicilianos, 'Countermeasures in Response to Grave Violations of Obligations Owed to the International Community' in Crawford and others, *Responsibility* (n 6) 1145; Elagab (n 7) 44; Ruys (n 7) 5; Pellet and Miron (n 15) [65]; Paparinskis, 'Countermeasures' (n 8) 269. On 'retorsion': Ruys (n 7) 5; Dawidowicz (n 32) 349–50; Dawidowicz (n 6) 27–31; White and Abass (n 7) 544; also Alland (n 6) 1131; Dupont, 'Unilateral' (n 114) 41–42, 45–46.

[115] Criddle (n 8) 584–86; similarly Matthew Happold, 'Targeted Sanctions and Human Rights' in Happold and Eden (n 114) 90; section III(A)(ii)(b). Other sanctions, including travel bans, are not considered: see, eg, Happold (n 115) 96–98; Marko Milanovic, 'Sayadi: The Human Rights Committee's Kadi (or a Pretty Poor Excuse for One . . .)' *EJIL:Talk!* (29 January 2009).

[116] ILC 'Draft conclusions on identification of customary international law, with commentaries' (2018) 2(2) ILCYB 122, Conc 8.

[117] ibid Conc 2, 124–25; Conc 9–10, 138–42.

[118] Authorities n 337. Generally Dawidowicz (n 6) 240–55; Dawidowicz (n 32) 414–15.

[119] Generally Pellet and Miron (n 15) [7]; Ruys (n 7) 1–3; White and Abass (n 7) 552–55; Vera Gowlland-Debbas, 'UN Sanctions and International Law: An Overview' in Gowlland-Debbas (n 70) 4; Georges Abi-Saab, 'The Concept of Sanction in International Law' in Gowlland-Debbas (n 70) 30–33, 39.

Nations (UN) Security Council framework.[120] Being permitted under the UN Charter, Security Council sanctions need not be otherwise justified.[121] Other sanctions may, however, potentially be justified as countermeasures where they respond to a State's wrongful conduct, aiming to induce its compliance with international obligations, and would otherwise themselves be internationally wrongful.[122]

The practice relating to sanctions is rapidly evolving, and so the following intends to only provide a broad overview of current sanctions regimes and related practice, outlining which States impose such sanctions; to what those sanctions respond; their content in terms of asset freezes; and which individuals are covered. Conclusions must necessarily be tentative, but the next section elaborates on the argument that such asset freezes could be considered countermeasures, responding to State conduct but implemented via a certain subset of individuals. If they are indeed countermeasures considered legitimate by the implementing States, those States must either judge that the covered individuals do not possess rights at all under the relevant treaties, so that the measures could not breach any third-party rights, or that the third-party rights approach does not otherwise apply to such individuals because they are not protected 'third parties' in this context.[123]

(i) Sanctions in practice

As at early 2023, a significant number of States had imposed asset freezes on individuals. Generally employed as part of a wider package of measures described as 'sanctions', they respond at least in part—as elaborated below—to alleged wrongdoing by States in various situations.[124] Sanctions regimes that are, or have been, 'autonomous'—imposed without UN Security Council authorisation[125]—include

[120] Noting use in this sense: eg, *ARSIWA*, 168; Alland (n 6) 1134, cf 1134–35; Pellet and Miron (n 15) [6]–[7], [62]–[65], cf [8]–[10]; Ruys (n 7) 1–2; Happold (n 115) 90–91; Ago (n 25) [78]–[79], cf [92]–[93]; Gowlland-Debbas (n 119) 4, cf 6; Crawford, 'Relationship' (n 70) 59–61; Crawford, *GP* (n 7) 292; Sicilianos (n 114) 1140; White and Abass (n 7) 552–53, cf 553–54; Abi-Saab (n 119) 37–38, cf 32; also Zoller (n 12) 107–8; cf Dawidowicz (n 6) 21–23.

[121] See UN Charter, arts 25, 103; Andreas Lowenfeld, 'Unilateral versus Collective Sanctions: An American's Perception' in Gowlland-Debbas (n 70) 97–98; Gowlland-Debbas (n 119) 16, 18–19; White and Abass (n 7) 556, cf 550; Ruys (n 7) 15–16; Milanovic, 'Sayadi' (n 115). Cf Happold (n 115) 87.

[122] Authorities nn 6–7, 189ff, particularly nn 198–99. This book assumes States may employ third-party (art 48) countermeasures: see Dawidowicz (n 6); Dawidowicz (n 32). Cf *ARSIWA*, art 54, 302–5; Guilfoyle, 'Countermeasures' (n 8) 72; Pellet and Miron (n 15) [57]–[59]; White and Abass (n 7) 547–50; Ruys (n 7) 22–26; also Sicilianos (n 114) 1137–40, 1144–45.

[123] Similarly authorities nn 107–10, 287; cf nn 37ff; Dawidowicz (n 6) 324–28.

[124] Generally, on various programmes discussed herein: Zia Ullah, 'Eversheds Sutherland Global Sanctions Guide (Third Edition)' (2021) <https://ezine.eversheds-sutherland.com/global-sanctions-guide/>; 'SanctionsWiki' <http://www.sanctionswiki.org/Main_Page>; Maya Lester and Michael O'Kane, 'European Sanctions' <https://www.europeansanctions.com/>; 'OpenSanctions' <https://www.opensanctions.org/>; Pellet and Miron (n 15) [62]; Ruys (n 7) 3; Dupont, 'Countermeasures' (n 112) 302, 308–10; Happold (n 115) 91–92; Dupont, 'Unilateral' (n 114) 38–39, 47–50; Criddle (n 8) 598, 607–10; Dawidowicz (n 32) 392–97; Dawidowicz (n 6) 195–237; Norman Eisen and others, 'The Brookings Sanctions Tracker' (2022) <https://www.brookings.edu/research/the-brookings-sanctions-tracker/>.

[125] Ruys (n 7) 3, 22; Happold (n 115) 91; Pellet and Miron (n 15) [62]–[63].

those vis-à-vis situations in Belarus, Crimea and Ukraine more generally, Guinea, Mali, Myanmar, Nicaragua, Syria, Tunisia, Turkey, Venezuela, and Zimbabwe. Others are partially 'autonomous', going beyond those authorised by the Security Council, including measures employed by certain States vis-à-vis Guinea-Bissau, the DRC, Lebanon, Libya, Iran, and North Korea.[126]

The practice of employing asset freezes targeted at individuals is not limited to a few Western States. Sanction-imposing States commonly include the twenty-seven European Union (EU) Member States, Australia, Canada, Japan, the UK, and the US.[127] Often the non-EU European Economic Area (EEA) States (Iceland, Liechtenstein and Norway) and former Yugoslavian States, and sometimes Armenia, Georgia, Moldova, Turkey, and Ukraine, 'align' with EU sanctions and impose similar measures.[128] Switzerland commonly takes a similar approach,[129] while States like New Zealand and Singapore have taken measures vis-à-vis certain situations.[130] Importantly for geographical diversity, as Dawidowicz observes, the League of Arab States, twenty-one States across Africa and the Middle East, imposed asset freezes on Syrian officials,[131] while the 'Group of Friends of the

[126] Distinguishing 'autonomous' and UNSC sanctions, eg: DFAT, 'Australia and sanctions' <https://www.dfat.gov.au/international-relations/security/sanctions/about-sanctions#types>; 'EU Sanctions Map' <https://www.sanctionsmap.eu/#/main>; also Lester and O'Kane (n 124); Ruys (n 7) 3; Dupont, 'Unilateral' (n 114) 47–50; Criddle (n 8) 607–10.

[127] Generally authorities n 124. See: <https://www.dfat.gov.au/international-relations/security/sanctions/about-sanctions> (Australia); <https://www.international.gc.ca/world-monde/international_relations-relations_internationales/sanctions/current-actuelles.aspx?lang=eng> (Canada); <https://www.consilium.europa.eu/en/policies/sanctions/> (EU); <https://www.mof.go.jp/policy/international_policy/gaitame_kawase/gaitame/economic_sanctions/list.htm> (Japan); <https://www.gov.uk/guidance/uk-sanctions> (UK); <https://www.treasury.gov/resource-center/sanctions/programs/pages/programs.aspx> (US).

[128] Eg: 'Declaration by the High Representative on behalf of the EU on the alignment of certain third countries concerning restrictive measures in respect of actions undermining or threatening the territorial integrity, sovereignty and independence of Ukraine' (30 March 2023) <https://www.consilium.europa.eu/en/press/press-releases/2023/03/30/statement-by-the-high-representative-on-behalf-of-the-eu-on-the-alignment-of-certain-third-countries-concerning-restrictive-measures-in-respect-of-actions-undermining-or-threatening-the-territorial-integrity-sovereignty-and-independ/>; similarly vis-à-vis Myanmar (18 July 2018) <https://www.consilium.europa.eu/en/press/press-releases/2018/07/18/declaration-by-the-high-representative-on-behalf-of-the-european-union-on-the-alignment-of-certain-countries-with-concerning-restrictive-measures-against-myanmar-burma/>; vis-à-vis Nicaragua (4 May 2020) <https://www.consilium.europa.eu/en/press/press-releases/2020/05/04/declaration-by-the-high-representative-josep-borrell-on-behalf-of-the-european-union-on-nicaragua/>; vis-à-vis Zimbabwe (PR 10202/1/10 REV1, 27 May 2010) <https://www.consilium.europa.eu/uedocs/cms_data/docs/pressdata/en/cfsp/114649.pdf>; see generally 'EU Third Countries' in 'SanctionsWiki' (n 124). Similarly Dawidowicz (n 6) 185, 195, 205, 223.

[129] See 'Secrétariat d'Etat à l'économie' <https://www.seco.admin.ch/seco/fr/home/Aussenwirtschaftspolitik_Wirtschaftliche_Zusammenarbeit/Wirtschaftsbeziehungen/exportkontrollen-und-sanktionen/sanktionen-embargos/aenderungen_im_2022.html>.

[130] 'Russian Sanctions' <https://www.mfat.govt.nz/en/countries-and-regions/europe/ukraine/russian-invasion-of-ukraine/sanctions> ('illegal invasion'); 'Sanctions and Restrictions Against Russia in Response to its Invasion of Ukraine' <https://www.mfa.gov.sg/Newsroom/Press-Statements-Transcripts-and-Photos/2022/03/20220305-sanctions#:~:text=In%20this%20regard%2C%20we%20will,Goods%20(Control)%20Order%202021> ('gross violation of international law').

[131] Dawidowicz (n 6) 225, referencing LAS Ministerial Resolution 7442 (27 November 2011); similarly 'Report of the Secretary-General on Unilateral Economic Measures as a Means of Political and Economic Coercion against Developing Countries' UN Doc A/72/307 (9 August 2017) 20.

Syrian People' has also endorsed asset freezes vis-à-vis Syrian regime members, at conferences where up to eighty-three States were represented.[132] In Africa, members of the Economic Community of West African States (ECOWAS), fifteen in total,[133] have imposed asset freezes in response to particular incidents.[134] So too have Russia[135] and Iran,[136] while China has employed individual sanctions, though apparently not including asset freezes.[137] Various States also appear to have been supportive of different sanctions regimes.[138]

These sanctions purport to respond, at least in part, to the internationally wrongful conduct of other States.[139] Sanctions vis-à-vis Russia concerning Crimea, and later Ukraine more generally, focus primarily on alleged violations of Ukraine's sovereignty and territorial integrity,[140] as do certain sanctions vis-à-vis

[132] See references Dawidowicz (n 6) 229–31, 243.

[133] Certain members were excluded at times: see 'ECOWAS Suspends Burkina Faso after Military Coup' *Al Jazeera* (28 January 2022) <https://www.aljazeera.com/news/2022/1/28/ecowas-suspends-burkina-faso-after-coup>.

[134] See 'West African Regional Bloc ECOWAS Imposes New Sanctions on Mali and Guinea' *France24* (8 November 2021) <https://www.france24.com/en/africa/20211108-west-african-regional-bloc-ecowas-imposes-new-sanctions-on-mali-and-guinea>; 'West African Bloc Sanctions Mali's Transitional Leaders' *Bloomberg* (7 November 2021) <https://www.bloomberg.com/news/articles/2021-11-07/west-african-bloc-sanctions-mali-s-transitional-leaders#xj4y7vzkg>; ECOWAS, 'Final Communique: Extraordinary Summit of the ECOWAS Authority of Heads of State and Government on the Situation in Mali, Guinea and Burkina Faso' (25 March 2022) <https://reliefweb.int/report/mali/final-communique-extraordinary-summit-ecowas-authority-heads-state-and-government>; ECOWAS, 'Communique: Extraordinary Session of the ECOWAS Authority of Heads of State and Government' (16 September 2021) <https://reliefweb.int/report/guinea/communique-extraordinary-session-ecowas-authority-heads-state-and-government-16>; Nigerian VP Office, 'ECOWAS Imposes Sanctions on Mali, Maintain Measures Against Military Takeover in Guinea' (8 November 2021) <https://statehouse.gov.ng/news/ecowas-imposes-sanctions-on-mali-maintain-measures-against-military-takeover-in-guinea/>.

[135] Asset freezes were imposed on Ukrainian individuals in 2018: see 'Russia' in Ullah (n 124); n 163.

[136] See 'Iran' in Ullah (n 124); n 164.

[137] 'Foreign Ministry Spokesperson Announces Sanctions on Relevant EU Entities and Personnel' (22 March 2021) <https://www.fmprc.gov.cn/mfa_eng/xwfw_665399/s2510_665401/2535_665405/202103/t20210322_9170814.html#:~:text=The%20Chinese%20side%20decides%20to,Lexmann%20of%20the%20European%20Parliament%2C>; 'Foreign Ministry Spokesperson Announces Sanctions on Relevant US and Canadian Individuals and Entity' (27 March 2021) <https://www.fmprc.gov.cn/mfa_eng/xwfw_665399/s2510_665401/2535_665405/202103/t20210327_9170817.html>. Further: Vladislav Djanic, 'European Parliament Puts Ratification . . .' *IA Rep* (21 May 2021). Sanctions seem limited to travel and business bans.

[138] Dawidowicz (n 6) 201–2, 210, 244–45. Cf nn 191–93.

[139] nn 140ff. Generally: ibid 192–202, 220–22, 232–33, 263–64; Dawidowicz (n 32) 392–97. There being additional reasons for action does not undermine that measures respond to alleged wrongs: Dawidowicz (n 6) 294–97; Tzanakopoulos (n 112) 188. Cf sanctions not apparently responding to State conduct: nn 340–341.

[140] Eg Australia: DFAT, 'Russia sanctions regime' <https://www.dfat.gov.au/international-relations/security/sanctions/sanctions-regimes/russia-sanctions-regime> ('threat to [Ukraine's] sovereignty and territorial integrity'); similarly Canada: 'Canadian Sanctions Related to Russia' <https://www.international.gc.ca/world-monde/international_relations-relations_internationales/sanctions/russia-russie.aspx?lang=eng>; EU: EU Dec 2014/145/CFSP (17 March 2014) [1] ('violation of Ukrainian sovereignty and territorial integrity by [Russia]'); EU Dec 2022/329 (25 February 2022) [8]–[10]; Japan: MFA, 'Statement on the Additional Measures over the Situation in Ukraine' (28 July 2014) <http://www.mofa.go.jp/press/release/press2e_000003.html> [1] ('Russia's . . . actions which violate [Ukraine's] sovereignty and territorial integrity'), [3]; 'Sanction Measures following the launch of military actions by Russia in Ukraine' (25 February 2022) <https://www.mofa.go.jp/press/release/press6e_000371.

Belarus.[141] Sanctions vis-à-vis Belarus otherwise,[142] as well as certain sanctions vis-à-vis the DRC,[143] Guinea,[144] Iran,[145] Libya,[146] Myanmar,[147] Nicaragua,[148] North Korea,[149] Syria,[150] Ukraine,[151] Venezuela,[152] and Zimbabwe,[153] respond—at

html>; New Zealand: n 130; Singapore: n 130; US: EO 13661 (16 March 2014) ('actions and policies of [Russia] … [*inter alia*] threaten [Ukraine's] peace, security, stability, sovereignty, and territorial integrity; and contribute to … misappropriation of its assets …'); EO 13662 (20 March 2014); EO 13685 (19 December 2014) ('Russian occupation'); UK: RussSEUER, reg 4; Dawidowicz (n 6) 232–33; Ruys (n 7) 4; Luca Pantaleo, 'Sanctions Cases in the European Courts' in Happold and Eden (n 114) 171. Cf Alexandra Hofer, 'The "Curiouser and Curiouser" Legal Nature of Non-UN Sanctions: The Case of US Sanctions against Russia' (2018) 23 JC & SL 75.

141 Canada: SEMBelR, art 2(a1); UK: BelSEUER, reg 4 ('cease actions … undermining or threatening [Ukraine's] territorial integrity, sovereignty or independence').

142 Canada: SEMBelR, preamble ('human rights violations'); EU: EU Dec 2012/642/CFSP (15 October 2012) ('lack of respect for human rights, democracy and the rule of law'); UK: BelSEUER, reg 4; US: EO 14038 (9 August 2021), preamble; EO 13405 (16 June 2006), preamble.

143 EU: EU Dec 2010/788/CFSP (20 December 2010), art 3(2)(b).

144 EU: EU Dec 2010/638/CFSP (25 October 2010) [1] ('violent crackdown by security forces on political demonstrators'); UK: GuineaSEUER, reg 4.

145 Australia: ASR, s 6, It 4 ('oppression'); EU: EU Council, 'Iran: EU restrictive measures' <http://www.consilium.europa.eu/en/policies/sanctions/iran/> ('persuade Iran to comply with its international obligations … serious human rights violations'); EU Reg 2011/235/CFSP (12 April 2011), art 2; US: EO 13553 (28 September 2010), s 1(a)(ii)(A); EO 13846 (6 August 2018), s 7.

146 US: EO 13566 (25 February 2011), preamble ('wanton violence against … civilians'), s 1; also EU: EU Reg 2016/44 (18 January 2016), art 6(2) (*inter alia* 'serious human rights abuses', though not apparently State-directed, see n 341); Criddle (n 8) 607; Dawidowicz (n 6) 220.

147 Australia: DFAT, 'Myanmar sanctions regime' <https://dfat.gov.au/international-relations/security/sanctions/sanctions-regimes/Pages/myanmar.aspx> ('human rights abuses'; 'coup d'état'); Canada: 'Canadian Sanctions Related to Myanmar' <https://www.international.gc.ca/world-monde/international_relations-relations_internationales/sanctions/myanmar.aspx?lang=eng>; EU: EU Dec 2018/655(CFSP) (26 April 2018) [2] ('grave human rights violations'); EU Dec 2018/900(CFSP) (25 June 2018) [2]; EU Dec (CFSP)2021/482 (22 March 2021), art 1(3); US: EO 14014 (9 August 2021), s 1(a)(ii)(C)-(D); USDOT, 'Treasury Sanctions Commanders and Units of the Burmese Security Forces for Serious Human Rights Abuses' (17 August 2018) <https://home.treasury.gov/news/press-releases/sm460>; Dawidowicz (n 6) 193–202.

148 EU: EU Dec 2019/1720 (14 October 2019) [1] ('repression … arbitrariness in detention and judicial procedures'), [2] ('deterioration of human rights and the rule of law'); also EU Council, 'Nicaragua: EU imposes sanctions on eight more individuals' (2 August 2021) <https://www.consilium.europa.eu/en/press/press-releases/2021/08/02/nicaragua-eu-imposes-sanctions-on-eight-more-individuals/> ('government to abide by … international human rights laws and standards'); UK: NicSEUER, reg 4; US: EO 13851 (27 November 2018).

149 US: EO 13687 (2 January 2015) ('serious human rights abuses'); EO 13810 (20 September 2017).

150 Eg, Australia: ASR, s 6, It 7 ('human rights abuses'); Canada: 'Canadian Sanctions related to Syria' <https://www.international.gc.ca/world-monde/international_relations-relations_internationales/sanctions/syria-syrie.aspx?lang=eng>; EU: EU Dec 2015/1836/CFSP (12 October 2015) [2] ('violent repression'; 'systematic violations of human rights'); US: EO 13572 (29 April 2011) ('Syria's human rights abuses'); similarly EO 13573 (18 May 2011) ('Syria's … violence against [Syrian] people'); Dawidowicz (n 6) 222–26.

151 EU: EU Dec 2014/119/CFSP (5 March 2014), art 1(1).

152 Canada: 'Canadian Sanctions Related to Venezuela' <https://www.international.gc.ca/world-monde/international_relations-relations_internationales/sanctions/venezuela.aspx?lang=eng> ('grave human rights abuses'); EU: EU Reg 2017/2063 (13 November 2017) [2] ('serious human rights violations'); US: EO 13692 (8 March 2015) ('human rights violations').

153 Australia: ASR, s 6, It 8; Canada: 'Canadian Sanctions Related to Zimbabwe' <https://www.international.gc.ca/world-monde/international_relations-relations_internationales/sanctions/zimbabwe.aspx?lang=eng> (*inter alia* 'human rights violations'); US: EO 13469 (25 July 2008) ('human rights abuses … public corruption'); Pantaleo (n 140) 171 ('persistent violations of fundamental rights'); Dawidowicz (n 6) 204–11.

least in part—to those States' alleged human rights abuses.[154] Sanctions vis-à-vis North Korea[155] and Iran additionally relate to those States' allegedly wrongful nuclear proliferation.[156] Sanctions vis-à-vis Turkey respond to its drilling activities in the Eastern Mediterranean, alleged to infringe Cypriot sovereignty.[157] Certain sanctions relating to Belarus, Crimea, Iran, Lebanon, Libya, Nicaragua, Tunisia, Ukraine, Venezuela, and Zimbabwe also respond in part to alleged corruption,[158] corruption being in violation of international law.[159] Sanctions concerning Guinea, Guinea-Bissau, and Mali respond to the failure to hold elections consequent on the overthrow of recognised governments,[160] which may arguably also be viewed as a breach of international law by the State represented by the new government.[161] Sanctions relating to the DRC and Lebanon similarly respond, in part, to alleged obstruction of the democratic process.[162] Sanctions imposed by Russia respond to the allegedly wrongful imposition of Ukrainian sanctions,[163] while those imposed by Iran respond to alleged terrorism, support thereof, and human rights violations.[164]

154 Generally Dawidowicz (n 6) 195–223.

155 Australia: ASR, s 6, It 1; EU: EU Reg 2017/1509 (30 August 2017), art 34; US: EO 13810, preamble.

156 Australia: ASR, s 6, It 4; Canada: SEMIR, s 2; EU: EU Reg 267/2012 (23 March 2012), art 23(2); EU Reg 2015/1861 (18 October 2015), art 1(13); US: EO 13846, preamble; Dupont, 'Unilateral' (n 114) 40, cf 55–58; Dupont, 'Countermeasures' (n 112) 311, cf 325–29, cited Ruys (n 7) 4; Pantaleo (n 140) 171.

157 EU: EU Dec CFSP 2019/1894 (11 November 2019) [1], [9]; also UK: UnDrillAEMedSEUER, reg 4.

158 Eg Belarus: EO 14038, s 1(a)(v)(E) ('public corruption'); EO 13405, s 1(a)(v)(E); Crimea: EO 13660 (6 March 2014), s 1(a)(i)(C) ('misappropriation'); Iran: EO 13846, s 7; Lebanon: EU Dec CFSP 2021/1277 (30 July 2021) [14] ('serious financial misconduct, including corruption'); Libya: EU Dec (CFSP) 2015/1333 (31 July 2015), art 9(2)(c)–(d); EO 13566, preamble; Nicaragua: EO 13851, s 1(a)(i)(D); Tunisia: EU Reg 101/2011 (4 February 2011), art 2 ('misappropriation'); Ukraine: EU Dec 2014/119/CFSP, art 1(1); Venezuela: EO 13692 ('public corruption'); Zimbabwe: EO 13469, s 1(a)(v). Further: Criddle (n 8) 587. Cf n 341 (apparent individual focus).

159 Eg, CAC, arts 4–12, 16–27, 30–31.

160 Guinea: 'Extraordinary ECOWAS Session Communique (16 September 2021)' (n 134) [7], [9](b) ('restore constitutional rule'), [10]; ECOWAS, 'Final Communique of the 3rd Extraordinary Summit of the ECOWAS Heads of State and Government on the Situation in Guinea and Mali' (7 November 2021) <https://old22.ecowas.int/wp-content/uploads/2021/11/Eng.Communiquei%CC%80-Final-Sommet-7-novembre-2021.pdf> [9] ('until constitutional order is restored'); Guinea-Bissau: EU Dec 2012/285/CFSP (31 May 2012) [2]–[3]; Mali: 'ECOWAS 3rd Summit Communique' (n 160) [13]–[16]; EU Dec CFSP 2021/2208 (13 December 2021) [6]–[7].

161 See analysis Jean d'Aspremont, 'Responsibility for Coups d'Etat in International Law' (2010) 18 Tul JICL 451, 455–73.

162 EU Dec 2010/788/CFSP, art 3(2)(a); EU Dec CFSP 2021/1277 [10]–[11].

163 See 'Decree on the Application of Special Economic Measures in Connection with Ukraine's Unfriendly Actions against Citizens and Legal Entities of the Russian Federation' (22 October 2018) <http://kremlin.ru/acts/news/58871>, cited Wikipedia, 'Russian sanctions against Ukraine' <https://en.wikipedia.org/wiki/Russian_sanctions_against_Ukraine#:~:text=Russian%20sanctions%20against%20Ukraine%20were,citizens%20and%2068%20Ukrainian%20companies>.

164 See MFA <https://en.mfa.ir/portal/viewpage/15045>; <https://en.mfa.ir/files/mfaen/s.pdf> (sanctions under the Countering Human Rights Violations and Adventurous and Terrorist Acts of The United States in The Region law (2017)). Further: 'Iran renews list of former and current US officials involved in terror acts and rights violations' *Tehran Times* (9 April 2022) <https://www.tehrantimes.com/news/471510/Iran-renews-list-of-former-and-current-U-S-officials-involved>.

Importantly, even while overwhelmingly responding to *State* conduct,[165] these sanctions include asset freezes,[166] which are measures 'targeted' at *individuals*,[167] and which restrict an individual's use of property.[168] States are apparently thus taking a similar approach to the UN Security Council when authorising sanctions,[169] the latter having recognised the necessity of not imposing country-wide economic sanctions but of 'modify[ing] and target[ing] sanctions more accurately on those who are really responsible—the leaders of the regimes, or non-State actors responsible.'[170]

In particular, the practice reveals that the following categories of persons tend to be covered by non-Security Council asset freezes:

- individuals *responsible* for, *implementing*, *engaging* in, *involved* in, *participating* in, *ordering*, *directing*, *controlling*, or *complicit* in, the relevant wrongful acts;[171]
- individuals *assisting*, *supporting*, *enabling*, *promoting*, *contributing* to, or *facilitating* such persons and/or acts;[172]

[165] See nn 139ff; Pantaleo (n 140) 177. Eg, *Rotenberg v Council* Case T-720/14 (30 November 2016) (EGC) [92] ('reaction to ... policies and activities of ... Russian authorities'), [176]; *Rosneft v Council* Case T-715/14 (13 September 2018) (EGC) [157]; *Al Assad v Council* Case T202/12 (12 March 2014) (EGC) [99] ('reaction to ... authorities of [Syria]'); also Dupont, 'Unilateral' (n 114) 40–41; Criddle (n 8) 598–99; Lester and O'Kane (n 124) for references to relevant case law. Cf nn 340–341 (sanctions seemingly responding to individuals).

[166] Eg Australia: ASR, ss 6, 14–15; Canada: SEMRR, s 3; Japan: MFA Japan (n 140) [3](1); MFA, 'Implementation of Measures to Freeze the Assets of President Bashar Al-Assad and His Related Individuals and Entities in Syria' (9 September 2011) <http://www.mofa.go.jp/announce/announce/2011/9/0909_02.html>, quoted 'Syria' in 'SanctionsWiki' (n 124); EU: EU Dec 2014/499/CFSP (25 July 2014), art 1(2) ('All funds and economic resources belonging to, owned, held or controlled by ... shall be frozen'); nn 163–64 (Russia/Iran); UK: BelSEUER, Pt 3(1); US: EO 13660, s 1(a) ('All property and interests in property ... are blocked and may not be transferred, paid, exported, withdrawn, or otherwise dealt in'); Dawidowicz (n 6) 195–201, 205–8, 217–18, 222–26, 233, 236.

[167] Happold (n 115) 87, 89–90; Pantaleo (n 140) 171–72, 177, see n 287; Ruys (n 7) 3; Criddle (n 8) 586.

[168] See *Kadi and Al Barakaat v Council and Commission* [2008] ECR I-6351 (GC) [92], [101], discussed nn207ff; also Happold (n 115) 89; Criddle (n 8) 586.

[169] Similarly Pantaleo (n 140) 177; Criddle (n 8) 607; Dawidowicz (n 6) 218–19.

[170] White and Abass (n 7) 558; also Pellet and Miron (n 15) [34]–[35]; Happold (n 115) 88–89. Thus, it 'adopt[s] so-called "intelligent" sanctions ... measures targeted at political elites or at the "trouble-makers"': Sicilianos (n 114) 1141; also Ruys (n 7) 3; Vera Gowlland-Debbas, 'Responsibility and the United Nations Charter' in Crawford and others, *Responsibility* (n 6) 130; Michael Bothe, 'Security Council's Targeted Sanctions against Presumed Terrorists' (2008) 6 JICJ 541, 544; ESCR Committee 'General Comment No. 8' (1997) UN Doc E/C.12/1997/8 [3], [4] ('governing élite'), [16], cited White and Abass (n 7) 546, 557. This avoids 'comprehensive sanctions ... affect[ing], sometimes very heavily, the innocent civilian population': Sicilianos (n 114) 1141; also Pantaleo (n 140) 196; Dawidowicz (n 6) 333–40; Lowenfeld (n 121) 103.

[171] Eg ASR (Australia), s 6, It 4 ('engaging in, is responsible for or is complicit in'), Its 7–9; SEMBelR (Canada), art 2(a) ('participated in'); MFA Japan (n 140) [3](1) ('directly involved in ... annexation ... and destabilization'); EU Dec 2014/499/CFSP, art 1(2) ('responsible for, actively supporting or implementing, actions or policies'); EU Reg 2016/44, art 6(2) ('involved ... complicit in ordering, controlling ... directing ... human rights abuses'); EU Reg 2011/235/CFSP, art 2 ('responsible for serious human rights violations'); EO 13722 (15 March 2016), s 2(iii) ('engaged in, facilitated ... responsible for'); EO 13660, s 1(a) (*inter alia* 'responsible for or complicit in, or ... engaged in ... actions or policies'); EO 13572, s 1(b)(i) ('responsible for', 'complicit in', 'ordering, controlling ... directing ... participat[ing] in ... human rights abuses'). Further: Criddle (n 8) 598–99, 607; Pantaleo (n 140) 171–72; Dawidowicz (n 6) 218–20, 233.

[172] Eg ASR (Australia), s 6, It 1 ('assisting' UNSCR 'evasion'), It 4 ('contributing to' nuclear/missile programs), Its 6–7 ('support'); SEMRR (Canada), s 2(a) ('engaged in activities ... directly or indirectly

- individuals *benefiting* from such persons;[173]
- individuals who are *associated* with such persons or acts,[174] sometimes expressly including family members;[175]
- individuals who are *owned*, *controlled*, or *act on behalf of* such persons;[176] and
- individuals who are involved in particular relevant *sectors*,[177] or operating in *disputed areas*.[178]

State or government officials are often expressly included,[179] sometimes identified as persons in 'positions of authority'.[180] However, even where not so identified, lists

facilitate, support, provide funding for or contribute to ... violation of [Ukraine's] sovereignty or territorial integrity'); EU Dec 2014/499/CFSP, art 1(2) ('supporting, materially or financially, actions' threatening Ukraine; 'actively supporting, materially or financially ... Russian decision-makers responsible for [Crimean] annexation'); EU Dec CFSP 2019/1894, art 2(1)(b) ('financial, technical or material support'); RSR (NZ), reg 3; EO 14038, s 1(a)(vi) ('materially assisted, sponsored, or provided financial, material, or technological support for, or goods or services to or in support of ... activity ... or ... person'); EO 13606 (22 April 2012), s 1(a)(ii)(A)-(B) (operating/directing 'technology ... that could assist ... or enable serious human rights abuses'; providing 'goods, services, or technology ... likely to be [so] used'); BelSEUER (UK), reg 6(2)(a)(vii) ('supporting [Belarussian] Government'); RussSEUER, regs 6(3)(a) ('provides support', 'promotes'), (b)–(c) (provid[ing] financial services, or mak[ing] available funds, economic resources, goods or technology').

173 Eg, EU Dec 2022/329, art 1 ('benefiting from Russian decision-makers ... benefiting from the Government'); EU Dec 2013/255/CFSP (31 May 2013), art 28(1) ('benefiting from ... the regime'); BelSEUER (UK), reg 6(2)(a)(vii) ('benefit from ... the Government').

174 Eg ASR (Australia), s 6, It 1 ('associated with' WMD/missile programmes), Its 5–6; SEMZR (Canada), s 2(b); EU Dec 2013/255/CFSP, art 28(1) ('persons and entities associated'); EU Dec (CFSP)2021/2208, art 1(4); EU Reg 267/2012, art 23(2)(a) ('directly associated with' proliferation); UnDrillAEMedSEUER (UK), reg 6(d).

175 Eg ASR (Australia), s 6, It 6A; SEMSR (Canada), s 2(b); 'ECOWAS 3rd Summit Communique' (n 160) [9], [15]; EU Dec 2015/1836, art 1(4) ('members of ... families'); RussSEUER (UK), reg 6(6)(b); EO 14014, s 1(a)(v) ('spouse ... adult child'); EO 13405, s 1(a)(ii)(C) ('family member').

176 Eg ASR (Australia), s 6, It 6; SEMSR (Canada), s 2(b); EU Dec 2012/642/CFSP, art 4(b) ('owned or controlled'); EU Dec 2011/137/CFSP (28 February 2011), art 6(1); EU Dec 2017/667(CFSP) (6 April 2017) ('persons or entities acting on their behalf or at their direction'); EO 13660, s 1(a)(v) ('owned or controlled by, or ... acted or purported to act for or on behalf of, directly or indirectly, any [relevant] person').

177 Eg ASR (Australia), s 6, It 6A ('engaging in an activity or performing a function ... of economic or strategic significance'); EU Dec 2022/329, art 1 ('leading businesspersons or legal persons, entities or bodies involved in economic sectors providing a substantial source of revenue to [Russian] Government'); EU Reg 267/2012, art 23(2)I (shipping); RussSEUER (UK), reg 6(4)(c) ('sector of strategic significance'); EO 14038, s 1(a)(iv) (defense; security; energy; potash; tobacco; construction; transportation); EO 13662, s 1(a)(i) (*inter alia* 'financial services, energy, metals and mining, engineering ... defense and related materiel'); EO 13846, ss 1–2 (shipping; automotive; petroleum); EO 13551 (1 September 2010), s 1 (*inter alia* arms); EO 13722, s 2(a)(i)–(ii)(industry); EO 14014, s 1(a)(i) (defense).

178 Eg, EU Dec 2022/329, art 1 (Crimea/Sevastopol where 'transferred contrary to Ukrainian law', 'conducting transactions with separatist groups'); RussSEUER (UK), reg 6(3)(f),(5); EO 13685, s 2(a)(i) ('operate in ... Crimea').

179 Eg ASR (Australia), s 6, It 6 (various officials), It 6A (Minister/'senior official'); SEMRR (Canada), s 2(b) (former/current 'senior official'); 'ECOWAS 3rd Summit Communique' (n 160) [9], [15] (*inter alia* junta members, 'Transition authorities'); EU Dec 2018/655(CFSP), art 6(1) (armed forces, police); EU Reg 314/2004, art 6(1) ('[government] members'); n 164 (Iran); LAS Ministerial Resolution 7442 ('top Syrian officials and figures'); EO 14038, s 1 (a)(ii)–(iii) ('political subdivision, agency or instrumentality', 'leader or official'); EO 13405, s 1(a)(ii)(C) ('senior-level official'); EO 13851, s 1(a)(iii) ('[Government] official'); RussSEUER (UK), reg 6(4A); also Dawidowicz (n 6) 197, 208, 217, 222, 224–26, 233.

180 Myanmar Sanctions (Canada) (n 147) ('officials ... occup[ying] positions of authority ... military operations').

of sanctioned individuals demonstrate that officials are captured in a given sanctions regime's other categories.[181]

(ii) Sanctions as countermeasures

Sanctions outside the Security Council framework are thus employed to respond to State conduct alleged to violate international law, but are aimed at particular related individuals. It certainly makes practical sense to influence the State's conduct through individuals whose actions determine how it behaves.[182] But is it legally relevant? More particularly, does it have any influence on the third-party rights approach to countermeasures discussed above?

It would only do so if these measures are indeed rightly characterised as countermeasures.[183] This requires that (1) the actions respond to a State's allegedly wrongful conduct; and (2) they would themselves otherwise be unlawful.[184] To be relevant to the third-party rights approach as it concerns *individual* claims, it would, moreover, be necessary that (3) State practice demonstrates the acceptability of violating *individual* rights in taking countermeasures in response to *State* conduct.[185] Only if it does so could the argument be made that customary international law allows countermeasures to be used as a good defence to breach of the rights of *both* the State and the relevant individuals, and any consequent overlapping claims.[186] In one investment case, undecided at the time of writing, it appears that a respondent State is indeed justifying sanctions taken in response to another State's allegedly wrongful conduct with impacts upon an investor as countermeasures, albeit not concerning asset freezes per se.[187] More generally, however, an indication of where the customary position may lie can be derived by addressing each point in turn.

First, that these actions purport to respond—at least in part—to the unlawful conduct of States, has been addressed above.[188] As to the second, freezes

[181] Eg consolidated lists: <https://dfat.gov.au/international-relations/security/sanctions/Pages/consolidated-list.aspx> (Australia); <https://data.europa.eu/euodp/data/dataset/consolidated-list-of-persons-groups-and-entities-subject-to-eu-financial-sanctions/resource/3a1d5dd6-244e-4118-82d3-db3be0554112> (EU); <https://www.gov.uk/government/publications/the-uk-sanctions-list> (UK); <https://www.treasury.gov/resource-center/sanctions/SDN-List/Pages/default.aspx> (US); also MFA Japan (n 166), quoted 'SanctionsWiki' (n 124); additional datasets: <https://www.opensanctions.org/datasets/sanctions/>.

[182] cf nn 170, 332.

[183] nn 112ff.

[184] Authorities nn 112–14.

[185] nn 94–97.

[186] cf nn 94–99.

[187] *VEB v Ukraine (Partial Award on Preliminary Objections)* SCC Case 2019/113, V2019/088 (31 January 2021) [76] (argument that even if measures breach BIT, 'they were taken in response to ongoing breaches by [Russia] of its international obligations owed to Ukraine ... the measures were thus taken for valid cause, were temporary in nature, and proportional to the injury caused by [Russia], which excludes any responsibility of Ukraine under international law').

[188] n 139.

of nationals' assets have long been regarded as a standard form of countermeasure,[189] and it would certainly appear that the freezes in these sanctions programmes might violate international law in various ways.[190] UN General Assembly resolutions have, for instance, condemned 'unilateral coercive economic measures' as contrary to international law,[191] while a 2017 Secretary-General's report collated responses from multiple States indicating that they generally regarded such measures, which included asset freezes,[192] as unlawful.[193] Indeed, the EU expressly acknowledges that its sanctions may breach international obligations, including vis-à-vis trade law.[194] The International Law Commission (ILC) apparently regarded early iterations of the EU's Myanmar sanctions, which included freezing of officials' assets, as countermeasures,[195] and the HRC's Special Rapporteur on the negative impact of unilateral coercive measures regarded countermeasures as the appropriate framework for evaluating such sanctions.[196] While focusing on illegality vis-à-vis States' jurisdictional immunities,[197] Dawidowicz emphasises that the practice vis-à-vis Syria is 'indicative of a willingness of a very large number of States to adopt *prima facie* unlawful unilateral coercive measures for which the justification can seemingly only be explained in legal terms by reference to third-party countermeasures'.[198]

[189] Elagab (n 7) 106–9, 111; Arnold McNair, *The Law of Treaties* (Clarendon 1961) 578 ('blocking of [nationals'] banking accounts'), quoted Elagab (n 7) 109; Gateano Arangio-Ruiz, 'Fourth Report on State Responsibility' (1992) 2(1) ILCYB 1 [37], [83], cited Silvia Borelli and Simon Olleson, 'Obligations Relating to Human Rights and Humanitarian Law' in Crawford and others, *Responsibility* (n 6) 1180; Crawford, 'SecondRep' (n 40) [368]; also Criddle (n 8) 595–97, cf 586; Zoller (n 12) 100, 102; Paparinskis, 'Countermeasures' (n 8) 277–78; ILC, 'Summary Records of the Meetings of the Fifty-Second Session' (2000) 1 ILCYB 1, 265–66, 285; White and Abass (n 7) 549; Dopagne (n 114) 181, 193; Dawidowicz (n 32) 387; Dawidowicz (n 6) 113, 254.

[190] Eg, Ruys (n 7) 10; Dupont, 'Unilateral' (n 114) 42, 44 (investment/immunities); Dawidowicz (n 32) 394–98; cf Dawidowicz (n 6) 113, 205, 222, 233 (apparently regarding freezing of officials' assets as relevant only vis-à-vis jurisdictional immunities), 233 (retorsion vis-à-vis lower-level officials); Criddle (n 8) 591–93 (non-intervention/investment); Dupont, 'Countermeasures' (n 112) 312–14 (investment/immunities).

[191] Eg GA resolutions 62/183 (19 December 2007), 64/189 (21 December 2009).

[192] SG Report (n 131) [12], also 11–13, 19.

[193] ibid 6 (Belarus/Cuba), 9–11 (Guatemala), 15 (Senegal/Sri Lanka/Syria). Further Ruys (n 7) 6 (South America).

[194] EU Council, 'Guidelines on Implementation and Evaluation of Restrictive Measures (Sanctions)' (4 May 2018) <https://data.consilium.europa.eu/doc/document/ST-5664-2018-INIT/en/pdf> [10]–[12], earlier version cited Dawidowicz (n 6) 25. On legality of trade measures under the EU–Russia PA and GATT: *Rosneft* (n 165) [165]–[183]. The EU apparently 'dismissed the legal characterization of [its] sanctions as countermeasures': Idriss Jazairy, 'Report of the Special Rapporteur on the Negative Impact of Unilateral Coercive Measures on the Enjoyment of Human Rights on His Mission to the EU' UN Doc A/HRC/39/54/Add.1 (17 July 2018) [18]. But, particularly given the acknowledgement that they might violate international law, as the Special Rapporteur noted, 'they require ... legal justification' as countermeasures: ibid [18]–[19]; similarly Ruys (n 7) 21 (if 'unlawful').

[195] As noted Dawidowicz (n 6) 195 (fn 523), citing ILC, 'Draft Articles on the Responsibility of International Organizations, with Commentaries' (2011) 2(2) ILCYB 46 (DARIO), 96.

[196] Jazairy (n 194) [18]–[20].

[197] See n 190.

[198] Dawidowicz (n 6) 231.

Other scholars similarly regard such measures as at least purporting to be countermeasures.[199]

Because this book is concerned with overlapping individual and interstate claims, and presently with whether countermeasures may preclude claims for breach of *individual* rights, we must specifically establish the third step, that these sanctions could violate obligations founding individual claims, rather than other obligations, like those relating to trade law or immunities. Accordingly, in line with recent scholarship, this section briefly considers potential resulting violations of human rights and investment law,[200] the two main fields in which individuals bring claims and also those in which individuals are said to hold their own rights.[201]

(a) Human rights

Because, as will be elucidated below, States could not in any event employ countermeasures to defend human rights violations,[202] a broad sketch of the issues arising from asset freezes with respect to human rights will suffice. Case law establishes that fair trial, effective remedy, and property rights are particularly relevant.[203] The former two are found in most multilateral human rights instruments,[204] while the last is found in certain instruments, including the European Convention on Human Rights (ECHR),[205] and all exist under EU law.[206]

In the well-known *Kadi* case,[207] the European Court of Justice (ECJ) held that an asset freeze violated 'rights of defence', 'the principle of effective judicial protection',[208] and the 'fundamental right to respect for property'.[209] Notably, notwithstanding that the asset freeze was 'temporary', it 'entail[ed] a restriction of the

[199] Criddle (n 8) 595–99, 609; Dupont, 'Investments' (n 67) 209; Dupont, 'Unilateral' (n 114) 40–41, 51, cf 54–61; Dopagne (n 114) 181, 193 (EU–FRY); van Aaken (n 8) 1–2; cf Dupont, 'Countermeasures' (n 112) 321–34; also Sicilianos (n 114) 1146 (FRY); Ruys (n 7) 11–14, 23–26.

[200] Similarly, eg, Ruys (n 7) 10–11, 17; van Aaken (n 8) 1 (FET/expropriation); Criddle (n 8) 584, 592 (investment); Dupont, 'Investments' (n 67); Dupont, 'Unilateral' (n 114) 42 (investment); Dupont, 'Countermeasures' (n 112) 312–13 (investment); Arangio-Ruiz (n 189) [83]; Elagab (n 7) 104–11.

[201] nn 94–99; Ch 2, n 10.

[202] nn 351–56.

[203] Happold (n 115) 94–96 (property), 98–109 (reputation/access/fair trial/remedy); Borelli and Olleson (n 189) 1186 (property); Pantaleo (n 140) 173 (fair trial/remedy), 175–77; nn 207ff. Further: *Sayadi v Belgium* Doc CCPR/C/94/D/1472/2006 (HRC, 29 December 2008) [10.13] (reputation).

[204] Generally Happold (n 115) 99; see ICCPR, arts 2(3), 14 (effective remedy/fair trial); similarly ECHR, arts 6, 13; AmCHR, arts 8, 25; AfCHPR, art 7 (fair trial); Godfrey Musial, 'The Right to an Effective Remedy under the African Charter on Human and Peoples' Rights' (2006) 6 AfHRLJ 441.

[205] ECHR Protocol 1, art 1; generally Martins Paparinskis, *The International Minimum Standard and Fair and Equitable Treatment* (OUP 2013) 228–37; Alice Ruzza, 'Expropriation and Nationalization' in *MPEPIL* (n 15) (2013) [16]; Elagab (n 7) 109–10.

[206] *Kadi (GC)* (n 168) [335]–[336], [355]–[356]. Cf Rachel Barnes, 'United States Sanctions: Delisting Applications, Judicial Review and Secret Evidence' in Happold and Eden (n 114) 202ff (US).

[207] Generally Happold (n 115) 91, 99–100 and authorities; Pantaleo (n 140) 174; White and Abass (n 7) 558.

[208] *Kadi (GC)* (n 168) [353].

[209] ibid [371].

exercise of [the] right to property' that was 'considerable, having regard to [its] general application . . . . and the fact that it ha[d] been applied' for some seven years.[210] The Court accepted that proportionate interferences in the 'public interest' were allowable,[211] observing that, in pursuing the aim of fighting terrorism,[212] the sanctions at issue 'might, in principle, be justified'.[213] However, the lack of procedural safeguards rendered them otherwise.[214]

In concluding his overview, Happold explains that 'asset freezes ... can[not] be said, in general, to infringe substantive human rights, at least when targeted at persons who actually fit the criteria established for the measures' imposition and provided the criteria themselves are not too widely drawn'.[215] However, questions of proportionality arise, including where the person's 'activities do not directly facilitate' the relevant wrongs,[216] as well as regarding sanctions' 'compatibility with procedural rights'.[217]

(b) *Investment law*

Only one case appears to have directly considered the legality of asset freezes vis-à-vis investment law obligations. The *Certain Iranian Assets* case, discussed below, concerned a US freeze on assets belonging to Iran and its instrumentalities, coupled with legislation authorising seizure of those assets to satisfy judgments against Iran for injuries resulting from its alleged support for terrorism,[218] measures which were challenged under the Treaty of Amity, which contains similar protections to those found in investment law.[219] Additionally, however, at least one case is pending in which investors allege that sanctions, which include an asset freeze, breach BIT obligations;[220] another alleges that Ukrainian sanctions (short of asset freezes) violate BIT protections;[221] while others concerning asset forfeiture proceedings—bearing some similarities to asset freezes—are either afoot or threatened.[222] Such cases demonstrate that challenges to asset freezes under investment law are by no means a merely theoretical possibility. Moreover, that States have

[210] ibid [358].
[211] ibid [355].
[212] ibid [363].
[213] ibid [366].
[214] ibid [368]–[370]. Generally Happold (n 115) 100.
[215] Happold (n 115) 92–93.
[216] ibid 99, referencing *Tay Za v Council* Case C-376/10P (13 March 2012) (GC), see [63]–[72].
[217] Happold (n 115) 99; also Paparinskis, *FET* (n 205) 231–37; Pantaleo (n 140) 177ff. Eg, *Akhras v Council* Case T-579/11 (12 February 2015) (EGC) [71]–[72] (reasons).
[218] *Certain Iranian Assets (Iran v USA)* ICJ Judgment of 30 March 2023 [24]–[29].
[219] See nn 251–56, 264–66, 274–76.
[220] Vladislav Djanic, 'Ukraine Is Looking for Counsel ...' *IA Rep* (1 February 2021); Damien Charlotin, 'Pierre Tercier Is Tapped ...' *IA Rep* (22 February 2022).
[221] Johanna Braun, 'Revealed: Tribunal in VEB v. Ukraine ...' *IA Rep* (22 September 2021), discussing *VEB* (n 187), see [75].
[222] Lisa Bohmer, 'Ukrainian Oligarchs to Lodge ...' *IA Rep* (23 May 2022); Vladislav Djanic, 'Two Russian Banks ...' *IA Rep* (12 May 2022). Cf nn 252–53.

invoked denial of benefits clauses under the Energy Charter Treaty (ECT) subsequent to the imposition of sanctions on numerous individuals relating to Russia's actions vis-à-vis Ukraine suggests a real concern that such entities might otherwise be entitled to investment protections thereunder.[223] Indeed, as will be seen, asset freezes might violate investment obligations in several ways.

For starters, BITs are in force as between numerous sanction-imposing and sanction-subject States, generally defining 'investment' as any asset invested in the former's territory.[224] Accordingly, nationals of sanction-subject States parties to such BITs may well have had such 'investments' frozen in sanction-imposing States.[225] Those BITs tend to contain provisions regarding non-expropriation,[226] fair and equitable treatment,[227] the free flow of funds,[228] and disposal of property.[229]

As to the first, expropriation involves the taking of property,[230] though it suffices that the action 'depriv[e] the owner of the substantial benefits of its

[223] See IEC, 'The United Kingdom denies advantages of Part III under Article 17 of the ECT' (29 September 2023), <https://www.energycharter.org/media/news/article/the-united-kingdom-denies-advantages-of-part-iii-under-article-17-of-the-ect/?tx_news_pi1%5Bcontroller%5D=News&tx_news_pi1%5Baction%5D=detail&cHash=c03e5fff166859c14b15efaa1f5cb8a3>, specifically mentioning sanctioned entities; 'Ukraine denies advantages under Article 17(2) of the ECT' (19 August 2022) <https://www.energycharter.org/media/news/article/ukraine-denies-advantages-under-article-172-of-the-ect/>, specifically mentioning sanctions. ECT, art 17, allows denial of benefits under Pt III on investment promotion and protection.

[224] Eg, Canada–Russia (1989), art I(b); Germany–Russia (1989), art 1; Japan–Russia (1998), art 1; UK–Russia (1989), art 1; Denmark–DPRK (1996), art 1; Germany–Iran (2002), art 1; France–Syria (1977), art 1; Germany–Syria (1977), art 1; Switzerland–Syria (2007), art 1; Turkey–Syria (2004), art 1(2); UK–Venezuela (1995), art 1; Zimbabwe–Germany (1995), art 1; Zimbabwe–Netherlands (1996), art 1; Switzerland–Zimbabwe (1996), art 1. Generally van Aaken (n 8) 1; Sebastián López Escarcena, *Indirect Expropriation in International Law* (Elgar 2014) 119–21; Rudolf Dolzer and Christoph Schreuer, *Principles of International Investment Law* (2nd edn, OUP 2012) 60ff; Ruzza (n 205) [17]–[20]; Zachary Douglas, *The International Law of Investment Claims* (CUP 2009) Ch 5.

[225] See particularly van Aaken (n 8) 1 (while 'sole bank account may not count as … "investment"', 'in most cases, especially if firms are targeted … satisfaction of this requirement … unproblematic'); Dupont, 'Investments' (n 67) 200–3; also Ruys (n 7) 10–11; Criddle (n 8) 592–93.

[226] Eg, Canada–Russia (1989), art VI; Germany–Russia (1989), art 4; Japan–Russia (1998), art 5; UK–Russia (1989), art 5; Denmark–DPRK (1996), art 5; Germany–Iran (2002), art 4(2); France–Syria (1977), art 5; Germany–Syria (1977), art 4(2); Switzerland–Syria (2007), art 7; Turkey–Syria (2004), art 4; UK–Venezuela (1995), art 5; Zimbabwe–Germany (1995), art 4(2); Zimbabwe–Netherlands (1996), art 6; Switzerland–Zimbabwe (1996), art 6.

[227] Eg, Canada–Russia (1989), art III; Japan–Russia (1998), art 3(3); UK–Russia (1989), art 2(2); Denmark–DPRK (1996), art 3(1); Germany–Iran (2002), art 2(3); France–Syria (1977), art 3; Germany–Syria (1977), art 2; Turkey–Syria (2004), art 2(2); Switzerland–Syria (2007), art 4; UK–Venezuela (1995), art 2(2); Zimbabwe–Germany (1995), art 2; Zimbabwe–Netherlands (1996), art 3(1); Switzerland–Zimbabwe (1996), art 4.

[228] Eg Canada–Russia (1989), art VII; Germany–Russia (1989), art 5; Japan–Russia (1998), art 8; UK–Russia (1989), art 6; France–Syria (1977), art 6; Germany–Syria (1977), art 5; Switzerland–Syria (2007), art 6; Turkey–Syria (2004), art 5; Denmark–DPRK (1996), art 7; Germany–Iran (2002), art 5; UK–Venezuela (1995), art 6; Zimbabwe–Germany (1995), art 5; Zimbabwe–Netherlands (1996), art 5; Switzerland–Zimbabwe (1996), art 5. Generally on BIT provisions potentially relevant in this context: Criddle (n 8) 592; also Ruys (n 7) 10–11; van Aaken (n 8) 1; Dupont, 'Investments' (n 67) 203–7.

[229] Eg, UK–Russia, art 2; Denmark–DPRK (1996), art 2(2); Turkey–Syria (2004), art 2(2); Switzerland–Syria (2007), art 4; UK–Venezuela (1995), art 2(2); Zimbabwe–Germany (1995), art 2(2); Zimbabwe–Netherlands (1996), art 3(1); Switzerland–Zimbabwe (1996), art 4(1).

[230] Dolzer and Schreuer (n 224) 101; Ruzza (n 205) [10].

ownership' ('indirect' expropriation).[231] Expropriation is generally lawful if non-discriminatory, for a 'public purpose', and compensated.[232] Asset freezes are, at the least, not compensated.[233] Nonetheless, international law accepts that States have 'regulatory powers that, by pursuing public needs, may legitimately justify restrictions of property rights without compensation' in certain circumstances.[234] In distinguishing such actions from indirect expropriation,[235] of relevance are, *inter alia*, the effects of the relevant measures[236]—including on the investor's control,[237] and taking account of how long it lasts[238]—and its 'nature',[239] including whether it is proportionate.[240]

Asset freezes like those considered here might have a legitimate purpose.[241] However, commentary suggests that '[w]henever [the economic] effect is substantial and lasts for a significant period of time, it will be assumed prima facie that a taking of the property has occurred'.[242] Measures such as those under discussion have been described as 'draconian',[243] placing 'considerable' restrictions on property rights,[244] and may be long-lasting: some of the sanctions noted above have been in place for twenty years;[245] others for closer to ten.[246] Admittedly, as noted above, certain courts applying human rights norms have considered that asset freezes are allowable where proportionate.[247] However, as one investment tribunal outlined, while human rights apply to all persons, it 'does not seem extraordinary' that foreign

[231] Ruzza (n 205) [13], also [11]; similarly Dolzer and Schreuer (n 224) 101; Dupont, 'Investments' (n 67) 203.

[232] Ruzza (n 205) [2]; Escarcena (n 224) 117; Dolzer and Schreuer (n 224) 99–100; Dupont, 'Investments' (n 67) 203.

[233] Similarly Dolzer and Schreuer (n 224) 100 (for 'indirect expropriation, illegality ... the rule, since ... no compensation'); cf Dupont, 'Investments' (n 67) 203.

[234] Ruzza (n 205) [8], also [14]; Criddle (n 8) 593; *Iranian Assets* (n 218) [185].

[235] Potentially difficult: Ruzza (n 205) [8], [14]; Dolzer and Schreuer (n 224) 102.

[236] Abba Kolo, 'Investor Protection vs Host State Regulatory Autonomy during Economic Crisis: Treatment of Capital Transfers and Restrictions under Modern Investment Treaties' (2007) 8 JWIT 457, 487; Dupont, 'Investments' (n 67) 203; Dolzer and Schreuer (n 224) 112–15.

[237] Dolzer and Schreuer (n 224) 117–18; also Kolo (n 236) 491–93.

[238] Dolzer and Schreuer (n 224) 124–25; also Kolo (n 236) 492–93.

[239] Kolo (n 236) 487; similarly Escarcena (n 224) 121.

[240] Dolzer and Schreuer (n 224) 123; Kolo (n 236) 487; Escarcena (n 224) 121.

[241] Eg, *Akhras (EGC)* (n 217) [146]–[147]; *Assad* (n 165) [116]; *Rotenberg* (n 165) [176].

[242] Dolzer and Schreuer (n 224) 112.

[243] Barnes (n 206) 198, referencing *Ahmed v HM Treasury* [2010] UKSC 2, see [5], [60], [192], also [38]–[39], [147].

[244] *Kadi (GC)* (n 168) [358], n 210; also Kolo (n 236) 489–90 (freeze arguably 'indirect expropriation' where 'deprived of any ability to use, enjoy or dispose of ... investment'), referencing Hober.

[245] Eg, vis-à-vis Zimbabwe: EO 13288 (6 March 2003); EU Reg 314/2004 (19 February 2004); DFAT, 'Zimbabwe sanctions regime' <https://www.dfat.gov.au/international-relations/security/sanctions/sanctions-regimes/zimbabwe-sanctions-regime> (2002).

[246] Eg, vis-à-vis Crimea/Ukraine: EU Dec 2014/145/CFSP (17 March 2014); EO 13660 (6 March 2014); Syria: EO 13572 (29 April 2011); EU Dec 2013/255/CFSP (31 May 2013); Tunisia: EU Reg 101/2011 (4 February 2011); Zimbabwe: SEMZR (Canada) (4 September 2008). Similarly Dawidowicz (n 6) 277.

[247] See nn 211, 215–17. While countermeasures must also be proportionate, the measure's impacts are compared with the State's breach, rather than the general interest: see *ARSIWA*, 294–96; cf n 211.

investors would be granted 'a higher standard of protection than nationals', given that investment treaties 'contain undertakings which are explicitly designed to induce foreigners to make investments in reliance upon them', persons who should not bear the same 'burden' in achieving 'regulatory objectives for the benefit of [that] national community'.[248] Accordingly, investment tribunals have been unprepared to afford States the same 'margin of appreciation' in implementing measures, including asset freezes, as the European Court of Human Rights (ECtHR).[249] There is therefore a good case that, as Criddle suggests, and dependent on circumstances, asset freezes 'deprive investors of the right to manage, use, and effectively control their property', and thus amount to expropriation.[250] Indeed, Iran challenged the US measures in the *Certain Iranian Assets* case on this basis.[251] The Court did not decide whether the asset freeze was expropriatory, given Iran's failure to identify impacted property within the Court's jurisdiction,[252] though it did conclude that the asset *seizures* amounted to expropriation due to their unreasonable breadth.[253]

The Court in *Certain Iranian Assets* also considered challenges based on rights to dispose of property.[254] No breach was established, because Iran had failed to identify property within the Court's jurisdiction impacted by the measure at issue.[255] Nonetheless, the Court observed that the terms of the asset freeze 'reflect[ed] a general prohibition of the disposal of property',[256] suggesting that challenges to the compatibility of such freezes with similar provisions might be a real possibility.

'Fair and equitable treatment' (FET) obligations, which 'may offer redress where the facts do not support a claim for expropriation'[257] and provide greater protection than the right to property,[258] have been described as 'concerned ... essentially with the host State's decision-making process',[259] encompassing due process.[260] FET also requires 'weighing' an investor's 'legitimate ... expectations' against the State's 'legitimate regulatory interests'.[261] Given the procedural concerns regarding

[248] *Quasar de Valores v Russia (Award)* SCC Case 24/2007 (20 July 2012) [21]–[23]. See Paparinskis, *FET* (n 205) 230; Ch 3, n 82.

[249] *Valores* (n 248) [125]–[128], [158], also referencing *RosInvest v Russia (Award)* SCC Case 79/2005 (12 September 2010) [567], [574]. See Paparinskis, *FET* (n 205) 230 (fn 101). Cf Peters (n 28) 447.

[250] Criddle (n 8) 592. Similarly Dupont, 'Investments' (n 67) 203; van Aaken (n 8) 1; Ruys (n 7) 10–11; Dupont, 'Countermeasures' (n 112) 313; Kolo (n 236) 489–91; also Paparinskis, 'Countermeasures' (n 8) 278.

[251] *Iranian Assets* (n 218) [170].

[252] ibid [188], [200].

[253] ibid [186]–[187].

[254] ibid [193].

[255] ibid [200]–[201].

[256] ibid [200].

[257] Dolzer and Schreuer (n 224) 132; also Kolo (n 236) 496.

[258] See Paparinskis, *FET* (n 205) 229–31. Further: Ch 3, n 82.

[259] Nicolas Angelet, 'Fair and Equitable Treatment' in *MPEPIL* (n 15) (2011) [2].

[260] See ibid [16], [21]–[22], [35]; Criddle (n 8) 592; Dolzer and Schreuer (n 224) 100, 154–56; Kolo (n 236) 497, 500–1; also Paparinskis, 'Countermeasures' (n 8) 329 (fair trial).

[261] *Saluka v Czech Republic (Partial Award)* PCA Case 2001-04 (17 March 2006) [306], cited Kolo (n 236) 479, also 493–94, 498–99; Dolzer and Schreuer (n 224) 145–49.

asset freezes already noted above vis-à-vis human rights,[262] similar circumstances might violate FET standards.[263]

Indeed, the Court in *Certain Iranian Assets* found that both the asset freeze and seizure violated protections against 'unreasonable ... measures that would impair [nationals'] legally acquired rights and interests',[264] considering the impairment 'manifestly excessive' given the measures' stated purpose.[265] Although concerned with a particular treaty standard, the Court observed that there was 'overlap' with more general FET standards, 'because fair and equitable treatment can encompass protection against unreasonable or discriminatory measures'.[266]

Finally, Ruffert remarks that 'clauses guaranteeing the free flow of capital are among the most important rules within [BITs]',[267] allowing investors to transfer funds to varying degrees.[268] Some, but not all, such provisions include restrictions,[269] or exceptions for domestic law or necessary measures.[270] Subject to such provisions, sanctions involving asset freezes 'impos[e] restrictions upon the transfer of capital' of those targeted,[271] and could thus violate such protections.[272] Indeed, and tellingly, in recent negotiations regarding a new free trade agreement, Australia and the UK reportedly planned to insert a 'provision confirming that economic sanctions are not impacted by the commitment to allow free transfers of funds by investors',[273] suggesting that sanctions may otherwise violate such provisions.

Admittedly, the Court in *Certain Iranian Assets* did not consider that the measures at issue violated obligations concerning the movement of funds.[274] However, it construed the provision in question narrowly as relating solely to exchange restrictions,[275] based on its particular content and context.[276] Provisions in BITs appear

[262] nn 208–17ff.

[263] Dupont, 'Investments' (n 67) 204; Criddle (n 8) 592–93, cf 593; van Aaken (n 8) 1; Ruys (n 7) 10–11.

[264] *Iranian Assets* (n 218) [144].

[265] ibid [156]–[157].

[266] ibid [144].

[267] Matthias Ruffert, 'Capital, Free Flow Of' in *MPEPIL* (n 15) (2014) [25]; also Dolzer and Schreuer (n 224) 212; Kolo (n 236) 471.

[268] Kolo (n 236) 471–74; Dolzer and Schreuer (n 224) 214.

[269] Dolzer and Schreuer (n 224) 214. Cf *Continental Casualty v Argentina (Award)* ICSID Case No ARB/03/9 (5 September 2008) [237]–[245] (no blocking of transfer 'related to an investment' within BIT's meaning).

[270] Kolo (n 236) 471–74; also Dolzer and Schreuer (n 224) 214–15; van Aaken (n 8) 1.

[271] Ruffert (n 267) [27] (vis-à-vis UNSC terrorism sanctions).

[272] Criddle (n 8) 592–93; also Kolo (n 236) 471–85. Similarly Ruys (n 7) 10, referencing Dupont, 'Countermeasures' (n 112) 312–16.

[273] 'UK-Australia FTA negotiations: agreement in principle' (Policy paper, 17 June 2021) <https://www.gov.uk/government/publications/uk-australia-free-trade-agreement-negotiations-agreement-in-principle/uk-australia-fta-negotiations-agreement-in-principle>, cited Johanna Braun, 'Australia and United Kingdom Announce "Agreement in Principle" ...' *IA Rep* (17 June 2021).

[274] *Iranian Assets* (n 218) [208].

[275] ibid [205]–[208]. Indeed, see [206] (first part of provision 'appear[ed] fairly broad on its face').

[276] ibid [206]–[207]. Noting that a 'prohibition of any restriction on the movement of capital' was unlikely to have been the Parties' intention, '[g]iven the treaty practice of States regarding movement of

generally to be in broader terms.[277] Moreover, in several cases before EU courts, sanctions vis-à-vis Russia have been challenged as contrary to the EU–Russia Partnership Agreement, including article 52 thereof, which contains provisions relating to free movement of capital.[278] EU courts have not denied that the sanctions *could* breach the Agreement, merely noting that even if they did, reliance could be placed on an exception clause thereunder.[279] Again some, but not all, BITs contain such exception clauses,[280] and it is worth highlighting that the Court in *Certain Iranian Assets* did not consider that the US could rely on such a clause to justify the asset freezes at issue.[281]

Asset freezes may thus violate BIT obligations in a variety of ways.

(iii) Conclusion: countermeasures, individual claims, and third-party rights

What, then, might this practice, in which many States purport to respond to the wrongful conduct of other States through asset freezes targeted at individuals, measures which could plausibly violate obligations owed to individuals under investment law, tell us?[282]

For starters, States are generally presumed not to act intentionally in violation of international law,[283] and indeed sanction-imposing States sometimes expressly assert their compliance with international legal obligations.[284] If these measures nonetheless plausibly *are* in breach of international law, then they will have to be justified as countermeasures.[285] And if the 'third-party rights approach' is correct, such countermeasures cannot preclude individual claims under investment law if

capital more generally': [207]. However, without further elaboration of practice, this is of limited assistance in interpreting other provisions.

[277] See eg Canada–Russia (1989), art VII; Germany–Russia (1989), art 5; France–Syria (1977), art 6; Germany–Syria (1977), art 5; Switzerland–Syria (2007), art 6; Turkey–Syria (2004), art 5; Denmark–DPRK (1996), art 7; Germany–Iran (2002), art 5 (notably with exceptions for, *inter alia*, criminal proceedings); UK–Venezuela (1995), art 6; Zimbabwe–Germany (1995), art 5; Zimbabwe–Netherlands (1996), art 5; Switzerland–Zimbabwe (1996), art 5. Cf Japan–Russia (1998), art 8; UK–Russia (1989), art 6.

[278] See *Rosneft* (n 165) [170]. See EU–Russia PA, art 52.

[279] *Rosneft* (n 165) [178]–[179], quoting *R (PJSC Rosneft Oil) v Her Majesty's Treasury* Case C-72/15 (28 March 2017) (GC) [110]–[117], discussing art 99 EU-Russia PA.

[280] Dupont, 'Investments' (n 67) 211–13; Criddle (n 8) 593; Ruys (n 7) 11; van Aaken (n 8) 1; Dupont, 'Countermeasures' (n 112) 313. Eg, *Continental* (n 269) [200]–[205] (necessity clause covered bank freeze).

[281] *Iranian Assets* (n 218) [102]–[103], [108]–[109].

[282] See section III(A)(ii); nn 90–98; Criddle, nn 108–10.

[283] Eg *Jurisdictional Immunities (Germany v Italy: Greece Intervening) (Judgment)* [2012] ICJ Rep 99 [138] ('good faith ... presumed'); similarly Dupont, 'Countermeasures' (n 112) 313.

[284] Eg, EU Council, 'How and when the EU adopts sanctions' <http://www.consilium.europa.eu/en/policies/sanctions/> ('[EU] measures ... are fully compliant with obligations under international law, including ... human rights', emphasis removed); EU Guidelines (n 194) [9]. Further Dawidowicz (n 6) 254; Dupont, 'Investments' (n 67) 214; Dupont, 'Unilateral' (n 114) 43; Dupont, 'Countermeasures' (n 112) 313; SG Report (n 131) 9.

[285] Similarly n 194.

individuals rely on their own rights.[286] In light of these considerations, two possible explanations emerge from the practice.

First, it does not appear from the practice that these individuals are regarded as "third parties", separate and unrelated to the State alleged to have been engaged in wrongdoing.[287] On the contrary, as was expressly acknowledged vis-à-vis one State's Zimbabwean sanctions, these individuals are apparently targeted precisely *because* of their 'connection' with the allegedly wrongdoing State.[288] In some cases, this is immediately apparent from the sanctions' wording: while since lifted, early EU asset freezes vis-à-vis the former Yugoslavia, for instance, covered the relevant governments' property,[289] but 'Government' was defined to include those 'acting or purporting to act for or on [its] behalf',[290] who were thus individually subject to sanctions.[291] In other cases, sanctions regimes expressly identify targeted individuals as State officials,[292] as figures of State authority,[293] or as 'acting on behalf of',[294] or supporting,[295] a particular State.

And certain case law emanating from sanction-imposing States underlies this focus on the individual-State relationship. The ECJ explained, for instance, in *Kadi*, that the relevant EU treaty provisions allowing for the imposition of sanctions 'concern the adoption of measures *vis-à-vis third countries*, since that concept *may include the rulers of such a country and also individuals and entities associated with or controlled, directly or indirectly, by them*.'[296] It held, similarly, vis-à-vis Syrian sanctions that:

[286] nn 89–90.

[287] See Pantaleo (n 140) 177 ('reasons justifying ... designation ... connected with [person's] role ... in the contested State's conduct'); nn 107–10, 322–32; cf discussion Dawidowicz (n 6) 326, referencing *inter alia* ILC, '52nd' (n 189) 273 (Pellet) ('utterly reject[ing] ... idea that individuals could be "third parties" in ... context of inter-State responsibility'); similarly Paparinskis, 'Countermeasures' (n 8) 333. Cf vis-à-vis UNSC: Pellet and Miron (n 15) [36]–[38]; Ruys (n 7) 15, 17; Happold (n 115) 89.

[288] OFAC, 'Zimbabwe Sanctions Program' (18 December 2013) <https://www.treasury.gov/resource-center/sanctions/Programs/Documents/zimb.pdf>, 4 ('persons ... targeted ... on the basis of their connection to ... Government'); similarly Syria Sanctions (Canada) (n 150) ('Syrian regime [members]'; those 'associated'); 'Japan Stands with Ukraine' (30 June 2022) <https://japan.kantei.go.jp/ongoingtopics/pdf/jp_stands_with_ukraine_eng.pdf> (*inter alia* 'persons related to [Russian] Government'); Pantaleo, n 287; Criddle, n 110.

[289] EU Reg 1294/1999 (15 June 1999) art 3. Further Dawidowicz (n 6) 183–85, 191–93.

[290] EU Reg 1294/1999, art 1(1)–(2).

[291] ibid art 2(1); Annex I.

[292] n 179.

[293] n 180.

[294] Eg EO 13553, s 1(a)(ii)(A) ('acting on behalf of ... [Iranian] Government'); similarly SEMSR (Canada), s 2(d); n 290.

[295] Eg ASR (Australia), s 6, It 7; EU Dec 2013/255/CFSP, art 28 ('supporting [Syrian] regime'); EO 13469, s 1(a)(vii) (supporting 'Government ... any senior official'); BelSEUER (UK), reg 6(2)(a)(vii) ('supporting ... Government'); also n 172.

[296] *Kadi (GC)* (n 168) [166] (emphasis added), also [172] (not covering 'persons ... in no way linked to ... governing regime of ... third country'). Cf *Tomana v Council* Case C-330/15P (28 July 2016) (ECJ) [45] (treaties now allowing measures 'against natural or legal persons and groups or non-State entities', referencing TFEU, art 215(2)). The point however, is that *when* measures are directed against States, that concept includes certain individuals. See Lester and O'Kane (n 124) for case law discussed herein.

> regarding restrictive measures *applying to a third country* ... the categories of natural persons at whom restrictive measures may be directed include those whose connection with the third country concerned is quite obvious, namely the leaders of third countries and individuals associated with them.[297]

In determining who is thus covered, EU courts require 'a set of indicia sufficiently specific, precise and consistent to establish that there is a sufficient link between the person subject to a measure freezing his funds and the [State] regime'.[298] Measures cannot simply 'be directed at persons ... present in a third country or associated with one'.[299]

EU courts have accepted that persons in 'senior posts' would be covered by such requirements,[300] as would persons supporting the relevant regime in an economic sense,[301] or through specific forms of facilitation.[302] Persons responsible for given acts have been regarded as 'associates' of a regime,[303] while a family member's inclusion was explained, in the Syrian context, as based on their being 'connected with the Syrian leaders ... particularly as the existence in that country of a tradition of the exercise of power by a family is a well-known fact'.[304] It could therefore be presumed 'that [the individual] profits from the Syrian regime and is associated with it'.[305] Even sanctions vis-à-vis individuals *benefiting* from persons or acts have been explained in terms of support, the European Court of Justice General Court (EGC) holding that 'recipients of those benefits cannot be unaware of the involvement of [the relevant] decision-makers' in the conduct at issue, 'and can expect their resources, derived at least in part from those benefits, to be targeted ... with

[297] *Assad* (n 165) [92] (emphasis added), referencing *Tay Za* (n 216) [68]; similarly *Tomana* (n 296) [76].

[298] *Akhras v Council* Case C-193/15P (7 April 2016) (ECJ) [61], citing *Anbouba v Council* Case C-630/13P (21 April 2015) (EGC) [53]. Vis-à-vis Zimbabwe: *Tomana* (n 296) [82]; also *Tay Za* (n 216) [61]–[63], referencing *Kadi (GC)* (n 168) [166]–[168]. Generally Pantaleo (n 140) 177–78, 191–94.

[299] *Tay Za* (n 216) [61].

[300] *Tomana* (n 296) [84], also [85]–[87].

[301] *Akhras (ECJ)* (n 298) [62] ('[businessman's] position ... providing economic support to ... Syrian regime or benefitting from it'); also *Akhras (EGC)* (n 217) [104] ('significant roles ... in ... Syrian business world ... links with ... person principally responsible for ... repression ... support ... to the regime'), [115]–[119], [127]–[133]; *Mayaleh v Council* Cases T-307/12 and T-408/13 (5 November 2014) (EGC) [141]–[142], [148] ('position of power and influence' regarding 'financial support of ... Syrian regime'); also *Anbouba* (n 298) [52]; cf *Chyzh v Council* Case T-276/12 (6 October 2015) (EGC), particularly [166]–[182] (prominent businessman insufficient without more); Pantaleo (n 140) 192.

[302] Eg, *Rotenberg* (n 165) [120]–[124] (construction), [128] ('public relations'); *R (Bredenkamp) v Secretary of State for Foreign and Commonwealth Affairs* [2013] EWHC 2480 (Admin) [4] ('assisting ... Mugabe regime'), discussed Lester and O'Kane (n 124). Control of another suffices: *Syrian Lebanese Commercial Bank v Council* Cases T-174/12 and T-80/13 (4 February 2014) (EGC) [101]–[114]; also *Mayaleh* (n 301) [148].

[303] *Tomana* (n 296) [48] ('persons whose activities seriously undermine [*inter alia*] ... human rights' 'constitute ... particular category of ... associates [of government members]').

[304] *Assad* (n 165) [96].

[305] ibid [97], also [99] ('leaders can easily circumvent ... measures' through 'relatives and associates'). Cf *Tay Za* (n 216) [61]–[71], discussed therein; Pantaleo (n 140) 191.

the aim of preventing them from being able to support the decision-makers in question'.[306]

Even the broadest sanctions—those aimed at whole sectors of a country's economy—could also be so regarded. Admittedly, the EGC held in *Rosneft*, a case concerned with measures against the Russian oil sector:

> that restrictive measures, by definition, have consequences which affect rights to property and the freedom to pursue a trade or business, thereby causing harm to persons who are *in no way responsible for the situation which led to the adoption of the sanctions*. That is a fortiori the case with respect to the consequences of targeted restrictive measures on the entities subject to those measures. . . .[307]

It noted there that:

> the objective of the restrictive measures at issue is not to penalise certain entities because of their links with the situation in Ukraine, but to impose economic sanctions on the Russian Federation, in order to increase the costs of its actions to undermine Ukraine's territorial integrity, sovereignty and independence, and to promote a peaceful settlement . . . .[308]

However, this case concerned measures other than asset freezes, notably restrictions on entities accessing capital markets and on exports to them.[309] Here, in considering the third-party rights approach, we are only interested in measures that might violate the international rights of individuals subject to those measures.[310] Indeed, as the ARSIWA note, 'indirect or consequential effects of countermeasures on third parties, which do not involve an independent breach of any obligation to those third parties' are not such as to render those countermeasures unlawful vis-à-vis those third parties.[311] Measures such as export controls clearly might have wide-ranging effects on industries in the target State,[312] but do not appear likely to violate the rights under investment law discussed above;[313] certainly not as obviously as asset freezes may do.[314] Indeed, when asset freezes were imposed on entities in the defence sector in the context of the Russia–Ukraine conflict, the Court's emphasis in evaluating the proportionality of those measures was very

306 *Rotenberg* (n 165) [91]. Similarly Pantaleo (n 140) 193.
307 *Rosneft* (n 165) [208] (emphasis added).
308 ibid [160]. Also [157], [205].
309 ibid [66], [79].
310 nn 89ff.
311 *ARSIWA*, 169, also citing *Cysne* (n 39) 1056–57 ('reprisals . . . may affect the nationals of an innocent State').
312 *Rosneft* (n 165) [208] (may 'harm [those] . . . in no way responsible').
313 Section III(A)(ii)(b).
314 Cf *Rosneft* (n 165) [207] (no breach of property rights).

different, notwithstanding similar arguments that the measures went beyond those 'directly responsible' for given actions:

> By applying also to persons and entities materially or financially supporting actions which undermine or threaten the territorial integrity, sovereignty and independence of Ukraine, the Council could legitimately expect that such actions cease or that they become more costly for those who undertake them, in order to promote a peaceful settlement of the crisis. . . .[315]

The focus is thus on the entity's *support* for the relevant wrongdoing, rather than mere involvement in a sector. In any event, notwithstanding the Court's views in *Rosneft* regarding the lack of connection between the allegedly wrongful acts and the entities' activities, those entities were part of an economic group 'predominantly owned by the Russian State'.[316] And in the practice relating to sanctions, it appears that either such a relationship, or involvement in particularly lucrative sectors, may be regarded as sufficient to demonstrate support for a regime. The UK's sanctions vis-à-vis both Russia and Belarus, for example, expressly define 'obtaining a benefit from or supporting the Government' as including not only carrying on, owning, controlling or working in certain positions for government-affiliated entities, but also carrying on businesses of either 'economic significance' or 'in a sector of or strategic significance' to the government.[317] The EU sanctions against Russia themselves also target 'leading businesspersons or legal persons, entities or bodies involved in economic sectors providing a substantial source of revenue to the [Russian] Government'.[318] From other sanctions, it appears that the basis for targeting 'goods which generate significant revenue for Russia' is that the revenue is 'thereby enabling its actions destabilising the situation in Ukraine'.[319] Similarly, in speaking of sanctions aimed at 'economic sectors that generate substantial revenue for the Russian regime', the Treasury Secretary said that the US would:

> make sure that Russian elites and the Kremlin's enablers are held accountable for their complicity in [the] war . . . the United States will also continue to choke off revenue and equipment underpinning Russia's unprovoked war in Ukraine.[320]

[315] *'Almaz-Antey' Air and Space Defence Corp v Council* Case T-255/15 (25 January 2017) (EGC) [105].

[316] *Rosneft* (n 165) [126].

[317] BelSEUER, reg 6(3A); RussSEUER, reg 6(4). Government affiliation and strategic significance are further defined: reg 6(4), reg 6(7) respectively.

[318] EU Dec 2022/329, art 1 (new art 2(1)(g)).

[319] EU Dec (CFSP)2022/578 (8 April 2022), arts 1(13), (20) (new arts 3(i), 4(k)).

[320] USDOT, 'Treasury Sanctions Elites and Companies in Economic Sectors that Generate Substantial revenue for the Russian Regime' (Pr Rel, 2 August 2022) <https://home.treasury.gov/news/press-releases/jy0905>.

The targeting of particular sectors in Iran is likewise justified on the basis of their 'facilitating' proliferation.[321] Such measures may thus also be viewed as based on the *support* those sectors provide, directly or indirectly, to the State's alleged wrong.

Individuals' assets are therefore frozen in practice precisely because those individuals are *not* regarded as third parties vis-à-vis the relevant State's allegedly wrongful conduct.[322] For certain persons, such as State officials, drawing such a link between the individual and State is unexceptional: States can 'only act through the institutions and agencies of the state, its officials and employees'[323] and rules of attribution exist precisely to treat individuals acting for the State as synonymous with it for State responsibility purposes.[324] Other persons are identified in the practice as *supporting* the State in some way.[325] The different categories of such support might generally be described in terms of 'complicity',[326] meaning 'participation in wrongdoing committed by another',[327] or providing 'aid or assistance' or 'means to enable or facilitate' an act.[328] Indeed, the term 'complicit' is sometimes expressly used in sanctions,[329] and was used in one sanctions-related case,[330] while another employed the terminology of 'collusion'.[331] Here too, however, the relevant individuals are not apparently treated as third parties: it is their 'connection' with the State that determines whether they are sanctioned.[332]

One possible explanation for the practice is therefore that States do not consider certain individuals having a 'connection' with, or complicit in, the State's wrongdoing as 'third parties' at all.[333] Given that only third-party rights cannot

[321] See USIFCPA, s 1244(a)(1) ('sectors ... facilitating ... nuclear proliferation activities'); similarly *Council v Kala Naft* Case C-348/12P (28 November 2013) (ECJ) [83] ('trading in key equipment and technology for ... gas and oil industry' potentially 'support for ... nuclear activities'), discussed Pantaleo (n 140) 193–94.

[322] Similarly, distinguishing measures where 'no connection ... with a third country' and 'inter-State smart sanctions': Pantaleo (n 140) 174–75, 177ff; quote n 287; also Criddle, nn 108–10; nn 107, 287.

[323] *Oppenheim's* (n 22) 540; see authorities Ch 1, n 8.

[324] nn 16–21. Similarly Criddle, nn 108–10.

[325] nn 172, 295, 301. Similarly distinguishing 'leadership' and 'private' support-based sanctions: Happold (n 115) 91. Although some describe attribution as holding States 'responsible for acts ... sufficiently linked to [them]' (Stern (n 71) 202; similarly Jackson (n 72) 178), resembling discussion of 'sufficient link' (n 298), complicity is insufficient for attribution: Jackson (n 72) 178–79; nn 481–82.

[326] Indeed, see n 320; similarly 'Further Russia and Belarus Sanctions' (Media Release, 18 May 2022), <https://www.foreignminister.gov.au/minister/marise-payne/media-release/further-russia-and-belarus-sanctions#:~:text=The%20Australian%20Government%20has%20imposed,who%20have%20supported%20the%20invasion> ('targeting those who share responsibility ... or hold levers of influence').

[327] Jackson (n 72) 10, discussion 11, 17–31. Further Chinkin (n 89) 297; n 482

[328] *Application of the Convention on the Prevention and Punishment of the Crime of Genocide (Bosnia and Herzegovina v Serbia and Montenegro) (Judgment)* [2007] ICJ Rep 43 [419]–[420] (referencing *ARSIWA*, art 16), cited Tams, 'Terrorists' (n 8) 387.

[329] n 171.

[330] Albeit UNSC: *Sayadi* (n 203) 31 (Diss Op Wedgewood).

[331] *Tomana* (n 296) [81].

[332] nn 297, 322, also n 287. Cf *Georg K v Interior Ministry* (1972) 71 ILR 284 (Adm Ct Austria) 290–91 (individual's conduct more likely affecting interstate relations where in authority); *Rosneft* (n 165) [208], n 307.

[333] nn 287–88, 296–97, 322–32. Similarly Criddle, nn 108–10; Peters/Roberts, n 107; Pantaleo, n 287.

be violated by countermeasures,[334] countermeasures against States could therefore also justify infringement of these individuals' rights,[335] and preclude any resulting claims.[336] Admittedly, not all States employ asset freezes in this manner, but, as noted above, a significant number have.[337] There is, on the other hand, limited practice suggesting that *all* individuals should be regarded as 'third parties' for countermeasures purposes.[338]

A second possible, alternative, explanation is that States simply do not think these measures are in breach of individual (third-party) rights. As noted in Chapter 5, States do not appear, in their practice relating to the amendment and termination of investment treaties, to regard individuals as having irrevocable rights thereunder.[339] Moreover, certain States aim sanctions, including asset freezes, at individuals allegedly involved in human rights abuses, terrorism, chemical weapons production, and cyberattacks, without any prima facie need for State involvement in the relevant conduct.[340] Even in some of the country-related sanctions regimes discussed above, the sanctions seem more directed at particular individuals than a State.[341] One could dismiss this practice as irrelevant here given that actions not responding to alleged *State* wrongdoing cannot amount to countermeasures.[342] But if this practice is taken to suggest that States are unconcerned with asset freezes being in violation of individual rights regardless of whether they could be justified as countermeasures, then this might undermine the argument regarding third-party rights made above, and suggest that States simply do not consider that such measures violate international law.

Of course, there may be reasons why measures taken in these particular fields are not in breach of international law, without needing to conclude that asset freezes are never wrongful. For starters, such measures are often taken in sectors in which States have international *obligations* to suppress certain activities. The Security Council has, for instance, mandated States to freeze the resources of those committing or attempting to commit terrorist acts, those participating in or facilitating

[334] nn 37–41.

[335] cf nn 37ff, 89ff; similarly: Criddle (n 8) 609–10; n 107.

[336] cf nn 25–41, 107–11.

[337] Similarly Dawidowicz (n 6) 243–44, 283; Dawidowicz (n 32) 410–12; see nn 127ff.

[338] Excepting the three cases nn 92–97, the literature is scholarly: nn 90ff. Cf *ADM* (n 7) [127]; [5], [15] (Op Rovine) (undisputed by Mexico), but cf Losari and Ewing-Chow (n 28) 289. Similarly: n 107 (Peters/Roberts); nn 107–10, 287.

[339] Ch 5, nn 382ff.

[340] Eg, ASR (Australia), s 6A; JVCFOA (Canada); EU Regs 2580/2001 (27 December 2001), 2018/1542 (15 October 2018), 2019/796 (17 May 2019), 2020/1998 (7 December 2020); Magnitsky Act (US), s 1263; EO 13818 (21 December 2017), s 1(a)(ii)(A); *Tomana* (n 296) [45]; cf *Kadi (GC)* (n 168) [167], [180].

[341] Eg DRC: EU Dec 2010/788/CFSP, art 3; Libya: EU Reg 2016/44, art 6(2); ASR, s 6, It 5 (including persons associated with *former* government); Yugoslavia/Balkans: EO 13304 (28 May 2003); EO 14033 (8 June 2021); ASR (Australia), s 6, It 2 (offences). Further: Dawidowicz (n 6) 181–93. Corruption sanctions tend also to be individual-focused.

[342] nn 15–22.

it, and related entities,[343] while obligations to criminalise terrorist financing, including through the freezing of funds, exist under the International Convention for the Suppression of the Financing of Terrorism.[344] Under the Convention against Corruption, States have obligations to prevent, criminalise and sanction corruption and money-laundering, including through asset seizure.[345] And under the Chemical Weapons Convention, States are to criminalise various activities relating to chemical weapons.[346] Almost all States are parties to these instruments.[347]

Moreover, the sanctions regimes in these fields generally appear to apply to limited numbers of persons, minimising the likelihood that investment protections would cover given individuals.[348] This is in stark contrast to country-based sanctions regimes generally, pursuant to which thousands of individuals' assets have been frozen.[349] And finally, even if the regimes prima facie cover any individuals, in practice, they often target State officials,[350] suggesting that the same argument regarding countermeasures being taken against States via certain individuals might be plausible here also.

Until a sanctions regime asset freeze is challenged before an international investment tribunal, which arguments will be pursued by respondent States, or ultimately accepted, is unknown. But the practice lends credence to the view that States do not accept the third-party rights approach to countermeasures vis-à-vis at least certain categories of individuals—whether because they consider that countermeasures taken against a State can legitimately target individuals complicit in the State's wrongdoing, or because they consider that individuals are only relying on the State's rights in bringing individual claims.

343 UNSC Resolution 1373 (2001) [1](c). Various States cite this resolution in explaining counter-terrorism sanctions: eg EU Sanctions Map (n 126); DFAT, 'Counter-Terrorism (UNSC 1373) sanctions regime' <https://www.dfat.gov.au/international-relations/security/sanctions/sanctions-regimes/Pages/counter-terrorism-unsc-1373-sanctions-regime>.

344 See ICSFT, art 8.

345 CAC, arts 15–17, 23, 26, 30–31, Ch 5.

346 CWC, arts I, VII.

347 See UN Treaty Collection: <https://treaties.un.org/Pages/ViewDetails.aspx?src=IND&mtdsg_no=XVIII-11&chapter=18>; <https://treaties.un.org/Pages/ViewDetails.aspx?src=TREATY&mtdsg_no=XVIII-14&chapter=18&clang=_en>; <https://treaties.un.org/pages/ViewDetails.aspx?src=TREATY&mtdsg_no=XXVI-3&chapter=26> (189, 189, and 193 Parties respectively).

348 Most of the human rights, cyber-attacks, chemical weapons and non-UN terrorism lists appear to cover tens of persons, with a couple covering hundreds: see the consolidated lists noted at n 181.

349 Total numbers can be gleaned from listings databases, but eg by mid-2023, the UK had sanctioned over 1,500 entities under its Ukraine-related regime alone: FCDO, 'UK Sanctions Following Russia's Invasion of Ukraine' (updated 8 June 2023) <https://www.gov.uk/government/collections/uk-sanctions-following-russias-invasion-of-ukraine>.

350 Eg many individuals sanctioned under EU and UK chemical weapons, human rights and anti-corruption sanctions appear to be current or former officials, as are some sanctioned for cyber-attack activities, while at least some under Australian human rights and anti-corruption and US human rights, anti-corruption and cyber-attack designations appear to be State-linked. See the consolidated lists at n 181. While counter-terrorism targets are often not State-related, action is Security Council-mandated: n 343.

One final point should be made. On either approach, as noted above, the ARSIWA underscore that countermeasures cannot impact 'fundamental human rights',[351] with cases continuing to be brought alleging, and sometimes finding, human rights violations resulting from the imposition of sanctions.[352] Human rights obligations are owed *erga omnes* (*partes*) to all or a group of States.[353] And *States* clearly *are* 'third parties' under international law in the countermeasures context.[354] Countermeasures would, accordingly, be precluded from affecting such obligations not because individual rights are in issue (though they may be),[355] but because the rights of *other* States would be violated.[356] The same would not, however, apply to investment law,[357] and it is therefore in this field that applying a different approach to countermeasures could be significant.[358]

IV. Self-defence, individuals, and third parties

Non-State actors, including terrorist groups, now have available the means to cause widescale damage and destruction.[359] With the UN Security Council not always functioning to address the threat, States are resorting to self-defence in response.[360] Many scholars nonetheless suggest that self-defence is exercisable only in response to State attacks.[361] Article 51 of the Charter, it is said, operates 'as an exception to the comprehensive ban on the *inter-state* use of force' in article 2(4), and thus only envisages 'armed attacks' by States.[362]

[351] *ARSIWA*, art 50(1)(b); also Dawidowicz (n 6) 308–9, 319–33; van Aaken (n 8) 2. "Fundamental" is unclear: see Paparinskis, 'Countermeasures' (n 8) 328–29; O'Keefe (n 10) 1164; Dawidowicz (n 6) 272, 328–29; cf DARIO, 94 (omitting).

[352] Eg, nn 208–14 (*Kadi*); *Assad* (n 165) [53]; nn 296ff (reasons/'substantive legality' separate).

[353] Ch 2, nn 211–16.

[354] nn 34–40.

[355] cf discussion Dawidowicz (n 6) 324–27, referencing *inter alia* James Crawford, 'Third Report on State Responsibility' (2000) 2(1) ILCYB 3 [312]; ILC, '52nd' (n 189) 266, 270–73, 293–94, 297–99, particularly 270 (Simma); cf Paddeu, *Justification* (n 8) 278–79.

[356] Dawidowicz (n 6) 309–12, 326–33; Paparinskis, 'Countermeasures' (n 8) 330–31, cf 332–34; Borelli and Olleson (n 189) 1185–86; also Raphaele Rivier, 'Inter-American Mechanisms' in Crawford and others, *Responsibility* (n 6) 745; BIICL Seminar, 'Sanctions, Countermeasures and Human Rights' (London, 12 June 2014); cf Paddeu, *Justification* (n 8) 278–79.

[357] Ch 2, n 148.

[358] Similarly Criddle (n 8) 598–99.

[359] Paddeu, 'Force' (n 49) 93–94; Greenwood, 'Self-Defence' (n 44) [18]; Tom Ruys and Sten Verhoeven, 'Attacks by Private Actors and the Right of Self-Defence' (2005) 10 JCSL 289, 289, 310; Ruys (n 21) 368–69, 488; Moir (n 70) 720.

[360] See Tams, 'Terrorists' (n 8) 365–67, 373–78, 392; Anne Peters and Christian Marxsen, 'Editors' Introduction: Self-Defence in Times of Transition' (2017) 77 ZfaöRV 3, 6.

[361] Eg authorities n 444; Olivier Corten, 'A Plea Against the Abusive Invocation of Self-Defence as a Response to Terrorism' *EJIL:Talk!* (14 July 2016); discussion Tams, 'Terrorists' (n 8) 367–69, 383–85; Jackson (n 72) 180–81; Ruys and Verhoeven (n 359) 290.

[362] Tams, 'Terrorists' (n 8) 385; similarly Corten, *War* (n 44) 162–69; Christian Tams, 'Note Analytique-Swimming with the Tide or Seeking to Stem It? Recent ICJ Rulings on the Law of

A. Dismissing the textual and jurisprudential arguments

We can derive two potential arguments against self-defence being available for use in response to attacks emanating from non-States.[363] The first is that individuals are simply unable to engage in 'armed attacks' within the meaning of article 51.[364] A textual analysis does not, however, get us far: article 51 says nothing regarding the attacker's identity, and certainly does not exclude that non-State actors could mount an 'armed attack'.[365] The *travaux prèparatoires* imply, if anything, the contrary.[366] Moreover, that self-defence excuses a violation of article 2(4) of the Charter does not dictate, logically-speaking, that only an interstate breach of article 2(4) can give rise to its exercise.[367]

It is often suggested that the ICJ established that self-defence can only operate where attacks are attributable to a State in its *Nicaragua*,[368] *Wall*,[369] and *Armed Activities*[370] decisions. But again, the rulings are not unequivocal, with scholars highlighting that the outcomes arguably depended on the factual situations at play.[371] Indeed, in *Armed Activities*, the Court explicitly declined to determine

Self-Defence' (2005) 18 Rev Queb DDI 275, 278–79; Trapp, 'Attack' (n 71) 680; Guy Keinan, 'Humanising the Right of Self-Defence' (2017) 77 ZfaöRV 57, 57.

[363] Similarly Keinan (n 362) 57–58; Lubell (n 48) 29–42; Karin Oellers-Frahm, 'Article 51—What Matters Is the Armed Attack, Not the Attacker' (2017) 77 ZfaöRV 49, 49.

[364] Authorities n 362.

[365] Lubell (n 48) 31–32; Christopher Greenwood, 'Historical Development and Legal Basis' in Dieter Fleck (ed), *The Handbook of International Humanitarian Law* (2nd edn, OUP 2008) 6; Greenwood, 'Self-Defence' (n 44) [17]; Tams, 'Terrorists' (n 8) 369, referencing *Wall* (n 58) 215 (Sep Op Higgins); Ruys (n 21) 369; Moir (n 70) 720; Trapp, 'Attack' (n 71) 684; Dinstein (n 47) [634]; Tams, 'Analytique' (n 362) 278; Ruys and Verhoeven (n 359) 290–91; Gray (n 44) 137, 207; Elizabeth Wilmshurst (ed), *Principles of International Law on Self-Defence* (Chatham House 2005) 11. Cf Corten, *War* (n 44) 162–64.

[366] Karl Zemanek, 'Armed Attack' in *MPEPIL* (n 15) (2013) [16]. Proposals to add the words 'by a State' after 'attack' were not renewed, but no explanation was given: Trapp, 'Attack' (n 71) 684–85; Ruys (n 21) 369.

[367] Marko Milanovic, 'Self-Defense and Non-State Actors: Indeterminacy and the Jus Ad Bellum' *EJIL:Talk!* (21 February 2010); Keinan (n 362) 58; similarly Ruys (n 21) 369–70; Dinstein (n 47) [634]. Cf Trapp, 'Attack' (n 71) 680.

[368] See *Nicaragua (Merits)* (n 44) [229]–[238], also [126], [130], [195], discussed, eg, Tams, 'Terrorists' (n 8) 368–69 ('effectively restricted self-defence to the inter-State context'), also referencing *Wall* (n 58) 215 (Sep Op Higgins), 229–30 (Sep Op Koojimans); Corten, *War* (n 44) 188, 466–67; Jackson (n 72) 179–80; Gray (n 44) 136–39; Ruys (n 21) 406–19; cf Trapp, 'Attack' (n 71) 686–88.

[369] *Wall* (n 58) [139] ('inherent right of self-defence in the case of armed attack by one State against another State'; no imputability shown), discussed, eg, Tams, 'Terrorists' (n 8) 384; Lubell (n 48) 31–32; Kimberley Trapp, 'Back to Basics: Necessity, Proportionality, and the Right of Self-Defence Against Non-State Terrorist Actors' (2007) 56 ICLQ 141, 143–44; Ruys (n 21) 473–76; Trapp, 'Attack' (n 71) 688; Jackson (n 72) 180; Tams, 'Analytique' (n 362) 283–84; Ruys and Verhoeven (n 359) 304–5; Greenwood, 'Self-Defence' (n 44) [16].

[370] *Armed Activities on the Territory of the Congo (DRC v Uganda) (Judgment)* [2005] ICJ Rep 168 [146]–[147] (self-defence not exercisable against DRC where non-State actor attacks not attributable), discussed, eg, Trapp, 'Attack' (n 71) 688–89; Trapp, 'Basics' (n 369) 144; Tams, 'Terrorists' (n 8) 384; Ruys (n 21) 481–85; Gray (n 44) 140–41; Tams, 'Analytique' (n 362) 285; Lubell (n 48) 33; Corten, *War* (n 44) 193, 468–69; Jörg Kammerhofer, 'The Resilience of the Restrictive Rules on Self-Defence' in Weller (n 70) 630–31.

[371] Eg, on *Nicaragua* and *Armed Activities*: Trapp, 'Attack' (n 71) 687–89; Trapp, 'Basics' (n 369) 142–45 (actions in purported self-defence aimed *at a State*, not non-State actors, explaining consequent

whether self-defence could generally be exercised in response to non-State actor attacks.[372]

B. Dismissing the third-party rights approach

(i) Self-defence and third-party rights: general propositions

In the absence of clarity emanating from a textual and jurisprudential analysis, it is more helpful to turn to the second argument, which explains *why*, on a policy level, those objecting to the use of force against non-State actors do so. Echoing the position vis-à-vis countermeasures,[373] scholars contend that self-defence only justifies violating the rights of an entity having committed an attack.[374] Even in attacking an individual in self-defence, force will be used against the State in which that individual is located, violating the prohibition on the use of force vis-à-vis that State,[375] and its territorial sovereignty.[376] Proponents of an 'inter-state reading of self-defence'[377] require the attack to be attributable to a State because

emphasis on attribution); see *Nicaragua (Merits)* (n 44) [156], [227]–[228], [237]; *Armed Activities* (n 370) [118], [147], [153]. Further: Ruys (n 21) 494 ('[s]ubstantial support' for distinction in practice), 495–96; Lubell (n 48) 32–33, 36, 40; Tams, 'Analytique' (n 362) 286; Moir (n 70) 723. Cf Tams, 'Rejoinder' (n 72) 1060. In *Wall*, the territory was occupied; with no other State in the picture, art 2(4) was not 'engage[d]' and self-defence 'inapplicable': Trapp, 'Attack' (n 71) 688; see *Wall* (n 58) [86]–[87], [139]; also Trapp, 'Basics' (n 369) 144; Tams, 'Analytique' (n 362) 283; Gray (n 44) 142 (no finding that self-defence applied '*only* in the case of an armed attack by one state against another' (original emphasis)); cf Corten, *War* (n 44) 147, 189–92; Dinstein (n 47) [648].

[372] *Armed Activities* (n 370) [147], discussed, eg, Tams, 'Terrorists' (n 8) 384; Tams, 'Analytique' (n 362) 285–86; Trapp, 'Basics' (n 369) 144–45; Trapp, 'Attack' (n 71) 688–89; Lubell (n 48) 33. Cf Ruys (n 21) 482–85; Corten, *War* (n 44) 193–95, 468–69; Jackson (n 72) 180–81.

[373] nn 34-40.

[374] See, eg, William O'Brien, 'Reprisals, Deterrence and Self-Defense in Counterterror Operations' (1990) 30 Virg JIL 421, 422, referencing Derek Bowett, 'Reprisals Involving Recourse to Armed Force' (1972) 66 AJIL 1, 3; also Bowett (n 47) 56.

[375] Tams, 'Terrorists' (n 8) 362, 364, 365, quoting Wilmshurst (n 365) 12 ('The right of states to defend themselves against ongoing attacks, even by private groups of non-state actors, is not generally questioned. What *is* questioned is the right to take action against the state that is the presumed source of such attacks, since ... an attack against a non-state actor within a state will inevitably constitute the use of force *on* the territorial state' (original emphasis)); Ruys (n 21) 377; Trapp, 'Basics' (n 369) 145–46; Lubell (n 48) 26–29; Gray (n 44) 210; Corten, *War* (n 44) 171–72.

[376] Tams, 'Terrorists' (n 8) 365, 367–68, 374, 385; Olivier Corten, 'Has Practice Led to an "Agreement Between the Parties" Regarding the Interpretation of Article 51 of the UN Charter?' (2017) 77 ZfaöRV 15, 15–16; Trapp, 'Basics' (n 369) 144–46; Trapp, 'Attack' (n 71) 680; Ruys (n 21) 377; Paddeu, *Justification* (n 8) 178, 219; Paddeu, 'Force' (n 49) 95–99; Kimberley Trapp, 'The Use of Force against Terrorists: A Reply to Christian J. Tams' (2009) 20 EJIL 1049, 1049–50; Tams, 'Rejoinder' (n 72) 1059; Corten, *War* (n 44) 172–73; Deeks (n 72) 491; Gray (n 44) 137, 226; also Lubell (n 48) 36ff. Cf n 386.

[377] For the terminology, eg Tams, 'Terrorists' (n 8) 383; similarly Jackson (n 72) 179; Trapp, 'Attack' (n 71) 680, 694; Trapp, 'Reply' (n 376) 1049.

the State is otherwise 'innocent'[378] and violation of its sovereignty cannot be excused.[379]

However, while countermeasures cannot justify violations of third-State rights,[380] the same does not hold true for self-defence. On the contrary, as Paddeu observes, the law of self-defence envisages possible third-party impacts.[381]

For starters, the obligation prohibiting the use of force is itself one that is owed *erga omnes*.[382] Consequently, *any* invocation of self-defence will necessarily excuse a use of force that would otherwise violate obligations owed to *every* other State.[383] 'Innocent' States thus have *these* rights affected when a State exercises self-defence, regardless of the target.[384] Indeed, even if one considers that self-defence is excluded altogether from the prohibition on the use of force,[385] the point stands that self-defence involves a use of force that—but for meeting the necessary conditions—would breach rights belonging to all States.

The legality of violating, through an invocation of self-defence, rights *other* than those concerning use of force, including rights to territorial sovereignty, must be considered vis-à-vis self-defence as a circumstance precluding wrongfulness.[386] The commentary to article 21 of the ARSIWA on self-defence acknowledges, in this respect, that exercising self-defence might affect third parties, including under the law of neutrality.[387] Relevantly for our purposes here, the law of neutrality allows

378 Eg Bowett (n 47) 10, 171; Michael Bothe, 'The Law of Neutrality' in Dieter Fleck (ed), *The Handbook of International Humanitarian Law* (3rd edn, OUP 2013) 559; Corten, *War* (n 44) 194; discussion Eliav Lieblich, 'Self-Defence Against Non-State Actors and The Myth of the Innocent State' [2019] <https://papers.ssrn.com/sol3/papers.cfm?abstract_id=3364163>, 4ff.

379 Trapp, 'Reply' (n 376) 1049–50, discussing Tams, 'Terrorists' (n 8) 385; similarly Trapp, 'Attack' (n 71) 680; Trapp, 'Basics' (n 369) 146; also Gray (n 44) 207, 210, 226; Paddeu, *Justification* (n 8) 178; Keinan (n 362) 57–58.

380 nn 34–40.

381 Paddeu similarly analyses self-defence effects on third-party rights, including vis-à-vis self-defence against non-State actors, and including discussion of neutrality: Paddeu, 'Force' (n 49) 103–6, 110–14; cf Paddeu, *Justification* (n 8) 180. Cf Lieblich (n 378) 12ff.

382 Eg *ARSIWA*, 278, citing *Barcelona Traction, Light and Power Company (Belgium v Spain)* [1970] ICJ Rep 3 [33] (aggression); Chinkin (n 89) 293–94.

383 See Ch 1, nn 124–33. Cf Paddeu, *Justification* (n 8) 221, also 178, 193–97; Paddeu, 'Force' (n 49) 100–2, 106–7; Crawford, 'Relationship' (n 70) 63–64, discussing Ch 1, n 132; James Crawford, 'Multilateral Rights and Obligations in International Law' (2006) 319 RdC 325, 443–44; cf *von Pezold*, n 406. Cf Crawford, 'SecondRep' (n 40) [240](b).

384 Similarly Paddeu, *Justification* (n 8) 178, 219; Paddeu, 'Force' (n 49) 102, 106–7. Cf n 378.

385 n 49. See Paddeu, 'Force' (n 49) 102, 106–7; Paddeu, *Justification* (n 8) 177, 194–97.

386 nn 50–52. Explaining why the violations must be considered separately: Paddeu, 'Force' (n 49) 99–105; Paddeu, *Justification* (n 8) 178, 192–98. While some scholars treat a violation of art 2(4) and sovereignty synonymously, they are not the same: ibid 178; see n 422. Indeed, use of force in self-defence may not require territorial violations: *Oppenheim's* (n 22) 419; Dinstein (n 47) [558], [565]–[571]; authorities nn 421–23.

387 *ARSIWA*, 167; similarly DAEAC, 118, also art 17. See Paddeu, 'Force' (n 49) 104–5, 110 and, considering neutrality's relevance to third-party issues in self-defence, and how self-defence itself addresses third parties: 110–14; cf n 426; and see sources nn 487–88. Generally Roberto Ago, 'Eighth Report on State Responsibility (Addendum)' (1980) 2(1) ILCYB 13, 34–36; Borchard (n 25) 113–14, 271–72; Cheng (n 20) 77–83; Bowett (n 47) 167–74; *Nuclear Weapons* (n 58) 501, 516–17 (Diss Op

States to restrict navigation through establishing blockades and inspecting vessels 'suspected of carrying contraband',[388] as well as to attack and destroy neutral vessels in certain circumstances.[389]

States have, in the post-Charter era, invoked self-defence to justify such impacts on navigation.[390] No State disputed, for instance, vis-à-vis an early post-1945 invocation of self-defence by Egypt, that rights of third States to freedom of navigation for their vessels in the Suez Canal could have consequently been impaired, only that the requirements of self-defence were met.[391] States have invoked self-defence to justify measures impacting neutrals since that time, including with respect to the Malvinas/Falklands and Iran–Iraq conflicts in the 1980s.[392] Significantly, the UN Panel of Inquiry concerning the 2010 *Mavi Marmara* flotilla incident accepted that a blockade—necessarily affecting navigational freedoms for third States' vessels[393]—was a justifiable measure of self-defence.[394]

The law of neutrality as it relates to impacts on a third State's *territory* is considered further below.[395] Other third-party impacts outside the law of neutrality may, however, be envisaged. For instance, in *Nuclear Weapons*, the ICJ recognised

Weeramantry, vis-à-vis non-belligerents); cf Jean-Marc Thouvenin, 'Self-Defence' in Crawford and others, *Responsibility* (n 6) 464; Paddeu, *Justification* (n 8) 175.

388 Paul Seger, 'The Law of Neutrality' in Clapham and Gaeta (n 60) 258–59; also IIHL, *San Remo Manual on International Law Applicable to Armed Conflicts at Sea* (Louise Doswald-Beck ed, CUP 1995) [93], [118], [125]; Natalie Klein, *Maritime Security and the Law of the Sea* (OUP 2012) 289–95; Bothe, 'Neutrality' (n 378) 571–72; Douglas Guilfoyle, 'The Proliferation Security Initiative: Interdicting Vessels in International Waters to Prevent the Spread of Weapons of Mass Destruction' (2005) 29 MULR 733, 744–47 (PSI). Neutrality law continues in existence post-1945: see Seger (n 388) 251–52, 261–62, 268; Bothe, 'Neutrality' (n 378) 551–54; Christopher Greenwood, 'The Concept of War in Modern International Law' (1987) 36 ICLQ 283, 299; also Judith Gardam, 'Role for Proportionality in the War on Terror' (2005) 74 Nord JIL 3, 21–22, referencing Chinkin (n 89), see particularly 302–3; Deeks (n 72) 497.

389 Klein (n 388) 289; IIHL (n 388) [67], [70], [151]; Bothe, 'Neutrality' (n 378) 571; Wolff von Heinegg, 'Maritime Warfare' in Clapham and Gaeta (n 60) 167, 178–80; generally Paddeu, 'Force' (n 49) 112; Bowett (n 47) 168.

390 Paddeu, 'Force' (n 49) 112, referencing Klein (n 388) 275. Explaining the need to view the law through the art 51 framework: Orakhelashvili (n 78) 192, citing Greenwood, 'War' (n 388) 298; Guilfoyle, 'PSI' (n 388) 743–44. Generally: Bowett (n 47) 71–75, 167–68; Cheng (n 20) 77–83; cf Paddeu, *Justification* (n 8) 358–59.

391 See *RPUNO* (1945–1954), vol 2, 432–33; Supp No 1 (1954–1955), vol 1, 360–61; UNYB (1951) 297–99; Greenwood, 'War' (n 388) 287–88, 292; Bowett (n 47) 191; also *Oppenheim's* (n 22) 422–23 (fn 21). Generally vis-à-vis ships: Cheng (n 20) 77–83, 94, citing *The Ralph* (1904) 39 US Ct Cl 204, 207–8; Bowett (n 47) 71–75.

392 See Paddeu, 'Force' (n 49) 112–13 and references; Gardam (n 388) 22–23; Guilfoyle, 'PSI' (n 388) 743, 748.

393 nn 388-390.

394 'Report of the Secretary-General's Panel of Inquiry on the 31 May 2010 Flotilla Incident' (2011) <http://www.un.org/News/dh/infocus/middle_east/Gaza_Flotilla_Panel_Report.pdf> [72], [160]. Doubts concerning the blockade's factual legality do not undermine the point: see discussion Douglas Guilfoyle, 'The Palmer Report on the Mavi Marmara Incident and the Legality of Israel's Blockade of the Gaza Strip' *EJIL:Talk!* (6 September 2011); also Klein (n 388) 275.

395 nn 425ff.

that the exercise of self-defence might justify breach of environmental law obligations.[396] This is so notwithstanding that such obligations are often also owed *erga omnes* and that breach thereof would, again therefore, affect the rights of *all* other States.[397] One might also imagine circumstances, not unknown in practice, in which self-defence is invoked against a civilian aircraft suspected of being used to launch an attack.[398] Such circumstances would implicate violations of the Chicago Convention vis-à-vis the State of registration of the aircraft, even if that State has nothing to do with the attack.[399]

The foregoing discussion has important implications for considering how self-defence might operate in the context of overlapping individual and interstate claims.

First, as Paddeu rightly concludes, at least in certain contexts, the exercise of self-defence envisages 'impairment of the rights of third states'.[400] Self-defence does not, apparently, therefore always operate according to the third-party rights approach outlined above in respect of countermeasures.[401]

Intuitively, this might sound surprising, for both countermeasures and self-defence prima facie respond to a 'wrong'—a breach of international law, or an armed attack—and so might be expected to operate similarly, with only the wrongdoing party bearing the consequences.[402] However, not all circumstances precluding wrongfulness fit this mould: necessity, for instance, is 'not dependent on the prior conduct of the injured State',[403] and, within 'strict' confines,[404] allows a State to take whatever actions are required—short of the use of force[405]—to protect that State's 'essential interests'.[406] An 'innocent' State must thus bear

[396] *Nuclear Weapons* (n 58) 242; also Gardam (n 388) 24. Treaty-based environmental obligations were not 'intended to deprive a State of the exercise of its right of self-defence under international law' (*Nuclear Weapons* (n 58) [30]), implying that they *could* be violated in the exercise thereof, though environmental considerations are relevant to necessity and proportionality: ibid [30].

[397] See *ARSIWA*, 277.

[398] For examples of self-defence being (mistakenly) invoked against civilian aircraft: *Oppenheim's* (n 22) 426–27; see also Kimberley Trapp, 'Uses of Force against Civil Aircraft' *EJIL:Talk!* (28 June 2011); Zemanek (n 366) [21], discussing 9/11 (n 477).

[399] See Trapp, 'Aircraft' (n 398).

[400] Paddeu, 'Force' (n 49) 113 (vis-à-vis navigation), cf 111 (not accepting use of force against neutral territory). Cf, vis-à-vis territory: Deeks (n 72) 497 and nn 486–88.

[401] nn 34–40. Similarly Paddeu, 'Force' (n 49) 109–10. Cf Bowett (n 47) 6–7, 9, 11.

[402] nn 373–79. See Paddeu, *Justification* (n 8) 86–87, 218–24, 276–77, 283–84; Paddeu, 'Force' (n 49) 109–10.

[403] *ARSIWA*, 178; also Paddeu, *Justification* (n 8) 87; Ago (n 387) 53; similarly in self-defence context: Wilmshurst (n 365) 12; Bowett (n 47) 173–74; also Elagab (n 7) 4; cf Ruys (n 21) 379–82 and authorities nn 408, 490–95.

[404] Ago (n 387) 19; *ARSIWA*, 178; also Ruys and Verhoeven (n 359) 309; Sarah Heathcote, 'Necessity' in Crawford and others, *Responsibility* (n 6) 492, 495–99; Crawford, *GP* (n 7) 306.

[405] See Ruys (n 21) 380–82; Ruys and Verhoeven (n 359) 309; Olivier Corten, 'Necessity' in Weller (n 70) 863–67; Corten, *War* (n 44) Ch 4; Ago (n 387) 21, 39, cf 39–42, 44; cf also Bowett (n 47) 56; Dinstein (n 47) [767] and summaries in Ruys (n 21) 379–81; Ruys and Verhoeven (n 359) 308–9.

[406] *ARSIWA*, art 25 (though other States' 'essential interest[s]' must not be impaired); generally Paddeu, *Justification* (n 8) 389, 397, 399–400, 401–13; Ch 4, n 526. Cf *von Pezold v Zimbabwe (Award)* ICSID Case No ARB/10/15 (28 July 2015) [648]–[657] (*erga omnes* obligations not violable, apparently equating with *jus cogens*), discussed Paddeu, *Justification* (n 8) 408–9.

the consequences of an invocation of necessity, and any resulting violations of its rights, even though it has done no wrong.[407] There is no barrier in principle to self-defence operating in the same way, without its use being 'dependent upon any prior breach of international law by the state in the territory of which defensive force is used'.[408] While both countermeasures and self-defence could be grounded theoretically in the idea of forfeiture—that the wrongdoer has lost their rights due to their wrongdoing[409]—it is also possible to conceive of self-defence as having a consequentialist rationale—that the interests of others give way to that of the attacked when this is essential to the latter's defence.[410] This kind of explanation, recognised as the basis for necessity,[411] can rationalise impacts on third-party rights.[412] And it is hardly an unknown approach to self-defence, with at least certain domestic systems recognising the possibility of using force against 'an innocent' in necessary self-defence.[413]

This position also reflects self-defence's historical origins, notably the *Caroline* incident, in which Britain famously invoked self-defence in response to non-State actors,[414] the US ultimately accepting that a violation of sovereignty would be allowable where 'the necessity of self-defence' was 'instant, overwhelming, leaving no choice of means, and no moment for deliberation'.[415] Self-defence could

[407] Eg Bowett (n 47) 10; Paddeu, *Justification* (n 8) 87–88. Cf Conclusion, nn 96ff; Crawford, *GP* (n 7) 319.

[408] Wilmshurst (n 365) 12; also Thouvenin (n 387) 464–65; Lubell (n 48) 40; authorities nn 490–95. Rejecting: Ago (n 387) 15, 53; Corten, 'Necessity' (n 405) 868; Bowett (n 47) 9–11, but cf 10 (necessity excuses 'innocent' State violation in self-defence), 56.

[409] Paddeu, *Justification* (n 8) 86–87, 218–24, 276–84.

[410] See ibid 206–10 (though doubting theory's explanatory power vis-à-vis aggressor), 87, 415–29 (necessity) and discussion Lieblich (n 378) 15–25. The original ILC definition required prior breach (see Stanimir Alexandrov, *Self-Defense Against the Use of Force in International Law* (Kluwer 1996) 182), but art 21 does not: Paddeu, 'Force' (n 49) 105, 110; Thouvenin (n 387) 464; cf Corten, *War* (n 44) 188.

[411] Paddeu, *Justification* (n 8) 414–21.

[412] See Bowett (n 47) 56, 173–74.

[413] ibid 173 and authorities (drawing the same 'parallel'). Discussing jurisdictions not apparently requiring that force only be used against aggressors, see Kevin Heller and Markus Dubber (eds), *The Handbook of Comparative Criminal Law* (Stan UP 2011) 67–68 (Australia), 115–16 (Canada), 191–92 (Egypt), 224–25 (France), 270–71 (Germany), 300–1 (India), 376–77 (Israel), 404 (Japan), 470 (South Africa), 542 (UK), also 509–10 (Spain), cf 154 (China), 427 (Russia); *Henwood v People* 54 Colo 188 (1913) 194 (if not careless), discussed Ian Henderson and Bryan Cavanagh, 'Self-Defence, Collateral Damage and Precautions in Attack' *Opinio Juris* (9 July 2014); cf Corten, *War* (n 44) 420–21, 473. For philosophical discussion: Suzanne Uniacke, *Permissible Killing: The Self-Defence Justification of Homicide* (CUP 1994) 67–82, 162–68, 177, 188–89, 191–92, 216–17, 229–30; Lieblich (n 378) 15–27; cf Paddeu, *Justification* (n 8) 178, 220–21.

[414] Greenwood, 'Self-Defence' (n 44) [17]; Greenwood, 'Development' (n 365) 6; Lubell (n 48) 34–35; Greenwood, 'Pre-Emptive' (n 70) 17, also 12; Bowett (n 47) 58–60; *Oppenheim's* (n 22) 420–22; Deeks (n 72) 502–3; Paddeu, 'Force' (n 49) 93. Generally Gray (n 44) 157–58; Ago (n 387) 39; Dinstein (n 47) [775].

[415] *Caroline Correspondence*, reproduced Eric Heinze and Malgosia Fitzmaurice, *Landmark Cases in Public International Law* (Kluwer 1998) 1254, cf ibid 1264 (disagreement whether met); further: 1246, 1250–51, 1253–54, 1256, 1258–61; Ago (n 387) 39–40 (fn 117); Crawford, *GP* (n 7) 310; Greenwood, 'Pre-Emptive' (n 70) 13; Brownlie (n 70) 42–43; Paddeu, *Justification* (n 8) 352–53, also 356, 359; Cheng (n 20) 87. The case is properly self-defence (Paddeu, *Justification* (n 8) 353–57; also Cheng

therefore apparently both respond to individual conduct, and allow necessary violations of third-party rights.[416] Thus, even if seeming counterintuitive at first blush, it is certainly plausible that self-defence and countermeasures need not operate identically—and indeed, the practice suggests that they do not, self-defence envisaging at least certain violations of third-party rights.[417]

(ii) Self-defence and third-party rights: is territorial sovereignty exempt from third-party impacts?

This leads us to the second, narrower point. Having accepted that *some* third-party rights are violable in self-defence, does this include a third State's right of territorial integrity, which would be violated in responding to an attack by a non-State actor from that State's territory (scenario (3) above)?[418] It bears emphasising that the critical issue here is not really whether non-State actors can be the 'source' of an attack,[419] because the same concerns about impacting an 'innocent' State's sovereignty would arise even if the attack coming from a third (including neutral) State's territory were by another *State*.[420] Moreover, scholars rarely object to self-defence being exercised against non-State actors located *outside* State territory (on the high seas for instance)[421] as violating the injunction in article 2(4),[422] even though such

(n 20) 87), though commonly considered necessity: eg Crawford, *GP* (n 7) 309–10 (fn 208); Ago (n 387) 39, 61–62; Ruys and Verhoeven (n 359) 308–9; Bowett (n 47) 58–60. Self-defence was then 'a corollary of the right of self-preservation': Paddeu, *Justification* (n 8) 363; generally 346–63; Cheng (n 20) Ch 2. Necessity as a circumstance precluding wrongfulness emerged later: Paddeu, *Justification* (n 8) 363ff. See nn 490ff.

416 Greenwood, 'Pre-Emptive' (n 70) 25; Bowett (n 47) 58–60; also Greenwood, 'Self-Defence' (n 44) [17]–[18] and authorities nn 408, 491ff. Cf Tams, 'Terrorists' (n 8) 368–69; Corten, *War* (n 44) 194.
417 Similarly Paddeu, 'Force' (n 49) 113.
418 Similarly ibid 110. See n 376 and Figure 6.2, nn 82–84.
419 Using such terminology: eg Greenwood, 'Self-Defence' (n 44) [15]–[18]; Wilmshurst (n 365) 11; also Ruys (n 21) 368ff; Tams, 'Analytique' (n 362) 275–76; Trapp, 'Attack' (n 71) 679; Lubell (n 48) 30–31; Corten, *War* (n 44) 126; Michael Wood, 'The Law on the Use of Force: Current Challenges' (2007) 11 SYBIL 1, 6. Making same point for different reasons: Tams, 'Terrorists' (n 8) 385, 392; and particularly Corten, 'Practice' (n 376) 15 ('largely irrelevant'), making point n 467.
420 See Deeks (n 72) 497, 503, 517; Lubell (n 48) 41–42; Kress (n 60) 251–52; Lieblich (n 378) 23; also Brownlie (n 70) 314–15; authorities nn 487–88.
421 See Tams, 'Terrorists' (n 8) 362; Ruys (n 21) 377; Corten, *War* (n 44) 170; Bowett (n 47) 21, 66–86; Dinstein (n 47) [570], [572]; Brownlie (n 70) 305, 375, 433; see sources n 376; cf Ruys and Verhoeven (n 359) 309 (necessity).
422 See Tams, 'Terrorists' (n 8) 362, 365 (force 'against individuals or groups [is] *as such* not sufficient to violate the prohibition', citing art 2(4)'s reference to 'international relations'), 374, 385; similarly Ruys and Verhoeven (n 359) 309; Ruys (n 21) 377, also 500–1; Milanovic, 'Indeterminacy' (n 367) (self-defence must violate sovereignty); Corten, *War* (n 44) 162–63, 169, also 127–28, 140. Similarly, noting art 2(4)'s banning force vis-à-vis 'territorial integrity or political independence': Trapp, 'Reply' (n 376) 1049–50; Trapp, 'Basics' (n 369) 145–46; Trapp, 'Attack' (n 71) 680; also Ruys and Verhoeven (n 359) 309; Corten, *War* (n 44) 170; Gray (n 44) 210, cf 226; Kammerhofer (n 370) 643. However, these terms do not limit the prohibition: eg, Ruys (n 21) 56–57; Guilfoyle, 'Countermeasures' (n 8) 79; Brownlie (n 70) 267; Lubell (n 48) 27–29; Tams, 'Terrorists' (n 8) 364; Corten, *War* (n 44) 149–51. Cf Bowett (n 47) 149–52. See n 386.

actions could also constitute prohibited uses of force.[423] This suggests that territorial sovereignty is the real concern.[424]

This being the case, two points may be made. The first relates to the law of neutrality, which—in addition to the allowances discussed above—permits States to target enemies on neutral *territory* where the neutral State is 'unable or unwilling' to prevent their attacks.[425] Some consider that, since the inclusion of article 2(4) in the UN Charter, such forcible action cannot be taken against neutral States unless they themselves have engaged in an 'armed attack'.[426] However, as noted above, the law of neutrality allows for both blockades and attacks on neutral vessels in the exercise of self-defence.[427] The former are a form of aggression (and would thus violate article 2(4)),[428] while the latter also amount to a prohibited use of force.[429] If such measures may, under the post-Charter law of neutrality, acceptably impact third States,[430] then it is not clear why the article 2(4) prohibition should rule out the application of other rules traditionally found in the law of neutrality.[431] Indeed, the *San Remo Manual Applicable to Armed Conflicts at Sea*, widely considered as reflecting customary international law,[432] recognises that States may use 'strictly necessary' force within a neutral State's waters where a belligerent poses 'a serious and immediate threat'.[433] States exercise sovereignty over these 'neutral waters'—internal waters, the territorial sea and archipelagic waters[434]—under international law.[435] It seems a stretch to accept that the article 2(4) prohibition impacted this branch of law such as to disallow use of force against *land* territory, while

[423] nn 398, 429; Ch 3, nn 131, 141; also Corten, *War* (n 44) 403; Dawidowicz (n 6) 149–50; and vis-à-vis attacks on certain State organs: Greenwood, 'Self-Defence' (n 44) [21]; Greenwood, 'Development' (n 365) 6; Dinstein (n 47) [574]; Ruys (n 21) 199–204; cf 500; Gray (n 44) 121, 204–5; Thomas Franck, *Recourse to Force* (CUP 2002) 66; also Corten, *War* (n 44) 403–4. Additionally, claims that attacks on nationals enliven self-defence cannot be ignored: eg, *Oppenheim's* (n 22) 422, 440–42; Bowett (n 47) Ch 5; Dinstein (n 47) [575]–[577], [723]–[733]; Greenwood, 'Development' (n 365) 6; Greenwood, 'Self-Defence' (n 44) [24]; Brownlie (n 70) 289, 296–301; Gray (n 44) 165–69; Ruys (n 21) 213–49. Cf Jessup (n 22) 158, 169–72; Tams, 'Terrorists' (n 8) 385.

[424] See authorities nn 376, 379, 419–20. Similarly Oellers-Frahm (n 363) 50.

[425] Cheng (n 20) 95–96, referencing *Caroline*, nn 414ff, also 84–92; Deeks (n 72) 499; Guideu (n 53) 222–24, 238. Similarly Bowett (n 47) 167–74 (necessity where no breach); Alston (n 54) [35]; also Brownlie (n 70) 309–16; sources nn 487–88 (relevance to non-State actors).

[426] Bothe, 'Neutrality' (n 378) 558–59, endorsed Paddeu, 'Force' (n 49) 111; also David Kretzmer, 'US Extra-Territorial Actions Against Individuals: Bin Laden, Al Awlaki, and Abu Khattalah—2011 and 2014' in Tom Ruys, Olivier Corten, and Alexandra Hofer (eds), *The Use of Force in International Law: A Case-Based Approach* (OUP 2018) 778, referencing Kress (n 60), see 248, 251–52.

[427] nn 388–94.

[428] Klein (n 388) 295, referencing GA Res 3314 (XXIX) (1974), art 3(c); Flotilla Report (n 394) [160].

[429] Greenwood, 'Development' (n 365) 6; Greenwood, 'Self-Defence' (n 44) [22]–[23]; Guilfoyle, 'Countermeasures' (n 8) 79–81; *Guyana v Suriname* (n 32) [446]; *Oil Platforms* (n 44) [61], [72], discussed Gray (n 44) 150–53; Dinstein (n 47) [574]; Brownlie (n 70) 382 (fn 3), 305; Ruys (n 21) 199–200, 204–13; Klein (n 388) 290; Greenwood, 'War' (n 388) 299; Bothe, 'Neutrality' (n 378) 571.

[430] See nn 382–84, 393.

[431] Indeed, see nn 487–88.

[432] Klein (n 388) 286 and references.

[433] IIHL (n 388) [22], cited von Heinegg (n 389) 173.

[434] IIHL (n 388) [14].

[435] See UNCLOS, art 2. Further: Greenwood, 'War' (n 388) 299.

continuing to allow *maritime* areas (including internal waters, actually *within* the State's territory) to be violated.[436] Accordingly, certain field manuals continue to explicitly endorse the acceptability of striking enemy forces on neutral territory where the State is 'unable or unwilling' to prevent their attacks.[437] If correct, then the argument for treating territorial sovereignty as exempt from the exercise of self-defence impacting third-State rights loses some of its persuasiveness.

The second point concerns the law outside of that relating to neutrality,[438] and the argument that the impossibility of violating a third State's territorial sovereignty in the exercise of self-defence is made clear in State practice surrounding the 'inherent right' of self-defence, referenced in article 51 and reflected in customary international law.[439] This practice, particularly as it relates to the invocation of self-defence against non-State actors, provides helpful insights in considering the question of whether the territorial sovereignty of 'innocent' third States really is completely inviolable in the self-defence context, because—as noted above—an attack against a non-State actor will almost always involve a simultaneous violation of a State's territory.[440]

The practice has been extensively studied in the literature.[441] No justice can be done here to the resulting analysis, nor the sharp divisions in conclusions that have been reached on the basis thereof.[442] This book shares the view that customary international law allows self-defence to be exercised in response to attacks by non-State actors, including where this necessitates a violation of the territorial sovereignty of the State in which they are located.[443] Others disagree.[444]

There can be little doubt that the practice is mixed.[445] So much is apparent from views expressed during an informal Security Council meeting in 2021 dedicated to

[436] On the maritime zones: UNCLOS, Pt II, s II; Pt IV.

[437] UKMOD, 'Manual of the Law of Armed Conflict' (2004) [1.43], cited Seger (n 388) 256; similarly USDOD, 'Law of War Manual' (2015) [13.3.1], [15.4.2], referencing also Australia, Canada, and Germany; similarly Deeks (n 72) 500; also Brownlie (n 70) 309. On US attacks in neutral Cambodia (1970s): Chinkin (n 89) 308–9; Guideu (n 53); Deeks (n 72) 526, 528.

[438] Similarly distinguishing neutrality and self-defence more generally: Paddeu, 'Force' (n 49) 110–14.

[439] *Nicaragua (Merits)* (n 44) [176], referenced Dinstein (n 47) [526]; Ruys (n 21) 59, cf 515; *Oppenheim's* (n 22) 418; also Bowett (n 47) 185, 187–88. Cf Kammerhofer (n 370) 639–46; Tams, 'Analytique' (n 362) 279–80 (subsequent practice), 289; Corten, 'Practice' (n 376) 15–17.

[440] nn 375–79. Cf Paddeu, *Justification* (n 8) 178.

[441] See particularly nn 442–44, 468.

[442] Eg on 'expansionists' versus 'restrictivists': Peters and Marxsen (n 360) 8, also 12; similarly: Corten, *War* (n 44) 6–27 ('extensive' versus 'restrictive' approaches); Kammerhofer (n 370) 628, 633; Bethlehem (n 72) 773; Corten, 'Plea' (n 361); Lieblich (n 378) 3; authorities nn 443–44.

[443] Eg Greenwood, 'Pre-Emptive' (n 70) 17, 21–25; Tams, 'Analytique' (n 362) 290; Lubell (n 48) 31 ('plentiful evidence ... provid[ing] solid support for ... contention'); Bethlehem (n 72) 774 ('reasonably clear and accepted'); Wilmshurst (n 365) 12; Wood (n 419) 6–7; Deeks (n 72) 493; *Oppenheim's* (n 22) 387, 419–21; Moir (n 70) 736; Jackson (n 72) 189; Franck (n 423) 54, 66–67; Bowett (n 47) 10, 56, 58; Kretzmer (n 426) 771; Dinstein (n 47) [645] [759], [763]; also Brownlie (n 70) 374–75, 434; Ruys (n 21), nn 448–49; discussion Kammerhofer (n 370) 629, 633; Tams, 'Terrorists' (n 8) 381–82.

[444] Eg Gray (n 44) 210, 226–27, 243–44, 248; Corten, *War* (n 44), particularly 161, 461–66; Corten, 'Plea' (n 361); also Ruys (n 21) 454–55; discussion Paddeu, 'Force' (n 49) 94–95; Peters and Marxsen (n 360) 8, 12.

[445] Similarly Corten, 'Practice' (n 376) 16.

the topic.[446] The majority of States intervening appeared to support the use of self-defence against non-State actors, at least in certain circumstances, but several States strongly objected thereto.[447] On the scholarly side, Ruys concludes, after a comprehensive review of the post-1945 situation, that a 'restrictive' approach to article 51 does not reflect current practice, even if that practice is 'far from coherent'.[448] His restrained conclusion is that no standard has yet 'replac[ed] the traditional one', but that self-defence against non-State actors is nonetheless 'not unambiguously illegal'.[449]

Many scholars seem to similarly assume that there was, at some point, such a 'traditional' rule precluding the exercise of self-defence against non-State actors.[450] Given, however, that (1) self-defence in the pre-Charter era certainly allowed self-defence to be employed against individual non-State actors even where that necessitated violations of third-party territorial sovereignty;[451] and (2) the wording of article 51 does not clearly mark a departure in this respect,[452] such scholars would need to demonstrate that customary international law, evidenced through State practice and *opinio juris*, changed in the post-1945 environment to disallow the use of self-defence against non-State actors.[453] Only then would advocates of the current legality of exercising self-defence in such a way need to demonstrate that customary international law has since changed yet again.[454]

Is such a change in the immediate post-1945 environment apparent? It was certainly not an obvious one.[455] States invoked self-defence in response to

[446] See UN Doc A/75/993-S/2021/247 (16 March 2021) and discussion Adil Ahmad Haque, 'Self-Defence Against Non-State Actors: All Over the Map' *Just Security* (24 March 2021).

[447] ibid. For discussion of previous practice whereby States expressly endorsed using self-defence vis-à-vis non-State actors: Ruys (n 21) 443–46; Tams, 'Terrorists' (n 8) 380–81; cf Corten, *War* (n 44) 167–68; Jackson (n 72) 185); also George Brandis, 'The Right of Self-Defence Against Imminent Armed Attack In International Law' *EJIL:Talk!* (25 May 2017); Jeremy Wright, 'The Modern Law of Self-Defence' *EJIL:Talk!* (11 January 2017); Dapo Akande, 'UK Parliamentary Inquiry into UK Policy on the Use of Drones for Targeted Killing' *EJIL:Talk!* (23 December 2015); Bethlehem (n 72) 771–72.

[448] Ruys (n 21) 485–86.

[449] ibid 486–87. Cf Paddeu, 'Force' (n 49) 95.

[450] Eg, Corten, *War* (n 44) 460–63, 493–94; Kammerhofer (n 370) 629 ('perceived pre-2001 orthodoxy'); Corten, 'Practice' (n 376) 17; Tams, 'Terrorists' (n 8) 363–64 ('dominant, restrictive, analysis'), 378; Paddeu, 'Force' (n 49) 94–95 ('traditional understanding'); Ruys and Verhoeven (n 359) 291, 298; Jackson (n 72) 183–84; also Trapp, 'Basics' (n 369) 149.

[451] See *Caroline*, nn 414–16. For further pre-1945 practice: Ago (n 387) 39–40 (necessity); Bowett (n 47) 38–41; Jessup (n 22) 166.

[452] nn 365–67.

[453] Greenwood, 'Self-Defence' (n 44) [17] (must otherwise show 'practice ... reflected widespread *opinio juris* that international law precluded resort to self-defence' against non-State actors); Greenwood, 'Pre-Emptive' (n 70) 25; also Kammerhofer (n 370) 633, 646; Christian Tams, 'Embracing the Uncertainty of Old: Armed Attacks by Non-State Actors Prior to 9/11' (2017) 77 ZfaöRV 61, 63. Cf nn 116–17.

[454] Suggesting such demonstration is needed, eg Corten, *War* (n 44) 161 ('new doctrine'), 175, 185, 455, 461–63, 465; Ruys (n 21) 486; also *Wall* (n 58) 230 (Sep Op Koojimans).

[455] cf Tams, 'Embracing' (n 453) 61–64; Greenwood, 'Pre-Emptive' (n 70) 25; Greenwood, 'Self-Defence' (n 44) [17]; also Lubell (n 48) 34 (discussing *Caroline*); Ruys (n 21) 404 (no real support either way 1960s–1980s); Corten, *War* (n 44) 456 (vis-à-vis 'indirect aggression', 'no decisive precedent ... one way or the other' in two decades post-Charter); Kammerhofer (n 370) 629, 632–34, 646 (and authorities); Gray (n 44) 242 (US position).

non-State actors soon after 1945,[456] with apparently limited objections.[457] Post-Charter scholars relied on *Caroline* as reflecting the law of self-defence,[458] as did the Nuremburg Tribunal.[459] Debates leading to the adoption of the Definition of Aggression in 1974, relied on by some as reflecting a stricter attitude,[460] seem rather to demonstrate only that the issue was controversial.[461] Certain States did indeed propose that aggression be limited to State action,[462] and suggest that self-defence was only available vis-à-vis attacks by States.[463] However, as Trapp outlines, other States argued that self-defence *could* be employed in response to non-State actors.[464] With the definition of aggression ultimately adopted, taken as indicative of an 'armed attack',[465] including so-called 'indirect aggression',[466] States apparently contemplated that non-State actors could be the *direct* aggressors, engaging in 'armed attacks'.[467]

456 See particularly Tams, 'Embracing' (n 453) 62, discussing, *inter alia*, India/Pakistan, 1948 (see UNYB (1947–1948) 387, admittedly, an accusation of State 'aggression' through support); Ruys (n 21) 394–99 (*inter alia* Israel/Egypt, 1956; Lebanon and Jordan/UAR, 1958, though noting emphasis on State links); cf Corten, *War* (n 44) 456.

457 Generally Tams, 'Embracing' (n 453) 62; Ruys (n 21) 394–99. The India/Pakistan discussion focused on Jammu/Kashmir: UNYB (1947–1948) 387–99. Israel's actions were considered disproportionate: Franck (n 423) 55; Ruys (n 21) 395. For Lebanon/UAR: Franck (n 423) 55; Ruys (n 21) 396–98.

458 Eg Hersch Lauterpacht, *Oppenheim's International Law*, vol 1 (8th edn, Longmans 1955) 298–99; JL Brierly, *The Law of Nations* (5th edn, OUP 1955) 315–16; Jessup (n 22) 163–64, 166, 168; cf Ruys (n 21) 370; Ruys and Verhoeven (n 359) 291. For State invocation: Corten, *War* (n 44) 438, cf 409–10; O'Brien (n 374) 453 (fn 160).

459 *In re Goering et al* (1946) 13 ILR 203 (IMT) 210; also Greenwood, 'Pre-Emptive' (n 70) 13; Bowett (n 47) 60, 142–44; Cheng (n 20) 87; cf Corten, *War* (n 44) 416–18.

460 Eg Ruys (n 21) 389, 418, 441, generally 382ff; Corten, *War* (n 44) 164, 445–50, 469; also Tams, 'Embracing' (n 453) 63; Gray (n 44) 207; cf Trapp, 'Attack' (n 71) 681–83.

461 See Trapp, 'Attack' (n 71) 682–83; also discussion Ruys (n 21) 383–90, differing conclusion: 389–90; cf Corten, *War* (n 44) 447.

462 See UN Doc A/AC.134/L.16, cited Ruys (n 21) 383; Trapp, 'Attack' (n 71) 681–82; Corten, *War* (n 44) 448.

463 See Ruys (n 21) 383, citing UN Doc A/AC.134/L.16, 384–85, with authorities; Corten, *War* (n 44) 447–49, with authorities; eg, UN Doc A/7620 [29], [62]; UN Doc A/8419 [56]; UN Doc A/AC.134/SR.52-66, 32, 117 (Uruguay), 55 (Ecuador), 57, cf 113 (Colombia), 86 (Mexico), 90, cf 119 (Cyprus), also 37 (Norway); UN Doc A/AC.134/SR.67-78, 112–13 (Uruguay).

464 Trapp, 'Attack' (n 71) 682, with authorities; also Ruys (n 21) 383–84, with authorities; eg, UN Doc A/7620 [65]; UN Doc A/8419 [27]–[28]; UN Doc A/AC.134/SR.52–66, 40–41 (Japan), 66, 68, 150–51 (US), also 20–21 (Italy), 115 (Indonesia), 154 (DRC), apparently 52 (USSR); UN Doc A/AC.134/SR.67-78, 7 (Japan), 114–15 (US); also Corten, *War* (n 44) 138–39. See UN DocA/AC.134/L.17 (aggression through '[o]rganizing, supporting or directing' non-State activities), cited Ruys (n 21) 383; Corten, *War* (n 44) 448; also Trapp, 'Attack' (n 71) 683.

465 *Nicaragua (Merits)* (n 44) [195], cited, eg Ruys (n 21) 407; Trapp, 'Attack' (n 71) 683; Ruys and Verhoeven (n 359) 303 and see, eg Gray (n 44) 137, 207 (supporting). Cf, on States not equating 'armed attack' with 'aggression': Trapp, 'Attack' (n 71) 682–83; similarly Ruys and Verhoeven (n 359) 302–3; see UN Doc A/8419 [38]; UN Doc A/AC.134/SR.67-78, 5–7, 8–9 (UK, Japan, Australia); also Greenwood, 'Self-Defence' (n 44) [10]; Bowett (n 47) 249–63; Corten, *War* (n 44) 404–5; Franck (n 423) 65.

466 Trapp, 'Attack' (n 71) 682; Ruys (n 21) 386–87, generally 371, 387–90; Corten, *War* (n 44) 445–50. See GA Res 3314(XXIX), art 3(g) (States' 'sending' individuals 'which carry out acts of armed force against another State of such gravity as to amount to [aggression]' 'or ... substantial involvement therein'), discussed eg Ruys (n 21) 387; Greenwood, 'Pre-Emptive' (n 70) 16; Corten, *War* (n 44) 445–50.

467 Corten, 'Practice' (n 376) 15 ('evident'); similarly Gray (n 44) 137; Trapp, 'Attack' (n 71) 683; Tams, 'Terrorists' (n 8) 368, 385; Tams, 'Embracing' (n 453) 63; also Ruys (n 21) 387.

And in actual practice, many States, across all geographic regions, have invoked self-defence in response to non-State actors in other States' territory since as early as the late 1940s, and consistently since,[468] most recently vis-à-vis ISIS within Syria.[469] There is no doubt that this practice was often, though not always, subject to strenuous objection.[470] But unlike the States actually exercising self-defence in this way—which must assume that consequent violations of another State's territorial sovereignty are justified,[471] where, under normal attribution standards, the territorial State did not commit an 'armed attack'[472]—when States dispute the legality of an exercise of self-defence, they may do so for diverse reasons,[473] including whether a response was necessary,[474] or proportionate.[475] They are not necessarily 'rejecting a right to respond to un-attributable armed attacks *in principle*'.[476] And in some circumstances, such objections have been absent, notably the near-universal support for the US' exercise of self-defence against Al-Qaeda post-9/11.[477]

[468] For extensive analysis see, eg, Ruys (n 21) 152–53, 157, 202, 394–405, 422–72; Gray (n 44) 128, 143–49, 163–64, 183, 191–95, 200–29, 237–48; Corten, *War* (n 44) 177–85, 456–61; Ruys and Verhoeven (n 359) 290, 292–98, 314–15, 317; Deeks (n 72) 486–87, 522, 524, 526–27, 532, 534ff, App I; Alexandrov (n 410) 168–71, 174–81, 184–86; Tams, 'Terrorists' (n 8) 367, 372, 378–80, 391, 393; *Oppenheim's* (n 22) 423–26; Franck (n 423) 55–59, 63–67; O'Brien (n 374) 427–28, 430–35, 446, 448–49, 454–57, 460–62; Trapp, 'Basics' (n 369) 147–55; Jackson (n 72) 181–87; Lubell (n 48) 29–30, 34, 36–37; Trapp, 'Attack' (n 71) 690–94; Moir (n 70) 728–34; Corten, 'Necessity' (n 405) 869; Tams, 'Embracing' (n 453) 62; Greenwood, 'Pre-Emptive' (n 70) 21–22; Tams, 'Analytique' (n 362) 280–81; Greenwood, 'Self-Defence' (n 44) [17]; Wood (n 419) 6; Dinstein (n 47) [645]–[647], [770]–[773]. Cf Gray (n 44) 125, 226.

[469] See Wright (n 447), Annex 1; Paddeu, 'Force' (n 49) 94. Suggesting a 'broad coalition' of 60 States: Gray (n 44) 190, generally 191–93, 237–43.

[470] See discussion Ruys (n 21) 395–404, 423–33, 447–53, 457–68, 486–87; Corten, *War* (n 44) 175, 179, 183–85, 455–66; Gray (n 44) 144–45, 202–6, 209–18, 224–27, 239–44; Corten, 'Plea' (n 361) (disagreement 'minimized'); Tams, 'Terrorists' (n 8) 367–68, 379–80; Franck (n 423) 66; Trapp, 'Attack' (n 71) 690–94; Trapp, 'Basics' (n 369) 149–50, 154.

[471] See nn 468–69; and eg, Ruys (n 21) 447; Franck (n 423) 64; Tams, 'Rejoinder' (n 72) 1061; Tams, 'Terrorists' (n 8) 367, 378–83; O'Brien (n 374) 461; Corten, *War* (n 44) 185–86; also Dinstein (n 47) [650]. Cf Gray (n 44) 125, 225–27.

[472] See Ruys (n 21) 428, 440, 453–57, 459; Ruys and Verhoeven (n 359) 313–14; Jackson (n 72) 181, 184, 187; discussion Tams, 'Terrorists' (n 8) 379–81, 385–87; Trapp, 'Reply' (n 376) 1050; Trapp, 'Basics' (n 369) 150; Greenwood, 'Pre-Emptive' (n 70) 24; Trapp, 'Attack' (n 71) 680, 690; also Corten, 'Practice' (n 376) 16. Cf Corten, *War* (n 44) 185–86 ('indirect ... attack'). Generally on attribution in this context: ibid 450–54; Ruys (n 21) 408–14; Ruys and Verhoeven (n 359) 300–4; Gray (n 44) 139–40; n 481.

[473] Ruys (n 21) 402–4, 455; Franck (n 423) 55, 67; Trapp, 'Attack' (n 71) 690–94; Gray (n 44) 121–22, 125, 127 ('may be limited to ... particular facts'); Tams, 'Embracing' (n 453) 62. On political considerations: Trapp, 'Attack' (n 71) 690; Deeks (n 72) 517–18; Ruys and Verhoeven (n 359) 293–94; Ruys (n 21) 403–4, 511–12; Tams, 'Terrorists' (n 8) 367–68; Trapp, 'Basics' (n 369) 153. Many statements relied on in the literature more recently appear to fail to distinguish different possible bases for objection.

[474] Eg actions criticised as reprisals: Tams, 'Terrorists' (n 8) 372 (fn 94); Ruys (n 21) 402 and authorities; Corten, *War* (n 44) 456, 486; also Gray (n 44) 205–6, 212; O'Brien (n 374) 436–37, 448–49, 453, 471.

[475] For examples: Tams, 'Terrorists' (n 8) 379; Ruys (n 21) 395, 402, 453; Trapp, 'Basics' (n 369) 154–55; Trapp, 'Attack' (n 71) 691; Gray (n 44) 163, 227–28; Corten, *War* (n 44) 457; O'Brien (n 374) 437, 456, 459, 464.

[476] Trapp, 'Attack' (n 71) 694; also Corten, *War* (n 44) 456. Indeed, noting difficulties in establishing clear practice see, eg, Ruys (n 21) 404, 427, 433, 447, 455, 462, 486–87; cf 425, 449; Corten, *War* (n 44) 184–85, 461–66, cf 185–86; Trapp, 'Attack' (n 71) 690–94; also Gray (n 44) 127–28 (UNSC), 242; cf O'Brien (n 374) 464 (fn 245).

[477] Gray (n 44) 200–1, 206; Tams, 'Terrorists' (n 8) 377–78; Tams, 'Analytique' (n 362) 280–81; Greenwood, 'Self-Defence' (n 44) [17]; Trapp, 'Attack' (n 71) 690; Greenwood, 'Pre-Emptive' (n

To be clear, there is no doubt that employing self-defence against non-State actors is controversial, and many States *do* clearly object to its use in this way.[478] But the point is that those suggesting that custom precluded use of self-defence against non-State actors in the post-1945 environment must bear the onus of demonstrating *enough* consistent practice in support, despite the fairly steady stream of invocations to the contrary; only then can those disagreeing with this view be saddled with the task of showing that the customary position does not remain thus.[479]

It bears mentioning that some have proposed an alternative explanation for the practice,[480] namely that action is actually taken against attacks by *States*, but under modified attribution standards.[481] Self-defence can, it is said, justify infringing a State's rights where a non-State attack occurs with that State's 'complicity' under an attribution standard akin to 'aiding and abetting'.[482] However, while States do commonly point to involvement in attacks by the State where the attackers are located,[483] as Ruys highlights, they also often make clear that they are responding to attacks by non-State actors, not States.[484] Perhaps more importantly, they often rely simply on another State's *failure* to prevent attacks as justifying their action.[485] Indeed, recent practice focuses on self-defence in response to non-State actor attacks where a State is 'unwilling or unable' to prevent those attacks.[486] The

70) 17–18; Trapp, 'Basics' (n 369) 151, 155–56; Jackson (n 72) 184; Wood (n 419) 6; Lubell (n 48) 34; Ruys and Verhoeven (n 359) 297; Dinstein (n 47) [645], [647]; Corten, 'Practice' (n 376) 16; Moir (n 70) 727; Milanovic, 'Indeterminacy' (n 367); Ruys (n 21) 434–40, cf 441–42; cf also Corten, *War* (n 44) 180–83, 460–61.

478 nn 447, 470. Similarly Gray (n 44) 206.

479 Authorities n 453.

480 See similarly summary Gray (n 44) 227; Paddeu, 'Force' (n 49) 107–10.

481 Tams, 'Terrorists' (n 8) 384–85; also Jackson (n 72) 181, 186–87; discussion Corten, *War* (n 44) 444ff; Milanovic, 'Indeterminacy' (n 367); Ruys (n 21) 490–93. Cf Paddeu, 'Force' (n 49) 108–9 (complicity not attribution); Gray (n 44) 247. For concerns regarding altering attribution standards: Ruys and Verhoeven (n 359) 299–300; Ruys (n 21) 491–93; Milanovic, 'Indeterminacy' (n 367); Jackson (n 72) 187–88; Trapp, 'Reply' (n 376) 1054–55; cf Tams, 'Rejoinder' (n 72) 1062.

482 Tams, 'Terrorists' (n 8) 385–86; similarly Ruys and Verhoeven (n 359) 315–17; discussion Ruys (n 21) 489–91; Paddeu, 'Force' (n 49) 107–9; Condorelli and Kress (n 18) 228; cf Gray (n 44) 226–27.

483 See Ruys (n 21) 394–402, 426, 428–29, 432, 435–36, 440, 447–48, 450–51, 453–54; Ruys and Verhoeven (n 359) 292–95, 312; Gray (n 44) 143–44; O'Brien (n 374) 461; Tams, 'Terrorists' (n 8) 385; Trapp, 'Basics' (n 369) 147–51; Corten, *War* (n 44) 463; also Paddeu, 'Force' (n 49) 96.

484 Ruys (n 21) 493; also Jackson (n 72) 187; Gray (n 44) 247.

485 See Gray (n 44) 143–44; Ruys and Verhoeven (n 359) 292–96, 317; Trapp, 'Attack' (n 71) 694–95; Ruys (n 21) 454, 459; Trapp, 'Basics' (n 369) 149–55; n 486; also Brownlie (n 70) 375. Unawareness is insufficient for complicity: Tams, 'Terrorists' (n 8) 386; Ruys and Verhoeven (n 359) 316; *Nicaragua (Merits)* (n 44) [157]. Cf Deeks (n 72) 522–24.

486 See Deeks (n 72) 485–87; Gray (n 44) 236–41, 247–48; Keinan (n 362) 57; Moir (n 70) 731–34; Paddeu, 'Force' (n 49) 96, 98; Dinstein (n 47) [768]. For earlier examples: Deeks (n 72) 486 ('century of state practice'); Ruys (n 21) 401, 431, 433, also 502–6. Supporting: Bethlehem (n 72) 776; Trapp, 'Basics' (n 369) 147; Deeks (n 72) 487–88, 504; also Wood (n 419) 7. Cf Gray (n 44) 243 (test 'controversial'), generally 236–48; similarly Theodore Christakis, 'Challenging the "Unwilling or Unable" Test' (2017) 77 ZfaöRV 19, 19–20; also Tams, 'Terrorists' (n 8) 385 ('radical'); Corten, 'Plea' (n 361). Cf Corten, *War* (n 44) 170 (inability 'purely theoretical'), also 171–72; Kretzmer (n 426) 777–78. No particular test need

origin of the 'unwilling or unable' approach lies in the law of neutrality discussed above,[487] which already envisages a State exercising self-defence impacting another State's sovereign areas where necessary to prevent third-State attacks.[488] However, whether such failures violate States' obligations to prevent attacks occurring from their territory or not,[489] what matters is that—as in the original conception of self-defence[490]—they may render self-defence *necessary*, and thus justify another State breaching the former State's territorial sovereignty.[491] That necessity will almost certainly be established where the State is complicit in the attacks,[492] and may exist where the State is otherwise 'unwilling or unable' to act.[493] This approach does not, contrary to criticism, use necessity to enlarge self-defence's operation.[494] Rather, it assumes, as noted above, that third-party effects are possible, but uses necessity to strictly limit these.[495]

(iii) Conclusion: self-defence, individuals, and third-party rights

Taken as a whole, it has been suggested here that it is at least plausible that self-defence *is* able to be employed both to respond to non-State actor attacks and to

be endorsed, as explained n 491. Similarly Paddeu, 'Force' (n 49) 98. Cf Gray (n 44) 243–44; Deeks (n 72) 488–89.

487 Deeks (n 72), particularly 496–503; similarly Ruys (n 21) 503; Greenwood, 'Pre-Emptive' (n 70) 24–25; Lubell (n 48) 41–42; also Cheng (n 20) 91–92, 95–96; nn 387–425.

488 nn 425–437. Applying to the non-State actor scenario: Deeks (n 72) 497, 503; Greenwood, 'Pre-Emptive' (n 70) 24–25; Lubell (n 48) 41–42; Ruys (n 21) 503. Cf, doubting 'analogy': Kress (n 60) 267.

489 Trapp, 'Reply' (n 376) 1054–55 (terrorism); also Lubell (n 48) 38–40; Ruys and Verhoeven (n 359) 305–7; Paddeu, 'Force' (n 49) 109. These are 'due diligence' obligations: Ruys and Verhoeven (n 359) 305–6, 318; Bowett (n 47) 49, 56; Christakis (n 486) 20. Generally Ruys (n 21) 374–77, also 454.

490 nn 414ff and authorities and see Greenwood, 'Pre-Emptive' (n 70) 25; Greenwood, 'Self-Defence' (n 44) [17]; Paddeu, *Justification* (n 8) 359, 361, 363; Lubell (n 48) 34–35; Dinstein (n 47) [776]; Cheng (n 20) 87, 95–96. Cf Ruys and Verhoeven (n 359) 309; Gray (n 44) 206; Brandis (n 447).

491 Trapp, 'Reply' (n 376) 1053; Deeks (n 72), particularly 493–95; Trapp, 'Basics' (n 369) 142, 146, 155; Trapp, 'Attack' (n 71) 695; Milanovic, 'Indeterminacy' (n 367); Lubell (n 48) 40–42; Dinstein (n 47) [766]–[767], [778] and particularly Greenwood, 'Self-Defence' (n 44) [18]: 'there is an understandable concern that a State ... the victim of an attack by a group unconnected with any other State should not inevitably be free to take action against that group in the territory of other States ... Only if the former State has shown itself to be unwilling (or, perhaps, unable) to act effectively against the group it can be said that military action in its territory ... meets the criterion of necessity.' Further: Brownlie (n 70) 375; *Oppenheim's* (n 22) 387, 419–21; Bethlehem (n 72) 775–76; Wood (n 419) 6–7; Greenwood, 'Pre-Emptive' (n 70) 24–25; Cheng (n 20) 87, 95–96; also Wilmshurst (n 365) 11–12; Michael Bothe, 'Terrorism and the Legality of Pre-Emptive Force' (2003) 14 EJIL 227, 233; even Corten, *War* (n 44) 171–72, cf 445–47. Cf Gray (n 44) 227, 247–48; Paddeu, 'Force' (n 49) 107–09; Ruys and Verhoeven (n 359) 308–9, 317–18.

492 Jackson (n 72) 188–89; Trapp, 'Reply' (n 376) 1053; Trapp, 'Basics' (n 369) 147, 150, 155; Moir (n 70) 735; Trapp, 'Attack' (n 71) 695; Ruys (n 21) 493–96, 502–6, 509–10; Deeks (n 72) 505; also Lubell (n 48) 41–42; apparently Bethlehem (n 72) 776. Cf Tams, 'Rejoinder' (n 72) 1061; Tams, 'Terrorists' (n 8) 385.

493 n 486; and see, eg, Trapp, 'Basics' (n 369) 147; Greenwood, 'Self-Defence' (n 44) [18]; Lubell (n 48) 41; Wilmshurst (n 365) 13; Moir (n 70) 735; generally nn 486–87.

494 Cf Paddeu, 'Force' (n 49) 108; Gray (n 44) 246; Kretzmer (n 426) 778–79. See nn 403–8.

495 See Ruys (n 21) 505–6, 509; also Kress (n 60) 250; Deeks (n 72) 495, 508, generally 506ff; Thouvenin (n 387) 464–65; cf discussion Corten, *War* (n 44) 471–72. See section IV(B)(i)–(ii), particularly n 408. Cf nn 426, 494.

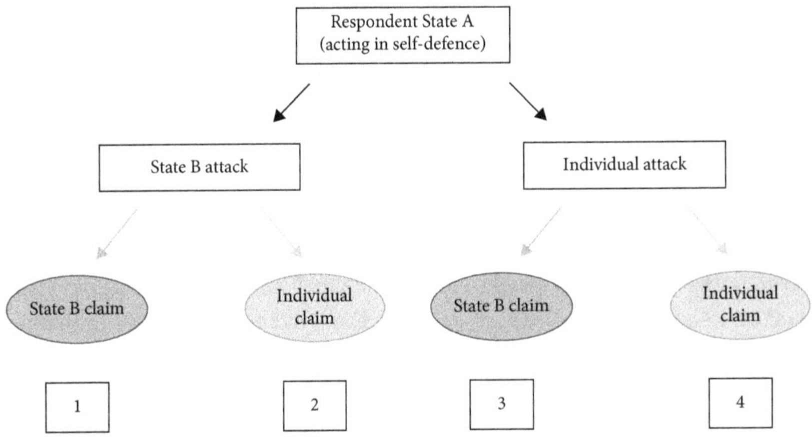

Figure 6.2 Potential overlapping individual and interstate claims resulting from a purported exercise of self-defence in response to an attack by either a State or an individual non-State actor

justify necessary violations of third-party rights. If correct, self-defence would therefore be able to be invoked in each of the four scenarios identified at the outset in Figure 6.2.

Scenario (1) is clear. If, as suggested, self-defence can—unlike countermeasures—respond directly to the actions of individual non-State actors, then scenario (4) comes into play, and (subject to violations which *cannot* be precluded[496]), self-defence could be invoked by a State to preclude the claims of individual attackers for any breach of international law arising from the actions taken in self-defence.[497] Apart from the one case noted above, self-defence does not appear to have been invoked in relation to individual claims.[498] Other circumstances precluding wrongfulness have, however, been so invoked: numerous investment tribunals have accepted, for instance, that States can rely on necessity to preclude individual claims arising from necessary measures.[499] Self-defence would appear likewise able to preclude individual claims arising out of a State's

[496] n 59.

[497] cf Paddeu, *Justification* (n 8) 407; Paparinskis, 'Countermeasures' (n 8) 342–43.

[498] n 53.

[499] Eg, *Union Fenosa v Egypt (Award)* ICSID Case No ARB/4/4 (31 August 2018) [8.1]–[8.4], [8.37]–[8.62]; *Urbaser v Argentina (Award)* ICSID Case No ARB/07/26 (8 December 2016) [709]–[718]; *Pezold* (n 406) [624]–[668]; *EDF International v Argentina (Final Award)* ICSID Case No ARB/03/23 (11 June 2012) [493]–[499], [1163]–[1181]; *Impregilo v Argentina (Award)* ICSID Case No ARB/07/17 (21 June 2011) [336]–[359]; *Suez v Argentina (Liability)* ICSID Case No ARB/03/17 (30 July 2010) [235]–[243]; *National Grid v Argentina (Award)* UNCITRAL Tribunal (3 November 2008) [254]–[262]; *LAFICO v Burundi* (1991) 96 ILR 279, 318–19, discussed Crawford, *GP* (n 7) 312. Generally discussion, eg, Tomka (n 69), with further authorities; Paddeu, *Justification* (n 8) 404–9; Paparinskis, 'New' (n 35) 632–35; Paparinskis, 'Countermeasures' (n 8) 342–43.

response to attacks by those individuals, where no question of third-party rights arises.

The possibility of self-defence operating to preclude claims in scenarios (2) and (3) depends on whether self-defence can, unlike countermeasures, justify third-party rights violations.[500] This book has suggested that there is a good argument that it can, both generally and in respect of territorial sovereignty. Self-defence would then operate like necessity as a circumstance precluding wrongfulness, and defend necessary violations of third-party rights.[501] Practice vis-à-vis necessity suggests that the effect would include the preclusion of an overlapping individual or interstate claim. For instance, as previously outlined, where individuals have claims so also must, at the least, their State of nationality.[502] Yet tribunals considering whether respondent States could rely on necessity to defend individual investment law claims did not consider that the inevitable violation of the rights of the individual's State of nationality prevented them from doing so, suggesting that overlapping States' claims would be equally precluded by the invocation of the defence.[503] Likewise, scholarly authority suggests that a State of nationality would be unable to exercise diplomatic protection vis-à-vis an individual targeted in self-defence.[504]

This being the case, it is plausible to suggest that individual claims could be precluded, under scenario (2), even if individuals invoke their own rights,[505] where the violation is necessary for a State to exercise self-defence in response to another State's armed attack.[506] Given the likelihood of individuals being harmed when a State exercises self-defence,[507] this could prove significant for self-defence's operation as a circumstance precluding wrongfulness. And under scenario (3), a State should expect to have its claims precluded—including any claim for violations of territorial sovereignty—where another State has responded in self-defence to an attack by individual non-State actor and the violation of the third State's rights proves necessary.

[500] See authorities nn 94–99; cf section III.
[501] nn 403–13.
[502] n 23; Ch 2, n 120.
[503] See *Suez (Liability)* (n 499) [239]; *Impregilo (Award)* (n 499) [354]. Cf *von Pezold*, n 406. See also *Torrey Canyon*, sometimes regarded as an example of necessity, where neither the individuals nor States protested: Ago (n 387) 28; also *Oppenheim's* (n 22) 417 (fn 2); Heathcote (n 404) 493; cf Paddeu, *Justification* (n 8) 401 (fn 456) (not necessity); Ruys (n 21) 381 (fn 65) (no art 2(4) breach). Similarly *Nachfolger*, discussed Heathcote (n 404) 493–94; *Oppenheim's* (n 22) 420 (fn 15).
[504] Bowett (n 47) 58 (treating as necessity), referencing Georg Schwarzenberger, 'The Fundamental Principles of International Law' (1955) 87 RdC 191, 332. The 'clean hands' doctrine could also be potentially relevant here, though its application to prevent diplomatic protection being exercised where the individual has committed a wrong is uncertain: see Chittharanjan Amerasinghe, *Diplomatic Protection* (OUP 2008) 217–21; John Dugard, 'Sixth Report on Diplomatic Protection' (2005) 2(1) ILCYB 1.
[505] cf nn 90ff.
[506] nn 490ff. Cf Paparinskis, 'Countermeasures' (n 8) 343.
[507] n 54.

V. Conclusion

This chapter addressed the operation of countermeasures and self-defence vis-à-vis overlapping individual and interstate claims. Four important points may be highlighted in conclusion. First, the distinction between breach (legal injury) and damage (factual injury), introduced in Chapter 1, is significant. Both countermeasures and self-defence taken against a State can apparently preclude individual claims for *damage* where the individual relies on the State's rights, and where the *legal* injury is thus done only to the State.[508] The controversy is whether they can preclude claims brought for breach of third-party (individual or State) rights and legal injury to those entities.[509]

However, second, just as the existence of separate State and individual rights does not, in and of itself, dictate the application of the other rules considered in this book, so too they do not necessarily render these circumstances precluding wrongfulness inapplicable to overlapping individual and interstate claims.[510] Even if individuals possess their own rights, the practice suggests that at least such certain individuals may not be regarded as third parties when countermeasures respond to State conduct.[511] Additionally, States arguably may, in necessary responses in self-defence to attacks by either individuals or States, violate third-party rights belonging to the other.[512] The allowability of both such actions may prove important in enabling these 'self-help' mechanisms[513] to function in today's world.[514]

Third, in determining *who* is liable to have their rights thus impacted in an overlapping individual-interstate claim scenario, the identity between the two entities may prove important.[515] Thus, State practice suggests that it is at least arguable that interstate countermeasures can preclude both States and individuals from invoking responsibility, even if the individual possesses its own rights, where that individual is *complicit* in the State's unlawful conduct.[516] For its part, self-defence was argued to justify violation of third-party rights when this is necessary.[517] Its operation vis-à-vis a State does not necessarily depend on any involvement in the relevant attack by that State—which may be simply 'unable' to act[518]—but, as

508 nn 25–32, 78.
509 nn 90ff, 374–79.
510 cf Conclusion, n 78.
511 Section III(A).
512 Section IV(A)–(B).
513 nn 8, 47; Dawidowicz (n 6) 20.
514 Similarly Bethlehem (n 72) 773–74; Deeks (n 72) 509; cf Gray (n 44) 138, discussing *Nicaragua (Merits)* (n 44) 544–45 (Diss Op Jennings); Parlett (n 8) 405 ('more nuanced approach . . . warranted in applying [ARSIWA] to investment treaty claims'); Peters/Roberts, n 107; generally nn 90, 108–10, 170, 360. Cf Bothe, 'Terrorism' (n 491) 239–40; Ruys and Verhoeven (n 359) 290, 310ff.
515 cf nn 107–10; Conclusion, n 10.
516 n 326.
517 nn 490ff.
518 n 493.

highlighted above, State involvement is common in cases in which self-defence is exercised vis-à-vis non-State actor attacks,[519] leading some to likewise suggest a standard of *complicity* in the individual's attacks.[520] In practice the 'connection' between the individual and the State is likely therefore to be relevant to the operation of both circumstances precluding wrongfulness vis-à-vis overlapping claims.[521]

Finally, however, human rights deserve particular consideration, as neither countermeasures nor self-defence can be invoked to justify violation of such rights.[522] Whether self-defence has been legitimately invoked may, however, be relevant to determining whether human rights have been violated.[523] As will be seen in the Conclusion to this book, human rights law provides an important tool for balancing the interests of States in employing these defences consistently with the law of State responsibility and the interests of individuals in pursuing their claims.

[519] n 483.

[520] n 482. This is not, however, relevant for scenario (2), where individuals may apparently suffer damage regardless of their involvement in an attack, in line with international humanitarian law. See generally n 58.

[521] n 332; cf Lubell (n 48) 36 ('connection' in a 'factual' sense); similarly Paddeu, 'Force' (n 49) 96; *ARSIWA*, 110 (individual–State 'factual relationship' for attribution). Cf Crawford, *GP* (n 7) 113 ('normative'), 113–15; similarly Condorelli and Kress (n 18) 225–28.

[522] nn 59, 351–56.

[523] nn 60–62.

Conclusion

The preceding chapters have undertaken a systematic survey of the potential for overlapping individual and interstate claims to arise, where both individuals and States are prima facie able to invoke the responsibility of the same respondent State for violations of international law arising in the same factual circumstances, and for various rules of preclusion to address resulting concerns.[1] The potential for such overlap is only likely to grow, with individual claims mechanisms continuing to emerge, increasing use of international courts generally, and domestic court involvement in international legal issues.[2]

While developments allowing individuals to bring claims for violations of international law against States provide such individuals with autonomy over claims concerning them, and free their States of nationality from entanglement in disputes,[3] the coexistence of individual claims mechanisms with more traditional means for interstate dispute settlement raises a myriad of concerns under the law of State responsibility.

These include concerns relating generally to multiplicity of claims: the injustice of subjecting a single respondent to repeated litigation, and uneasiness surrounding wastefulness and inconsistent decisions.[4] However, there are also broader implications for the traditional freedoms of States: the prospect of individual claims imperils the possibility for States to settle disputes, including those concerning large numbers of nationals, *inter se*, while uncertainties regarding how far circumstances precluding wrongfulness also preclude individual claims may lead to hesitation in States exercising countermeasures, self-defence, and consent on the interstate level.[5]

With the Articles on Responsibility of States for Internationally Wrongful Acts (ARSIWA) leaving largely unaddressed the application of the law of State responsibility to overlapping individual and interstate claims, this book aimed to bring some much-needed clarity to this area of the law.[6] The overarching question addressed was how far the law of State responsibility allows the action of a State or

[1] Introduction, nn 24, 60ff, 81; Ch 2(III).
[2] Introduction, nn 8–9, 32–27; Ch 2. Similarly Yuval Shany, *The Competing Jurisdictions of International Courts and Tribunals* (OUP 2003) 5–8, 74, 77.
[3] Introduction, nn 11–13
[4] Introduction, nn 40–46.
[5] Introduction, nn 49, 51–59.
[6] Introduction, nn 27–29.

Overlapping Individual and Interstate Claims in International Law. Jessica Howley, Oxford University Press.
 DOI: 10.1093/oso/9780192871466.003.0008

an individual to preclude the other from successfully invoking State responsibility where the claims of those two entities overlap.

This Conclusion briefly summarises the findings made regarding the rules and principles of international law considered in the foregoing chapters that may limit the bringing of such overlapping claims, and thereby offset the concerns such overlap raises. It then considers how States might manage the operation of such rules in future, in view of the complex policy considerations at stake.

I. Operation of rules of preclusion

Chapters 3–6 demonstrated that the conduct of both individuals and States can enliven rules of State responsibility relating to the invocation of responsibility, breach, and reparation, that can preclude the successful bringing of an overlapping claim by the other. While some of the rules are unidirectional, with potential operation to preclude only the claims of States,[7] or of individuals,[8] most of the rules have at least some potential to work in both directions, responding to the conduct of either a State or individual, and precluding overlapping claims belonging to the other.

Unfairness would result if *every* overlapping claim were able to be precluded through the action of another entity, undermining the autonomy of both States and individuals in bringing their own claims.[9] The main requirement limiting the over-zealous application of the rules considered herein, and which acts as a common thread running through them, is one of *identity*; that is, to what extent these rules might operate to block overlapping individual and interstate claims depends largely on the identity between those claims.[10] As in respect of *res judicata*, that identity may be categorised in three ways:[11]

(1) *legal injury*, meaning whether both a State and individual are claiming for breach of the same *rights*;
(2) *factual injury*, meaning whether both a State and individual are claiming for the same *damage*;
(3) *party identity*, meaning whether the *same entities* are bringing the overlapping claims, and for breach of *their* rights.[12]

[7] Only individuals can consent to arbitration enlivening ICSID's article 27, or fail to exhaust local remedies, with potential impacts on a State's claim: Ch 3, nn 17, 33.

[8] Only States can impact an individual's claim under article 222(c) of the CARICOM Treaty; certain *res judicata*-like provisions restrict only individual claims; and countermeasures can only respond to State conduct, with potential impacts on individual claims: Ch 3, n 16; Ch 4, n 123; Ch 6, nn 15–22.

[9] Shany (n 2) 23–24, 115, 121, 155.

[10] Similarly ibid 22ff, 155; Yuval Shany, *Regulating Jurisdictional Relations Between National and International Courts* (OUP 2007) 3 ('required degree of similarity'), 114, 125, 131–33, 194; André Nollkaemper, *National Courts and the International Rule of Law* (OUP 2011) 251; see Ch 4(IV).

[11] See Ch 4, n 113; similarly Shany (n 10) 133ff ('same parties'/'same issues').

[12] See Ch 4, nn 113–15, 145–59, 210–11, 246–47, generally section IV(A)–(C).

Determining when the necessary identity is present for the purposes of these rules requires precision in distinguishing between State and individual rights—substantive, procedural, international, and domestic—and between 'direct' and 'derivative' claims made for breach of the same or distinct substantive rights,[13] as well as in appreciating the complexities surrounding when overlapping individual and interstate claims are being brought for the same damage. Chapter 3 laid the foundation for understanding these issues through a rigorous analysis of the distinction between diplomatic protection, 'direct', and 'mixed' interstate claims.[14]

While each of the rules of preclusion considered in this book depends, for its application, on some level of identity between the overlapping individual and interstate claims at issue, we have seen that the degree of required identity varies. The prohibition on double recovery requires only, for instance, that the *damage* in two claims be the same.[15] Other rules appear, at least prima facie, to depend on identity of *persons*: rules concerning waiver, consent, countermeasures, and, at least on one view, self-defence, cannot affect third-party rights. This means that they cannot prima facie operate to preclude claims of an entity relying on its own rights and not providing the waiver or being responsible for the conduct giving rise to the exercise of the relevant defence.[16] For their part, the local remedies rule, and the provisions of the Convention on the Settlement of Investment Disputes between States and Nationals of Other States (ICSID) and the Revised Treaty of Chaguaramas Establishing the Caribbean Community (CARICOM Treaty), do not require party identity to operate,[17] but because they are only applicable where the interstate claim is one of diplomatic protection, there needs to be identity in the *damage* claimed, and at least a degree of similarity in the *breach* alleged, across the claims.[18] And *res judicata* requires prima facie identity across all three categories.[19]

Even with these requirements, however, we should not underestimate the extent to which an entity's actions might, in the application of these rules in practice, affect the other's claims.[20] Indeed, the foregoing chapters have demonstrated the potential breadth in application of the rules considered therein to preclude one or both of overlapping individual and interstate claims.

First, because diplomatic protection claims can be brought for *any* violation of international law causing individual damage, the category of claims potentially precluded by the local remedies rule, and the ICSID and CARICOM treaty

13 See particularly Peters (n 137) 284–317 ('procedural'/'substantive'/'direct'/'derivative' rights), generally authorities Ch 4, n 158; also Ch 5, n 131.

14 Ch 3. Similarly Shany (n 10) 139–40.

15 Ch 4, nn 58–65.

16 Ch 5, nn 18–21, 40–41; Ch 6, nn 89ff, 373ff.

17 See Shany, Ch 3, n 9; André Nollkaemper, 'Conversations among Courts: Domestic and International Adjudicators' in Cesare Romano, Karen Alter, and Yuval Shany (eds), *The Oxford Handbook of International Adjudication* (OUP 2014) 529; Ch 3(I)(A)–(B).

18 Ch 3, nn 32, 188–92, 206–10; Ch 4, nn 372ff. Cf Shany (n 10) 30 (no 'formal similarity').

19 Ch 4, nn 113–15.

20 cf Ch 4, nn 143–44, 167, 260–61, 386, 612, 647.

provisions, is much broader than those who focus on whose rights are violated, or the nature of that right, might acknowledge.[21]

Second, Chapter 4 demonstrated that the prohibition on double recovery has almost certain application as between individual and interstate claims for the same damage, regardless of which entity receives that reparation, and whether through settlement, or before a domestic or international tribunal.[22] Once it is understood that almost all interstate claims are brought either solely or partially for damage done to an individual's person or property (through diplomatic protection or 'mixed' claims),[23] the scope for this rule to preclude the second of two overlapping individual and interstate reparation claims—the State's *or* the individual's—is astonishingly broad. Indeed, its application extends, vis-à-vis an overlapping individual claim, to interstate claims for individual damage where many persons are affected, where the State's other interests are involved, where only limited sums are ultimately paid in compensation (including on a lump-sum basis), and where the State claims for damage *reflecting* that done to an individual.[24]

While the same chapter demonstrated that the potential application of *res judicata* is more complicated, it suggested that there is good reason to consider that the principle should apply to preclude the second of two overlapping individual and interstate claims where the relevant individuals and States are claiming for the same damage, resulting from similar violations, and in the same interest.[25] Notably, this would capture many diplomatic protection claims overlapping with individual claims, as well as, potentially, 'mixed' claims, similar to class actions, brought for widescale damage to a State's citizens.[26]

Third, Chapter 5 demonstrated that the rights *to claim* considered herein belong to States and individuals respectively, meaning that they cannot be waived by the other. Nonetheless, interstate claims commonly depend on damage to an individual's person or property, which may also presuppose a violation of the individual's rights under *domestic* law. Individual waivers of such rights or damage may prevent a State from establishing individual injury, undermining the basis for an overlapping interstate claim.[27] Moreover, while States may not apparently *waive* individual claims brought before international and domestic courts per se, they appear to have significant capabilities to remove the capacity of those individuals to bring claims altogether. They can certainly do so vis-à-vis claims before their own domestic courts,[28] and practice suggests that they also consider themselves able, through interstate consent, to do so vis-à-vis individual *international*

21 Ch 3, n 202, generally Ch 3(II).
22 Ch 4(II).
23 Ch 3, nn 206–12, 248–49.
24 Ch. 4(V)(A)(i), Ch 4(V)(B)(i).
25 Ch 4(V)(A)(ii), Ch 4(V)(B)(ii), Ch 4(VI), particularly nn 372ff, 581ff, 608–13, 637ff.
26 Ch 4(V)(A)(ii), Ch 4(V)(B)(ii).
27 Ch 5(II).
28 Ch 5(III)(B).

claims procedures before, and possibly even after, claims have been instituted.[29] This marks a significant potential intrusion into claims brought by individuals and a notable reserve of power to the State to settle claims on an interstate basis.[30]

Finally, Chapter 6 demonstrated the scope for a respondent State to invoke countermeasures and self-defence to preclude overlapping individual and interstate claims from being successfully brought. At least where an individual claimant is not relying on its own substantive rights under international law, a respondent State may apparently rely on these defences to preclude both the claims of the State to whose conduct the relevant measure responds and the individual's overlapping claim.[31] Where there are, at least arguably, individual rights under international law involved, Chapter 6 suggested that one should not jump to the conclusion that a respondent could not rely on such defences to preclude individual claims. Questioning the mainstream 'third-party rights' approach, it examined State practice pertaining to sanctions and exercises of self-defence against non-State actors, suggesting that there is scope to argue that overlapping individual and interstate claims can, where both entities are sufficiently connected to the conduct giving rise to the defence, be precluded through the exercise of countermeasures and self-defence, regardless of whether those entities invoke distinct rights.[32]

In sum, the possibilities resulting from the application of these rules for States to preclude their nationals' claims, and, by contrast, for individuals to interfere with the exercise of traditional powers of States under the law of State responsibility, are substantial. The mere fact of individual claims mechanisms having been provided does not guarantee that individuals will be able to claim unimpeded.[33] At the same time, in enabling individuals to bring claims under international law, States have restricted their own ability to bring, defend, and conclusively settle claims on the interstate level.[34]

II. Policy considerations: striking the right balance

Having reached conclusions regarding the actual and potential operation of these rules to overlapping individual and interstate claims, we may consider whether those conclusions appear satisfactory. As noted in the Introduction, the complex policy considerations at play cannot be identified in this book either comprehensively or in a way that would be free from contestation. However, from this book's

[29] Ch 5(III)(C).
[30] Similarly Anthea Roberts, 'State-to-State Investment Treaty Arbitration: A Hybrid Theory of Interdependent Rights and Shared Interpretative Authority' (2014) 55 Harv ILJ 1, 28; authorities n 44.
[31] Ch 6, nn 32, 78–79.
[32] Ch 6(III)–(IV).
[33] Similarly Roberts (n 30) 28; authorities n 44.
[34] Similarly Robert McCorquodale, 'The Individual and the International Legal System' in Malcolm Evans (ed), *International Law* (4th edn, OUP 2014) 301; Roberts (n 30) 28.

consideration of the existence, development, and application of the law of State responsibility, rules of preclusion, individual claims mechanisms, and human rights, we may at least derive considerations concerning (1) respondent States (protection from multiple claims; preservation of freedom to act consistently with the law of State responsibility); (2) applicant States (respect for role in settling claims that concern them, including claims of their nationals); (3) individuals (protection of interests in claims concerning them); and (4) the system of international dispute settlement more broadly (ensuring functioning in a cost-effective and cohesive manner).[35]

Correctly understood, some of the rules appear to be reasonably unproblematic. Ensuring that the local remedies rule is applied to all cases of diplomatic protection properly so-called allows the individual and State to attempt to settle their differences before the dispute is escalated to the international level, in line with the rule's longstanding policy objectives.[36] Situations in which it is unreasonable to expect the individual to exhaust remedies are catered for by exceptions.[37] For the applicant State, any unresolved claim can proceed, and the prospect of being forced to delay a 'mixed' claim, concerning also its own damage, awaiting the individual's exhaustion, is remote in practice.[38] However, properly applying these rules requires an analysis beginning from the correct premise, as this book has shown.[39]

Turning to the other rules, the picture appears less rosy for some. The principles of *res judicata* and particularly that precluding double recovery have potentially far-reaching effects on overlapping claims, especially where diplomatic protection and 'mixed' interstate claims are concerned. As noted in Chapter 4, the prejudice to an applicant State nonetheless appears limited: it is not unreasonable that the individual 'direct' victim of a given measure should be able to dispose of claims concerning themselves and their damage, leaving the State unable to claim for damage only "fictionally" incurred by it.[40] Indeed, that outcome is consistent with that resulting from the application of other rules considered herein: diplomatic protection claims would be equally precluded where an individual has successfully exhausted local remedies, or waived the damage they have suffered.[41] And where the State has suffered distinct damage, the State's claim for that damage rightly survives.[42]

[35] Similarly authorities Introduction, nn 40–46, 49, 57–59; Roberts (n 30) 7–10; Amerasinghe, n 38.

[36] Ch 3, n 191; Chittharanjan Amerasinghe, *Local Remedies in International Law* (2nd edn, CUP 2004) 59–62, 74, and see 22–37 for the history.

[37] Ch 3, nn 112, 380ff.

[38] Ch 3(IV)(C)(i) and see Hugh Thirlway, *The Law and Procedure of the International Court of Justice: Fifty Years of Jurisprudence* (OUP 2013) 1554. Similarly on the State/individual interests underlying the local remedies rule: Amerasinghe (n 35) 59–64.

[39] Similarly Stephan Wittich, 'Direct Injury and the Incidence of the Local Remedies Rule' (2000) 5 Aust Rev I & EL 121, 136, 142.

[40] Ch 4, nn 617–21. Cf n 620 (possible State prejudice).

[41] Ch 4, n 621; Ch 5(II).

[42] Ch 4(V)(B), particularly nn 399, 593–96.

Indeed, to some extent, applicant States may wish for *greater* certainty that the principle of *res judicata*, in particular, would preclude individuals from bringing overlapping claims in circumstances in which such States have themselves already claimed. An applicant State may have concerns about being unable to engage in litigation on a holistic basis with a respondent State, particularly where a large number of its citizens have been affected, for fear that claims will nonetheless continue to be brought by such individuals.[43] However, as Chapter 5 demonstrated, States have at their disposal a significant arsenal of possibilities to preclude their nationals from bringing both domestic and international claims, through the exercise of waiver and consent, and in practice make use of those possibilities to enter into settlement agreements *inter se*. Despite the promise of a more cosmopolitan understanding of international law, individuals remain greatly reliant therefore on State action.[44]

While the protective function of the principles of *res judicata* and that precluding double recovery for a respondent State thus appears adequately balanced with the interests of a potential applicant State, the same cannot be said for the individual. Individuals should rightly be alarmed at the prospect of claims for reparation being blocked by their State of nationality pursuing an overlapping claim first, including where the State engages in a class action-like settlement of claims on behalf of numerous citizens.[45] There is, after all, no guarantee that the State will pass any reparation on to the affected individuals, rather than using those sums in other ways, such as for reconstruction in a post-conflict environment.[46]

Finally, for countermeasures and self-defence, one might consider their application to overlapping claims potentially both over- and under-inclusive. If one shares the view that, with the exception of human rights, individuals do not hold substantive rights in the fields in which they claim (including under investment law), then respondent States are free to take countermeasures or exercise self-defence in response to State conduct, with individuals obliged to bear any resulting negative consequences for themselves.[47] On the other hand, if one views individuals as holding their own substantive rights in these fields, and accepts that both countermeasures and self-defence cannot affect third-party rights, then potential respondent States are in a bind: in exercising their rights, they risk being pursued on the individual level for damage caused through otherwise legitimate actions against the State.[48] And for self-defence, States will struggle to respond to attacks

[43] Ch 4, n 623.

[44] Similarly Kate Parlett, *The Individual in the International Legal System: Continuity and Change in International Law* (CUP 2011) 359–62, 367, 370–72; McCorquodale (n 34) 284 ('participation ... dependent on State consent'), cf 286, 301; cf Anne Peters, *Beyond Human Rights: The Legal Status of the Individual in International Law* (Jonathan Huston tr, CUP 2016) 409–35. Cf Introduction, nn 7–9.

[45] Ch 4, nn 554ff, 646–48.

[46] See Ch 4, nn 509, 513.

[47] Ch 6, nn 24ff, 78–79.

[48] See Introduction, nn 51–59; generally Ch 6(III)–(IV).

by non-State actors given the almost inevitable infringement of third State (territorial) rights in doing so.[49]

Where should the balance lie in the application of all of these rules between the interest of individuals in pursuing their own claim, that of the State in settling, perhaps on a global basis, the claims of its citizens, and those of respondent States exercising their rights under the law of State responsibility?[50] With the present law seeming to allow States significant leeway in impeding individual claims, it is suggested here that human rights law provides the foundation for a fitting counterbalance and should be the prism through which the appropriateness of State action is judged.[51]

The context for this proposal is the risk that States run, in exercising their powers to prevent their nationals' claims being brought before domestic and international fora, of secondary claims being brought by the individuals affected for breach of their rights.[52] One can envisage two commonly recognised rights being of particular pertinence.[53]

First, human rights instruments and domestic constitutional provisions often protect property rights.[54] Domestic and international courts have recognised that private claims can amount to property,[55] and investment tribunals have also sometimes recognised claims as 'investments',[56] including international claims such as those before the Southern African Development Community Tribunal (SADCT).[57] Domestic courts have, in several decisions, considered whether a purported waiver or settlement of claims on the interstate level, such as those

[49] Ch 6, nn 373–79, 514; generally Ch 6(IV).

[50] Similarly Anthea Roberts, 'Triangular Treaties: The Extent and Limits of Investment Treaty Rights' (2015) 56 Harv ILJ 353, 396–97; n 35.

[51] cf Roberts (n 50) 397–99 and see nn 52ff.

[52] Similarly Roberts (n 50) 398, 411–14; also Gerald Fitzmaurice, 'Fourth Report on the Law of Treaties' [1959] 2 ILCYB 37 [159]. For 'secondary' language, eg: Luke Eric Peterson, 'Singapore Judge Sees Investors . . .' *IA Rep* (17 August 2017).

[53] Similarly Andrea Gattini, 'A Trojan Horse for Sudeten Claims? On Some Implications of the Prince of Liechtenstein v Germany' (2002) 13 EJIL 513, 525–26. Further: *Julian and Drake v New Zealand* (1997) 118 ILR 223 (HRC) 227–28 (waiver-related claims: denying remedy/discrimination); *Kandyrine v France* Recueil Lebon 303678, ILDC 2734 (FR 2011) (Cons d'Etat, 23 December 2011) [23].

[54] ECHR Protocol 1, art 1 ('possessions'); AfCHPR, art 14; AmCHR, art 21. On domestic law, n 58; generally Robert Jennings and Arthur Watts, *Oppenheim's International Law*, vol 1 (9th edn, Longman 1992) 539.

[55] Eg, *Dames and Moore v Regan* (1981) 453 US 654 (USSC) 688–89; *Draon v France* (2006) 42 EHRR 40 [65] (where 'sufficient basis in national law'); *BTS Holding v Slovakia (Merits)* App 55617/17 (ECtHR, 30 June 2022) [49] ('if . . . sufficiently established to be enforceable'), n 61; also *Beaumartin v France* (1995) 19 EHRR 485, n 46; cf *Breitung's Estate v USA (The Seguranca)* (1939) 10 ILR 598 (Arbitration) 604–5 (no individual claim under interstate agreement).

[56] See cases referenced Damien Charlotin, 'Singapore Appeal Court Grapples . . .' *IA Rep* (29 November 2018); Peterson, 'Singapore' (n 52): eg *Mondev v US (Award)* (2002) 6 ICSID Rep 192 [80]–[83].

[57] Luke Eric Peterson, 'In New Ruling . . .' *IA Reporter* (14 July 2016); cf Peterson, 'Singapore' (n 52), also discussing *ATA Construction v Jordan (Award)* ICSID Case No ARB/08/2 (18 May 2010) [125]–[126] ('right to arbitration . . . asset').

considered in Chapter 5, expropriates such rights.[58] More recently, the European Court of Human Rights (ECtHR) held that a State had violated the right to property in refusing to enforce an arbitral award before its domestic courts, holding, *inter alia*, that even if the refusal had been in the public interest, it was not proportionate, having 'taken no account of the requirements of the protection of the applicant company's fundamental rights and the need for a fair balance to be struck between them and the general interest of the community rights'.[59]

There is no reason in principle why human rights or similar domestic actions would not also be available to provide some recourse against a State that precludes its nationals' claims through operation of *res judicata* or the rule precluding double recovery and fails to share any reparation.[60] Indeed, although the facts of the case were quite particular, the ECtHR in *Beaumartin* found that an interstate lump-sum settlement agreement, in providing that France was responsible for apportioning the sum among the beneficiaries, 'proclaimed the principle of the right to compensation of certain categories of expropriated persons', who thus had a property right thereunder that France could not refuse to recognise.[61]

Second, various human rights instruments recognise rights to a fair hearing.[62] As a purported waiver or other settlement of claims generally involves States' barring claims before their own courts and other fora, this right might be thereby engaged.[63] Likewise, in investment law, one tribunal found Lesotho to have committed a denial of justice by participating in suspending the SADCT when a case was pending against it.[64] The South African Constitutional Court criticised South Africa's involvement in that suspension for, in part, similar reasons,[65] while an African Commission on Human and Peoples' Rights (ACommHPR) case was also brought but dismissed.[66] Another investment tribunal held a State responsible to provide reparation consequent on breach of the dispute settlement provision of a

[58] See *German Assets in Switzerland Case* (1957) 24 ILR 542 (BVerfG) 544–46 (no expropriation); similarly *Togen Akiyama v State* (1963) 32 ILR 233 (Tokyo DC) 235; *Austrian State Treaty Case* (1961) 40 ILR 184 (SC Austria) 186 (no unconstitutional taking); *German-Portuguese Assets Case* (1968) 51 ILR 401 (BVerfG)) 411–14; *Ryuichi Shimoda v Japan* (1963) 32 ILR 626 (Tokyo DC) 642 (no taking); *Aris Gloves v United States* (1970) 56 ILR 536 (US Ct Cl) 542–43; cf *Ditta Pomante v Germany* (1960) 40 ILR 64 (L'Aquila Civ Ct) 71 (unclear); *Restitution of Household Effects Belonging to Jews Deported from Hungary* (1965) 44 ILR 301 (CA, Berlin) 302, 312 (compensation required); also Ch 5, n 164. Cf *Haas v Humphrey* (1957) 24 ILR 316 (USCA) 317–18. Generally Roberts (n 50) 398. Cf *Dames* (n 55) 688–89.

[59] *BTS* (n 55) [71]. See Damien Charlotin, 'European Court of Human Rights Finds …' *IA Rep* (1 July 2022).

[60] Similarly Roberts (n 30) 51. See Ch 4, n 513.

[61] *Beaumartin* (n 55) [28], discussed Parlett (n 44) 89. Similarly *Irresberger v Austria* (1953) 20 ILR 433 (Landesgericht Austria) 433–34 (domestic law).

[62] ICCPR, art 14(1); ECHR, art 6(1); AmCHR, art 8(1); AfCHPR, art 7(1).

[63] nn 64–66, 73ff; also *M v United Nations and Belgium* (1969) 69 ILR 139 (CA, Brussels) 143.

[64] Luke Eric Peterson, 'Arbitrators Hold State Liable …' *IA Rep* (14 July 2016).

[65] Jarrod Hepburn, 'South African Court Finds Fault …' *IA Rep* (2 March 2018).

[66] *Tembani v Angola* et al Comm 409/12 (ACommHR, Oct/Nov 2013) [138]–[142], [144], [146], cited Erika de Wet, 'Reactions to the Backlash: Trying to Revive the SADC Tribunal through Litigation' *EJIL:Talk!* (5 August 2016).

bilateral investment treaty (BIT), and the 'right to arbitrate' found therein, through actions taken domestically to prevent the claimant from bringing its claims.[67]

Naturally, the success of such claims by an individual depends on whether there are forums—domestic or international—available to hear them.[68] Moreover, even where such fora exist, it does not follow that individual claims may never be impaired, for most human rights may be limited to some extent,[69] and individuals have no absolute right to reparation for international law violations.[70] Indeed, in a post-war or other emergency environment, it may be a laudable aim to sacrifice nationals' assets to secure peace.[71] Thus, both domestic and international courts have generally been prepared to accept that barring individual claims does not infringe property rights where that action is proportionate and done in pursuit of a legitimate interest.[72] For instance, concerning rights to a hearing, in what later developed into the *Certain Property Case*, the ECtHR considered a post-war treaty clause that prevented Germany from admitting claims against persons who had

[67] *Dunkeld v Belize (Award)* PCA Case 2010-13 (28 June 2016) [336]–[337], see [9], [29] (anti-suit injunctions).

[68] See nn 53ff; similarly Frits Kalshoven, 'Expert Opinion' in Hisakazu Fujita, Isomi Suzuki, and Kantaro Nagano (eds), *War and the Rights of Individuals: Renaissance of Individual Compensation* (Nippon Hyoron-sha 1999) 41–42. Non-nationals might claim under different BITs: eg *Azurix v Argentina (Annulment)* ICSID Case No ARB/01/12 (1 September 2009) [109], while human rights are jurisdiction-based (Frédéric Mégret, 'Nature of Obligations' in Daniel Moeckli and others (eds), *International Human Rights Law* (3rd edn, OUP 2018) 89; James Crawford, *Brownlie's Principles of Public International Law* (8th edn, OUP 2012) 651–53; Gateano Arangio-Ruiz, 'Fourth Report on State Responsibility' [1992] 2(1) ILCYB 1 [134]; ALI, *Restatement of the Law: The Foreign Relations Law of the United States*, vol II (3rd edn, ALI Publishers 1987) 179), meaning individuals can claim even if their States are non-parties: McCorquodale (n 34) 290–91; eg *Pad v Turkey (Admissibility)* App 60167/00 (ECtHR, 28 June 2007); Ch 5, nn 351–52.

[69] Eg, *Legal Consequences of the Construction of a Wall in the Occupied Palestinian Territory (Advisory Opinion)* [2004] ICJ Rep 136 [136]; also Peters (n 44) 487.

[70] See *Jurisdictional Immunities (Germany v Italy: Greece Intervening) (Judgment)* [2012] ICJ Rep 99 [94]; Christian Tomuschat, 'Individuals' in James Crawford and others (eds), *The Law of International Responsibility* (OUP 2010) 988–89; also *Prosecutor v Lubanga (Judgment on the appeals against the "Decision establishing the principles and procedures to be applied to reparations" of 7 August 2012)* Case ICC-01/04-01/06AA2A3 (3 March 2015) [155] (no 'internationally recognized human right to a consideration of *individual* applications for reparations').

[71] See Ch 5, nn 49–51; Gattini (n 53) 541; also Peters (n 44) 175 (State claim treated 'preferentially'), 212-13, 216. Generally, on sacrificing individual interests: Bin Cheng, *General Principles of Law as Applied by International Courts and Tribunals* (Stevens & Sons 1953) 47–48; Edwin Borchard, *The Diplomatic Protection of Citizens Abroad: Or, the Law of International Claims* (Banks 1915) 31, 351; Philip Jessup, *A Modern Law of Nations* (Archon 1968) 138; Paul Weis, *Nationality and Statelessness in International Law* (2nd edn, Sijthoff & Noordhoff 1979) 33–34; N Jansen Calamita, 'International Human Rights and the Interpretation of International Investment Treaties: Constitutional Considerations' in Freya Baetens (ed), *Investment Law within International Law: Integrationist Perspectives* (CUP 2013) 174–75. Cf Eduardo Jiménez de Aréchaga, 'International Responsibility' in Max Sørensen (ed), *Manual of Public International Law* (Macmillan 1968) 563 and authorities (amnesties).

[72] See *Belk v US* (1988) 858 F 2d 706 (USCA) 709 (impairment/public interest); *Draon* (n 55) [77], [78]–[86] (disproportionate *in casu*); *German Assets* (n 58) 545; also *State Treaty* (n 58) 186 (no ECHR compensation); *Kandyrine* (n 53) [23]; *Akiyama* (n 58) 237; n 74; Gattini (n 53) 541; Hans van Houtte, Bart Delmartino, and Iasson Yi, *Post-War Restoration of Property Rights Under International Law*, vol 1 (CUP 2008) 28; Peters (n 44) 216; Eyal Benvenisti, 'Individual Remedies for Victims of Armed Conflicts in the Context of Mass Claims Settlements' in Holger Hestermeyer and others (eds), *Coexistence, Cooperation and Solidarity: Liber Amicorum Rüdiger Wolfrum* (Martinus Nijohoff 2012) 1102–3.

received property confiscated for reparations purposes.[73] The Court examined whether Germany could, relying on this clause, deprive an individual claiming restitution of property of his right to a hearing.[74] Ultimately, the Court considered that Germany had the 'legitimate aim' of regaining its sovereignty in the 'vital public interest', and its actions were not therefore 'disproportionate'.[75]

In the case of self-defence and countermeasures as circumstances precluding wrongfulness, it is suggested that human rights provide an appropriate limitation on the actions of *both* a respondent State invoking such a defence and the individual claimant's State of nationality.

As to respondent States, the risk of taking a 'third-party rights' approach to countermeasures and self-defence in the modern world is that it limits the capacity of such States to rely on such defences in protecting their interests.[76] Even if such a State could rely on the defence vis-à-vis the wrongdoing actor (for countermeasures, the State; for self-defence, either a State or individual non-State actor), if an overlapping claim could nonetheless be brought by the other, particularly in circumstances in which effects on that other are difficult to avoid, then the respondent loses, at least partly, the benefit of such a defence.[77]

This book suggested that these considerations render a strict 'third-party rights' approach undesirable. For countermeasures, a concentration on 'third-party' rights, including whether individuals hold 'direct' or 'derivative' rights, appears to place insufficient focus on *party identity* in determining when they may be employed.[78] Just as rules of attribution recognise that certain individuals *are* the State for State responsibility purposes,[79] so too would it be possible not to regard individuals as 'third parties' for countermeasures purposes where they are *complicit* in the State's wrongdoing.[80] An explosion of recent State practice regarding sanctions targeted at such persons does not definitively establish the acceptability of treating

[73] *Prince Hans-Adam II of Liechtenstein v Germany* ECHR 2001-VIII 7 [29]; also *Certain Property (Liechtenstein v Germany) (Preliminary Objections)* [2005] ICJ Rep 6 [14]; discussion Michael Winn, 'Peace Treaty Claim Waivers: The Case of Price Hans-Adam II of Liechtenstein and the "Scene at a Roman Well"' (2006) 38 Geo Wash ILR 807, 809–10, 816. See also on impeding court access to comply with obligations concerning immunity: eg, *Waite and Kennedy v Germany* (1999) 118 ILR 121 [58], [63], [67]-[73]; *Al-Adsani v UK* (2002) 34 EHRR 11 [54]–[56]; *Association SOS Attentats and De Boëry v France* ECHR 2006-XIV 375 [38]–[39], discussed Ch 5(III)(C)(iii); Gattini (n 53) 530; also Nollkaemper (n 10) 22, 29–30.

[74] *Prince Hans-Adam* (n 73) [51]–[52]; Winn (n 73) 813.

[75] *Prince Hans-Adam* (n 73) [69]; discussion Winn (n 73) 813–15; Gattini (n 53) 532.

[76] Ch 6, n 514. Consent is, however, strictly relational. See Federica Paddeu, *Justification and Excuse in International Law* (CUP 2018) 170–72, cf 93; generally Ch 5, nn 18–21, 40–42.

[77] Introduction, nn 57–59. The reparation owed to the overlapping claimant may be significantly more than would otherwise be due to the wrongdoing actor, eg, where third-State damage is caused in exercising self-defence vis-à-vis an individual attack: see Ch 6(IV)(B)(ii).

[78] See Ch 6(III). Similarly suggesting moving beyond the 'direct'/'derivative' debate: Criddle, Ch 6, nn 108–9; Peters (n 44) 329–31; Roberts (n 50) 356, 399–402.

[79] Ch 1, nn 8–11; Ch 6, nn 322–38.

[80] Ch 6, nn 333, 482.

countermeasures against a State as also effective to preclude claims for violation of those individuals' rights—but it certainly suggests that the argument is plausible.[81]

For self-defence, this book suggested that a focus on third-party rights is to misunderstand the nature of this circumstance precluding wrongfulness, which envisages the possibility of infringing such rights where necessary to respond to an 'armed attack'.[82] It argued for the view that States can respond to attacks by both States and individuals in self-defence, meaning that both State and individual claims could be precluded by a respondent's invocation of self-defence due to the conduct of the other.[83] Again, however, the relationship between those entities may prove important in determining how far an invocation of self-defence can, in practice, affect the claims of both, with requirements of necessity and proportionality greatly limiting impacts on unrelated third parties.[84]

Accepting some flexibility in the application of these defences provides a means for balancing individual rights with the freedom of respondent States to exercise these 'self-help' mechanisms in a manner suited to global realities.[85] Countermeasures could target individuals who are sufficiently involved in, and whose actions will most likely affect, the wrongdoing State's conduct.[86] And with attacks increasingly coming from individual non-State actors rather than State authorities, States could employ self-defence to realistically protect themselves, within the bounds of what is necessary and proportionate.[87]

Human rights law will nonetheless continue to provide an appropriate limitation in both cases. Countermeasures cannot affect human rights, being *erga omnes* in nature,[88] and human rights claims against sanction-imposing States underscore their continued importance in ensuring States do not overstep the mark.[89] For its part, while an exercise of self-defence *may* infringe third-party rights, respect for human rights is built into the substantive rule.[90] Even if, as suggested in this book, there is a strong argument that individuals do not possess rights irrevocable by States outside of the human rights field (although certain international tribunals have disagreed),[91] human rights law would therefore continue to provide a means of redress against a respondent State's excesses in employing these defences.

[81] Ch 6(III)(A).
[82] Ch 6(IV)(B).
[83] Ch 6(IV)(B).
[84] Ch 6, nn 517–21 and Peters, Ch 6, n 107.
[85] Ch 6, nn 513–14.
[86] Ch 6, n 182.
[87] Ch 6, nn 45, 359–60, 514.
[88] Ch 6, nn 351–53, 356.
[89] Generally Idriss Jazairy, 'Report of the Special Rapporteur on the Negative Impact of Unilateral Coercive Measures on the Enjoyment of Human Rights' UN Doc A/HRC/33/48 (2 August 2016) [31]–[66]; eg, Ch 6, nn 207–14.
[90] Ch 6, nn 59, 522–23, Ch 6(IV)(B).
[91] Ch 5(III)(C)(viii); cf Ch 6, nn 94–97.

Additionally, as for other rules of preclusion considered above, human rights and domestic law may provide redress against the individual's *own* State for its actions leading to a respondent State's invocation of circumstances precluding wrongfulness. Thus, at least one claim was brought against a State based on, *inter alia*, individual rights to property, where that State's wrongful conduct resulted in *another State's* retaliatory action and consequent individual losses,[92] a situation that bears a strong resemblance to the countermeasures scenario considered in this book.[93] That claim was rejected, *inter alia* because there was no right to property in a market share and individuals were taken to be aware that circumstances, including retaliation within the World Trade Organization (WTO) framework, might affect their business.[94] Nonetheless, the bringing of the case highlights the possibilities for human rights actions in such situations.[95]

Additionally, individuals and third States affected by the invocation of self-defence against non-State actors could potentially found a compensation claim on the principle reflected in ARSIWA article 27, which provides that reliance on a circumstance precluding wrongfulness is 'without prejudice' to 'compensation for any material loss [thereby] caused'.[96] Allowing for the possibility of compensation being awarded notwithstanding invocation of a circumstance precluding wrongfulness avoids, notes the commentary, a State 'shift[ing] the burden of the defence of its own interests or concerns on to an innocent third State'.[97] Here, the distinction between justification and excuse becomes potentially relevant, with Paddeu noting that several factors related to that distinction, including whether a given response is lawful, play into the question of whether compensation should be paid.[98] While Paddeu considers that the justification/excuse distinction has no bearing on compensation to *third* parties, as a matter pertaining 'exclusively [to] the bilateral relations between the state invoking the defence and the state against which the defence is invoked',[99] as Lowe explains,

[92] Marco Bronckers and Sophie Goelen, 'Financial Liability of the EU for Violations of WTO Law—A Legislative Proposal Benefiting Innocent Bystanders' in Marise Cremona and others (eds), *Reflections on the Constitutionalisation of International Economic Law: Liber Amicorum for Ernst-Ulrich Petersmann* (Martinus Nijhoff 2014) 173–89, referencing *inter alia FIAMM v Council* [2005] ECR II-5393 (CFI) (EU law claims resulting from WTO retaliation); similarly Junianto Losari and Michael Ewing-Chow, 'A Clash of Treaties: The Lawfulness of Countermeasures in International Trade Law and International Investment Law' (2015) 16 JWIT 274, 304–5; Roberts (n 50) 402.

[93] cf Losari and Ewing-Chow (n 92) 305; Bronckers and Goelen (n 92) 178–81. On the causal connection between the EU's conduct and the US' retaliatory action: *FIAMM* (n 92) [177]–[191], cf [202]–[214].

[94] *FIAMM v Council* [2008] ECR 1-06513 (ECJ) [185]-[186].

[95] nn 88, 92–94.

[96] James Crawford, *The International Law Commission's Articles on State Responsibility: Introduction, Text and Commentaries* (CUP 2002) (*ARSIWA*), art 27, see 189–90; generally Paddeu (n 76) 77–94; James Crawford, *State Responsibility: The General Part* (CUP 2013) 318; Sandra Szurek, 'The Notion of Circumstances Precluding Wrongfulness' in Crawford and others, *Responsibility* (n 70) 436–37.

[97] *ARSIWA*, 190; also Paddeu (n 76) 89–90.

[98] Paddeu (n 76) 94, generally section 2.5.

[99] ibid 93.

through hypothetical examples, if there is no wrongful conduct, then it is difficult to account for a duty to compensate *anyone* for any damage thereby caused, including unrelated third parties, but if the conduct remains wrongful, then it is at least possible for international law to limit the scope of the excuse such that third parties are protected.[100]

Although article 27 was apparently intended to cover third-party effects of countermeasures and self-defence,[101] if the latter is, as argued in this book, more akin to necessity, generally recognised as an *excuse* under international law,[102] then the argument for its application vis-à-vis third party effects may be stronger than in respect of countermeasures, generally considered a justification.[103] And indeed, it is in cases of necessity that the principle has been recognised in practice,[104] including, importantly, concerning the impact of necessity on *individual* claims under investment law.[105] In any event, as Paddeu notes, the existence of an actual rule requiring payment of compensation in the circumstances to which article 27 applies is uncertain,[106] and any such a claim might therefore remain speculative.[107] The principle behind article 27 may, however, also serve as a means of balancing the interests of a respondent State and those affected by the invocation of a circumstance precluding wrongfulness.[108] And adopting the approach to countermeasures and self-defence advocated in this book would ensure the possibility of recouping for damage is appropriately limited: if the policy behind the rule is to limit impacts on 'innocent' 'third' entities,[109] it is questionable whether it would cover circumstances of complicity or involvement by those entities in the relevant conduct leading to an invocation of countermeasures or self-defence.[110] It would, however, provide a reasonable basis for protecting the interests of individuals or States which are truly 'innocent'.

[100] Vaughan Lowe, 'Precluding Wrongfulness or Responsibility: A Plea for Excuses' (1999) 10 EJIL 405, 410–11.

[101] Paddeu (n 76) 79, 92–93; also Crawford, *GP* (n 7) 319–20, discussing ILC, 'Summary Records of the Meetings of the Fifty-First Session' (1999) 1 ILCYB 1, 174.

[102] See Paddeu (n 76) Ch 8, particularly 414.

[103] ibid Ch 6.4, and see 87–92, 223.

[104] *ARSIWA*, 190; Paddeu (n 76) 87–88, cf 422–24.

[105] Eg, *CMS Gas v Argentina (Award)* ICSID Case No ARB/01/8 (12 May 2005) [383], [388], [390]–[394]; also *LG&E v Argentina (Liability)* ICSID Case No ARB/02/1 (3 October 2006) [260]; *Sempra Energy v Argentina (Award)* ICSID Case No ARB/02/16 (28 September 2007) [394], cases cited UNLS, *Materials on the Responsibility of States for Internationally Wrongful Acts* (UN 2012) 190–93; also Paddeu (n 76) 78; Ch 6, n 499.

[106] Paddeu (n 76) 78–79, 85–88, 93–94, 422–25. Similarly DW Bowett, *Self-Defence in International Law* (MUP 1958) 174; Martins Paparinskis, 'Investment Treaty Arbitration and the (New) Law of State Responsibility' (2013) 24 EJIL 617, 633–34.

[107] Paddeu (n 76) 93–4; also *ARSIWA*, 190 (agreement).

[108] cf n 97.

[109] n 97.

[110] nn 80, 84. Cf Peters (n 44) 331.

III. The way forward

Overlapping individual and interstate claims are only likely to increase as time goes on. This book has provided clarity regarding the relationship between such claims, outlining when individual or interstate claims are liable to be precluded, under the law of State responsibility, through the actions of the other entity possessing an overlapping claim. Nonetheless, there remain uncertainties regarding how some of the rules and principles considered herein will operate in practice, including how far international courts and tribunals will accept actions by States intended to block individual claims.

In the interests of legal certainty, the ideal situation would be for the relationship between individual and interstate claims, including vis-à-vis the use of circumstances precluding wrongfulness, to be made clear at the time an individual treaty-based claims mechanism is established.[111] There are both historic examples[112] and current treaties, including the ICSID and CARICOM treaties, that address how overlapping claims are to be handled.[113] By building limitations into the claims mechanism in advance, individuals are made aware of potential future restraints and not taken by surprise when States attempt to resolve disputes without their involvement.[114] Litigation regarding States' treaty powers exercised after the event, as has occurred in practice and may be looming vis-à-vis attempts to dismantle the intra-EU BIT system, would thereby be minimised.[115]

Human rights law will, in any event, continue to provide protections to individual claimants from the overzealous actions of States, coverage which should be broadened to the extent possible, domestically and internationally.[116] In the meantime, however, the chapters in this book will assist States, individuals, and international tribunals in understanding the relationship between overlapping individual and interstate claims under international law, and place all parties concerned in a more certain position going forward.

[111] cf Martins Paparinskis, 'Investment Arbitration and the Law of Countermeasures' (2008) 79 BYBIL 264, 351; Roberts (n 50) 357–58, 388; Shany (n 2) Ch 7; Ch 5, nn 357–65.

[112] See OECD, 'Draft Convention on the Protection of Foreign Property' (1967) art 7, discussed Roberts (n 30) 43–44; Paparinskis (n 110) 282; Louis Sohn and R Baxter (eds), *Convention on the International Responsibility of States for Injuries to Aliens* (HLS 1961) art 23(1), 201; Prize Court Convention, discussed Ch 5, n 359.

[113] See Ch 3(I)(A).

[114] cf Ch 5, nn 364–65, 379–80.

[115] cf Ch 5(III)(C)(vi), nn 418, 429–38.

[116] cf John Dugard, 'First report on diplomatic protection' (2000) 2(1) ILCYB 205 [22]–[32].

IV. The way forward

Bibliography

Books, chapters and entries

Abi-Saab G, 'The Concept of Sanction in International Law' in Vera Gowlland-Debbas (ed), *United Nations Sanctions and International Law* (Kluwer 2001)

Alexandrov S, *Self-Defense Against the Use of Force in International Law* (Kluwer 1996)

ALI, *Restatement of the Law: The Foreign Relations Law of the United States* (2nd edn, ALI Publishers 1965)

ALI, *Restatement of the Law: The Foreign Relations Law of the United States*, vol II (3rd edn, ALI Publishers 1987)

Alland D, 'The Definition of Countermeasures' in James Crawford and others (eds), *The Law of International Responsibility* (OUP 2010)

Amerasinghe C, *Local Remedies in International Law* (2nd edn, CUP 2004)

Amerasinghe C, *Diplomatic Protection* (OUP 2008)

Angelet N, 'Fair and Equitable Treatment' in Rüdiger Wolfrum (ed), *MPEPIL (Online)* (OUP 2011)

Antkowiak T, 'The Americas' in Daniel Moeckli and others (eds), *International Human Rights Law* (3rd edn, OUP 2018)

Barboza J, 'Legal Injury: The Tip of the Iceberg in the Law of State Responsibility?' in Maurizio Ragazzi (ed), *International Responsibility Today: Essays in Memory of Oscar Schachter* (Martinus Nijhoff 2005)

Barker J, 'Compensation' in James Crawford and others (eds), *The Law of International Responsibility* (OUP 2010)

Barnes R, 'United States Sanctions: Delisting Applications, Judicial Review and Secret Evidence' in Paul Eden and Matthew Happold (eds), *Economic Sanctions and International Law* (Hart 2016)

Barnett P, *Res Judicata, Estoppel, and Foreign Judgments* (OUP 2001)

Baudenbacher C and Clifton M-J, 'Courts of Regional Economic and Political Integration Agreements' in Cesare Romano, Karen Alter, and Yuval Shany (eds), *The Oxford Handbook of International Adjudication* (OUP 2014)

Ben Mansour A, 'Consent' in James Crawford and others (eds), *The Law of International Responsibility* (OUP 2010)

Benvenisti E, 'Individual Remedies for Victims of Armed Conflicts in the Context of Mass Claims Settlements' in Holger Hestermeyer and others (eds), *Coexistence, Cooperation and Solidarity: Liber Amicorum Rüdiger Wolfrum* (Martinus Nijohoff 2012)

Berman F, 'The Relevance of the Law on Diplomatic Protection in Investment Arbitration' in Federico Ortino and others (eds), *Investment Treaty Law, Current Issues II* (BIICL 2007)

Bollecker-Stern B, *Le Préjudice Dans La Théorie de La Responsibilité Internationale* (Pedone 1973)

Borchard E, *The Diplomatic Protection of Citizens Abroad: Or, the Law of International Claims* (Banks 1915)

Borelli S and Olleson S, 'Obligations Relating to Human Rights and Humanitarian Law' in James Crawford and others (eds), *The Law of International Responsibility* (OUP 2010)

Bothe M, 'The Law of Neutrality' in Dieter Fleck (ed), *The Handbook of International Humanitarian Law* (3rd edn, OUP 2013)

Bottini G, 'Indirect Shareholder Claims' in Meg Kinnear and others (eds), *Building International Investment Law: The First 50 Years of ICSID* (Kluwer 2016)

Bowett DW, *Self-Defence in International Law* (MUP 1958)

Brierly JL, *The Law of Nations* (5th edn, OUP 1955)

Bronckers M and Goelen S, 'Financial Liability of the EU for Violations of WTO Law—A Legislative Proposal Benefiting Innocent Bystanders' in Marise Cremona and others (eds), *Reflections on the Constitutionalisation of International Economic Law: Liber Amicorum for Ernst-Ulrich Petersmann* (Martinus Nijhoff 2014)

Brower C and Henin P, 'Res Judicata' in Meg Kinnear and others (eds), *Building International Investment Law: The First 50 Years of ICSID* (Kluwer 2016)

Brown C, *A Common Law of International Adjudication* (OUP 2007)

Brown LN and Bell JS, *French Administrative Law* (5th edn, Clarendon 1998)

Brownlie I, *International Law and the Use of Force by States* (OUP 1963)

Brownlie I, *System of the Law of Nations: State Responsibility, Part I* (Clarendon 1983)

Brownlie I, *Principles of Public International Law* (4th edn, OUP 1990)

Brownlie I, *Principles of Public International Law* (7th edn, OUP 2008)

Brunnée J, 'Consent' in Rüdiger Wolfrum (ed), *MPEPIL (Online)* (OUP 2010)

Burgorgue-Larsen, L and Úbeda de Torres, A, *The Inter-American Court of Human Rights: Case Law and Commentary* (Rosalind Greenstein tr, OUP 2011)

Calamita NJ, 'International Human Rights and the Interpretation of International Investment Treaties: Constitutional Considerations' in Freya Baetens (ed), *Investment Law within International Law: Integrationist Perspectives* (CUP 2013)

Campbell K, 'Legal Rights' in Edward Zalta (ed), *The Stanford Encyclopedia of Philosophy* (2017) <https://plato.stanford.edu/archives/win2016/entries/legal-rights/>

Caron D, 'The Place of the Environment in International Tribunals' in Jay Austin and Carl Bruch (eds), *The Environmental Consequences of War: Legal, Economic, and Scientific Perspectives* (CUP 2000)

Caron D, 'International Claims and Compensation Bodies' in Cesare Romano, Karen Alter, and Yuval Shany (eds), *The Oxford Handbook of International Adjudication* (OUP 2014)

Cashman, P *Class Action Law and Practice* (Federation Press 2007)

Chappez J, *La Règle de l'épuisement Des Voies Des Recours Interns* (Pedone 1972)

Cheng B, *General Principles of Law as Applied by International Courts and Tribunals* (Stevens & Sons 1953)

Chinkin C, *Third Parties in International Law* (OUP 1993)

Chinkin C, 'Monism and Dualism: The Impact of Private Authority on the Dichotomy Between National and International Law' in Janne Nijman and André Nollkaemper (eds), *New Perspectives on the Divide Between National and International Law* (OUP 2007)

Clapham A (ed), *Brierly's Law of Nations: An Introduction to the Role of International Law in International Relations* (7th edn, OUP 2012)

Cohen M, 'The Politics of Reparations at the International Criminal Court' in Holly Cullen, Philipp Kastner, and Sean Richmond (eds), *The Politics of International Criminal Law* (Brill Nijhoff 2020)

Condorelli L and Kress C, 'The Rules of Attribution: General Considerations' in James Crawford and others (eds), *The Law of International Responsibility* (OUP 2010)

Connors J, 'United Nations' in Daniel Moeckli and others (eds), *International Human Rights Law* (3rd edn, OUP 2018)

Corten O, *The Law against War: The Prohibition on the Use of Force in Contemporary International Law* (Christopher Sutcliffe tr, Hart 2010)

Corten O, 'The Obligation of Cessation' in James Crawford and others (eds), *The Law of International Responsibility* (OUP 2010)

Corten O, 'Necessity' in Marc Weller (ed), *The Oxford Handbook of the Use of Force in International Law* (OUP 2015)

Craig P, *Administrative Law* (8th edn, Sweet & Maxwell 2016)

Crawford J, 'The Relationship between Sanctions and Countermeasures' in Vera Gowlland-Debbas (ed), *United Nations Sanctions and International Law* (Kluwer 2001)

Crawford J, *International Law as an Open System* (Cameron May 2002)

Crawford J, *The International Law Commission's Articles on State Responsibility: Introduction, Text and Commentaries* (CUP 2002)

Crawford J, 'Overview of Part Three of the Articles on State Responsibility' in James Crawford and others (eds), *The Law of International Responsibility* (OUP 2010)

Crawford J, *Brownlie's Principles of Public International Law* (8th edn, OUP 2012)

Crawford J, *State Responsibility: The General Part* (CUP 2013)

Crawford J, 'The International Law Commission's Articles on Diplomatic Protection Revisited' in Tiyanjana Maluwa, Max du Plessis, and Dire Tladi (eds), *The Pursuit of a Brave New World in International Law: Essays in Honour of John Dugard* (Brill Nijhoff 2017)

Das H and van Houtte H, *Post-War Restoration of Property Rights under International Law*, vol 2 (CUP 2008)

Dawidowicz M, *Third-Party Countermeasures in International Law* (CUP 2017)

de Aréchaga EJ, 'International Responsibility' in Max Sørensen (ed), *Manual of Public International Law* (Macmillan 1968)

de Preux J, 'Article 91 - Responsibility' in Yves Sandoz, Christophe Swinarski, and Bruno Zimmerman (eds), *Commentary on the Additional Protocols* (ICRC, Martinus Nijhoff 1987)

Delbrück J, '"Laws in the Public Interest" - Some Observations on the Foundations and Identification of *Erga Omnes* Norms in International Law' in Volkmar Götz, Peter Selmer, and Rüdiger Wolfrum (eds), *Liber amicorum Günther Jaenicke—Zum 85. Geburtstag* (Springer 1998)

Dimitrakopoulos I, *Individual Rights and Liberties Under the U.S. Constitution: The Case Law of the U.S. Supreme Court* (Martinus Nijhoff 2007)

Dinstein Y, *War, Aggression and Self-Defence* (6th edn, CUP 2017)

Dolzer R and Schreuer C, *Principles of International Investment Law* (2nd edn, OUP 2012)

Donner R, *The Regulation of Nationality in International Law* (2nd edn, Transnational 1994)

Dopagne F, 'Sanctions and Countermeasures by International Organizations: Diverging Lessons for the Idea of Autonomy' in Richard Collins and Nigel White (eds), *International Organizations and the Idea of Autonomy* (Routledge 2011)

Dörr O and Randelzhofer A, 'Article 2(4)' in Bruno Simma and others (eds), *The Charter of the United Nations: A Commentary* (3rd edn, OUP 2012)

Douglas Z, *The International Law of Investment Claims* (CUP 2009)

Dugard J, 'Diplomatic Protection' in Rüdiger Wolfrum (ed), *MPEPIL (Online)* (OUP 2009)

Dugard J, 'Diplomatic Protection' in James Crawford and others (eds), *The Law of International Responsibility* (OUP 2010)

Dupont P-E, 'The Arbitration of Disputes Related to Foreign Investments Affected by Unilateral Sanctions' in Ali Marossi and Marisa Bassett (eds), *Economic Sanctions under International Law: Unilateralism, Multilateralism, Legitimacy and Consequences* (Asser 2015)

Dupont P-E, 'Unilateral European Sanctions as Countermeasures: The Case of the EU Measures Against Iran' in Matthew Happold and Paul Eden (eds), *Economic Sanctions and International Law* (Hart 2016)

Ebobrah S, 'International Human Rights Courts' in Cesare Romano, Karen Alter, and Yuval Shany (eds), *The Oxford Handbook on International Adjudication* (OUP 2014)

Elagab O, *The Legality of Non-Forcible Counter-Measures in International Law* (Clarendon 1988)

Elliott M and Varuhas JN, *Administrative Law: Text and Materials* (5th edn, OUP 2017)

Endicott T, *Administrative Law* (4th edn, OUP 2018)

Escarcena SL, *Indirect Expropriation in International Law* (Edward Elgar 2014)

Evans C, *The Right to Reparation in International Law for Victims of Armed Conflict* (CUP 2012)

Feichtner I, 'Waiver' in Rüdiger Wolfrum (ed), *MPEPIL (Online)* (OUP 2012)

Fitzmaurice G, *The Law and Procedure of the International Court of Justice* (Grotius 1986)

Franck T, *Recourse to Force* (CUP 2002)

Gaja G, 'Is a State Specially Affected When Its Nationals' Human Rights Are Infringed?' in Lal Chand Vohrah and others (eds), *Man's Inhumanity to Man: Essays on International Law in Honour of Antonio Cassese* (Kluwer 2003)

Gaja G, 'States Having an Interest in Compliance with the Obligation Breached' in James Crawford and others (eds), *The Law of International Responsibility* (OUP 2010)

Gaja G, 'The Concept of an Injured State' in James Crawford and others (eds), *The Law of International Responsibility* (OUP 2010)

Garner B, *Black's Law Dictionary* (10th edn, Thomson Reuters 2014)

Gattini A, 'Compensation to Victims' in Antonio Cassese (ed), *The Oxford Companion to International Criminal Justice* (OUP 2009)

Gherari H, 'African Mechanisms' in James Crawford and others (eds), *The Law of International Responsibility* (OUP 2010)

Gomula J, 'Responsibility and the World Trade Organization' in James Crawford and others (eds), *The Law of International Responsibility* (OUP 2010)

Gourgourinis A, 'Reviewing the Administration of Domestic Regulation in WTO and Investment Law: The International Minimum Standard as "One Standard to Rule Them All"?' in Freya Baetens (ed), *Investment Law Within International Law: Integrationist Perspectives* (CUP 2013)

Gowlland-Debbas V, 'Introduction' in Vera Gowlland-Debbas (ed), *United Nations Sanctions and International Law* (Kluwer 2001)

Gowlland-Debbas V, 'Responsibility and the United Nations Charter' in James Crawford and others (eds), *The Law of International Responsibility* (OUP 2010)

Gray C, 'Restitution' in James Crawford and others (eds), *The Law of International Responsibility* (OUP 2010)

Gray C, 'Remedies' in Cesare Romano, Karen Alter, and Yuval Shany (eds), *The Oxford Handbook of International Adjudication* (OUP 2014)

Gray C, *International Law and the Use of Force* (4th edn, OUP 2018)

Greenwood C, 'Historical Development and Legal Basis' in Dieter Fleck (ed), *The Handbook of International Humanitarian Law* (2nd edn, OUP 2008)

Greenwood C, 'Self-Defence' in Rüdiger Wolfrum (ed), *MPEPIL (Online)* (OUP 2011)

Greer S, 'Europe' in Daniel Moeckli and others (eds), *International Human Rights Law* (3rd edn, OUP 2018)

Handley K, *Spencer Bower and Handley: Res Judicata* (4th edn, LexisNexis 2009)

Happold M, 'Targeted Sanctions and Human Rights' in Matthew Happold and Paul Eden (eds), *Economic Sanctions and International Law* (Hart 2016)

Heathcote S, 'Necessity' in James Crawford and others (eds), *The Law of International Responsibility* (OUP 2010)

Heinze E and Fitzmaurice M, *Landmark Cases in Public International Law* (Kluwer 1998)

Heller K and Dubber M (eds), *The Handbook of Comparative Criminal Law* (Stan UP 2011)

Henkin L, *Foreign Affairs and the United States Constitution* (2nd edn, Clarendon 1996)

Hernández G, 'The Interaction between Investment Law and the Law of Armed Conflict in the Interpretation of Full Protection and Security Clauses' in Freya Baetens (ed), *Investment Law Within International Law: Integrationist Perspectives* (CUP 2013)

Heyns C and Killander M, 'Africa' in Daniel Moeckli and others (eds), *International Human Rights Law* (3rd edn, OUP 2018)

Higgins R, *Problems and Processes: International Law and How We Use It* (Clarendon 1994)

Higgins R, *Themes and Theories* (OUP 2009)

Hohfeld WN, *Fundamental Legal Conceptions as Applied in Judicial Reasoning and Other Legal Essays* (Yale UP 1923)

Holtzmann H, 'Mass Claims' in Rüdiger Wolfrum (ed), *MPEPIL (Online)* (OUP 2008)

Holtzmann H and Kristjánsdóttir E, *International Mass Claims Processes: Legal and Practical Perspectives* (OUP 2007)

ICRC, 'Introduction', *Customary IHL Database* <https://ihl-databases.icrc.org/customary-ihl/eng/docs/v1_cha_chapterin_in>

ICRC, 'Practice Relating to Rule 150: Reparation', *Customary IHL Database* <https://ihl-databases.icrc.org/customary-ihl/eng/docs/v2_rul_rule150>

ICRC, 'Rule 51: Public and Private Property in Occupied Territory', *Customary IHL Database* <https://ihl-databases.icrc.org/customary-ihl/eng/docs/v1_rul_rule51>

ICSID, *Convention on the Settlement of Investment Disputes between States and Nationals of Other States: Documents Concerning the Origin and the Formulation of the Convention*, vol II (1968)

International Institute of Humanitarian Law (IIHL), *San Remo Manual on International Law Applicable to Armed Conflicts at Sea* (Louise Doswald-Beck ed, CUP 1995)

Jackson M, *Complicity in International Law* (OUP 2015)

Jakab A, 'Trianon Peace Treaty (1920)' in Rüdiger Wolfrum (ed), *MPEPIL (Online)* (OUP 2015)

Jennings R and Watts A, *Oppenheim's International Law*, vol 1 (9th edn, Longman 1992)

Jessup P, *A Modern Law of Nations* (Archon 1968)

Jinks D, 'International Human Rights Law in Time of Armed Conflict' in Andrew Clapham and Paola Gaeta (eds), *The Oxford Handbook of International Law in Armed Conflict* (OUP 2014)

Juillard P, 'Calvo Doctrine/Calvo Clause' in Rüdiger Wolfrum (ed), *MPEPIL (Online)* (OUP 2007)

Kalshoven F, 'Expert Opinion' in Hisakazu Fujita, Isomi Suzuki, and Kantaro Nagano (eds), *War and the Rights of Individuals: Renaissance of Individual Compensation* (Nippon Hyoron-sha 1999)

Kammerhofer J, 'The Resilience of the Restrictive Rules on Self-Defence' in Marc Weller (ed), *The Oxford Handbook of the Use of Force in International Law* (OUP 2015)

Kato N, 'The Role of Diplomatic Protection in the Implementation Process of Public Interests' in Teruo Komori and Karel Wellens (eds), *Public Interest Rules of International Law: Towards Effective Implementation* (Ashgate 2009)

Kaufmann-Kohler G, 'Non-Disputing State Submissions in Investment Arbitration: Resurgence of Diplomatic Protection?' in Laurence Boisson de Chazournes, Marcelo Kohen, and Jorge Viñuales (eds), *Diplomatic and Judicial Means of Dispute Settlement* (Martinus Nijhoff 2013)

Kaye P, *European Case Law on the Judgements Convention* (Wiley & Sons 1998)

Kerbrat Y, 'Interaction Between the Forms of Reparation' in James Crawford and others (eds), *The Law of International Responsibility* (OUP 2010)

Kjos HE, *Applicable Law in Investor-State Arbitration: The Interplay Between National and International Law* (OUP 2013)

Klein N, *Maritime Security and the Law of the Sea* (OUP 2012)

Kramer M, Simmonds NE, and Steiner H, *A Debate over Rights: Philosophical Enquiries* (OUP 2000)

Kretzmer D, 'US Extra-Territorial Actions Against Individuals: Bin Laden, Al Awlaki, and Abu Khattalah—2011 and 2014' in Tom Ruys, Olivier Corten, and Alexandra Hofer (eds), *The Use of Force in International Law: A Case-Based Approach* (OUP 2018)

Lange D, *The Doctrine of Res Judicata in Canada* (Butterworths 2000)

Lauterpacht H, *Oppenheim's International Law*, vol 1 (8th edn, Longmans 1955)

Lauterpacht H, *International Law: Being the Collected Papers of Hersch Lauterpacht* (Elihu Lauterpacht ed, CUP 1970)

Layton A and others, *European Civil Practice*, vol 1 (2nd edn, Sweet & Maxwell 2004)

Leathley C, *International Dispute Resolution in Latin America: An Institutional Overview* (Kluwer 2007)

Lectures on International Law and the United Nations (Univ Mich 1957)

Levine J, 'The Interaction of International Investment Arbitration and the Rights of Indigenous Peoples' in Freya Baetens (ed), *Investment Law within International Law: Integrationist Perspectives* (CUP 2013)

Lesaffre H, 'Countermeasures' in James Crawford and others (eds), *The Law of International Responsibility* (OUP 2010)

Lillich R and Weston B, *International Claims: Their Settlement By Lump Sum Agreements*, vol I (Virginia UP 1975)

Lillich R and Weston B, *International Claims: Their Settlement By Lump Sum Agreements*, vol II (Virginia UP 1975)

Lowenfeld A, 'Unilateral versus Collective Sanctions: An American's Perception' in Vera Gowlland-Debbas (ed), *United Nations Sanctions and International Law* (Kluwer 2001)

Lubell N, *Extraterritorial Use of Force Against Non-State Actors* (OUP 2010)

Mackenzie R and others, *Manual on International Courts and Tribunals* (OUP 2010)

Mazzeschi RP, 'Impact on the Law of Diplomatic Protection' in Menno Kamminga and Martin Scheinin (eds), *The Impact of Human Rights Law on General International Law* (OUP 2009)

McCorquodale R, 'The Individual and the International Legal System' in Malcolm Evans (ed), *International Law* (4th edn, OUP 2014)

McDermott P, *Res Judicata and Double Jeopardy* (Butterworths 1999)

McGregor H and others, *McGregor on Damages* (19th edn, Sweet & Maxwell 2014)

McLachlan C, Shore L, and Weiniger M, *International Investment Arbitration: Substantive Principles* (2nd edn, OUP 2017)

McNair A, *The Law of Treaties: British Practice and Opinions* (Clarendon 1938)

McNair A, *Legal Effects of War* (3rd edn, CUP 1948)

McNair A, *International Law Opinions*, vol II (OUP 1956)

McNair A, *The Law of Treaties* (Clarendon 1961)

McNair A, *Legal Effects of War* (4th edn, CUP 1966)

Mégret F, 'Nature of Obligations' in Daniel Moeckli and others (eds), *International Human Rights Law* (3rd edn, OUP 2018)

Merrills J, *The Development of International Law by the European Court of Human Rights* (2nd edn, Manchester UP 1993)

Moir L, 'Action Against Host States of Terrorist Groups' in Marc Weller (ed), *The Oxford Handbook of the Use of Force in International Law* (OUP 2015)
Momtaz, D 'Attribution of Conduct to the State: State Organs and Entities Empowered to Exercise Elements of Governmental Authority' in James Crawford and others (eds), *The Law of International Responsibility* (OUP 2010)
Morss J, *International Law as the Law of Collectives* (Ashgate 2013)
Mugerwa N, 'Subjects of International Law' in Max Sørensen (ed), *Manual of Public International Law* (Macmillan 1968)
Mulheron R, *The Class Action in Common Law Legal Systems: A Comparative Perspective* (Hart 2004)
Murphy S, 'International Judicial Bodies for Resolving Disputes between States' in Cesare Romano, Karen Alter, and Yuval Shany (eds), *The Oxford Handbook of International Adjudication* (OUP 2014)
Murphy S, Kidane W, and Snider T, *Litigating War: Arbitration of Civil Injury by the Eritrea-Ethiopia Claims Commission* (OUP 2013)
Nagareda R, *The Law of Class Actions and Other Aggregate Litigation* (Foundation 2009)
Nollkaemper A, *National Courts and the International Rule of Law* (OUP 2011)
Nollkaemper A, 'Conversations among Courts: Domestic and International Adjudicators' in Cesare Romano, Karen Alter, and Yuval Shany (eds), *The Oxford Handbook of International Adjudication* (OUP 2014)
Nowak JE and Rotunda RD, *Constitutional Law* (6th edn, West 2000)
OHCHR, *Frequently Asked Questions on a Human Rights-Based Approach to Development Cooperation* (UN 2006)
O'Keefe R, 'Proportionality' in James Crawford and others (eds), *The Law of International Responsibility* (OUP 2010)
Oppenheim L, *International Law: A Treatise*, vol II (Longmans 1905)
Ouguergouz F, *The African Charter on Human and Peoples' Rights* (Martinus Nijhoff 2003)
Paddeu F, *Justification and Excuse in International Law* (CUP 2018)
Palmeter D and Mavroidis P, *Dispute Settlement in the World Trade Organization* (CUP 2004)
Pantaleo L, 'Sanctions Cases in the European Courts' in Matthew Happold and Paul Eden (eds), *Economic Sanctions and International Law* (Hart 2016)
Paparinskis M, *The International Minimum Standard and Fair and Equitable Treatment* (OUP 2013)
Paparinskis M, 'Analogies and Other Regimes of International Law' in Zachary Douglas, Joost Pauwelyn, and Jorge Viñuales (eds), *The Foundations of International Investment Law* (OUP 2014)
Paparinskis M and Howley J, 'Article 5: Submission by a Non-Disputing Party to the Treaty' in Dimitrij Euler, Markus Gehring, and Maxi Scherer (eds), *Transparency in International Investment Arbitration* (CUP 2015)
Parlett K, *The Individual in the International Legal System: Continuity and Change in International Law* (CUP 2011)
Parlett K, 'The Application of the Rules on Countermeasures in Investment Claims' in Christine Chinkin and Freya Baetens (eds), *Sovereignty, Statehood and State Responsibility* (CUP 2015)
Parry C, 'Of Treaties' in Peter Feuerstein and Clive Parry (eds), *Multum non Multa: Festschrift für Kurt Lipstein* (CF Müller 1980)
Paulsson J, *Denial of Justice in International Law* (CUP 2005)
Pellet A, 'The Definition of Responsibility in International Law' in James Crawford and others (eds), *The Law of International Responsibility* (OUP 2010)

Pellet A, 'The ILC's Articles on State Responsibility for Internationally Wrongful Acts and Related Texts' in James Crawford and others (eds), *The Law of International Responsibility* (OUP 2010)

Pellet A and Miron A, 'Sanctions' in Rüdiger Wolfrum (ed), *MPEPIL (Online)* (OUP 2013)

Peters A, *Beyond Human Rights: The Legal Status of the Individual in International Law* (Jonathan Huston tr, CUP 2016)

Petrović D, 'The UN Compensation Commission' in James Crawford and others (eds), *The Law of International Responsibility* (OUP 2010)

Phillipson C, *Termination of War and Treaties of Peace* (Unwin 1916)

Portmann R, *Legal Personality in International Law* (CUP 2010)

Potestà M, 'State-to-State Dispute Settlement Pursuant to Bilateral Investment Treaties: Is There Potential?' in Nerina Boschiero and others (eds), *International Courts and the Development of International Law: Essays in Honour of Tullio Treves* (Asser 2013)

Potestà M, 'Towards a Greater Role for State-to-State Arbitration in the Architecture of Investment Treaties?' in Shaheeza Lalani and Rodrigo Polanco Lazo (eds), *The Role of the State in Investor-State Arbitration* (Brill Nijhoff 2015)

Ragazzi M, *The Concept of International Obligations* Erga Omnes (Clarendon 1997)

Ralston J, *International Arbitral Law and Procedure* (Ginn 1910)

Recanati M, 'Diplomatic Intervention and State-to-State Arbitration as Alternative Means for the Protection of Foreign Investments and Host States' General Interests: The Italian Experience' in Giorgio Sacerdoti and others (eds), *General Interests of Host States in International Investment Law* (CUP 2014)

Reinder C and Schreuer C, 'Human Rights and International Investment Arbitration' in Pierre-Marie Dupuy, Ernst-Ulrich Petersmann, and Francesco Francioni (eds), *Human Rights in International Investment Law and Arbitration* (OUP 2009)

Ripinsky S and Williams K, *Damages in International Investment Law* (BIICL 2008)

Rivier R, 'Inter-American Mechanisms' in James Crawford and others (eds), *The Law of International Responsibility* (OUP 2010)

Romano C, Alter K, and Shany Y (eds) *The Oxford Handbook on International Adjudication* (OUP 2014)

Roucounas E, 'Non-State Actors: Areas of International Responsibility in Need of Further Exploration' in Maurizio Ragazzi (ed), *International Responsibility Today: Essays in Memory of Oscar Schachter* (Martinus Nijhoff 2005)

Ruedin X-B, *Exécution Des Arrêts de La Cour Européenne Des Droits de l'homme* (Helbing Lichtenhahn 2009)

Ruffert M, 'Capital, Free Flow Of' in Rüdiger Wolfrum (ed), *MPEPIL (Online)* (OUP 2014)

Ruys T, *'Armed Attack' and Article 51 of the UN Charter* (CUP 2010)

Ruzza A, 'Expropriation and Nationalization' in Rüdiger Wolfrum (ed), *MPEPIL (Online)* (OUP 2013)

Sacerdoti G, 'Diplomatic Conciliation of Investment Disputes: The Italian-Swiss Controversy on Secondary Residences in Engadine (1990–1992) and Its Lessons' in Marise Cremona and others (eds), *Reflections on the Constitutionalisation of International Economic Law: Liber Amicorum for Ernst-Ulrich Petersmann* (Martinus Nijhoff 2014)

Sacerdoti G, 'The Role of Lawyers in the WTO Dispute Settlement System' in Rufus Yerxa and Bruce Wilson (eds), *Key Issues in WTO Dispute Settlement: The first ten years* (CUP 2005)

Salles LE, *Forum Shopping in International Adjudication: The Role of Preliminary Objections* (CUP 2014)

Schabas W, *The European Convention on Human Rights: A Commentary* (OUP 2015)

Schreuer C, *Decisions of International Institutions Before Domestic Courts* (Oceana 1981)
Schreuer C, *The ICSID Convention: A Commentary* (2nd edn, CUP 2009)
Schreuer C, 'Interaction of International Tribunals and Domestic Courts in Investment Law' in Arthur W Rovine (ed), *Contemporary Issues in International Arbitration and Mediation* (Martinus Nijhoff 2011)
Schreuer C, 'The Protection of Investments in Armed Conflict' in Freya Baetens (ed), *Investment Law within International Law: Integrationist Perspectives* (CUP 2013)
Schreuer C, 'Investment Arbitration' in Cesare Romano, Karen Alter, and Yvual Shany (eds), *The Oxford Handbook of International Adjudication* (OUP 2014)
Seger P, 'The Law of Neutrality' in Andrew Clapham and Paola Gaeta (eds), *The Oxford Handbook of International Law in Armed Conflict* (OUP 2014)
Shah O (ed), *Class Actions: A Global Guide from Practical Law* (Thomson Reuters 2015)
Shany Y, *The Competing Jurisdictions of International Courts and Tribunals* (OUP 2003)
Shany Y, *Regulating Jurisdictional Relations Between National and International Courts* (OUP 2007)
Sicilianos L-A, 'Countermeasures in Response to Grave Violations of Obligations Owed to the International Community' in James Crawford and others (eds), *The Law of International Responsibility* (OUP 2010)
Simma B and Pulkowski D, '*Leges Speciales* and Self-Contained Regimes' in James Crawford and others (eds), *The Law of International Responsibility* (OUP 2010)
Simmonds N, *Central Issues in Jurisprudence* (3rd edn, Sweet & Maxwell 2008)
Singh MP, *German Administrative Law in Comparative Perspective* (Springer 2001)
Sohn L and Baxter R (eds), *Convention on the International Responsibility of States for Injuries to Aliens* (HLS 1961)
Sornarajah M, *Foreign Investment* (4th edn, CUP 2017)
Stephens W, *Revisions of the Treaty of Versailles* (Columbia UP 1939)
Stern B, 'A Plea for "Reconstruction" of International Responsibility Based on the Notion of Legal Injury' in Maurizio Ragazzi (ed), *International Responsibility Today: Essays in Memory of Oscar Schachter* (Martinus Nijhoff 2005)
Stern B, 'The Elements of an Internationally Wrongful Act' in James Crawford and others (eds), *The Law of International Responsibility* (OUP 2010)
Strong S, *Class, Mass, and Collective Arbitration in National and International Law* (OUP 2013)
Szurek S, 'The Notion of Circumstances Precluding Wrongfulness' in James Crawford and others (eds), *The Law of International Responsibility* (OUP 2010)
Tams C, *Enforcing Obligations* Erga Omnes *in International Law* (CUP 2005)
Tams C, 'Waiver, Acquiescence, and Extinctive Prescription' in James Crawford and others (eds), *The Law of International Responsibility* (OUP 2010)
Thirlway H, *The Law and Procedure of the International Court of Justice: Fifty Years of Jurisprudence* (OUP 2013)
Thomas J, *Public Rights, Private Relations* (OUP 2015)
Thouvenin J-M, 'Self-Defence' in James Crawford and others (eds), *The Law of International Responsibility* (OUP 2010)
Time for Action: Report of the West Indian Commission (West Indian Commission 1992)
Tomka P, 'Defences Based on Necessity under Customary International Law and on Emergency Clauses in Bilateral Investment Treaties' in Meg Kinnear and others (eds), *Building International Investment Law: The First 50 Years of ICSID* (Kluwer 2016)
Tomuschat C, 'Individuals' in James Crawford and others (eds), *The Law of International Responsibility* (OUP 2010)

Tomuschat C, 'Article 36' in Andreas Zimmerman and others (eds), *The Statute of the International Court of Justice: A Commentary* (OUP 2012)

Trapp K, 'Can Non-State Actors Mount an Armed Attack?' in Marc Weller (ed), *The Oxford Handbook of the Use of Force in International Law* (OUP 2015)

Tribe LH, *American Constitutional Law*, vol 1 (3rd edn, Foundation Press 2000)

Tzanakopoulos A, *Disobeying the Security Council: Countermeasures Against Wrongful Sanctions* (OUP 2011)

Unberath, H *Transferred Loss: Claiming Third Party Loss in Contract Law* (Hart 2003)

Uniacke S, *Permissible Killing: The Self-Defence Justification of Homicide* (CUP 1994)

United Nations Legislative Series (UNLS), *Materials on the Responsibility of States for Internationally Wrongful Acts* (2012), ST./LEG/SER.B/25

US DoS, *Conference for the Conclusion and Signature of the Treaty of Peace with Japan: Record of Proceedings* (US Govt 1951)

Vallat F, *International Law and the Practitioner* (Manchester UP 1966)

van Houtte H, Das H, and Delmartino B, 'The United Nations Compensation Commission' in Pablo de Greiff (ed), *The Handbook of Reparations* (OUP 2006)

van Houtte H, Delmartino B, and Yi I, *Post-War Restoration of Property Rights Under International Law*, vol 1 (CUP 2008)

Varuhas JN, *Damages and Human Rights* (Hart 2016)

Vattel E de, *The Law of Nations, or, Principles of the Law of Nature Applied to the Conduct and Affairs of Nations and Sovereigns* (T & JW Johnson 1867)

Verzijl JHW, *International Law in Historical Perspective*, vol VIII (AW Sijthoff 1976)

Viñuales J, 'Sovereignty in Foreign Investment Law' in Zachary Douglas, Joost Pauwelyn, and Jorge Viñuales (eds), *The Foundations of International Investment Law* (OUP 2014)

von Heinegg W, 'Maritime Warfare' in Andrew Clapham and Paola Gaeta (eds), *The Oxford Handbook of International Law in Armed Conflict* (OUP 2014)

Wälde T and Sabahi B, 'Compensation, Damages, and Valuation' in Peter Muchlinski, Federico Ortino, and Christoph Schreuer (eds), *The Oxford Handbook of International Investment Law* (OUP 2008)

Wehland H, *The Coordination of Multiple Proceedings in Investment Treaty Arbitration* (OUP 2013)

Weis P, *Nationality and Statelessness in International Law* (2nd edn, Sijthoff & Noordhoff 1979)

Weiss F, 'Trade and Investment Law: What Relations?' in Giorgio Sacerdoti and others (eds), *General Interests of Host States in International Investment Law* (CUP 2014)

Weston B, Lillich R, and Bederman D, *International Claims: Their Settlement By Lump Sum Agreements, 1975–1995* (Transnational Publishers 1999)

White N and Abass A, 'Countermeasures and Sanctions' in Malcolm Evans (ed), *International Law* (4th edn, OUP 2014)

Whiteman M, *Damages in International Law* (US Government 1937)

Wilken S and Ghaly K, *The Law of Waiver, Variation, and Estoppel* (3rd edn, OUP 2012)

Wilmshurst E (ed), *Principles of International Law on Self-Defence* (Chatham House 2005)

Wisner R, 'Derivative Actions and Indirect Claims' in Federico Ortino and others (eds), *Investment Treaty Law: Current Issues II* (BIICL 2007)

Wittich S, 'Compensation' in Rüdiger Wolfrum (ed), *MPEPIL (Online)* (OUP 2012)

Wühler N, 'Mixed Arbitral Tribunals' in Rudolf Bernhardt (ed), *Encyclopedia of Public International Law* (Elsevier 1997)

Wyler E and Papaux A, 'Satisfaction' in James Crawford and others (eds), *The Law of International Responsibility* (OUP 2010)

Zemanek K, 'Armed Attack' in Rüdiger Wolfrum (ed), *MPEPIL* (OUP 2013)
Zoller E, *Peacetime Unilateral Remedies: An Analysis of Countermeasures* (Transational 1984)
Zwaak L (revisor), 'The Procedure Before the European Court of Human Rights' in Pieter van Dijk and others (eds), *Theory and Practice of the European Convention on Human Rights* (4th edn, Intersentia 2006)
Zwart T, *The Admissibility of Human Rights Petitions* (Martinus Nijhoff 1994)

Journal articles, presentations, and papers

Alter K, Gathii J, and Helfer L, 'Backlash against International Courts in West, East and Southern Africa: Causes and Consequences' (2016) 27 EJIL 293
Berman F, 'International Treaties and British Statutes' (2005) 26 Stat L Rev 1
Bethlehem D, 'Self-Defense Against an Imminent or Actual Armed Attack by Nonstate Actors' (2012) 106 AJIL 769
Blühdorn R, 'Le Fonctionnement et La Jurisprudence Des Tribunaux Arbitraux Mixtes Créés Par Les Traités de Paris' (1932) 41 RdC 137
Bothe M, 'Terrorism and the Legality of Pre-Emptive Force' (2003) 14 EJIL 227
Bothe M, 'Security Council's Targeted Sanctions against Presumed Terrorists' (2008) 6 JICJ 541
Borchard E, 'Protection of Citizens Abroad and Change of Original Nationality' (1934) 20 YLJ 359
Bowett D, 'Reprisals Involving Recourse to Armed Force' (1972) 66 AJIL 1
Brierly JL, 'The Theory of Implied State Complicity in International Claims' (1928) 9 BYBIL 42
Caplan RL, 'Parens Patriae Antitrust Suits by Foreign Nations' (1977) 6 Denv J Intl L & Pol 705
Choi W-M, 'The Present and Future of The Investor-State Dispute Settlement Paradigm' (2007) 10 JIEL 725
Chinkin C, 'A Critique of the Public/Private Dimension' (1999) 10 EJIL 387
Christakis T, 'Challenging the "Unwilling or Unable" Test' (2017) 77 ZfaöRV 19
Cogan JK, 'The Regulatory Turn in International Law' (2011) 52 Harv ILJ 321
Contreras Garduño D, 'Defining Beneficiaries of Collective Reparations: The Experience of the IACtHR' (2012) 4 AmsLF 40
Contreras Garduño D, 'Collective Reparations: Tensions and Dilemmas Between Collective Reparations and the Individual Right to Receive Reparations' (2018) Utrecht University Human Rights Research Series, vol 84 <https://dspace.library.uu.nl/handle/1874/369720>
Corten O, 'Has Practice Led to an "Agreement Between the Parties" Regarding the Interpretation of Article 51 of the UN Charter?' (2017) 77 ZfaöRV 15
Cowell F, 'The Death of the Southern African Development Community Tribunal's Human Rights Jurisdiction' (2013) 13 HRLR 1
Cox P, 'Public Enforcement Compensation and Private Rights' (2016) 100 Minn LR 2313
Crawford J, 'Responsibility to the International Community as a Whole' (2001) 8 Ind JGLS 303
Crawford J, 'The ILC's Articles on Responsibility of States for Internationally Wrongful Acts: A Retrospect' (2002) 96 AJIL 874
Crawford J, 'The ILC's Articles on Diplomatic Protection' (2006) 31 SAYIL 19
Crawford J, 'Multilateral Rights and Obligations in International Law' (2006) 319 RdC 325

Crawford J, 'Chance, Order, Change: The Course of International Law' (2013) 365 RdC 9

Criddle E, 'Humanitarian Financial Intervention' (2013) 24 EJIL 583

Cucos D, 'The Position of the Individual in Post-Codification Diplomatic Protection' (2014) 5 CYBP & PIL 181

Curtis G, 'The Checkered Career of *Parens Patriae*: The State as Parent or Tyrant?' (1976) 25 DePaul LR 895

d'Aspremont J, 'Responsibility for Coups d'Etat in International Law' (2010) 18 Tul JICL 451

Daugirdas K and Mortenson J (eds), 'Contemporary Practice of the United States Relating to International Law' (2016) 110 AJIL 789

Dawidowicz M, 'Public Law Enforcement without Public Law Safeguards? An Analysis of State Practice on Third-Party Countermeasures and Their Relationship to the UN Security Council' (2007) 77 BYBIL 333

Deeks A, '"Unwilling or Unable": Toward a Normative Framework for Extraterritorial Self-Defense' (2012) 52 Virg JIL 483

Demirkol B, 'Does an Investment Treaty Tribunal Need Special Consent for Mass Claims?' (2013) 2 Camb JI & CL 612

Dodge W, 'National Courts and International Arbitration: Exhaustion of Remedies and Res Judicata Under Chapter Eleven of NAFTA' (2000) 23 Hast I & CLR 357

Dolzer R, 'The Settlement of War-Related Claims: Does International Law Recognize a Victim's Private Right of Action? Lessons after 1945' (2002) 20 Berk JIL 296

Douglas Z, 'The Hybrid Foundations of Investment Treaty Arbitration' (2004) 74 BYBIL 151

Dupont P-E, 'Countermeasures and Collective Security: The Case of the EU Sanctions Against Iran' (2012) 17 JC & SL 301

Ewing-Chow M, 'Thesis, Antithesis and Synthesis: Investor Protection in BITs, WTO and FTAs' (2007) 30 UNSWLJ 548

Gaja G, 'The Protection of General Interests in the International Community' (2012) 364 RdC 9

Gaillard E, 'Abuse of Process in International Arbitration' (2017) 32 ICSID Rev-FILJ 17

Gaja G, 'The Position of Individuals in International Law: An ILC Perspective' (2010) 21 EJIL 11

Garcia-Amador FV, 'State Responsibility: Some New Problems' (1958) 94 RdC 365

Gardam J, 'Role for Proportionality in the War on Terror' (2005) 74 Nord JIL 3

Gattini A, 'A Trojan Horse for Sudeten Claims? On Some Implications of the Prince of Liechtenstein v Germany' (2002) 13 EJIL 513

Gattini A, 'To What Extent Are Immunity and Non-Justiciability Major Hurdles to Individuals' Claims for War Damages?' (2003) 1 JICJ 348

Gourgourinis A, 'The Distinction Between Interpretation and Application of Norms in International Adjudication' (2011) 2 JIDS 31

Graefrath B, 'Responsibility and Damages Caused: Relationship between Responsibility and Damages' (1984) 185 RdC 9

Greenwood C, 'International Law and the Pre-Emptive Use of Force: Afghanistan, Al-Qaida, and Iraq' (2003) 4 SDILJ 7

Greenwood C, 'The Concept of War in Modern International Law' (1987) 36 ICLQ 283

Guideu T, 'Defending America's Cambodian Incursion' (1994) 11 Ariz JICL 215

Guilfoyle D, 'The Proliferation Security Initiative: Interdicting Vessels in International Waters to Prevent the Spread of Weapons of Mass Destruction' (2005) 29 MULR 733

Guilfoyle D, 'Interdicting Vessels to Enforce the Common Interest: Maritime Countermeasures and the Use of Force' (2007) 56 ICLQ 69

Hanna G, 'The Helicopter State: Misuse of Parens Patriae Unconstitutionally Precludes Individual and Class Claims' (2017) 92 Wash LR 1955

Harrison J, 'The Life and Death of BITs: Legal Issues Concerning Survival Clauses and the Termination of Investment Treaties' (2012) 13 JWIT 928

Hartmann S, 'When Two International Regimes Collide: An Analysis of the Tobacco Plain Packaging Disputes and Why Overlapping Jurisdiction of the WTO and Investment Tribunals Does Not Result in Convergence of Norms' (2017) 21 UCLAJILFA 204

Hawkes LM, '*Parens Patriae* and the Union Carbide Case: The Disaster at Bhopal Continues' (1988) 21 Corn ILJ 181

Henckels C, 'Investment Treaty Security Exceptions, Necessity and Self-Defence in the Context of Armed Conflict' (March 2018), available: <https://papers.ssrn.com/sol3/papers.cfm?abstract_id=3136191&download=yes>

Henin P and others, 'Innovating International Investment Agreements: A Proposed Green Investment Protocol for Climate Change Mitigation and Adaptation' (2019) 36 Arb Int 37

Hensler D, 'The Globalization of Class Actions: An Overview' (2009) 662 Annals AAPSS 7

Hess B, 'The Private-Public Divide in International Dispute Resolution' (2018) 388 RdC 49

Hessick FA, 'Standing, Injury in Fact and Private Rights' (2008) 93 Corn LR 275

Himes JL, 'State *Parens Patriae* Authority: The Evolution of the State Attorney General's Authority' (ILEP Symposium: Protecting the Public: The Role of Private and Public Attorneys' General, Miami, 23–24 April 2004)

Hobér K, 'Res Judicata and Lis Pendens in International Arbitration' (2014) 366 RdC 99

Hofer A, 'The "Curiouser and Curiouser" Legal Nature of Non-UN Sanctions: The Case of US Sanctions against Russia' (2018) 23 JC & SL 75

Hofman R and Riemann F, 'ILA Committee on Compensation for Victims of War: Background Report' (2004)

IDI, 'The Protection of Human Rights and the Principle of Non-Intervention in Internal Affairs of States' (1989) 63(II) IDIA 338

Juratowich B, 'The Relationship between Diplomatic Protection and Investment Treaties' (2008) 23 ICSID Rev-FILJ 10

Kanner A, 'The Public Trust Doctrine, *Parens Patriae*, and the Attorney General as the Guardian of the State's Natural Resources' (2005) 16 Duke Env L & Pol For 57

Kaufmann-Kohler G and Potestà M, 'Investor-State Dispute Settlement and National Courts: Current Framework and Reform Options' [2020] EYBIEL (Special Issue)

Keinan G, 'Humanising the Right of Self-Defence' (2017) 77 ZfaöRV 57

Kelsen H, 'Opinion Concerning the Claims of the Italian Owners of the Ship "Fausto"' (1986) 37 ÖZ 1

Kokott J, 'The Exhaustion of Local Remedies' (2004) 69 ILA Rep Conf 606

Kolo A, 'Investor Protection vs Host State Regulatory Autonomy during Economic Crisis: Treatment of Capital Transfers and Restrictions under Modern Investment Treaties' (2007) 8 JWIT 457

Kress C, 'Some Reflections on the International Legal Framework Governing Transnational Armed Conflicts' (2010) 15 JC & SL 245

Lemos M, 'Aggregate Litigation Goes Public: Representative Suits by State Attorneys General' (2012) 126 Harv LR 486

Lieblich E, 'Self-Defence Against Non-State Actors and The Myth of the Innocent State' (2 April 2019), available: <https://papers.ssrn.com/sol3/papers.cfm?abstract_id=3364163>

Losari J and Ewing-Chow M, 'A Clash of Treaties: The Lawfulness of Countermeasures in International Trade Law and International Investment Law' (2015) 16 JWIT 274

Lowe V, '*Res Judicata* and the Rule of Law in International Arbitration' (1996) 8 AfJICL 38

Lowe V, 'Precluding Wrongfulness or Responsibility: A Plea for Excuses' (1999) 10 EJIL 405

MacDonald C, 'NAFTA Cross-Border Trucking: Mexico Retaliates After Congress Stops Mexican Trucks at the Border' (2009) 42 VJTL 1631

Meron T, 'The Incidence of the Rule of Exhaustion of Local Remedies' (1959) 35 BYBIL 83
Meron T, 'The Insurer and the Insured under International Claims Law' (1974) 68 AJIL 628
Metz BE, 'Reconstitutionalizing *Parens Patriae*: How Federal *Parens Patriae* Doctrine Appropriately Permits State Damages Suits Aggregating Private Tort Claims', available: <http://www.law.columbia.edu/sites/default/files/microsites/career-services/Reconstitutionalizing%20Parens%20Patriae.pdf>
Milano E, 'Diplomatic Protection and Human Rights before the International Court of Justice: Re-Fashioning Tradition' (2004) 35 Neth YBIL 85
Moehlecke C, 'The Chilling Effect of International Investment Disputes: Limited Challenges to State Sovereignty' (2020) 64 ISQ 1
Murphy S, 'Liability and the WHO Framework Convention on Tobacco Control' (2003) 5 Int L Forum 62
Musial G, 'The Right to an Effective Remedy under the African Charter on Human and Peoples' Rights' (2006) 6 AHRLJ 441
Nathan L, 'The Disbanding of the SADC Tribunal: A Cautionary Tale' (2013) 35 HRQ 870
Note, 'State Protection of Its Economy and Environment: Parens Patriae Suits for Damages' (1970) 6 Colum JL & Soc Probs 411
O'Brien W, 'Reprisals, Deterrence and Self-Defense in Counterterror Operations' (1990) 30 Virg JIL 421
Oellers-Frahm K, 'Article 51 - What Matters Is the Armed Attack, Not the Attacker' (2017) 77 ZfaöRV 49
Orakhelashvili A, 'Overlap and Convergence: The Interaction between Jus Ad Bellum and Jus in Bello' (2007) 12 JC & SL 157
Orrego Vicuna F, 'The Changing Law of Nationality of Claims' (2000) 69 ILA Rep Conf 631
Paddeu F, 'Self-Defence as a Circumstance Precluding Wrongfulness: Understanding Article 21 of the Articles on State Responsibility' (2015) 85 BYBIL 90
Paddeu F, 'Use of Force against Non-State Actors and the Circumstance Precluding Wrongfulness of Self-Defence' (2017) 30 Leid JIL 93
Paparinskis M, 'Investment Arbitration and the Law of Countermeasures' (2008) 79 BYBIL 264
Paparinskis M, 'Investment Treaty Arbitration and the (New) Law of State Responsibility' (2013) 24 EJIL 617
Pauwelyn J, 'A Typology of Multilateral Treaty Obligations: Are WTO Obligations Bilateral or Collective in Nature?' (2003) 14 EJIL 907
Pauwelyn J, 'Adding Sweeteners to Softwood Lumber: The WTO-NAFTA "Spaghetti Bowl" Is Cooking' (2006) 9 JIEL 197
Pauwelyn J and Salles LE, 'Forum Shopping Before International Tribunals: (Real) Concerns, (Im)Possible Solutions' (2009) 42 Corn ILJ 77
Pellet A, 'The Second Death of Euripide Mavrommatis? Notes on the International Law Commission's Draft Articles on Diplomatic Protection' (2008) 7 LPICT 33
Perotti A, 'Los Particulares y Las Controversias En El Mercosur' (2008) 122 Cuestión Logística 46
Peters A and Marxsen C, 'Editors' Introduction: Self-Defence in Times of Transition' (2017) 77 ZfaöRV 3
Potestà M, 'Republic of Italy v Republic of Cuba' (2012) 106 AJIL 341
Radjai N, Halonen L, and Kyriakou P, 'An Analysis of the Compensation Regime Applicable to Claims Arising from Armed Conflicts Affecting Investments in MENA' (2016) 3 BCDRIAR 219

Ratliff J, '*Parens Patriae:* An Overview' (2000) 74 Tul LR 1847
Reich A, 'The Effectiveness of the WTO Dispute Settlement System: A Statistical Analysis' *EUI Working Paper LAW 2017/11*, available: <https://cadmus.eui.eu/bitstream/handle/1814/47045/LAW_2017_11.pdf>
Reinisch A, 'The Use and Limits of *Res Judicata* and *Lis Pendens* as Procedural Tools to Avoid Conflicting Dispute Settlement Outcomes' (2004) 3 LPICT 37
Requejo Isidro M and Hess B, 'The Mixed Arbitral Tribunals in the Peace Treaties of 1919–1922' *MPI for Procedural Law Research Paper Series No 2018(5)*
Reuter A, 'Taking Investors' Rights Seriously: The Achmea and CETA Rulings of the European Court of Justice Do Not Bar Intra-EU Investment Arbitration' (2021) 36 ICSID Rev-FILJ 33.
Roberts A, 'Power and Persuasion in Investment Treaty Interpretation: The Dual Role of States' (2010) 104 AJIL 179
Roberts A, 'State-to-State Investment Treaty Arbitration: A Hybrid Theory of Interdependent Rights and Shared Interpretative Authority' (2014) 55 Harv ILJ 1
Roberts A, 'Triangular Treaties: The Extent and Limits of Investment Treaty Rights' (2015) 56 Harv ILJ 353
Ruys T, 'Sanctions, Retorsions and Countermeasures: Concepts and International Legal Framework' [2016], available: <https://papers.ssrn.com/sol3/papers.cfm?abstract_id=2760853>
Ruys T and Verhoeven S, 'Attacks by Private Actors and the Right of Self-Defence' (2005) 10 JCSL 289
Sainati T, 'Human Rights Class Actions: Rethinking the Pilot-Judgment Procedure at the European Court of Human Rights' (2015) 56 Harv ILJ 147
Sattorova M, 'Investor Rights under EU Law and International Investment Law' (2016) 17 JWIT 895
Schaerer E, 'A Rose by Any Other Name: Why a Parens Patriae Action Can Be a Mass Action under the Class Action Fairness Act' (2013) 16 NYUJ Legis & Pub Pol 39
Schmid, 'Anmerkung: Societe Petrol Block' (1929) I ZfaöRV 102
Schwarzenberger G, 'The Fundamental Principles of International Law' (1955) 87 RdC 191
Simma B, 'From Bilateralism to Community Interest in International Law' (1994) 250 RdC 217
Simpson M, 'Chopping Away at Chapter 11: The Softwood Lumber Agreement's Effect on the NAFTA Investor-State Dispute Resolution Mechanism' (2007) 22 AUILR 479
Sloane R, 'On the Use and Abuse of Necessity in the Law of State Responsibility' (2012) 106 AJIL 447
Sloss D, 'Using International Court of Justice Advisory Opinions to Adjudicate Secessionist Claims' (2001) 42 SCLR 357
Sotomayer A, 'The Rule Against Duplication of Procedures in the Regional Systems of Human Rights Protection' [2009] Notre Dame Working Paper 2, available: <http://www.nd.edu/~ndlaw/cchr/papers/Andres_%20Duplication_Procedures.pdf>
Spiermann O, 'Individual Rights, State Interests and the Power to Waive ICSID Jurisdiction under Bilateral Investment Treaties' (2004) 20 Arb Int 179
Stephens B, 'The Curious History of the Alien Tort Statute' (2014) 89 NDLR 1467
Tams C, 'All's Well That Ends Well: Comments on the ILC's Articles on State Responsibility' (2002) 62 ZfaöRV 759
Tams C, 'Note Analytique—Swimming with the Tide or Seeking to Stem It? Recent ICJ Rulings on the Law of Self-Defence' (2005) 18 Rev Queb DDI 275
Tams C, 'The Use of Force against Terrorists' (2009) 20 EJIL 359

Tams C, 'The Use of Force against Terrorists: A Rejoinder to Federico Sperotto and Kimberley N Trapp' (2009) 20 EJIL 1057
Tams C, 'Embracing the Uncertainty of Old: Armed Attacks by Non-State Actors Prior to 9/11' (2017) 77 ZfaöRV 61
Tejera Perez V, 'Diplomatic Protection Revival for Failure to Comply with Investment Arbitration Awards' (2012) 3 JIDS 445
Thomas M, 'Parens Patriae and The States' Historic Police Power' (2016) 69 SMULR 759
Titi C, 'Most-Favoured-Nation Treatment: Survival Clauses and Reform of International Investment Law' (2016) 33 JIA 425
Tladi D, 'The Constitutional Court's Judgment in the SADC Tribunal Case: International Law Continues to Befuddle' (2020) 10 CCR 129
Tomka P, Howley J, and Proulx V-J, 'International and Municipal Law before the World Court: One or Two Legal Orders?' (2015) XXXV Pol YBIL 11
Trapp K, 'Back to Basics: Necessity, Proportionality, and the Right of Self-Defence Against Non-State Terrorist Actors' (2007) 56 ICLQ 141
Trapp K, 'The Use of Force against Terrorists: A Reply to Christian J. Tams' (2009) 20 EJIL 1049
Trevino C, 'State-to-State Investment Treaty Arbitration and the Interplay with Investor-State Arbitration Under the Same Treaty' (2014) 5 JIDS 199
Tropper J and Reinisch A, 'The 2020 Termination Agreement of Intra-EU BITs and Its Effect on Investment Arbitration in the EU: A Public International Law Analysis of the Termination Agreement' (2022) 16 Aust YBIA 301
Tzanakopoulos A, 'Domestic Courts in International Law: The International Judicial Function of National Courts' (2011) 34 Loy LAI & CLR 133
Vermeer-Künzli A, 'A Matter of Interest: Diplomatic Protection and State Responsibility *Erga Omnes*' (2007) 56 ICLQ 553
Vermeer-Künzli A, 'As If: The Legal Fiction in Diplomatic Protection' (2007) 18 EJIL 37
Vermeer-Künzli A, 'Unfinished Business: Concurrence of Claims Presented before a Human Rights Court or Treaty Body and through Diplomatic Protection' (2010) 10 HRLR 269
Vladimirovich Kochenov D and Lavranos N, 'Achmea versus the Rule of Law: CJEU's Dogmatic Dismissal of Investors' Rights in Backsliding Member States of the European Union' (2021) 14 Hague JRL 195
Voon T and Mitchell A, 'Denunciation, Termination and Survival: The Interplay of Treaty Law and Investment Law' (2016) 31 ICSID Rev-FILJ 413
Weinstock R, 'The Lorax State: Parens Patriae and the Provision of Public Goods' (2009) 109 Colum LR 798
Weiss EB, 'Invoking State Responsibility in the Twenty-First Century' (2002) 96 AJIL 798
Winn M, 'Peace Treaty Claim Waivers: The Case of Price Hans-Adam II of Liechtenstein and the "Scene at a Roman Well"' (2006) 38 Geo Wash ILR 807
Wittich S, 'Direct Injury and the Incidence of the Local Remedies Rule' (2000) 5 Aust Rev I & EL 121
Wood M, 'The Law on the Use of Force: Current Challenges' (2007) 11 SYBIL 1
Wu E, 'Addressing Multiplicity of Shareholder Claims in ICSID Arbitrations Under Bilateral Investment Treaties: A "Tiered Approach" to Prioritising Claims?' (2010) 6 AIAJ 134

Reports and related documents

Alston P, 'Study on Targeted Killings' UN Doc A/HRC/124/24/Add.6 (28 May 2010)
ESCR Committee 'General Comment No. 8' (1997) UN Doc E/C.12/1997/8

EU Council, 'Guidelines on Implementation and Evaluation of Restrictive Measures (Sanctions)' (4 May 2018), available: <https://data.consilium.europa.eu/doc/document/ST-5664-2018-INIT/en/pdf>
HRC, 'General Comment No. 24' (1994) UN Doc CCPR/C/21/Rev.1/Add.6
HRC, 'General Comment No. 26: Continuity of Obligations' UN Doc CCPR/C/21/Rev.1/Add.8/Rev.1 (8 December 1997)
HRC, 'General Comment No. 33' (2008) UN Doc CCPR/C/GC/33
HRC, 'General Comment No. 36' UN Doc CCPR/C/GC/36 (3 September 2019)
ILA, 'Interim Report on *Res Judicata* and Arbitration' (2004) 25 Arb Int 35
ILA, 'Toronto Conference Report: Diplomatic Protection of Persons and Property' (2006) 72 ILA Rep Conf 353
ILA, 'Final Report on Res Judicata and Arbitration' (2009) 25 Arb Int 67
Jazairy I, 'Report of the Special Rapporteur on the Negative Impact of Unilateral Coercive Measures on the Enjoyment of Human Rights', UN Doc A/HRC/33/48 (2 August 2016)
Jazairy I, 'Report of the Special Rapporteur on the Negative Impact of Unilateral Coercive Measures on the Enjoyment of Human Rights on His Mission to the EU', UN Doc A/HRC/39/54/Add.1 (17 July 2018)
'Notification by the Democratic People's Republic of Korea', Communication from the Secretary-General of the UN, C.N.467.1997.TREATIES-10 (Depository Notification), available: <https://treaties.un.org/doc/Publication/CN/1997/CN.467.1997-Eng.pdf>
OECD, 'Draft Convention on the Protection of Foreign Property' (1967)
Report of the Secretary-General's Panel of Inquiry on the 31 May 2010 Flotilla Incident (2011), available: <https://www.un.org/News/dh/infocus/middle_east/Gaza_Flotilla_Panel_Report.pdf>
UNCTAD, 'UNCTAD's Reform Package for the International Investment Regime' (2017)
UNSG, 'Unilateral Economic Measures as a Means of Political and Economic Coercion against Developing Countries', UN Doc A/72/307 (9 August 2017)
Yip KL, 'Written Contribution to the General Discussion' (14 July 2015), available: <https://www.ohchr.org/Documents/HRBodies/CCPR/Discussion/2015/KaLokYip.doc>

ILC documents

Ago R, 'Eighth Report on State Responsibility' (1979) 2(1) ILCYB 3
Ago R, 'Eighth Report on State Responsibility (Addendum)' (1980) 2(1) ILCYB 13
Arangio-Ruiz G, 'Second Report on State Responsibility' (1989) 2(1) ILCYB 1
Arangio-Ruiz G, 'Fourth Report on State Responsibility' (1992) 2(1) ILCYB 1
Bennouna M, 'Preliminary Report on Diplomatic Protection' (1998) 2(1) ILCYB 309
Crawford J, 'First Report on State Responsibility' (1997) 2(1) ILCYB 1
Crawford J, 'Second Report on State Responsibility' (1999) 2(1) ILCYB 1
Crawford J, 'Third Report on State Responsibility' (2000) 2(1) ILCYB 3
Crawford J, 'Fourth Report on State Responsibility' (2001) 2(1) ILCYB 1
Dugard J, 'First Report on Diplomatic Protection' (2000) 2(1) ILCYB 205
Dugard J, 'Second Report on Diplomatic Protection' (2001) 2(1) ILCYB 97
Dugard J, 'Third Report on Diplomatic Protection' (2002) 2(1) ILCYB 49
Dugard J, 'Fifth Report on Diplomatic Protection' (2004) 2(1) ILCYB 43
Dugard J, 'Sixth Report on Diplomatic Protection' (2005) 2(1) ILCYB 1
Fitzmaurice G, 'Second Report on the Law of Treaties' (1957) 2 ILCYB 16
Fitzmaurice G, 'Fourth Report on the Law of Treaties' (1959) 2 ILCYB 37
Garcia-Amador FV, 'International Responsibility: Report' (1956) 2 ILCYB 173

Garcia-Amador FV, 'Sixth Report on State Responsibility' (1961) 2 ILCYB 1
ILC, 'Diplomatic Protection' (1997) 2(2) ILCYB 60
ILC, 'Diplomatic Protection: Comments and observations received from Governments' (2006) UN Doc A/CN.4/561
ILC, 'Draft Articles on Diplomatic Protection with commentaries' (2006) 2(2) ILCYB 22
ILC, 'Draft articles on the effects of armed conflicts on treaties, with commentaries' (2011) 2(2) ILCYB 108
ILC, 'Draft Articles on the Responsibility of International Organizations, with commentaries' (2011) 2(2) ILCYB 46
ILC, 'Draft conclusions on identification of customary international law, with commentaries' (2018) 2(2) ILCYB 122
ILC, 'State Responsibility: Comments and observations received from Governments' (1998) UN Doc A/CN.4/488; Add 1-3
ILC, 'State Responsibility: Comments and observations received from Governments' (2001) UN Doc A/CN.4/515
ILC, 'Report of the ILC on the Work of its Thirty-First Session' (1979) 2 ILCYB 1
ILC, 'Summary Records of the Meetings of the Fiftieth Session' (1998) 1 ILCYB 1
ILC, 'Summary Records of the Meetings of the Fifty-First Session' (1999) 1 ILCYB 1
ILC, 'Summary Records of the Meetings of the Fifty-Second Session' (2000) 1 ILCYB 1
ILC, 'Summary Records of the Meetings of the Fifty-Third Session' (2001) 1 ILCYB 1
ILC, 'Summary Records of the Meetings of the Fifty-Fourth Session' (2002) 1 ILCYB 1
ILC, 'Summary Records of the Meetings of the Fifty-Fifth Session' (2003) 1 ILCYB 1
Riphagen W, 'Third Report on State Responsibility' (1982) ILCYB 22
Waldock H, 'Third Report on the Law of Treaties' (1964) 2 ILCYB 5

Newspaper articles, blogs, podcasts, policy papers, press releases, and other online materials

'ECOWAS Suspends Burkina Faso after Military Coup' *Al Jazeera* (28 January 2022), available: <https://www.aljazeera.com/news/2022/1/28/ecowas-suspends-burkina-faso-after-coup>
'Iran renews list of former and current US officials involved in terror acts and rights violations' *Tehran Times* (9 April 2022), available: <https://www.tehrantimes.com/news/471510/Iran-renews-list-of-former-and-current-U-S-officials-involved>
'Qatar and Saudi Arabia Agree to Suspend Proceedings before the WTO's Appellate Body' *IA Reporter* (10 January 2022)
'[Updated] Dutch Real Estate Investor Lodges ICSID Claim against Romania' *IA Reporter* (5 June 2022)
'UK-Australia FTA negotiations: agreement in principle' (Policy paper, 17 June 2021), available:<https://www.gov.uk/government/publications/uk-australia-free-trade-agreement-negotiations-agreement-in-principle/uk-australia-fta-negotiations-agreement-in-principle>
'West African Regional Bloc ECOWAS Imposes New Sanctions on Mali and Guinea' *France24* (8 November 2021), available: <https://www.france24.com/en/africa/20211108-west-african-regional-bloc-ecowas-imposes-new-sanctions-on-mali-and-guinea>
'West African Bloc Sanctions Mali's Transitional Leaders' *Bloomberg* (7 November 2021), available: <https://www.bloomberg.com/news/articles/2021-11-07/west-african-bloc-sanctions-mali-s-transitional-leaders#xj4y7vzkg>

Akande D, 'UK Parliamentary Inquiry into UK Policy on the Use of Drones for Targeted Killing' *EJIL:Talk!* (23 December 2015)

Batura J and Risini I, 'Of Parties, Third Parties, and Treaty Interpretation: Ukraine v. Russia (X) before the European Court of Human Rights' *EJIL:Talk!* (26 September 2022).

Bernasconi-Osterwalder N, 'State-State Dispute Settlement in Investment Treaties' *IISD Best Practices Series* (October 2014)

Bohmer L, 'In Now-Public Decision, Reasoning of German Federal Supreme Court on Set Aside of BIT Award Is Clarified' *IA Reporter* (11 November 2018)

Bohmer L, 'Analysis: In Gosling v. Mauritius, Majority Saw No Treaty Violation, Stressing the Absence of a Right to Build a Real Estate Development on UNESCO World Heritage Site; Stanimir Alexandrov Disagreed' *IA Reporter* (24 February 2020)

Bohmer L, 'Breaking: EU Member States Sign Plurilateral Treaty to Terminate Intra-EU BITs' *IA Reporter* (6 May 2020)

Bohmer L, 'Analysis: In Previously Unseen Turkey-Syria BIT Award, Majority Imports a More Favourable War-Losses Clause; in Dissent Ziade Warns of "Exorbitant" Implications of Majority Reading' *IA Reporter* (31 November 2020)

Bohmer L, 'Easing of Qatar-Saudi Arabia Tensions Could Affect Treaty-Based Arbitrations' *IA Reporter* (14 January 2021)

Bohmer L, 'Tribunal in Lion Mexico v. Mexico Finds First Known Denial of Justice under NAFTA, as Claimant Was Not given the Opportunity to Defend Itself against a Complex Private Fraud Leading to the Cancellation of Its Debt Instruments' *IA Reporter* (24 September 2021)

Bohmer L, 'Vilnius Court Decides That the Courts of the Respondents' Domicile Have Jurisdiction over Claims Based on the Plurilateral Termination Agreement – Once Again Throwing out Lithuania's Attempt to Seek Damages from Investors Involved in Parallel ICSID and SCC Arbitrations' *IA Reporter* (14 February 2022)

Bohmer L, 'Ukrainian Oligarchs to Lodge Third Treaty Claim against the US' *IA Reporter* (23 May 2022)

Bohmer L, 'Breaking: Parties Reach Agreement in Principle on Modernizing Energy Charter Treaty, Including Carve-Outs for Fossil Fuels and Intra-EU Disputes, Stricter Definitions and Standards of Protection, and Application of 2014 UNCITRAL Rules on Transparency' *IA Reporter* (24 June 2022)

Brandis G, 'The Right of Self-Defence Against Imminent Armed Attack In International Law' *EJIL:Talk!* (25 May 2017)

Braun J, 'Analysis: On Quantum, Deutsche Telekom v. India Tribunal Opts for Sunk Costs Approach, Departing from Parallel Indian Satellite Spectrum Cases' *IA Reporter* (23 April 2021)

Braun J, 'Australia and United Kingdom Announce "Agreement in Principle" on a New FTA, Including an Investment Chapter, but No ISDS Mechanism' *IA Reporter* (17 June 2021)

Braun J, 'Revealed: Tribunal in VEB v. Ukraine Upholds Jurisdiction over Russian State-Owned Claimant, but Declines to Import More Favourable Standards of Treatment through the Underlying Treaty's MFN Clause' *IA Reporter* (22 September 2021)

Bray D and Kapoor S, 'Agreement on the Termination of Intra-EU BITs: Sunset in Stone?' *Kluwer Arbitration Blog* (4 November 2020)

Brouwer E, 'Planned Vote on Modernised ECT Is Postponed, as EU Member States and Institutions Discuss Way Forward' *IA Reporter* (28 April 2023)

Brouwer E, 'Analysis: Investment Protocol to the African Continental Free Trade Area Agreement Emphasises Sustainable Development, Setting Narrow Standards of Protection and Introducing Obligations on Foreign Investors' *IA Reporter* (25 May 2023)

Charlotin D, 'Twin Arbitrations Started against Spain in Wake of Banco Popular's Resolution' *IA Reporter* (24 August 2018)

Charlotin D, 'Singapore Appeal Court Grapples with Various Investment Treaty Arbitration Concepts Including "Related to", Estoppel, Unilateral Declarations, Territorial Nexus and Exhaustion of Remedies' *IA Reporter* (29 November 2018)

Charlotin D, 'Iberdrola Tribunal Applies Res Judicata Effect of Prior Award, and Finds That Previous Recourse to ICSID Proceedings Precludes a Subsequent UNCITRAL Arbitration' *IA Reporter* (2 September 2020)

Charlotin D, 'Analysis: In WTO Ruling, McRae-Chaired Panel Finds That Measures by Saudi Arabia Breached beIN's IP Rights – but Some Measures Fall within Essential Security Exception' *IA Reporter* (3 September 2020)

Charlotin D, 'Pierre Tercier Is Tapped to Chair Under-the-Radar UNCITRAL BIT Arbitration Brought by Chinese Claimants' *IA Reporter* (22 February 2022)

Charlotin D, 'European Court of Human Rights Finds That Failure by Slovakia to Enforce ICC Award Amounts to Breach of Right to Property' *IA Reporter* (1 July 2022)

Charlotin D, Perez Aznar F, and Peterson LE, 'Looking Back: Long-Confidential Benhamou v. Uruguay Award Is Unearthed, Revealing First Known Attempt at State-to-State BIT Consultations over Interpretive Question, and Tribunal's Handling of Claims by Beneficiary of Trust' *IA Reporter* (2 April 2018)

Corten O, 'A Plea Against the Abusive Invocation of Self-Defence as a Response to Terrorism' *EJIL:Talk!* (14 July 2016)

Dahlquist J, 'Investigation: European Commission's Push for Termination of Intra-EU Investment Treaties Shifts to Multilateral Plane, but Member-States at Odds over Scope of Effort' *IA Reporter* (15 November 2018)

Dahlquist J and Peterson LE, 'European Commission's Infringement Arguments Come into Focus, as the Push to Dismantle Intra-EU BITs Also Shows Signs of Broadening' *IA Reporter* (10 September 2015)

de Wet E, 'Reactions to the Backlash: Trying to Revive the SADC Tribunal through Litigation' *EJIL:Talk!* (5 August 2016)

Debevoise & Plimpton, '23 EU Member States Sign Treaty to Terminate Intra-EU Bilateral Investment Treaties' *Debevoise In Depth* (11 May 2020), available: <https://www.debevoise.com/-/media/files/insights/publications/2020/05/2020051123-eu-member-states-sign-treaty-to-termina.pdf>

Debevoise & Plimpton, 'The Future of Investment Law in the EU: A Practical Perspective' *Debevoise Update* (8 December 2021), available: <https://www.debevoise.com/-/media/files/insights/publications/2021/12/20211208-the-future-of-investment-law-in-the-eu.pdf>

'Declaration by the High Representative on behalf of the European Union on the alignment of certain third countries with the Council Decision 2010/92/CFSP extending restrictive measures against Zimbabwe' (PR 10202/1/10 REV1, 27 May 2010), available: <https://www.consilium.europa.eu/uedocs/cms_data/docs/pressdata/en/cfsp/114649.pdf>

'Declaration by the High Representative on behalf of the EU on the alignment of certain third countries concerning restrictive measures against Myanmar/Burma' (18 July 2018), available: <https://www.consilium.europa.eu/en/press/press-releases/2018/07/18/declaration-by-the-high-representative-on-behalf-of-the-european-union-on-the-alignment-of-certain-countries-with-concerning-restrictive-measures-against-myanmar-burma/>

'Declaration by the High Representative Josep Borrell, on behalf of the European Union, on Nicaragua' (4 May 2020), available: <https://www.consilium.europa.eu/en/press/

press-releases/2020/05/04/declaration-by-the-high-representative-josep-borrell-on-behalf-of-the-european-union-on-nicaragua/>

'Declaration by the High Representative on behalf of the EU on the alignment of certain third countries concerning restrictive measures in respect of actions undermining or threatening the territorial integrity, sovereignty and independence of Ukraine' (30 March 2023), available: <https://www.consilium.europa.eu/en/press/press-releases/2023/03/30/statement-by-the-high-representative-on-behalf-of-the-eu-on-the-alignment-of-certain-third-countries-concerning-restrictive-measures-in-respect-of-actions-undermining-or-threatening-the-territorial-integrity-sovereignty-and-independ/>

Djanic V, 'Qatar Airways Lodges Treaty-Based Arbitration Cases against Four Middle Eastern States' IA Reporter (22 July 2020)

Djanic V, 'Ukraine Is Looking for Counsel in 3.5 Billion USD Treaty-Based Dispute, as Sanctions Are Imposed on Chinese Investors' *IA Reporter* (1 February 2021)

Djanic V, 'European Parliament Puts Ratification of China Investment Agreement on Hold in Light of Chinese Sanctions' *IA Reporter* (21 May 2021)

Djanic V, 'Looking Back: High-Profile Tribunal Hearing One of Venezuela's Earliest ICSID Cases Discussed Foreign Control Requirement, Force Majeure, Lost Profit, and Compound Interest' *IA Reporter* (2 September 2021)

Djanic V, 'Two Russian Banks Threaten Treaty Arbitration against Ukraine Following Seizure of Their Assets in the Context of the Ongoing Russia-Ukraine War' *IA Reporter* (12 May 2022)

'ECHR Communicates to Russia New Inter-State Case Concerning Events in Crimea and Eastern Ukraine' *ECHR Pr Rel 296/15* (1 October 2015)

'ECHR Deals with Cases Concerning Crimea and Eastern Ukraine' *ECHR Pr Rel 345/14* (26 November 2014)

'ECHR to Adjourn Some Individual Applications on Eastern Ukraine Pending Grand Chamber Judgment in Related Inter-State Case' *ECHR Pr Rel 432* (17 December 2018)

ECtHR, 'Decisions of 24 September 2015' *ECHR Pr Rel 286/15* (24 September 2015)

ECtHR, 'ECHR Gives Notification to Russia of Cases Brought by Relatives of People Killed in the Downing of Malaysian Airlines Flight MH-17' *ECHR Pr Rel 121* (4 April 2019)

ECtHR, 'Q&A on Inter-State Cases' (April 2022), available: <https://echr.coe.int/Documents/Press_Q_A_Inter-State_cases_ENG.pdf>

ECtHR, 'Inter-State Case Ukraine v. Russia (X): Receipt of Completed Application Form and Notification to Respondent State' *ECHR Pr Rel 220* (28 June 2022)

Eisen N and others, 'The Brookings Sanctions Tracker' (2022) <https://www.brookings.edu/research/the-brookings-sanctions-tracker/>

'EU Sanctions Map', available: <https://www.sanctionsmap.eu/#/main>

Gaja G, 'The International Court of Justice's Approach to Injuries Suffered by Individuals' (Oxford, 8 May 2014), available: <https://podcasts.ox.ac.uk/international-court-justices-approach-injuries-suffered-individuals>

Guilfoyle D, 'The Palmer Report on the Mavi Marmara Incident and the Legality of Israel's Blockade of the Gaza Strip' *EJIL:Talk!* (6 September 2011)

Haque AA, 'Self-Defence Against Non-State Actors: All Over the Map' *Just Security* (24 March 2021)

'Hearing in the Inter-State Case Georgia v. Russia (II) Concerning the 2008 Armed Conflict between the Two Countries' *ECHR Pr Rel* (22 September 2011)

Henderson I and Cavanagh B, 'Self-Defence, Collateral Damage and Precautions in Attack' *Opinio Juris* (9 July 2014)

Hepburn J, 'Palm Oil Company Sees BIT Claim Registered against Indonesia at ICSID' *IA Reporter* (11 August 2016)

Hepburn J, 'South African Court Finds Fault with Former President's Role in Neutering of a Regional Tribunal; Ruling Comes on the Heels of Arbitral Finding That Sanctioned Lesotho for Its Role in Same Events' *IA Reporter* (2 March 2018)

Hepburn J, 'Investor-State Arbitration Opt-Outs Proliferate in Newly-Disclosed Trans-Pacific Partnership Agreement Side Letters' *IA Reporter* (8 March 2018)

Hepburn J, 'European Court of Human Rights Dismisses Investor Claim, Citing Substantial Similarity to Parallel BIT Arbitration That Had Netted Partial Recovery' *IA Reporter* (30 April 2018)

Hepburn J, 'Saudi Arabia Faces $1 Billion Claim by Qatari Media Firm under OIC Investment Agreement, amidst Gulf Diplomatic Crisis' *IA Reporter* (1 October 2018)

Hepburn J, 'South Korean Supreme Court Ruling That Has Held Japanese Companies Liable for Forced Labour Could Give Rise to Chevron-Ecuador Type Investment Treaty Arbitration' *IA Reporter* (31 October 2018)

Hepburn J, 'Relying on Investment Treaty Case-Law, the European Court of Human Rights Permits Crimea-Related Case to Proceed' *IA Reporter* (1 February 2021)

Hepburn J and Kabra R, 'Investigation: Further Russia Investment Treaty Decisions Uncovered, Offering Broader Window into Arbitrators' Approaches to Crimea Controversy' *IA Reporter* (17 November 2017)

IEC, 'The United Kingdom denies advantages of Part III under Article 17 of the ECT' (29 September 2023), available: <https://www.energycharter.org/media/news/article/the-united-kingdom-denies-advantages-of-part-iii-under-article-17-of-the-ect/?tx_news_pi1%5Bcontroller%5D=News&tx_news_pi1%5Baction%5D=detail&cHash=c03e5fff166859c14b15efaa1f5cb8a3>

IEC, 'Ukraine denies advantages under Article 17(2) of the ECT' (19 August 2022), available: <https://www.energycharter.org/media/news/article/ukraine-denies-advantages-under-article-172-of-the-ect/>

Keane D, 'ICERD and Palestine's Inter-State Complaint', *EJIL:Talk!* (30 April 2018)

Keane D, 'CERD Reaches Historic Decisions in Inter-State Communications' *EJIL:Talk!* (6 September 2019)

Lester M and O'Kane M, 'European Sanctions', available: <https://www.europeansanctions.com/>

Lester S, 'Ending the WTO Dispute Settlement Crisis: Where to from Here?' *IISD Policy Analysis* (2 March 2022)

Lostal M, 'The Ntaganda Reparations Order: A Marked Step towards a Victim-Centred Reparations Legal Framework at the ICC' *EJIL:Talk!* (24 May 2021)

McCabe Centre for Law and Cancer, 'Australia's Plain Packaging Laws at the WTO: Progress to Date', available: <http://untobaccocontrol.org/kh/legal-challenges/australias-plain-packaging-laws-wto/> (3 October 2017)

Milanovic M, 'Sayadi: The Human Rights Committee's Kadi (or a Pretty Poor Excuse for One . . .)' *EJIL:Talk!* (29 January 2009)

Milanovic M, 'More on Drones, Self-Defense, and the Alston Report on Targeted Killings' *EJIL:Talk!* (5 June 2010)

Milanovic M, 'Self-Defense and Non-State Actors: Indeterminacy and the Jus Ad Bellum' *EJIL:Talk!* (21 February 2010)

Milanovic M, 'Russia Files Interstate Complaint Against Ukraine in Strasbourg' *EJIL:Talk!* (26 July 2021)

Milanovic M, 'The European Court's Admissibility Decision in Ukraine and the Netherlands v Russia: The Good, the Bad and the Ugly – Part II' *EJIL:Talk!* (26 January 2023)

Milanovic M and Shah S, 'Ukraine and the Netherlands v. Russia (Nos 8019/16, 43800/14, 28525/20, 11055/22): Amicus Curiae Brief' (2023), available: <https://papers.ssrn.com/sol3/papers.cfm?abstract_id=4427214>

Moorehead A, 'Brazil's Robust Defense of the Legal Prohibition on the Use of Force and Self Defence' *Just Security* (20 April 2018)

'OpenSanctions', available: <https://www.opensanctions.org/>

Peterson LE, 'U.S. Financial Firm Discontinues Argentine Claim, but Reserves Rights to Take Part in Any Future Settlement Talks' *IA Reporter* (2 April 2009)

Peterson LE, 'UNCITRAL Claim by U.S. Hedge Fund Clears Jurisdictional Hurdle in Fight over Ecuador Electricity Investments; Ecuador Sought to Deny Benefits of U.S. Investment Treaty' *IA Reporter* (16 December 2010)

Peterson LE, 'Czech Republic Terminates Investment Treaties in Such a Way as to Cast Doubt on Residual Legal Protection for Existing Investments' *IA Reporter* (1 February 2011)

Peterson LE, 'Indonesia Ramps up Termination of BITs – and Kills Survival Clause in One Such Treaty – but Faces New $600 Mil. Claim from Indian Mining Investor' *IA Reporter* (20 November 2015)

Peterson LE, 'Arbitrators Hold State Liable For A Denial Of Justice Occurring In Relation To Actions Taken In International Forums; "Rule Of Law" Treaty Obligation Also Breached' *IA Reporter* (14 July 2016)

Peterson LE, 'In New Ruling On Covered Investors And Investments, A Pair Of Arbitrators Deem Southern African Development Community's Finance And Investment Protocol To Have Expansive Scope' *IA Reporter* (14 July 2016)

Peterson LE, 'INVESTIGATION: Lesotho Is Held Liable for Investment Treaty Breach Arising out of Its Role in Hobbling a Regional Tribunal That Had Been Hearing Expropriation Case' *IA Reporter* (14 July 2016)

Peterson LE, 'Multilateral Investment Treaty's Exhaustion of Remedies Requirement Does Not Hobble Case Because Local Courts Couldn't Offer Same Relief Available before International Tribunal' *IA Reporter* (14 July 2016)

Peterson LE, 'Singapore Judge Sees Investors as Clearing Temporal Jurisdiction Hurdle in Fight with Lesotho, but Disagrees That Right to Claim before SADC Standing Tribunal Was a Protected Investment' *IA Reporter* (17 August 2017)

Peterson LE, 'Analysis: What Have We Learned from the First Wave of Post-Denunciation ICSID Claims against Venezuela – and Why Do Investors Keep Suing Venezuela There?' *IA Reporter* (30 November 2017)

Peterson LE, 'NAFTA Parties Unveil Text of New Agreement' *IA Reporter* (1 October 2018)

PICT, *Courts and Tribunals* (13 November 2017), available: <http://www.pict-pcti.org/>

Risini I and Ulfstein G, 'The Netherlands' Inter-State Application against Russia Six Years after MH 17' *EJIL:Talk!* (14 August 2020)

'SanctionsWiki', available: <http://www.sanctionswiki.org/Main_Page>

Smit Duijzentkunst B, 'Of Rights and Powers: Waiving Investment Treaty Protection' *EJIL:Talk!* (9 December 2013)

Steven L and Thornton N, 'Two Roads-Two Tribunals: Recent "Fork-in-the-Road" Interpretations' *Kluwer Arbitration Blog* (16 December 2009)

Trapp K, 'Uses of Force against Civil Aircraft' *EJIL:Talk!* (28 June 2011)

Ulfstein G and Risini I, 'Inter-State Applications under the European Convention on Human Rights: Strengths and Challenges' *EJIL:Talk!* (24 January 2020)

Ullah Z, Eversheds Sutherland Global Sanctions Guide (Third Edition)' (2021), available: <https://ezine.eversheds-sutherland.com/global-sanctions-guide/>

Vaccaro-Incisa GM, 'Crimea Investment Disputes: Are Jurisdictional Hurdles Being Overcome Too Easily?' *EJIL:Talk!* (9 May 2018)

Van Aaken A, 'International Investment Law and Decentralized Targeted Sanctions: An Uneasy Relationship' (2016) 164 Columbia FDI Perspectives, available: <http://ccsi.columbia.edu/files/2013/10/No-164-van-Aaken-FINAL.pdf>

Venema V, 'The Sahara Memorial Seen From Space' *BBC World Service* (22 January 2014), available: <https://www.bbc.co.uk/news/magazine-25643103>

Wierzbowski K and Szostak A, 'Extinguishing Intra-EU Bilateral Investment Treaties: Recent Developments' *CPR Speaks* (19 January 2021), available: <https://blog.cpradr.org/2021/01/19/exinguishing-intra-eu-bilateral-investment-treaties-recent-developments/>

Wikipedia, 'Russian sanctions against Ukraine' available: <https://en.wikipedia.org/wiki/Russian_sanctions_against_Ukraine#:~:text=Russian%20sanctions%20against%20Ukraine%20were,citizens%20and%2068%20Ukrainian%20companies>

Wisehart D, 'The Crisis in Ukraine and the Prohibition of the Use of Force: A Legal Basis for Russia's Intervention?' *EJIL:Talk!* (4 March 2014)

Wong E, 'US Imposes Sanctions on Myanmar Over Rohinga Atrocities' *New York Times* (17 August 2018)

Wright J, 'The Modern Law of Self-Defence' *EJIL:Talk!* (11 January 2017)

Yanos A and Ramos-Mrosovsky C, 'Intra-EU Investment Treaty Disputes in US Courts: Achmea, Micula and Beyond' *GAR* (12 August 2021)

Index

Introductory Note:

References such as '178–9' indicate (not necessarily continuous) discussion of a topic across a range of pages. Wherever possible in the case of topics with many references, these have either been divided into sub-topics or only the most significant discussions of the topic are listed. Because the entire work is about 'overlapping individual and State claims', the use of this term (and certain others which occur consistently throughout the book) as an entry point has been restricted. Information will be found under the corresponding detailed topics. Cross-references in a form such as 'courts; see also *individual courts*' direct the reader to headings in a particular class (e.g. in this case 'International Court of Justice (ICJ)') rather than a specific '*individual courts*' entry.

For the benefit of digital users, indexed terms that span two pages (e.g., 52–53) may, on occasion, appear on only one of those pages.

The manufacturer's authorised representative in the EU for product safety is Oxford University Press España S.A. of el Parque Empresarial San Fernando de Henares, Avenida de Castilla, 2 – 28830 Madrid (www.oup.es/en or product.safety@oup.com). OUP España S.A. also acts as importer into Spain of products made by the manufacturer.

www.ingramcontent.com/pod-product-compliance
Lightning Source LLC
LaVergne TN
LVHW011821200926
848484LV00005B/1273